CLYMER®
MANUALS

HARLEY-DAVIDSON
FLH/FLT TWIN CAM 88 & 103 • 1999-2005

WHAT'S IN YOUR TOOLBOX?

You Tube™

More information available at Clymer.com
Phone: 805-498-6703

Haynes Publishing Group
Sparkford Nr Yeovil
Somerset BA22 7JJ England

Haynes North America, Inc
861 Lawrence Drive
Newbury Park
California 91320 USA

ISBN 10: 1-59969-016-0
ISBN-13: 978-1-59969-016-2
Library of Congress: 2005910540

Author: Ed Scott

Technical Photography: *Ed Scott, with assistance by Jordan Engineering, Oceanside, California.*
Additional assistance courtesy San Diego Harley-Davidson (sandiegoharley.com)
and Patrick Racing (www.patrickracing.com).

Technical Illustrations: *Errol and Mitzi McCarthy*

Cover: *Mark Clifford Photography, Los Angeles, California (www.markclifford.com)*
2003 Road Glide courtesy of Gary Sullivan, Thousand Oaks, California.

© **Haynes North America, Inc. 2005**
With permission from J.H. Haynes & Co. Ltd.
Clymer is a registered trademark of Haynes North America, Inc.
Printed in the U.S.A.

All rights reserved. No part of this book may be reproduced or transmitted in any form or by any means, electronic or mechanical, including photocopying, recording or by any information storage or retrieval system, without permission in writing from the copyright holder.

While every attempt is made to ensure that the information in this manual is correct, no liability can be accepted by the authors or publishers for loss, damage or injury caused by any errors in, or omissions from, the information given.

Common spark plug conditions

NORMAL

Symptoms: Brown to grayish-tan color and slight electrode wear. Correct heat range for engine and operating conditions.
Recommendation: When new spark plugs are installed, replace with plugs of the same heat range.

WORN

Symptoms: Rounded electrodes with a small amount of deposits on the firing end. Normal color. Causes hard starting in damp or cold weather and poor fuel economy.
Recommendation: Plugs have been left in the engine too long. Replace with new plugs of the same heat range. Follow the recommended maintenance schedule.

CARBON DEPOSITS

Symptoms: Dry sooty deposits indicate a rich mixture or weak ignition. Causes misfiring, hard starting and hesitation.
Recommendation: Make sure the plug has the correct heat range. Check for a clogged air filter or problem in the fuel system or engine management system. Also check for ignition system problems.

ASH DEPOSITS

Symptoms: Light brown deposits encrusted on the side or center electrodes or both. Derived from oil and/or fuel additives. Excessive amounts may mask the spark, causing misfiring and hesitation during acceleration.
Recommendation: If excessive deposits accumulate over a short time or low mileage, install new valve guide seals to prevent seepage of oil into the combustion chambers. Also try changing gasoline brands.

OIL DEPOSITS

Symptoms: Oily coating caused by poor oil control. Oil is leaking past worn valve guides or piston rings into the combustion chamber. Causes hard starting, misfiring and hesitation.
Recommendation: Correct the mechanical condition with necessary repairs and install new plugs.

GAP BRIDGING

Symptoms: Combustion deposits lodge between the electrodes. Heavy deposits accumulate and bridge the electrode gap. The plug ceases to fire, resulting in a dead cylinder.
Recommendation: Locate the faulty plug and remove the deposits from between the electrodes.

TOO HOT

Symptoms: Blistered, white insulator, eroded electrode and absence of deposits. Results in shortened plug life.
Recommendation: Check for the correct plug heat range, over-advanced ignition timing, lean fuel mixture, intake manifold vacuum leaks, sticking valves and insufficient engine cooling.

PREIGNITION

Symptoms: Melted electrodes. Insulators are white, but may be dirty due to misfiring or flying debris in the combustion chamber. Can lead to engine damage.
Recommendation: Check for the correct plug heat range, over-advanced ignition timing, lean fuel mixture, insufficient engine cooling and lack of lubrication.

HIGH SPEED GLAZING

Symptoms: Insulator has yellowish, glazed appearance. Indicates that combustion chamber temperatures have risen suddenly during hard acceleration. Normal deposits melt to form a conductive coating. Causes misfiring at high speeds.
Recommendation: Install new plugs. Consider using a colder plug if driving habits warrant.

DETONATION

Symptoms: Insulators may be cracked or chipped. Improper gap setting techniques can also result in a fractured insulator tip. Can lead to piston damage.
Recommendation: Make sure the fuel anti-knock values meet engine requirements. Use care when setting the gaps on new plugs. Avoid lugging the engine.

MECHANICAL DAMAGE

Symptoms: May be caused by a foreign object in the combustion chamber or the piston striking an incorrect reach (too long) plug. Causes a dead cylinder and could result in piston damage.
Recommendation: Repair the mechanical damage. Remove the foreign object from the engine and/or install the correct reach plug.

CONTENTS

QUICK REFERENCE DATA

MOTORCYCLE DATA

MODEL:_____ YEAR:_____

VIN NUMBER:_____

ENGINE SERIAL NUMBER:_____

CARBURETOR SERIAL NUMBER OR I.D. MARK:_____

Record the numbers here for your reference.

MODEL DESIGNATION

FLHT/FLHTI Electra Glide Standard (1999-2005)
FLHTC/FLHTCI Electra Glide Classic (1999-2005)
FLHTCUI Classic Electra Glide (1999-2005)
FLHTCSE2 Screamin' Eagle Electra Glide 2 (2005)
FLHR/FLHRI Road King (1999-2005)
FLHRCI Road King Classic (1999-2005)
FLHRS/FLHRSI Road King Custom (2004-2005)
FLTR/FLTRI Road Glide (1999-2005)

TIRE INFLATION PRESSURE (COLD)*

Model	kPa	PSI
Front wheels		
Rider only	248	36
Rider and passenger	248	36
Rear wheels		
Rider only	248	36
Rider and passenger	275	40

*Tire pressure for original equipment tires. Aftermarket tires may require different inflation pressure.

ENGINE OIL SPECIFICATIONS

Type	HD rating	Viscosity	Ambient operating temperature
HD Multi-grade	HD360	SAE 10W/40	Below 40° F
HD Multi-grade	HD360	SAE 20W/50	Above 40° F
HD Regular heavy	HD360	SAE 50	Above 60° F
HD Extra heavy	HD360	SAE 60	Above 80° F

ENGINE AND PRIMARY DRIVE/TRANMSSION OIL CAPACITIES

Oil tank refill capacity	3.5 U.S. qts. (3.3 L, 2.9 lmp. qts.)
Primary chain case (dry)	32 U.S. oz. (946 ml., 26.6 lmp. oz.)
Transmission	
Oil change	20-24 U.S. oz. (591-709 ml, 19-23 lmp. oz.)
Rebuild (dry)	24 U.S. oz. (709 ml, 23 lmp. oz.)

RECOMMENDED LUBRICANTS AND FLUIDS

Brake fluid	
1999-2004 models	DOT 5
2005 models	DOT 4
Clutch fluid	DOT 4
Front fork oil	HD Type E or an equivalent
Fuel	91 pump octane or higher leaded or unleaded
Transmission	HD Transmission Lubricant or an equivalent
Primary chaincase	HD Primary Chaincase Lubricant or an equivalent

MAINTENANCE AND TUNE-UP TORQUE PECIFICATIONS

Item	ft.-lb.	in.-lb.	N•m
Air filter			
Cover screw	–	36-60	4-7
Torx screws	–	20-40	2-4
Clutch adjusting screw locknut	–	72-120	8-14
Clutch inspection cover screws	–	84-108	10-12
Crankcase oil plug	–	120-144	14-16
Engine oil drain plug	14-21	–	19-28
Front fork cap bolt	11-22	–	15-30
Spark plug	11-18	–	15-24
Primary chaincase			
Inspection cover screws	–	50-70	6-8
Chain adjuster shoe nut	21-29	–	29-39
Oil tank drain plug	14-21	–	19-29
Front axle nut	50-55	–	68-75
Rear axle nut			
1999-2001	60-65	–	81-88
2002-2005	95-105	–	129-142
Transmission drain plug	14-21	–	19-28
Front fork			
Drain plug	–	72-96	8-11
Air connection hex	8-12	–	11-16

AIR SUSPENSION ADJUSTMENTS (1991-2001 MODELS)

Load	Recommended pressure PSI (kPa)	
	Front fork	Rear shock absorbers
Rider weight		
Up to 150 lbs. (68 kg)	–	–
For each additional		
25 lbs. (11kg)	1.0 (7)	1.0 (7)
Passenger weight for each		
additional 50 lbs. (23 kg)	–	1.5 (10)
Luggage weight for each		
additional 10 lbs. (6 kg)	1.0 (7)	3.0 (21)
Maximum pressure	25 (172)	25 (172)

AIR SUSPENSION ADJUSTMENTS (2002-2005 MODELS)[1]

Load	Recommended pressure PSI (kPa)	
	Standard shock shock absorber	Low profile shock absorber[2]
Solo rider weight		
Up to 150 lbs. (68 kg)	0 (0)	0-5 (0-35)
150-200 lbs. (68-91 kg)	0-10 (0-69)	0-10 (0-69)
200-250 lbls. (91-113 kg)	5-15 (35-103)	5-10 (35-69)
Rider with passenger		
Up to 150 lbs. (66 kg)	10-15 (69-103)	20-30 (138-207)
Up to 200 lbs. (91 kg)	20-25 (138-172)	25-35 (172-241)
Maximum GVWR	20-35 (138-241)	40-50 (276-345)

1. The front fork on 2002-2005 models is not equipped with air suspension.
2. Equipped on FLHRS and FLHRSI models only.

FRONT FORK OIL CAPACITY/OIL LEVEL

Model	Capacity/level (each fork leg)
Fork oil capacity	
Non-cartridge type	
1999-2001 models	9.7 U.S. oz. (287 ml, 8.08 lmp. oz.)
2002-2005 models	11.1 U.S. oz. (328 ml, 9.24 lmp. oz.)
Cartridge type	11.1 U.S. oz. (328 ml, 9.24 lmp. oz.)[1]
Fork oil level (cartridge type)	
2002 models	4.4 in. (111.8 mm)[2]
2003-2005 models	4.21 in. (107 mm)[2]

1. The fork oil capacity is approximately this amount. The fork oil level must be at the specified level.
2. From the top surface of the fork tube

MAINTENANCE AND TUNE-UP SPECIFICATIONS

Item	Specification
Engine compression	90 psi (620kN/m^2)
Spark plugs	HD No. 6R12*
Gap	0.038-0.043 in. (0.097-1.09 mm)
Idle speed	950-1050 rpm
Ignition timing	Non-adjustable
Drive belt deflection	5/16-3/8 in. (8-10 mm)
Brake pad minimum thickness	
1999 models	1/16 in. (1.6 mm)
2000-2005 models	0.04 in. (1.02 mm)
Clutch cable free play	1/16-1/8 in. (1.6-3.2 mm)

*Harley-Davidson recommends that no other type of spark plug be substituted for the recommended H-D type.

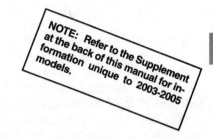
NOTE: Refer to the Supplement at the back of this manual for information unique to 2003-2005 models.

CHAPTER ONE

GENERAL INFORMATION

This detailed and comprehensive manual covers Harley-Davidson FLH and FLT Twin Cam 88 and 103 models from 1999-on. Over a thousand original photos and illustrations based on a complete disassembly of the machine, combined with the hands on text, provide the detail necessary to carry out any procedure safely and efficiently.

A shop manual is a reference tool and as in all Clymer manuals, the chapters are thumb tabbed for easy reference. Important items are indexed at the end of the manual. All procedures, tables and figures are designed for the reader who may be working on the motorcycle for the first time. Frequently used specifications and capacities from individual chapters are summarized in the *Quick Reference Data* at the front of the book.

Tables 1-11 are at the end of this chapter.
Table 1 lists model designation.
Table 2 lists general dimensions.
Table 3 lists motorcycle weight.

Table 4 lists motorcycle weight ratings.
Table 5 lists fuel tank capacity.
Table 6 lists decimal and metric equivalents.
Table 7 lists general torque specifications.
Table 8 lists conversion tables.
Table 9 lists technical abbreviations.
Table 10 lists American tap and drill sizes.
Table 11 lists special tools.

MANUAL ORGANIZATION

This chapter provides general information on shop safety, tool use, service fundamentals and shop supplies. The tables at the end of the chapter include general motorcycle information.

Chapter Two provides methods for quick and accurate diagnosis of problems. Troubleshooting procedures present typical symptoms and logical methods to pinpoint and repair the problem.

Chapter Three explains all routine maintenance necessary to keep the motorcycle running well. Chapter Three also includes recommended tune-up procedures, eliminating the need to constantly consult other chapters on the various assemblies.

Subsequent chapters describe specific systems such as engine, transmission, clutch, drive system, fuel and exhaust systems, suspension and brakes. Each disassembly, repair and assembly procedure is given in step-by-step form.

Some of the procedures in this manual specify special tools. In most cases, the tool is illustrated in use. Well-equipped mechanics may be able to substitute similar tools or fabricate a suitable replacement. In some cases, specialized equipment or expertise may make it impractical for the home mechanic to attempt the procedure. Such operations are identified in the text with the recommendation to have a dealership or specialist perform the task. It may be less expensive to have a professional perform these jobs, especially when considering the cost of the equipment.

WARNINGS, CAUTIONS AND NOTES

The terms, WARNING, CAUTION and NOTE have specific meanings in this manual.

A WARNING emphasizes areas where injury or even death could result from negligence. Mechanical damage may also occur. WARNINGS *are to be taken seriously.*

A CAUTION emphasizes areas where equipment damage could occur. Disregarding a CAUTION could cause permanent mechanical damage, though injury is unlikely.

A NOTE provides additional information to make a step or procedure easier or clearer. Disregarding a NOTE could cause inconvenience, but would not cause equipment damage or personal injury.

SAFETY

Professional mechanics can work for years and never sustain a serious injury or mishap. Follow these guidelines and practice common sense to safely service the motorcycle.

1. Do not operate the motorcycle in an enclosed area. The exhaust gasses contain carbon monoxide, an odorless, colorless and tasteless poisonous gas.

Carbon monoxide levels build quickly in small enclosed areas and can cause unconsciousness and death in a short time. Make sure the work area is properly ventilated or operate the motorcycle outside.

2. *Never* use gasoline or extremely flammable liquid to clean parts. Refer to *Cleaning Parts* and *Handling Gasoline Safely* in this chapter.

3. *Never* smoke or use a torch in the vicinity of flammable liquids, such as gasoline or cleaning solvent.

4. Before welding or brazing on the motorcycle, remove the fuel tank, carburetor and shocks to a safe distance at least 50 ft. (15 m) away.

5. Use the correct type and size of tools to avoid damaging fasteners.

6. Keep tools clean and in good condition. Replace or repair worn or damaged equipment.

7. When loosening a tight fastener, be guided by what would happen if the tool slips.

8. When replacing fasteners, make sure the new fasteners are the same size and strength as the original ones.

9. Keep the work area clean and organized.

10. Wear eye protection *anytime* the safety of the eyes is in question. This includes procedures involving drilling, grinding, hammering, compressed air and chemicals.

11. Wear the correct clothing for the job. Tie up or cover long hair so it can not get caught in moving equipment.

12. Do not carry sharp tools in clothing pockets.

13. Always have an approved fire extinguisher available. Make sure it is rated for gasoline (Class B) and electrical (Class C) fires.

14. Do not use compressed air to clean clothes, the motorcycle or the work area. Debris may be blown into the eyes or skin. *Never* direct compressed air at anyone. Do not allow children to use or play with any compressed air equipment.

15. When using compressed air to dry rotating parts, hold the part so it can not rotate. Do not allow the force of the air to spin the part. The air jet is capable of rotating parts at extreme speed. The part may be damaged or disintegrate and cause serious injury.

16. Do not inhale the dust created by brake pad and clutch wear. These particles may contain asbestos. In addition, some types of insulating materials and

gaskets may contain asbestos. Inhaling asbestos particles is hazardous to health.

17. Never work on the motorcycle while someone is working under it.

18. When placing the motorcycle on a stand, make sure it is secure before walking away.

Handling Gasoline Safely

Gasoline is a volatile flammable liquid and is one of the most dangerous items in the shop. Because gasoline is used so often, many people forget that it is hazardous. Only use gasoline as fuel for gasoline internal combustion engines. When working on a motorcycle, keep in mind that gasoline is always present in the fuel tank, fuel line and carburetor. To avoid a disastrous accident when working around the fuel system, carefully observe the following precautions:

1. *Never* use gasoline to clean parts. See *Cleaning Parts* in this chapter.

2. When working on the fuel system, work outside or in a well-ventilated area.

3. Do not add fuel to the fuel tank or service the fuel system while the motorcycle is near open flames, sparks or where someone is smoking. Gasoline vapor is heavier than air, it collects in low areas and is more easily ignited than liquid gasoline.

4. Allow the engine to cool completely before working on any fuel system component.

5. When draining the carburetor, catch the fuel in a plastic container and pour it into an approved gasoline storage devise.

6. Do not store gasoline in glass containers. If the glass breaks, a serious explosion or fire may occur.

7. Immediately wipe up spilled gasoline with rags. Store the rags in a metal container with a lid until they can be properly disposed of, or place them outside in a safe place for the fuel to evaporate.

8. Do not pour water onto a gasoline fire. Water spreads the fire and makes it more difficult to put out. Use a class B, BC or ABC fire extinguisher to extinguish the fire.

9. Always turn off the engine before refueling. Do not spill fuel onto the engine or exhaust system. Do not overfill the fuel tank. Leave an air space at the top of the tank to allow room for the fuel to expand due to temperature fluctuations.

Cleaning Parts

Cleaning parts is one of the more tedious and difficult service jobs performed in the home garage. There are many types of chemical cleaners and solvents available for shop use. Most are poisonous and extremely flammable. To prevent chemical exposure, vapor buildup, fire and serious injury, note the following:

1. Read and observe the entire product label before using any chemical. Always know what type of chemical is being used and whether it is poisonous and/or flammable.

2. Do not use more than one type of cleaning solvent at a time. When mixing chemicals, measure the proper amounts according to the manufacturer.

3. Work in a well-ventilated area.

4. Wear chemical-resistant gloves.

5. Wear safety glasses.

6. Wear a vapor respirator if the instructions call for it.

7. Wash hands and arms thoroughly after cleaning parts.

8. Keep chemical products away from children and pets.

9. Thoroughly clean all oil, grease and cleaner residue from any part that must be heated.

10. Use a nylon brush when cleaning parts. Metal brushes may cause a spark.

11. When using a parts washer, only use the solvent recommended by the manufacturer. Make sure the parts washer is equipped with a metal lid that will lower in case of fire.

Warning Labels

Most manufacturers attach information and warning labels to the motorcycle. These labels contain instructions that are important to personal safety when operating, servicing, transporting and storing the motorcycle. Refer to the owner's manual for the description and location of labels. Order replacement labels from the manufacturer if they are missing or damaged.

SERIAL NUMBERS

Serial numbers are stamped in various locations on the frame, engine, transmission and carburetor. Record these numbers in the *Quick Reference Data* section in the front of the manual. Have these numbers available when ordering parts.

The frame serial number (**Figure 1**) is stamped on the right side of the frame down tube.

The VIN number label (**Figure 2**) is located just below the frame number on the right side frame down tube.

The engine serial number is stamped on a pad on the left side of the crankcase (**Figure 3**) and the right side of the crankcase (**Figure 4**).

The transmission serial number (**Figure 5**) is stamped on a pad on the right side of the transmission case next to the side door.

The carburetor serial number (**Figure 6**) is located on the side of the carburetor body next to the accelerator pump linkage.

Table 1 lists model designation.

FASTENERS

Proper fastener selection and installation is important to ensure the motorcycle operates as designed and can be serviced efficiently. The choice of original equipment fasteners is not arrived at by chance. Make sure that replacement fasteners meet all the same requirements as the originals.

Threaded Fasteners

Threaded fasteners secure most of the components on the motorcycle. Most are tightened by turning them clockwise (right-hand threads). If the normal rotation of the component being tightened would loosen the fastener, it may have left-hand threads. If a left-hand threaded fastener is used, it is noted in the text.

Two dimensions are required to match the threads of the fastener: the number of threads in a given distance and the outside diameter of the threads.

Two systems are currently used to specify threaded fastener dimensions: the U.S. Standard system and the metric system (**Figure 7**). Pay particular attention when working with unidentified fasteners; mismatching thread types can damage threads.

> *CAUTION*
> *To ensure the fastener threads are not mismatched or cross-threaded, start all fasteners by hand. If a fastener is*

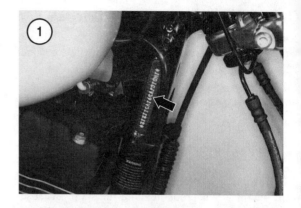

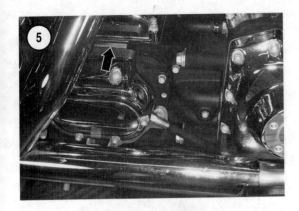

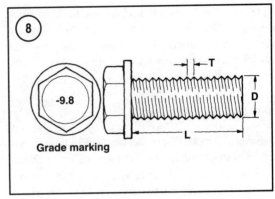

Grade marking

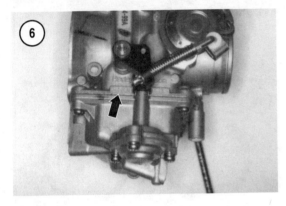

ric screws and bolts. A typical bolt may be identi-fied by the numbers, 8–1.25 × 130. This indicates the bolt has diameter of 8 mm, the distance between thread crests is 1.25 mm and the length is 130 mm. Always measure bolt length as shown in **Figure 8** to avoid purchasing replacements of the wrong length.

The numbers located on the top of the fastener (**Figure 8**) indicate the strength of metric screws and bolts. The higher the number, the stronger the fastener. Unnumbered fasteners are the weakest.

Many screws, bolts and studs are combined with nuts to secure particular components. To indicate the size of a nut, manufacturers specify the internal diameter and the thread pitch.

The measurement across two flats on a nut or bolt indicates the wrench size.

WARNING
Do not install fasteners with a strength classification lower than what was originally installed by the manufacturer. Doing so may cause equipment failure and/or damage.

Torque Specifications

The materials used in the manufacture of the mo-torcycle may be subjected to uneven stresses if the fasteners of the various subassemblies are not in-stalled and tightened correctly. Fasteners that are improperly installed or work loose can cause exten-sive damage. It is essential to use an accurate torque wrench, described in this chapter, with the torque specifications in this manual.

Specifications for torque are provided in New-ton-meters (N•m), foot-pounds (ft.-lb.) and inch-pounds (in.-lb.). Refer to **Table 7** for general torque specifications. To use **Table 7**, first deter-

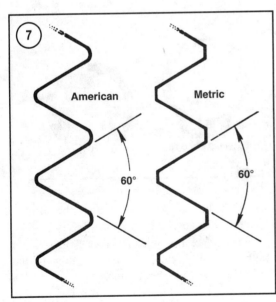

hard to start or turn, determine the cause before tightening with a wrench.

The length (L, **Figure 8**), diameter (D) and dis-tance between thread crests (pitch) (T) classify met-

mine the size of the fastener as described in *Fasteners* in this chapter. Torque specifications for specific components are at the end of the appropriate chapters. Torque wrenches are covered in the *Basic Tools* section.

Self-Locking Fasteners

Several types of bolts, screws and nuts incorporate a system that creates interference between the two fasteners. Interference is achieved in various ways. The most common type is the nylon insert nut and a dry adhesive coating on the threads of a bolt.

Self-locking fasteners offer greater holding strength than standard fasteners, which improves their resistance to vibration. Most self-locking fasteners cannot be reused. The materials used to form the lock become distorted after the initial installation and removal. It is a good practice to discard and replace self-locking fasteners after their removal. Do not replace self-locking fasteners with standard fasteners.

Washers

There are two basic types of washers: flat washers and lockwashers. Flat washers are simple discs with a hole to fit a screw or bolt. Lockwashers are used to prevent a fastener from working loose. Washers can be used as spacers and seals, or to help distribute fastener load and to prevent the fastener from damaging the component.

As with fasteners, when replacing washers, make sure the replacement washers are of the same design and quality.

Cotter Pins

A cotter pin is a split metal pin inserted into a hole or slot to prevent a fastener from loosening. In certain applications, such as the rear axle on an ATV or motorcycle, the fastener must be secured in this way. For these applications, a cotter pin and castellated (slotted) nut is used.

To use a cotter pin, first make sure the diameter is correct for the hole in the fastener. After correctly tightening the fastener and aligning the holes, insert the cotter pin through the hole and bend the ends over the fastener (**Figure 9**). Unless instructed to do so, never loosen a torqued fastener to align the

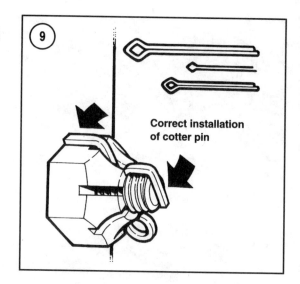

Correct installation of cotter pin

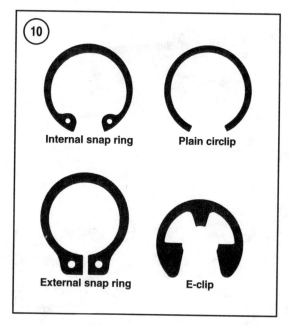

Internal snap ring   Plain circlip

External snap ring   E-clip

holes. If the holes do not align, tighten the fastener just enough to achieve alignment.

Cotter pins are available in various diameters and lengths. Measure length from the bottom of the head to the tip of the shortest pin.

Snap Rings and E-clips

Snap rings (**Figure 10**) are circular-shaped metal retaining clips. They are required to secure parts and gears in place on parts such as shafts, pins or rods. External type snap rings are used to retain

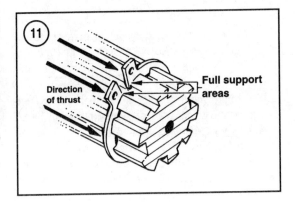

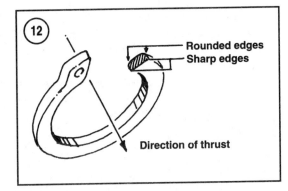

items on shafts. Internal type snap rings secure parts within housing bores. In some applications, in addition to securing the component(s), snap rings of varying thickness also determine endplay. These are usually called selective snap rings.

Two basic types of snap rings are used: machined and stamped snap rings. Machined snap rings (**Figure 11**) can be installed in either direction, since both faces have sharp edges. Stamped snap rings (**Figure 12**) are manufactured with a sharp edge and a round edge. When installing a stamped snap ring in a thrust application, install the sharp edge facing away from the part producing the thrust.

Remove E-clips with a flat blade screwdriver by prying between the shaft and E-clip. To install an E-clip, center it over the shaft groove and push or tap it into place.

Observe the following when installing snap rings:
1. Remove and install snap rings with snap ring pliers. See *Snap Ring Pliers* in this chapter.
2. In some applications, it may be necessary to replace snap rings after removing them.
3. Compress or expand snap rings only enough to install them. If overly expanded, they lose their retaining ability.

4. After installing a snap ring, make sure it seats completely.
5. Wear eye protection when removing and installing snap rings.

SHOP SUPPLIES

Lubricants and Fluids

Periodic lubrication helps ensure a long service life for any type of equipment. Using the correct type of lubricant is as important as performing the lubrication service, although in an emergency the wrong type is better than none. The following section describes the types of lubricants most often required. Make sure to follow the manufacturer's recommendations for lubricant types.

Engine oils

Engine oil is classified by two standards: the American Petroleum Institute (API) service classification and the Society of Automotive Engineers (SAE) viscosity rating. This information is on the oil container label. Two letters indicate the API service classification. The number or sequence of numbers and letter (10W-40 for example) is the oil's viscosity rating. The API service classification and the SAE viscosity index are not indications of oil quality.

The service classification indicates that the oil meets specific lubrication standards. The first letter in the classification (*S*) indicates that the oil is for gasoline engines. The second letter indicates the standard the oil satisfies.

Always use an oil with a classification recommended by the manufacturer. Using an oil with a different classification can cause engine damage.

Viscosity is an indication of the oil's thickness. Thin oils have a lower number while thick oils have a higher number. Engine oils fall into the 5- to 50-weight range for single-grade oils.

Most manufacturers recommend multigrade oil. These oils perform efficiently across a wide range of operating conditions. Multigrade oils are identified by a (*W*) after the first number, which indicates the low-temperature viscosity.

Engine oils are most commonly mineral (petroleum) based; however, synthetic and semi-synthetic types are used more frequently. When selecting engine oil, follow the manufacturer's recommendation for type, classification and viscosity.

Greases

Grease is lubricating oil with thickening agents added to it. The National Lubricating Grease Institute (NLGI) grades grease. Grades range from No. 000 to No. 6, with No. 6 being the thickest. Typical multipurpose grease is NLGI No. 2. For specific applications, manufacturers may recommend water-resistant type grease or one with an additive such as molybdenum disulfide (MoS_2).

Brake fluid

Brake fluid is the hydraulic fluid used to transmit hydraulic pressure (force) to the wheel brakes. Brake fluid is classified by the Department of Transportation (DOT). Current designations for brake fluid are DOT 3, DOT 4 and DOT 5. This classification appears on the fluid container.

Each type of brake fluid has its own definite characteristics. Harley-Davidson FLH/FLT models use silicone based DOT 5 brake fluid. Do not intermix DOT 3 or DOT 4 with DOT 5 type brake fluid as this may cause brake system failure since the DOT 5 brake fluid is not compatible with other brake fluids. When adding brake fluid, *only* use the fluid recommended by the manufacturer.

Brake fluid will damage any plastic, painted or plated surface it contacts. Use extreme care when working with brake fluid and clean up spills immediately with soap and water.

Hydraulic brake systems require clean and moisture free brake fluid. Never reuse brake fluid. Keep containers and reservoirs properly sealed.

WARNING
Never put a mineral-based (petroleum) oil into the brake system. Mineral oil will cause rubber parts in the system to swell and break apart, resulting in complete brake failure.

Cleaners, Degreasers and Solvents

Many chemicals are available to remove oil, grease and other residue from the motorcycle. Before using cleaning solvents, consider how they will be used and disposed of, particularly if they are not water-soluble. Local ordinances may require special procedures for the disposal of many types of cleaning chemicals. Refer to *Safety and Cleaning Parts* in this chapter for more information on their use.

Use brake parts cleaner to clean brake system components when contact with petroleum-based products will damage seals. Brake parts cleaner leaves no residue. Use electrical contact cleaner to clean electrical connections and components without leaving any residue. Carburetor cleaner is a powerful solvent used to remove fuel deposits and varnish from fuel system components. Use this cleaner carefully, as it may damage finishes.

Generally, degreasers are strong cleaners used to remove heavy accumulations of grease from engine and frame components.

Most solvents are designed to be used in a parts washing cabinet for individual component cleaning. For safety, use only nonflammable or high flash point solvents.

Gasket Sealant

Sealants are used with a gasket or seal and are occasionally used alone. Follow the manufacturer's recommendation when using sealants. Use extreme care when choosing a sealant different from the type originally recommended. Choose sealants based on their resistance to heat and various fluids, and their sealing capabilities.

One of the most common sealants is RTV, or room temperature vulcanizing sealant. This sealant cures at room temperature over a specific time period. This allows the repositioning of components without damaging gaskets.

Moisture in the air causes the RTV sealant to cure. Always install the tube cap as soon as possible after applying RTV sealant. RTV sealant has a limited shelf life and will not cure properly if the shelf life has expired. Keep partial tubes sealed and discard them if they have surpassed the expiration date.

Applying RTV sealant

Clean all old gasket residue from the mating surfaces. Remove all gasket material from blind threaded holes; it can cause inaccurate bolt torque. Spray the mating surfaces with aerosol parts cleaner

and wipe with a lint-free cloth. The area must be clean for the sealant to adhere.

Apply RTV sealant in a continuous bead 2-3 mm (0.08-0.12 in.) thick. Circle all the fastener holes unless otherwise specified. Do not allow any sealant to enter these holes. Assemble and tighten the fasteners to the specified torque within the time frame recommended by the RTV sealant manufacturer.

Gasket Remover

Aerosol gasket remover can help remove stubborn gaskets. This product can speed up the removal process and prevent damage to the mating surface that may be caused by using a scraping tool. Most of these types of products are very caustic. Follow the gasket remover manufacturer's instructions for use.

Threadlocking Compound

A threadlocking compound is a fluid applied to the threads of fasteners. After the fastener is tightened, the fluid dries and becomes a solid filler between the threads. This makes it difficult for the fastener to work loose from vibration, or heat expansion and contraction. Some threadlocking compounds also provide a seal against fluid leakage.

Before applying threadlocking compound, remove any old compound from both thread areas and clean them with aerosol parts cleaner. Use the compound sparingly. Excess fluid can run into adjoining parts.

Threadlocking compounds are available in different strengths. Follow the particular manufacturer's recommendations regarding compound selection.

Two manufacturers of threadlocking compound are ThreeBond and Loctite. They both offer a wide range of compounds for various strength, temperature and repair applications.

BASIC TOOLS

Most of the procedures in this manual can be carried out with simple hand tools and test equipment familiar to the home mechanic. Always use the correct tools for the job at hand. Keep tools organized and clean. Store them in a tool chest with related tools organized together.

Quality tools are essential. The best are constructed of high-strength alloy steel. These tools are light, easy to use and resistant to wear. Their working surface is devoid of sharp edges and the tool is carefully polished. They have an easy-to-clean finish and are comfortable to use. Quality tools are a good investment.

When purchasing tools to perform the procedures covered in this manual, consider the tool's potential frequency of use. If a tool kit is just now being started, consider purchasing a basic tool set (**Figure 13**) from a large tool supplier. These sets are available in many tool combinations and offer substantial savings when compared to individually purchased tools. As work experience grows and tasks become more complicated, specialized tools can be added.

Screwdrivers

Screwdrivers of various lengths and types are mandatory for the simplest tool kit. The two basic types are the slotted tip (flat blade) and the Phillips tip. These are available in sets that often include an assortment of tip sizes and shaft lengths.

As with all tools, use a screwdriver designed for the job. Make sure the size of the tip conforms to the size and shape of the fastener. Use them only for driving screws. Never use a screwdriver for prying or chiseling metal. Repair or replace worn or damaged screwdrivers. A worn tip may damage the fastener, making it difficult to remove.

Torx Drivers

Many of the components on the Harley-Davidson models covered in this manual are secured with internal Torx fasteners. These fasteners require specific Torx drivers for removal and installation. These fasteners reduce cam-out and fastener damage, and allow high torque transmission due to the complete enclosure of the driver within the fastener.

Torx screwdrivers in individual sizes, or screwdrivers that accept various bit sizes are available. However, the most practical application is a Torx bit set that accepts various drive types and sizes. A typical set contains T-10 through T40 bits that accept 1/4 and 3/8 in. drive attachments.

Wrenches

Open-end, box-end and combination wrenches (**Figure 14**) are available in a variety of types and sizes.

The number stamped on the wrench refers to the distance between the work areas. This size must match the size of the fastener head.

The box-end wrench is an excellent tool because it grips the fastener on all sides. This reduces the chance of the tool slipping. The box-end wrench is designed with either a 6- or 12-point opening. For stubborn or damaged fasteners, the 6-point provides superior holding ability by contacting the fastener across a wider area at all six edges. For general use, the 12-point works well. It allows the wrench to be removed and reinstalled without moving the handle over such a wide arc.

An open-end wrench is fast and works best in areas with limited overhead access. It contacts the fastener at only two points, and is subject to slipping under heavy force, or if the tool or fastener is worn. A box-end wrench is preferred in most instances, especially when breaking a fastener loose and applying the final tightness to a fastener.

The combination wrench has a box-end on one end and an open-end on the other. This combination makes it a very convenient tool.

Adjustable Wrenches

An adjustable wrench or Crescent wrench (**Figure 15**) can fit nearly any nut or bolt head that has clear access around its entire perimeter. Adjustable wrenches are best used as a backup wrench to keep a large nut or bolt from turning while the other end is being loosened or tightened with a box-end or socket wrench.

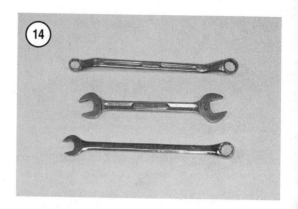
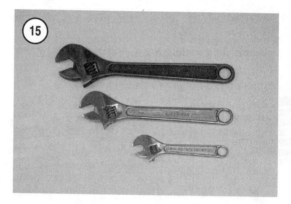
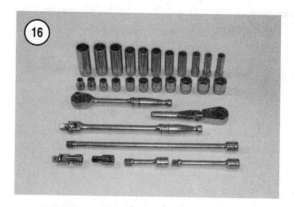

Adjustable wrenches contact the fastener at only two points, which makes them more subject to slipping off the fastener. The fact that one jaw is adjustable and may loosen only aggravates this shortcoming. Make certain the solid jaw is the one transmitting the force.

Socket Wrenches, Ratchets and Handles

Sockets that attach to a ratchet handle (**Figure 16**) are available with 6-point (A, **Figure 17**) or 12-point

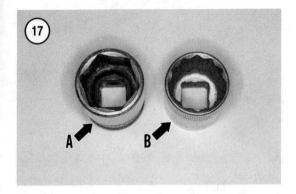

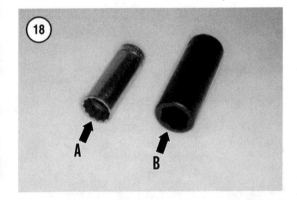

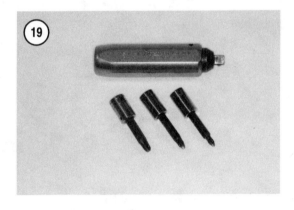

ness of a 19-mm hand socket (A, **Figure 18**) and the 19-mm impact socket (B). Use impact sockets when using an impact driver or air tools. Use hand sockets with hand-driven attachments.

WARNING
Do not use hand sockets with air or impact tools as they may shatter and cause injury. Always wear eye protection when using impact or air tools.

Various handles are available for sockets. The speed handle is used for fast operation. Flexible ratchet heads in varying lengths allow the socket to be turned with varying force, and at odd angles. Extension bars allow the socket setup to reach difficult areas. The ratchet is the most versatile. It allows the user to install or remove the nut without removing the socket.

Sockets combined with any number of drivers make them undoubtedly the fastest, safest and most convenient tool for fastener removal and installation.

Impact Driver

An impact driver provides extra force for removing fasteners by converting the impact of a hammer into a turning motion. This makes it possible to remove stubborn fasteners without damaging them. Impact drivers and interchangeable bits (**Figure 19**) are available from most tool suppliers. When using a socket with an impact driver, make sure the socket is designed for impact use. Refer to *Socket Wrenches, Ratchets and Handles* in this section.

WARNING
Do not use hand sockets with air or impact tools as they may shatter and cause injury. Always wear eye protection when using impact or air tools.

Allen Wrenches

Allen or setscrew wrenches (**Figure 20**) are used on fasteners with hexagonal recesses in the fastener head. These wrenches are available in L-shaped bar, socket and T-handle types. A metric set is required when working on most motorcycles. Allen bolts are sometimes called socket bolts.

(B) openings and different drive sizes. The drive size indicates the size of the square hole that accepts the ratchet handle. The number stamped on the socket is the size of the work area and must match the fastener head.

As with wrenches, a 6-point socket provides superior holding ability, while a 12-point socket needs to be moved only half as far to reposition it on the fastener.

Sockets are designated for either hand or impact use. Impact sockets are made of thicker material for more durability. Compare the size and wall thick-

Torque Wrenches

A torque wrench is used with a socket, torque adapter or similar extension to tighten a fastener to a measured torque. Torque wrenches come in several drive sizes (1/4, 3/8, 1/2 and 3/4) and have various methods of reading the torque value. The drive size indicates the size of the square drive that accepts the socket, adapter or extension. Common methods of reading the torque value are the deflecting beam, the dial indicator and the audible click (**Figure 21**).

When choosing a torque wrench, consider the torque range, drive size and accuracy. The torque specifications in this manual indicate the range required.

A torque wrench is a precision tool that must be properly cared for to remain accurate. Store torque wrenches in cases or separate padded drawers within a toolbox. Follow the manufacturer's instructions for their care and calibration.

Torque Adapters

Torque adapters or extensions extend or reduce the reach of a torque wrench. The torque adapter shown in **Figure 22** is used to tighten a fastener that cannot be reached due to the size of the torque wrench head, drive and socket. If a torque adapter changes the effective lever length (**Figure 23**), the torque reading on the wrench will not equal the actual torque applied to the fastener. It is necessary to recalibrate the torque setting on the wrench to compensate for the change of lever length. When a torque adapter is used at a right angle to the drive head, calibration is not required since the effective length has not changed.

To recalculate a torque reading when using a torque adapter, use the following formula and refer to **Figure 23**.

$$TW = \frac{TA \times L}{L + A}$$

TW is the torque setting or dial reading on the wrench.

TA is the torque specification and the actual amount of torque that will be applied to the fastener.

A is the amount that the adapter increases (or in some cases reduces) the effective lever length as measured along the centerline of the torque wrench (**Figure 23**).

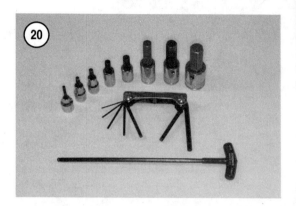

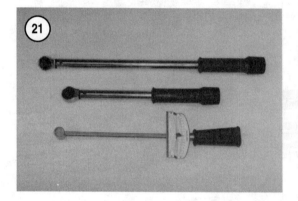

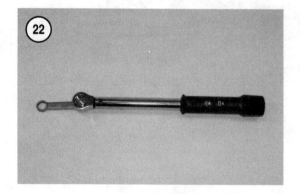

L is the lever length of the wrench as measured from the center of the drive to the center of the grip.

The effective length is the sum of L and A (**Figure 23**).

Example:

TA = 20 ft.-lb.

A = 3 in.

L = 14 in.

$$TW = \frac{20 \times 14}{14 + 3} = \frac{280}{17} = 16.5 \text{ ft. lb.}$$

In this example, the torque wrench would be set to the recalculated torque value (TW = 16.5 ft.-lb.) .

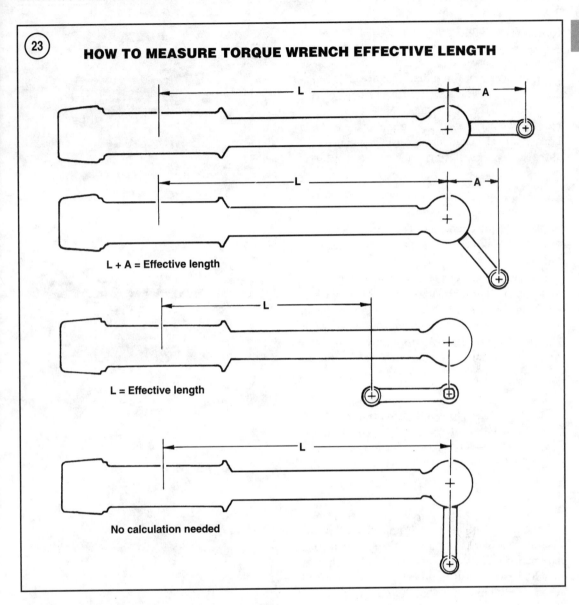

HOW TO MEASURE TORQUE WRENCH EFFECTIVE LENGTH

L + A = Effective length

L = Effective length

No calculation needed

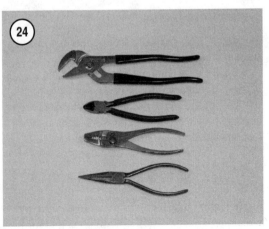

When using a beam-type wrench, tighten the fastener until the pointer aligns with 16.5 ft.-lb. In this example, although the torque wrench is pre-set to 16.5 ft.-lb., the actual torque is 20 ft.-lb.

Pliers

Pliers come in a wide range of types and sizes. Pliers are useful for holding, cutting, bending and crimping. Do not use them to turn fasteners. **Figure 24** and **Figure 25** show several types of useful pliers. Each design has a specialized function. Slip-joint pliers are general-purpose pliers used for gripping and bending. Diagonal cutting pliers are needed to cut wire and can be used to remove cotter pins. Needlenose pliers are used to hold or bend small objects. Locking pliers (**Figure 25**), sometimes called Vise-grips, are used to hold objects very tightly. They have many uses ranging from holding two parts together, to gripping the end of a broken stud. Use caution when using locking pliers, as the sharp jaws will damage the objects they hold.

Snap Ring Pliers

Snap ring pliers are specialized pliers with tips that fit into the ends of snap rings to remove and install them.

Snap ring pliers are available with a fixed action (either internal or external) or convertible (one tool works on both internal and external snap rings). They may have fixed tips or interchangeable ones of various sizes and angles. For general use, select a convertible type pliers with interchangeable tips.

WARNING
Snap rings can slip and fly off when they are being removed and installed. Also, the snap ring pliers tips may break. Always wear eye protection when using snap ring pliers.

Hammers

Various types of hammers (**Figure 26**) are available to fit a number of applications. A ball-peen hammer is used to strike another tool, such as a punch or chisel. Soft-faced hammers are required when a metal object must be struck without damaging it. *Never* use a metal-faced hammer on engine and suspension components, as damage will occur in most cases.

Always wear eye protection when using hammers. Make sure the hammer face is in good condition and the handle is not cracked. Select the correct hammer for the job and make sure to strike the object squarely. Do not use the handle or the side of the hammer to strike an object.

SPECIAL TOOLS

Many of the procedures in this manual require special tools. These are described in the appropriate

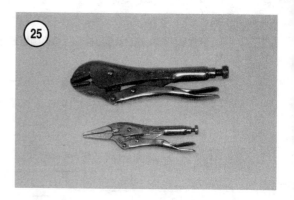

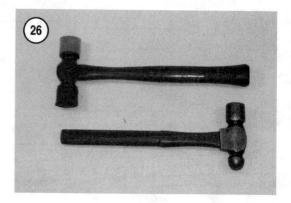

chapter and are available from either the manufacturer or a tool supplier. See **Table 11**.

In many cases, an acceptable substitute may be found in an existing tool kit. Another alternative is to make the tool. Many schools with a machine shop curriculum welcome outside work that can be used as practical shop applications for students.

PRECISION MEASURING TOOLS

The ability to accurately measure components is essential to successfully rebuild an engine. Equip-

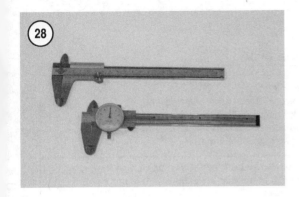

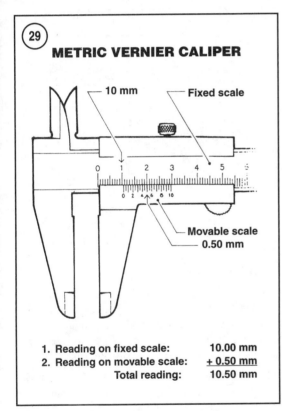

METRIC VERNIER CALIPER

10 mm — Fixed scale

Movable scale
0.50 mm

1. Reading on fixed scale: 10.00 mm
2. Reading on movable scale: + 0.50 mm
         Total reading: 10.50 mm

ment using another tool. A standard gauge is usually provided with measuring tools to check accuracy and calibrate the tool if necessary.

Precision measurements can vary according to the experience of the person performing the procedure. Accurate results are only possible if the mechanic possesses a feel for using the tool. Heavy-handed use of measuring tools will produce less accurate results. Hold the tool gently by the fingertips so the point at which the tool contacts the object is easily felt. This feel for the equipment will produce more accurate measurements and reduce the risk of damaging the tool or component. Refer to the following sections for specific measuring tools.

Feeler Gauge

The feeler or thickness gauge (**Figure 27**) is used for measuring the distance between two surfaces.

A feeler gauge set consists of an assortment of steel strips of graduated thickness. Each blade is marked with its thickness. Blades can be of various lengths and angles for different procedures.

A common use for a feeler gauge is to measure valve clearance. Wire (round) type gauges are used to measure spark plug gap.

Calipers

Calipers (**Figure 28**) are excellent tools for obtaining inside, outside and depth measurements. Although not as precise as a micrometer, they allow reasonable precision, typically to within 0.05 mm (0.001 in.). Most calipers have a range up to 150 mm (6 in.).

Calipers are available in dial, vernier or digital versions. Dial calipers have a dial readout that provides convenient reading. Vernier calipers have marked scales that must be compared to determine the measurement. The digital caliper uses an LCD to show the measurement.

Properly maintain the measuring surfaces of the caliper. There must not be any dirt or burrs between the tool and the object being measured. Never force the caliper closed around an object; close the caliper around the highest point so it can be removed with a slight drag. Some calipers require calibration. Always refer to the manufacturer's instructions when using a new or unfamiliar caliper.

To read a vernier caliper, refer to **Figure 29**. The fixed scale is marked in 1 mm increments. Ten indi-

ment is manufactured to close tolerances, and obtaining consistently accurate measurements is essential to determining which components require replacement or further service.

Each type of measuring instrument is designed to measure a dimension with a certain degree of accuracy and within a certain range. When selecting the measuring tool, make sure it is applicable to the task.

As with all tools, measuring tools provide the best results if cared for properly. Improper use can damage the tool and result in inaccurate results. If any measurement is questionable, verify the measure-

DECIMAL PLACE VALUES*

0.100	Indicates 1/10 (one tenth of an inch or millimeter)
0.010	Indicates 1/100 (one one-hundreth of an inch or millimeter)
0.001	Indicates 1/1,000 (one one-thousandth of an inch or millimeter)

*This chart represents the values of figures placed to the right of the decimal point. Use it when reading decimals from one-tenth to one one-thousandth of an inch or millimeter. It is not a conversion chart (for example: 0.001 in. is not equal to 0.001 mm).

vidual lines on the fixed scale equal 1 cm. The moveable scale is marked in 0.05 mm (hundredth) increments. To obtain a reading, establish the first number by the location of the 0 line on the movable scale in relation to the first line to the left on the fixed scale. In this example, the number is 10 mm. To determine the next number, note which of the lines on the movable scale align with a mark on the fixed scale. A number of lines will seem close, but only one will align exactly. In this case, 0.50 mm is the reading to add to the first number. The result of adding 10 mm and 0.50 mm is a measurement of 10.50 mm.

Micrometers

A micrometer is an instrument designed for linear measurement using the decimal divisions of the inch or meter (**Figure 30**). While there are many types and styles of micrometers, most of the procedures in this manual call for an outside micrometer. The outside micrometer is used to measure the outside diameter of cylindrical forms and the thickness of materials.

A micrometer's size indicates the minimum and maximum size of a part that it can measure. The usual sizes (**Figure 31**) are 0-1 in. (0-25 mm), 1-2 in. (25-50 mm), 2-3 in. (50-75 mm) and 3-4 in. (75-100 mm).

Micrometers that cover a wider range of measurements are available. These use a large frame with interchangeable anvils of various lengths. This type of micrometer offers a cost savings; however, its overall size may make it less convenient.

Reading a Micrometer

When reading a micrometer, numbers are taken from different scales and added together. The following sections describe how to read the measurements of various types of outside micrometers.

For accurate results, properly maintain the measuring surfaces of the micrometer. There cannot be any dirt or burrs between the tool and the measured object. Never force the micrometer closed around an object. Close the micrometer around the highest point so it can be removed with a slight drag. **Figure 32** shows the markings and parts of a standard inch micrometer. Be familiar with these terms before using a micrometer in the follow sections.

Standard inch micrometer

The standard inch micrometer is accurate to one-thousandth of an inch or 0.001. The sleeve is marked in 0.025 in. increments. Every fourth sleeve

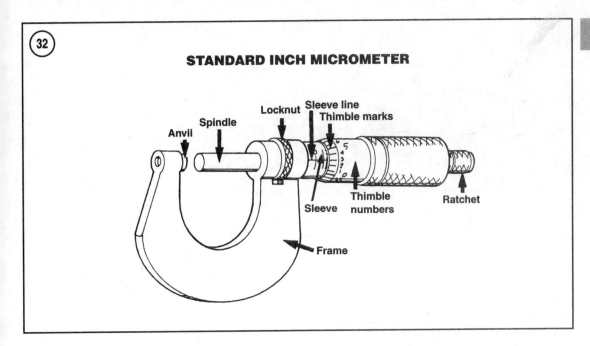

STANDARD INCH MICROMETER

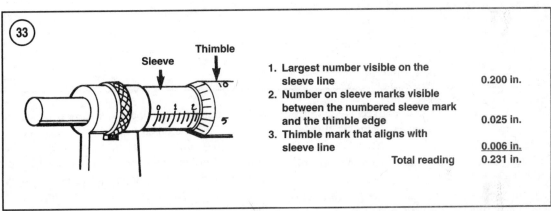

1. Largest number visible on the sleeve line   0.200 in.
2. Number on sleeve marks visible between the numbered sleeve mark and the thimble edge   0.025 in.
3. Thimble mark that aligns with sleeve line   0.006 in.

                 Total reading   0.231 in.

mark is numbered 1, 2, 3, 4, 5, 6, 7, 8, 9. These numbers indicate 0.100, 0.200, 0.300, and so on.

The tapered end of the thimble has twenty-five lines marked around it. Each mark equals 0.001 in. One complete turn of the thimble will align its zero mark with the first mark on the sleeve or 0.025 in.

To read a standard inch micrometer, perform the following steps and refer to **Figure 33**.

1. Read the sleeve and find the largest number visible. Each sleeve number equals 0.100 in.

2. Count the number of lines between the numbered sleeve mark and the edge of the thimble. Each sleeve mark equals 0.025 in.

3. Read the thimble mark that aligns with the sleeve line. Each thimble mark equals 0.001 in.

NOTE
If a thimble mark does not align exactly with the sleeve line, estimate the amount between the lines. For accurate readings in ten-thousandths of an inch (0.0001 in.), use a vernier inch micrometer.

4. Add the readings from Steps 1-3.

Vernier inch micrometer

A vernier inch micrometer is accurate to one ten-thousandth of an inch or 0.0001 in. It has the same marking as a standard inch micrometer with an additional vernier scale on the sleeve. The ver-

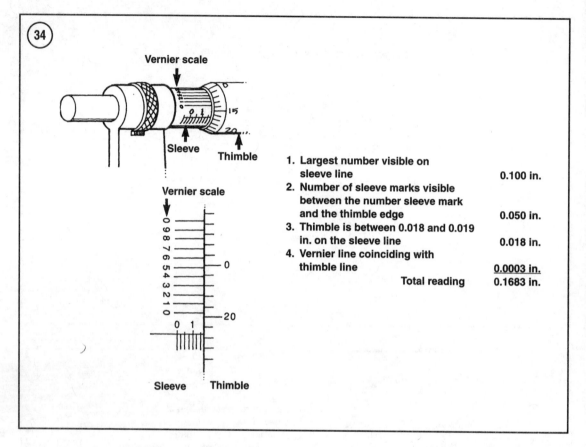

(34)

Vernier scale

Sleeve

Thimble

Vernier scale

Sleeve   Thimble

1. Largest number visible on
   sleeve line   0.100 in.
2. Number of sleeve marks visible
   between the number sleeve mark
   and the thimble edge   0.050 in.
3. Thimble is between 0.018 and 0.019
   in. on the sleeve line   0.018 in.
4. Vernier line coinciding with
   thimble line   0.0003 in.
                              Total reading   0.1683 in.

nier scale consists of 11 lines marked 1-9 with a 0 on each end. These lines run parallel to the thimble lines and represent 0.0001 in. increments.

To read a vernier inch micrometer, perform the following steps and refer to **Figure 34**.

1. Read the micrometer in the same way as a standard micrometer. This is the initial reading.

2. If a thimble mark aligns exactly with the sleeve line, reading the vernier scale is not necessary. If they do not align, read the vernier scale in Step 3.

3. Determine which vernier scale mark aligns with one thimble mark. The vernier scale number is the amount in ten-thousandths of an inch to add to the initial reading from Step 1.

Metric micrometer

The standard metric micrometer (**Figure 35**) is accurate to one one-hundredth of a millimeter (0.01-mm). The sleeve line is graduated in millimeter and half millimeter increments. The marks on the upper half of the sleeve line equal 1.00 mm. Every fifth mark above the sleeve line is identified

with a number. The number sequence depends on the size of the micrometer. A 0-25 mm micrometer, for example, will have sleeve marks numbered 0 through 25 in 5 mm increments. This numbering sequence continues with larger micrometers. On all metric micrometers, each mark on the lower half of the sleeve equals 0.50 mm.

The tapered end of the thimble has fifty lines marked around it. Each mark equals 0.01 mm. One complete turn of the thimble aligns its 0 mark with the first line on the lower half of the sleeve line or 0.50 mm.

To read a metric micrometer, add the number of millimeters and half-millimeters on the sleeve line to the number of one one-hundredth millimeters on the thimble. Perform the following steps and refer to **Figure 36**.

1. Read the upper half of the sleeve line and count the number of lines visible. Each upper line equals 1 mm.

2. See if the half-millimeter line is visible on the lower sleeve line. If so, add 0.50 mm to the reading from Step 1.

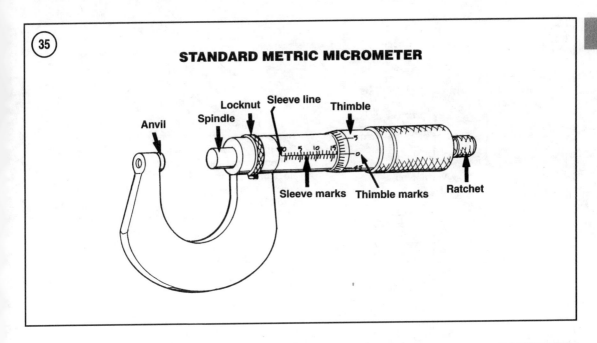

STANDARD METRIC MICROMETER

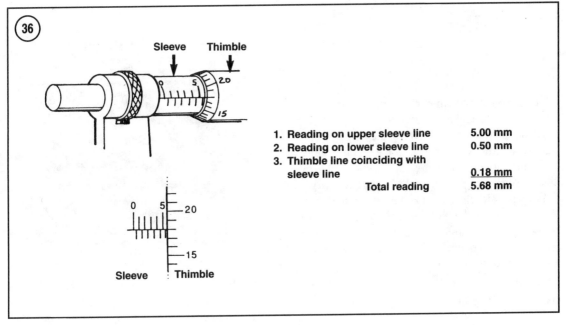

1. Reading on upper sleeve line   5.00 mm
2. Reading on lower sleeve line   0.50 mm
3. Thimble line coinciding with
   sleeve line   0.18 mm
                        Total reading   5.68 mm

3. Read the thimble mark that aligns with the sleeve line. Each thimble mark equals 0.01 mm.

NOTE
If a thimble mark does not align exactly with the sleeve line, estimate the amount between the lines. For accurate readings in two-thousandths of a millimeter (0.002 mm), use a metric vernier micrometer.

4. Add the readings from Steps 1-3.

Metric vernier micrometer

A metric vernier micrometer is accurate to two-thousandths of a millimeter (0.002-mm). It has the same markings as a standard metric micrometer with the addition of a vernier scale on the sleeve. The vernier scale consists of five lines marked 0, 2,

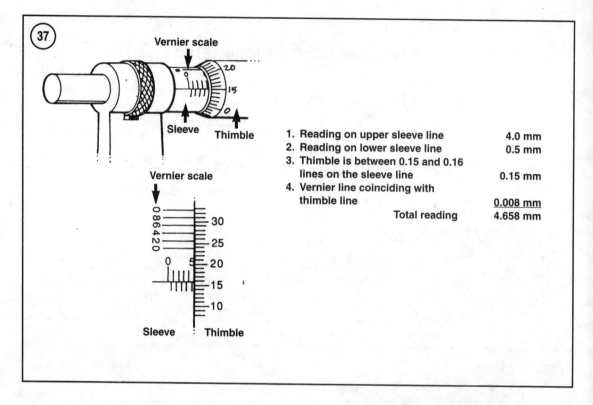

Vernier scale

Sleeve Thimble

Vernier scale

Sleeve : Thimble

1. Reading on upper sleeve line 4.0 mm
2. Reading on lower sleeve line 0.5 mm
3. Thimble is between 0.15 and 0.16
   lines on the sleeve line 0.15 mm
4. Vernier line coinciding with
   thimble line 0.008 mm
   Total reading 4.658 mm

4, 6, and 8. These lines run parallel to the thimble lines and represent 0.002-mm increments.

To read a metric vernier micrometer, perform the following steps and refer to **Figure 37**.

1. Read the micrometer in the same way as a standard metric micrometer. This is the initial reading.

2. If a thimble mark aligns exactly with the sleeve line, reading the vernier scale is not necessary. If they do not align, read the vernier scale in Step 3.

3. Determine which vernier scale mark aligns exactly with one thimble mark. The vernier scale number is the amount in two-thousandths of a millimeter to add to the initial reading from Step 1.

Micrometer Adjustment

Before using a micrometer, check its adjustment as follows.

1. Clean the anvil and spindle faces.

2A. To check a 0-1 in. or 0-25 mm micrometer:
   a. Turn the thimble until the spindle contacts the anvil. If the micrometer has a ratchet stop, use it to ensure the proper amount of pressure is applied.
   b. If the adjustment is correct, the 0 mark on the thimble will align exactly with the 0 mark on

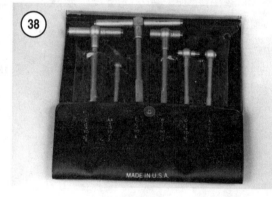

the sleeve line. If the marks do not align, the micrometer is out of adjustment.
   c. Follow the manufacturer's instructions to adjust the micrometer.

2B. To check a micrometer larger than 1 in. or 25 mm, use the standard gauge supplied by the manufacturer. A standard gauge is a steel block, disc or rod that is machined to an exact size.
   a. Place the standard gauge between the spindle and anvil, and measure its outside diameter or length. If the micrometer has a ratchet stop, use it to ensure the proper amount of pressure is applied.

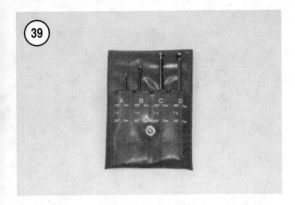

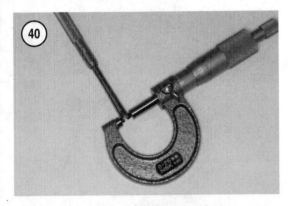

1. Store micrometers in protective cases or separate padded drawers in a toolbox.

2. When in storage, make sure the spindle and anvil faces do not contact each other or an other object. If they do, temperature changes and corrosion may damage the contact faces.

3. Do not clean a micrometer with compressed air. Dirt forced into the tool will cause wear.

4. Lubricate micrometers with WD-40 to prevent corrosion.

Telescoping and Small Bore Gauges

Use telescoping gauges (**Figure 38**) and small hole gauges (**Figure 39**) to measure bores. Neither gauge has a scale for direct readings. An outside micrometer must be used to determine the reading.

To use a telescoping gauge, select the correct size gauge for the bore. Compress the movable post and carefully insert the gauge into the bore. Carefully move the gauge in the bore to make sure it is centered. Tighten the knurled end of the gauge to hold the movable post in position. Remove the gauge and measure the length of the posts. Telescoping gauges are typically used to measure cylinder bores.

To use a small-bore gauge, select the correct size gauge for the bore. Carefully insert the gauge into the bore. Tighten the knurled end of the gauge to carefully expand the gauge fingers to the limit within the bore. Do not overtighten the gauge, as there is no built-in release. Excessive tightening can damage the bore surface and damage the tool. Remove the gauge and measure the outside dimension (**Figure 40**). Small hole gauges are typically used to measure valve guides.

b. If the adjustment is correct, the 0 mark on the thimble will align exactly with the 0 mark on the sleeve line. If the marks do not align, the micrometer is out of adjustment.

c. Follow the manufacturer's instructions to adjust the micrometer.

Micrometer Care

Micrometers are precision instruments. They must be used and maintained with great care. Note the following:

Dial Indicator

A dial indicator (**Figure 41**) is a gauge with a dial face and needle used to measure variations in dimensions and movements. Measuring brake rotor runout is a typical use for a dial indicator.

Dial indicators are available in various ranges and graduations, and with three basic types of mounting bases: magnetic, clamp, or screw-in stud. When purchasing a dial indicator, select the magnetic stand type with a continuous dial.

Cylinder Bore Gauge

A cylinder bore gauge is similar to a dial indicator. The gauge set shown in **Figure 42** consists of a dial indicator, handle and different length adapters (anvils) to fit the gauge to various bore sizes. The bore gauge is used to measure bore size, taper and out-of-round. When using a bore gauge, follow the manufacturer's instructions.

Compression Gauge

A compression gauge (**Figure 43**) measures combustion chamber (cylinder) pressure, usually in psi or kg/cm^2. The gauge adapter is either inserted or screwed into the spark plug hole to obtain the reading. Disable the engine so it will not start and hold the throttle in the wide-open position when performing a compression test. An engine that does not have adequate compression cannot be properly tuned. See Chapter Three.

Multimeter

A multimeter (**Figure 44**) is an essential tool for electrical system diagnosis. The voltage function indicates the voltage applied or available to various electrical components. The ohmmeter function tests circuits for continuity, or lack of continuity, and measures the resistance of a circuit.

Some manufacturers'specifications for electrical components are based on results using a specific test meter. Results may vary if using a meter not recommend by the manufacturer is used. Such requirements are noted when applicable.

Ohmmeter (analog) calibration

Each time an analog ohmmeter is used or if the scale is changed, the ohmmeter must be calibrated.

Digital ohmmeters do not require calibration.
1. Make sure the meter battery is in good condition.
2. Make sure the meter probes are in good condition.
3. Touch the two probes together and observe the needle location on the ohms scale. The needle must align with the 0 mark to obtain accurate measurements.
4. If necessary, rotate the meter ohms adjust knob until the needle and 0 mark align.

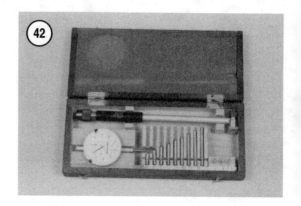

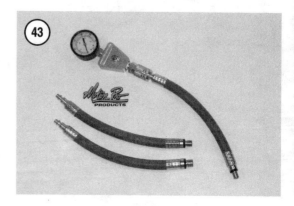

ELECTRICAL SYSTEM FUNDAMENTALS

A thorough study of the many types of electrical systems used in today's motorcycles is beyond the scope of this manual. However, an understanding of electrical basics is necessary to perform simple diagnostic tests.

Voltage

Voltage is the electrical potential or pressure in an electrical circuit and is expressed in volts. The more pressure (voltage) in a circuit, the more work that can be performed.

Direct current (DC) voltage means the electricity flows in one direction. All circuits powered by a battery are DC circuits.

Alternating current (AC) means the electricity flows in one direction momentarily then switches to the opposite direction. Alternator output is an example of AC voltage. This voltage must be changed or rectified to direct current to operate in a battery powered system.

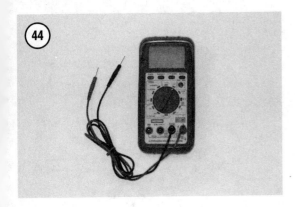

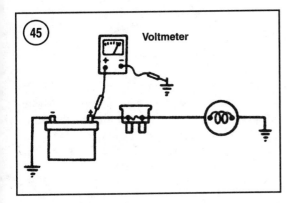

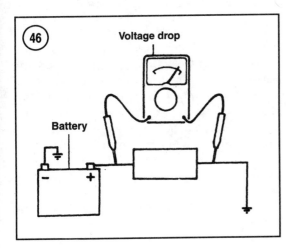

Measuring voltage

Unless otherwise specified, perform all voltage tests with the electrical connectors attached. When measuring voltage, select the meter range that is one scale higher than the expected voltage of the circuit to prevent damage to the meter. To determine the actual voltage in a circuit, use a voltmeter. To simply check if voltage is present, use a test light.

NOTE
When using a test light, either lead can be attached to ground.

1. Attach the negative meter test lead to a good ground (bare metal). Make sure the ground is not insulated with a rubber gasket or grommet.
2. Attach the positive meter test lead to the point being checked for voltage (**Figure 45**).
3. Turn on the ignition switch. The test light should light or the meter should display a reading. The reading should be within one volt of battery voltage. If the voltage is less, there is a problem in the circuit.

Voltage drop test

Resistance causes voltage to drop. This resistance can be measured in an active circuit by using a voltmeter to perform a voltage drop test. A voltage drop test compares the difference between the voltage available at the start of a circuit to the voltage at the end of the circuit while the circuit is operational. If the circuit has no resistance, there will be no voltage drop. The greater the resistance, the greater the voltage drop will be. A voltage drop of one volt or more indicates excessive resistance in the circuit.
1. Connect the positive meter test lead to the electrical source (where electricity is coming from).
2. Connect the negative meter test lead to the electrical load (where electricity is going). See **Figure 46**.
3. If necessary, activate the component(s) in the circuit.
4. A voltage reading of 1 volt or more indicates excessive resistance in the circuit. A reading equal to battery voltage indicates an open circuit.

Resistance

Resistance is the opposition to the flow of electricity within a circuit or component and is measured in ohms. Resistance causes a reduction in available current and voltage.

Resistance is measured in a inactive circuit with an ohmmeter. The ohmmeter sends a small amount of current into the circuit and measures how difficult it is to push the current through the circuit.

An ohmmeter, although useful, is not always a good indicator of a circuit's actual ability under operating conditions. This is due to the low voltage (6-9 volts) that the meter uses to test the circuit. The voltage in an ignition coil secondary winding can be several thousand volts. Such high voltage can cause the coil to malfunction, even though it tests acceptable during a resistance test.

Resistance generally increases with temperature. Perform all testing with the component or circuit at room temperature. Resistance tests performed at high temperatures may indicate high resistance readings and result in the unnecessary replacement of a component.

Measuring resistance and continuity testing

> *CAUTION*
> *Only use an ohmmeter on a circuit that has no voltage present. The meter will be damaged if it is connected to a live circuit. An analog meter must be calibrated each time it is used or the scale is changed. See **Multimeter** in this chapter.*

A continuity test can determine if the circuit is complete. This type of test is performed with an ohmmeter or a self-powered test lamp.
1. Disconnect the negative battery cable.
2. Attach one test lead (ohmmeter or test light) to one end of the component or circuit.
3. Attach the other test lead to the opposite end of the component or circuit (**Figure 47**).
4. A self-powered test light will come on if the circuit has continuity or is complete. An ohmmeter will indicate either low or no resistance if the circuit has continuity. An open circuit is indicated if the meter displays infinite resistance.

Amperage

Amperage is the unit of measurement for the amount of current within a circuit. Current is the actual flow of electricity. The higher the current, the more work that can be performed up to a given point. If the current flow exceeds the circuit or component capacity, the system will be damaged.

Measuring amps

An ammeter measures the current flow or amps of a circuit (**Figure 48**). Amperage measurement re-

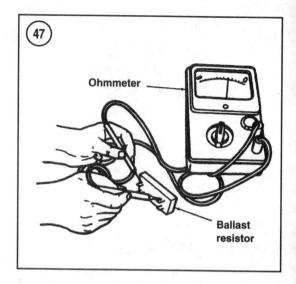

quires that the circuit be disconnected and the ammeter be connected in series to the circuit. Always use an ammeter that can read higher than the anticipated current flow to prevent damage to the meter. Connect the red test lead to the electrical source and the black test lead to the electrical load.

BASIC SERVICE METHODS

Most of the procedures in this manual are straightforward and can be performed by anyone reasonably competent with tools. However, consider personal capabilities carefully before attempting any operation involving major disassembly of the engine.
1. Front, in this manual, refers to the front of the motorcycle. The front of any component is the end closest to the front of the motorcycle. The left and right sides refer to the position of the parts as viewed by the rider sitting on the seat facing forward.
2. Whenever servicing an engine or suspension component, secure the motorcycle in a safe manner.
3. Tag all similar parts for location and mark all mating parts for position. Record the number and thickness of shims as they are removed. Identify parts by placing them in sealed and labeled plastic sandwich bags.
4. Tag disconnected wires and connectors with masking tape and a marking pen. Do not rely on memory alone.
5. Protect finished surfaces from physical damage or corrosion. Keep gasoline and other chemicals off painted surfaces.

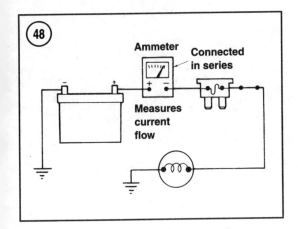

6. Use penetrating oil on frozen or tight bolts. Avoid using heat where possible. Heat can warp, melt or affect the temper of parts. Heat also damages the finish of paint and plastics.

7. When a part is a press fit or requires a special tool for removal, the information or type of tool is identified in the text. Otherwise, if a part is difficult to remove or install, determine the cause before proceeding.

8. To prevent objects or debris from falling into the engine, cover all openings.

9. Read each procedure thoroughly and compare the illustrations to the actual components before starting the procedure. Perform the procedure in sequence.

10. Recommendations are occasionally made to refer service to a dealership or specialist. In these cases, the work can be performed more economically by the specialist than by a home mechanic.

11. The term *replace* means to discard a defective part and replace it with a new part. *Overhaul* means to remove, disassemble, inspect, measure, repair and/or replace parts as required to recondition an assembly.

12. Some operations require the use of a hydraulic press. If a press is not available, have these operations performed by a shop equipped with the necessary equipment. Do not use makeshift equipment that may damage the motorcycle.

13. Repairs are much faster and easier if the motorcycle is clean before starting work. Degrease the motorcycle with a commercial degreaser; follow the directions on the container for the best results. Clean all parts with cleaning solvent as they are removed.

CAUTION
Do not direct high-pressure water at steering bearings, carburetor hoses, wheel bearings, and suspension and electrical components. The water will force the grease out of the bearings and possibly damage the seals.

14. If special tools are required, have them available before starting the procedure. When special tools are required, they will be described at the beginning of the procedure.

15. Make diagrams of similar-appearing parts. For instance, crankcase bolts are often not the same lengths. Do not rely on memory alone. It is possible that carefully laid out parts will become disturbed, making it difficult to reassemble the components correctly without a diagram.

16. Make sure all shims and washers are reinstalled in the same location and position.

17. Whenever rotating parts contact a stationary part, look for a shim or washer.

18. Use new gaskets if there is any doubt about the condition of old ones.

19. If self-locking fasteners are used, replace them with new ones. Do not install standard fasteners in place of self-locking ones.

20. Use grease to hold small parts in place if they tend to fall out during assembly. Do not apply grease to electrical or brake components.

Removing Frozen Fasteners

If a fastener cannot be removed, several methods may be used to loosen it. First, apply penetrating oil such as Liquid Wrench or WD-40. Apply it liberally and let it penetrate for 10-15 minutes. Rap the fastener several times with a small hammer. Do not hit it hard enough to cause damage. Reapply the penetrating oil if necessary.

For frozen screws, apply penetrating oil as described, then insert a screwdriver in the slot and rap the top of the screwdriver with a hammer. This loosens the rust so the screw can be removed in the normal way. If the screw head is too damaged to use this method, grip the head with locking pliers and twist the screw out.

Avoid applying heat unless specifically instructed, as it may melt, warp or remove the temper from parts.

Removing Broken Fasteners

If the head breaks off a screw or bolt, several methods are available for removing the remaining portion. If a large portion of the remainder projects out, try gripping it with locking pliers. If the projecting portion is too small, file it to fit a wrench or cut a slot in it to fit a screwdriver (**Figure 49**).

If the head breaks off flush, use a screw extractor. To do this, centerpunch the exact center of the remaining portion of the screw or bolt. Drill a small hole in the screw and tap the extractor into the hole. Back the screw out with a wrench on the extractor (**Figure 50**).

Repairing Damaged Threads

Occasionally, threads are stripped through carelessness or impact damage. Often the threads can be repaired by running a tap (for internal threads on nuts) or die (for external threads on bolts) through the threads (**Figure 51**). To clean or repair spark plug threads, use a spark plug tap.

If an internal thread is damaged, it may be necessary to install a Helicoil or some other type of thread insert. Follow the manufacturer's instructions when installing their insert.

If it is necessary to drill and tap a hole, refer to **Table 8** for American tap and drill sizes.

Stud Removal/Installation

A stud removal tool is available from most tool suppliers. This tool makes the removal and installation of studs easier. If one is not available, thread two nuts onto the stud and tighten them against each other. Remove the stud by turning the lower nut (**Figure 52**).

1. Measure the height of the stud above the surface.
2. Thread the stud removal tool onto the stud and tighten it, or thread two nuts onto the stud.
3. Remove the stud by turning the stud remover or the lower nut.
4. Remove any threadlocking compound from the threaded hole. Clean the threads with an aerosol parts cleaner.
5. Install the stud removal tool onto the new stud or thread two nuts onto the stud.
6. Apply threadlocking compound to the threads of the stud.

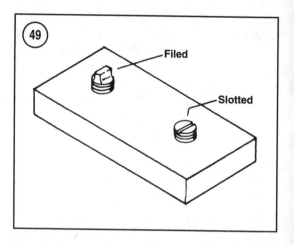

Filed

Slotted

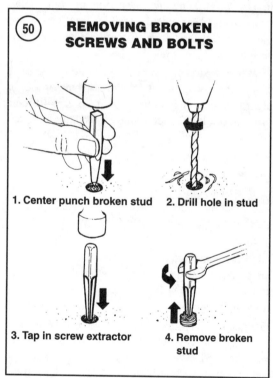

REMOVING BROKEN SCREWS AND BOLTS

1. Center punch broken stud

2. Drill hole in stud

3. Tap in screw extractor

4. Remove broken stud

7. Install the stud and tighten with the stud removal tool or the top nut.
8. Install the stud to the height noted in Step 1 or its torque specification.
9. Remove the stud removal tool or the two nuts.

Removing Hoses

When removing stubborn hoses, do not exert excessive force on the hose or fitting. Remove the hose clamp and carefully insert a small screwdriver

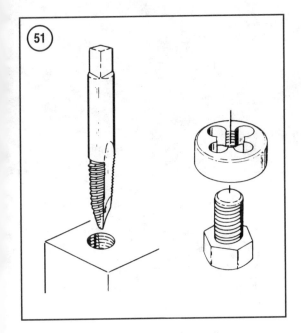

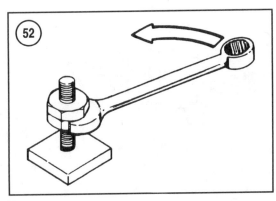

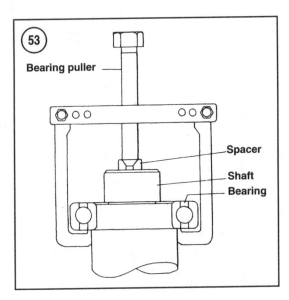

Bearing puller

Spacer

Shaft

Bearing

or pick tool between the fitting and hose. Apply a spray lubricant under the hose and carefully twist the hose off the fitting. Clean the fitting of any corrosion or rubber hose material with a wire brush. Clean the inside of the hose thoroughly. Do not use any lubricant when installing the hose (new or old). The lubricant may allow the hose to come off the fitting, even with the clamp secure.

Bearings

Bearings are used in the engine and transmission assembly to reduce power loss, heat and noise caused by friction. Because bearings are precision parts, they must be maintained by proper lubrication and maintenance. If a bearing is damaged, replace it immediately. When installing a new bearing, take care to prevent damaging it. Bearing replacement procedures are included in the individual chapters where applicable; however, use the following sections as a guideline.

NOTE
Unless otherwise specified, install bearings with the manufacturer's mark or number facing outward.

Removal

While bearings are normally removed only when damaged, there may be times when it is necessary to remove a bearing that is in good condition. However, improper bearing removal will damage the bearing and maybe the shaft or case half. Note the following when removing bearings.

1. When using a puller to remove a bearing from a shaft, take care that the shaft is not damaged. Always place a piece of metal between the end of the shaft and the puller screw. In addition, place the puller arms next to the inner bearing race. See **Figure 53**.

2. When using a hammer to remove a bearing from a shaft, do not strike the hammer directly against the shaft. Instead, use a brass or aluminum rod between the hammer and shaft (**Figure 54**) and make sure to support both bearing races with wooden blocks as shown.

3. The ideal method of bearing removal is with a hydraulic press. Note the following when using a press:

a. Always support the inner and outer bearing races with a suitable size wooden or aluminum ring (**Figure 55**). If only the outer race is supported, pressure applied against the balls and/or the inner race will damage them.

b. Always make sure the press arm (**Figure 55**) aligns with the center of the shaft. If the arm is not centered, it may damage the bearing and/or shaft.

c. The moment the shaft is free of the bearing, it will drop to the floor. Secure or hold the shaft to prevent it from falling.

Installation

1. When installing a bearing in a housing, apply pressure to the *outer* bearing race (**Figure 56**). When installing a bearing on a shaft, apply pressure to the *inner* bearing race (**Figure 57**).

2. To install a bearing as described in Step 1, some type of driver is required. Never strike the bearing directly with a hammer or the bearing will be damaged. When installing a bearing, use a piece of pipe or a driver with a diameter that matches the bearing race. **Figure 58** shows the correct way to use a driver and hammer to install a bearing.

3. Step 1 describes how to install a bearing in a case half or over a shaft. However, to install a bearing over a shaft and into a housing at the same time, a tight fit will be required for both outer and inner bearing races. In this situation, install a spacer underneath the driver tool so that pressure is applied evenly across both races. See **Figure 59**. If the outer race is not supported as shown in **Figure 59**, the balls will push against the outer bearing race and damage it.

Interference fit

1. Follow this procedure to install a bearing over a shaft. When a tight fit is required, the bearing inside diameter will be smaller than the shaft. In this case, driving the bearing on the shaft using normal methods may cause bearing damage. Instead, heat the bearing before installation. Note the following:

a. Secure the shaft so it is ready for bearing installation.

b. Clean all residues from the bearing surface of the shaft. Remove burrs with a file or sandpaper.

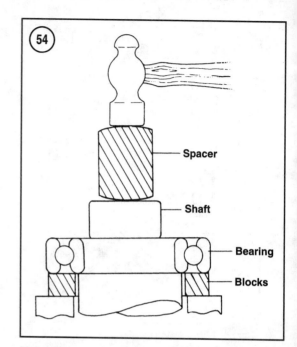

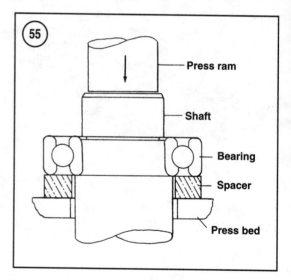

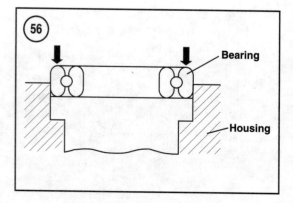

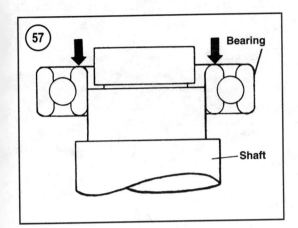

57

Bearing

Shaft

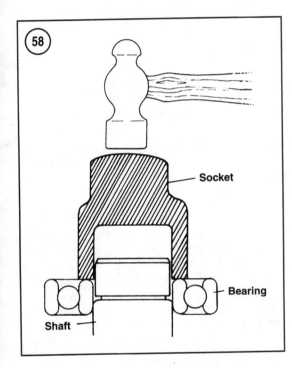

58

Socket

Bearing

Shaft

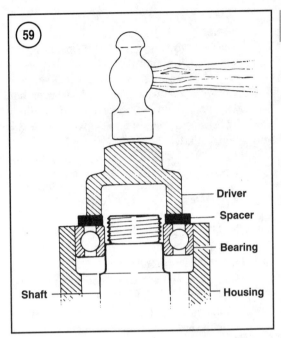

59

Driver

Spacer

Bearing

Shaft

Housing

and tap the bearing into place. As the bearing chills, it will tighten on the shaft, so installation must be done quickly. Make sure the bearing is installed completely.

2. Follow this step to install a bearing in a housing. Bearings are generally installed in a housing with a slight interference fit. Driving the bearing into the housing using normal methods may damage the housing or cause bearing damage. Instead, heat the housing before the bearing is installed. Note the following:

CAUTION
Before heating the housing in this procedure, wash the housing thoroughly with detergent and water. Rinse and rewash the cases as required to remove all traces of oil and other chemical deposits.

a. Heat the housing to approximately 212° F (100° C) in an oven or on a hot plate. An easy way to check that it is the proper temperature is to place tiny drops of water on the housing; if they sizzle and evaporate immediately, the temperature is correct. Heat only one housing at a time.

CAUTION
Do not heat the housing with a propane or acetylene torch. Never bring

c. Fill a suitable pot or beaker with clean mineral oil. Place a thermometer rated above 120° C (248° F) in the oil. Support the thermometer so that it does not rest on the bottom or side of the pot.

d. Remove the bearing from its wrapper and secure it with a piece of heavy wire bent to hold it in the pot. Hang the bearing in the pot so it does not touch the bottom or sides of the pot.

e. Turn the heat on and monitor the thermometer. When the oil temperature rises to approximately 120° C (248° F), remove the bearing from the pot and quickly install it. If necessary, place a socket on the inner bearing race

a flame into contact with the bearing or housing. The direct heat will destroy the case hardening of the bearing and will likely warp the housing.

b. Remove the housing from the oven or hot plate, and hold onto the housing with a kitchen potholder, heavy gloves or heavy shop cloth. It is hot!

NOTE
Remove and install the bearings with a suitable size socket and extension.

c. Hold the housing with the bearing side down and tap the bearing out. Repeat for all bearings in the housing.
d. Before heating the bearing housing, place the new bearing in a freezer if possible. Chilling a bearing slightly reduces its outside diameter while the heated bearing housing assembly is slightly larger due to heat expansion. This will make bearing installation easier.

NOTE
Always install bearings with the manufacturer's mark or number facing outward.

e. While the housing is still hot, install the new bearing(s) into the housing. Install the bearings by hand, if possible. If necessary, lightly tap the bearing(s) into the housing with a socket placed on the outer bearing race (**Figure 57**). Do not install new bearings by driving on the inner-bearing race. Install the bearing(s) until it seats completely.

Seal Replacement

Seals (**Figure 60**) are used to contain oil, water, grease or combustion gasses in a housing or shaft. Improper removal of a seal can damage the housing or shaft. Improper installation of the seal can damage the seal. Note the following:
1. Prying is generally the easiest and most effective method of removing a seal from a housing. However, always place a rag underneath the pry tool (**Figure 61**) to prevent damage to the housing.
2. Pack waterproof grease in the seal lips before the seal is installed.

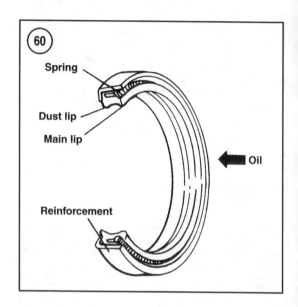

3. In most cases, install seals with the manufacturer's numbers or marks face out.
4. Install seals with a socket placed on the outside of the seal as shown in **Figure 62**. Drive the seal squarely into the housing. Never install a seal by hitting against the top of the seal with a hammer.

STORAGE

Several months of non-use can cause a general deterioration of the motorcycle. This is especially true in areas of extreme temperature variations. This deterioration can be minimized with careful preparation for storage. A properly stored motorcycle will be much easier to return to service.

Storage Area Selection

When selecting a storage area, consider the following:
1. The storage area must be dry. A heated area is best, but not necessary. It should be insulated to minimize extreme temperature variations.
2. If the building has large window areas, mask them to keep sunlight off the motorcycle.
3. Avoid buildings in industrial areas where corrosive emissions may be present. Avoid areas close to saltwater.
4. Consider the area's risk of fire, theft or vandalism. Check with an insurer regarding motorcycle coverage while in storage.

Preparing the Motorcycle for Storage

The amount of preparation a motorcycle should undergo before storage depends on the expected length of non-use, storage area conditions and personal preference. Consider the following list the minimum requirement:

1. Wash the motorcycle thoroughly. Make sure all dirt, mud and road debris are removed.
2. Start the engine and allow it to reach operating temperature. Drain the engine oil and transmission oil, regardless of the riding time since the last service. Fill the engine and transmission with the recommended type of oil.
3. Drain all fuel from the fuel tank, run the engine until all the fuel is consumed from the lines and carburetor.
4. Remove the spark plugs and pour a teaspoon of engine oil into the cylinders. Place a rag over the openings and slowly turn the engine over to distribute the oil. Reinstall the spark plugs.
5. Remove the battery. Store the battery in a cool and dry location.
6. Cover the exhaust and intake openings.
7. Reduce the normal tire pressure by 20%.
8. Apply a protective substance to the plastic and rubber components, including the tires. Make sure to follow the manufacturer's instructions for each type of product being used.
9. Place the motorcycle on a stand or wooden blocks, so the wheels are off the ground. If this is not possible, place a piece of plywood between the tires and the ground. Inflate the tires to the recommended pressure if the motorcycle can not be elevated.
10. Cover the motorcycle with old bed sheets or something similar. Do not cover it with plastic material that will trap moisture.

Returning the Motorcycle to Service

The amount of service required when returning a motorcycle to service after storage depends on the length of non-use and storage conditions. In addition to performing the reverse of the above procedure, make sure the brakes, clutch, throttle and engine stop switch work properly before operating the motorcycle. Refer to Chapter Three and evaluate the service intervals to determine which areas require service.

Table 1 MODEL DESIGNATION

1999-2003
　FLHT Electra Glide Standard
　FLHTC/FLHTCI* Electra Glide Classic
　FLHTCUI* Ultra Classic Electra Glide
　FLHR/FLHRI* Road King
　FLHRCI* Road King Classic
　FLTR/FLTRI* Road Glide

*The I designation indicates fuel injected models.

Table 2 GENERAL DIMENSIONS

Item/model	in.	mm
Wheelbase		
FLHT	63.50	1612.9
FLHTC/FLHTCI	63.50	1612.9
FLHTCUI ULTRA	63.50	1612.9
FLHR/FLHRI	63.50	1612.9
FLHRCI	63.50	1612.9
FLTR/FLTRI	63.50	1612.9
Overall length		
FLHT	93.7	2379.98
FLHTC/FLHTCI	97.5	2476.50
FLHTCUI ULTRA	98.3	2496.82
FLHR/FLHRI	93.70	2379.98
FLHRC	93.70	2379.98
FLTR/FLTRI	93.70	2379.98
Overall width		
FLHT	39.0	990.6
FLHTC/FLHTCI	39.0	990.6
FLHTCUI ULTRA	39.0	990.6
FLHR/FLHRI	34.45	875.03
FLHRC	34.45	875.03
FLTR/FLTRI	35.75	908.05
Road clearance		
FLHT	5.12	130.01
FLHTC/FLHTCI	5.12	130.01
FLHTCUI ULTRA	5.12	130.01
FLHR/FLHRI	5.12	130.01
FLHRCI	5.12	130.01
FLTR/FLTRI	5.12	130.01
Overall height		
FLHT	61.0	1549.4
FLHTC/FLHTCI	61.0	1549.4
FLHTCUI ULTRA	61.0	1549.4
FLHR/FLHRI	55.06	1398.5
FLHRCI	55.06	1398.5
FLTR/FLTRI	55.0	1397.0
Saddle height		
FLHT	27.25	692.15
FLHTC/FLHTCI	27.25	692.15
FLHTCUI ULTRA	27.25	692.15
FLHR/FLHRI	27.25	692.15
FLHRC	26.94	684.27
FLTR/FLTRI	26.94	684.27

Table 3 MOTORCYCLE WEIGHT (DRY)

Model	lbs.	kg
FLHT	742	337
FLHTC/FLHTCI	760	345
FHTCUI ULTRA	772	350
FLHR/FLHRI	707	321
FLHRCI	694	315
FLTR/FLTRI	715	324

Table 4 GROSS VEHICLE WEIGHT RATINGS

	lbs.	kg
Gross vehicle weight rating (GVWR)*	1329	603
Gross axle weight rating (GAWR)		
Front axle	500	227
Rear axle	829	376

*GVWR is the maximum allowable vehicle weight. This includes combined motorcycle, rider(s) and accessory weight.

Table 5 FUEL TANK CAPACITY

Model	U.S. gal	Liters	Imp. gal
Total	5.0	18.9	4.16
Reserve	0.9	3.4	0.75

Table 6 DECIMAL AND METRIC EQUIVALENTS

Fractions	Decimal in.	Metric mm	Fractions	Decimal in.	Metric mm
1/64	0.015625	0.39688	33/64	0.515625	13.09687
1/32	0.03125	0.79375	17/32	0.53125	13.49375
3/64	0.046875	1.19062	35/64	0.546875	13.89062
1/16	0.0625	1.58750	9/16	0.5625	14.28750
5/64	0.078125	1.98437	37/64	0.578125	14.68437
3/32	0.09375	2.38125	19/32	0.59375	15.08125
7/64	0.109375	2.77812	39/64	0.609375	15.47812
1/8	0.125	3.1750	5/8	0.625	15.87500
9/64	0.140625	3.57187	41/64	0.640625	16.27187
5/32	0.15625	3.96875	21/32	0.65625	16.66875
11/64	0.171875	4.36562	43/64	0.671875	17.06562
3/16	0.1875	4.76250	11/16	0.6875	17.46250
13/64	0.203125	5.15937	45/64	0.703125	17.85937
7/32	0.21875	5.55625	23/32	0.71875	18.25625
15/64	0.234375	5.95312	47/64	0.734375	18.65312
1/4	0.250	6.35000	3/4	0.750	19.05000
17/64	0.265625	6.74687	49/64	0.765625	19.44687
9/32	0.28125	7.14375	25/32	0.78125	19.84375
19/64	0.296875	7.54062	51/64	0.796875	20.24062
5/16	0.3125	7.93750	13/16	0.8125	20.63750
21/64	0.328125	8.33437	53/64	0.828125	21.03437
11/32	0.34375	8.73125	27/32	0.84375	21.43125
23/64	0.359375	9.12812	55/64	0.859375	22.82812
3/8	0.375	9.52500	7/8	0.875	22.22500
25/64	0.390625	9.92187	57/64	0.890625	22.62187
13/32	0.40625	10.31875	29/32	0.90625	23.01875
27/64	0.421875	10.71562	59/64	0.921875	23.41562
7/16	0.4375	11.11250	15/16	0.9375	23.81250
29/64	0.453125	11.50937	61/64	0.953125	24.20937
15/32	0.46875	11.90625	31/32	0.96875	24.60625
31/64	0.484375	12.30312	63/64	0.984375	25.00312
1/2	0.500	12.70000	1	1.00	25.40000

Table 7 GENERAL TORQUE SPECIFICATIONS

Type[2]	1/4	5/16	3/8	7/16	1/2	9/16	5/8	3/4	7/8	1
SAE 2	6	12	20	32	47	69	96	155	206	310
SAE 5	10	19	33	54	78	114	154	257	382	587
SAE 7	13	25	44	71	110	154	215	360	570	840
SAE 8	14	29	47	78	119	169	230	380	600	700

1. Convert ft.-lb. specification to N•m by multiplying by 1.3558.
2. Fastener strength of SAE bolts can be determined by the bolt head grade markings. Unmarked bolt heads and cap screws are usually mild steel. More grade markings indicate higher fastener quality.

| SAE 2 | SAE 5 | SAE 7 | SAE 8 |

Table 8 CONVERSION TABLES

Multiply	By:	To get the equivalent of:
Length		
Inches	25.4	Millimeter
Inches	2.54	Centimeter
Miles	1.609	Kilometer
Feet	0.3048	Meter
Millimeter	0.03937	Inches
Centimeter	0.3937	Inches
Kilometer	0.6214	Mile
Meter	3.281	Mile
Fluid volume		
U.S. quarts	0.9463	Liters
U.S. gallons	3.785	Liters
U.S. ounces	29.573529	Milliliters
Imperial gallons	4.54609	Liters
Imperial quarts	1.1365	Liters
Liters	0.2641721	U.S. gallons
Liters	1.0566882	U.S. quarts
Liters	33.814023	U.S. ounces
Liters	0.22	Imperial gallons
Liters	0.8799	Imperial quarts
Milliliters	0.033814	U.S. ounces
Milliliters	1.0	Cubic centimeters
Milliliters	0.001	Liters
Torque		
Foot-pounds	1.3558	Newton-meters
Foot-pounds	0.138255	Meters-kilograms
Inch-pounds	0.11299	Newton-meters
Newton-meters	0.7375622	Foot-pounds
Newton-meters	8.8507	Inch-pounds
Meters-kilograms	7.2330139	Foot-pounds

(continued)

Table 8 CONVERSION TABLES (continued)

Multiply	By:	To get the equivalent of:
Volume		
Cubic inches	16.387064	Cubic centimeters
Cubic centimeters	0.0610237	Cubic inches
Temperature		
Fahrenheit	(F -32°) × 0.556	Centigrade
Centigrade	(C × 1.8) + 32	Fahrenheit
Weight		
Ounces	28.3495	Grams
Pounds	0.4535924	Kilograms
Grams	0.035274	Ounces
Kilograms	2.2046224	Pounds
Pressure		
Pounds per square inch	0.070307	Kilograms per square centimeter
Kilograms per square centimeter	14.223343	Pounds per square inch
Kilopascals	0.1450	Pounds per square inch
Pounds per square inch	6.895	Kilopascals
Speed		
Miles per hour	1.609344	Kilometers per hour
Kilometers per hour	0.6213712	Miles per hour

Table 9 TECHNICAL ABBREVIATIONS

ABDC	After bottom dead center
ATDC	After top dead center
BBDC	Before bottom dead center
BDC	Bottom dead center
BTDC	Before top dead center
C	Celsius (Centigrade)
cc	Cubic centimeters
cid	Cubic inch displacement
CDI	Capacitor discharge ignition
CKP	Crankshaft position sensor
CMP	Camshaft position sensor
cu. in.	Cubic inches
F	Fahrenheit
ft.	Feet
ft.-lb.	Foot-pounds
gal.	Gallons
H/A	High altitude
hp	Horsepower
in.	Inches
in.-lb.	Inch-pounds
I.D.	Inside diameter
kg	Kilograms
kgm	Kilogram meters
km	Kilometer
kPa	Kilopascals
L	Liter
m	Meter
MAG	Magneto
MAP	Manifold absolute pressure
ml	Milliliter

(continued)

Table 9 TECHNICAL ABBREVIATIONS (continued)

mm	Millimeter
N•m	Newton-meters
O.D.	Outside diameter
OE	Original equipment
oz.	Ounces
psi	Pounds per square inch
PTO	Power take off
pt.	Pint
qt.	Quart
rpm	Revolutions per minute
TSSM	Turn signal/security module
TSM	Turn signal module

Table 10 AMERICAN TAP AND DRILL SIZES

Tap thread	Drill size	Tap thread	Drill size
#0-80	3/64	1/4-28	No. 3
#1-64	No. 53	5/16-18	F
#1-72	No. 53	5/16-24	I
#2-56	No. 51	3/8-16	5/16
#2-64	No. 50	3/8-24	Q
#3-48	5/64	7/16-14	U
#3-56	No. 46	7/16-20	W
#4-40	No. 43	1/2-13	27/64
#4-48	No. 42	1/2-20	29/64
#5-40	No. 39	9/16-12	31/64
#5-44	No. 37	9/16-18	33/64
#6-32	No. 36	5/8-11	17/32
#6-40	No. 33	5/18-18	37/64
#8-32	No. 29	3/4-10	21/32
#8-36	No. 29	3/4-16	11/16
#10-24	No. 25	7/8-9	49/64
#10-32	No. 21	7/8-14	13/16
#12-24	No. 17	1-8	7/8
#12-28	No. 15	1-14	15/16
1/4-20	No. 8		

Table 11 SPECIAL TOOLS

Tool description	Part No.	Manufacturer
Belt tension gauge	HD-355381	H-D
Camshaft bearing puller	1280	JIMS
Camshaft remove and installer	1277	JIMS
Camshaft chain tensioner tool	1283	JIMS
Camshaft inner bearing installer	1278	JIMS
Camshaft inner bearing remover tool	1279	JIMS
Camshaft/crankshaft sprocket lock tool	1285	JIMS
Connecting rod bushing tool	1051	JIMS
Connecting rod clamping tool	HD-95952-33B	H-D
Connecting rod bushing hone	HD-422569	H-D
Crankcase bearing snap ring remover and installer	1710	JIMS
Crankshaft assembly removing tool	1047-TP	JIMS
Crankshaft bearing tool	1275	JIMS
Crankshaft bushing tool	1281	JIMS

(continued)

Table 11 SPECIAL TOOLS (continued)

Tool description	Part No.	Manufacturer
Crankshaft guide	1288	JIMS
Cylinder chamfering cone	2078	JIMS
Cylinder stand	HD-39782-A	H-D
Cylinder torque plates	1287	JIMS
Cylinder head stand	HD-39782	H-D
Driver handle and remover	HD-34740	H-D
Drive sprocket lock	2260	JIMS
Engine stand/Twin Cam 88	1022	JIMS
Exhaust valve seat adapter	HD-39782A-4	H-D
Fork seal/cap installer	2046	JIMS
Fork oil level gauge	08-0121	Motion Pro
Hydraulic brake bleeder	–	Mityvac
Intake valve adapter	HD-39782A-3	H-D
Mainshaft bearing race puller and installer	34902-84	JIMS
Motor sprocket shaft seal installer tool	39361-69	JIMS
Retaining ring pliers	J-5586	H-D
Rocker arm bushing retainer	94804-57	JIMS
Rocker arm shaft reamer	94804-57	JIMS
Spark tester	08-0122	Motion Pro
Sprocket shaft bearing cone installer	HD-997225-55B	H-D
Sprocket shaft bearing installation tool	97225-55	JIMS
Sprocket shaft bearing race tool set	94547-80A	JIMS
Timken bearing race installer	2246	JIMS
Transmission bearing and race installer tool handle	33416-80	JIMS
Transmission main drive gear tool set	35316-80	JIMS
Transmission main drive gear bearing tool	37842-91	JIMS
Transmission main bearing remover set	1720	JIMS
Vacuum hose identifier kit	74600	Lisle
Valve cutter set Neway	HD-35758A	H-D
Valve guide brush	HD-34751	H-D
	HD-34751-A	H-D
Valve guide driver	HD-34740	H-D
	B-45524-1	H-D
Valve guide installation sleeve	HD-34731	H-D
Valve guide installer sleever	B-45524-2A	H-D
Valve guide reamer	HD-39932	H-D
	B-45523	H-D
Valve guide reamer T-handle	HD-39847	H-D
Valve guide reamer and honing lubricant	HD-39064	H-D
	HD-39964	H-D
Valve guide hone	HD-34723	H-D
	B-45525	H-D
Valve seat installation tool	HD-34643A	H-D
Valve seat driver handle	HD-34740	H-D
Wheel bearing race remover and installer	33461	JIMS
Wrist pin bushing reamer tool	1726	JIMS

CHAPTER TWO

TROUBLESHOOTING

The troubleshooting procedures described in this chapter provide typical symptoms and logical methods for isolating the cause(s). There may be several ways to solve a problem, but only a systematic approach will be successful in avoiding wasted time and possibly unnecessary parts replacement.

Gather as much information as possible to aid in diagnosis. Never assume anything and do not overlook the obvious. Make sure there is fuel in the tank. On carbureted models, make sure the fuel shutoff valve is in the ON position. If the motorcycle has been sitting for any length of time, fuel deposits may have gummed up the carburetor jets or plugged the injector nozzles on fuel-injected models. Gasoline loses its volatility after standing for long periods and water condensation may have diluted it. Drain the old gas and start with a new tank full. Make sure the engine stop switch is in the RUN po-

sition. Make sure the spark plug wires are attached to the spark plugs.

If a quick check does not reveal the problem, proceed with one of the troubleshooting procedures described in this chapter. After defining the symptoms, follow the procedure that most closely relates to the condition(s).

In most cases, expensive and complicated test equipment is not needed to determine whether repairs can be performed at home. A few simple checks could prevent an unnecessary repair charge and lost time while the motorcycle is at a dealership's service department. On the other hand, be realistic and do not attempt repairs beyond personal capabilities. Many service departments will not take work that involves the reassembly of damaged or abused equipment. If they do, expect the cost to be high.

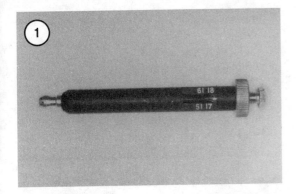

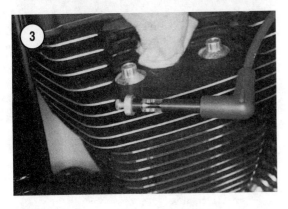

If the motorcycle does require the attention of a professional, describe the symptoms, conditions and previous repair attempts accurately and fully. The more information a technician has available, the easier it will be to diagnose.

By following the lubrication and maintenance schedule described in Chapter Three, the need for troubleshooting can be reduced by eliminating potential problems before they occur. However, even with the best of care the motorcycle may require troubleshooting.

Refer to **Tables 1-4**, at the end of this chapter, for electrical specifications and diagnostic trouble codes.

OPERATING REQUIREMENTS

An engine needs three basics to run properly: correct fuel/air mixture, compression and a spark at the right time. If one basic requirement is missing, the engine will not run. Four-stroke engine operating principles are described in Chapter Four under *Engine Principles*.

ENGINE STARTING

NOTE
*On fuel injected models, do **not** open the throttle when starting either a cold or warm engine. The electronic control module automatically adjusts the fuel mixture to the conditions.*

Engine Fails to Start (Spark Test)

Perform the following spark test to determine if the ignition system is operating properly.

CAUTION
Before removing the spark plugs in Step 1, clean all dirt and debris away from the plug base. Dirt that falls into the cylinder causes rapid engine wear.

1. Disconnect the spark plug wire and remove the spark plug as described in Chapter Three.

NOTE
*A spark tester is a useful tool for testing spark output. **Figure 1** shows the Motion Pro Ignition System Tester (part No. 080122). This tool is inserted in the spark plug cap and its base is grounded against the cylinder head. The tool's air gap is adjustable, and it allows the visual inspection of the spark while testing the intensity of the spark. This tool is available through motorcycle repair shops.*

2. Cover the spark plug hole with a clean shop cloth to reduce the chance of gasoline vapors being emitted from the hole.

3. Insert the spark plug (**Figure 2**), or spark tester (**Figure 3**), into its plug cap and ground the spark

plug base against the cylinder head. Position the spark plug so the electrode is visible.

> *WARNING*
> *Mount the spark plug, or tester, away from the spark plug hole in the cylinder so that the spark plug or tester cannot ignite the gasoline vapors in the cylinder. If the engine is flooded, do not perform this test. The firing of the spark plug can ignite fuel that is ejected through the spark plug hole.*

> *NOTE*
> *If a spark plug is used, perform this test with a new spark plug.*

4. Turn the ignition switch to the ON position.

> *WARNING*
> *Do **not** hold the spark plug, wire or connector, or a serious electrical shock may result.*

5. Turn the engine over with the electric starter. A crisp blue spark should be evident across the spark plug electrode or spark tester terminals. If there is strong sunlight on the plug, shade the plug by hand to better see the spark.
6. If the spark is good, check for one or more of the following possible malfunctions:
   a. Obstructed fuel line or fuel filter.
   b. Malfunctioning fuel pump (EFI models).
   c. Low compression or engine damage.
   d. Flooded engine.
   e. Incorrect ignition timing

> *NOTE*
> *If the engine backfires during starting, the ignition timing may be incorrect due to a defective ignition component. Refer to **Ignition Timing** in Chapter Three for more information.*

7. If the spark is weak or if there is no spark, refer to *Engine is Difficult to Start* in this chapter.

Engine is Difficult to Start

Check for one or more of the following possible malfunctions.
1. Fouled spark plug(s).

2. Improperly adjusted enricher valve (carbureted models).
3. Intake manifold air leak.
4. A plugged fuel tank filler cap.
5. Clogged fuel line.
6. Contaminated fuel system.
7. An improperly adjusted carburetor (carbureted models).
8. Malfunctioning fuel pump (EFI models).
9. A defective ignition module.
10. A defective ignition coil.
11. Damaged ignition coil primary and secondary wires.
12. Incorrect ignition timing.
13. Low engine compression.
14. Engine oil too heavy (winter temperatures).
15. Discharged battery.
16. A defective starter motor.
17. Loose or corroded starter and/or battery cables.
18. A loose ignition sensor and module electrical connector.
19. Incorrect pushrod length (intake and exhaust valve pushrods interchanged).

Engine Will Not Crank

Check for one or more of the following possible malfunctions.
1. Ignition switch turned OFF.
2. A faulty ignition switch.
3. Engine run switch in OFF position.
4. A defective engine run switch.
5. Loose or corroded starter and battery cables (solenoid chatters).
6. Discharged or defective battery.
7. A defective starter motor.
8. A defective starter solenoid.
9. A defective starter shaft pinion gear.
10. Slipping overrunning clutch assembly.
11. A seized piston(s).
12. Seized crankshaft bearings.
13. A broken connecting rod.

ENGINE PERFORMANCE

The following check lists assume the engine runs, but is not operating at peak performance. This will serve as a starting point from which to isolate a performance malfunction.

Fouled Spark Plugs

If the spark plugs continually foul, check for the following:
1. Severely contaminated air filter element.
2. Incorrect spark plug heat range. See Chapter Three.
3. Rich fuel mixture.
4. Worn or damaged piston rings.
5. Worn or damaged valve guide oil seals.
6. Excessive valve stem-to-guide clearance.
7. Incorrect carburetor float level (carbureted models).

Engine Runs but Misfires

1. Fouled or improperly gapped spark plugs.
2. Damaged spark plug cables.
3. Incorrect ignition timing.
4. Defective ignition components.
5. An obstructed fuel line or fuel shutoff valve (carbureted models).
6. Obstructed fuel filter.
7. Clogged carburetor jets (carbureted models).
8. Malfunctioning fuel pump (fuel injected models).
9. Loose battery connection.
10. Wiring or connector damage.
11. Water or other contaminates in the fuel.
12. Weak or damaged valve springs.
13. Incorrect camshaft/valve timing.
14. A damaged valve(s).
15. Dirty electrical connections.
16. Intake manifold or carburetor air leak (carbureted models).
17. Induction module air leak (fuel injected models).
18. A plugged carburetor vent hose.
19. Plugged fuel tank vent system.

Engine Overheating

1. Incorrect carburetor adjustment or jet selection.
2. Incorrect ignition timing or defective ignition system components.
3. Improper spark plug heat range.
4. Damaged or blocked cooling fins.
5. Low oil level.
6. Oil not circulating properly.
7. Leaking valves.

8. Heavy engine carbon deposits.

Engine Runs Rough with Excessive Exhaust Smoke

1. Clogged air filter element.
2. Rich carburetor adjustment (carbureted models).
3. Choke not operating correctly (carbureted models).
4. Water or other fuel contaminants.
5. Clogged fuel line and/or filter.
6. Spark plugs fouled.
7. A defective ignition coil.
8. A defective ignition module or sensor(s).
9. Loose or defective ignition circuit wire.
10. Short circuits from damaged wire insulation.
11. Loose battery cable connections.
12. Incorrect camshaft/valve timing.
13. Intake manifold or air filter air leaks.

Engine Lacks Power

1. Incorrect carburetor adjustment (carbureted models).
2. Engine overheating.
3. Incorrect ignition timing.
4. Incorrectly gapped spark plugs.
5. An obstructed muffler(s).
6. Dragging brake(s).

Engine Lacks Acceleration

1. Incorrect carburetor adjustment (carbureted models).
2. Clogged fuel line.
3. Incorrect ignition timing.
4. Dragging brake(s).

Valve Train Noise

1. A bent pushrod(s).
2. A defective hydraulic lifter(s).
3. A bent valve.
4. Rocker arm seizure or damage (binding on shaft).
5. Worn or damaged camshaft gear bushing(s).
6. Worn or damaged camshaft gear(s).

STARTING SYSTEM

The starting system consists of the battery, starter motor, starter relay, solenoid, start switch, starter mechanism and related wiring.

When the ignition switch is turned on and the start button is pushed in, current is transmitted from the battery to the starter relay. When the relay is activated, it activates the starter solenoid that mechanically engages the starter with the engine.

Starting system problems are most often related to a loose or corroded electrical connection.

Refer to **Figure 4** for starter motor and solenoid terminal identification.

Troubleshooting Preparation

Before troubleshooting the starting system, check for the following:

1. The battery is fully charged.
2. Battery cables are the proper size and length. Replace damaged or undersized cables.
3. All electrical connections are clean and tight. High resistance caused from dirty or loose connectors can affect voltage and current levels.
4. The wiring harness is in good condition, with no worn or frayed insulation or loose harness sockets.
5. The fuel tank is filled with an adequate supply of fresh gasoline.
6. The spark plugs are in good condition and properly gapped.
7. The ignition system is working correctly.

Voltage Drop Test

Before performing the steps listed under *Troubleshooting*, perform this voltage drop test. These steps help find weak or damaged electrical components that may be causing the starting system problem. A voltmeter is required to test voltage drop.

1. To check voltage drop in the solenoid circuit, connect the positive voltmeter lead to the positive battery terminal. Connect the negative voltmeter lead to the solenoid (**Figure 5**).

> *NOTE*
> *The voltmeter lead must not touch the starter-to-solenoid terminal. **Figure 6** shows the solenoid terminal with the starter/solenoid removed to better illustrate the step.*

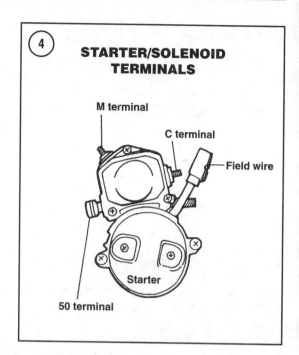

(4) STARTER/SOLENOID TERMINALS

M terminal
C terminal
Field wire
Starter
50 terminal

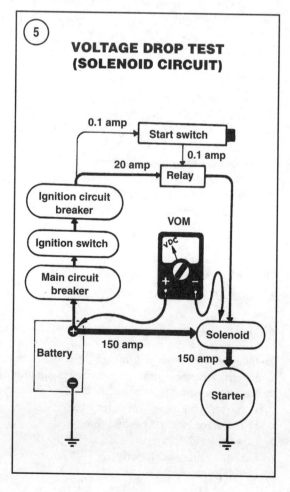

(5) VOLTAGE DROP TEST (SOLENOID CIRCUIT)

0.1 amp
Start switch
0.1 amp
20 amp
Relay
Ignition circuit breaker
VOM
Ignition switch
Main circuit breaker
Battery
150 amp
Solenoid
150 amp
Starter

⑥

3. To check the starter motor ground circuit, connect the negative voltmeter lead to the negative battery terminal. Connect the positive voltmeter lead to the starter motor housing (**Figure 7**).

4. Turn the ignition switch ON and push the starter button while reading the voltmeter scale. The voltage drop must not exceed 0.2 volts. If it does, check the ground connections between the meter leads.

5. If the problem is not found, refer to *Troubleshooting* in the following section.

> *NOTE*
> *Steps 3 and 4 check the voltage drop across the starter motor ground circuit. To check any ground circuit in the starting circuit, repeat this test and leave the negative voltmeter lead connected to the battery and connect the positive voltmeter lead to the ground in question.*

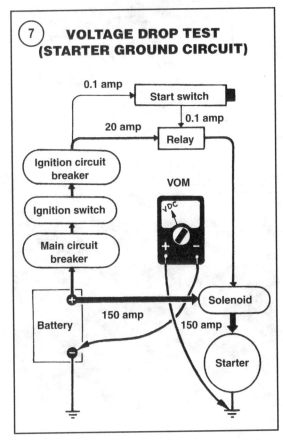

⑦ **VOLTAGE DROP TEST (STARTER GROUND CIRCUIT)**

Troubleshooting

The basic starter related troubles are:

1. Starter motor does not spin.
2. Starter motor spins but does not engage.
3. The starter motor will not disengage after the start button is released.
4. Loud grinding noises when starter motor turns.
5. Starter motor stalls or spins too slowly.

> *CAUTION*
> *Never operate the starter motor for more than 30 seconds at a time. Allow the starter to cool before reusing it. Failing to allow the starter motor to cool after continuous starting attempts can damage the starter.*

Starter motor does not spin

2. Turn the ignition switch ON and push the starter button while reading the voltmeter scale. Note the following:

    a. The circuit is operating correctly if the voltmeter reading is 2 volts or less. A voltmeter reading of 12 volts indicates an open circuit.

    b. A voltage drop of more than 2 volts shows a problem in the solenoid circuit.

    c. If the voltage drop reading is correct, continue with Step 3.

1. Turn the ignition switch ON and push the starter button while listening for a click at the starter relay in the electrical panel. Turn the ignition switch OFF and note the following:

    a. If the starter relay clicks, test the starter relay as described under *Component Testing* in this section. If the starter relay test readings are correct, continue with Step 2.

    b. If the solenoid clicks, go to Step 3.

    c. If there was no click, go to Step 6.

2. Check the wiring connectors between the starter relay and solenoid. Note the following:

    a. Repair any dirty, loose fitting or damaged connectors or wiring.

    b. If the wiring is in good condition, remove the starter motor as described in Chapter Eight. Perform the solenoid and starter motor bench tests described in this section.

3. Perform a voltage drop test between the battery and solenoid terminals as described under *Voltage Drop Test* in this section. The normal voltage drop is less than 2 volts. Note the following:

    a. If the voltage drop is less than 2 volts, perform Step 4.

    b. If the voltage drop is more than 2 volts, check the solenoid and battery wires and connections for dirty or loose fitting terminals; clean and repair as required.

4. Remove the starter motor as described in Chapter Eight. Momentarily connect a fully charged 12-volt battery to the starter motor as shown in **Figure 8**. If the starter motor is operational, it will turn when connected to the battery. Disconnect the battery and note the following:

    a. If the starter motor turns, perform the solenoid pull-in and hold-in tests as described under *Solenoid Testing (Bench Tests)* in this section.

    b. If the starter motor does not turn, disassemble the starter motor as described in Chapter Eight, and check it for opens, shorts and grounds.

5. If the problem is not evident after performing Steps 3 and 4, check the starter shaft to see if it is binding at the jackshaft. Check the jackshaft for binding or damage. Refer to *Starter Jackshaft* in Chapter Five.

6. If there is no click when performing Step 1, measure voltage between the starter button and the starter relay. The voltmeter must read battery voltage. Note the following:

    a. If battery voltage is noted, continue with Step 7.

    b. If there is no voltage, go to Step 8.

7. Check the starter relay ground at the starter relay. Note the following:

    a. If the starter relay is properly grounded, test the starter relay as described in this section.

    b. If the starter relay is not grounded, check the ground connection. Repair the ground connection, then retest.

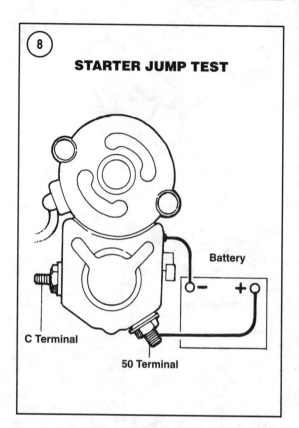

(8)

STARTER JUMP TEST

Battery

C Terminal

50 Terminal

(9)

A

B

(10)

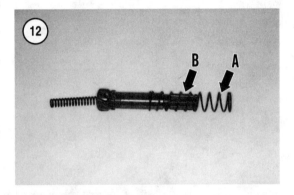

***Starter motor spins
but does not engage***

If the starter motor spins but the pinion gear does not engage the ring gear, perform the following:

1. Remove the outer primary cover as described in Chapter Five.

2. Check the pinion gear (A, **Figure 9**) mounted on the end of the jackshaft. If the teeth are chipped or worn, inspect the clutch ring gear (B, **Figure 9**) for the same problems. Note the following:

    a. If the pinion gear and ring gear are damaged, service these parts as described in Chapter Five.

    b. If the pinion gear and ring gear are not damaged, continue with Step 3.

3. Remove and disassemble the starter motor as described in Chapter Eight. Then check the overrunning clutch assembly (**Figure 10**) for the following.

    a. Roller damage (**Figure 11**).

    b. Compression spring damage (A, **Figure 12**).

    c. Excessively worn or damaged pinion teeth.

    d. Pinion does not run in overrunning direction.

    e. Damaged clutch shaft splines (B, **Figure 12**).

    f. Damaged overrunning clutch assembly (**Figure 13**).

4. Replace worn or damaged parts as required.

***Starter motor will not disengage
after the start button is released***

1. A sticking solenoid, caused by a worn solenoid compression spring (A, **Figure 12**), can cause this problem. Replace the solenoid if damaged.

2. On high-mileage motorcycles, the pinion gear (A, **Figure 9**) can jam on a worn clutch ring gear (B). Unable to return, the starter will continue to run. This condition usually requires ring gear replacement.

3. Check the start switch and starter relay for internal damage. Test the start switch as described under *Switches* in Chapter Eight. Test the starter relay as described in this chapter.

***Loud grinding noises when
the starter motor turns***

Incorrect pinion gear and clutch ring gear engagement (B, **Figure 9**) or a broken overrunning clutch mechanism (**Figure 13**) can cause this problem. Remove and inspect the starter motor as described in Chapter Eight.

8. Check for voltage at the starter button. Note the following:

    a. If there is voltage at the starter button, test the starter relay as described in this section.

    b. If there is no voltage at the starter button, check continuity across the starter button. If there is voltage leading to the starter button but no voltage leaving the starter button, replace the button switch and retest. If there is no voltage leading to the starter button, check the starter button wiring for dirty or loose-fitting terminals or damaged wiring; clean and/or repair as required.

Starter motor stalls or spins too slowly

1. Perform a voltage drop test between the battery and solenoid terminals as described under *Voltage Drop Test* in this section. The normal voltage drop is less than 2 volts. Note the following:
   a. If the voltage drop is less than 2 volts, continue with Step 2.
   b. If the voltage drop exceeds 2 volts, check the solenoid and battery wires and connections for dirty or loose-fitting terminals; clean and repair as required.
2. Perform a voltage drop test between the solenoid terminals and the starter motor. The normal voltage drop is less than 2 volts. Note the following:
   a. If the voltage drop is less than 2 volts, continue with Step 3.
   b. If the voltage drop exceeds 2 volts, check the solenoid and starter motor wires and connections for dirty or loose-fitting terminals; clean and repair as required.
3. Perform a voltage drop test between the battery ground wire and the starter motor as described under *Voltage Drop Tests* in this section. The normal voltage drop is less than 0.2 volts. Note the following:
   a. If the voltage drop is less than 0.2 volts, continue with Step 4.
   b. If the voltage drop exceeds 0.2 volts, check the battery ground wire connections for dirty or loose-fitting terminals; clean and repair as required.
4. Perform the *Starter Current Draw Tests* in this section. Note the following:
   a. If the current draw is excessive, check for a damaged starter motor or starter drive assembly. Remove the starter motor as described in Chapter Eight and test the current as described in this section.
   b. If the current draw reading is correct, continue with Step 5.
5. Remove the outer primary cover as described in Chapter Five. Check the pinion gear (A, **Figure 9**). If the teeth are chipped or worn, inspect the clutch ring gear (B, **Figure 9**) for the same problem.
   a. If the pinion gear and ring gear are damaged, service these parts as described in Chapter Five.
   b. If the pinion gear and ring gear are not damaged, continue with Step 6.

6. Remove and disassemble the starter motor as described in Chapter Eight. Check the disassembled starter motor for opens, shorts and grounds.

Component Testing

The following sections describe how to test individual starting system components. Refer to Chapter Eight for starter service.

Starter Relay Removal/Testing/Installation

Check the starter relay operation with an ohmmeter, jumper wires and a fully charged 12-volt battery.
1. Remove the left side saddlebag as described in Chapter Fourteen.
2. Remove the frame left side cover.
3. Carefully pull the fuse block assembly (**Figure 14**) from the frame mounting tabs.
4. Raise the top cover latches slightly and remove the cover from the fuse blocks.
5. Pull straight up and remove the starter relay (**Figure 15**) from the rear fuse block.

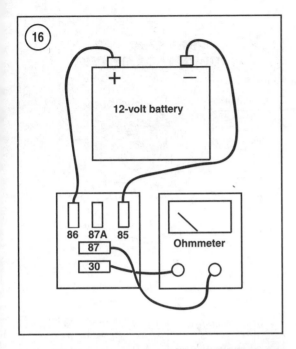

12-volt battery

86 87A 85

87

30

Ohmmeter

CAUTION
*The negative battery lead **must** be connected to the relay terminal No. 85 to avoid internal diode damage.*

6. Connect an ohmmeter and 12-volt battery between the relay terminals shown in **Figure 16**. This setup will energize the relay for testing.

7. Check for continuity through the relay contacts using an ohmmeter while the relay coil is energized. The correct reading is 0 ohm. If resistance is excessive or if there is no continuity, replace the relay.

8. If the starter relay passes this test, reconnect the relay.

9. Install the starter relay (**Figure 15**) into the rear fuse block. Press it in until it bottoms.

10. Install the top cover onto the front and rear fuse block. Press it on until the top cover latches correctly.

11. Reposition the fuse block assembly (**Figure 17**) onto the frame mounting tabs.

12. Install the frame left side cover.

13. Install the left side saddlebag as described in Chapter Fourteen.

Starter Motor Current Draw Tests

The following current draw test measures the current (amperage) the starter circuit requires to crank the engine. Refer to **Table 1** for current draw specifications.

A short circuit in the starter motor or a damaged pinion gear assembly can cause excessive current draw. If the current draw is low, suspect an undercharged battery or an open circuit in the starting circuit.

Current draw test (starter motor installed)

NOTE
This test requires a fully charged battery and an inductive ammeter.

1. Shift the transmission into NEUTRAL.

2. Disconnect the two spark plug caps from the spark plugs. Then ground the plug caps with two extra spark plugs. Do *not* remove the spark plugs from the cylinder heads.

3. Connect an inductive ammeter between the starter motor terminal and positive battery terminal (**Figure 18**). Connect a jumper cable from the negative battery terminal to ground (**Figure 18**).

4. Turn the ignition switch ON and press the start button for approximately 10 seconds. Note the ammeter reading.

NOTE
The current draw is high when the start button is first pressed, then it will drop and stabilize at a lower reading. Refer to the lower stabilized reading during this test.

5. If the current draw exceeds the specification in **Table 1**, check for a defective starter or starter drive mechanism. Remove and service these components as described in Chapter Eight.

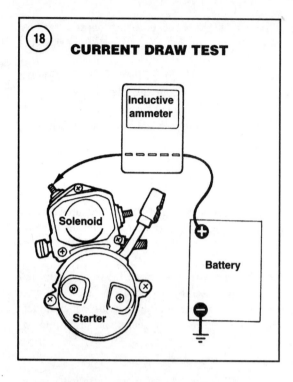

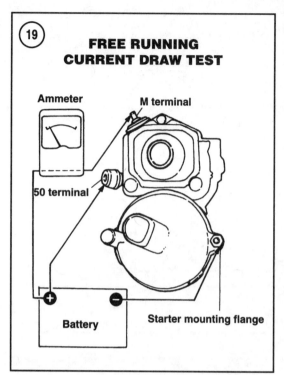

6. Disconnect the ammeter and jumper cables.

Current draw test (starter motor removed)

This test requires a fully charged 12-volt battery, an inductive ammeter, a jumper wire (14 gauge minimum) and three jumper cables (6-gauge minimum).
1. Remove the starter motor as described in Chapter Eight.

NOTE
The solenoid must be installed on the starter motor during the following tests.

2. Mount the starter motor in a vise with soft jaws.
3. Connect the 14-gauge jumper cable between the positive battery terminal and the solenoid 50 terminal (**Figure 19**).
4. Connect a jumper cable (6-gauge minimum) between the positive battery terminal and the ammeter (**Figure 19**).
5. Connect the second jumper cable between the ammeter and the M terminal on the starter solenoid (**Figure 19**).
6. Connect the third jumper cable between the battery ground terminal and the starter motor mounting flange (**Figure 19**).

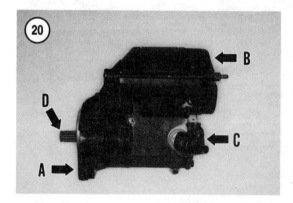

7. Read the ammeter; the correct ammeter reading is 90 amps. A damaged pinion gear assembly will cause an excessively high current draw reading. If the current draw reading is low, check for an undercharged battery, or an open field winding or armature in the starter motor.

Solenoid Testing (Bench Tests)

This test requires a fully charged 12-volt battery and three jumper wires.

1. Remove the starter motor (A, **Figure 20**) as described in Chapter Eight.

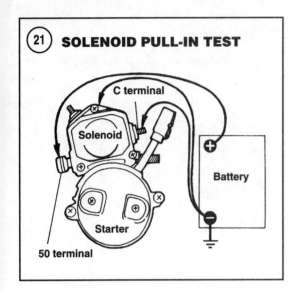

(21) **SOLENOID PULL-IN TEST**

C terminal

Solenoid

Battery

Starter

50 terminal

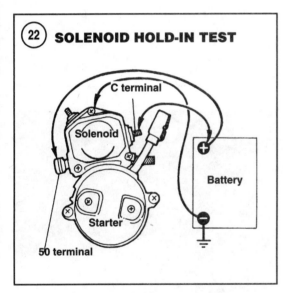

(22) **SOLENOID HOLD-IN TEST**

C terminal

Solenoid

Battery

Starter

50 terminal

NOTE
*The solenoid (B, **Figure 20**) must be installed on the starter motor during the following tests.*

2. Disconnect the C field wire terminal (C, **Figure 20**) from the solenoid before performing the following tests. Insulate the end of the wire terminal so that it cannot short out on any of the test connectors.

CAUTION
Because battery voltage is being applied directly to the solenoid and starter in the following tests, do not leave the jumper cables connected to

the solenoid for more than 3-5 seconds; otherwise, the voltage will damage the solenoid.

NOTE
Thoroughly read the following procedure to become familiar with and understand the procedures and test connections, then perform the tests in the order listed and without interruption.

3. Perform the solenoid pull-in test as follows:
    a. Connect one jumper wire from the negative battery terminal to the solenoid C terminal (**Figure 21**).
    b. Connect one jumper wire from the negative battery terminal to the solenoid housing (ground) (**Figure 21**).
    c. Touch a jumper wire from the positive battery terminal to the starter 50 terminal (**Figure 21**). The pinion shaft (D, **Figure 20**) should pull into the housing.
    d. Leave the jumper wires connected and continue with Step 4.
4. To perform the solenoid hold-in test, perform the following:
    a. With the pinion shaft pulled in (Step 3), disconnect the C terminal jumper wire from the negative battery terminal and connect it to the positive battery terminal (**Figure 22**). The pinion shaft should remain in the housing. If the pinion shaft returns to its normal position, replace the solenoid.
    b. Leave the jumper wires connected and continue with Step 5.
5. To perform the solenoid return test, perform the following:
    a. Disconnect the jumper wire from the starter 50 terminal (**Figure 23**); the pinion shaft must return to its out position.
    b. Disconnect all of the jumper wires from the solenoid and battery.
6. Replace the solenoid if the starter shaft failed to operate as described in Steps 3-5. See *Solenoid Replacement* in Chapter Eight.

CHARGING SYSTEM

The charging system consists of the battery, alternator and a solid state rectifier/voltage regulator.

The alternator generates alternating current (AC) which the rectifier converts to direct current (DC). The regulator maintains the voltage to the battery and load (lights, ignition and accessories) at a constant voltage despite variations in engine speed and load.

A malfunction in the charging system generally causes the battery to remain undercharged.

Service Precautions

Before servicing the charging system, observe the following precautions to prevent damage to any charging system component.

1. Never reverse battery connections.
2. Do not short across any connection.
3. Never start the engine with the alternator disconnected from the voltage regulator/rectifier unless instructed to do so during testing.
4. Never attempt to start or run the engine with the battery disconnected.
5. Never attempt to use a high-output battery charger to help start the engine.
6. Before charging the battery, remove it from the motorcycle as described in Chapter Eight.
7. Never disconnect the voltage regulator/rectifier connector with the engine running. The voltage regulator/rectifier (**Figure 24**) is mounted on the front frame cross member.
8. Do not mount the voltage regulator/rectifier unit in another location.
9. Make sure the negative battery terminal is connected to the engine and frame.

Troubleshooting Sequence

If the battery is discharged, perform the following procedures as listed.

1. Test the battery as described in Chapter Eight. Charge the battery if necessary. If the battery will not hold a charge while riding, perform the *Charging System Output Test*.
2. If the charging system output is with specification, determine the total amount of current demand by the electrical system and all accessories as described under *Electrical System Current Load Test*.
3. If the charging system output exceeds the current demand and the battery continues to not hold a charge, perform the *Current Drain Test*.

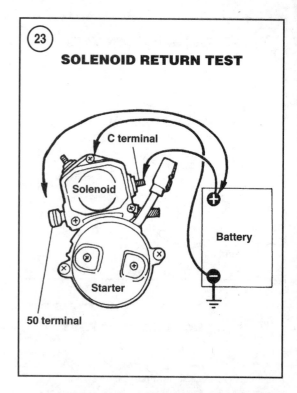

(23)

SOLENOID RETURN TEST

C terminal

Solenoid

Starter

50 terminal

Battery

(24)

4. If the charging system output is not within specification, test the stator and voltage regulator as described in this section.

5. If the battery will not hold a charge when the motorcycle is not in use, perform the *Current Drain Test*.

Charging System Output Test

This test requires a load tester.

1. To perform this test, the battery must be fully charged.

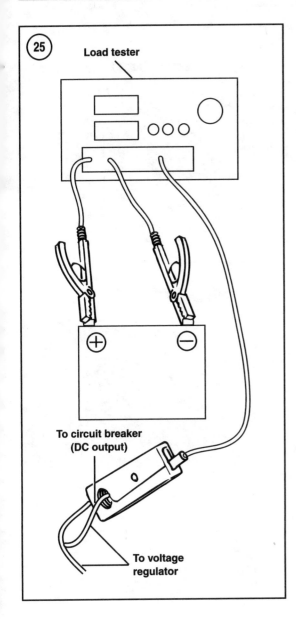

Load tester

To circuit breaker
(DC output)

To voltage
regulator

CAUTION
When using a load tester, refer to the manufacturer's instructions. To prevent tester damage caused by overheating, do not leave the load switch ON for more than 20 seconds at a time.

2. Connect the load tester negative and positive leads to the battery terminals. Then place the load tester's inductive pickup over the circuit breaker to voltage regulator wire (**Figure 25**).

3. Start the engine and slowly bring the speed up to 3000 rpm while reading the load tester scale. With the engine running at 3000 rpm, operate the load tester switch until the voltage scale reads 13.0 volts. The tester should show an alternator current output reading as follows:

    a. Carbureted models: 34-40 amps.

    b. Fuel injected models: 41-48 amps.

4. With the engine still running at 3000 rpm, turn the load switch off and read the load tester voltage scale. Battery voltage should not exceed 15 volts. Turn the engine off and disconnect the load tester from the motorcycle.

5. Perform the *Stator Test* described in this chapter. If the stator tests acceptable, a defective voltage regulator/rectifier or a wiring short circuit is indicated.

Make sure to eliminate the possibility of a poor connection or damaged wiring before replacing the voltage regulator/rectifier.

Electrical System Current Load Test

This test, requiring a load tester, measures the total current load of the electrical system and any additional accessories while the engine is running. Perform this test if the battery keeps being discharged, yet the charging system output is within specifications.

If aftermarket electrical components have been added to the motorcycle, the increased current demand may exceed the charging systems capacity and result in a discharged battery.

CAUTION
When using a load tester, refer to the manufacturer's instructions. To prevent tester damage caused by overheating, do not leave the load switch ON for more than 20 seconds at a time.

1. Connect a load tester to the battery as shown in **Figure 26**.

2. Turn the ignition switch ON but do not start the engine. Then turn on *all* electrical accessories and switch the headlight beam to HIGH.

3. Read the ampere reading (current draw) on the load tester and compare it to the test results obtained in the *Charging System Output Test* in this chapter. The charging system output test results (current reading) must exceed the current draw by

3.5 amps for the battery to remain sufficiently charged.

4. If aftermarket accessories have been added to the motorcycle, disconnect them and repeat Step 2. If the current draw is now within the specification, the problem is with the additional accessories.

5. If no accessories have been added to the motorcycle, a short circuit may be causing the battery to discharge.

Stator Test

1. With the ignition switch turned OFF, disconnect the regulator/rectifier connector from the crankcase (**Figure 27**).

2. Switch an ohmmeter to its R × 1 scale. Then connect it between either stator socket at the crankcase and ground (**Figure 28**). The correct ohmmeter reading is infinity. Any other reading suggests a grounded stator. Repeat this test for the other stator socket.

3. Switch an ohmmeter to its R × 1 scale. Then connect it between both stator sockets at the crankcase. The correct ohmmeter reading should be less than 0.5 ohm. If the resistance is not as specified, replace the stator.

4. Check stator AC voltage output as follows:
   a. Connect an AC voltmeter across the stator pins as shown in **Figure 29**.
   b. Start the engine and slowly increase engine speed to 2000 rpms. The AC output on carburetted models is 16-20 VAC per 1000 rpm. The AC output on fuel injected models is 19-26 VAC per 1000 rpm.

> *NOTE*
> ***Figure 30*** *is shown with the primary chain housing removed to better illustrate the step.*

   c. If the AC voltage output reading is below the specified range, the problem is probably a defective stator (**Figure 30**) or rotor. If these parts are not damaged, perform the *Charging System Output Test* in this section.

5. Reconnect the regulator/rectifier connector.

Voltage Regulator Ground Test

The voltage regulator base (**Figure 24**) must be grounded to the frame for proper operation.

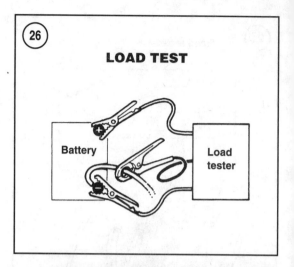

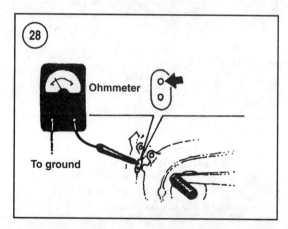

1. Switch an ohmmeter to the R × 1 scale.

2. Connect one ohmmeter lead to a good engine or frame ground and the other ohmmeter lead to the regulator base. Read the ohmmeter scale. The correct reading is 0 ohm. Note the following:
   a. If there is low resistance (0 ohm), the voltage regulator is properly grounded.

29 CHECKING ALTERNATOR OUTPUT

AC voltmeter

30

31

b. If there is high resistance, remove the voltage regulator and clean its frame mounting points.

3. Check the voltage regulator connector plug. Cut the wire clamp, lower the connector and make sure it is (**Figure 31**) is clean and tightly connected. Re-

position the connector onto the frame and secure it with a new wire clamp.

Voltage Regulator Bleed Test

> *NOTE*
> *Figure 27 is shown with the primary chain case removed to better illustrate the step.*

1. Disconnect the voltage regulator connector from the engine crankcase (**Figure 27**).

> *NOTE*
> *Do not disconnect the wire from the voltage regulator to the circuit breaker.*

2. Connect one probe of a 12-volt test lamp to a good frame or engine ground.
3. Connect the other test lamp probe to one of the voltage regulator pins, then to the other pin.
4. If the test lamp lights, replace the voltage regulator.
5. If the voltage regulator passes this test, reconnect the voltage regulator connector at the engine crankcase.

Current Drain Test

This test measures the current draw or drain on the battery when all electrical systems and accessories are off. Perform this test if the battery will not hold a charge when the motorcycle is not being used. A current draw that exceeds 7 mA will discharge the battery. The ECM (1 mA), voltage regulator (2 mA) and radio memory (4 mA) account for the 7 mA current draw. The battery must be fully charged to perform this test.

1. Disconnect the negative battery cable from the battery.
2. Connect an ammeter between the negative battery terminal and the battery ground cable as shown in **Figure 32**.
3. With the ignition switch, lights and all accessories turned off, read the ammeter. If the current drain exceeds 7 mA, continue with Step 4.
4. Refer to the wiring diagrams at the end of the manual for the necessary model. Check the charging system wires and connectors for shorts or other damage.

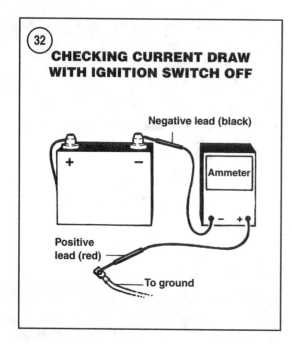

CHECKING CURRENT DRAW WITH IGNITION SWITCH OFF

5. Unplug each electrical connector separately and check for a change in the meter reading. If the meter reading changes after a connector is disconnected, the damaged circuit has been found. Check the electrical connectors carefully before testing individual components.

6. After completing the test, disconnect the ammeter and reconnect the negative battery cable.

IGNITION SYSTEM

All models are equipped with a transistorized ignition system. This solid-state system uses no contact breaker points to trigger the ignition. Refer to the wiring diagrams at the end of this book for the necessary model and year.

Because of the solid-state design, problems with the transistorized system are rare. If a problem occurs, it generally causes a weak spark or no spark at all. An ignition system with a weak spark or no spark is relatively easy to troubleshoot. It is difficult, however, to troubleshoot an ignition system that only malfunctions when the engine is hot or under load.

Ignition System Precautions

The following measures must be taken to protect the ignition system.

1. Never disconnect any of the electrical connectors while the engine is running.

2. Apply dielectric grease to all electrical connectors prior to reconnecting them. This will help seal out moisture.

3. Make sure all electrical connectors are free of corrosion and are completely coupled to each other.

4. The ignition control module must always be mounted securely to the backside of the electrical panel.

Troubleshooting Preparation

1. Refer to the wiring diagrams at the end of this book for the specific model.

2. Check the wiring harness for visible signs of damage.

3. Make sure all connectors are properly attached to each other and locked in place.

4. Check all electrical components for a good ground to the engine.

5. Check all wiring for short circuits or open circuits.

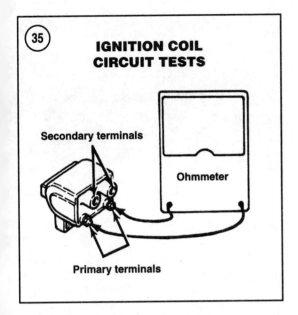

(35)

IGNITION COIL CIRCUIT TESTS

Secondary terminals

Ohmmeter

Primary terminals

(36)

Ignition Module or Electronic Control Module Testing and Replacement

If the ignition module, or electronic control module, is suspected of being defective, have it tested by a H-D dealership before purchasing a replacement. The cost of the test will not exceed the cost of replacing an ignition module, or electronic control module, that may not repair the problem. Most parts suppliers will not accept returns on electrical components.

Ignition Coil Testing

Use an ohmmeter to check the ignition coil secondary and primary resistance. Test the coil twice: first when it is cold (room temperature), then at normal operating temperature. If the engine will not start, heat the coil with a hair dryer, then test with the ohmmeter.

1. Remove the seat as described in Chapter Fourteen.
2. Remove the fuel tank as described in Chapter Seven.
3. Disconnect the primary wire connector (A, **Figure 34**) and the secondary wires (B) from the ignition coil.

NOTE
When switching between ohmmeter scales in the following tests, always cross the test leads and zero the needle to assure a correct reading (analog meter only).

4. Set an ohmmeter on R × 1. Measure the ignition coil primary resistance between the coil primary terminals (**Figure 35**). Compare the reading to the specification in **Table 2**. Replace the ignition coil if the reading is not within specification.
5. Set the ohmmeter on its highest scale. Measure the resistance between the secondary terminals (**Figure 35**). Compare the reading to the specification in **Table 2**. Replace the ignition coil if the reading is not within specification.

Ignition Coil Cables and Caps Inspection

All models are equipped with resistor- or suppression-type spark plug cables (**Figure 36**, typical). These cables reduce radio interference. The

6. Remove the seat as described in Chapter Fourteen.

7. Check for a damaged ignition circuit breaker (**Figure 33**) located under the seat.

8. Make sure the fuel tank has an adequate supply of fresh gasoline.

9. Check the spark plug cable routing and the connections at the spark plugs. If there is no spark or only a weak one, repeat the test with new spark plugs. If the condition remains the same with new spark plugs and if all external wiring connections are good, the problem is most likely in the ignition system. If a strong spark is present, the problem is probably not in the ignition system. Check the fuel system.

10. Remove the spark plugs and examine them as described in Chapter Three.

cable's conductor consists of a carbon-impregnated fabric core material instead of solid wire.

If a plug cable becomes damaged, due to either corrosion or conductor breaks, its resistance increases. Excessive cable resistance will cause engine misfire and other ignition or driveability problems.

When troubleshooting the ignition system, inspect the spark plug cables (**Figure 37**, typical) for:

1. Corroded or damaged connector ends.

2. Breaks in the cable insulation that could allow arcing.

3. Split or damaged plug caps that could allow arcing to the cylinder heads.

4. Replace damaged or questionable spark plug cables.

ENGINE MANAGEMENT SYSTEM DIAGNOSTIC CODES

All models covered in this manual are equipped with an on-board diagnostic system that identifies and stores faults as a two-digit diagnostic code. The retrieved code(s) indicate in which system a fault(s) has occurred.

Troubleshooting is limited to code retrieval. Further diagnosis and clearing of codes requires specific Harley-Davidson test equipment that is *only* available to dealership personnel.

If a diagnostic code has been set, the check-engine light will be activated. During normal operation, the check engine light illuminates for approximately four seconds when the ignition is turned ON. The check-engine light then turns off and remains off. If a diagnostic code(s) has been set, the check-engine light turns on for four seconds, turns off, then turns back on for eight seconds or longer.

Diagnostic codes are by counting the number of times the check-engine light flashes.

Carbureted Models

NOTE
Diagnostic codes can only be cleared
by a Harley-Davidson dealership.

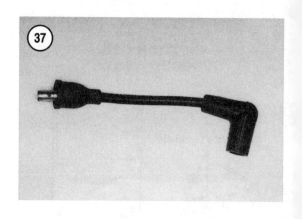

Diagnostic code retrieval

Diagnostic trouble codes are displayed as a series of flashes at the check-engine light on the speedometer face. To retrieve the stored codes, a jumper wire made of 18-gauge wire and two Deutsch sockets (H-D part No. 72191-94), shown in **Figure 38**, are required.

To retrieve the diagnostic code(s), perform the following:

1. Remove the seat as described in Chapter Fourteen.

2. Remove the right side saddlebag as described in Chapter Fourteen.

3. Remove the frame right side cover.

4. Lift the data link connector (A, **Figure 39**) up and off the mounting bracket.

5. Remove the protective cover (B, **Figure 39**) from the data link connector.

6. Install the jumper wire onto pins No. 1 (green/red) and No. 2 (black) on the data link connector.

7. Turn the ignition/light key switch to the IGNITION position. After approximately eight seconds, the different systems enter the diagnostic codes:

   a. The check engine light begins with a ready signal, which is a series of six rapid flashes, approximately three per second. The ready signal indicates the check engine light is ready to flash a diagnostic code.

   b. The ready signal is followed by a two-second pause.

   c. Then the system flashes the first digit of the stored diagnostic code. The check-engine light will illuminate for one second then turn off for one second. Record the number of

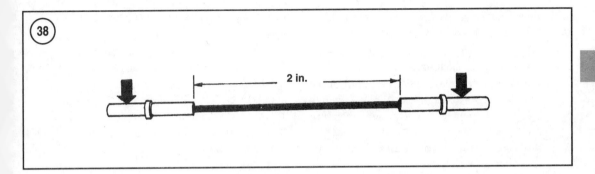

2 in.

flashes. For example, two flashes indicate the first digit is two.

d. The system pauses for two seconds then flashes the second digit of the diagnostic code. Record the number of flashes. For example, five flashes indicate the second digit is five. In this example, the first code is twenty five, or a problem with the rear ignition coil.

e. If more than one code is present, the system will pause for two seconds then flash the ready signal, which is a series of six rapid flashes.

f. The system pauses for two seconds, then flashes the first digit of the next diagnostic code, followed by the second digit.

8. The system displays the stored codes sequentially until each diagnostic code has been displayed. Then the system repeats the codes. The check-engine light repeats the stored codes until the jumper wire is disconnected. When the codes repeat, all stored codes have been displayed. Turn the ignition switch to the OFF position and remove the jumper wire from the data link connector.

9. Refer to diagnostic codes in **Table 3** to locate the problem.

10. Install the protective cover (B, **Figure 39**) onto the data link connector (A) and fit the data link connector onto the mounting bracket.

11. Install the frame right side cover.

12. Install the right side saddlebag as described in Chapter Fourteen.

13. Install the seat as described in Chapter Fourteen.

Fuel Injected Models

NOTE
Diagnostic codes can only be cleared
by a Harley-Davidson dealership.

Diagnostic code retrieval

Diagnostic codes are displayed as a series of flashes by the check-engine light on the speedometer face. To retrieve the diagnostic code(s), perform the following:

1. Turn the ignition/light key switch to the IGNITION position for three seconds.

2. Pause for one second after the fuel pump stops running.

3A. On FLHTCI, FLHTCUI and FLTRI models, turn the ignition/light key switch back to the OFF position for three seconds.

3B. On FLHRI and FLHRCI models, turn the ignition/light key switch back to the LOCK position for three seconds.

4. Repeat Steps 1-3 once.

5. Turn the ignition/light key switch to the IGNITION position. In approximately eight seconds, the check engine light will start to flash as follows:

a. The check engine light begins with a ready signal, which is a series of six rapid flashes, approximately three per second. The ready signal indicates the check engine light is ready to flash a diagnostic code.

b. The ready signal is followed by a two-second pause in which the light is off.

c. Then the system flashes the first digit of the stored diagnostic code. The check-engine light will illuminate for one second, then turn off for one second. Record the number of flashes. For example, two flashes indicate the first digit is two.

d. The system pauses for two seconds, then flashes the second digit of the diagnostic code. Record the number of flashes. For example, five flashes indicate the second digit is five. In this example, the first code is 25, or a problem with the rear ignition coil.

e. If more than one code is present, the system will pause for two seconds, then flash the ready signal, which is a series of six rapid flashes.

f. The system pauses for two seconds, then flashes the first digit of the next diagnostic code, followed by the second digit.

6. The system displays the stored codes sequentially until each diagnostic code has been displayed. Then the system repeats the codes until the ignition/light key switch is turned to the following position:

a. On FLHTCI, FLHTCUI and FLTRI models, turn the ignition/light key switch back to the LOCK position.

b. On FLHRI and FLHRCI models, turn the ignition/light key switch back to the OFF position.

c. Wait for ten seconds for the ECM relay to click. After the click, the motorcycle can be started.

7. Refer to diagnostic codes in **Table 3** to locate the problem.

CRUISE CONTROL SYSTEM DIAGNOSTIC CODES

NOTE
The diagnostic codes can only be cleared by a Harley-Davidson dealership.

The on-board diagnostic system identifies faults within the system and stores this information as a three-digit diagnostic trouble code. The diagnostic system can store a maximum of eight trouble codes.

Diagnostic codes are displayed as a series of flashes by the cruise control engagement *C* light on the face of tachometer. To retrieve the diagnostic code(s), perform the following:

1. Turn the engine off.
2. On the front fairing cap, turn the cruise ON/OFF rocker switch to the OFF position. The light in the rocker switch is off.
3. On the right side handlebar switch, push the cruise SET/RESUME switch to SET and hold it.
4. Turn the ignition key switch to IGNITION, but do not start the engine.
5. On the right side handlebar switch, release the cruise SET/RESUME switch from the SET position and look at the cruise control engagement *C* light. The light will begin transmitting the diagnostic codes. Each code consists of three digits.
6. The system flashes the first digit of the stored diagnostic code. The cruise control engagement *C* light illuminates for about 1/4 of a second, then turns off for about 1/4 of a second. Record the number of flashes. For example, three flashes indicate the first digit is three.
7. The system pauses for one second, then flashes the second digit of the diagnostic code. Record the number of flashes. For example, five flashes indicate the second digit is five.
8. The system pauses again for one second, then flashes the third digit of the diagnostic code. Record the number of flashes. For example, three flashes indicate the third digit is three. In this example, the first code is three hundred fifty three, or an internal failure.
9. If more than one code is present, the system will pause for two seconds, then flash the ready signal, which is a series of six rapid flashes. The system will flash the other trouble codes after the ready signal.
10. Refer to diagnostic codes in **Table 4** to locate the problem.
11. To exit the diagnostic mode, turn the ignition key switch to the OFF position.

FUEL SYSTEM (CARBURETED MODELS)

Begin fuel system troubleshooting with the fuel tank and work through the system, reserving the

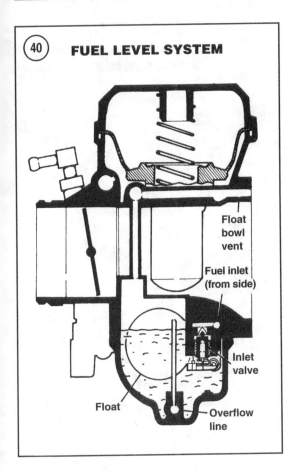

40 **FUEL LEVEL SYSTEM**

Float bowl vent

Fuel inlet (from side)

Inlet valve

Float

Overflow line

carburetor as the final point. Most fuel system problems result from an empty fuel tank, a plugged fuel filter or fuel valve, sour fuel, a dirty air filter or clogged carburetor jets. Do not assume the carburetor is the problem. Unnecessary carburetor adjustment can compound the problem.

Identifying Carburetor Conditions

Refer to the following conditions to identify whether the engine is running lean or rich.

Rich

1. Fouled spark plugs.
2. Engine misfires and runs rough under load.
3. Excessive exhaust smoke as the throttle is increased.
4. An extreme rich condition causes a choked or dull sound from the exhaust and an inability to clear the exhaust with the throttle held wide open.

Lean

1. Blistered or very white spark plug electrodes.
2. Engine overheats.
3. Slow acceleration and engine power is reduced.
4. Flat spots on acceleration that are similar in feel to when the engine starts to run out of gas.
5. Engine speed fluctuates at full throttle.

Troubleshooting

Isolate fuel system problems to the fuel tank, fuel shutoff valve and filter, fuel hoses, external fuel filter (if used) or carburetor. In the following procedures, it is assumed that the ignition system is working properly and is correctly adjusted.

Fuel level system

The fuel level system is shown in **Figure 40**. Proper carburetor operation depends on a constant and correct carburetor fuel level. As fuel is drawn from the float bowl during engine operation, the float level in the bowl drops. As the float drops, the fuel valve moves from its seat and allows fuel to flow through the seat into the float bowl. Fuel entering the float bowl causes the float to rise and push against the fuel valve. When the fuel level reaches a predetermined level, the fuel valve is pushed against the seat to prevent the float bowl from overfilling.

If the fuel valve fails to close, the engine will run too rich or flood with fuel. Symptoms of this problem are rough running, excessive black smoke and poor acceleration. This condition will sometimes clear up when the engine is run at wide-open throttle and the fuel is being drawn into the engine before the float bowl can overfill. As the engine speed is reduced, however, the rich running condition returns.

Several things can cause fuel overflow. In most instances, a small piece of dirt is trapped between the fuel valve and seat, or the float level is incorrect. If fuel is flowing out of the overflow tube connected to the bottom of the float bowl, the fuel valve inside the carburetor is being held open. First check the position of the fuel shutoff valve lever. Turn the fuel shutoff valve lever OFF. Then lightly tap on the carburetor float bowl and turn the fuel shutoff valve lever ON. If the fuel flow stops running out of the overflow tube, whatever was holding the fuel valve off of its seat has been dislodged. If fuel continues to flow from the overflow tube, remove and service the carburetor. See Chapter Seven.

NOTE
Fuel will not flow from the vac-uum-operated fuel shutoff valve until the engine is running.

Starting enrichment (choke) system

A cold engine requires a rich mixture to start and run properly. On all models, a cable-actuated starter enrichment valve is used for cold starting.

If the engine is difficult to start when cold, check the starting enrichment (choke) cable adjustment described in Chapter Three.

Accelerator pump system

During sudden acceleration, the diaphragm type accelerator pump system (**Figure 41**) provides additional fuel to the engine. Without this system, the carburetor would not be able to provide a sufficient amount of fuel.

The system consists of a spring loaded neoprene diaphragm that is compressed by the pump lever during sudden acceleration. This causes the diaphragm to force fuel from the pump chamber, through a check valve and into the carburetor venturi. The diaphragm spring returns the diaphragm to the uncompressed position, which allows the chamber to refill with fuel.

If the engine hesitates during sudden acceleration, check the operation of the accelerator pump system. Carburetor service is covered in Chapter Seven.

Vacuum-operated fuel shutoff valve testing

All models are equipped with a vacuum-operated fuel shutoff valve. A vacuum hose is connected between the fuel shutoff valve diaphragm and the carburetor. When the engine is running, vacuum is applied to the fuel shutoff valve through this hose. For fuel to flow through the fuel valve, a vacuum must be present with the fuel shutoff valve handle in the ON or RES position. The following steps troubleshoot the fuel shutoff valve by applying a vac-

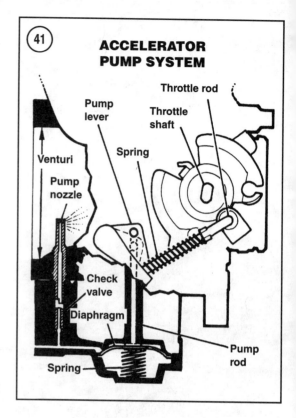

(41) **ACCELERATOR PUMP SYSTEM**

Throttle rod

Pump lever

Throttle shaft

Venturi

Spring

Pump nozzle

Check valve

Diaphragm

Spring

Pump rod

uum from a separate source. A Mity-Vac hand-operated vacuum pump (**Figure 42**), gas can, drain hose that is long enough to reach from the fuel valve to the gas can, and hose clamp are required for this test.

WARNING
Gasoline is highly flammable. When servicing the fuel system in the following sections, work in a well-ventilated area. Do not expose gasoline and gasoline vapors to sparks or other ignition sources.

1. Disconnect the negative battery cable.
2. Visually check the amount of fuel in the tank. Add fuel if necessary.
3. Turn the fuel shutoff valve to the OFF position (A, **Figure 43**, typical) and disconnect the fuel hose (B) from the fuel shutoff valve. Plug the open end of the hose.
4. Connect the drain hose to the fuel shutoff valve and secure it with a hose clamp. Insert the end of the drain hose into a gas can.
5. Disconnect the vacuum hose from the fuel shutoff valve.

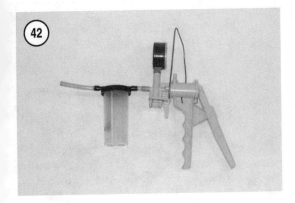

6. Connect a hand-operated vacuum pump to the fuel shutoff valve vacuum hose nozzle.

7. Turn the fuel shutoff valve lever to the ON position.

CAUTION
In Step 8, do not apply more than 25 in. (635 mm) Hg vacuum or the fuel shutoff valve diaphragm will be damaged.

8. Apply 25 in. Hg of vacuum to the valve. Fuel should flow through the fuel shutoff valve when the vacuum is applied.

9. With the vacuum still applied, turn the fuel shutoff valve lever to the RES position. Fuel should continue to flow through the valve.

10. Release the vacuum and make sure the fuel flow stops.

11. Repeat Steps 8-10 five times. Fuel should flow with vacuum applied and stop flowing when the vacuum is released.

12. Turn the fuel shutoff valve OFF. Disconnect the vacuum pump and drain hoses.

13. Reconnect the fuel hose (B, **Figure 43**) to the fuel shutoff valve.

14. If the fuel valve failed this test, replace the fuel shutoff valve as described in Chapter Seven.

FUEL SYSTEM (FUEL INJECTED MODELS)

The fuel injection system is controlled by the engine management system via the ignition control module. Troubleshooting this system, due to the specialized equipment required, must be performed by a Harley-Davidson dealership.

However, most fuel system problems result from an empty tank, a plugged filter, fuel pump failure, contaminated fuel or a restricted air filter element. Begin any fuel system troubleshooting with these items first. Refer to the *Engine Starting* and *Engine Performance* procedures in this chapter.

ENGINE NOISES

1. Knocking or pinging during acceleration can be caused by using a lower octane fuel than recommended or a poor grade of fuel. Incorrect carburetor jetting (carbureted models) and an incorrect spark plug heat range (too hot) can cause pinging. Refer to *Spark Plug Heat Range* in Chapter Three. Check also for excessive carbon buildup in the combustion chamber or a defective ignition module.

2. Slapping or rattling noise at low speed or during acceleration can be caused by excessive piston-to-cylinder wall clearance. Also check for a bent connecting rod(s) or worn piston pin and/or piston pin hole in the piston(s).

3. Knocking or rapping during deceleration is usually caused by excessive rod bearing clearance.

4. Persistent knocking and vibration or other noises are usually caused by worn main bearings. If the main bearings are in good condition, consider the following:

   a. Loose engine mounts.
   b. Cracked frame.
   c. Leaking cylinder head gasket(s).
   d. Exhaust pipe leakage at cylinder head(s).
   e. Stuck piston ring(s).
   f. Broken piston ring(s).
   g. Partial engine seizure.
   h. Excessive connecting rod bearing clearance.
   i. Excessive connecting rod side clearance.

j. Excessive crankshaft runout.

5. Rapid on-off squeal indicates a compression leak around the cylinder head gasket or spark plug.

6. For valve train noise, check for the following:
   a. Bent pushrod(s).
   b. Defective lifter(s).
   c. Valve sticking in guide.
   d. Worn cam gears and/or cam.
   e. Damaged rocker arm or shaft. Rocker arm may be binding on shaft.

ENGINE LUBRICATION

An improperly operating engine lubrication system will quickly lead to serious engine damage. Check the engine oil level as described in Chapter Three weekly. Oil pump service is covered in Chapter Four.

Low Oil Warning Light

The low oil warning light, mounted on the indicator light panel, should come on when the ignition switch is turned ON before the engine is started. After the engine is started, the oil light should turn off when the engine speed is above idle.

If the low oil warning light does not come on when the ignition switch is turned ON and the engine is not running, check for a defective light bulb as described in Chapter Eight. If the bulb is working, check the oil pressure switch, or sensor, (**Figure 44**) as described in Chapter Eight.

If the oil light remains on when the engine speed is above idle, turn the engine OFF and check the oil level in the oil tank. If the oil level is correct, oil may not be returning to the oil tank from the return line. Check for a clogged or damaged return line or a damaged oil pump. If the motorcycle is being operated in conditions where the ambient temperature is below freezing, ice and sludge may be blocking the oil feed pipe.

Oil Consumption High or Engine Smokes Excessively

1. Worn valve guides.
2. Worn valve guide seals.
3. Worn or damaged piston rings.
4. Oil pan overfilled.
5. Oil filter restricted.

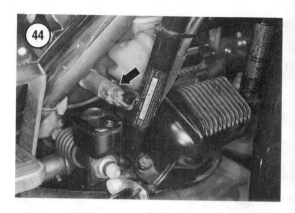

6. Leaking cylinder head surfaces.

Oil Fails to Return to Oil Tank

1. Oil lines or fittings restricted or damaged.
2. Oil pump damaged or operating incorrectly.
3. Oil tank pan empty.
4. Oil filter restricted.
5. Damaged oil feed pump.

Engine Oil Leaks

1. Clogged air filter breather hose.
2. Restricted or damaged oil return line to oil tank.
3. Loose engine parts.
4. Damaged gasket sealing surfaces.
5. Oil pan tank overfilled.
6. Restricted oil filter.
7. Plugged air filter-to-breather system hose.

CLUTCH

Clutch diagnosis, except adjustment, requires partial clutch disassembly to identify and correct the problem. Refer to Chapter Five for clutch service procedures.

Clutch Chatter or Noise

Clutch chatter or noise is usually caused by worn or warped clutch plates.

Clutch Slippage

1. Incorrect clutch adjustment.
2. Worn friction plates.

3. Weak or damaged diaphragm spring.
4. Damaged pressure plate.

Clutch Dragging

1. Incorrect clutch adjustment.
2. Warped clutch plates.
3. Worn or damaged clutch shell or clutch hub.
4. Worn or incorrectly assembled clutch ball and ramp mechanism.
5. Incorrect primary chain alignment.
6. Weak or damaged diaphragm spring.

TRANSMISSION

Transmission symptoms are sometimes hard to distinguish from clutch symptoms. Refer to Chapter Six for transmission service procedures.

Gears Will Not Stay Engaged

1. Worn or damaged shifter parts.
2. Incorrect shifter rod adjustment.
3. Incorrect shifter drum adjustment.
4. Severely worn or damaged gears and/or shift forks.

Difficult Shifting

1. Worn or damaged shift forks.
2. Worn or damaged shifter clutch dogs.
3. Weak or damaged shifter return spring.
4. Clutch drag.

Excessive Gear Noise

1. Worn or damaged bearings.
2. Worn or damaged gears.
3. Excessive gear backlash.

LIGHTING SYSTEM

If bulbs burn out frequently, check for excessive vibration, loose connections that permit sudden current surges, or the installation of the wrong type of bulb.

Most light and ignition problems are caused by loose or corroded ground connections. Check these prior to replacing a bulb or electrical component.

EXCESSIVE VIBRATION

Excessive vibration is usually caused by loose engine mounting hardware. A bent axle shaft or loose suspension component causes high-speed vibration problems. Vibration can also be caused by the following conditions:

1. Cracked or broken frame.
2. Severely worn primary chain.
3. Tight primary chain links.
4. Loose, worn or damaged engine stabilizer link.
5. Loose or damaged rubber mounts.
6. Improperly balanced wheel(s).
7. Defective or damaged wheel(s).
8. Defective or damaged tire(s).
9. Internal engine wear or damage.
10. Loose or worn steering head bearings.
11. Loose swing arm pivot shaft nut.

FRONT SUSPENSION
AND STEERING

Poor handling may be caused by improper tire inflation pressure, a damaged or bent frame or front steering components, worn wheel bearings, or dragging brakes. Possible causes for suspension and steering malfunctions are listed below.

Irregular or Wobbly Steering

1. Loose wheel axle nut(s).
2. Loose or worn steering head bearings.
3. Excessive wheel bearing play.
4. Damaged cast wheel.
5. Spoked wheel out of alignment.
6. Unbalanced wheel assembly.
7. Incorrect wheel alignment.
8. Incorrect suspension-to-engine alignment. Refer to *Motorcycle Alignment* in Chapter Nine.
9. Bent or damaged steering stem or frame at steering neck.
10. Tire incorrectly seated on rim.
11. Excessive front end load from nonstandard equipment.

Stiff Steering

1. Low front tire air pressure.
2. Bent or damaged steering stem or frame.
3. Loose or worn steering head bearings.

Stiff or Heavy Fork Operation

1. Incorrect fork springs.
2. Incorrect fork oil viscosity.
3. Excessive amount of fork oil.
4. Bent fork tubes.
5. Incorrect fork air pressure.

Poor Fork Operation

1. Worn or bent fork tubes.
2. Leaking fork seals.
3. Contaminated fork oil.
4. Incorrect fork springs.
5. Excessive front end load from nonstandard equipment.
6. Incorrect fork air pressure.

Poor Rear Shock Absorber Operation

1. Weak or worn springs.
2. Damper unit leaking.
3. Shock shaft worn or bent.
4. Incorrect rear shock springs.
5. Rear shocks adjusted incorrectly.
6. Excessive rear end load from nonstandard equipment.
7. Incorrect loading.
8. Incorrect rear shock air pressure.

BRAKE SYSTEM

All models are equipped with front and rear disc brakes. Good brakes are vital to the safe operation of any motorcycle. Perform the maintenance procedures in Chapter Three to minimize brake system problems. Brake system service is covered in Chapter Twelve. To refill the front and rear master cylinders, only use DOT 5 silicone-based brake fluid.

Insufficient Braking Power

Worn brake pads or discs, air in the hydraulic system, glazed or contaminated pads, low brake fluid level, or a leaking brake line or hose can cause this problem. Visually check for leaks. Check for worn brake pads. Also check for a leaking or damaged primary cup seal in the master cylinder. Bleed and adjust the brakes. Rebuild a leaking master cylinder or brake caliper. Brake drag causes excessive heat and brake fade. See *Brake Drag* in this section.

Spongy Brake Feel

Spongy brake feel is generally caused by air in the hydraulic system. Bleed and adjust the brakes.

Brake Drag

Check the brake adjustment, while checking for insufficient brake pedal and/or hand lever free play. Also check for worn, loose or missing parts in the brake calipers. Check the brake disc for excessive runout.

Brakes Squeal or Chatter

Check brake pad thickness and disc condition. Make sure the caliper antirattle springs are properly installed and in good condition. Clean off any dirt on the pads. Loose components can also cause this problem. Check for:
1. Warped brake disc.
2. Loose brake disc.
3. Loose caliper mounting bolts.
4. Loose front axle nut.
5. Worn wheel bearings.
6. Damaged hub.

Table 1 STARTER MOTOR TEST SPECIFICATIONS	
Minimum no-load speed @ 11.5 volts	3000 rpm
Maximum no-load current @ 11.5 volts	90 amps
Current draw	
Normal	160-180 amps
Maximum	200 amps
Brush length (minimum)	0.433 in. (11.0 mm)
Commutator diameter (minimum)	1.141 in. (28.981 mm)

Table 2 ELECTRICAL SPECIFICATIONS

Item	Specification
Battery capacity	
1999	12 volts, 30 amp hour @ 10 hour rate
2000-on	12 volts, 28 amp hour @ 20 hour rate
Alternator	
AC voltage output	14.3-14.7 @ 3600 rpm
Amperes	
FLHR, FLHRI, FLHRCI, FLHT, FLHTC, FLTR	38 amps
FLHTCI, FLHTCUI, FLLTRI	45 amps
Stator coil resistance	NA
Voltage regulator	
Voltage output @ 3600 rpm	14.3-14.7 @ 75° F (24° C)
Amps @ 3000 rpm	
FLHR, FLHRI, FLHRCI, FLHT, FLHTC, FLTR	34-40 amps
FLHTCI, FLHTCUI, FLLTR	41-48 amps
Ignition coil	
Primary resistance	0.5-0.7 ohms
Secondary resistance	5500-7500 ohms

Table 3 ENGINE MANAGEMENT DIAGNOSTIC CODES

Diagnostic code No.	Fault condition
11	Throttle position sensor (EFI)
12	MAP sensor (carbureted)
12	Barometric pressure sensor (EFI)
14	Engine temperature sensor (EFI)
15	Intake air temperature sensor (EFI)
16	Battery positive voltage
23	Front cylinder fuel injector (EFI)
24	Front cylinder ignition coil
25	Rear cylinder ignition coil
32	Rear cylinder fuel injector (EFI)
33	Fuel pump relay (EFI)
35	Tachometer (except FLHR, FLHRCI)
41	Crankshaft position sensor
42	Camshaft position sensor
44	Bank angle sensor
52	RAM error or failure
53	ROM error or failure
54	EPROM error or failure
55	Ignition module failure
56	Camshaft position sensor and crankshaft position sensor timing or signal error

Table 4 CRUISE CONTROL DIAGNOSTIC CODES

Diagnostic code No.	Fault condition
111	No code recorded
112	Throttle roll off
113	Cruise control switch turned OFF
121	Short between wiring harness SET/RESUME
122	Application of front or rear brakes
	(continued)

Table 4 CRUISE CONTROL DIAGNOSTIC CODES (continued)

Diagnostic code No.	Fault condition
211	Coast (S/C button engaged) interval longer than six seconds
212	Speed drops below 30 mph (48 k/ph) while in coast (S/C button engaged)
213	Speed drops below 26 mph (42 k/ph) or exceeds 90 mph (144 k/ph)
221	Speed drops 15 mph (24 k/ph) below set speed (such in climbing a steep hill)
222	Speed decreases greater than 20 mph (32 k/ph) per second
223	Vehicle speed sensor input
231	Engine speed over 5000 rpm
232	Loss of tachometer signal
242	High rate of RPM change detected (such as when contacting a slippery surface)
311	Internal failure
312	Internal failure
313	Internal failure
321	Internal failure
323	Internal failure
331	Internal failure
332	Internal failure
333	Internal failure
341	Low voltage
342	Internal failure
343	Internal failure
351	Internal failure
352	Internal failure
353	Internal failure
361	Internal failure
362	Internal failure
363	Internal failure
371	Internal failure
423	Internal failure
432	Internal failure
777	Internal failure

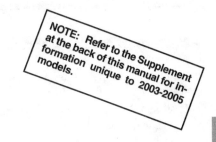

CHAPTER THREE

LUBRICATION, MAINTENANCE
AND TUNE-UP

This chapter covers lubrication, maintenance and tune-up procedures. If a procedure requires more than minor disassembly, reference to the appropriate chapter is listed. Maintenance intervals, capacities, recommendations and specification are in **Tables 1-9** at the end of this chapter.

To maximize the service life of the motorcycle, and gain maximum safety and performance, it is necessary to perform periodic inspections and maintenance. Minor problems found during routine service can be corrected before they develop into major ones.

Consider the maintenance schedule a guide. Harder than normal use and exposure to mud, water or high humidity indicates the need for more frequent servicing to most maintenance items.

ROUTINE SAFETY CHECKS

Pre-ride Inspection

1. Check wheel and tire condition. Check tire pressure. Refer to *Tires and Wheels* in this chapter.
2. Make sure all lights work. Refer to *Lights and Horn* in this chapter.
3. Check engine, transmission and primary drive for oil leakage. If necessary, add oil as described in this chapter.
4. Check brake fluid level and condition. If necessary, add fluid as described in this chapter.

5. Check the operation of the front and rear brakes.
6. Check clutch operation. If necessary, adjust the clutch as described in this chapter.
7. Check the throttle operation. The throttle should move smoothly and return quickly when released. If necessary, adjust throttle free play as described in this chapter.
8. Inspect the front and rear suspension. They should have a solid feel with no looseness.
9. Check the exhaust system for leakage or damage.
10. Inspect the fuel system for leakage.
11. Check the fuel level in fuel tank.
12. Check drive belt tension as described in this chapter.

CAUTION
When checking the tightness of the exposed fasteners, do not check the cylinder head bolts without following the procedure described in Chapter Four.

Lights and Horn

With the ignition ON, check the following:
1. Pull the front brake lever and make sure the brake light works.
2. Push the rear brake pedal down and check that the brake light comes on soon after the pedal has been depressed.

3. Make sure the headlight and taillight work.

4. Move the dimmer switch up and down between the high and low positions, and make sure both headlight elements are working.

5. Push the turn signal switch to the left and right positions, and make sure all four turn signal lights are working.

6. Make sure all accessory lights work properly, if so equipped.

7. Check the horn button operation.

8. If the horn or any light fails to work properly, refer to Chapter Eight.

TIRES AND WHEELS

Tire Pressure

Check the tire pressure often to maintain tire profile, traction and handling, and to get the maximum life out of the tire. Carry a tire gauge in the motorcycle's tool kit. **Table 2** lists the cold tire pressures for the original equipment tires.

> *NOTE*
> *After checking and adjusting the air pressure, reinstall the air valve caps. These caps prevent debris from collecting in the valve stems and causing air leakage or incorrect tire pressure readings.*

Tire Inspection

Inspect the tires periodically for excessive wear, deep cuts and imbedded objects such as stones or nails. If a nail or other object is found in a tire, mark its location with a light crayon prior to removing it. This will help locate the hole for repair.

Measure the depth with a tread depth gauge (**Figure 1**) or a small ruler as shown in **Figure 2**. As a guideline, replace tires when the tread depth is 5/16 in. (8. 0 mm.) or less. Refer to Chapter Nine for tire changing and repair information.

Spoke Tension

On models with laced wheels, check for loose or damaged spokes. Refer to Chapter Nine for spoke service.

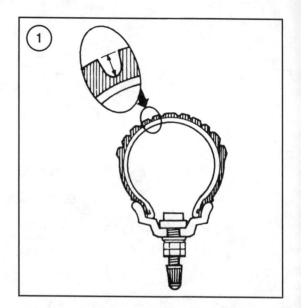

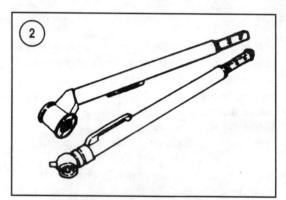

Rim Inspection

Check the wheel rims for cracks and other damage. If they are damaged, a rim can make the motorcycle handle poorly. Refer to Chapter Nine for wheel service.

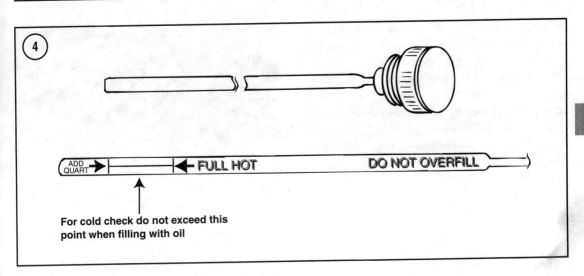

For cold check do not exceed this
point when filling with oil

PERIODIC LUBRICATION

Engine Oil Level Check

Check the engine oil level with the dipstick/oil
filler cap (**Figure 3**) in the transmission/oil tank
case cover.

> *NOTE*
> *Check both vent hoses and intercon-*
> *necting oil hoses for swelling, cracks*
> *or damage. Replace damaged hoses*
> *immediately. Check each hose con-*
> *nection and make sure the hose*
> *clamps are secure.*

1. Start and run the engine for approximately 10
minutes or until the engine has reached normal operating temperature. Then turn the engine off and
allow the oil to settle in the tank.
2. Place the motorcycle on a level surface and park
it on its jiffy stand.

> *CAUTION*
> *Holding the motorcycle straight up*
> *will result in an incorrect oil level*
> *reading.*

3. Wipe the area around the oil filler cap with a
clean rag. Then pull the oil filler cap (**Figure 3**) out
of the transmission case. Wipe the dipstick with a
clean rag and reinsert the filler cap all the way into
the oil tank until it bottoms. Withdraw the filler cap
and check the oil level on the dipstick. The oil level
should be at the FULL HOT mark on the dipstick
(**Figure 4**). If the oil level is even with or below the
ADD QUART mark, continue with Step 4. If the oil
level is correct, go to Step 5.
4. Add the recommended engine oil listed in **Table
3**.

> *CAUTION*
> *Do not overfill the oil level in the*
> *transmission or the oil filler cap will*
> *pop out when the oil gets hot.*

5. Check the O-ring (**Figure 5**) for cracks or other
damage. Replace the O-ring if necessary.
6. Reinstall the oil filler cap and push it down until
it bottoms.

Engine Oil and Filter Change

Regular oil and filter changes contribute more to
engine longevity than any other maintenance performed. **Table 1** lists the recommended oil and filter
change intervals for motorcycles operated in mod-
erate climates. If the motorcycle is operated under

dusty conditions, the oil becomes contaminated more quickly and should be changed more frequently than recommended.

Use a motorcycle oil with an API classification of *SF* or *SG*. The classification is printed on the container. Always use the same brand of oil at each change. Refer to **Table 3** for correct oil viscosity to use under anticipated ambient temperatures, not engine oil temperature. Using oil additives is not recommended as they may cause clutch slippage.

> *WARNING*
> *Contact with oil may cause skin cancer. Wash oil from hands with soap and water as soon as possible after handling engine oil.*

> *CAUTION*
> *Do not use the current SH and SJ rated automotive oils in motorcycle engines. The SH and SJ rated oils contain friction modifiers that reduce frictional losses on engine components. Specifically designed for automotive engines, these oils can damage motorcycle engines and clutches.*

> *NOTE*
> *The engine oil tank is an integral part of the transmission case and is connected to the rear of the crankcase with two hoses. The oil level dipstick is on the upper right side of the transmission/oil tank case (**Figure 3**).*

> *NOTE*
> *Never dispose of motor oil in the trash, on the ground or down a storm drain. Many service stations and oil retailers accept used oil for recycling. Do not combine other fluids with motor oil to be recycled. To locate a recycler, contact the American Petroleum Institute (API) at www.recycleoil.org.*

1. Start and run the engine for approximately 10 minutes or until the engine has reached normal operating temperature. Turn the engine off and allow the oil to settle in the transmission case. Support the motorcycle so that the oil can drain completely.

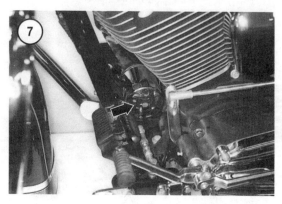

> *NOTE*
> *Before removing the oil filler cap, clean off all dirt and debris around it.*

2. Remove the oil filler cap (**Figure 3**) to speed up the flow of oil.

> *NOTE*
> *The transmission/oil tank case is equipped with two drain plugs. Remove only the engine oil drain plug (A, **Figure 6**). Do not remove the transmission drain plug (B, **Figure 6**).*

3. Place a drain pan underneath the transmission/oil tank pan, and remove the engine oil drain plug and O-ring (A, **Figure 6**) from the left side of the pan.

4. Allow the oil to drain completely.

5. To replace the oil filter (**Figure 7**), perform the following:

   a. Temporarily install the drain bolt and O-ring, and tighten the bolt finger-tight. Then move the drain pan underneath the oil filter.

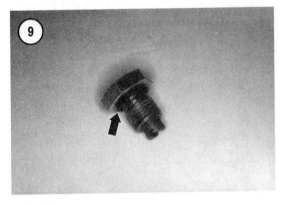

b. At the front of the engine, install a socket type oil filter wrench squarely over the oil filter and loosen it *counterclockwise*. Quickly remove the oil filter as oil will begin to run out.

c. Hold the filter over the drain pan and pour out the remaining oil. Place the filter in a plastic bag, seal the bag and dispose of it properly.

d. Remove the drain plug and gasket. Wipe the drain plug sealing surface on the oil pan with a clean, lint-free cloth.

e. Coat the neoprene gasket (**Figure 8**) on the new filter with clean oil.

CAUTION
Tighten the oil filter by hand. Do not overtighten.

f. Screw the oil filter onto its mount by hand and tighten it until the filter gasket touches the sealing surface, then tighten the filter by hand an additional 3/4 turn.

6. Replace the engine oil drain plug O-ring (**Figure 9**) if it is leaking or damaged.

7. Lubricate the O-ring with clean engine oil before installing it. Then screw in the drain plug and O-ring, and tighten to the specification in **Table 6**.

8. Inspect the oil plug at the base of the right side crankcase for leakage. If leakage has occurred, remove the oil plug, clean the threads thoroughly in solvent and dry. Apply Loctite Pipe Sealant, or an equivalent, to the threads and reinstall the oil plug. Tighten the plug to the specification in **Table 6**.

CAUTION
*Do not overfill the engine in Step 9. **Table 4** lists two engine oil refill capacities. One capacity is for an oil and filter change, and the other is for after the engine is rebuilt. If too much oil is added, the oil filler cap will be forced out of the transmission case cover when the oil gets hot.*

9. Add the correct viscosity (**Table 3**) and quantity (**Table 4**) of oil to the transmission/oil tank case. Insert the oil filler cap into the case and push it down until it bottoms.

NOTE
*After oil has been added, the oil level will register above the FULL HOT dipstick mark (**Figure 4**) until the engine runs and the filter fills with oil. To obtain a correct reading after adding oil and installing a new oil filter, follow the procedure in Step 10.*

10. After changing the engine oil and filter, check the oil level as follows:

a. Start and run the engine for 1 minute, then shut it off.

b. Check the oil level on the dipstick as described in this chapter.

c. If the oil level is correct, it will register in the dipstick's safe operating level range. If so, *do not* top off or add oil to bring it to the FULL HOT level on the dipstick.

11. Check the oil filter and drain plug for leaks.

12. Dispose the used oil properly.

Transmission Oil Level Check

Table 1 lists the recommended transmission oil inspection intervals. When checking the transmission oil level, do not allow any dirt or debris to enter the transmission/oil tank case opening.

> *WARNING*
> *Contact with oil may cause skin cancer. Wash oil from hands with soap and water as soon as possible after handling engine oil.*

> *NOTE*
> *The transmission oil tank is an integral part of the transmission case. The oil level dipstick is on the forward portion of the clutch release cover attached to the side of the transmission/oil tank case.*

1. Ride the motorcycle for approximately 10 minutes and shift through all five gears until the transmission oil has reached normal operating temperature. Turn the engine off and allow the oil to settle in the tank. Park the motorcycle on a level surface and have an assistant support it so that it is standing straight up.

> *CAUTION*
> *Do not check the oil level with the motorcycle supported on its jiffy stand or the reading will be incorrect.*

2. Clean the area around the transmission filler cap/dipstick (**Figure 10**).

3. Wipe the dipstick and reinsert it into the clutch release cover housing. Do not screw the cap/dipstick into place. Rest it on the housing, then withdraw it. The oil level is correct when it registers between the two dipstick marks (**Figure 11**).

> *CAUTION*
> *Do not add engine oil. Add only the recommended transmission oil listed in Table 5.*

4. If the oil level is low, add the recommended type of transmission oil listed in **Table 5**. Do not overfill.

5. Inspect the filler cap O-ring. Replace it if it is worn or damaged.

6. Install the oil filler cap/dipstick and tighten it securely.

7. Wipe any spilled oil off the clutch release cover housing.

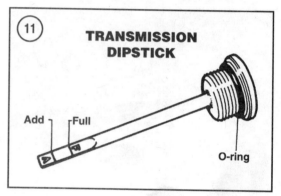

Transmission Oil Change

Table 1 lists the recommended transmission oil change intervals.

1. Ride the motorcycle for approximately 10 minutes and shift through all five gears until the transmission oil has reached normal operating temperature. Turn off the engine and allow the oil to settle in the tank. Park the motorcycle on a level surface and have an assistant support it so that it is standing straight up.

2. Clean the area around the transmission filler cap/dipstick (**Figure 10**). Unscrew and remove the cap.

> *NOTE*
> *The oil tank pan is equipped with two drain plugs. Remove the transmission oil drain plug (B, **Figure 6**) and not the engine oil drain plug (A).*

3. Place a drain pan underneath the transmission/oil tank pan and remove the transmission oil drain plug and O-ring (B, **Figure 6**).

4. Check the drain plug O-ring (**Figure 9**) for damage and replace it if necessary.

5. The drain plug is magnetic. Check the plug for metal debris that may indicate transmission damage, then wipe the plug off. Replace the plug if it is damaged.

6. Install the transmission drain plug and gasket, and tighten to the specification in **Table 6**.

CAUTION
*Do not add engine oil. Only add the recommended transmission oil in **Table 5**. Be sure to add the oil to the correct oil filler hole.*

7. Refill the transmission through the filler cap/ dipstick hole with the recommended quantity (**Table 4**) and type (**Table 5**) of transmission oil.

8. Install the transmission filler cap/dipstick cap and O-ring (**Figure 11**), and tighten securely.

9. Remove the oil drain pan and dispose of the oil as outlined under *Engine Oil and Filter Change* in this chapter.

10. Ride the motorcycle until the transmission oil reaches normal operating temperature. Then shut the engine off.

11. Check the transmission drain plug for leaks.

12. Check the transmission oil level as described in this chapter. Readjust the level if necessary.

Primary Chaincase Oil Level Check

The primary chaincase oil lubricates the clutch, primary chain and sprockets. **Table 1** lists the intervals for checking the chaincase oil level. When checking the primary chaincase oil level, do not allow any dirt or debris to enter the housing.

1. Park the motorcycle on a level surface and support it so that it is standing straight up. Do not support it on the jiffy stand.

CAUTION
Do not check the oil level with the motorcycle supported on its jiffy stand or the reading will be incorrect.

2. Remove the screws securing the clutch inspection cover and O-ring (**Figure 12**). Remove the cover.

3. The oil level is correct when it is even with the bottom of the clutch opening or at the bottom of the clutch diaphragm spring (**Figure 13**).

CAUTION
*Do not add engine oil. Only add the recommended primary chaincase lubricant listed in **Table 5**.*

4. If necessary, add the recommended type of primary chaincase lubricant listed in **Table 5** through the opening to correct the level.

5. Install the clutch inspection cover O-ring (**Figure 12**) onto the primary chain case cover.

6. Install the clutch inspection cover and tighten the screws to the specification in **Table 6**.

Primary Chaincase Oil Change

Table 1 lists the recommended primary chaincase lubricant replacement intervals.

1. Ride the motorcycle for approximately 10 minutes and shift through all five gears until the transmission oil has reached normal operating temperature. Turn off the engine and allow the oil to settle. Park the motorcycle on a level surface and have an assistant support it so that it is standing straight up. Do not support it with its jiffy stand.

2. Place a drain pan under the chaincase and re-move the drain plug (**Figure 14**).

3. Allow the oil to drain for at least 10 minutes.

4. The drain plug is magnetic. Check the plug for metal debris that may indicate drive component or clutch damage, then wipe the plug off. Replace the plug if it is damaged.

5. Reinstall the drain plug and tighten it securely.

6. Remove the screws securing the clutch inspec-tion cover and O-ring (**Figure 12**). Remove the cover.

> *CAUTION*
> *Do not add engine oil. Only add the recommended primary chaincase lu-bricant listed in **Table 5**.*

7. Refill the primary chaincase through the clutch opening with the recommended quantity (**Table 4**) and type (**Table 5**) of primary chaincase oil. Do not overfill. The oil level must be even with the bottom of the clutch opening or at the bottom of the clutch diaphragm spring (**Figure 13**).

8. Install the clutch inspection cover O-ring (**Fig-ure 12**) onto the primary chain case cover.

9. Install the clutch inspection cover and tighten the screws to the specification in **Table 6**.

10. Ride the motorcycle until the primary chaincase oil reaches normal operating tempera-ture. Then shut the engine off.

11. Check the primary chaincase drain plug for leaks.

Front Fork Oil Change (Except Left Side Fork on 2002 FLHR and FLHRI Models)

> *NOTE*
> *The cartridge fork installed on the left side of the 2002 FLHR and FLHRI models must be partially disassem-bled for fork oil replacement. Refer to* ***Front Fork Disassembly and Assem-bly (2002 FLHR and FLHRI Left Side) in Chapter Ten.*** *The right side fork leg oil can be changed using this procedure, **Table 1** lists the recom-mended fork oil change intervals.*

1. Disconnect the negative battery cable as de-scribed in Chapter Eight

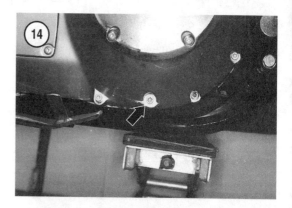

2A. On FLHT, FLHTC, FLHTCI and FLHTCUI models, remove the outer fairing and radio. On FLHT models, also remove the storage box. Refer to Chapter Fourteen.

2B. On FLHR, FLHRI and FLHRCI models, re-move the headlight nacelle. Refer to Chapter Four-teen.

2C. On FLTR and FLTRI models, remove the in-strument nacelle. Refer to Chapter Fourteen.

3. Remove the right side saddlebag as described in Chapter Fourteen.

WARNING
Wear eye protection and use caution when releasing the air from the front fork air valve. Moisture and/or fork oil may spurt out when the air pressure is released.

4. Cover the rear brake assembly and wheel prior to releasing the compressed air from the front air valve. If necessary, wipe off any oil residue that may have been ejected from the air valve.

5. On 1999-2001 models, remove the cap from the front fork air valve (**Figure 15**), then slowly depress the air valve to release the air from the front fork air pipe system. Unscrew and remove the core from the air valve. Place the air valve core and cap in a reclosable plastic bag to avoid misplacing them.

6. Place a drain pan beside one fork tube, then remove the drain screw and washer (**Figure 16**) from the slider.

7. Straddle the motorcycle and apply the front brake lever. Push down on the fork and release. Repeat to force as much oil out of the fork tube as possible.

CAUTION
Do not allow the fork oil to come in contact with the brake components.

8. Replace the drain screw washer if it is damaged.
9. Repeat Steps 6-8 for the opposite fork tube.
10. Support the motorcycle on a stand or floor jack. See *Motorcycle Stands* in Chapter Nine.
11. Unscrew and remove the hex bolt (**Figure 17**) securing the banjo fitting to the top of each fork tube.
12. Carefully move the air pipe assembly from the top of the fork tubes.
13. After the fork oil has thoroughly drained, install the drain screw and washer onto the fork slider. Tighten the drain screw to the specification in **Table 6**.
14. Insert a clear plastic tube into the fork cap bolt opening (**Figure 18**). Attach a funnel to the plastic tube and refill each fork leg with the correct viscosity and quantity of fork oil. Refer to **Table 5** and **Table 8**. Remove the funnel and plastic tube.
15. Repeat Steps 10-14 for the opposite fork tube.
16. Install the valve core and tighten it securely onto the front fork air valve (**Figure 15**).
17. Apply clean fork oil to new O-rings on the banjo fittings, then install them onto the banjo fitting.
18. Carefully install the air pipe assembly onto the top of the fork tubes.
19. Slowly screw the hex bolt (**Figure 17**) securing the banjo fitting to the top of the fork tube. Hold the air pipe assembly to keep it from turning, then tighten the hex bolt to the specification in **Table 6**.
20. On 1999-2000 models, pressurize the front fork tubes to the air pressure in **Table 7**.
21. Install all items removed in Steps 2 and 3.
22. Reconnect the negative battery cable as described in Chapter Eight.
23. Road test the motorcycle and check for leaks.

Control Cables

Lubricate the control cables at the intervals in **Table 1**, or when they become stiff or sluggish. When lubricating the control cables, inspect each cable for fraying and cable sheath damage. Cables are relatively inexpensive and should be replaced if they are faulty. Lubricate the cables with a cable lubricant.

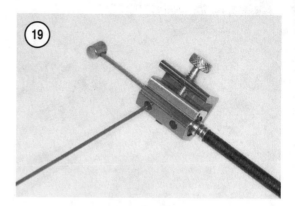

> *CAUTION*
> *If the original equipment cables have been replaced with nylon-lined cables, do not lubricate them as described in this procedure. Oil and most cable lubricants will cause the cable liner to expand, pushing the liner against the cable sheath. Nylon-lined cables are normally used dry. When servicing nylon-lined and other aftermarket cables, follow the manufacturer's instructions.*

> *CAUTION*
> *Do not use chain lubricant to lubricate control cables.*

> *CAUTION*
> *The starting enrichment valve (choke) cable is designed to operate with a certain amount of cable resistance. Do **not** lubricate the enrichener cable or its conduit.*

> *NOTE*
> *The major cause of cable breakage or cable stiffness is improper lubrication. Maintaining the cables as described in this section will ensure long service life.*

1A. Disconnect the clutch cable ends as described under *Clutch Cable Replacement* in Chapter Five.

1B. Disconnect both throttle cable ends as described under *Throttle and Idle Cables* in Chapter Seven.

2. Attach a lubricator tool to the cable following the tool manufacturer's instructions (**Figure 19**).

> *NOTE*
> *Place a shop cloth at the end of the cable to catch all excess lubricant.*

3. Insert the lubricant nozzle tube into the lubricator, press the button on the can and hold it down until the lubricant begins to flow out of the other end of the cable. If the lubricant squirts out from around the lubricator, it is not clamped to the cable properly. Loosen and reposition the cable lubricator.

> *NOTE*
> *If the lubricant does not flow out of the other end of the cable, check the cable for fraying, bending or other damage. Replace damaged cables.*

4. Remove the lubricator tool and wipe off both ends of the cable.

5A. Reconnect the clutch cable ends as described under *Clutch Cable Replacement* in Chapter Five.

5B. Reconnect both throttle cable ends as described under *Throttle and Idle Cable Replacement* in Chapter Seven.

6. Adjust the cables as described in this chapter.

Throttle Control Grip Lubrication

Table 1 lists the recommended throttle control grip lubrication intervals. To remove and install the throttle grip (**Figure 20**), refer to *Throttle and Idle Cable Replacement* in Chapter Seven. Lubricate the throttle control grip where it contacts the handlebar with graphite.

Steering Head Lubrication

Lubricate the steering head bearings at the interval in **Table 1**. Complete lubrication requires removal of the steering head assembly. Refer to Chapter Ten.

Wheel Bearings (1999 Models)

Lubricate the wheel bearings at the interval in **Table 1**. Complete lubrication requires removal of the wheel bearing assemblies. Refer to Chapter Nine.

Swing Arm Bearings

Lubricate the swing arm at the interval in **Table 1**. Refer to Chapter Eleven for procedures.

Front Brake Lever Pivot Pin Lubrication

Inspect the front brake lever pivot pin for lubricant at the intervals in **Table 1**. If the pin is dry, lubricate it with a light weight oil. To service the pivot pin, refer to *Front Master Cylinder* in Chapter Twelve.

Clutch Lever Pivot Pin Lubrication

Inspect the clutch lever pivot pin at the intervals in **Table 1**. Lubricate the pin with a light weight oil. To service the pivot pin, refer to *Clutch Cable Replacement* in Chapter Five.

PERIODIC MAINTENANCE

This section describes the periodic inspection, adjustment and replacement of various operational items. Perform these procedures at the intervals in **Table 1**, or earlier if necessary.

Primary Chain Adjustment

As the primary chain stretches and wears, its free play movement increases. Excessive free play causes premature chain and sprocket wear and increases chain noise. If the free play is adjusted too tight, the chain wears prematurely.

> *NOTE*
> *On models so equipped, always disarm the optional TSSM security system prior to disconnecting the battery or the siren will sound.*

1. Disconnect the negative battery cable as described in Chapter Eight.
2. Support the motorcycle with the rear wheel off the ground.

> *NOTE*
> *Note the location of the inspection cover screws. There are two different length screws and they must be reinstalled in the correct location.*

3. Remove the primary chain inspection cover and gasket (**Figure 21**).
4. Turn the primary chain to find the tightest point on the chain. Measure chain free play at this point.

> *NOTE*
> ***Figure 22** is shown with the primary chaincase removed to better illustrate the steps.*

5. Check primary chain free play at the upper chain run midway between the sprockets (**Figure 22**). If the primary chain free play is incorrect, continue with Step 6. If the free play is correct, go to Step 7.

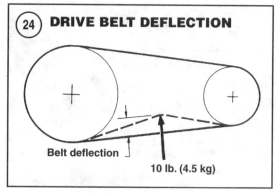

DRIVE BELT DEFLECTION

Belt deflection

10 lb. (4.5 kg)

The correct primary chain free play specifications are:

    a. Cold engine: 5/8 to 7/8 in. (15.9-22. 3 mm).

    b. Hot engine: 3/8 to 5/8 in. (9.5-15.9 mm).

6A. On 1999-2000 models, perform the following:

    a. Loosen the primary chain adjuster shoe nut.

    b. Move the shoe assembly up or down to correct free play.

    c. Tighten the primary chain adjuster shoe nut to the torque specification in **Table 6**, then recheck free play.

6B. On 2001-on models, perform the following:

    a. Loosen the primary chain adjuster shoe nut (**Figure 23**).

    b. Move the shoe assembly up or down to correct free play.

    c. Tighten the primary chain adjuster shoe nut (**Figure 23**) to the specification in **Table 6**, then recheck free play.

7. Install the primary chain inspection cover and a *new* gasket (**Figure 21**). Tighten the cover screws to the specification in **Table 6**.

8. Lower the motorcycle to the ground.

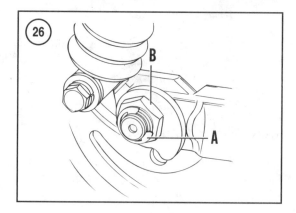

Final Drive Belt Deflection and Alignment

Inspect drive belt deflection and rear axle alignment at the intervals in **Table 1**. If the drive belt is severely worn, or if it is wearing incorrectly, refer to Chapter Eleven for inspection and replacement procedures.

> *NOTE*
> *Check the drive belt deflection and axle alignment when the belt is cold.*

1. Support the motorcycle with the rear wheel off the ground. Then turn the rear wheel and check the drive belt for its tightest point. When this point is located, turn the wheel so the belt's tight spot is on the lower belt run, midway between the front and rear sprockets.

2. Lower the motorcycle to the ground.

3. Position the motorcycle so both wheels are on the ground. When checking and adjusting drive belt deflection in the following steps, have an assistant sit on the seat facing forward.

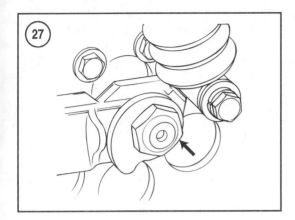

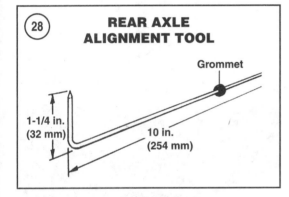

REAR AXLE
ALIGNMENT TOOL

Grommet

1-1/4 in.
(32 mm)

10 in.
(254 mm)

NOTE
Use the Harley-Davidson belt tension gauge (part No. HD-35381) or equivalent to apply pressure against the drive belt in Step 4.

4. Apply a force of 10 lb. (4.5 kg) to the middle of the lower belt strand while measuring the belts deflection measurement at the same point (**Figure 24**). Compare the correct belt deflection measurement with the specification in **Table 9**. If the belt deflection measurement is incorrect, continue with Step 5. If the deflection measurement is correct, go to Step 7.

5. Support the bike with the rear wheel off the ground.

6A. On 1999-2001 models, perform the following:

a. Remove the spring clip and loosen the rear axle nut.

b. Turn the axle adjuster (**Figure 25**) in equal amounts to adjust belt deflection while maintaining rear wheel alignment. Recheck drive belt deflection as described in Step 4.

6B. On 2002 models, perform the following:

a. On the right side, remove the E-clip (A, **Figure 26**) from the rear axle groove.

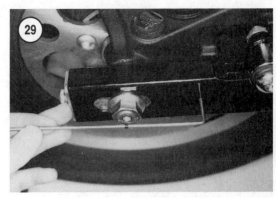

b. Loosen the rear axle nut (B, **Figure 26**) and then tighten it to 15-20 ft-lbs. (20-27 N•m).

c. On the left side, rotate the rear axle (**Figure 27**) in either direction to adjust belt deflection. Recheck drive belt deflection as described in Step 4.

NOTE
The adjuster cams are located on each side of the rear axle.

d. Make sure the adjuster cam on each side is against the weld nub on the frame.

e. Hold onto the rear axle and tighten the axle nut to the torque specification in **Table 6**.

f. With the flat side facing out, install the E-clip onto the rear axle groove. Make sure the E-clip is correctly seated in the rear axle groove.

NOTE
On 2002 models, rear wheel alignment is not necessary.

7. On 1999-2001 models, when the drive belt deflection measurement is correct, check axle alignment as follows:

a. To make the alignment tool shown in **Figure 28**, refer to *Motorcycle Alignment* in Chapter Nine.

b. Support the motorcycle with the rear wheel off the ground.

c. Insert the alignment tool into the swing arm index hole. Then hold it parallel to the rear axle and slide the grommet on the tool until it aligns with the axle center point (**Figure 29**).

d. Remove the alignment tool without disturbing the position of the grommet and insert the tool into the opposite side of the swing arm. Compare the axle center point with the position of the grommet. Axle alignment is correct if the two measurements are within .032 in. (0.8 mm) of each other.

　e. If the axle alignment is incorrect, adjust the axle with the axle adjusters (**Figure 26**) while maintaining the correct drive belt deflection measurement.

8. When the drive belt deflection and axle alignment adjustments are correct, tighten the rear axle nut to the torque specification in **Table 6**. Install the spring clip through the axle nut and rear axle.

9. Lower the rear wheel to the ground.

Brake Pad Inspection

1. Without removing the front or rear brake calipers, inspect the brake pads for damage.

2. Measure the thickness of each brake pad lining (**Figure 30**) with a ruler. Replace the brake pad if its thickness is worn to the minimum thickness in **Table 9**. Replace the brake pads as described in Chapter Twelve.

Disc Brake Fluid Level

1. To check the front master cylinder, perform the following:

　a. Turn the handlebar straight ahead so the master cylinder is level.

　b. Observe the brake fluid level by looking at the sight glass (**Figure 31**) on the master cylinder reservoir top cover. If the fluid level is correct, the sight glass will be dark purple. If the level is low, the sight glass will have a lightened, clear appearance.

> *NOTE*
> *Access to the rear master cylinder is restricted by the exhaust system. Checking the fluid level and replenishing the fluid is easier with the front cylinder's muffler removed. Refer to Chapter Seven.*

2. To check the rear master cylinder, perform the following:

　a. Support the motorcycle so the rear master cylinder is level.

　b. Observe the brake fluid level by looking at the sight glass (A, **Figure 32**) on the master cylinder reservoir top cover. If the fluid level

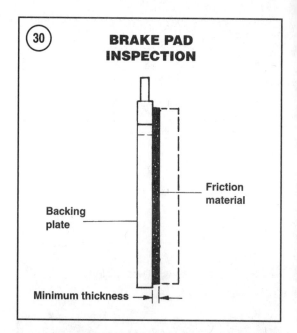

BRAKE PAD INSPECTION

Friction material

Backing plate

Minimum thickness

is correct, the sight glass will be dark purple. If the level is low, the sight glass will have a lightened, clear appearance.

> *WARNING*
> *Do not use brake fluid labeled **DOT 5.1**. This is a glycol-based fluid that is **not compatible** with silicone based DOT 5. DOT 5 brake fluid is purple while DOT 5.1 is an amber/clear color. Do not intermix these different types of brake fluid, as doing so will lead to brake component damage and possible brake failure.*

> *CAUTION*
> *Be careful when handling brake fluid. Do not spill it on painted or plastic surfaces, as it damages them. Wash*

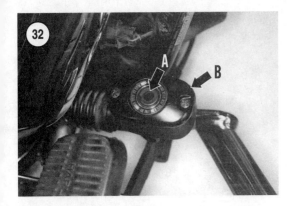

the area immediately with soap and water, and thoroughly rinse it.

NOTE
To control the flow of brake fluid, punch a small hole in the seal of a new container of brake fluid next to the edge of the pour spout. This helps prevent fluid spillage, especially while adding fluid to the small reservoir.

3. If the brake fluid level is low, perform the following:

  a. Clean any dirt from the master cylinder cover prior to removing it.

  b. Remove the top cover (B, **Figure 32**) and lift the diaphragm out of the reservoir.

  c. Add fresh DOT 5 brake fluid to correct the level.

  d. Reinstall the diaphragm and top cover. Tighten the screws securely.

NOTE
If the brake fluid level is low enough to allow air in the hydraulic system,

bleed the brakes as described in Chapter Twelve.

Front and Rear Brake Disc Inspection

Visually inspect the front and rear brake discs (**Figure 33**, typical) for scoring, cracks or other damage. Measure the brake disc thickness and, if necessary, service the brake discs as described in Chapter Twelve.

Disc Brake Lines and Seals

Check the brake lines between each master cylinder and each brake caliper. If there is any leakage, tighten the connections and bleed the brakes as described in Chapter Twelve.

Disc Brake Fluid Change

Every time the reservoir cover is removed, a small amount of dirt and moisture enters the brake fluid. The same thing happens if there is a leak or if any part of the hydraulic system is loosened or disconnected. Dirt can clog the system and cause unnecessary wear. Water in the fluid vaporizes at high temperatures, impairing the hydraulic action and reducing brake performance.

To change brake fluid, follow the brake bleeding procedure in Chapter Twelve. Continue adding new fluid to the master cylinder until the fluid leaving the caliper is clean and free of contaminants and air bubbles.

WARNING
*Do not use brake fluid labeled **DOT 5.1**. This is a glycol-based fluid that is **not compatible** with silicone based DOT 5. DOT 5 brake fluid is purple while DOT 5.1 is an amber/clear color. Do not intermix these different types of brake fluid, as doing so will lead to brake component damage and possible brake failure.*

Front Disc Brake Adjustment

The front disc brake does not require periodic adjustment.

Rear Disc Brake Adjustment

The rear disc brake does not require periodic adjustment.

Clutch Adjustment

> *CAUTION*
> *Because the clutch cable adjuster clearance increases with engine temperature, adjust the clutch when the engine is cold. If the clutch is adjusted when the engine is hot, insufficient pushrod clearance can cause the clutch to slip.*

1. Remove the clutch inspection cover and O-ring (**Figure 12**).
2. Slide the rubber boot (**Figure 34**) off the clutch in-line cable adjuster.
3. Loosen the adjuster locknut (A, **Figure 35**) and turn the adjuster (B) to provide maximum cable slack.
4. Make sure the clutch cable seats squarely in its perch (**Figure 36**) at the handlebar.
5. At the clutch mechanism, loosen the clutch adjusting screw locknut (A, **Figure 37**) and turn the adjusting screw (B) *clockwise* until it is lightly seated.
6. Squeeze the clutch lever three times to verify the clutch balls are seated in the ramp release mechanism located behind the transmission side cover.

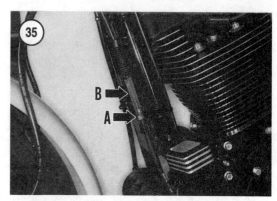

7. Back out the adjusting screw (B, **Figure 37**) *counterclockwise* 1/2 to 1 turn. Then hold the adjusting screw (B, **Figure 37**) and tighten the locknut (A) to the specification in **Table 6**.
8. Once again, squeeze the clutch lever to its maximum limit three times to set the clutch ball and ramp release mechanism.
9. Check the free play as follows:
   a. At the in-line cable adjuster, turn the adjuster away from the locknut until slack is eliminated at the clutch hand lever.

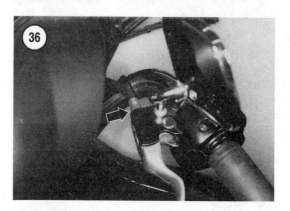

   b. Pull the clutch cable sheath away from the clutch lever, then turn the clutch cable adjuster to obtain the free play (**Figure 38**) in **Table 9**.
   c. When the adjustment is correct, tighten the clutch in-line cable locknut and slide the rubber boot over the cable adjuster.
10. Install the clutch inspection cover O-ring onto the primary chain case cover.

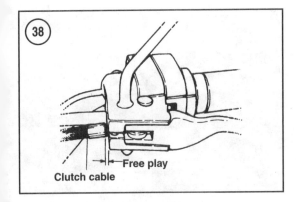

Free play
Clutch cable

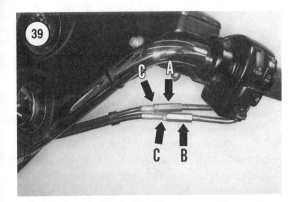

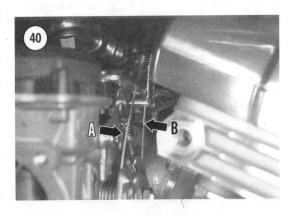

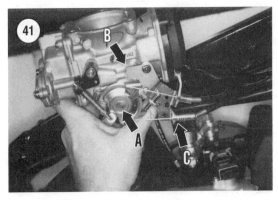

11. Install the clutch inspection cover (**Figure 12**) and tighten the screws to the specification in **Table 6**.

Throttle Cables Inspection

Inspect the throttle cables from the grip to the carburetor or the fuel injector module. Make sure they are not kinked or chafed. Replace them if necessary as described in Chapter Seven.

Make sure the throttle grip rotates smoothly from fully closed to fully open. Check with the handlebar at the center, full left and full right positions.

Throttle Cables Adjustment (Carbureted Models)

There are two different throttle cables. At the throttle grip, the front cable is the throttle control cable (A, **Figure 39**) and the rear cable is the idle control cable (B). At the carburetor, the outboard cable is the throttle control cable (A, **Figure 40**) and the inboard cable is the idle control cable (B).

1. Remove the air filter and backing plate as described in Chapter Seven.
2. At the handlebar, loosen both control cable adjuster locknuts (C, **Figure 39**), then turn the cable adjusters (A and B) *clockwise* as far as possible to increase cable slack.
3. Turn the handlebars so the front wheel points straight ahead. Then turn the throttle grip to open the throttle completely and hold it in this position.

> *NOTE*
> *Figure 41 is shown with the carburetor body removed to better illustrate the steps.*

4. At the handlebar, turn the throttle control cable adjuster (A, **Figure 39**) *counterclockwise* until the throttle cam (A, **Figure 41**) stop just touches the stop boss (B) on the carburetor body. Then tighten the throttle cable adjuster locknut and release the throttle grip.
5. Turn the front wheel all the way to the full right lock position and hold it there.
6. At the handlebar, turn the idle cable adjuster (B, **Figure 39**) until the lower end of the idle control cable just contacts the spring in the carburetor cable guide (C, **Figure 41**). Tighten the idle cable locknut.

7. Shift the transmission into NEUTRAL and start the engine.

8. Increase engine speed several times. Release the throttle and make sure the engine speed returns to idle. If the engine speed does not return to idle, at the handlebar, loosen the idle control cable adjuster locknut and turn the cable adjuster *clockwise* as required. Tighten the idle control cable adjuster locknut.

9. Allow the engine to idle in NEUTRAL. Then turn the handlebar from side to side. Do not operate the throttle. If the engine speed increases when the handlebar assembly is turned, the throttle cables are routed incorrectly or damaged. Turn off the engine. Recheck cable routing and adjustment.

> *WARNING*
> *Do not ride the motorcycle until the throttle cables are properly adjusted. Also, the cables must not catch or pull when the handlebar is turned from side to side. Improper cable routing and adjustment can cause the throttle to stick open. This could cause loss of control and a possible crash. Recheck this adjustment before riding the motorcycle.*

Throttle Cables Adjustment (Fuel Injected Models)

The throttle cable adjustment *must* be performed by a Harley-Davidson dealership equipped with a Scanalyzer tool.

Starting Enrichment Valve (Choke) Cable Adjustment (Carbureted Models)

The starting enrichment (choke) knob (**Figure 42**) should move from fully open to fully closed position without binding. The knob should also stay in its fully closed or fully open position without creeping. If the knob does not stay in position, adjust tension on the cable by turning the plastic knurled nut behind the knob (**Figure 43**) as follows:

> *CAUTION*
> *The starting enrichment (choke) cable must have sufficient cable resistance to work properly. Do not lubricate the enrichment cable or its conduit.*

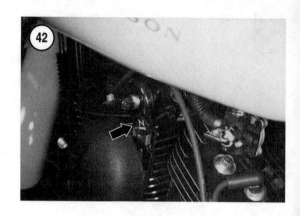

1. Loosen the hex nut behind the mounting bracket. Then move the cable to free it from its mounting bracket slot.

2. Hold the cable across its flats with a wrench and turn the knurled plastic nut *counterclockwise* to reduce cable resistance. The knob must slide inward freely.

3. Turn the knurled plastic nut (**Figure 43**) *clockwise* to increase cable resistance. Continue adjustment until the knob remains stationary when it is pulled all the way out. The knob must move without any roughness or binding.

4. Reinstall the cable into the slot in its mounting bracket with the star washer located between the bracket and hex nut. Tighten the hex nut securely.

5. Recheck the knob movement and readjust if necessary.

Fuel Line Inspection

Inspect the fuel lines from the fuel tank to the carburetor or fuel injection module. Replace leaking or damaged fuel lines. Make sure the hose clamps are in place and holding securely. Check the hose fittings for looseness.

> *WARNING*
> *A damaged or deteriorated fuel line can cause a fire or explosion if fuel spills onto a hot engine or exhaust pipe.*

Exhaust System

Check all fittings for exhaust leakage. Do not forget the crossover pipe connections. Tighten all bolts and nuts. Replace gaskets as necessary. See Chapter Seven for removal and installation procedures.

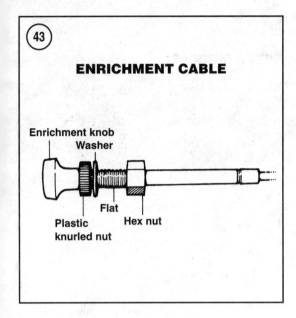

ENRICHMENT CABLE

Enrichment knob
Washer
Flat
Plastic
knurled nut
Hex nut

Steering Play

Check the steering head bearing adjustment (Chapter Ten) at the intervals in **Table 1**.

Rear Swing Arm Pivot Bolt

Check the rear swing arm pivot bolt tightness (Chapter Eleven) at the intervals specified in **Table 1**.

Rear Shock Absorbers

Check the rear shock absorbers for oil leakage or damaged bushings. Check the shock absorber mounting bolts and nuts for tightness. Refer to *Shock Absorbers* in Chapter Eleven for procedures.

Engine Mounts and Stabilizer

Check the stabilizer and the engine and frame mounts for loose or damaged parts. Refer to Chapter Four for procedures.

Fasteners

CAUTION
Special procedures must be used to tighten the cylinder head mounting
bolts. To accurately check these bolts for tightness, refer to **Cylinder Head Installation** *in Chapter Four. Tightening these bolts incorrectly can cause an oil leak or cylinder head warp.*

Constant vibration can loosen many fasteners on a motorcycle. Check the tightness of all fasteners, especially those on:
1. Engine mounting hardware.
2. Engine and primary covers.
3. Handlebar and front fork.
4. Gearshift lever.
5. Sprocket bolts and nuts.
6. Brake pedal and lever.
7. Exhaust system.
8. Lighting equipment.

Electrical Equipment and Switches

Check all of the electrical equipment and switches for proper operation.

TUNE-UP

Perform the following tune-up procedures at the intervals in **Table 1**. Perform a complete tune-up in the following order:
1. Clean or replace the air filter element.
2. Check engine compression.
3. Check or replace the spark plugs.
4. On carbureted models, adjust the idle speed.

Air Filter Element Removal/Installation

Remove and inspect the air filter at the interval in **Table 1**. If necessary, clean the element. Replace the element if it is damaged or starting to deteriorate.

The air filter removes dust and abrasive particles before the air enters the carburetor, or fuel injection module, and the engine. Without the air filter, very fine particles will enter the engine and cause rapid wear of the piston rings, cylinder bores and bearings. Particles also might clog small passages in the carburetor. Never run the motorcycle without the element installed.

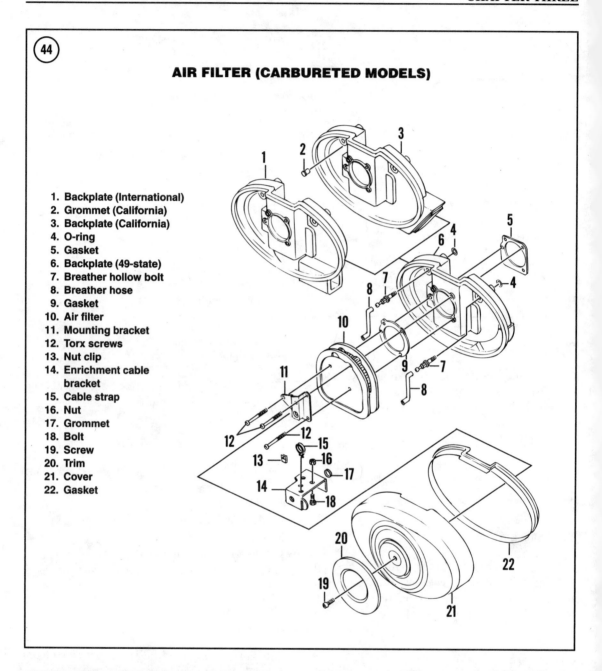

AIR FILTER (CARBURETED MODELS)

1. Backplate (International)
2. Grommet (California)
3. Backplate (California)
4. O-ring
5. Gasket
6. Backplate (49-state)
7. Breather hollow bolt
8. Breather hose
9. Gasket
10. Air filter
11. Mounting bracket
12. Torx screws
13. Nut clip
14. Enrichment cable bracket
15. Cable strap
16. Nut
17. Grommet
18. Bolt
19. Screw
20. Trim
21. Cover
22. Gasket

Refer to **Figure 44** (carbureted models) or **Figure 45** (fuel injected models).

1. Remove the air filter cover screw (A, **Figure 46**) and remove the cover (B).

2. Remove the Torx screws and mounting bracket (**Figure 47**) from the air filter element.

3. Gently pull the air filter element from the backplate and disconnect the two breather hoses (A, **Figure 48**) from the breather hollow bolts on the backplate. Remove the air filter element (B, **Figure 48**).

4. Clean the air filter as described in the following procedure.

5. Inspect the gasket (A, **Figure 49**) for damage. Replace it if necessary.

6. Inspect the breather hoses (B, **Figure 49**) for tears or deterioration. Replace them if necessary.

NOTE
Figure 50 is shown with the air filter backplate removed to better illustrate the step.

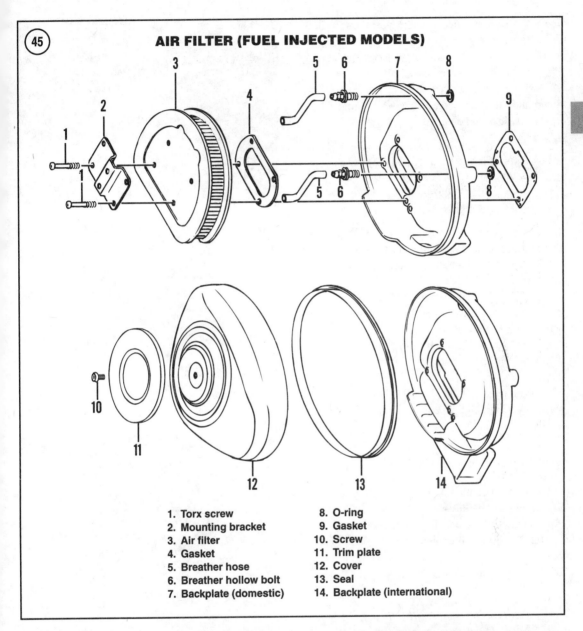

AIR FILTER (FUEL INJECTED MODELS)

1. Torx screw
2. Mounting bracket
3. Air filter
4. Gasket
5. Breather hose
6. Breather hollow bolt
7. Backplate (domestic)
8. O-ring
9. Gasket
10. Screw
11. Trim plate
12. Cover
13. Seal
14. Backplate (international)

7. On California models, make sure the trap door swings freely (**Figure 50**).

8. If they were removed, install a new gasket (A, **Figure 49**) and breather hoses (B).

9. Position the element with the flat side facing down and attach the breather hoses (**Figure 51**) to the backside of the element.

> *NOTE*
> *If an aftermarket air filter element is being installed, position it onto the backplate following the manufacturer's instructions.*

10. Move the element into position (B, **Figure 48**) and install the mounting bracket (**Figure 47**) and the Torx screws. Tighten the screws to the torque specification in **Table 6**.

11. Apply a drop of ThreeBond TB1342 (blue) or an equivalent threadlocking compound to the cover screw prior to installation.

12. Inspect the seal ring (**Figure 52**) on the air filter cover for hardness or deterioration. Replace it if necessary.

13. Install the air filter cover (B, **Figure 46**) and the screw (A). Tighten the screw to the specification in **Table 6**.

Air Filter Element Cleaning

The air filter element is a paper/wire type (**Figure 51**). If an aftermarket element is installed, refer to the manufacturer's cleaning instructions.

1. Remove the air filter element as described in this chapter.

2. Replace the air filter if damaged.

> *WARNING*
> *Do not clean the air filter in solvent. Never clean the air filter element in gasoline or low flash point solvent. The residual solvent or vapors may cause a fire or explosion after the filter is reinstalled.*

> *CAUTION*
> *Do not tap or strike the air filter element on a hard surface to dislodge dirt. Doing so will damage the element.*

3. Place the air filter in a pan filled with lukewarm water and mild detergent. Move the air filter ele-

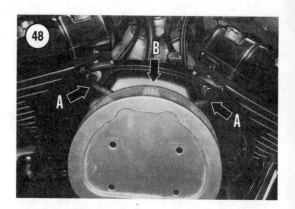

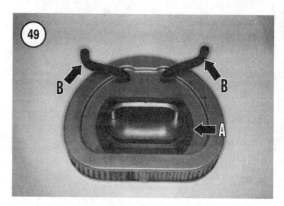

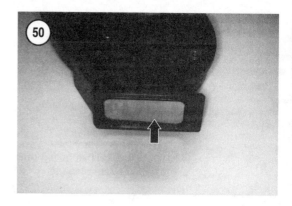

ment back and forth to help dislodge trapped dirt. Thoroughly rinse it in clean water to remove all detergent residue.

4. Hold the air filter up to a strong light. Check the filter pores for dirt and oil. Repeat Step 3 until there is no dirt and oil in the filter pores. If the air filter cannot be cleaned, or if the filter is saturated with oil or other chemicals, replace it.

> *CAUTION*
> *Do not use high air pressure to dry the filter, as this will damage it.*

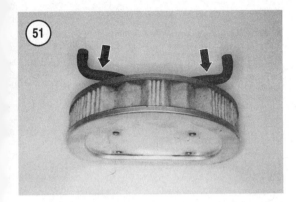

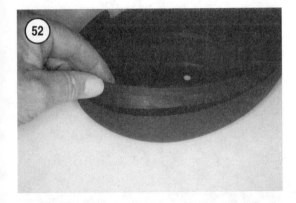

3

> *CAUTION*
> *In the next step, do not blow compressed air through the outer surface of the air filter element. Doing so can force dirt trapped on the outer filter surface deeper into the air filter element, restricting airflow and damaging the air filter element.*

5. Gently apply compressed air through the inside surface of the air filter element to remove loosened dirt and dust trapped in the filter.

6. Inspect the air filter element. Replace it if it is torn or damaged. Do not ride the motorcycle with a damaged filter element as it will allow dirt to enter the engine.

7. Clean the breather hoses in the same lukewarm water and mild detergent. Make sure both hoses are clean and clear. Clean them out with a pipe cleaner if necessary.

8. Wipe the inside of the cover and backplate with a clean damp shop rag.

> *CAUTION*
> *Air will not pass through a wet or damp filter. Make sure the filter is dry before installing it.*

9. Allow the filter to dry completely, then reinstall it as described in this chapter.

Compression Test

A compression check is one of the most effective ways to check the condition of the engine. If possible, check the compression at each tune-up, and record and compare it with the readings at subsequent tune-ups. This will help spot any developing problems.

1. Prior to starting the compression test, check for the following:

    a. The cylinder head bolts (**Figure 53**) are tightened as specified in Chapter Four.

    b. The battery is fully charged to ensure proper engine cranking speed.

2. Warm the engine to normal operating temperature. Shut off the engine.

3. Remove the spark plugs (**Figure 54**) and reinstall them in their caps. Place the spark plugs against the cylinder head to ground them.

4. Connect the compression tester (**Figure 55**) to one cylinder following its manufacturer's instructions.

5. Place the throttle in the wide-open position.

6. On carburetted models, make sure the starting enrichment (choke) knob (**Figure 42**) is pushed in to the fully OFF position.

7. Crank the engine over until there is no further rise in pressure.

8. Record the reading and remove the tester.

9. Repeat Steps 4-8 for the other cylinder.

10. Reinstall the spark plugs and reconnect their caps.

Results

When interpreting the results, actual readings are not as important as the difference between the readings. **Table 9** lists the standard engine compression reading. Pressure must not vary between the cylinders by more than 10 percent. Greater differences indicate worn or broken rings, leaky or sticky valves, a blown head gasket or a combination of all.

If compression readings do not differ between cylinders by more than 10 percent, the rings and valves are in good condition. A low reading (10 percent or more) on one cylinder indicates valve or ring trouble. To determine which, pour about a teaspoon of engine oil into the spark plug hole. Turn the engine over once to distribute the oil, then take another compression test and record the reading. If the compression increases significantly, the valves are good but the rings are defective on that cylinder. If compression does not increase, the valves require servicing.

NOTE
An engine cannot be tuned to maximum performance with low compression.

Spark Plug Removal

CAUTION
Whenever the spark plug is removed, dirt around it can fall into the plug hole. This can cause serious engine damage.

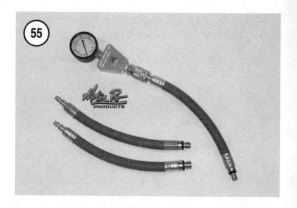

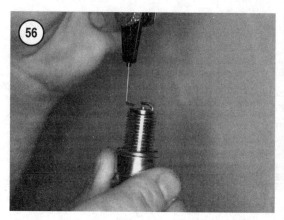

1. Blow away loose dirt or debris that may have accumulated around the base of the spark plug (**Figure 54**) and could fall into the cylinder head.

2. Grasp the spark plug lead and twist it from side to side to break the seal. Then pull the cap off the spark plug. If the cap is stuck to the plug, twist it slightly to break it loose.

NOTE
Use a spark plug socket equipped with a rubber insert that holds the spark plug. This type of socket allows both removal and installation of the recessed spark plugs.

3. Install the spark plug socket onto the spark plug. Make sure it is correctly seated. Install an open-end wrench or socket handle and remove the spark plug. Mark the spark plug with the cylinder number from which it was removed.

4. Repeat Steps 1-3 for the remaining spark plug.

5. Thoroughly inspect each plug. Look for broken center porcelain, excessively eroded electrodes and excessive carbon or oil fouling.

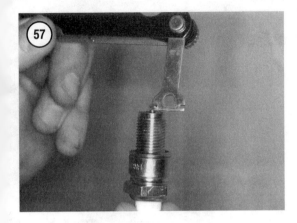

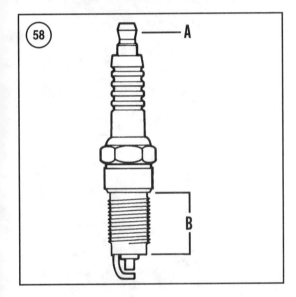

6. Inspect the spark plug caps and secondary wires for damage or hardness. If any portion is damaged, replace the cap and secondary wire as an assembly. The front and rear cylinder assemblies have different part numbers.

Spark Plug Gapping and Installing

Carefully gap the spark plugs to ensure a reliable, consistent spark. Use a special spark plug gapping tool and a wire feeler gauge.

1. Insert a wire feeler gauge between the center and side electrode of the plug (**Figure 56**). The correct gap is in **Table 9**. If the gap is correct, a slight drag will be felt as the wire gauge is pulled through. If there is no drag, or the gauge will not pass through, bend the side electrode with a gapping tool (**Figure 57**) to adjust to the proper gap in **Table 9**.

2. Install the terminal nut (A, **Figure 58**).
3. Apply a *light coat* of antiseize lubricant on the threads of the spark plug before installing it. Do *not* use engine oil on the plug threads.

> *CAUTION*
> *The cylinder head is aluminum and the spark plug hole is easily damaged if the spark plug is cross-threaded.*

4. Slowly screw the spark plug into the cylinder head by hand until it seats. Very little effort is required. If force is necessary, the plug is cross-threaded; unscrew it and try again.

> *NOTE*
> *Do not overtighten. This will only distort the gasket and destroy its sealing ability.*

5. Hand-tighten the plug until it seats against the cylinder head, then tighten it to the specification in **Table 6**.
6. Install the spark plug cap and lead to the correct spark plug. Rotate the cap slightly in both directions and make sure it is attached to the spark plug.
7. Repeat for the other spark plug.

Spark Plug Heat Range

Spark plugs are available in various heat ranges that are hotter or colder than the plugs originally installed by the manufacturer.

Select a plug with a heat range designed for the loads and conditions under which the motorcycle will be operated. A plug with an incorrect heat range can foul, overheat and cause piston damage.

In general, use a hot plug for low speeds and low temperatures. Use a cold plug for high speeds, high engine loads and high temperatures. The plug should operate hot enough to burn off unwanted deposits, but not so hot that it is damaged or causes preignition. To determine if plug heat range is correct, remove each spark plug and examine the insulator.

Do not change the spark plug heat range to compensate for adverse engine or carburetion conditions.

When replacing plugs, make sure the reach or thread length (B, **Figure 58**) is correct. A longer than standard plug could interfere with the piston and cause engine damage.

Refer to **Table 8** for recommended spark plugs.

SPARK PLUG CONDITION

NORMAL

GAP BRIDGED

CARBON FOULED

OVERHEATED

OIL FOULED

SUSTAINED PREIGNITION

Spark Plug Reading

Reading the spark plugs can provide information regarding engine performance. Reading plugs that have been in use indicates spark plug operation, air/fuel mixture composition and engine conditions (such as oil consumption or pistons). Before checking the spark plugs, operate the motorcycle under a medium load for approximately 6 miles (10 km). Avoid prolonged idling before shutting off the engine. Remove the spark plugs as described in this chapter. Examine each plug and compare it to those in **Figure 59**. Refer to the following sections to determine the operating conditions.

If the plugs are being inspected to determine if carburetor jetting is correct, start with new plugs and operate the motorcycle at the load that corresponds to the jetting information desired. For example, if the main jet is in question, operate the motorcycle at full throttle, shut the engine off and coast to a stop.

Normal condition

If the plug has a light tan or gray deposit and no abnormal gap wear or erosion, good engine, air/fuel mixture and ignition conditions are good. The plug in use is of the proper heat range, and may be serviced and returned to use.

Carbon fouled

Soft, dry, sooty deposits covering the entire firing end of the plug are evidence of incomplete combustion. Even though the firing end of the plug is dry, the plug's insulation decreases when in this condition. An electrical path is formed that bypasses the electrodes and causes a misfire condition. Carbon fouling can be caused by one or more of the following:

1. Rich fuel mixture.
2. Cold spark plug heat range.
3. Clogged air filter.
4. Improperly operating ignition component.
5. Ignition component failure.
6. Low engine compression.
7. Prolonged idling.

Oil fouled

The tip of an oil-fouled plug has a black insulator tip, a damp oily film over the firing end and a carbon layer over the entire nose. The electrodes are not worn. Oil-fouled spark plugs may be cleaned in an emergency, but it is better to replace them. Correct the cause of fouling before returning the engine to service. Common causes for this condition are:

1. Incorrect air/fuel mixture.
2. Low idle speed or prolonged idling.
3. Ignition component failure.
4. Cold spark plug heat range.
5. Engine still being broken in.
6. Valve guides worn.
7. Piston rings worn or broken.

Gap bridging

Plugs with gap bridging have gaps shorted out by combustion deposits between the electrodes. If this condition is encountered, check for excessive carbon or oil in the combustion chamber. Be sure to locate and correct the cause of this condition.

Overheating

Badly worn electrodes, premature gap wear and a gray or white blistered porcelain insulator surface are signs of overheating. The most common cause is a spark plug of the wrong heat range (too hot). If the spark plug is the correct heat range and is overheated, consider the following causes:

1. Lean air/fuel mixture.
2. Improperly operating ignition component.
3. Engine lubrication system malfunction.
4. Cooling system malfunction.
5. Engine air leak.
6. Improper spark plug installation (overtightened).
7. No spark plug gasket.

Worn out

Corrosive gases formed by combustion and high voltage sparks have eroded the electrodes. A spark plug in this condition requires more voltage to fire under hard acceleration. Replace it with a new spark plug.

Preignition

If the electrodes are melted, preignition is almost certainly the cause. Check for intake air leaks at the manifold and carburetor, or throttle body, and advanced ignition timing. It is also possible that the plug is the wrong heat range (too hot). Find the cause of the preignition before returning the engine to service. For additional information refer to *Engine Performance* in Chapter Two.

Ignition Timing

The engine is equipped with a fully transistorized ignition system and is controlled by the ignition module or electronic control module. This solid-state system uses no breaker points to trigger the ignition. Problems with the transistorized system are rare and there are no means of adjusting ignition timing. Harley-Davidson does not provide any ignition timing procedures. If an ignition related problem is suspected, inspect the ignition components as described in Chapter Eight.

Incorrect ignition timing can cause a drastic loss of engine performance and efficiency. It may also cause overheating.

IDLE SPEED ADJUSTMENT

Carbureted Models

1. Start the engine and warm it to normal operating temperature. Shut off the engine.
2. Make sure the starting enrichment (choke) valve (**Figure 42**) is pushed all the way to the OFF position.
3. On models without a tachometer, connect a portable tachometer to the engine following the manufacturer's instructions.

NOTE
Figure 60 is shown with the air filter assembly removed to better illustrate the step.

4. Start the engine and with the engine idling, compare the tachometer reading to the idle speed specification in **Table 9**. If the tachometer reading is incorrect, adjust the idle speed with the carburetor throttle stop screw (**Figure 60**).

NOTE
The idle mixture is set and sealed by the manufacturer and is not adjustable.

5. Accelerate the engine a couple of times and release the throttle. The idle speed should return to the speed set in Step 4. If necessary, readjust the idle speed by turning the throttle stop screw (**Figure 60**). Shut off the engine.
6. If a portable tachometer is installed, disconnect and remove it.

Fuel Injected Models

Idle speed adjustments on fuel injected models *must* be performed by a Harley-Davidson dealership equipped with a Scanalyzer tool.

Table 1 MAINTENANCE AND LUBRICATION SCHEDULE[1]

Pre-ride check
  Check tire condition and inflation pressure
  Check wheel rim condition
  Check light and horn operation
  Check engine oil level; add oil if necessary
  Check brake fluid level and condition; add fluid if necessary
  Check the operation of the front and rear brakes lever
  Check throttle operation
  Check clutch lever operation
  Check fuel level in fuel tank; top off if necessary
  Check fuel system for leaks
  Check drive belt tension
Initial 500 miles (800 km)
  Change engine oil and filter
  Check battery condition; clean cable connections if necessary
  Check brake fluid level and condition; add fluid if necessary
  Check front and rear brake pads and discs for wear
  Check tire condition and inflation pressure
  Check primary chain deflection; adjust if necessary
  Check drive belt tension; adjust if necessary
  Change primary chaincase lubricant
  Change transmission lubricant
  Check clutch lever operation; adjust if necessary
  Check drive belt and sprockets condition
  Inspect spark plugs
  Inspect air filter element
  Lubricate front brake and clutch lever pivot pin
  Lubricate clutch cable if necessary
  Check throttle operation
  Check enrichment (choke) cable operation (carbureted models)
  Check engine idle speed; adjust if necessary
  Check fuel system for leaks
  Check electrical switches and equipment for proper operation
  Check oil and brake lines for leakage
  Check all fasteners for tightness**
  Road test the bike
Every 2500 miles (4000 km)
  Check transmission lubricant level; add lubricant if necessary
  Check drive belt tension; adjust if necessary
  Inspect air filter element; clean or replace if necessary
  Check throttle operation
  Check enrichment (choke) cable operation (carbureted models)
  Check fuel system for leaks
  Check oil and brake lines for leakage
  Check electrical switches and equipment for proper operation
  Road test the bike
Every 5000 miles (8000 km)
  Change engine oil and filter
  Check battery condition; clean cable connections if necessary
  Check brake fluid level and condition; add fluid if necessary
  Check front and rear brake pads and discs for wear
  Check tire condition and inflation pressure
  Check wire wheel spoke nipple tightness; adjust if necessary (models so equipped)
  Check primary chain deflection; adjust if necessary
  Check drive belt tension; adjust if necessary
  Change primary chaincase lubricant
  Change transmission lubricant
  Check clutch lever operation; adjust if necessary
  Check drive belt and sprockets condition

(continued)

Table 1 MAINTENANCE AND LUBRICATION SCHEDULE[1] (continued)

Every 5000 miles (8000 km)
  Check steering head bearing adjustment; adjust if necessary
  Inspect spark plugs
  Inspect air filter element; clean or replace if necessary
  Lubricate front brake and clutch lever pivot pin
  Lubricate clutch cable if necessary
  Check throttle operation
  Check enrichment (choke) cable operation (carbureted models)
  Check engine idle speed; adjust if necessary
  Check fuel system for leaks
  Check electrical switches and equipment for proper operation
  Check oil and brake lines for leakage
  Check all fasteners for tightness[2]
  Road test the bike
Every 10,000 miles (16,000 km)
  Replace spark plugs
  Perform a compression test
  Lubricate steering head bearings
  Lubricate rear swing arm bearings
  Inspect engine mounts for wear or damage; replace if necessary
Every 20,000 miles (32,000 km)
  Change front fork oil
  Inspect fuel tank filter, replace if necessary
  Inspect fuel supply valve filter screen

1. Consider this maintenance schedule a guide to general maintenance and lubrication intervals. Harder than normal use and exposure to mud, water and high humidity indicates more frequent servicing to most of the maintenance items.
2. Except cylinder head bolts. Cylinder head bolts must be tightened following the procedure listed in Chapter Four. Improper tightening of the cylinder head bolts may cause cylinder gasket damage and/or cylinder head leakage.

Table 2 TIRE INFLATION PRESSURE (COLD)*

Model	kPa	PSI
Front wheels		
Rider only	248	36
Rider and passenger	248	36
Rear wheels		
Rider only	248	36
Rider and passenger	275	40

*Tire pressure for original equipment tires. Aftermarket tires may require different inflation pressure.

Table 3 ENGINE OIL SPECIFICATIONS

Type	HD rating	Viscosity	Ambient Operating temperature
HD Multi-grade	HD360	SAE 10W/40	Below 40° F
HD Multi-grade	HD360	SAE 20W/50	Above 40° F
HD Regular heavy	HD360	SAE 50	Above 60° F
HD Extra heavy	HD360	SAE 60	Above 80° F

Table 4 ENGINE AND PRIMARY DRIVE/TRANSMISSION OIL CAPACITIES

Oil tank refill capacity	3.5 U.S. qts. (3.3 L, 2.9 Imp. qts.)
Primary chain case (dry)	32 U.S. ozs. (946 ml., 26.6 Imp. ozs.)
Transmission	
Oil change	20-24 U.S. oz. (591-709 ml, 19-23 Imp. oz.)
Rebuild (dry)	24 U.S. oz. (709 ml, 23 Imp.oz.)

Table 5 RECOMMENDED LUBRICANTS AND FLUIDS

Brake fluid	DOT 5 silicone
Front fork oil	HD Type E or an equivalent
Fuel	91 pump octane or higher leaded or unleaded
Transmission	HD Transmission Lubricant or an equivalent
Primary chaincase	HD Primary Chaincase Lubricant or an equivalent

Table 6 MAINTENANCE AND TUNE-UP TORQUE SPECIFICATIONS

Item	ft.-lb.	in.-lb.	N•m
Air filter			
Cover screw	–	36-60	4-7
Torx screws	–	20-40	2-4
Clutch adjusting screw locknut	–	72-120	8-14
Clutch inspection cover screws	–	84-108	10-12
Crankcase oil plug	–	120-144	14-16
Engine oil drain plug	14-21	–	19-28
Front fork cap bolt	11-22	–	15-30
Spark plug	11-18	–	15-24
Primary chaincase			
Inspection cover screws	–	50-70	6-8
Chain adjuster shoe nut	21-29	–	29-39
Oil tank drain plug	14-21	–	19-28
Front axle nut	50-55	–	68-75
Rear axle nut			
1999-2001	60-65	–	81-88
2002	95-105	–	129-142
Transmission drain plug	14-21	–	19-28
Front fork			
Drain plug	–	72-96	8-11
Air connection hex	8-12	–	11-16

Table 7 AIR SUSPENSION ADJUSTMENTS

Load	Recommended pressure PSI (kPa)	
	Front fork*	Rear shock absorbers
Rider weight		
Up to 150 lbs. (68 kg)	–	–
For each additional		
25 lbs. (11kg)	1.0 (7)	1.0 (7)
Passenger weight for each		
additional 50 lbs. (23 kg)	–	1.5 (10)
Luggage weight for each		
additional 10 lbs. (6 kg)	1.0 (7)	3.0 (21)
Maximum pressure	25 (172)	25 (172)

*The front fork on 2002 models is not equipped with air suspension.

Table 8 FRONT FORK OIL CAPACITY/OIL LEVEL

Model	Capacity/level (each fork leg)
Fork oil capacity	
Non-cartridge type	
1999-2001 models	9.7 U.S. oz. (287 ml, 8.08 Imp. oz.)
2002-2005 models	11.1 U.S. oz. (328 ml, 9.24 Imp. oz.)
Cartridge type	11.1 U.S. oz. (328 ml, 9.24 Imp. oz.)[1]
Fork oil level (cartridge type)	
2002 models	4.4 in. (111.8 mm)[2]
2003-2005 models	4.21 in. (107 mm)[2]

1. The fork oil capacity is approximately this amount. The fork oil level must be at the specified level.
2. From the top surface of the fork tube

Table 9 MAINTENANCE AND TUNE-UP SPECIFICATIONS

Item	Specification
Engine compression	90 psi (620 kPa)
Spark plugs	HD No. 6R12*
Gap	0.038-0.043 in. (0.097-1.09 mm)
Idle speed	950-1050 rpm
Ignition timing	Non-adjustable
Drive belt deflection	5/16-3/8 in. (8-10 mm)
Brake pad minimum thickness	
1999 models	1/16 in. (1.6 mm)
2000-2005 models	0.04 in. (1.02 mm)
Clutch cable free play	1/16-1/8 in. (1.6-3.2 mm)

*Harley-Davidson recommends that no other type of spark plug be substituted for the recommended H-D type.

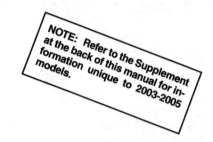
NOTE: Refer to the Supplement at the back of this manual for information unique to 2003-2005 models.

CHAPTER FOUR

ENGINE

This chapter provides complete service and overhaul procedures, including information for disassembly, removal, inspection, service and engine reassembly.

Refer to **Tables 1-6** at the end of the chapter for specifications. Refer to the Supplement at the back of this manual for information regarding the Twin Cam 103 engine.

All models covered in this manual are equipped with the Twin Cam 88 or 103 engine, an air-cooled four-stroke, overhead-valve V-twin engine. The engine consists of three major assemblies: engine, crankcase and gearcase. Viewed from the engine's right side, engine rotation is clockwise.

Both cylinders fire once in 720° of crankshaft rotation. The rear cylinder fires 315° after the front cylinder. The front cylinder fires again in another 405°. Note that one cylinder is always on its exhaust stroke when the other fires on its compression stroke.

Refer to **Figure 1** for basic engine operating principles.

SERVICE PRECAUTIONS

Before servicing the engine, note the following:

1. Review the *Basic Service Methods* and *Precision Measuring Tools* sections in Chapter One. Accurate measurements are critical to a successful engine rebuild.

2. Throughout the text there are references to the left and right side of the engine. This refers to the engine as it is mounted in the frame, not how it may sit on the workbench.

3. Always replace worn or damaged fasteners with those of the same size, type and torque requirements. Make sure to identify each bolt before replacing it. Lubricate bolt threads with engine oil, unless otherwise specified, before tightening them. If a specific torque value is not listed in **Table 4**, refer to the general torque specifications in Chapter One.

> *CAUTION*
> *The engine is assembled with hardened fasteners. Do not install fasteners with a lower strength grade classification.*

4. Use special tools where noted. Refer to **Table 11** in Chapter One.

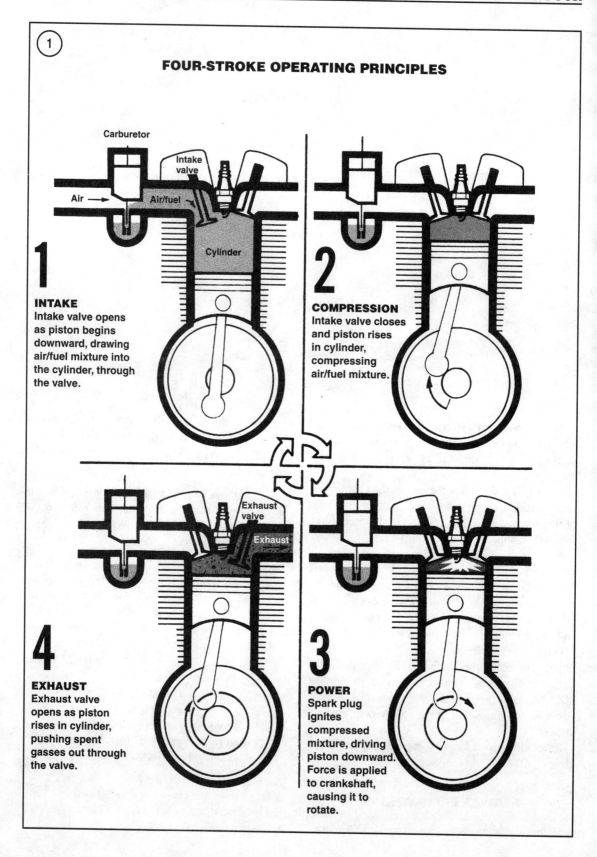

① **FOUR-STROKE OPERATING PRINCIPLES**

1

INTAKE
Intake valve opens
as piston begins
downward, drawing
air/fuel mixture into
the cylinder, through
the valve.

2

COMPRESSION
Intake valve closes
and piston rises
in cylinder,
compressing
air/fuel mixture.

4

EXHAUST
Exhaust valve
opens as piston
rises in cylinder,
pushing spent
gasses out through
the valve.

3

POWER
Spark plug
ignites
compressed
mixture, driving
piston downward.
Force is applied
to crankshaft,
causing it to
rotate.

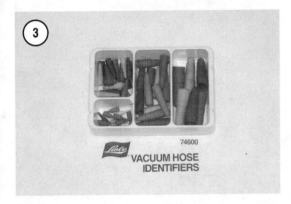

VACUUM HOSE
IDENTIFIERS
74600

5. Store parts in boxes, plastic bags and containers (**Figure 2**). Use masking tape and a permanent, waterproof marking pen to label parts.

6. Use a box of assorted size and color vacuum hose identifiers, such as those shown in **Figure 3** (Lisle part No. 74600), to identify hoses and fittings during engine removal and disassembly.

7. Use a vise with protective jaws to hold parts.

8. Use a press or special tools when force is required to remove and install parts. Do not try to pry, hammer or otherwise force them on or off.

9. Replace all O-rings and oil seals during reassembly. Apply a small amount of grease to the inner lips of each new seal to prevent damage when the engine is first started.

10. Record the location, position and thickness of all shims as they are removed.

SPECIAL TOOLS

Engine service requires a number of special tools. These tools and their part numbers are listed with the individual procedures. For a complete list of the special tools mentioned in this manual, refer to **Ta-**

ble 11 in Chapter One. The engine tools used in this chapter are either Harley-Davidson or JIMS special tools. JIMS special tools are available through some Harley-Davidson dealerships or many aftermarket motorcycle suppliers.

When purchasing special tools, make sure to specify that the tools required are for the 1999-on FLHT, FLHR or FLTR series Twin-Cam 88 models. Many of the tools are specific to this engine. Tools for other engine models may be slightly different.

SERVICING ENGINE IN FRAME

Many components can be serviced while the engine is mounted in the frame:

1. Rocker arm cover and rocker arms.
2. Cylinder heads.
3. Cylinders and pistons.
4. Camshafts.
5. Gearshift mechanism.
6. Clutch.
7. Transmission.
8. Carburetor or fuel injection induction module.
9. Starter motor and gears.
10. Alternator and electrical systems.

ENGINE

Removal

Refer to **Figure 4**.

1. Thoroughly clean the engine of all dirt and debris.

2. Remove the seat as described in Chapter Fourteen.

> *NOTE*
> *Always disarm the optional TSSM security system prior to disconnecting the battery or the siren will sound.*

3. Disconnect the negative battery cable as described Chapter Eight.

4. Support the motorcycle on a stand or floor jack. See *Motorcycle Stands* in Chapter Nine.

5. Remove the fuel tank as described in Chapter Seven.

6. Remove both saddlebags as described in Chapter Fourteen.

7. Remove both frame side covers.

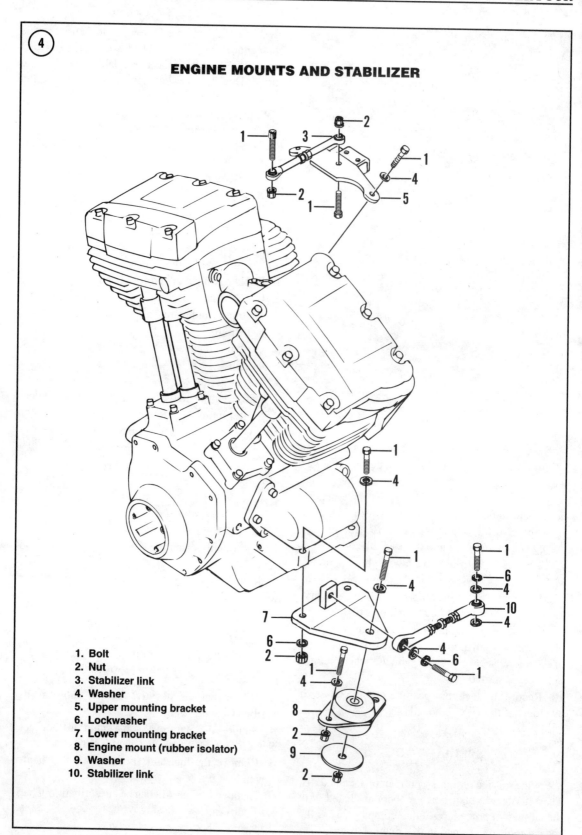

ENGINE MOUNTS AND STABILIZER

1. Bolt
2. Nut
3. Stabilizer link
4. Washer
5. Upper mounting bracket
6. Lockwasher
7. Lower mounting bracket
8. Engine mount (rubber isolator)
9. Washer
10. Stabilizer link

8. On FLHTCUI models, remove the front fairing lower cover on each side as described in Chapter Fourteen.

9. Remove the air filter and backing plate as described in Chapter Seven.

10A. On carbureted models, remove the carburetor as described in Chapter Seven.

10B. On fuel injected models, remove the fuel injection induction module as described in Chapter Seven.

11. Remove the exhaust system as described in Chapter Seven.

12. Remove the rear brake pedal as described in Chapter Twelve.

13. Remove all four footboards as described in Chapter Fourteen.

14. Drain the engine oil as described in Chapter Three.

15. Remove the bolts securing the oil line cover and remove the cover (**Figure 5**).

16. Disconnect the three oil lines from the crankcase. Plug the oil lines to prevent dirt from entering the hoses.

17. Remove the camshaft position sensor as described in Chapter Eight.

18. Disconnect the following electrical connectors:
   a. Crankshaft position sensor (**Figure 6**).
   b. Alternator stator and voltage regulator (**Figure 7**).
   c. Oil pressure switch or sending unit (**Figure 8**).
   d. MAP sensor on carbureted models.
   e. Engine temperature sensor (**Figure 9**).

19. Remove the ignition coil and spark plug assembly as described in Chapter Eight.

20. Remove the primary chain case assembly, including the inner housing, as described in Chapter Five.

21. Remove the engine oil cap/dipstick.

22. Remove the alternator rotor as described in Chapter Eight.

23. Disconnect the hose from the breather cover and move the hose behind the transmission flange.

24A. On 1999-2001 models, on the right side, cut the cable clamp securing the voltage regulator connector to the lower frame rail. Lower the connector and disconnect it (**Figure 10**).

24B. On 2002 models, perform the following:

  a. Locate the voltage regulator connector attached to the bottom of the voltage regulator.

  b. Slide the connector toward the left side to release the groove on the connector from the bracket ridge (**Figure 11**).

  c. Raise the external latch and use a rocking motion, separate the connector's pin and socket halves.

25. Remove the alternator stator assembly as described in Chapter Eight.

26. Remove the flange locknuts securing the voltage regulator to the frame front cross tube studs. Lift the voltage regulator up and off the studs, and remove it and the wiring harness.

27. Remove the clutch cable from the lower portion of the crankcase as described under *Clutch Cable Replacement* in Chapter Five.

28. On the left side of the engine stabilizer, refer to **Figure 4** and perform the following:

  a. Remove the bolt and nut securing the inboard end of the stabilizing link (A, **Figure 12**) to the frame.

  b. Remove the two bolts and washers (B, **Figure 12**) securing the upper mounting bracket to the cylinder heads.

  c. Remove the stabilizer link and upper mounting bracket assembly from the frame and engine.

29. Wrap the frame front down tubes with protective tape to prevent surface damage in the following steps.

30. Support the transmission case with a jack or wooden blocks. Apply sufficient jack pressure on the transmission prior to removing the engine-to-transmission mounting bolts.

31. Using a ratchet strap, secure the transmission to the frame so it will not shift after the engine is removed.

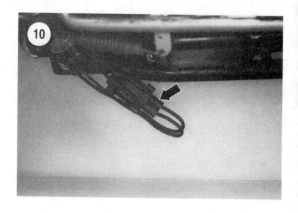

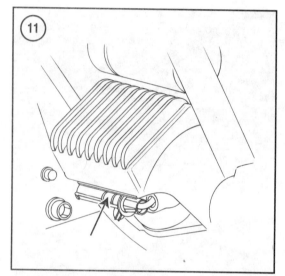

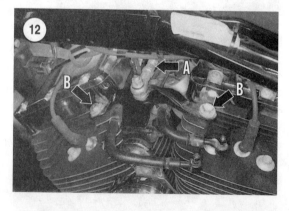

32. Remove the two bolts and washers (**Figure 13**) on each side securing the engine to the transmission.

33. Support the engine with a floor jack (**Figure 14**). Apply enough jack pressure on the crankcase to support it prior to removing the engine mounting bolts.

34. Remove the two bolts and washers (**Figure 15**) securing the engine to the front lower mounting bracket.

35. Cover both rocker covers with foam padding to protect the finish.

36. Check the engine to make sure all wiring, hoses and other related components have been disconnected from the engine. Make sure nothing will interfere with the removal of the engine from the right side of the frame.

4

NOTE
Due to the weight of the engine assembly, a minimum of two people are required to safely remove the engine from the frame.

37. Slide the engine assembly forward to clear the two locating dowels on the lower engine-to-transmission mounting bolt locations. The dowels stick out approximately 1/2 in. (12.7 mm). The engine may have to be rotated slightly to clear the dowels.

38. Remove the engine from the right side of the frame.

39. Mount the engine in the twin cam 88 engine stand (JIMS part No. 1022) (**Figure 16**) or an equivalent.

40. Service the front engine mount, if necessary. Refer to **Figure 4**.

41. Clean the front and rear engine mount bolts and washers in solvent and dry thoroughly.

42. Replace leaking or damaged oil hoses.

Installation

CAUTION
Due to the weight of the engine assembly, a minimum of two people are required to safely install the engine into the frame.

1. If removed, install the two lower locating dowels in the transmission case (**Figure 17**).

2. Make sure all wiring, hoses and other related components are out of the way and will not interfere with engine installation.

3. Correctly position a floor jack and piece of wood under the frame to support the engine when it is installed into the frame.

4. Install the engine from the right side of the frame and place it on the floor jack. Apply enough jack

pressure on the crankcase to support it prior to installing the engine mounting bolts.

5. Slide the engine assembly toward the rear and onto the two transmission locating dowels. The engine may have to be rotated slightly to accept the dowels.

6. Install the four engine-to-transmission bolts and washers hand-tight at this time.

7. Install the two bolts and washers securing the engine to the lower mounting bracket front isolator. Tighten finger-tight at this time.

8. Tighten the engine-to-transmission bolts in a criss-cross pattern in the following sequence:
   a. Tighten to 15 ft.-lb. (20 N•m).
   b. Tighten to 30-35 ft.-lb. (41-47 N•m).

9. Tighten the engine-to-lower bracket bolts to the specification in **Table 4**.

10. Remove the ratchet strap from the transmission and frame.

11. Remove the floor jack.

NOTE
Step 12 is shown with the engine removed from the frame to better illustrate the procedure.

12. Install the oil filter mount as follows:
   a. Install *new* O-ring seals (**Figure 18**) onto the mount.
   b. Apply Three Bond TB1342 or an equivalent to the bolt threads prior to installing them onto the *new* lockplate.
   c. Install the oil filter mount onto the crankcase and install the lockplate, three bolts and washers (**Figure 19**).
   d. Tighten the bolts to the specification in **Table 4**.
   e. Bend down the locking tab against the top and bottom bolt heads.
   f. Install the oil filter.

13. Remove the protective tape from the frame front down tubes.

14. Remove the foam padding from the rocker covers.

15. Install the clutch cable onto the lower portion of the crankcase as described under *Clutch Cable Replacement* in Chapter Five.

16. On the left side of the engine stabilizer, refer to **Figure 4** and perform the following:
   a. Install the stabilizer link and upper mounting bracket assembly onto the frame and engine.

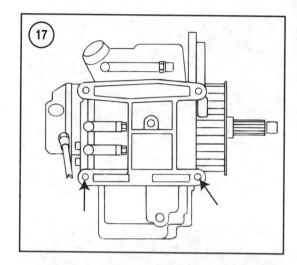

   b. Install the two bolts and washers (B, **Figure 12**) securing the upper mounting bracket to the cylinder heads. Tighten to the specification in **Table 4**

   c. Install the bolt and nut securing the inboard end of the stabilizing link (A, **Figure 12**) to the frame and tighten securely

CAUTION
When installing the voltage regulator onto the threaded studs, make sure its electrical wires are not trapped between the frame and the base of the voltage regulator. If the wires are trapped, it will cause a short that may damage the electrical harness.

17. Install the voltage regulator onto the frame front cross tube studs. Install the flange locknuts (**Figure 20**) and tighten them to the specification in **Table 4**.

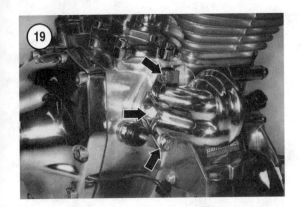

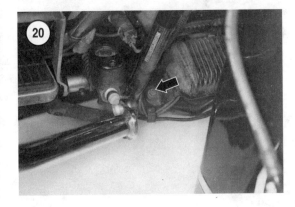

18. Install the alternator stator assembly as described in Chapter Eight.

19A. On 1999-2001 models, on the right side, connect the voltage regulator connector (**Figure 10**). Raise it up against the lower frame rail and secure it with a new cable clamp.

19B. On 2002 models, perform the following:

   a. Connect the pin and voltage regulators socket halves together until the latches click together.

   b. Slide the connector toward the right side of the motorcycle until the connector groove fully engages the bracket ridge (**Figure 11**).

20. Connect the hose onto the transmission breather cover.

21. Install the alternator rotor as described in Chapter Eight.

22. Install the engine oil cap/dipstick.

23. Install the primary chain case inner housing and assembly as described in Chapter Five.

24. Adjust the clutch and primary chain as described in Chapter Three.

25. Install the primary chain outer housing as described in Chapter Five.

26. Install the ignition coil and spark plug assembly as described in Chapter Eight.

27. Connect the following electrical connectors:

   a. Crankshaft position sensor (**Figure 6**).

   b. Alternator stator and voltage regulator (**Figure 7**).

   c. Oil pressure switch or sending unit (**Figure 8**).

   d. MAP sensor on carburetted models.

   e. Engine temperature sensor (**Figure 9**).

28. Install the camshaft position sensor as described in Chapter Eight.

29. Connect the three oil lines onto the crankcase and install new hose clamps.

30. Install the oil line cover and bolts. Tighten the bolts to the specification in **Table 4**.

31. Install all four footboards as described in Chapter Fourteen.

32. Install the exhaust system as described in Chapter Seven.

33. Install the rear brake pedal as described in Chapter Twelve.

34A. On carbureted models, install the carburetor as described in Chapter Seven.

34B. On fuel injected models, install the fuel injection induction module as described in Chapter Seven.

35. Install the air filter backing plate and air filter as described in Chapter Seven.

36. Install the fuel tank as described in Chapter Seven.

37. On FLHTCUI models, install the front fairing lower cover on each side as described in Chapter Fourteen.

38. Install both saddlebags as described in Chapter Fourteen.

39. Install both frame side covers.

40. Remove the stand from under the motorcycle and place the motorcycle on the jiffystand.

41. Connect the negative battery cable as described in Chapter Eight.

42. Install the seat.

43. Refill the engine oil as described in Chapter Three.

44. Check the motorcycle alignment as described in Chapter Nine.

45. Start the engine and check for leaks.

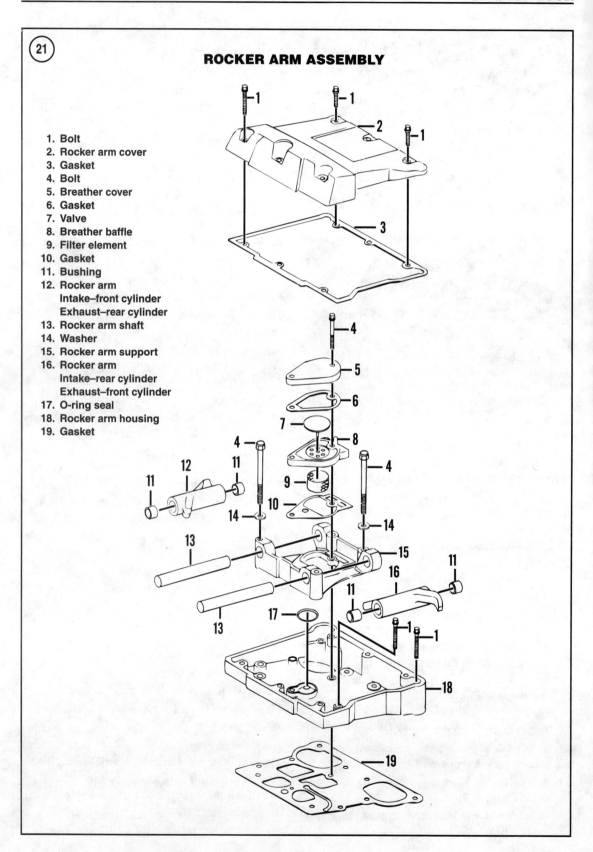

(21)

ROCKER ARM ASSEMBLY

1. Bolt
2. Rocker arm cover
3. Gasket
4. Bolt
5. Breather cover
6. Gasket
7. Valve
8. Breather baffle
9. Filter element
10. Gasket
11. Bushing
12. Rocker arm
    Intake–front cylinder
    Exhaust–rear cylinder
13. Rocker arm shaft
14. Washer
15. Rocker arm support
16. Rocker arm
    Intake–rear cylinder
    Exhaust–front cylinder
17. O-ring seal
18. Rocker arm housing
19. Gasket

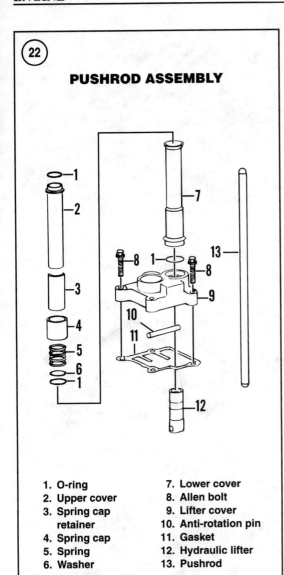

PUSHROD ASSEMBLY

1. O-ring
2. Upper cover
3. Spring cap retainer
4. Spring cap
5. Spring
6. Washer
7. Lower cover
8. Allen bolt
9. Lifter cover
10. Anti-rotation pin
11. Gasket
12. Hydraulic lifter
13. Pushrod

ROCKER ARMS AND PUSHRODS

Refer to **Figure 21** and **Figure 22**.

The rocker arm and pushrod procedures are shown with the rear cylinder. The same procedures also apply to the front cylinder. Any differences are noted.

NOTE
The rocker arms and pushrod procedures are shown with the engine removed to better illustrate the steps.

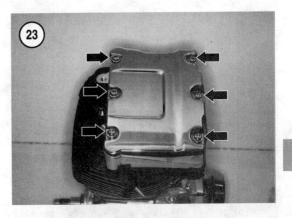

Removal

1. If the engine is mounted in the frame, perform the following:
   a. Perform Steps 1-10 under *Engine Removal* in this chapter.
   b. Remove the upper cylinder head mounting bracket.
2. Using a crisscross pattern, loosen and remove the rocker arm cover bolts (**Figure 23**).
3. Remove the rocker arm cover and gasket.

NOTE
On 2002 models, the breather is a one-piece unit and is removed as an assembly.

4. On 1999-2001 models, disassemble the breather as follows:
   a. Remove the bolts (A, **Figure 24**) and remove the cover (B) and gasket.
   b. Remove the breather baffle (A, **Figure 25**), valve (B) and gasket (**Figure 26**).
   c. Install *new* gaskets during installation.

5. Remove both spark plugs as described in Chapter Three to make it easier to rotate the engine by hand.

> *CAUTION*
> *Do not rotate the engine using the camshaft sprocket mounting bolt. Doing so may break the bolt and damage the camshaft.*

> *CAUTION*
> *The piston must be at top dead center (TDC) to avoid damage to the pushrods and rocker arms in the following steps.*

6A. *With the primary chain cover in place,* position the piston for the cylinder being worked on at top dead center (TDC) on the compression stroke as follows:

a. Support the motorcycle on a stand with the rear wheel off the ground. See *Motorcycle Stands* in Chapter Nine.
b. Shift the transmission into fifth gear.
c. Rotate the rear wheel in the direction of normal rotation.
d. Stop rotating the rear wheel when the intake and exhaust valves are closed.
e. Wiggle both rocker arms. There should be free play which indicates that both valves are closed and the piston is at top dead center (TDC) on the compression stroke. Also, the push rods are in the unloaded position.
f. Look into the spark plug hole with a flashlight and verify that the piston is at TDC.

6B. *With the primary chain cover removed,* position the piston for the cylinder being worked on at top dead center (TDC) on the compression stroke as follows:

a. Shift the transmission into NEUTRAL.
b. Install the sprocket shaft nut onto the end of the left side of the crankshaft.
c. Place a socket or wrench on the compensating sprocket shaft nut.
d. Rotate the compensating sprocket shaft *counterclockwise* until the intake and exhaust valves are closed.
e. Wiggle both rocker arms. There should be free play which indicates that both valves are closed and the piston is at top dead center (TDC) on the compression stroke. Also, the push rods are in the unloaded position.

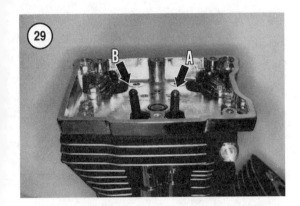

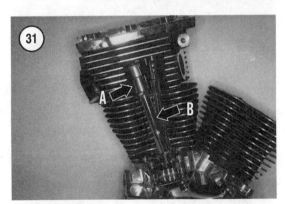

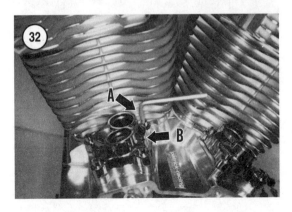

f. Look into the spark plug hole with a flashlight and verify that the piston is at TDC.

7. Using a crisscross pattern, loosen, then remove the four bolts and washers (**Figure 27**) securing the rocker arm support. Remove the support.

8. Remove the O-ring seal (**Figure 28**) from the rocker arm housing.

9. Mark each pushrod with its top and bottom position. Then its operating position in the cylinder head.

NOTE
When removing the pushrods in the following steps, do not intermix the parts from each set. When reinstalling the original pushrods, install them so each end faces in its original operating position. The pushrods develop a set wear pattern and installing them upside down may cause rapid wear to the pushrod, lifter and rocker arm.

10. Remove the intake (A, **Figure 29**) and exhaust (B) pushrods up through the cylinder head.

11. Remove the pushrod covers as follows:

a. Using a screwdriver, pry the spring cap retainer (**Figure 30**) from between the cylinder head and spring cap.

b. Slide the upper cover down (A, **Figure 31**) and remove the pushrod cover assembly (B) from the cylinder head and the lifter cover.

c. Repeat substeps a and b for the opposite pushrod cover.

NOTE
To clear the cylinder's lower cooling fins, loosen the lifter cover's two inner Allen bolts with a short 90° Allen wrench (A, Figure 32) or a ball-end straight Allen wrench.

12. Remove the lifter cover mounting bolts and remove the cover (B, **Figure 32**).

13. Remove the lifter cover gasket from the crankcase.

NOTE
Do not intermix the lifters when removing them in Step 14. Mark them so they can be installed in their original positions.

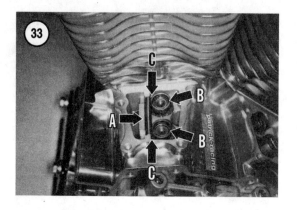

14. Remove the antirotation pin (A, **Figure 33**), then remove both hydraulic lifters (B).

15. Cover the crankcase opening with duct tape (**Figure 34**) to prevent the entry of debris.

16. Loosen the rocker arm housing six bolts (**Figure 35**) 1/8 turn at a time in the pattern shown in **Figure 36**.

17. Tap the rocker arm housing with a rubber mallet to free it, then lift it off the cylinder head.

18. Remove the rocker arm housing gasket.

Installation

1. Position the *new* rocker arm housing gasket onto the cylinder head so the breather channel (**Figure 37**) is covered and install the gasket (**Figure 38**).

2. Install the rocker arm housing onto the cylinder head.

3. Apply ThreeBond TB1342, or an equivalent, threadlocking compound to the bolt threads. Install the rocker arm housing six bolts (**Figure 35**) and tighten them 1/8 turn at a time in the pattern shown in **Figure 36**. Tighten them to the specification in **Table 4**.

4. Install a *new* O-ring seal (**Figure 28**) onto the rocker arm housing. Apply a light coat of clean engine oil to the O-ring.

5. Install the hydraulic lifters (B, **Figure 33**) into the correct crankcase receptacles with both flat surfaces facing toward the front and rear of the engine. This is necessary for installation of the antirotation pin in the next step.

CAUTION
Failure to install the antirotational pin will allow the lifter to rotate off the camshaft lobe and cause severe internal engine damage.

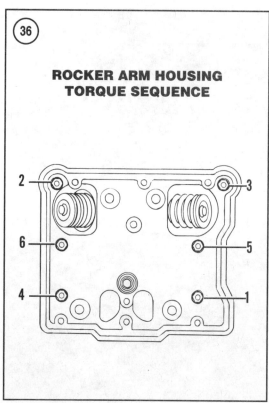

ROCKER ARM HOUSING TORQUE SEQUENCE

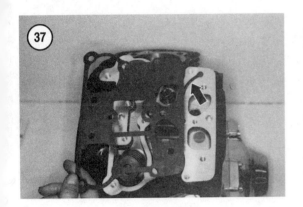

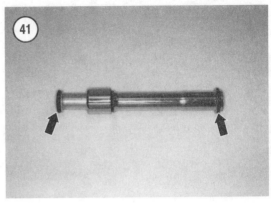

4

6. Install the antirotation pin (A, **Figure 33**) and make sure it is seated correctly within the crankcase receptacle and against the flats on both hydraulic lifters (C, **Figure 33**).

7. Rotate the engine until both lifters for the cylinder head being serviced seat onto the camshaft's lowest position (base circle). The lifter's top surface will be flush with the top surface of the crankcase surface as shown in **Figure 39**.

8. Install a *new* lifter cover gasket (**Figure 40**) onto the crankcase.

NOTE
To clear the cylinder's lower cooling fins, tighten the lifter cover two inner Allen bolts with a short 90° Allen wrench (A, Figure 32).

9. Install the lifter cover and the mounting bolts (B, **Figure 32**). Tighten the bolts to the specification in **Table 4**.

10. Install *new* O-ring seals (**Figure 41**) onto each end of the pushrod covers. Apply a light coat of clean engine oil to the O-rings.

11. If the pushrod cover assembly was disassembled, reassemble it as described under *Pushrods* in this chapter.

CAUTION
The pushrod covers and the pushrods must be installed in the correct location in the cylinder head and pushrod cover as indicated in Table 3.

12. Compress the pushrod cover and install it into the correct location in the lifter cover and cylinder

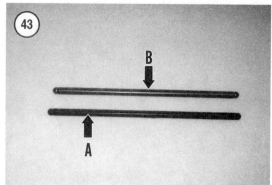

head (**Figure 42**). Do not install the spring cap retainer at this time.

13. Repeat Step 11 and Step 12 for the other pushrod cover.

14. Install the pushrods as follows:

> *CAUTION*
> *Two different length pushrods are used in the Twin Cam 88 engine. The black exhaust pushrods (A, **Figure** 43) are longer than the silver intake pushrods (B).*

a. When installing the existing pushrods, install each pushrod in its original position and in the correct orientation. Refer to A, **Figure 29** for intake and B, **Figure 29** for exhaust.

> *NOTE*
> *Because new pushrods are symmetrical, they can be installed with either end facing up.*

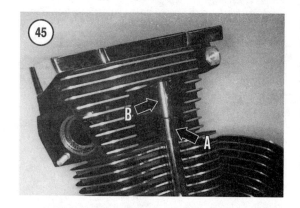

b. Make sure the pushrod is centered into its respective lifter.

15. Install the rocker arm support assembly and bolts (**Figure 44**).

> *CAUTION*
> *To avoid damaging a pushrod, rocker arms or valves, tighten the rocker arm support mounting bolts evenly and in a crisscross pattern. When tightening the mounting bolts, spin each pushrod by hand to ensure the rocker arm support is being tightened evenly. If one or both pushrods cannot be rotated, loosen the mounting bolts and determine the cause.*

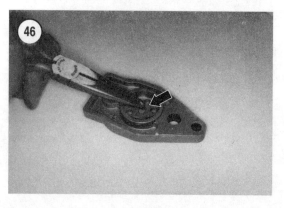

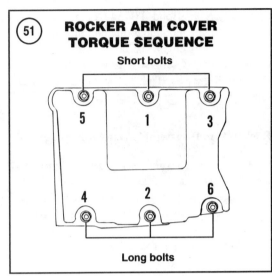

ROCKER ARM COVER TORQUE SEQUENCE

Short bolts

5   1   3

4   2   6

Long bolts

16. Tighten the rocker arm support assembly and bolts evenly in a crisscross pattern to the specification in **Table 4**.

17. Make sure the pushrod cover O-rings are correctly seated in the cylinder head and lifter cover. Depress the spring cap (A, **Figure 45**) and install the spring cap retainer (B). Make sure the spring cap retainer is correctly seated. Repeat for the remaining pushrod covers.

18A. On 1999-2001 models, assemble the breather as follows:

  a. If removed, install the valve onto the breather baffle and pull the tip through from the other side (**Figure 46**) to seat it.

  b. Install a *new* gasket (**Figure 47**).

  c. Install a *new* filter element.

  d. Hold the filter element in place and install the breather baffle (**Figure 48**).

  e. Install the cover and bolts (**Figure 49**) and tighten securely.

18B. On 2002 models, perform the following:

  a. Install a *new* filter element.

  b. Hold the filter element in place and install the breather assembly.

  c. Install the bolts and tighten securely.

19. Install a *new* rocker arm cover gasket (**Figure 50**).

20. Install the rocker arm cover.

NOTE
*There are two different length bolts (**Figure 51**) securing the rocker arm cover.*

21. Apply ThreeBond TB1342 or an equivalent threadlocking compound to the bolt threads. Install the rocker arm cover six bolts (**Figure 52**) and tighten them 1/8 turn at a time in the sequence shown in **Figure 51**. Tighten them to the specification in **Table 4**.

Rocker Arm Disassembly/Assembly

1. Before removing the rocker arms (**Figure 53**), measure the rocker arm end clearance as follows:
   a. Insert a feeler gauge between the rocker arm and the rocker arm support as shown in **Figure 54**.
   b. Record the measurement.
   c. Repeat for each rocker arm.
   d. Replace the rocker arm and/or the rocker arm support if the end clearance is not within the specification in **Table 2**.
2. Prior to disassembling the rocker arms, mark each one with an IN (intake) or EX (exhaust) (**Figure 55**) to ensure they are installed in their original positions.
3. Remove the rocker arm shafts (A, **Figure 56**) and remove the rocker arms (B).
4. Clean all parts in solvent. Blow compressed air through all oil passages.
5. Install the rocker arm shaft (A, **Figure 57**) part way into the rocker arm support (B) in its original position.
6. Install a rocker arm (C, **Figure 57**) into its original position and push the shaft part way through the rocker arm.
7. Align the notch in the rocker arm shaft (A, **Figure 58**) with the mating bolt hole (B) in the support and install the shaft all the way. Check for correct alignment (**Figure 59**).
8. Repeat Step 6 and Step 7 for the remaining rocker arm and shaft.

Rocker Arm Component Inspection

When measuring the rocker arm components, compare the actual measurements to the specifications in **Table 2**. Replace any part that is damaged or out of specification as described in this section.
1. Inspect the rocker arm pads and ball sockets (**Figure 60**) for pitting and excessive wear.
2. Examine the rocker arm shaft (**Figure 61**) for scoring, ridge wear or other damage. If these condi-

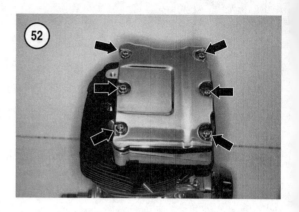

tions are present, replace the rocker arm shaft. If the shaft does not show any wear or damage, continue with Step 8.
3. Check the rocker arm bushing (**Figure 62**) for wear or scoring.
4. Measure the rocker arm shaft diameter (**Figure 63**) where it contacts the rocker arm bushing and rocker arm housing. Measure both ends of the shaft. Record each measurement.
5. Measure the rocker arm bushing inside diameter (**Figure 64**) and the rocker arm support bore diameter. Record each measurement.
6. Subtract the measurements taken in Step 4 from those taken in Step 5 to obtain the following rocker arm shaft measurements:
   a. Shaft-to-rocker arm support.
   b. Shaft-to-rocker arm bushing.
7. Replace the rocker arm, the bushings or the rocker arm support if the clearance exceeds the specifications in **Table 2**. Rocker arm bushing replacement is described in this chapter.
8. Inspect the rocker arm shaft contact surfaces in the rocker arm support (**Figure 65**) for wear or elongation.
9. Inspect the gasket surface of the rocker arm cover for damage or warp.
10. Inspect the rocker arm support (**Figure 66**) for damage or warp.
11. Inspect both gasket surfaces of the rocker arm housing for damage or warp.

Rocker Arm Bushing Replacement

Each rocker arm is equipped with two bushings (**Figure 62**). Replacement bushings must be reamed after installation. Use the rocker arm bushing line

---

4

ROCKER ARM ASSEMBLY

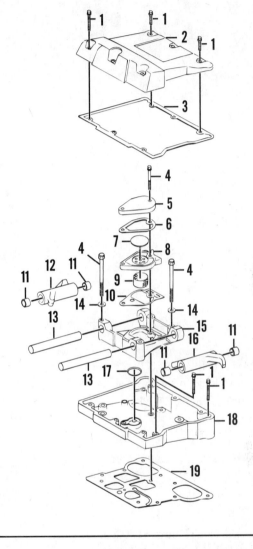

1. Bolt
2. Rocker arm cover
3. Gasket
4. Bolt
5. Breather cover
6. Gasket
7. Valve
8. Breather baffle
9. Filter element
10. Gasket
11. Bushing
12. Rocker arm
    Intake–front cylinder
    Exhaust–rear cylinder
13. Rocker arm shaft
14. Washer
15. Rocker arm support
16. Rocker arm
    Intake–rear cylinder
    Exhaust–front cylinder
17. O-ring seal
18. Rocker arm housing
19. Gasket

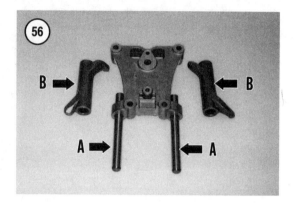

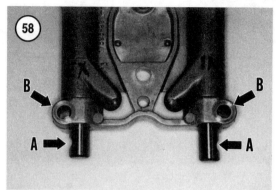

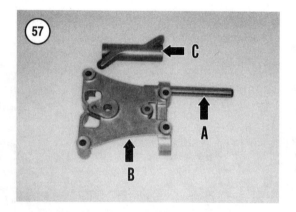

reamer (JIMS part No. 94804-57). If the correct size reamer is unavailable, have the bushings replaced by a Harley-Davidson dealership.

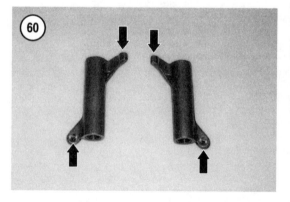

NOTE
Since the new bushings must be reamed, remove one bushing at a time. The opposite bushing is then used as a guide to ream the first bushing.

1. Press one bushing (**Figure 62**) out of the rocker arm. Do not remove the second bushing. If the bushing is difficult to remove, perform the following:

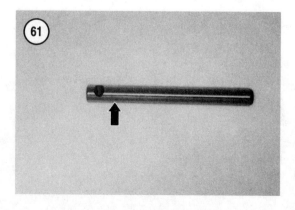

   a. Thread a 9/16 × 18 tap into the bushing.
   b. Support the rocker arm in a press so the tap is at the bottom.
   c. Insert a mandrel through the top of the rocker arm and seat it on top of the tap.
   d. Press on the mandrel to force the bushing and tap out of the rocker arm.
   e. Remove the tap from the bushing and discard the bushing.

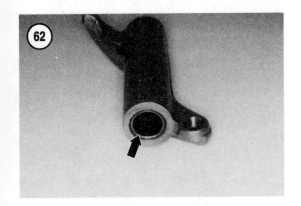

4

2. Position the new bushing with the split portion facing toward the top of the rocker arm.

3. Press the new bushing into the rocker arm until the bushing's outer surface is flush with the end of rocker arm bore.

4. Ream the new bushing with the bushing line reamer as follows:

    a. Mount the rocker arm in a vise with soft jaws so the new bushing is at the bottom.

CAUTION
Only turn the reamer clockwise. Do not rotate the reamer counterclockwise or the reamer and bushing will be damaged.

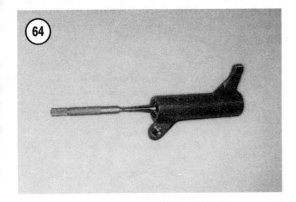

    b. Mount a tap handle on top of the reamer and insert the reamer into the bushing. Turn the reamer *clockwise* until it passes through the new bushing and remove it from the bottom side.

5. Remove the rocker arm from the vise and repeat Steps 1-3 to replace the opposite bushing. The first bushing now serves as a guide to ream the second bushing.

6. After installing and reaming both bushings, clean the rocker arm assembly in solvent. Then clean it with hot, soapy water and rinse it with clear, cold water. Dry it with compressed air.

7. Measure the inside diameter of each bushing. When properly reamed, the bushings must provide the shaft clearance listed in **Table 2**.

Pushrod Inspection

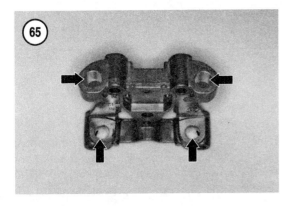

1. Clean the pushrods in solvent and dry them with compressed air.

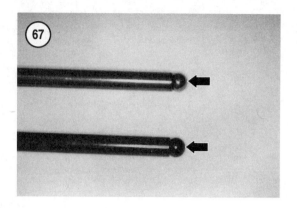

2. Check the pushrods for bending, cracks and worn or damaged ball heads (**Figure 67**).
3. Replace any damaged pushrods.

CYLINDER HEAD

The cylinder head procedures are shown on the rear cylinder (**Figure 68**). The same procedures also relate to the front cylinder. Any differences are noted.

NOTE
The following procedures are shown with the engine removed to better illustrate the steps.

Removal

1. Remove the rocker arm assemblies and pushrods as described in this chapter.
2. Using a crisscross pattern, loosen the four cylinder head bolts (**Figure 69**) 1/8 turn at a time. Remove the four bolts and note the position of the short and long bolts.
3. Tap the cylinder head with a rubber mallet to free it, then lift it off the cylinder.
4. Remove the cylinder head gasket.
5. Remove the two O-rings and the cylinder head dowel pins (**Figure 70**).
6. Repeat these steps to remove the opposite cylinder head.

Inspection

1. Thoroughly clean the outside of the cylinder head. Use a stiff brush, soap and water to remove all debris from the cooling fins (**Figure 71**). If neces-

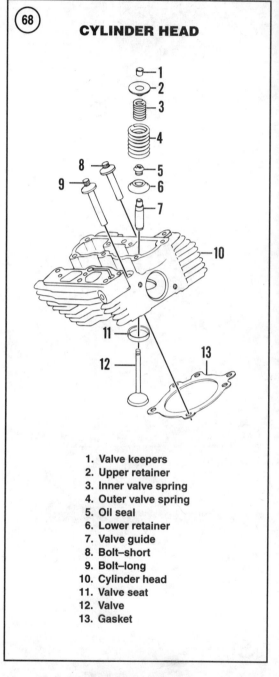

CYLINDER HEAD

1. Valve keepers
2. Upper retainer
3. Inner valve spring
4. Outer valve spring
5. Oil seal
6. Lower retainer
7. Valve guide
8. Bolt–short
9. Bolt–long
10. Cylinder head
11. Valve seat
12. Valve
13. Gasket

sary, use a piece of wood and scrape away any lodged dirt. Clogged cooling fins can cause overheating and lead to engine damage.
2. *Without removing the valves*, use a wire brush to remove all carbon deposits from the combustion chamber. Use a fine wire brush dipped in solvent or make a scraper from hardwood. Be careful not to damage the head, valves or spark plug threads.

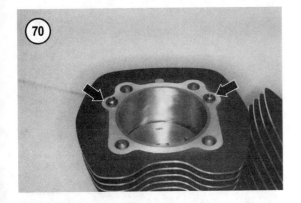

CAUTION
Cleaning the combustion chamber
with the valves removed can damage
the valve seat surfaces. A damaged or
even slightly scratched valve seat will
cause poor valve seating.

3. Examine the spark plug threads in the cylinder head for damage. If there is minor damage or if the threads are dirty or clogged with carbon, use a spark plug thread tap (**Figure 72**) to clean the threads following the manufacturer's instructions. If there is severe thread damage, restore the threads by installing a steel thread insert. Purchase thread insert kits at automotive supply stores or have them installed by a Harley-Davidson dealership or machine shop.

NOTE
When using a tap to clean spark plug
threads, coat the tap with an aluminum tap-cutting fluid or kerosene.

NOTE
Aluminum spark plug threads are
commonly damaged due to galling,
cross-threading and over-tightening.
To prevent galling, apply an antiseize
compound on the plug threads before
installation and do not overtighten.

4. After all carbon is removed from the combustion chambers and valve ports, and if the spark plug thread hole has been repaired, clean the entire head in solvent. Dry it with compressed air.
5. Examine the crown on the piston (**Figure 73**). The crown should show no signs of wear or damage. If the crown appears pecked or spongy-looking, also check the spark plug, valves and combustion chamber for aluminum deposits. If these deposits are found, the cylinder has over-

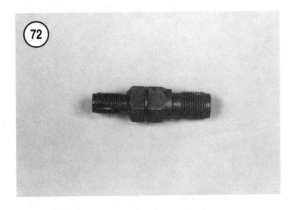

heated. Check for a lean fuel mixture or other conditions that could cause preignition.

6. Check for cracks in the combustion chamber, the intake port (**Figure 74**) and the exhaust port (**Figure 75**). Replace a cracked head if welding can not repair it.

7. Inspect the exhaust pipe mounting bolts (**Figure 76**) for damage. Repair the threads with a tap if they are damaged.

> *NOTE*
> *If the cylinder head is bead-blasted, clean the head thoroughly with solvent, then with hot soapy water. Residual grit seats in small crevices and other areas, and can be hard to get out. Also run a tap through each exposed thread to remove grit from the threads. Residue grit left in the engine will cause premature wear.*

8. Thoroughly clean the cylinder head.

9. Measure for warp by placing a straightedge across the gasket surface at several points and attempting to insert a feeler gauge between the straightedge and cylinder head at each location (**Figure 77**). Maximum allowable warp is in **Table 2**. Distortion or nicks in the cylinder head surface could cause an air leak and overheating. If warp exceeds the limit, resurface or replace the cylinder head. Consult a Harley-Davidson dealership or machine shop experienced in this type of work.

10. Check the rocker arm housing mating surfaces for warp (**Figure 78**) using the procedure in Step 9.

11. Make sure the breather channel is clear at each end (**Figure 79**).

12. Check the valves and valve guides as described under *Valves and Valve Components* in this chapter.

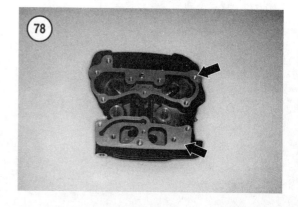

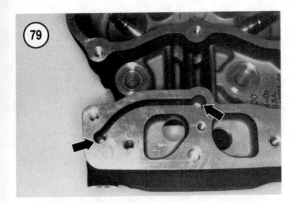

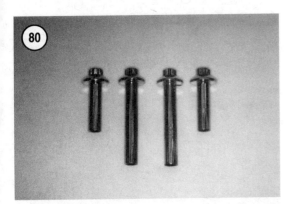

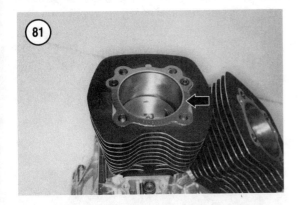

4

Installation

1. If removed, install the piston and cylinder as described in this chapter.

2. Lubricate the cylinder studs and cylinder head bolts as follows:

    a. Clean the cylinder head bolts in solvent and dry with compressed air.

    b. Apply clean engine oil to the cylinder head bolt threads and to the flat shoulder surface on each bolt (**Figure 80**). Wipe excess oil from the bolts, leave only an oil film on these surfaces.

3. Install the two dowel pins (**Figure 70**) into the top of the cylinder.

4. Install a *new* O-ring over each dowel pin. Apply a light coat of clean engine oil to the O-rings.

> *CAUTION*
> *Because the O-rings center the head gasket on the cylinder, install them before installing the head gasket.*

5. Install a *new* cylinder head gasket (**Figure 81**) onto the cylinder.

> *CAUTION*
> *Do not use sealer on the cylinder head gasket. For an aftermarket head gasket, follow the manufacturer's instructions for gasket installation.*

> *NOTE*
> *The cylinder heads are **not** identical. Refer to the FRONT or REAR mark (**Figure 82**) cast into top surface of the cylinder head.*

6. Install the cylinder head (**Figure 83**) onto the cylinder and the dowel pins. Position the head care-

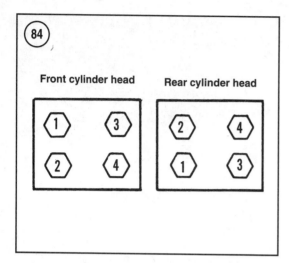

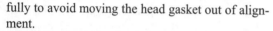

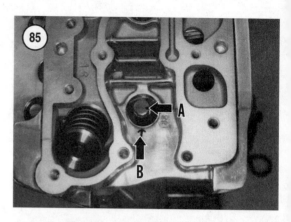

fully to avoid moving the head gasket out of alignment.

7. Install and finger-tighten the cylinder head bolts. Make sure the short bolts are on the spark plug side.

CAUTION
Failure to follow the torque pattern and sequence in Step 8 may cause cylinder head distortion and gasket leakage.

8. Refer to **Figure 84** for the front and rear cylinder head bolt tightening sequence. Torque the cylinder head bolts as follows:

    a. Starting with bolt No. 1, tighten each bolt in order to 84-108 in.-lb. (9-12 N•m).

    b. Starting with bolt No. 1, tighten each bolt in order to 144-168 in.-lb. (16-19 N•m).

    c. Make a vertical mark with a permanent marker on each bolt head (A, **Figure 85**). Make another mark on the cylinder head (B, **Figure 85**) at a 90° angle, or 1/4 turn from the mark on the bolt head.

    d. Use the marks as a guide and tighten each bolt head 90°, or 1/4 turn, clockwise until the marks are aligned (**Figure 86**).

9. Install the rocker arm assemblies and pushrods as described in this chapter.

VALVES AND VALVE COMPONENTS

Complete valve service requires a number of special tools, including a valve spring compressor, to

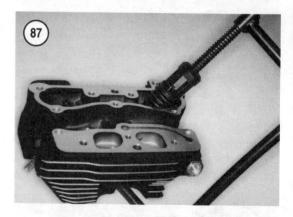

remove and install the valves. The following procedures describe how to check for valve component wear and to determine what type of service is required.

Valve Removal

1. Remove the cylinder head as described in this chapter.

4

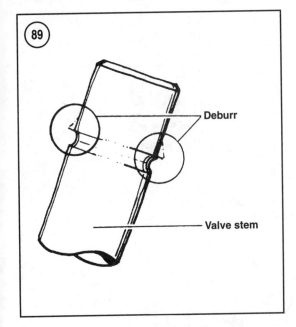

2. Install the valve spring compressor (**Figure 87**) squarely over the valve spring upper retainer (**Figure 88**) and against the valve head.

CAUTION
To avoid loss of spring tension, compress the spring only enough to remove the valve keepers.

3. Tighten the valve spring compressor until the valve keepers separate from the valve stem. Lift the valve keepers out through the valve spring compressor with a magnet or needlenose pliers.

4. Gradually loosen the valve spring compressor and remove it from the cylinder head.

5. Remove the spring retainer and the valve springs.

CAUTION
Remove any burrs from the valve stem groove before removing the valve (Figure 89); otherwise the valve guide will be damaged as the valve stem passes through it.

6. Remove the valve from the cylinder while rotating it slightly.

7. Remove the valve spring lower retainer.

8. Remove the valve guide oil seal.

CAUTION
Keep the components of each valve assembly together by placing each set in a divided carton, or into separate small boxes or small reclosable plastic bags. Identify the components as either intake or exhaust. If both cylinders are disassembled, also label the components as front and rear. Do not intermix components from the valves or excessive wear may result.

9. Repeat Steps 3-8 to remove the remaining valve.

Valve Inspection

When measuring the valves and valve components in this section, compare the actual measurements to the new and wear limit specifications in **Table 2**. Replace parts that are out of specification or are damaged as described in this section.

1. Clean valves in solvent. Do not gouge or damage the valve seating surface.

2. Inspect the valve face. Minor roughness and pitting (**Figure 90**) can be removed by lapping the valve as described in this chapter. Excessive un-

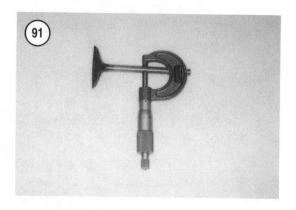

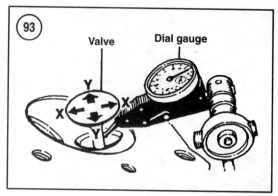

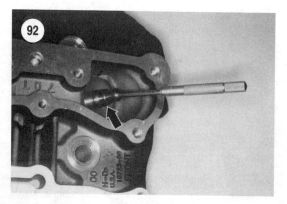

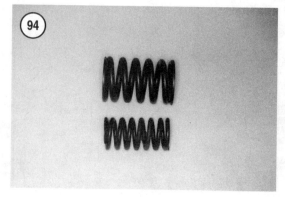

evenness to the contact surface indicates the valve is not serviceable.

3. Inspect the valve stem for wear and roughness. Then measure the valve stem outside diameter with a micrometer (**Figure 91**).

4. Remove all carbon and varnish from the valve guides with a stiff spiral wire brush before measuring wear.

5. Measure the valve guide inside diameter with a small hole gauge (**Figure 92**). Measure at the top, center and bottom positions. Then measure the small hole gauge.

6. Determine the valve stem-to-valve guide clearance by subtracting the valve stem outside diameter from the valve guide inner diameter. Compare this measurement to the specification in **Table 2**.

7. If a small hole gauge is not available, insert each valve into its guide. Attach a dial indicator to the valve stem next to the head (**Figure 93**). Hold the valve slightly off its seat and rock it sideways in both directions 90° to each other. If the valve rocks more than slightly, the guide is probably worn. Take the cylinder head to a Harley-Davidson dealership or machine shop and have the valve guides measured.

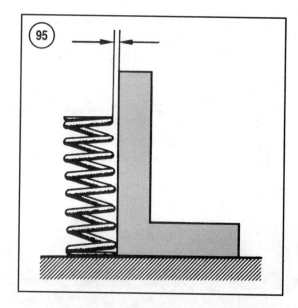

8. Check the inner and outer valve springs as follows:

   a. Inspect each of the valve springs (**Figure 94**) for visual damage.

   b. Use a square to visually check the spring for distortion or tilt (**Figure 95**).

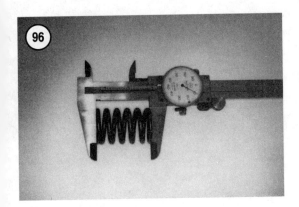

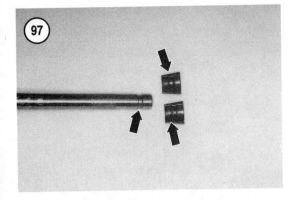

c. Measure the valve spring free length with a vernier caliper (**Figure 96**) and compare it to the dimension in **Table 2**.

d. Repeat substeps a-c for each valve spring.

e. Replace defective springs as a set (inner and outer).

9. Check the valve spring upper and lower retainers seats for cracks or other damage.

10. Check the fit of valve keepers on the valve stem end (**Figure 97**). They should index tightly into the valve stem groove.

11. Inspect the valve seats (**Figure 98**) in the cylinder head. If they are worn or burned, they can be reconditioned as described in this chapter. Seats and valves in near-perfect condition can be reconditioned by lapping with fine carborundum paste.

a. Clean the valve seat and corresponding valve mating areas with contact cleaner.

b. Coat the valve seat with layout fluid.

c. Install the valve into its guide and tap it against its seat. Do not rotate the valve.

d. Lift the valve out of the guide and measure the seat width at various points around the seat with a vernier caliper.

e. Compare the seat width with the specification in **Table 2**. If the seat width is less than specified or uneven, resurface the seats as described in this chapter.

f. Remove all layout fluid residue from the seats and valves.

Valve Installation

1. Clean the end of the valve guide.

2. Install the spring lower retainer (**Figure 99**). Push it down until it is seated on the cylinder head surface (**Figure 100**).

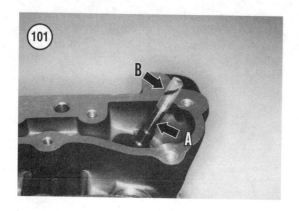

3. Coat a valve stem with Torco MPZ, molybdenum disulfide paste or equivalent. Install the valve part way into the guide. Then slowly turn the valve as it enters the oil seal and continue turning it until the valve is installed all the way.

4. Work the valve back and forth in the valve guide to ensure the lubricant is distributed evenly within the valve guide.

5. Withdraw the valve and apply an additional coat of the lubricant.

6. Reinstall the valve into the valve guide but do not push the valve past the top of the valve guide.

7. Use isopropyl alcohol and thoroughly clean all lubricant from the outer surface of the valve guide.

CAUTION
Do not allow any of the retaining compound to enter the valve guide bore.

8. Apply Loctite Retaining Compound RC/620 or an equivalent to the oil seal seating surface and to the outer surface of the valve guide.

9. Push the valve all the way into the cylinder head until it bottoms (A, **Figure 101**).

CAUTION
The oil seal will be torn as it passes the valve stem keeper groove if the plastic capsule is not installed in Step 10. The capsule is included in the top end gasket set.

10. Hold the valve in place and install the plastic capsule (B, **Figure 101**) onto the end of the valve stem. Apply a light coat of clean engine oil to the outer surface of the capsule.

11. With the valve held in place, install the oil seal (**Figure 102**) onto the valve stem.

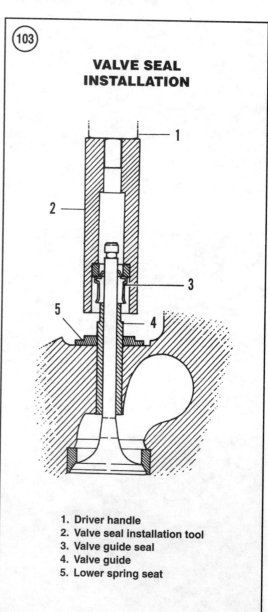

VALVE SEAL INSTALLATION

1. Driver handle
2. Valve seal installation tool
3. Valve guide seal
4. Valve guide
5. Lower spring seat

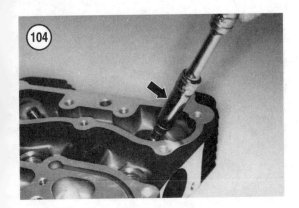

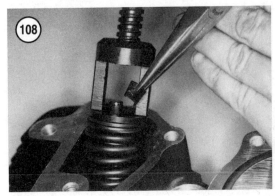

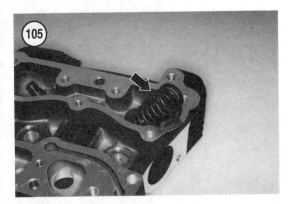

12A. If special tools are used, use the Harley-Davidson valve seal installation tool (part No. HD-34643A) and driver handle (part No. HD-34740) (**Figure 103**) to push the oil seal down until it bottoms on the cylinder head surface.

12B. If special tools are not used, use an appropriate-size deep socket (**Figure 104**) to push the oil seal down until it bottoms on the cylinder head surface.

13. Remove the plastic capsule from the valve stem. Keep the capsule as it will be used on the remaining valves.

14. Install the inner valve spring (**Figure 105**) and make sure it is properly seated on the lower spring retainer.

15. Install the outer valve spring (**Figure 106**) and make sure it is properly seated on the lower spring retainer.

16. Install the upper spring retainer (**Figure 107**) on top of the valve springs.

> *CAUTION*
> *To avoid loss of spring tension, only compress the springs enough to install the valve keepers.*

17. Compress the valve springs with a valve spring compressor (**Figure 87**) and install the valve keepers (**Figure 108**).

18. Make sure both keepers are seated around the valve stem prior to releasing the compressor.

19. Slowly release tension from the compressor and remove it. After removing the compressor, inspect the valve keepers to make sure they are properly seated (**Figure 109**). Tap the end of the valve stem with a *soft-faced* hammer to ensure the keepers are properly seated.

20. Repeat Steps 1-19 for the remaining valves.

21. Install the cylinder head as described in this chapter.

Valve Guide Replacement

Tools

The following tools or their equivalents are required to replace the valve guides.
1. Driver handle and remover (HD-34740).
2. Valve guide installation sleeve (HD-34741).
3. Valve guide reamer (HD-39932) and T-handle (HD-39847).
4. Valve guide reamer (HD-39964) and honing lubricant.
5. Valve guide hone (HD-34723).
6. Valve guide brush (HD-34751).

Procedure

1. Place the cylinder head on a wooden surface with the combustion chamber side facing down.
2. Shoulderless valve guides (**Figure 110**) are used. Before the valve guides are removed, note and record the shape of the guide that projects into the combustion chamber. If the valve guide installation tool is *not* going to be used, measure the distance from the face of the guide to the cylinder head surface with a vernier caliper (**Figure 111**). Record the distance for each valve guide. The new valve guides must be installed to this *exact* height dimension.
3. Remove the valve guides as follows:

> **CAUTION**
> *Use the correct size valve guide removal tool to remove the valve guides or the tool may expand the end of the guide. An expanded guide will widen and damage the guide bore in the cylinder head as it passes through it.*

> **NOTE**
> *The valve guides can either be pressed out or driven out. Pressing the guides out is recommended since it lessens the chance of cylinder head damage.*

a. Support the cylinder head so the combustion chamber faces down.
b. To drive the guides out, place the cylinder on a piece of wood.

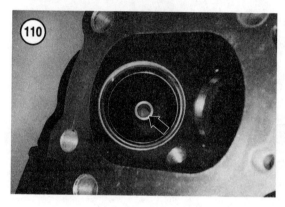

c. To press the guides out, support the cylinder head in the press with a cylinder head stand (JIMS part No. 39782) so the valve guide is perpendicular to the press table.
d. Insert the driver handle and remover into the top of the valve guide.
e. Press or drive the valve guide out through the combustion chamber.
f. Repeat substeps a-e for the remaining valve guides.
4. Clean the valve guide bores in the cylinder head.
5. Because the valve guide bores in the cylinder head may have enlarged during removal of the old guides, measure each valve guide bore prior to purchasing the new guides. Then purchase the new valve guides to match their respective bore diameters. Determine the bore diameter as follows:

a. Measure the valve guide bore diameter in the cylinder head with a bore gauge or snap gauge. Record the bore diameter.
b. The new valve guide outside diameter must be 0.0020-0.0033 in. (0.050-0.084 mm) larger than the guide bore in the cylinder head. When purchasing new valve guides,

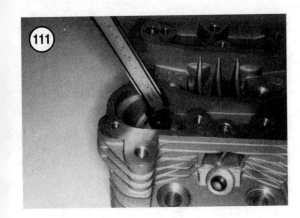

measure the new guide's outside diameter with a micrometer. If the new guide's outside diameter is not within this specification, install oversize valve guide(s). See a Harley-Davidson dealership for available sizes.

6. Apply a thin coat of molylube or white grease to the entire outer surface of the valve guide before installing it in the cylinder head.

CAUTION
When installing oversize valve guides, make sure to match each guide to its respective bore in the cylinder head.

7. Install the new guide using the driver handle and valve guide installation tools. Press or drive the guide into the cylinder head until the valve guide installation tool bottoms out on the cylinder head surface. When the tool bottoms on the cylinder head surface, the valve guide is installed to the correct height. If the driver handle tool is not used, install the valve guide to the same height recorded prior to removal. Measure the valve guide's installed height using a vernier caliper (**Figure 111**) during installation.

NOTE
Replacement valve guides are sold with a smaller inside diameter than the valve stem. Ream the guide to fit the valve stem.

8. Ream the new valve guide as follows:
   a. Apply a liberal amount of reamer lubricant to the ream bit and to the valve guide bore.
   b. Start the reamer straight into the valve guide bore.

CAUTION
Only apply pressure to the end of the drive socket. If pressure is applied to the T-handle, the bore will be uneven, rough cut and tapered.

   c. Apply thumb pressure to the end of the drive socket portion of the T-handle while rotating the T-handle *clockwise*. Only *light* pressure is required. Apply additional lubricant to the reamer and into the valve guide while rotating the reamer.
   d. Continue to rotate the reamer until the entire bit has traveled through the valve guide and the shank of the reamer rotates freely.

CAUTION
Never back the reamer out through the valve guide as the guide will be damaged.

   e. Remove the T-handle from the reamer. Remove the reamer from the combustion chamber side of the cylinder head.
   f. Apply low-pressure compressed air to clean out the small shavings from the valve guide bore. Then clean the valve guide bore with the small spiral brush.

9. Hone the valve guide as follows:
   a. Install the valve guide hone into a high-speed electric drill.
   b. Lubricate the valve guide bore and hone stones with the reamer lubricant—*do not use motor oil.*
   c. Carefully insert the hone stones into the valve guide bore.
   d. Start the drill and move the hone back and forth in the valve guide bore for 10 to 12 complete strokes to obtain a 60° crosshatch pattern.

10. Repeat Steps 8 and 9 for each valve guide.

11. Soak the cylinder head in a container filled with hot, soapy water. Then clean the valve guides with a valve guide brush or an equivalent bristle brush. *Do not use a steel brush.* Do not use cleaning solvent, kerosene or gasoline as these chemicals will not remove all of the abrasive particles produced during the honing operation. Repeat this step until all of the valve guides are thoroughly cleaned. Then rinse the cylinder head and valve guides in clear, cold water and dry them with compressed air.

12. After cleaning and drying the valve guides, apply clean engine oil to the guides to prevent rust.

13. Resurface the valve seats as described in *Valve Seat Reconditioning* in this chapter.

Valve Seat Inspection

1. Remove all carbon residue from each valve seat. Then clean the cylinder head as described under *Valve Inspection* in this chapter.

> *NOTE*
> *Machinist's dye is the most accurate method of checking the valve seat width and position.*

2. Check the valve seats in their original locations with machinist's dye as follows:
   a. Thoroughly clean the valve face and valve seat with contact cleaner.
   b. Spread a thin layer of Prussian blue or machinist's dye evenly on the valve face.
   c. Insert the valve into its guide.
   d. Support the valve by hand (**Figure 112**) and tap the valve up and down in the cylinder head. Do not rotate the valve or the reading will be false.
   e. Remove the valve and examine the impression left by the machinist's dye. The impressions on the valve and the seat should be even around their circumferences and the width (**Figure 113**) should be within the specifications in **Table 2**. If the width is beyond the specification or if the impression is uneven, recondition the valve seats.

3. Closely examine the valve seat in the cylinder head (**Figure 98**). It should be smooth and even with a polished seating surface.

4. If the valve seat is in good condition, install the valve as described in this chapter.

5. If the valve seat is not correct, recondition the valve seat as described in this chapter.

Valve Seat Reconditioning

Valve seat reconditioning requires considerable expertise and special tools. In most cases, it is more economical and practical to have these procedures performed by an experienced machinist.

The following procedure is provided for those equipped to perform the task. A valve seat cutter set

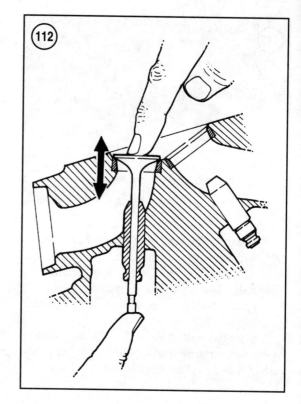

(HD-35758A) or equivalent is required. Follow the manufacturer's instructions.

Refer to **Figure 114** for valve seat angles. While the valve seat angles for both the intake and exhaust valves are the same, different cutter sizes are required. Also note that a 45° seat angle is specified to grind the seats, while a 46° seat angle is specified to cut the seats.

1. Clean the valve guides as described under *Inspection* in this chapter.

2. Carefully rotate and insert the solid pilot into the valve guide. Make sure the pilot is correctly seated.

> *CAUTION*
> *Valve seat accuracy depends on a correctly sized and installed pilot.*

3. Using the 45° grinding stone or 46° cutter, descale and clean the valve seat with one or two turns.

> *CAUTION*
> *Measure the valve seat contact area in the cylinder head (**Figure 113**) after each cut to make sure its size and area are correct. Over-grinding will lower the valves into the cylinder head and*

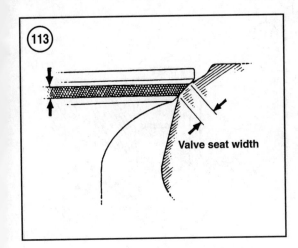

113

Valve seat width

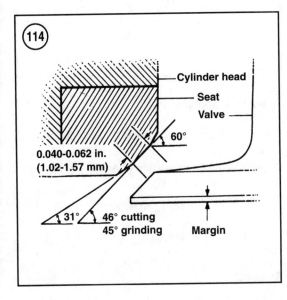

114

Cylinder head
Seat
Valve
60°
0.040-0.062 in.
(1.02-1.57 mm)
31° / 46° cutting
45° grinding   Margin

the valve seat will have to be replaced.

4. If the seat is still pitted or burned, turn the cutter until the surface is clean. Work slowly and carefully to avoid removing too much material from the valve seat.

5. Remove the pilot from the valve guide.

6. Apply a small amount of valve lapping compound to the valve face and install the valve. Rotate the valve against the valve seat using a valve lapping tool. Remove the valve.

7. Measure the valve seat with a vernier caliper (**Figure 113** and **Figure 114**). Record the measurement to use as a reference point when performing the following steps.

CAUTION
The 31° cutter removes material quickly. Work carefully and check the progress often.

8. Reinsert the solid pilot into the valve guide. Make sure the pilot is properly seated. Install the 31° cutter onto the solid pilot and lightly cut the seat to remove 1/4 of the existing valve seat.

9. Install the 60° cutter onto the solid pilot and lightly cut the seat to remove the lower 1/4 of the existing valve seat.

10. Measure the valve seat with a vernier caliper. Then fit the 45° grinding stone or 46° cutter onto the solid pilot and cut the valve seat to the specified seat width in **Table 2**.

11. When the valve seat width is correct, check valve seating as follows:

12. Remove the solid pilot from the cylinder head.

13. Inspect the valve seat-to-valve face impression as follows:

   a. Clean the valve seat with contact cleaner.

   b. Spread a thin layer of Prussian Blue or machinist's dye evenly on the valve face.

   c. Insert the valve into its guide.

   d. Support the valve with two fingers and turn it with the valve lapping tool.

   e. Remove the valve and examine the impression left by the Prussian blue or machinist's dye.

   f. Measure the valve seat width (**Figure 113** and **Figure 114**). Refer to **Table 2** for the correct seat width.

   g. The valve seat contact area must be in the center of the valve face area.

14. If the contact area is too high or too wide on the valve, cut the seat with the 31° cutter. This will remove part of the top valve seat area to lower or narrow the contact area.

15. If the contact area is too low or too wide on the valve, use the 60° cutter and remove part of the lower area to raise and widen the contact area.

16. After obtaining the desired valve seat position and angle, use the 45° grinding stone or the 46° cutter and *lightly* clean off any burrs caused by the previous cuts.

17. When the contact area is correct, lap the valve as described in this chapter.

18. Repeat Steps 1-17 for the remaining valve seats.

19. Thoroughly clean the cylinder head and all valve components in solvent, then clean them with detergent and hot water, and rinse in cold water. Dry them with compressed air. Then apply a light coat of engine oil to all non-aluminum surfaces to prevent rust formation.

Valve Lapping

If valve wear or distortion is not excessive, attempt to restore the valve seal by lapping the valve to the seat.

After lapping the valves, install the valve assemblies and test each valve seat for a good seal by pouring solvent into the ports (**Figure 115**). If the seal is good, no solvent will leak past the seat surface. If solvent leaks past any seat, the combustion chamber will appear wet. Disassemble the leaking valve and repeat the lapping procedure or recondition the valve as described in this chapter.

1. Smear a light coat of fine grade valve lapping compound on the seating surface of the valve.

2. Insert the valve into the head.

3. Wet the suction cup of the lapping tool and stick it onto the head of the valve. Lap the valve to the seat by spinning the tool between both hands while lifting and moving the valve around the seat 1/4 turn at a time.

4. Wipe off the valve and seat frequently to check the progress. Lap only enough to achieve a precise seating ring around the valve head.

5. Closely examine the valve seat in the cylinder head. The seat must be smooth and even with a polished seating ring.

6. Thoroughly clean the valves and cylinder head in solvent to remove all grinding compound residue. Compound left on the valves or the cylinder head will cause rapid engine wear.

7. After installing the valves into the cylinder head, test each valve for proper seating. Pour solvent into the intake and exhaust ports. Solvent should not leak past the valve seats. If the solvent leaks, the combustion chamber will appear wet. If solvent leaks past any of the seats, disassemble that valve assembly and repeat the lapping procedure until there is no leakage.

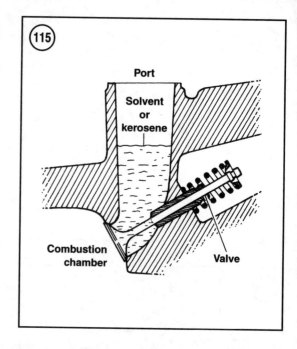

Valve Seat Replacement

Valve seat replacement requires considerable experience and equipment. Refer this work to a Harley-Davidson dealership or machine shop.

CYLINDER

Refer to **Figure 116**.

Removal

1. Remove the cylinder head as described in this chapter.

2. Remove all dirt and debris from the cylinder base.

3. Remove the two dowel pins and O-rings (**Figure 117**) from the top of the cylinder if they are still in place.

4. Turn the crankshaft until the piston is at bottom dead center (BDC).

> *NOTE*
> *The front and rear cylinders are identical (same part number). Mark each cylinder so they will be reinstalled in their original positions.*

5. Pull the cylinder straight up and off the piston and cylinder studs. If necessary, tap around the per-

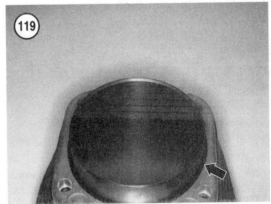

PISTON/CYLINDER ASSEMBLY

1. Upper compression ring
2. Lower compression ring
3. Upper oil ring
4. Spacer
5. Lower oil ring
6. Retaining ring
7. Piston
8. Connecting rod bushing
9. Connecting rod
10. Piston pin
11. O-ring
12. Locating dowel
13. Cylinder
14. O-ring seal

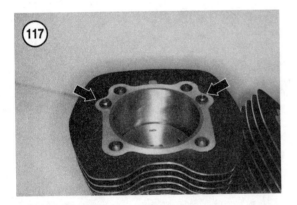

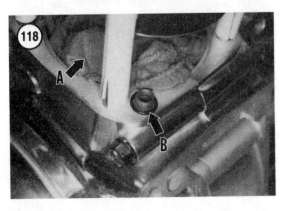

imeter of the cylinder with a rubber or plastic mallet.

6. Place clean shop rags (A, **Figure 118**) into the crankcase opening to prevent objects from falling undetected into the crankcase.

7. Remove the O-ring seal (B, **Figure 118**) from the locating dowel. Leave the locating dowels in place unless they are loose.

8. Remove the O-ring (**Figure 119**) from the base of the cylinder.

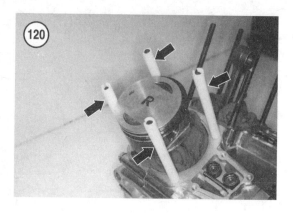

9. Install a vinyl or rubber hose over each stud (**Figure 120**). This will protect both the piston and the studs from damage.

> *CAUTION*
> *After removing the cylinder, be careful when working around the cylinder studs to avoid bending or damaging them. The slightest bend could cause the stud to fail.*

10. Repeat these steps to remove the other cylinder.

Inspection

To obtain an accurate cylinder bore measurement, the cylinder must be torqued between torque plates (JIMS part No. 1287). Measurements made without the torque plates will be inaccurate and may vary by as much as 0.001 in. (0.025 mm). Refer this procedure to a shop equipped and experienced with this procedure if the tools are not available. The cylinder bore must be thoroughly clean and at room temperature to obtain accurate measurements. Do not measure the cylinder immediately after it has been honed as it will still be warm. Measurements can vary by as much as 0.002 in. (0.051 mm) if the cylinder block is not at room temperature.

1. Thoroughly clean the outside of the cylinder. Use a stiff brush, soap and water to clean all debris from the cooling fins (**Figure 121**). If necessary, use a piece of wood to scrape away lodged dirt. Clogged cooling fins can cause overheating and lead to possible engine damage.

2. Carefully remove all gasket residue from the top and bottom cylinder block gasket surfaces.

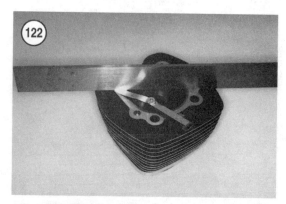

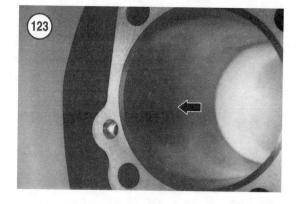

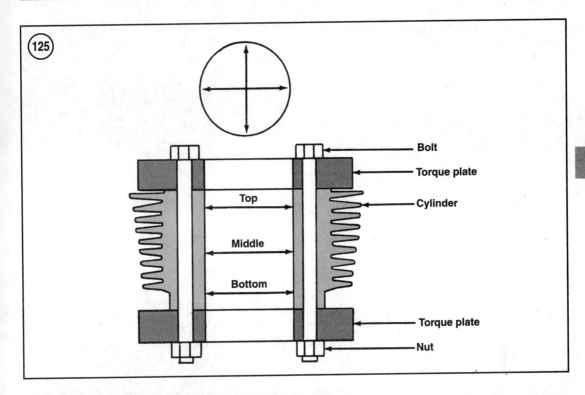

Top

Middle

Bottom

Bolt

Torque plate

Cylinder

Torque plate

Nut

4

3. Thoroughly clean the cylinder with solvent and dry it with compressed air. Lightly oil the cylinder block bore to prevent rust.

4. Check the top and bottom cylinder gasket surfaces with a straightedge and feeler gauge (**Figure 122**). Replace the cylinder if warp exceeds the limit in **Table 2**.

5. Check the cylinder bore (**Figure 123**) for scuff marks, scratches or other damage.

6. Install the torque plate onto the cylinder (**Figure 124**) following the manufacturer's instructions.

7. Measure the cylinder bore with a bore gauge or inside micrometer at the positions indicated in **Figure 125**. Perform the first measurement 0.500 in. (12.7 mm) below the top of the cylinder (**Figure 126**). Do not measure areas where the rings do not travel.

8. Measure in two axes aligned with the piston pin and at 90° to the pin. If the taper or out-of-round measurements exceed the service limits in **Table 2**, bore both cylinders to the next oversize and install oversize pistons and rings. Confirm the accuracy of all measurements and consult with a parts supplier on the availability of replacement parts before having the cylinder serviced.

9. Remove the torque plates.

10. If the cylinders were serviced, wash each cylinder in hot, soapy water to remove the fine grit material left from the boring or honing process. Run a clean white cloth through the cylinder bore. If the cloth shows traces of grit or oil, the bore is not clean. Wash the cylinder until the cloth passes through cleanly. When the bore is clean, dry it with compressed air, then lubricate it with clean engine oil to prevent the bore from rusting.

CAUTION
Only hot, soapy water will completely clean the cylinder bore. Solvent and kerosene cannot wash fine grit out of the cylinder crevices. Abrasive grit left in the cylinder will cause premature engine wear.

Cylinder Studs and Cylinder Head Bolts Inspection and Cleaning

The cylinder studs and cylinder head bolts must be in good condition and properly cleaned before the cylinder and cylinder heads are installed. Damaged or dirty studs may cause cylinder head distortion and gasket leaks.

> **CAUTION**
> *The cylinder studs, cylinder head bolts and washers consist of hardened material. Do not substitute them with parts made of a lower grade material. If replacement is required, purchase the parts from the manufacturer.*

1. Inspect the cylinder head bolts. Replace any that are damaged.
2. Examine the cylinder studs (A, **Figure 127**) for bending, looseness or damage. Replace studs as described under *Cylinder Stud Replacement* in this chapter. If the studs are in good condition, perform Step 3.
3. Cover both crankcase openings with shop rags (B, **Figure 127**) to prevent debris from falling into the engine.
4. Remove all carbon residue from the cylinder studs and cylinder head bolts as follows:
   a. Apply solvent to the cylinder stud and mating cylinder head bolt threads, and thread the bolt onto the stud.
   b. Turn the cylinder head bolt back and forth to loosen and remove the carbon residue from the threads. Remove the bolt from the stud. Wipe off the residue with a shop rag moistened in cleaning solvent.
   c. Repeat substeps a and b until both thread sets are free of carbon residue.
   d. Spray the cylinder stud and cylinder head bolt with an aerosol parts cleaner and allow them to dry.
   e. Set the clean bolt aside and install it on the same stud when installing the cylinder head.
5. Repeat Step 4 for each cylinder stud and cylinder head bolt set.

Installation

> **NOTE**
> *When a cylinder has been bored oversize, the inner lead-in angle at the base*

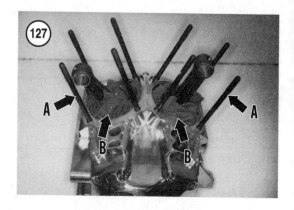
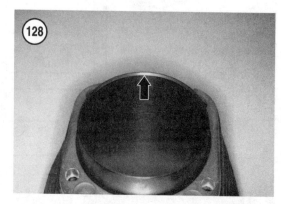
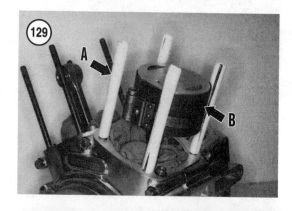

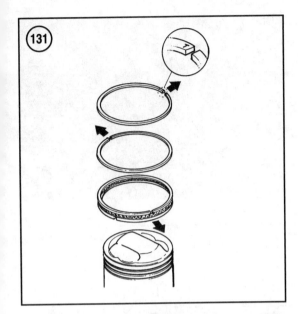

*of the bore skirt (**Figure 128**) has been eliminated. This lead-in angle is necessary for the piston rings to safely enter the cylinder bore. If necessary, use a chamfering cone (JIMS part No. 2078) or a hand grinder with a fine*

stone to make in a new lead-in angle. The finished surface must be smooth so it will not catch and damage the piston rings during installation.

1. If removed, install the pistons and rings as described in this chapter.

2. Remove gasket residue and clean the cylinder as described under *Inspection* in this chapter.

3. Remove the vinyl or rubber hose from each stud (A, **Figure 129**).

4. Install a *new* O-ring onto the base of the cylinder. Apply a light coat of clean engine oil to the O-ring.

5. If removed, install the locating dowels (**Figure 130**) into the crankcase.

6. Install a *new* O-ring seal (B, **Figure 118**) onto the locating dowel. Apply a light coat of clean engine oil to the O-ring.

7. Turn the crankshaft until the piston is at top dead center (TDC).

8. Lubricate the cylinder bore, piston and piston rings liberally with clean engine oil.

9. Position the top compression ring gap so it is facing the intake port. Then stagger the remaining piston ring end gaps as shown in **Figure 131**.

10. Compress the piston rings with a ring compressor (B, **Figure 129**).

NOTE
Install the cylinder in its original position as noted during removal.

11. Carefully align the cylinder (front facing forward) with the cylinder studs and slide it down (**Figure 132**) until it is over the top of the piston. Continue sliding the cylinder down past the rings (**Figure 133**). Remove the ring compressor once the piston rings enter the cylinder bore. Remove the shop rag from the crankcase opening.

12. Continue to slide the cylinder down until it bottoms out on the crankcase.

13. Repeat Steps 1-12 to install the other cylinder.

14. Install the cylinder heads as described in this chapter.

PISTONS AND PISTON RINGS

Refer to **Figure 116**.

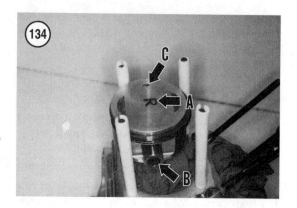

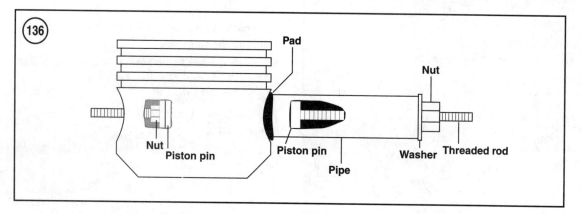

Pad

Nut

Nut
Piston pin

Piston pin

Pipe

Washer Threaded rod

Piston and Piston Rings Removal

1. Remove the cylinder as described in this chapter.
2. Cover the crankcase with clean shop rags.
3. Lightly mark the pistons with F (front) or R (rear) (A, **Figure 134**).

> *WARNING*
> *The piston pin retaining rings may spring out of the piston during removal. Wear safety glasses when removing them in Step 4.*

4. Using an awl, pry the piston pin retaining rings (**Figure 135**) out of the piston. Place a thumb over the hole to help keep the rings from flying out during removal.

> *NOTE*
> *Mark the piston pins so they can be reinstalled into their original pistons.*

5. Support the piston and push out the piston pin (B, **Figure 134**). If the piston pin is difficult to remove, use a piston pin removal tool (**Figure 136**).
6. Remove the piston from the connecting rod.

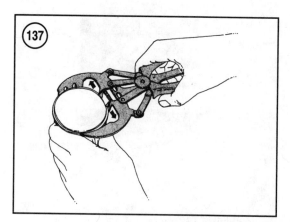

7. Remove the piston rings by using a ring expander tool (**Figure 137**) or spreading them by hand (**Figure 138**).
8. Inspect the pistons, piston pins and pistons rings as described in this chapter.

Piston Inspection

1. If necessary, remove the piston rings as described in this chapter.

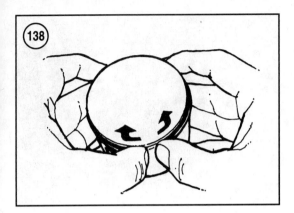

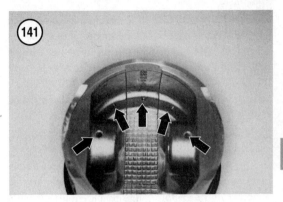

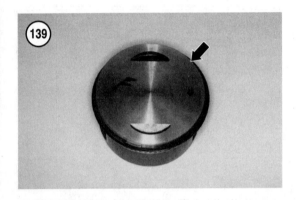

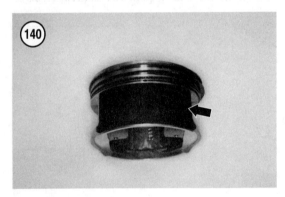

or from the cylinder bore near the top. Removal of carbon from these two areas may cause increased oil consumption.

CAUTION
The pistons have a special coating on the skirt (Figure 140). Do not scrape or use any type of abrasive on this surface as it will be damaged.

3. After cleaning the piston, examine the crown. The crown should show no signs of wear or damage. If the crown appears pecked or spongy-looking, check the spark plug, valves and combustion chamber for aluminum deposits. If aluminum deposits are found, the engine is overheating.

4. Examine each ring groove for burrs, dented edges or other damage. Pay particular attention to the top compression ring groove as it usually wears more than the others. The oil rings and grooves generally wear less than compression rings and their grooves. If the of oil ring groove is worn or if the oil ring assembly is tight and difficult to remove, the piston skirt may have collapsed due to excessive heat and is permanently deformed. Replace the piston.

5. Check the oil control holes (**Figure 141**) in the piston for carbon or oil sludge buildup. Clean the holes with wire and blow them out with compressed air.

6. Check the piston skirt (**Figure 140**) for cracks or other damage. If a piston shows signs of partial seizure such as aluminum build-up on the piston skirt, replace the piston to reduce the possibility of engine noise and further piston seizure.

NOTE
If the piston skirt is worn or scuffed unevenly from side-to-side, the connecting rod may be bent or twisted.

2. Carefully clean the carbon from the piston crown (**Figure 139**) with a soft scraper. Large carbon accumulations reduce piston cooling and cause detonation and piston damage. Make sure the piston remains properly identified.

CAUTION
Be very careful not to gouge or otherwise damage the piston when removing carbon. Never use a wire brush to clean the piston ring grooves. Do not attempt to remove carbon from the sides of the piston above the top ring

7. Check the circlip groove (**Figure 142**) on each side for wear, cracks or other damage. If the grooves are questionable, check the circlip fit by installing a new circlip into each groove, then attempt to move the circlip from side-to-side. If the circlip has any side play, the groove is worn and the piston must be replaced.

8. Measure piston-to-cylinder clearance as described under *Piston Clearance* in this chapter.

9. If the piston needs to be replaced, select a new piston as described under *Piston Clearance* in this chapter. If the piston, rings and cylinder are not damaged and are dimensionally correct, they can be reused.

Piston Pin Inspection and Clearance

1. Clean the piston pin in solvent and dry it thoroughly.

2. Inspect the piston pin for chrome flaking or cracks. Replace if necessary.

3. Oil the piston pin and install it in the connecting rod (**Figure 143**). Slowly rotate the piston pin and check for radial play.

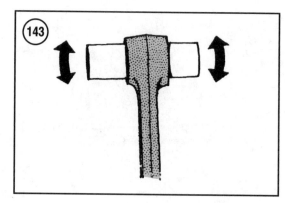

4. Oil the piston pin and install it in the piston (**Figure 144**). Check the piston pin for excessive play.

5. To measure piston pin-to-piston clearance, perform the following:

   a. Measure the piston pin outer diameter with a micrometer (**Figure 145**).

   b. Measure the inside diameter of the piston pin bore (**Figure 146**) with a snap gauge. Measure the snap gauge with a micrometer.

   c. Subtract the piston pin outer diameter from the piston pin bore to obtain the clearance dimension. Check it against the specification in **Table 2**.

   d. If it is out of specification, replace the piston and/or the piston pin.

6. Replace the piston pin and/or piston or connecting rod if necessary.

Piston Clearance

1. Make sure the piston skirt and cylinder bore is clean and dry.

2. Measure the cylinder bore with a bore gauge (**Figure 126**) as described under *Cylinder Inspection* in this chapter.

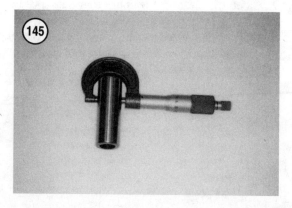

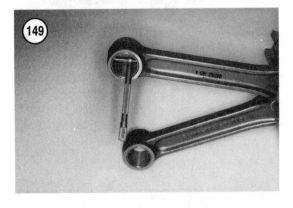

3. Measure the piston diameter with a micrometer as follows:

    a. Hold the micrometer at the bottom of the piston skirt at a right angle to the piston pin bore (**Figure 147**). Adjust the micrometer so the spindle and anvil just touch the skirt.

    b. Start below the bottom ring and slowly move the micrometer toward the bottom of the skirt.

    c. The micrometer will be loose, then tight at about 0.5 in. (12.7 mm) from the bottom, then loose again.

    d. Measure the piston skirt at the tightest point.

4. Subtract the piston diameter from the largest bore diameter; the difference is piston-to-cylinder clearance. If the clearance exceeds the specification in **Table 2**, the pistons should be replaced and the cylinders bored oversize and then honed. Purchase the new pistons first. Measure their diameter and add the specified clearance to determine the proper cylinder bore diameter.

Piston Pin Bushing in Connecting Rod Inspection and Replacement

The piston pin bushings are reamed to provide correct piston pin-to-bushing clearance. This clearance is critical in preventing pin knock and top end damage.

1. Inspect the piston pin bushings (**Figure 148**) for excessive wear or damage such as pit marks, scoring or wear grooves. Then make sure the bushing is not loose. The bushing must be a tight fit in the connecting rods.

2. Measure the piston pin diameter (**Figure 145**) where it contacts the bushing.

3. Measure the piston pin bushing diameter using a snap gauge (**Figure 149**).

4. Subtract the piston pin outer diameter from the bushing inner diameter to determine piston pin clearance. Replace the pin and bushing if they are worn to the service limit in **Table 2**.

Piston Pin Bushing Replacement

Tools

The following special tools are required to replace and ream the piston pin bushings. The clamp tool is only required if the bushing is being replaced with the crankcase assembled. If these tools are not available, have a shop with the proper equipment perform the procedure.

1. Connecting rod clamp tool (HD-95952-33B).
2. Connecting rod bushing tool (JIMS 1051).
3. Bushing reamer tool (JIMS 1726-3).
4. Connecting rod bushing hone (HD-422569).

Procedure

1. Remove two of the plastic hoses protecting the cylinder studs.
2. Install the connecting rod clamping tool as follows:
   a. Install the clamp portion of the connecting rod clamping tool over the connecting rod so the slots engage the cylinder head studs. Do not scratch or bend the studs.
   b. Position the threaded cylinders with the knurled end facing up and install the cylinders onto the studs. Tighten the clamp securely.
   c. Alternately tighten the thumbscrews on the side of the connecting rod. Do not turn only one thumbscrew, as this will move the connecting rod off center and tightening the other thumbscrew will cause the connecting rod to flex or bend.
3. Cover the crankcase opening to keep bushing particles from falling into the engine.

> *NOTE*
> *When installing the new bushing, align the oil slot in the bushing with the oil hole in the connecting rod.*

4. Replace the bushing using the connecting rod bushing tool (**Figure 150**) following the tool manufacturer's instructions. The new bushing must be flush with both sides of the connecting rod.
5. Ream the piston pin with the bushing reamer tool (**Figure 151**) following the manufacturer's instructions.
6. Hone the new bushing to obtain the piston pin clearance in **Table 2**. Use honing oil, not engine oil, when honing the bushing to size.
7. Install the piston pin through the bushing. The pin should move through the bushing smoothly. Confirm pin clearance using a micrometer and bore gauge.
8. Carefully remove all metal debris from the crankcase.

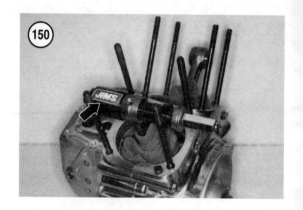

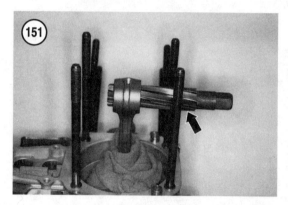

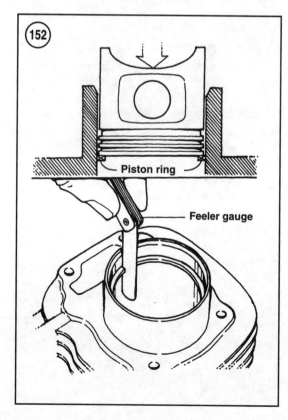

Piston ring

Feeler gauge

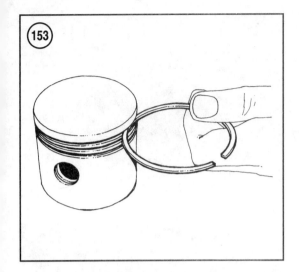

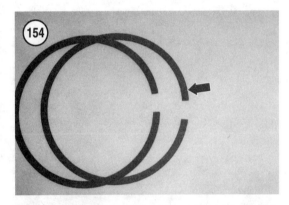

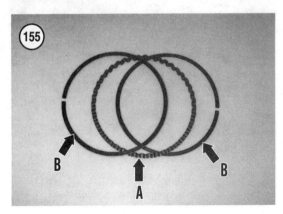

3. Insert one piston ring into the top of its cylinder and tap it down approximately .50 in. (12.7 mm), using the piston to square it in the bore. Measure the ring end gap (**Figure 152**) with a feeler gauge and compare it with the specification in **Table 2**. Replace the piston rings as a set if any one ring end gap measurement is excessive. Repeat Step 3 for each ring.

4. Roll each compression ring around its piston groove as shown in **Figure 153**. The ring should move smoothly with no binding. If a ring binds in its groove, check the groove for damage. Replace the piston if necessary.

Piston Ring Installation

Each piston is equipped with three piston rings: two compression rings and one oil ring assembly. The top compression ring is not marked. The lower compression ring is marked with a dot (**Figure 154**).

Harley-Davidson recommends that *new* piston rings be installed every time the piston is removed. Always lightly hone the cylinder before installing new piston rings.

1. Wash the piston in hot, soapy water. Then rinse it with cold water and dry it with compressed air. Make sure the oil control holes in the lower ring groove are clear.

2. Install the oil ring assembly as follows:
   a. The oil ring consists of three rings: a ribbed spacer ring (A, **Figure 155**) and two steel rings (B).
   b. Install the spacer ring into the lower ring groove. Butt the spacer ring ends together. Do not overlap the ring ends.
   c. Insert one end of the first steel ring into the lower groove so it is below the spacer ring. Then spiral the other end over the piston crown and into the lower groove. To prevent the ring end from scratching the side of the piston, place a piece of shim stock or a thin, flat feeler gauge between the ring and piston.
   d. Repeat substep c to install the other steel ring above the spacer ring.

NOTE
*To install the compression rings, use a ring expander as shown in **Figure 137**. Do not expand the rings any more than necessary to install them.*

Piston Ring Inspection

1. Clean the piston ring grooves as described under *Piston Inspection*.

2. Inspect the ring grooves for burrs, nicks, or broken or cracked lands. Replace the piston if necessary.

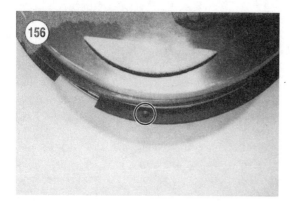

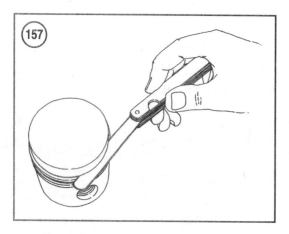

3. Install the lower compression ring with the dot facing up (**Figure 156**).

4. Install the *new* top compression ring with either side facing up.

5. Check the ring side clearance with a feeler gauge as shown in **Figure 157**. Check the side clearance in several spots around the piston. If the clearance is larger than the service limit in **Table 2**, replace the piston.

6. Stagger the ring gaps around the piston as shown in **Figure 131**.

Piston Installation

1. Cover the crankcase openings to avoid dropping a retaining ring into the engine.

2. Install a *new* piston pin retaining ring into one groove in the piston. Make sure the ring seats in the groove completely.

3. Coat the connecting rod bushing and piston pin with assembly oil.

4. Slide the piston pin into the piston until its end is flush with the piston pin boss (**Figure 158**).

NOTE
The piston markings described in Step 5 are for Harley-Davidson pistons. For aftermarket pistons, follow their manufacturer's directions for piston alignment and installation.

5. Place the piston over the connecting rod with its arrow mark (C, **Figure 134**) facing toward the front of the engine. Install used pistons on their original connecting rods; refer to the marks made on the pistons during removal.

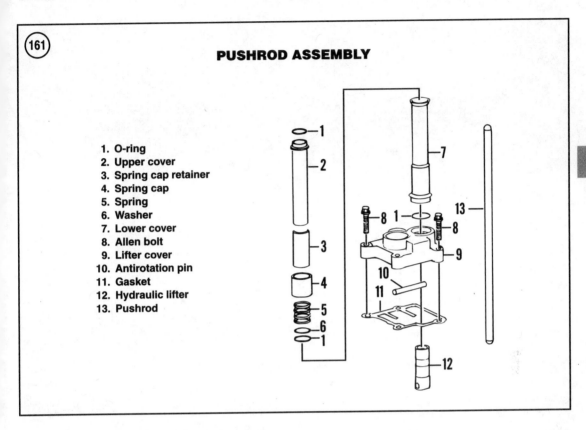

161

PUSHROD ASSEMBLY

1. O-ring
2. Upper cover
3. Spring cap retainer
4. Spring cap
5. Spring
6. Washer
7. Lower cover
8. Allen bolt
9. Lifter cover
10. Antirotation pin
11. Gasket
12. Hydraulic lifter
13. Pushrod

4

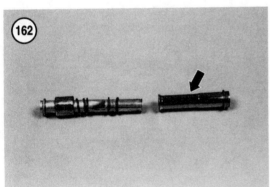

162

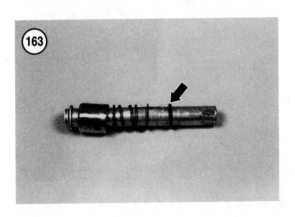

163

6. Push the piston pin (B, **Figure 134**) through the connecting rod bushing and into the other side of the piston. Push the piston pin in until it bottoms on the retaining ring.

7. Install the other *new* piston pin retaining ring (**Figure 159**) into the piston groove. Make sure it seats properly in the piston groove (**Figure 160**).

8. Repeat Steps 1-7 for the other piston.

9. Install the cylinders as described in this chapter.

PUSHRODS

Removal/Installation

Remove and install the pushrods as described under *Rocker Arm Cover and Cylinder Head Removal* in this chapter.

Inspection

1. Disassemble the pushrod assembly (**Figure 161**) as follows:

    a. Remove the lower pushrod cover (**Figure 162**).

    b. Remove the O-ring (**Figure 163**).

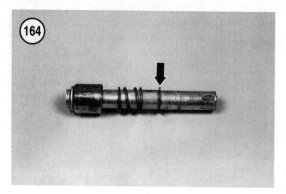

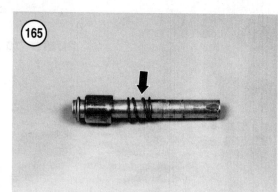

   c. Remove the spacer (**Figure 164**).
   d. Remove the spring (**Figure 165**).
   e. Remove the spring cap (**Figure 166**).
2. Check the pushrod cover assembly (**Figure 167**) as follows:
   a. Check the spring for sagging or cracking.
   b. Check the spacer for deformation or damage.
   c. Check the pushrod covers for cracking or damage.
3. Check the pushrod ends (**Figure 168**) for wear.
4. Roll the pushrods on a surface plate or plate glass, and check for bending.
5. Replace all worn or damaged parts. Install *new* O-rings.
6. Reverse Step 1 to assemble the pushrod assembly. Push the lower pushrod cover (A, **Figure 169**) into the spring cap (B) to seat the O-ring.

VALVE LIFTERS

Figure 161 shows a valve lifter in relation to its pushrod and valve lifter cover. The valve lifters and covers are installed on the right side of the engine. During engine operation, the lifters are pumped full with engine oil, thus taking up all play in the valve train. When the engine is turned off, the lifters leak down after a period of time as some of the oil drains out. When the engine is started, the lifters click until they completely refill with oil. The lifters are working properly when they stop clicking after the engine is run for a few minutes. If the clicking persists, there may be a problem with the lifter(s).

Removal

During removal, store lifters in proper sequence so they will be installed in their original position in the crankcase.

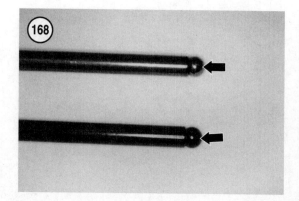

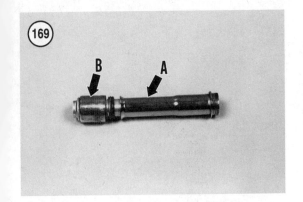

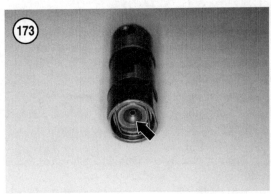

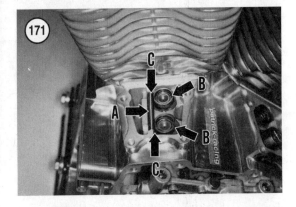

1. Remove the pushrods as described under *Rocker Arm Cover and Cylinder Head Removal* in this chapter.

NOTE
*In Step 2, loosen the two inner lifter cover Allen bolts with a short 90° Allen wrench, as shown in A, **Figure 170**, or a ball-end straight Allen wrench.*

2. Remove the lifter cover mounting bolts and remove the cover (B, **Figure 170**).
3. Remove the lifter cover gasket from the crankcase.

NOTE
Do not intermix the lifters in Step 4. Mark them so they will be installed in their original position.

4. Remove the antirotation pin (A, **Figure 171**) and both hydraulic lifters (B).
5. Cover the crankcase opening (**Figure 172**) to prevent the entry of small parts.
6. If the lifters are not going to be inspected as described in the following section, store them upright in a container filled with clean engine oil until installation.
7. Remove the lifter cover gasket.

Inspection

NOTE
Place the lifters on a clean, lint-free cloth during inspection. Place inspected lifters in a container of clean engine oil.

1. Check the pushrod socket (**Figure 173**) in the top of the lifter for wear or damage.

2. Check the lifter roller (**Figure 174**) for pitting, scoring, galling or excessive wear. If the rollers are worn excessively, check the mating cam lobes for the same wear condition.

3. Clean the lifter rollers with contact cleaner. Then measure the roller fit and end clearance, and compare them to the specification in **Table 2**. Replace the lifter assembly if either part is worn to the service limit.

4. Determine the lifter-to-crankcase bore clearance as follows:

    a. Measure the lifter bore receptacle in the crankcase and record the measurement.

    b. Measure the lifter outside diameter (**Figure 175**) and record the measurement.

    c. Subtract substep b from substep a to determine the lifter-to-crankcase bore clearance, then compare the measurement to the service limit in **Table 2**. Replace the lifter or crankcase if the clearance is worn to the service limit.

5. If a lifter does not show visual damage, it may be contaminated with dirt or have internal damage. If so, replace it. The lifters are not serviceable and must be replaced as a unit.

6. After inspecting the lifters, store them in a container filled with clean engine oil until installation.

7. If most of the oil has drained out of the lifter, refill it with a pump-type oil can through the oil hole in the side of the lifter.

8. Clean all gasket material from the mating surfaces of the crankcase and the lifter cover.

Installation

1. Remove two of the lifters from the oil-filled container and keep them vertical.

2. Install the hydraulic lifters (B, **Figure 171**) into the crankcase receptacles with the flat surfaces facing toward the front and rear of the engine.

> *CAUTION*
> *Failure to install the antirotation pin will allow the lifter to rotate off the camshaft lobe, and cause severe internal engine damage.*

3. Install the antirotation pin (A, **Figure 171**). Make sure it is seated correctly within the crankcase receptacle and against the flats on both hydraulic lifters (C, **Figure 171**).

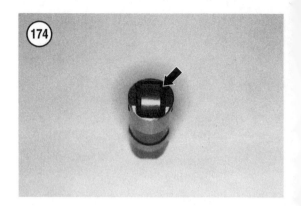

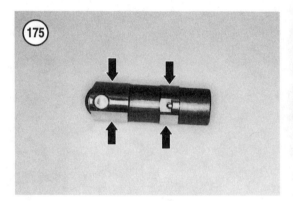

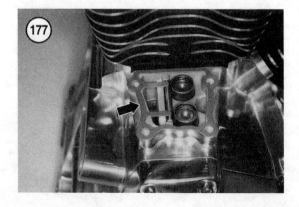

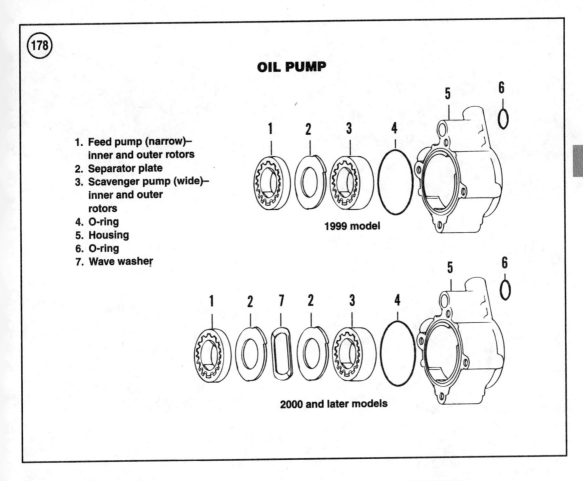

(178)

OIL PUMP

1. Feed pump (narrow)–
   inner and outer rotors
2. Separator plate
3. Scavenger pump (wide)–
   inner and outer
   rotors
4. O-ring
5. Housing
6. O-ring
7. Wave washer

1999 model

2000 and later models

4. Rotate the engine until both lifters for the cylinder head being serviced seat onto the cam's lowest position (base circle). The lifter's top surface will be flush with the top surface of the crankcase surface as shown in **Figure 176**.

5. Install a *new* lifter cover gasket (**Figure 177**) onto the crankcase.

> NOTE
> In Step 2, tighten the two inner lifter cover Allen bolts with a short 90-degree Allen wrench as shown in A, *Figure 170* or ball-end straight Allen wrench.

6. Install the lifter cover and the mounting bolts (B, **Figure 170**). Tighten the bolts to the specification in **Table 4**.

7. Repeat Steps 1-6 to install the other set of lifters.

8. Install the pushrods as described under *Rocker Arm Cover and Cylinder Head Installation* in this chapter.

OIL PUMP

The oil pump is mounted to the right side of the crankcase under the camshaft support plate. The oil pump consists of two sections: a feed pump (narrow rotors) which supplies oil under pressure to the engine components and a scavenger pump (wide rotors) which returns the oil from the engine to the oil pan in the base of the transmission case. The oil travels from the engine to the oil pan through two interconnecting hoses.

Disassembly/Removal

The oil pump can be removed with the engine in the frame. This procedure is shown with the engine removed and partially disassembled to better illustrate the steps. Refer to **Figure 178**.

> NOTE
> The oil pump on 1999 models is slightly different from the 2000-on

models. Both assemblies are covered in the following procedure. Differences between the two types are identified. Parts are not interchangeable between the two types.

1. Drain the engine oil as described in Chapter Three.

2. Remove the camshaft support plate assembly as described under *Camshaft Support Plate Removal* in this chapter.

4

3. Remove the feed pump inner (**Figure 179**) and outer rotors (**Figure 180**).

4A. On 1999 models, remove the separator plate (**Figure 181**).

4B. On 2000-on models, remove the outer separator plate (**Figure 182**), wave washer (**Figure 183**) and the inner separator plate (**Figure 184**).

5. Remove the scavenger pump outer and inner rotors (**Figure 185**).

6. Carefully pull the oil pump body (**Figure 186**) straight off the crankshaft.

7. Remove the O-ring (**Figure 187**) from the backside of the oil pump.

Inspection

1. Clean all parts thoroughly in solvent and place them on a clean, lint-free cloth. Refer to **Figure 188** for 1999 models or **Figure 189** for 2000-on models.

2. Inspect both sets of inner and outer rotors (**Figure 190**) for scratches and abrasion.

3. Inspect the oil pump housing (**Figure 191**) for scratches caused by the rotors.

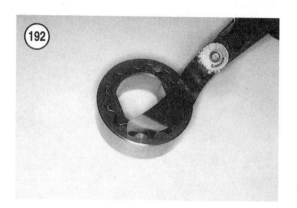

4. Inspect the interior passageways of the oil pump housing. Make sure all oil sludge and debris is removed. Blow low-pressure compressed air through all oil pump housing passages.

5. Install the inner rotor into the outer rotor. Check the clearance between the inner tip and outer rotor (**Figure 192**) with a flat feeler gauge. Replace the rotors as a set if the clearance exceeds the dimension in **Table 2**. Also measure the other set of rotors.

6. Measure the thickness of the inner (**Figure 193**) and outer (**Figure 194**) rotors. Both rotors should be the same thickness. If they are not, replace them as a complete set. Also measure the other set of rotors.

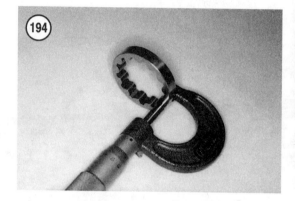

Reassembly/Installation

> *NOTE*
> *Position both inner and outer rotor sets with the punch marks (**Figure 195**) facing out.*

1. Install a *new* O-ring (**Figure 187**) onto the backside of the oil pump. Apply clean engine oil to the O-ring.

2. Carefully push the oil pump body (**Figure 186**) straight onto the crankshaft. Align the O-ring and fitting to the crankcase fitting (**Figure 196**). Push it on until it bottoms. Make sure the O-ring seats correctly in the crankcase fitting

3. Install the scavenge outer rotor (**Figure 197**) into the oil pump housing.

4. Align the flat on the scavenge inner rotor with the flat on the crankshaft and install the inner rotor (**Figure 198**). Push it on until it is meshed with the outer rotor.

5A. On 1999 models, align the tangs on the separator plate with the oil pump grooves and install the separator plate (**Figure 181**).

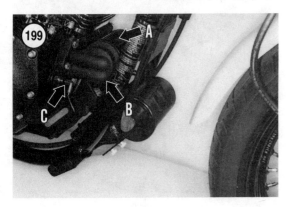

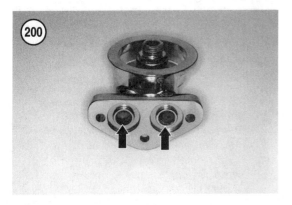

5B. On 2000-on models, perform the following:

   a. Align the tangs on the inner separator plate with the oil pump grooves and install the inner separator plate (**Figure 184**).

   b. Install the wave washer (**Figure 183**).

   c. Align the tangs on the outer separator plate with the oil pump grooves and install the outer separator plate (**Figure 182**).

6. Install the feed pump outer rotor (**Figure 180**) into the oil pump housing.

7. Align the flat on the feed pump inner rotor with the flat on the crankshaft and install the inner rotor (**Figure 179**). Push it on until it is meshed with the outer rotor.

8. Install the camshaft support plate assembly as described under *Camshaft Support Plate Installation* in this chapter.

9. Refill the engine oil as described in Chapter Three.

OIL FILTER MOUNT

The oil filter mount is on the front right side of the engine and can be removed with the engine in the frame.

Removal

1. Park the motorcycle on a level surface.

2. Remove the front cylinder's exhaust pipe as described in Chapter Seven.

3. Drain the engine oil and remove the oil filter (A, **Figure 199**) as described in Chapter Three.

4. Place several shop cloths under the oil filter mount for residual oil that will drain out in the next step.

5. Straighten the lockplate tabs and remove the three bolts, oil filter and oil filter mount (B, **Figure 199**) from the crankcase.

Inspection

1. Clean the oil filter mount in solvent and dry it with compressed air.

2. Inspect the oil filter mount for damage that could lead to an oil leak.

3. Make sure the oil passageways (**Figure 200**) are clear.

4. Check the oil filter mounting surface (A, **Figure 201**) and oil filter mounting threads (B) for wear or damage.

Installation

1. Thoroughly clean the crankcase mating surface.
2. Install *new* O-ring seals (**Figure 202**) onto the mount.
3. Apply Three Bond TB1342, or an equivalent, to the threads of the three prior to installing them onto the *new* lockplate.
4. Install the oil filter mount onto the crankcase. Install the lockplate, and three bolts and washers (**Figure 203**).
5. Tighten the bolts to the specification in **Table 4**.
6. Bend the locking tab against the top and bottom bolt heads.
7. Install a *new* oil filter (A, **Figure 199**).
8. Disconnect the electrical connector from the oil pressure switch (C, **Figure 199**). Thoroughly clean the electrical connector and the switch terminal with an aerosol parts cleaner to remove oil that may have come in contact with these parts.
9. Install the front cylinder's exhaust pipe as described in Chapter Seven.
10. Start the engine and check for leaks.

CAMSHAFT SUPPORT PLATE

A camshaft and crankshaft sprocket lock (JIMS part No. 1285), and a camshaft chain tensioner tool (JIMS part No. 1283) are required to remove and install the camshaft support plate.

> *NOTE*
> *Two types of methods are used to secure the rear camshaft sprocket. Early 1999 models use a Woodruff key as shown in 24, **Figure 204**. Later 1999-on models are splined as shown in 29, **Figure 205**.*

Removal

> *NOTE*
> *This procedure can be performed with the engine mounted in the frame. This procedure is shown with the engine removed and partially disassembled to better illustrate the steps.*

1. Remove the exhaust system as described in Chapter Seven.
2. Remove the pushrods, lifters and lifter covers as described in this chapter.

> *CAUTION*
> *On 1999-2001 models, the cam position sensor wiring (**Figure 206**) is routed through the camshaft cover. Move the cover out of the way and secure it to the frame with a piece of wire. Do not hang the cover by the wiring.*

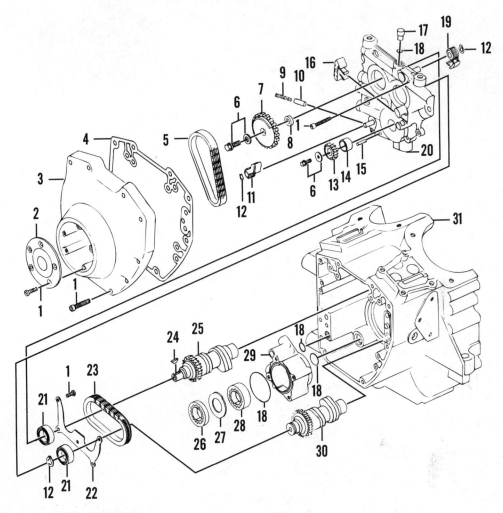

CAMSHAFTS AND COVER (1999 MODELS)

1. Screw
2. Cover
3. Camshaft cover
4. Gasket
5. Camshaft primary drive chain
6. Bolt and washer
7. Rear cylinder camshaft drive sprocket (34 teeth)
8. Spacer
9. Oil pump relief spring
10. Oil pump relief valve
11. Primary chain tensioner
12. Snap ring
13. Front camshaft drive sprocket (17 teeth)
14. Bushing
15. Roll pin
16. Chain guide
17. Plug
18. O-ring
19. Secondary chain tensioner
20. Camshaft support plate
21. Bearing
22. Bearing retainer plate
23. Camshaft secondary drive chain
24. Woodruff key
25. Camshaft–rear cylinder
26. Oil pump feed rotors
27. Separator plate
28. Oil pump scavenger rotors
29. Oil pump housing
30. Camshaft–front cylinder
31. Crankcase half–right side

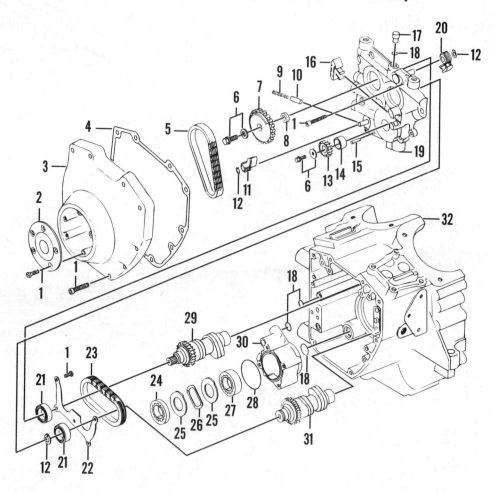

CAMSHAFTS AND COVER (2000-ON MODELS)

1. Screw
2. Cover
3. Camshaft cover
4. Gasket
5. Camshaft primary drive chain
6. Bolt and washer
7. Rear cylinder camshaft drive sprocket
8. Spacer
9. Oil pump relief spring
10. Oil pump relief valve
11. Primary chain tensioner
12. Snap ring
13. Crankshaft sprocket
14. Bushing
15. Roll pin
16. Chain guide
17. Plug
18. O-ring
19. Camshaft support plate
20. Secondary chain tensioner
21. Bearing
22. Bearing retainer plate
23. Camshaft secondary drive chain
24. Oil pump feed rotors
25. Separator plate
26. Wave washer
27. Oil pump scavenger rotors
28. O-ring
29. Camshaft–rear cylinder
30. Oil pump housing
31. Camshaft–front cylinder
32. Crankcase half–right side

4

3. Using a crisscross pattern, loosen then remove the bolts securing the camshaft cover (**Figure 207**), and remove the cover and gasket.

4. On 1999-2001 models, remove the bolt securing the crankshaft position sensor (**Figure 208**) and remove the sensor from the crankcase.

5. To ensure the camshaft primary drive chain is reinstalled in the same direction of travel, mark one of the link plates with a permanent marking pen or a scribe.

6. Relieve the tension on the camshaft primary drive chain as follows:

    a. Install the camshaft chain tensioner tool (A, **Figure 209**) onto the camshaft primary chain tensioner.

    b. Using a wrench, rotate the tool counterclockwise and insert the hold pin (B, **Figure 209**) through the hole in the tensioner and into the hole in the support plate. Push the hold pin in until it bottoms.

    c. Remove the wrench and tensioner tool from the tensioner.

7. Install and mesh the camshaft and crankshaft sprocket lock (A, **Figure 210**) between the sprockets.

8. Loosen the bolt securing the crankshaft sprocket (B, **Figure 210**).

NOTE
*The rear camshaft sprocket bolt is secured with a threadlocking compound. Attempt to loosen the bolt with an impact driver or air impact wrench. If this is not successful, evenly heat the bolt head with a propane torch. Use caution, as excessive heat may damage the tensioner assembly. Do **not** use excessive force to remove the bolt. If necessary, have a Harley-Davidson dealership remove the bolt.*

9. Loosen the bolt securing the rear camshaft sprocket (C, **Figure 210**).

10. Remove the special tool installed in Step 7.

11. Remove camshaft sprocket bolt (A, **Figure 211**) and the crankshaft sprocket bolt and washer (B).

NOTE
If it is difficult to loosen either sprocket from its respective shaft, use a small pry bar and gently loosen the sprocket(s) from the shaft.

12. Remove the rear camshaft drive sprocket (A, **Figure 212**), the crankshaft sprocket (B) and the primary camshaft drive chain (C) as an assembly. Pull the assembly straight off the shafts.

13. On models so equipped, remove the Woodruff key from the rear camshaft.

14. Remove the sprocket spacer (**Figure 213**) from the rear camshaft.

15. Squeeze the tabs and remove the camshaft chain guide (**Figure 214**).

16. Loosen the camshaft support plate Allen bolts in the following sequence:

   a. Using a crisscross pattern, loosen and remove the four Allen bolts (A, **Figure 215**) securing the support plate to the oil pump assembly.

   b. Using a crisscross pattern, loosen and remove the remaining six Allen bolts securing the support plate (B, **Figure 215**) to the crankcase.

17. Withdraw the camshaft support plate assembly from the crankcase. If necessary, carefully pry the plate loose from the crankcase in the areas where the locating dowels are located (**Figure 216**).

18. Remove the O-ring (A, **Figure 217**) from the oil pump assembly and the lower O-ring (B).

19. On 2000-on models, remove the upper O-ring (C, **Figure 217**).

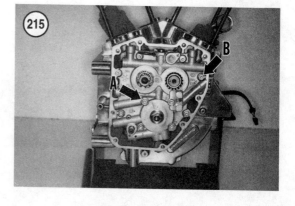

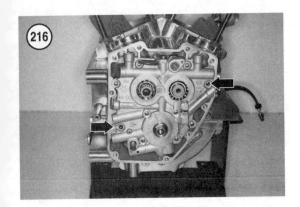

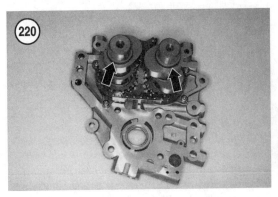

20. If necessary, disassemble and remove the camshafts as described in this chapter.

Installation

> *NOTE*
> *Release the secondary chain tension to install the camshaft inner ends into the crankcase bearings (D, **Figure 217**). If the tension is not released, the inner ends of the camshafts will be pulled together and out of alignment with the bearings, making installation difficult.*

1. Release the tension on the camshaft secondary chain tension as follows:

    a. Install the camshaft chain tensioner tool onto the camshaft secondary chain tensioner.

    b. Using a wrench, rotate the tool counterclockwise and insert the hold pin (**Figure 218**) through the hole in the outer surface of the support plate and into the hole in the tensioner. Push the hold pin in until it bottoms.

    c. Remove the wrench and tensioner tool from the tensioner.

2. Push on the oil pump assembly to make sure it is correctly seated against the crankcase.

3. Install a *new* O-ring (A, **Figure 217**) onto the oil pump assembly and a *new* O-ring (B) onto the lower location. Apply a light coat of clean engine oil to the O-rings.

4. On 2000-on models, install a new upper O-ring (C, **Figure 217**). Apply a light coat of clean engine oil to the O-ring.

5. Lubricate the camshaft needle bearing (**Figure 219**) in the crankcase and the camshaft bearing surfaces (**Figure 220**) with clean engine oil.

6. If the camshafts were removed from the support plate, make sure the timing marks (**Figure 221**) on each camshaft are aligned with each other. If the marks are not aligned, reposition the camshafts prior to installing the assembly into the crankcase.

CAUTION
Do not force the camshaft support plate assembly into the crankcase. During installation, the camshaft ends may not be correctly aligned with the needle bearings. If force is applied, the needle bearing(s) will be damaged.

7. If removed, install the two locating dowels (E, **Figure 217**) onto the crankcase.

8. Slowly install the camshaft support plate assembly into the crankcase. Guide the camshaft ends into the crankcase needle bearings. If necessary, slightly rotate and/or wiggle the end of the rear cylinder camshaft (**Figure 222**) to assist in the alignment.

CAUTION
When properly aligned, the camshaft support plate assembly fits snugly against the crankcase mating surface. If they do not meet correctly, do not attempt to pull the parts together with the mounting bolts. Separate the camshaft support plate assembly and determine the cause of the interference.

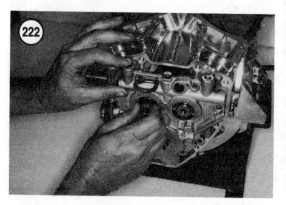

9. Push the camshaft support plate assembly onto the crankcase until it bottoms on the two locating dowels and the crankcase mating surface.

10. Make sure the timing marks (**Figure 223**) on each camshaft are still aligned. If they are not aligned, correct the problem at this time.

11. Tighten the six camshaft support plate-to-crankcase Allen bolts in the following sequence:

   a. Install and loosely tighten the Allen bolts (B, **Figure 215**).

   b. Tighten the Allen bolts in a crisscross pattern to the specification in **Table 4**.

12. Tighten the four camshaft support plate-to-oil pump Allen bolts in the following sequence:

   a. Install the Allen bolts (A, **Figure 215**). Tighten the bolts until they just contact the support plate, then back them out 1/4 turn.

   b. Rotate the engine until the oil pump is in neutral center with no load on it.

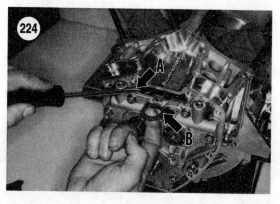

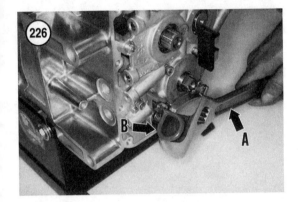

c. Tighten the bolts until they are snug against the support plate. Then tighten the Allen bolts in a crisscross pattern to the specification in **Table 4**.

13. After all ten Allen bolts are tightened, check the perimeter of the support plate to make sure it is seated against the crankcase mating surface.

14. Install an angled pick into the crankcase opening and against the secondary camshaft chain tensioner shoe (A, **Figure 224**). *Slowly* release the hold pin (B) and allow the tensioner shoe to gradually contact the chain surface. If it is released too fast, the shoe surface will slam against the chain and be damaged.

15. Squeeze the camshaft chain guide tabs and install it (**Figure 214**) onto the two posts.

NOTE
Step 16 is not necessary if the original camshaft support plate, both camshafts, rear camshaft sprocket, crankshaft drive sprocket and the crankshaft assembly are reused. If any of these components have been replaced, Step 16 is necessary to ensure correct alignment between the rear camshaft sprocket and the crankshaft drive sprocket. If the alignment is incorrect, the primary drive chain and both sprockets will bind and cause premature wear.

16. If new parts have been installed, perform the alignment procedure described under *Rear Camshaft Sprocket and Crankshaft Drive Sprocket Alignment*. If all original parts have been installed, proceed to Step 17.

17. Relieve the tension on the camshaft primary drive chain as follows:

    a. Install the camshaft chain tensioner tool (**Figure 225**) onto the camshaft primary chain tensioner.

    b. Using a wrench (A, **Figure 226**), rotate the tool counterclockwise and insert the hold pin (B) through the hole in the tensioner and into the hole in the support plate. Push the hold pin in until it bottoms.

    c. Remove the wrench and tensioner tool from the tensioner.

18. Install the sprocket spacer (**Figure 213**) onto the rear camshaft with the manufacturer's marks facing the crankcase.

NOTE
Refer to the mark made prior to removal and position the camshaft primary drive chain so it will travel in the same direction. If it is installed incorrectly, the drive chain will wear prematurely.

19. Assemble the rear camshaft sprocket, the crankshaft drive sprocket and the primary drive chain as an assembly. Align the index mark on both sprockets so they face each other as shown in **Figure 227**.

20. On models so equipped, install the Woodruff key onto the rear camshaft.

21. Install the rear camshaft drive sprocket (A, **Figure 212**), the crankshaft sprocket (B), and the primary camshaft drive chain (C) as an assembly onto the crankshaft and rear camshaft. Align the flat on the crankshaft sprocket with the flat on the crankshaft (A, **Figure 228**). Check the alignment of the index mark on both sprockets, and make sure they face each other as shown in B, **Figure 228**. Realign the sprocket index marks if necessary.

22. Apply clean engine oil to the underside of both *new* sprocket bolts prior to installation.

23. Apply a small amount of ThreeBond TB1360, or an equivalent, threadlocking compound to the threads of the *new* rear camshaft sprocket bolt. Do not apply the locking agent to the crankshaft bolt.

24. Install a *new* camshaft sprocket bolt (A, **Figure 211**) and *new* crankshaft sprocket bolt and washer (B). Tighten the bolts finger-tight at this time.

25. Install and mesh the camshaft and crankshaft sprocket lock (**Figure 229**) between the sprockets.

26. Place a flat blade screwdriver (A, **Figure 230**) between the primary camshaft drive chain and the tensioner. Slowly release the hold pin (B), then slowly withdraw the screwdriver and allow the tensioner to gradually contact the chain surface. If it is released too fast, the shoe surface will slam against the chain and be damaged.

27. Tighten both bolts as follows:
   a. Tighten both bolts to 15 ft.-lb. (20 N•m).
   b. Loosen both bolts one complete revolution (360°).
   c. Tighten the rear camshaft bolt to 34 ft.-lb. (46 N•m).
   d. Tighten the crankshaft bolt to 24 ft.-lb. (33 N•m).

28. Remove the tool installed in Step 25.

29. On 1999-2001 models, install the crankshaft position sensor (**Figure 208**) into the crankcase and tighten the bolt securely.

30. Install a *new* camshaft cover gasket (**Figure 231**) onto the crankcase.

31. Install the camshaft cover onto the crankcase. Make sure the cam position sensor wiring (**Figure 206**) is correctly positioned. Install the bolts and tighten them securely in a crisscross pattern.

32. Install the lifter covers, lifters and pushrods as described in this chapter.

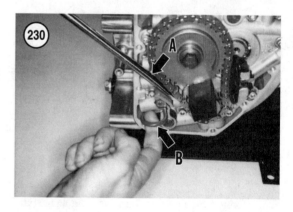

33. Install the exhaust system as described in Chapter Seven.

Rear Camshaft Sprocket and Crankshaft Drive Sprocket Alignment

This procedure is required if the camshaft support plate, either or both camshafts, the rear camshaft sprocket, the crankshaft drive sprocket and/or the crankshaft assembly have been replaced.

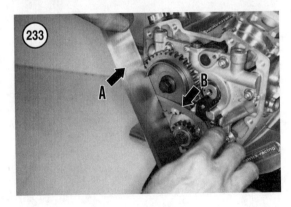

If alignment between the rear camshaft sprocket and the crankshaft drive sprocket is incorrect, the primary drive chain and both sprockets will bind and cause premature wear.

1. Install the sprocket spacer (**Figure 213**) onto the rear camshaft with the manufacturer's marks facing the crankcase.

2. On models so equipped, install the Woodruff key onto the rear camshaft.

3. Apply clean engine oil to the camshaft splines (or Woodruff key) and to the rear camshaft sprocket splines.

4. Install the rear camshaft sprocket onto the camshaft. Install the *used* mounting bolt and flat washer (A, **Figure 232**). Tighten the bolt finger-tight at this time.

NOTE
Use a smaller outer diameter washer in Step 5 to allow room for the straightedge to be placed against the flat surface of the crankshaft sprocket face.

5. Install the crankshaft sprocket (B, **Figure 232**) onto the crankshaft. Install the *used* mounting bolt and a *washer with a smaller outer diameter* (C). Tighten the bolt finger-tight at this time.

6. Install and mesh the camshaft and crankshaft sprocket lock (**Figure 229**) between the sprockets.

7. Tighten both bolts as follows:
   a. Tighten both bolts to 15 ft.-lb. (20 N•m).
   b. Loosen both bolts one complete revolution (360°).
   c. Tighten the rear camshaft bolt to 34 ft.-lb. (46 N•m).
   d. Tighten the crankshaft bolt to 24 ft.-lb. (33 N•m).

8. Remove the special tool from the sprockets.

9. Place a straightedge (A, **Figure 233**) against the face of both sprockets. Push the straightedge against the *crankshaft sprocket* and hold it there.

10. Try to insert a 0.005 in. (0.127 mm) feeler gauge (B, **Figure 233**) between the straightedge and the camshaft sprocket face.

11A. If the 0.005 in. (0.127 mm) feeler gauge can be inserted, the sprockets are correctly aligned. Remove both sprockets and proceed with Step 17 of *Camshaft Support Plate Installation* in the previous procedure.

11B. If a different thickness feeler gauge can be inserted, indicating a height difference other than 0.005 in. (0.127 mm), the rear camshaft spacer must be changed. Continue to insert feeler gauges of different thicknesses until the dimension is determined. Record this dimension as it will be used to choose a new spacer.

12. Remove the rear camshaft sprocket bolt, washer and sprocket.

13. Remove the existing sprocket spacer (**Figure 213**) from the rear camshaft. Compare the part num-

ber stamped on the spacer with the part numbers in **Table 5** to determine the thickness.

14A. If the crankshaft sprocket is more than 0.005 in. (0.127 mm) above the camshaft sprocket, install the next *thicker* size spacer under the camshaft sprocket.

14B. If the crankshaft sprocket is less than 0.005 in. (0.127 mm) above the camshaft sprocket, install the next *thinner* size spacer under the camshaft sprocket.

15. Install a new spacer and repeat this procedure until the height difference is 0.005 in. (0.127 mm).

16. After the correct spacer thickness is established, proceed with Step 17 of *Camshaft Support Plate Installation*.

Camshaft Support Plate and Camshafts

A hydraulic press, camshaft chain tensioner tool (JIMS part No. 1283) and camshaft remover and installer (JIMS part No. 1277) are required to perform the following procedure.

Disassembly

1. Remove the camshaft support plate as described in this chapter.

2. Remove the snap ring (**Figure 234**) from the front cylinder camshaft.

3. Release the tension on the camshaft secondary chain tension as follows:

    a. Install the camshaft chain tensioner tool onto the camshaft secondary chain tensioner.

    b. Using a wrench, rotate the tool counterclockwise and insert the hold pin (**Figure 235**) through the hole in the outer surface of the support plate and into the hole in the tensioner. Push the hold pin in until it bottoms.

    c. Remove the wrench and tensioner tool from the tensioner.

4. Loosen and remove the four T20 Torx screws (**Figure 236**) securing the bearing retainer plate. Remove the bearing retainer plate (**Figure 237**).

5. Press the camshafts and secondary drive chain out of the camshaft support plate as follows:

    a. Turn the camshaft support cover face up on two support blocks in a press bed. Make sure the support blocks are tall enough to allow the

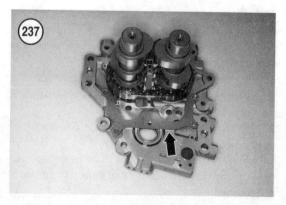

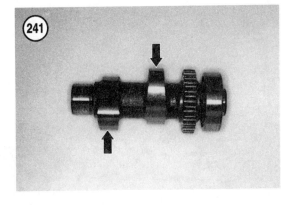

complete removal of the camshafts from the cover.

   b. Install the cups of the camshaft remover and installer onto the top of the camshafts (**Figure 238**) following the manufacturer's instructions.

   c. Center the press ram over the center of the tool (**Figure 239**).

   d. Slowly press the assembly out of the support cover.

   e. Remove the assembly, cover and special tool from the press bed.

6. To ensure the camshaft secondary drive chain is reinstalled in the same direction of travel, mark one of the link plates (**Figure 240**) on the bearing side with a permanent marking pen or scribe.

7. Separate the camshafts from the secondary drive chain.

Inspection

There are no manufacturer's specifications available for the camshaft. The following procedure is a visual inspection to determine if the camshafts require replacement.

1. Check the camshaft lobes (**Figure 241**) for wear. The lobes should not be scored and the edges should be square.

2. Inspect the drive chain sprocket (**Figure 242**) for broken or chipped teeth. Also check the teeth for cracking or rounding. If the sprocket is damaged or severely worn, replace the camshaft.

3. If the camshaft sprockets are worn, check the camshaft secondary drive chain (**Figure 243**) for damage.

4A. On early models, inspect the Woodruff key and key slot in the rear cylinder's camshaft for wear or damage.

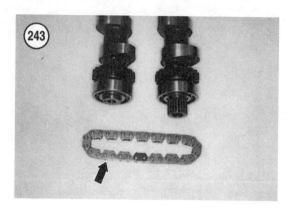

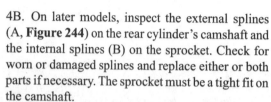

4B. On later models, inspect the external splines (A, **Figure 244**) on the rear cylinder's camshaft and the internal splines (B) on the sprocket. Check for worn or damaged splines and replace either or both parts if necessary. The sprocket must be a tight fit on the camshaft.

5. Check the snap ring groove (**Figure 245**) on the front cylinder's camshaft for wear or damage.

6. Inspect and rotate the ball bearing (**Figure 246**) on each camshaft. They should rotate smoothly with no roughness. If they are damaged, replace the ball bearings as described in this section.

Assembly

> *NOTE*
> *This procedure is shown with the ball bearings in place on the camshafts.*

1. Prior to installing the camshaft assembly, relieve the tension on the secondary cam chain tensioner as follows.

   a. Install the camshaft chain tensioner tool (**Figure 247**) onto the camshaft secondary chain tensioner.

   b. Using a wrench, rotate the tool counterclockwise (**Figure 248**) and insert the hold pin through the hole in the tensioner and into the hole in the support plate. Push the hold pin in until it bottoms (**Figure 249**).

   c. Remove the wrench and tensioner tool from the tensioner.

2. Assemble the camshafts and the secondary drive chain as follows:

   a. Locate the index marks on the front of the camshafts (**Figure 250**). Transfer these marks to the backside of the sprockets, in the same location with a permanent marking pen or

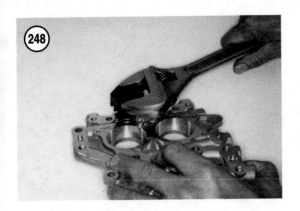

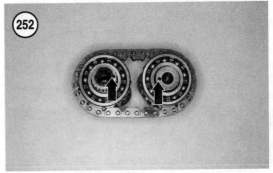

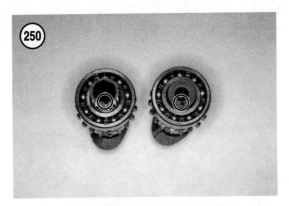

scribe (**Figure 251**). These marks will be used for proper alignment of the camshaft as it is pressed into the camshaft support plate.

NOTE
*Refer to the mark made on one of the link plates in **Disassembly** Step 6 and position the camshaft secondary drive chain so it travels in the same direction as noted prior to removal. If it is installed incorrectly, the drive chain will wear prematurely.*

b. Position the camshafts with the index marks facing directly opposite each other (**Figure 252**).

c. Position the secondary chain with the marked link plate facing up (**Figure 240**) and install the secondary chain onto both camshafts.

d. Rotate the camshafts in either direction several times and recheck the alignment of the index marks. If necessary, readjust one of the camshafts to achieve correct alignment (**Figure 252**).

3. Apply a light coat of clean engine oil, or press lube, to the camshaft ends and to the bearing receptacles in the camshaft support plate.

4. Place the camshaft support plate on the press bed with the bearing receptacles facing up (**Figure 253**).

5. Position the camshaft assembly on the camshaft support plate with the rear cylinder camshaft (**Figure 254**) located toward the back of the support plate. Align the bearings with the support plate receptacles and hold the assembly in place.

NOTE
*Prior to pressing the camshaft assembly into place, make sure the camshaft index marks on the backside of the sprockets align (**Figure 255**). If they are out of alignment, remove the assembly and correct this alignment.*

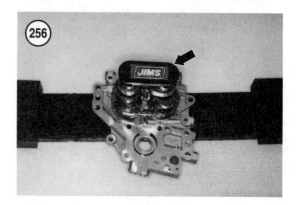

6. Install the cups of the camshaft remover and installer onto the top of the camshafts (**Figure 256**) following the manufacturer's instructions.

7. Center the press ram over the center of the tool (**Figure 257**).

8. Slowly press the assembly into the support cover until it bottoms.

9. Remove the assembly and special tool from the press bed.

10. Turn the assembly over and make sure the camshaft index marks are still correctly aligned as shown in **Figure 258**.

11. Rotate the camshafts several complete revolutions and check for binding.

12. Install the retainer plate (**Figure 237**).

13. Apply a small amount of ThreeBond TB1342 or an equivalent threadlocking compound to the Torx screw threads. Install the four T20 Torx screws (**Figure 236**) and tighten them securely.

14. Place a flat blade screwdriver between the secondary camshaft drive chain and the tensioner. Slowly release the hold pin (**Figure 235**), then slowly withdraw the screwdriver and allow the tensioner to gradually contact the chain surface. If it

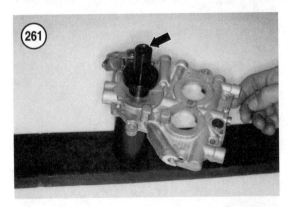

is released too fast, the shoe surface will slam against the chain and be damaged.

15. Install the snap ring (**Figure 259**) onto the front cylinder camshaft. Make sure the snap ring is correctly seated in the camshaft groove.

16. Install the camshaft support plate as described in this chapter.

Bushing replacement

A crankshaft bushing tool (JIMS part No. 1281) is required to remove and install the crankshaft bushing.

1. Place the bushing support tool on the press bed.

NOTE
The crankshaft bushing edge is knurled on the side that faces the primary chain side.

2. Position the camshaft support plate with the primary chain side facing up. Place the camshaft support plate onto the bushing support tool and center the bushing over the tool (**Figure 260**).

3. Install the *remove side* of the driver (**Figure 261**) through the bushing and into the support tool until the shoulder of the driver contacts the edge of the bushing.

4. Press the bushing out of the support plate until the driver collar contacts the support plate.

5. If the bushing support tool was removed, place it on the press bed.

6. Position the camshaft support plate with the secondary chain side facing up. Place the camshaft support plate onto the bushing support tool.

7. Apply a light coat of clean engine oil, or press lube, to the outer surface of the bushing and to the support plate bushing receptacle.

8. Position the bushing into the receptacle with the knurled side facing up.

9. Install the *install side* of the driver (**Figure 262**) through the bushing and into the support tool until the driver contacts the edge of the bushing.

10. Press the bushing into the support plate until the driver collar contacts the support plate.

11. Remove the special tools and the support plate from the press bed.

Camshaft Bearing Replacement

Ball bearings

A hydraulic press, camshaft bearing puller (JIMS part No 1280), and camshaft remover and installer (JIMS part No. 1277) are required to remove and install the camshaft ball bearings.

1. Install the camshaft bearing puller tool onto the camshaft ball bearing (**Figure 263**) and remove the camshaft ball bearing following the manufacturer's instructions.

2. Repeat Step 1 for the other camshaft bearing.

> *NOTE*
> *The ball bearing is installed in the camshaft support plate, not on the camshaft(s).*

3. Install the ball bearing(s) into the camshaft support plate using the camshaft remover and installer as follows:

   a. Place the support block on the press bed.

   b. Place the camshaft support plate (A, **Figure 264**) onto a support block. Make sure the support plate is indexed correctly into the support block.

   c. Apply a light coat of clean engine oil, or press lube, to the outer surface of the ball bearing and to the support plate bearing receptacle.

   d. Place the ball bearing onto the support plate (B, **Figure 264**).

   e. Install the bearing pilot (**Figure 265**) into the ball bearing.

   f. Press the bearing straight into the support plate until it bottoms.

   g. Remove the pilot from the bearing and remove the support plate from the press bed.

Needle bearings

> *NOTE*
> *The camshaft needle bearings can be removed with the engine mounted in the frame and the camshaft support plate removed. This procedure is shown with the engine removed and partially disassembled to better illustrate the steps.*

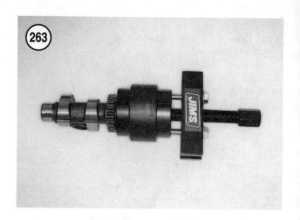

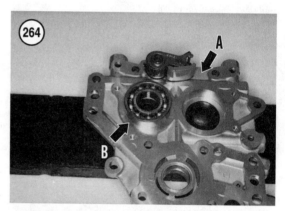

> *NOTE*
> *Replace both needle bearings as a set even if only one need to be replacement.*

A twin cam 88 engine stand (JIMS part No. 1022) and flywheel press (JIMS part No. 1047-TP) were used in the following procedure.

1. Remove the camshaft support plate assembly from the engine as described in this chapter.

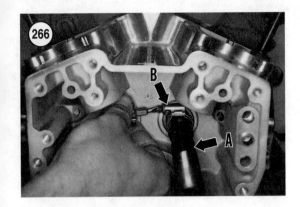

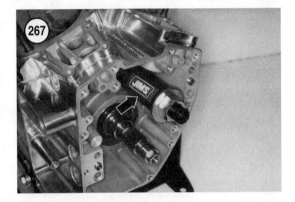

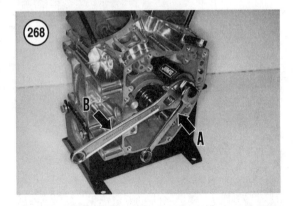

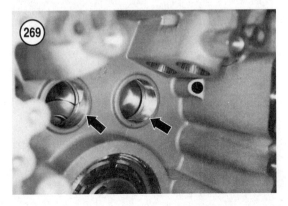

2. Install the puller portion of the tool set (A, **Figure 266**) part way into the needle bearing. Install a small hose clamp (B) onto the end that is closest to the needle bearing and tighten it. This closes the end of the tool so it can pass through the needle bearing. Push the puller all the way through the needle bearing and remove the hose clamp.

3. Assemble the remainder of the tool components onto the puller portion (**Figure 267**) following the manufacturer's instructions.

4. Place a 5/8 in. wrench on the flats of the puller (A, **Figure 268**).

5. Place a 1 1/8 in. wrench, or an adjustable wrench, on the large nut (B, **Figure 268**).

CAUTION
Do not turn the 5/8 in. wrench as this will damage the special tool and the crankcase receptacle.

6. Hold onto the 5/8 in. wrench to keep the puller from rotating. Turn the 1 1/8 in. wrench *clockwise* on the large nut. Tighten the large nut and pull the needle bearing out of the crankcase receptacle.

7. Disassemble the special tool and remove the needle bearing from it.

8. Repeat Steps 2-7 for the other needle bearing.

9. Apply a light coat of clean engine oil, or press lube, to the outer surface of the needle bearings and to the crankcase needle bearing receptacles (**Figure 269**).

NOTE
The following photographs are shown with the crankcase disassembled to better illustrate the steps.

10. Apply a light coat of clean engine oil to the threads of the screw portion and to the installer plate.

11. Insert the screw portion of the special tool part way into the installer plate.

12. Push the installer onto the screw until it locks into place.

13. Position the new bearing with the manufacturer's marks facing out on the installer (**Figure 270**).

14. Position the installer plate onto the crankcase, aligning the tool to the bearing receptacle (A, **Figure 271**).

15. Position the thumb screws through the installer plate (B, **Figure 271**) and onto the crankcase threaded holes. Tighten the thumb screws securely.

16. Slowly tighten the screw until the bearing starts to enter the crankcase receptacle. Continue to tighten it until the installer contacts the crankcase surface. This will correctly position the needle bearing within the crankcase.

17. Remove the special tools.

18. Repeat Steps 10-17 for the other needle bearing.

**Oil Pressure Relief Valve
Removal/Installation**

> *NOTE*
> *This procedure is shown with the camshaft assembly removed to better illustrate the steps.*

1. Remove the camshaft support plate assembly from the engine as described in this chapter.

2A If the camshaft assembly is still in place, secure the camshaft support plate in a vise with soft jaws.

2B. If the camshaft assembly has been removed, place the camshaft support plate on a piece of soft wood.

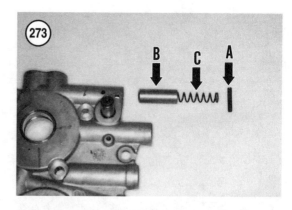

3. Use a 1/8 in. punch to drive out the roll pin (**Figure 272**) securing the valve body and spring. Discard the roll pin (A, **Figure 273**).

4. Remove the valve body (B, **Figure 273**) and spring (C) from the bypass port of the camshaft support plate.

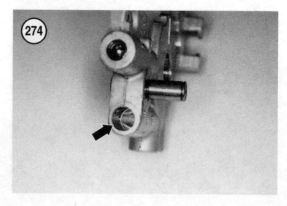

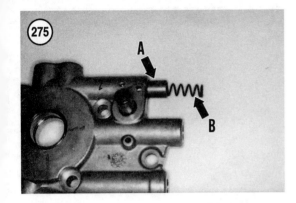

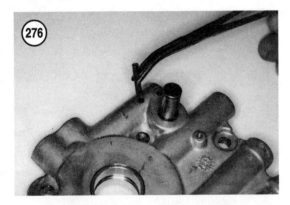

5. Inspect the valve body, spring and bypass port (**Figure 274**) for wear or damage. Replace as necessary.

6. Apply a light coat of clean engine oil to the bypass port and to the valve body.

7. Position the valve body (A, **Figure 275**) with the closed end going into the bypass port first.

8. Install the spring (B, **Figure 275**) into the valve body.

9. Push the valve body and spring into the bypass port, hold them in place and install a *new* roll pin (**Figure 276**). Tap the roll pin in until it bottoms (**Figure 272**).

Cleaning Plug Removal/Installation

NOTE
This procedure is shown with the camshaft assembly removed to better illustrate the steps.

1. Remove the camshaft support plate assembly from the engine as described in this chapter.

2A. If the camshaft assembly is still in place, secure the camshaft support plate in a vise with soft jaws.

2B. If the camshaft assembly has been removed, place the camshaft support plate on piece of soft wood.

3. Use a pair of pliers to carefully remove the cleaning plug (**Figure 277**) from the camshaft support plate. Remove the O-ring.

4. Thoroughly clean the cleaning plug receptacle and support plate in solvent. Dry them with compressed air.

5. Apply low-pressure compressed air to the cleaning plug receptacle (**Figure 278**) to blow out any debris. Make sure the oil hole is clear.

6. Install a *new* O-ring onto the cleaning plug and install the cleaning plug. Press it in until it bottoms.

Camshaft Primary and Secondary Chain Tensioner Removal/Inspection/Installation

NOTE
The following illustrations show the primary chain tensioner. They also apply to the secondary chain tensioner.

1. Remove the camshaft primary and/or secondary chain as described in this chapter.

2. Remove the snap ring (**Figure 279**) securing the chain tensioner to the mounting post.

3. Slide the chain tensioner (A, **Figure 280**) off the mounting post.

4. Inspect the chain tensioner pad (A, **Figure 281**) for wear. If the pad surface is worn halfway through (A, **Figure 282**) or chipped (B), replace the assembly.

5. Check the spring (B, **Figure 281**) for sagging or damage. Replace the assembly if necessary.

6. Install the chain tensioner onto the mounting post and insert the spring end into the receptacle in the cover (B, **Figure 280**). Push the chain tension on until it bottoms.

7. Install a *new* snap ring (**Figure 283**). Make sure it is correctly seated in the mounting post groove.

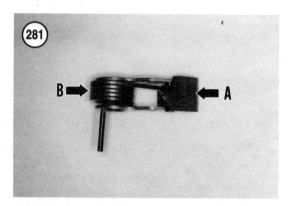

CRANKCASE AND CRANKSHAFT

Disassembly

A twin cam 88 engine stand (JIMS part No. 1022) and flywheel press (JIMS part No. 1047-TP) were used in the following procedure.

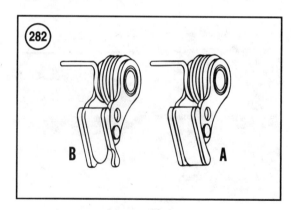

> *CAUTION*
> *Prior to disassembling the crankcase, measure the crankshaft end play as described in **Crankshaft End Play Inspection**.*

Refer to **Figure 284**.

1. Remove the engine from the frame as described in this chapter.

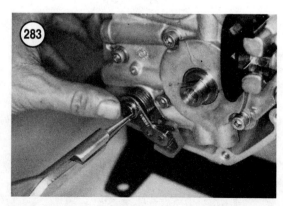

> *CAUTION*
> *Do not lift the crankcase assembly by the cylinder studs. Bent or damaged*

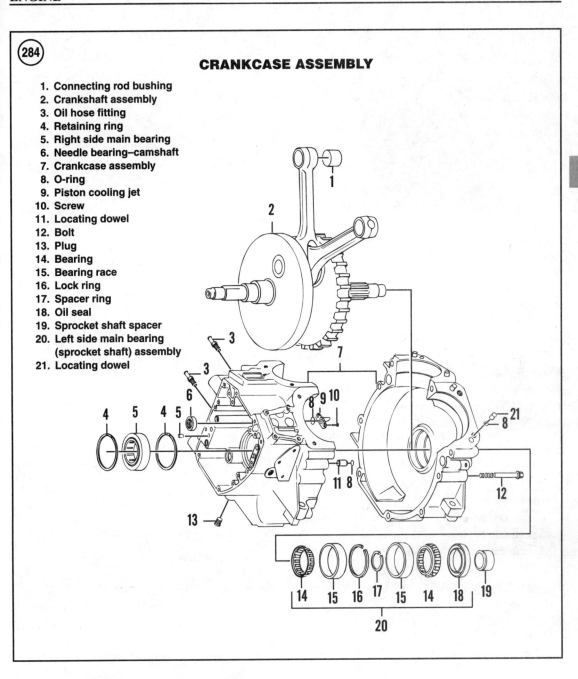

CRANKCASE ASSEMBLY

1. Connecting rod bushing
2. Crankshaft assembly
3. Oil hose fitting
4. Retaining ring
5. Right side main bearing
6. Needle bearing–camshaft
7. Crankcase assembly
8. O-ring
9. Piston cooling jet
10. Screw
11. Locating dowel
12. Bolt
13. Plug
14. Bearing
15. Bearing race
16. Lock ring
17. Spacer ring
18. Oil seal
19. Sprocket shaft spacer
20. Left side main bearing
    (sprocket shaft) assembly
21. Locating dowel

4

cylinder studs may cause the engine to leak oil.

2. Remove the following components as described in this chapter:

   a. Cylinder heads and cylinders.
   b. Pistons.
   c. Pushrods and valve lifters.
   d. Camshaft assembly.
   e. Oil pump.
   f. Alternator rotor and stator assembly (Chapter Eight).

NOTE
Leave the bolts for the left side off so the case halves can be separated in the following steps.

3. Attach the crankcase assembly to an engine stand (**Figure 285**) following the manufac-

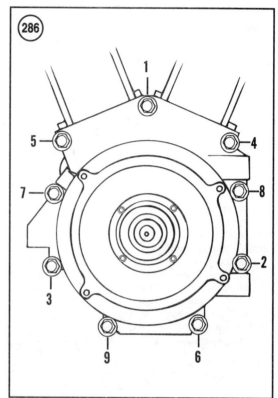

turer's instructions. Make sure the stand is attached so the case can be separated in the following steps.

4. Secure the engine stand to the workbench.

5. Using the torque pattern shown in **Figure 286**, loosen the bolts in two to three stages and remove them from the left side of the crankcase (**Figure 287**).

6. Place the crankcase assembly on wooden blocks with the camshaft cover (left side) facing up. Use wooden blocks thick enough so the right side of the crankshaft clears the workbench surface (**Figure 288**).

7. Tap around the perimeter of the crankcase with a plastic mallet and remove the left crankcase half (**Figure 289**).

8. If the crankcase halves will not separate easily, perform the following:

   a. Install a flywheel press (A, **Figure 290**) onto the left side of the crankcase following the manufacturer's instructions.

   b. Make sure the right side engine stand bolts (A, **Figure 291**) are not installed onto the crankcase half.

   c. Apply clean engine oil, or press lube, to the end of the center screw and install it into the tool.

CAUTION
Do not use a hand impact driver or air impact wrench on the center screw. They will damage the crankcase halves and the tool.

   d. Slowly turn the center screw with a wrench (B, **Figure 290**) 1/2 turn at a time. After each turn, tap on the end of the center screw with a

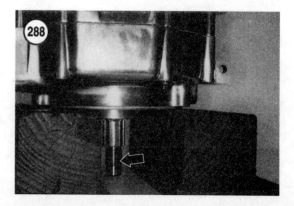

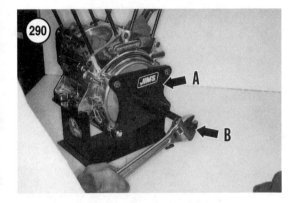

brass mallet to relieve the stress on the center screw and the tool.

   e. Repeat substep d until the center screw turns freely and the crankcase halves begin to separate (B, **Figure 291**).

   f. Remove the crankcase from the engine stand.

   g. Remove the right side crankcase half (**Figure 292**).

   h. Remove the special tool from the left side crankcase unless the crankshaft is going to be removed in Step 10.

9. Remove the locating dowels and O-rings (**Figure 293**) from the right side crankcase.

WARNING
Wear safety glasses to press out the crankshaft.

CAUTION
Do not drive the crankshaft out of the crankcase with a hammer.

10A. If a hydraulic press is available, press the crankshaft out of the right crankcase half as follows:

   a. Support the right crankcase half on wooden blocks in a press with the outer surface facing up.

   b. Center the press ram on the end of the crankshaft, then press the crankshaft out of the right crankcase half. Have an assistant support the crankshaft as it is being pressed out.

   c. Remove the crankshaft.

   d. Remove the right crankcase half from the press bed and place it on a workbench for further service.

10B. If a hydraulic press is not available, perform the following:

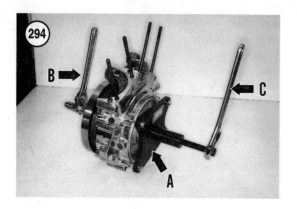

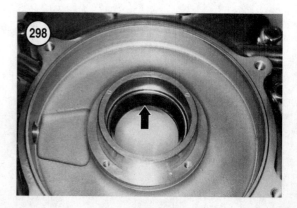

a. Install a flywheel press (A, **Figure 294**) onto the left side of the crankcase following the manufacturer's instructions.

b. Apply clean engine oil, or press lube, to the end of the center screw and install it into the tool.

CAUTION
Do not use a hand impact driver or air impact wrench on the center screw, as they will damage the crankcase and the tool.

c. Secure the right side of the crankshaft with a wrench (B, **Figure 294**) to prevent it from rotating in the following step.

d. Slowly turn the center screw with a wrench (C, **Figure 294**) 1/2 turn at a time. After each turn, tap on the end of the center screw with a brass mallet to relieve the stress on the center screw and the tool.

e. Repeat substep d until the center screw pushes the crankshaft out of the left side crankcase half.

f. Remove the special tool from the left side crankcase half.

11. To remove the left side crankshaft outer roller bearing and oil seal assembly, perform the following:

a. Place the left side crankcase on the workbench with the outer surface facing up.

b. Carefully pry the sprocket shaft spacer out of the oil seal.

c. Carefully pry the oil seal out of the crankcase using a wide-blade screwdriver. Support the screwdriver with a rag to prevent damage to the crankcase.

d. Lift the outer roller bearing from the crankcase.

Crankcase Cleaning and Inspection

1. Clean both case halves in solvent and dry them with compressed air.

2. Apply a light coat of oil to the races to prevent rust.

3. Inspect the right side (**Figure 295**) and left side (**Figure 296**) case halves for cracks or other damage.

4. Inspect the case studs (**Figure 297**) for bending, cracks or other damage. If necessary, replace studs as described under *Cylinder Stud Replacement* in this chapter.

5. Inspect the left side main bearing races. Refer to **Figure 298** for the outer bearing race and **Figure 299** for the inner bearing race. Also, check the roller bearings for wear or damage. The bearings should turn smoothly with no roughness. If any of these parts are worn, replace the bearing assembly as described under *Left Side Main Bearing Assembly Replacement* in this chapter.

6. Inspect the right side main needle bearing (**Figure 300**) for wear or damage. The bearing should turn smoothly with no roughness. If it is damaged, replace the bearing assembly as described under *Right Side Main Bearing Replacement* in this chapter.

7. Inspect the camshaft needle bearings (**Figure 301**) in the right side crankcase for damage. To replace this bearing, refer to *Camshaft Support Plate* in this chapter.

8. Inspect the valve lifter bore receptacles (**Figure 302**) for wear or damage. Refer to *Valve Lifters* in this chapter.

NOTE
If the original piston cooling jets are being reinstalled, apply Loctite No. 222 (purple) or an equivalent thread-locking compound to the screw threads prior to installation.

9. Make sure the piston cooling jets (**Figure 303**) are clear. If necessary, remove the T20 Torx mounting screws, cooling jets and O-rings. Clean the oil jets with compressed air. Install *new* O-rings and tighten the screws securely.

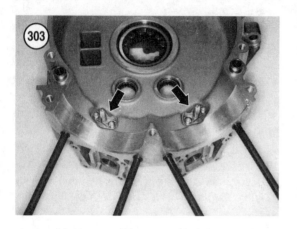

Crankshaft and Connecting Rods Cleaning and Inspection

If any portion of the crankshaft and/or connecting rods are worn or damaged, replace them as one assembly. If necessary, have the crankshaft overhauled by a Harley-Davidson dealership.

1. Clean the crankshaft assembly in solvent and dry it thoroughly with compressed air.

2. Hold the shank portion of each connecting rod where it attaches to the crankshaft (**Figure 304**). Pull up and down on each connecting rod. Any amount of up and down movement indicates excessive lower bearing wear. If there is movement, have the crankshaft overhauled.

3. Measure connecting rod sideplay with a feeler gauge (**Figure 305**) and compare it to the service limit in **Table 2**.

4. Inspect the right side (pinion shaft) (**Figure 306**) and the left side (sprocket shaft) (**Figure 307**) for excessive wear or damage.

5. Support the crankshaft on a truing stand or in a lathe and check the runout at the flywheel outer rim (A, **Figure 308**) and the shaft adjacent to the flywheel (B) with a dial indicator. If the runout exceeds the service limit in **Table 2**, have the crankshaft trued or overhauled.

6. Inspect the crankshaft position sensor timing teeth (**Figure 309**) on the left side flywheel for damaged or missing teeth.

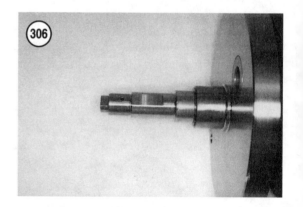

7. On 2001-on models only, make sure the retaining ring (**Figure 310**) is secure on the right side of the crankshaft.

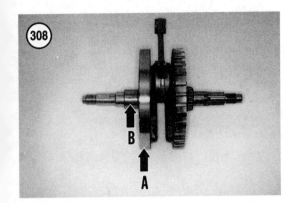

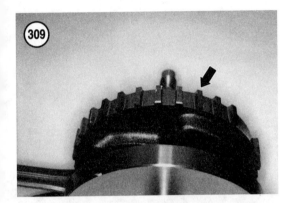

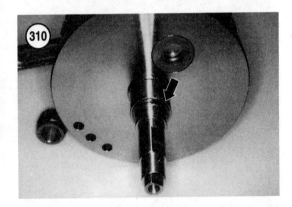

4

Right Side Main Bearing Replacement

A hydraulic press and a crankshaft bearing remover and installer (JIMS part No. 1275) are required for the following procedure.

Removal

1. Remove the main bearing retaining ring (**Figure 311**) from one side of the bearing as follows:
   a. Insert a small screwdriver under one end of the retaining ring.
   b. Push the end toward the bearing bore.
   c. Raise the end of the ring up and out of the crankcase groove.
   d. Work around the circumference of the ring and pull it out of the groove.
   e. Discard the retaining ring as it *cannot* be reused.
2. Turn the crankcase half over and repeat Step 1 to remove the remaining retaining ring (A, **Figure 312**). Discard the retaining ring as it *cannot* be reused.

> *NOTE*
> *The JIMS support tube is marked with either REMOVER or INSTALLER side.*

3. Place the support tube on the press bed with the side marked REMOVER facing up.
4. Position the right side crankcase with the outer surface facing up and position the bearing directly over the support tube on the press bed.
5. Install the pilot shaft (**Figure 313**) through the bearing and into the support tube.
6. Center the press driver over the pilot shaft.
7. Hold the crankcase half parallel to the press bed and have an assistant slowly apply pressure on the

pilot shaft until the bearing is free from the case half.

8. Remove the case half and special tools from the press bed.

Installation

1. Apply a light coat of clean engine oil to the outer surface of the bearing and to the crankcase receptacle.

2. Position the right side crankcase with the outer surface facing up on the press bed.

3. Position the new bearing with the manufacturer's marks facing up (B, **Figure 312**) and place it over the crankcase receptacle.

4. Place the support tube (**Figure 314**) on the new bearing with the side marked INSTALLER facing up.

5. Center the press driver over the support tube.

6. Slowly apply press pressure to the support tube and press the bearing into the crankcase. Apply pressure until the support tube contacts the crankcase surface. This will correctly position the bearing within the crankcase (A, **Figure 315**). Remove the support tube (B).

7. Remove the crankcase from the press bed.

8. Check each side of the crankcase to make sure the bearing is centered within the receptacle. The retaining ring groove must be visible on each side of the bearing. If it is not, reposition the bearing until it is centered correctly.

> *WARNING*
> *The edges of the new retaining rings are sharp. Wear shop gloves.*

> *CAUTION*
> *Both new retaining rings must be installed correctly to properly secure the bearing in the crankcase half.*

9. Install a *new* retaining ring (**Figure 311**) onto each side of the new bearing as follows:
   a. Position the new retaining ring with the center of the closed end going into the ring groove.
   b. Press the center of the closed end into the groove and hold it there to keep it within the ring groove.
   c. Using a small screwdriver and alternating from side to side, press the retaining ring into

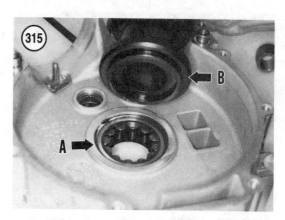

the ring groove. Work with a small section at a time.
   d. Continue to work around the circumference until the retaining ring is completely installed in the ring groove. Make sure the retaining ring is correctly seated in the ring groove.

10. Turn the crankcase half over and repeat Step 9 for the other retaining ring (A, **Figure 312**).

11. Make sure the bearing rotates smoothly.

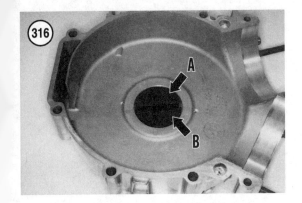

Left Side Main Bearing Assembly Replacement

Replace the left main bearing assembly as a complete set even if one bearing or race is damaged.

Tools

The following tools or their equivalents are required to remove and install the left side main bearing:

1. Hydraulic press.

2. Sprocket shaft bearing race tool (JIMS part No. 94547-80A).

3. Race and bearing installation tool handle (JIMS part No. 33416-80).

4. Snap ring removal and installation tool (JIMS part No. 1710).

5. Sprocket bearing race installation tool (JIMS part No. 2246).

Inner and outer bearing race replacement

NOTE
When replacing the bearing races in the following steps, do not remove the lock ring installed between the inner and outer bearing races. This ring is under heavy tension and will damage the bearing bore as it passes through it.

1. Place the crankcase on the workbench with the inboard surface facing up.
2. Install half of the bearing race remover tool into the crankcase and push it against the inner bearing race (A, **Figure 316**).
3. Install the other half of the bearing race remover tool into the crankcase and push it against the inner bearing race (B, **Figure 316**).
4. Hold the bearing race remover tools in place and turn the crankcase over.
5. Insert the tool handle into the center of both race remover tools. Press it in until the ring (**Figure 317**) is locked into both bearing race remover tools (**Figure 318**).
6. Support the left crankcase half on the press bed with wooden blocks and with the tool handle facing up.
7. Center the press ram directly over the tool handle and slowly press the inner bearing race out of the crankcase.
8. Remove the crankcase and special tools from the press bed.
9. Place the crankcase on the workbench with the outboard surface facing up.
10. Install half of the bearing race remover tool into the crankcase and push it against the outer bearing race (A, **Figure 319**).
11. Install the other half of the bearing race remover tool into the crankcase and push it against the outer bearing race (B, **Figure 319**).

12. Hold the bearing race remover tools in place and turn the crankcase over.

13. Insert the tool handle into the race remover tools. Press it in until the ring (**Figure 317**) is locked into both bearing race remover tools (**Figure 320**).

14. Support the left crankcase half on the press bed with wooden blocks and with the tool handle facing up.

15. Center the press ram directly over the tool handle and slowly press the outer bearing race out of the crankcase.

16. Remove the crankcase and special tools from the press bed.

17. Clean the crankcase half in solvent and dry it with compressed air.

18. Check the lock ring (**Figure 321**) for looseness or damage. If the lock ring is loose or damaged, perform the following:

   a. Place the crankcase on a workbench with the outboard side facing up.

   b. With the gap of the lock ring at the 12 o'clock position, install the special tool clamps onto each side of the lock ring at the 10 o'clock and 2 o'clock positions.

   c. Securely tighten the 9/16 in. Allen screws securing the clamps to the lock ring.

   d. Use snap ring pliers to compress the lock ring and withdraw it from the crankcase groove.

   e. Remove the clamps from the old lock ring and install them onto the new lock ring.

   f. Squeeze the pliers (**Figure 322**) and insert the lock ring into the crankcase groove.

   g. Make sure the lock ring gap is centered with the crankcase oil hole as shown in **Figure 321**.

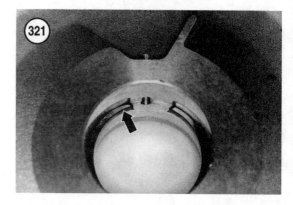

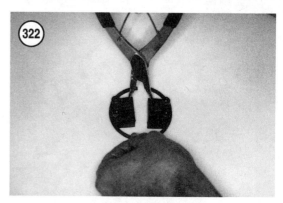

NOTE
Install both races with their larger di-ameter sides facing out. Install the bearing races with the same tool used to remove the old ones.

19. Apply clean engine oil, or press lube, to the bearing receptacles in the crankcase and to the outer surface of the inner bearing races.
20. Place the installer base on the press bed with the large end facing up.
21. Position the crankcase with the outboard surface facing up.
22. Install the crankcase onto the installer base (**Figure 323**) so the crankcase retaining ring rests on top of the installer base.
23. Install the outboard outer race onto the crankcase receptacle.
24. Apply clean engine oil, or press lube, to the shaft of the pressing plug and install the pressing plug into the installer base (**Figure 324**). Push it down onto the bearing outer race.
25. Center the press ram directly over the pressing plug and slowly press the outer bearing race into the outboard surface of the crankcase until it touches the retaining ring (**Figure 325**).
26. Remove the crankcase and special tools from the press.
27. Turn the crankcase over and repeat Steps 23-26 for the inboard outer bearing race.

Crankshaft inner sprocket shaft bearing replacement

A sprocket shaft bearing cone installer (part No. HD-997225-55B) is required to install the sprocket shaft bearing (**Figure 326**).
1. Support the crankshaft with the bearing side facing up.
2. Install the bearing splitter under the bearing (**Figure 327**) and tighten it securely.
3. Attach a bearing puller to the splitter (**Figure 328**).
4. Slowly tighten the center screw and withdraw the bearing from the crankshaft shoulder.
5. Remove the bearing remover, splitter and bearing from the crankshaft.
6. Clean the sprocket shaft with contact cleaner. Check the sprocket shaft for cracks or other damage. If it is damaged, refer service to a Harley-Davidson dealership.

7. Slide the new bearing over the sprocket shaft.

8. Refer to **Figure 329** and press the new bearing into place as follows:

   a. Apply clean graphite lubricant to the installer's pilot shaft threads, flat washer and bearing.

   b. Thread the pilot shaft (A) onto the crankshaft until it contacts the crankshaft shoulder.

   c. Slide the sleeve (B) over the pilot shaft until it contacts the bearing inner race.

   d. Install the tool's bearing (C) and washer (D) over the pilot shaft and onto the top of the sleeve.

   e. Thread the handle (E) onto the pilot shaft (A).

   f. Slowly tighten the handle clockwise until the bearing bottoms on the crankshaft shoulder.

   g. Unscrew and remove all parts of the bearing installer.

Crankshaft End Play Inspection

The crankshaft end play *must* be between 0.001-0.005 in. (0.025-0.127 mm). End play is determined by the thickness of the shim between the inner and outer bearings on the left side. **Table 6** lists the shim part numbers and thickness.

If the end play was measured before disassembly and was within specification, and if the same components are reinstalled, then the same size shim can be reinstalled as a starting point.

Carefully measure the end play as described in Step 11. If there is *any* doubt about your abilities to properly set up the crankshaft end play, refer this procedure to a Harley-Davidson dealership.

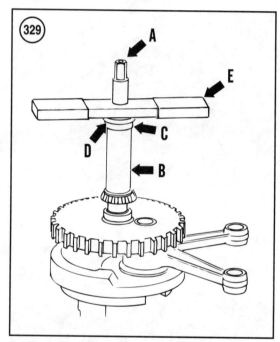

Tools

The following tools or their equivalents are required to assemble the crankcase halves:

1. Sprocket shaft bearing installation tool (JIMS part No. 97225-55).

2. Crankshaft guide (JIMS part No. 1288).

3. Engine stand (JIMS part No. 1022).

Procedure

1. Position the crankshaft (**Figure 330**) with the left side facing up.

2. Apply clean engine oil or assembly lube to the inner bearing and to the left side crankcase inner bearing race.

3. Install the shim of the specified thickness (see *Crankshaft End Play Inspection*) onto the inner bearing race.

4. Place the left crankcase half over the crankshaft sprocket and onto the inner bearing.

5. Make sure the connecting rods are positioned within the crankcase openings as shown in **Figure 331**.

6. Make sure the crankcase is located correctly on the crankshaft inner bearing.

7. Install the outer roller bearing onto the crankshaft (**Figure 332**) and push it into the outer bearing race.

8. Install the sprocket shaft bearing installation tool onto the crankshaft following the manufacturer's instructions.

CRANKCASE ASSEMBLY

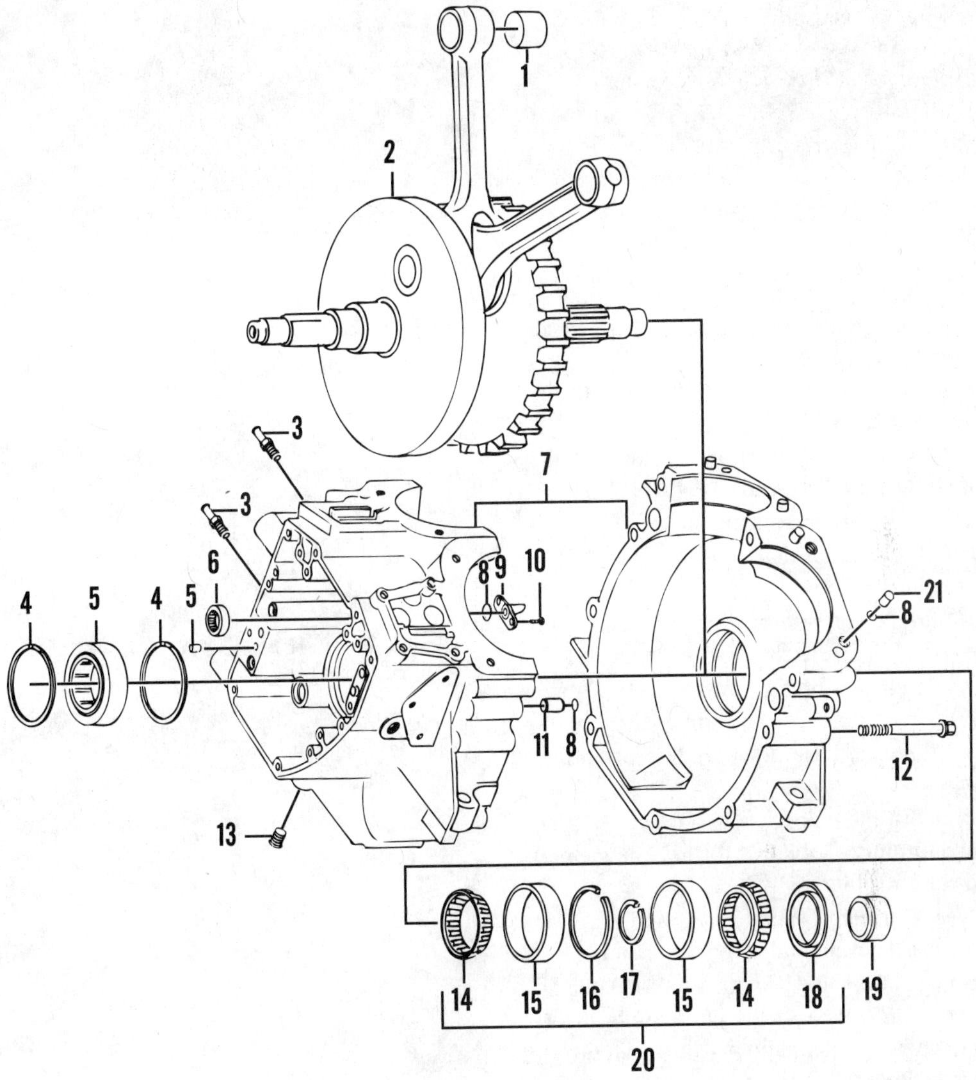

1. Connecting rod bushing
2. Crankshaft assembly
3. Oil hose fitting
4. Retaining ring
5. Right side main bearing
6. Needle bearing–camshaft
7. Crankcase assembly
8. O-ring
9. Piston cooling jet
10. Screw
11. Locating dowel
12. Bolt
13. Plug
14. Bearing
15. Bearing race
16. Lockring
17. Spacer ring
18. Oil seal
19. Sprocket shaft spacer
20. Left side main bearing (sprocket shaft) assembly
21. Locating dowel

9. Hold onto the handle of the installation tool (A, **Figure 333**) and tighten the large nut with a wrench (B). Tighten the large nut until the outer bearing is seated correctly and makes firm contact with the shim installed in Step 3.

10. Remove the special tools and make sure the outer bearing is seated correctly (**Figure 334**).

11. Check crankshaft end play as follows:

   a. Securely attach a dial indicator to the left crankcase half.

   b. Position the dial indicator contact pointer on the end of the crankshaft (A, **Figure 335**).

   c. Push down hard on the crankcase (B, **Figure 335**) while turning it back and forth.

   d. Hold the crankcase down and zero the dial gauge.

   e. Pull up on the crankcase as far as it will go while turning it back and forth. Note the dial indicator reading.

   f. Repeat this step several times and note the readings. They should all be the same.

   g. The end play should be within 0.001-0.005 in. (0.025-0.127 mm). If the end play is incorrect, replace the shim with a shim of a different thickness. **Table 6** lists the various thickness shims and their part numbers.

   h. Remove the dial indicator.

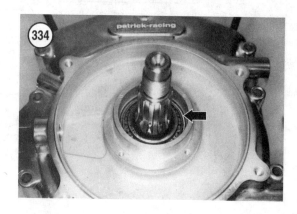

12. Turn the crankcase assembly over and place it on wooden blocks (**Figure 336**) thick enough so the left side of the crankshaft clears the workbench surface.

13. Install the locating dowels and *new* O-rings (**Figure 337**) into both locations (**Figure 338**) in the right crankcase half. Apply clean engine oil to the O-rings.

14. Install the crankshaft guide (**Figure 339**) over the crankshaft.

4

15. Thoroughly clean and dry both crankcase gasket surfaces before applying gasket sealer in Step 16.

16. Apply a thin coat of a non-hardening gasket sealant to the crankcase mating surfaces. Use one of the following gasket sealants:

   a. Harley-Davidson crankcase sealant (part No. HD-99650-81).

   b. 3M #800 sealant.

   c. ThreeBond Liquid Gasket 1104.

17. Align the crankcase halves and carefully lower the right crankcase half onto the crankshaft and left crankcase half (**Figure 340**). Press it down until it is seated correctly on the locating dowels. If necessary, carefully tap the perimeter of the right crankcase half until it is seated around the entire perimeter (**Figure 341**).

CAUTION
When properly aligned, the crankcase halves will fit snugly against each other around the entire perimeter. If they do not meet correctly, do not attempt to pull the case halves together with the mounting bolts. Separate the crankcase assembly and investigate the cause of the interference.

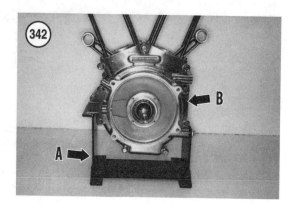

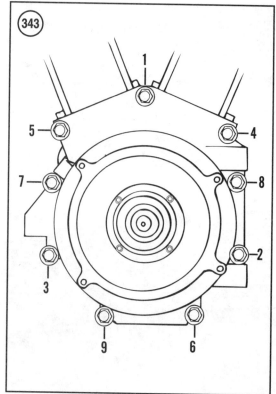

18. Place the crankcase assembly in an engine stand (A, **Figure 342**). Secure the engine stand to the workbench.

19. Install the nine crankcase bolts into the left crankcase half (**Figure 342**) and tighten them as follows:

    a. Alternately tighten the nine bolts finger-tight.

    b. Using the torque pattern shown in **Figure 343**, tighten the bolts to 10 ft.-lb. (14 N•m).

    c. Using the same sequence, tighten the bolts to 15-19 ft.-lb. (20-26 N•m).

20. Install the left crankcase oil seal as described in the following procedure.

21. Apply clean engine oil to the outer surface of the sprocket shaft spacer and install it onto the crankshaft and into the oil seal (**Figure 344**).

22. Install the following components as described in this chapter:

    a. Alternator rotor and stator assembly (Chapter Eight).

    b. Oil pump.

    c. Camshaft assembly.

    d. Pushrods and valve lifters.

    e. Pistons.

    f. Cylinder heads and cylinders.

23. Install the engine into the frame as described in this chapter.

Crankcase Left Side Oil Seal Replacement

A sprocket shaft seal installer tool (JIMS part No. 39361-69 or equivalent) is required to install the oil seal.

1. Remove the sprocket shaft spacer (**Figure 344**) from the crankshaft and the oil seal.

2. Carefully pry the old oil seal (**Figure 345**) out of the bearing bore.

4

3. Position the *new* oil seal with the open side facing out.

4. Install the oil seal onto the crankshaft (A, **Figure 346**) and center it within the bearing bore.

5. Apply clean engine oil or press lube to the installer tool threads, both washers and the radial bearing.

6. Install the main body onto the crankshaft and screw it on until it stops (B, **Figure 346**).

7. Install the shaft seal installer tool following the manufacturer's instructions.

8. Hold onto the handle (A, **Figure 347**) of the main body and tighten the large nut (B) with a wrench. Tighten the large nut slowly and make sure the oil seal (**Figure 348**) is entering straight into the bearing bore.

9. Tighten the large nut until the shaft seal installer tool contacts the crankcase surface (**Figure 349**).

10. Remove the special tools.

11. Apply clean engine oil to the outer surface of the sprocket shaft spacer and install it onto the crankshaft and into the oil seal (**Figure 344**).

Cylinder Stud Replacement

Replace bent or damaged cylinder studs (**Figure 350**) to prevent cylinder block and cylinder head leaks.

1. If the engine lower end is assembled, block off the lower crankcase opening with clean shop cloths.

2A. If the stud has broken off with the top surface of the crankcase, remove it with a stud remover. Refer to Chapter One.

2B. If the stud is still in place, perform the following:

    a. Thread a 3/8 in.-16 nut onto the top of the stud.

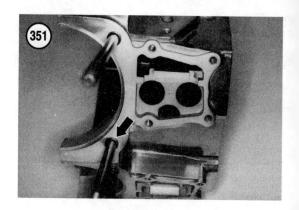

b. Thread an additional nut onto the stud and tighten it against the first nut so they are locked.

c. Turn the bottom nut counterclockwise and unscrew the stud.

3. Clean the stud threads in the crankcase with a spiral brush, then clean them with an aerosol parts cleaner. If necessary, clean the threads with an appropriate size tap.

NOTE
If the new studs have a threadlocking compound patch already applied to the lower stud threads, do not apply any additional locking compound.

4. If the new stud does not have the threadlocking compound patch, apply ThreeBond TB1360 or an equivalent to the lower stud threads.

NOTE
The cylinder studs have a shoulder on one end. This end must be installed next to the crankcase surface.

5. Place a 0.313 in. diameter steel ball (H-D part No. 8860) into a cylinder head bolt, then thread the bolt onto the end of the new stud without the collar.

6. Position the stud with the shoulder end going in first and hand-thread the new stud into the crankcase.

CAUTION
Do not use a breaker bar, ratchet or similar tool to install the studs. These tools may bend the stud and cause the engine to leak oil.

7. Hold the air impact wrench directly in-line with the stud. *Slowly* tighten the new stud with an air im-

pact wrench until the stud shoulder just contacts the top surface of the crankcase (**Figure 351**).

8. Tighten the stud to the torque specification in **Table 4** by hand.

9. Remove the cylinder head bolt and steel ball from the cylinder stud.

10. Repeat Steps 2-9 for any additional studs.

ENGINE BREAK-IN

Following cylinder service such as boring, honing and installing new rings, or major lower end work, break-in the engine as though it were new. The service and performance life of the engine depends on the break-in.

1. For the first 50 mi. (80 km), maintain engine speed below 2500 rpm in any gear. However, do not lug the engine. Do not exceed 50 mph during this period.

2. From 50-500 mi. (80-804 km), vary the engine speed. Avoid prolonged steady running at one engine speed. During this period, increase engine speed to 3000 rpm. Do not exceed 55 mph.

3. After the first 500 mi. (804 km), the engine break-in is complete.

Table 1 GENERAL ENGINE SPECIFICATIONS

Item	Specifications
Engine type	4-stroke, 45° OHV V twin, Twin Cam 88
Bore and stroke	3.75 × 4.00 in. (95.25 × 101.6 mm)
Displacement	88 cubic inch (1450 cc)
Compression ratio	9.0 to 1
Torque	82 ft. lb. (111 N•m) @ 3500 rpm
Maximum sustained engine speed	5600 rpm
Engine weight	165 lbs. (74.8 kg)
Cooling system	Air cooled

Table 2 ENGINE SERVICE SPECIFICATIONS

Item	New in. (mm)	Service limit in. (mm)
Cylinder head		
Warp	–	0.006 (0.15)
Valve guide fit in head	0.0020-0.0033 (0.051-0.084)	0.002 (0.051)
Valve seat fit in head	0.003-0.0045 (0.076-0.114)	0.002 (0.051)
Rocker arm		
Shaft fit in bushing	0.0005-0.0020 (0.013-0.051)	0.0035 (0.089)
Bushing fit in rocker arm	0.002-0.004 (0.051-0.102)	–
End clearance	0.003-0.013 (0.08-0.033)	0.025 (0.635)
Shaft fit in rocker arm support	0.0007-0.0022 (0.018-0.056)	0.0035 (0.089)
Valves		
Valve stem-to-guide clearance		
Intake	0.0008-0.0026 (0.020-0.066)	–
Exhaust	0.0015-0.0033 (0.038-0.084)	–
Seat width	0.040-0.062 (1.02-1.58)	–
Valve stem protrusion	1.990-2.024 (50.55-51.41)	–
Valve springs		
Free length		
Outer	2.105-2.177 (53.47-55.3)	–
Inner	1.926-1.996 (48.9-50.7)	–
Piston-to-cylinder clearance	0.0006-0.0017 (0.015-0.043)	0.0016 (0.041)
Piston pin fit in piston	0.0003-0.0005 (0.008-0.013)	0.001 (0.25)
Piston rings		
Compression ring end gap		
Top ring	0.010-0.020 (0.25-0.51)	0.030 (0.76)
Second ring	0.014-0.024 (0.36-0.61)	0.034 (0.86)
Oil control ring end gap	0.010-0.050 (0.25-1.27)	0.050 (1.27)
Compression ring side clearance		
Top ring	0.0012-0.0037 (0.030-0.094)	0.0045 (0.11)
Second ring	0.0012-0.0037 (0.030-0.094)	0.0045
Oil control ring side clearance	0.0031-0.0091 (0.079-0.23)	0.010 (0.25)
Cylinder		
Taper	–	0.002 (0.05)
Out of round	–	0.003 (0.08)
Warp		
At top (cylinder head)	–	0.006 (0.15)
At base (crankcase)	–	0.008 (0.20)
Cylinder bore		
Standard	–	3.753 (95.326)
Oversize 0.005 in	–	3.758 (95.453)
Oversize 0.010 in.	–	3.763 (95.580)
Oversize 0.020 in.	–	3.773 (95.834)
Oversize 0.030 in.	–	3.783 (96.088)
Connecting rod		
Connecting rod-to-crankpin clearance	0.0004-0.0012 (0.0102-0.0305)	0.002 (0.05)
Piston pin clearance in connecting rod	0.0003-0.0007 (0.008-0.018)	0.002 (0.05)
Connecting rod side play	0.005-0.015 (0.13-0.38)	0.020 (0.51)
Hydraulic lifters		
Fit in guide	0.0008-0.0020 (0.02-0.05)	0.003 (0.076)
Roller fit	–	0.0015 (0.038)
Roller end clearance	–	0.015 (0.38)
Camshaft support plate		
Camshaft chain tensioner shoe	–	0.080-0.090 (2.03-2.29)*
Camshaft support plate warp	–	0.010 (0.25)
Camshaft bushing fit	–	0.0008-0.001 (0.0203-0.0254)
Oil pump rotor tip clearance	–	0.004 (0.10)

(continued)

Table 2 ENGINE SERVICE SPECIFICATIONS (continued)

Item	New in. (mm)	Service limit in. (mm)
Sprocket shaft Timken bearing		
Cup fit in crankcase	0.003-0.005 (0.08-0.13)	–
Cone fit on shaft	0.005-0.0015 (0.13-0.038)	–
Crankshaft		
Runout (at flywheel rim)	0.000-0.010 (0.0-0.25)	0.015 (0.38)
Runout (at pinion shaft)	0.000-0.002 (0.0-0.05)	0.003 (0.08)
End play	0.001-0.005 (0.03-0.13)	0.002 (0.05)

*One-half the thickness of the shoe.

Table 3 PUSH ROD AND LIFTER LOCATION

Cylinder	Lifter bore	Cylinder head/rocker housing bore
Front		
Intake	Inside	Rear
Exhaust	Outside	Front
Rear		
Intake	Inside	Front
Exhaust	Outside	Rear

Table 4 ENGINE TORQUE SPECIFICATIONS

Item	ft.-lb.	in.-lb.	N•m
Bearing retainer plate screws	–	20-30	2-3
Breather cover bolts	–	90-120	10-14
Camshaft cover screws	–	90-120	10-14
Camshaft support plate Allen bolts	–	90-120	10-14
Camshaft position sensor cover screw	–	20-30	2-3
Camshaft position sensor screw	–	50-80	6-9
Crankshaft position sensor screw	–	90-120	10-14
Crankshaft sprocket bolt	Refer to text		
Crankcase bolts	15-19	–	20-26
Cylinder head bolts	Refer to text		
Cylinder head bracket bolts	28-35	–	38-47
Cylinder stud	10-20	–	14-27
Engine oil drain plug	14-21	–	19-28
Engine mount (rubber isolator) bolts	21-27	–	28-37
Engine-to-lower bracket bolts	33-38	–	45-52
Lower bracket-to-engine mount bolt	35-45	–	47-61
Left side footpeg bracket screws	25-30	–	34-41
Lifter cover bolts	–	90-120	10-14
Oil filter mount bolts			
1999-2001	–	90-120	10-14
2002	–	130-150	15-17
Oil fitting	–	120-144	14-16
Oil line cover bolts	–	90-108	10-12
Oil pump screws	–	90-120	10-14
Oil pan screws	–	84-120	9-14

(continued)

Table 4 ENGINE TORQUE SPECIFICATIONS (continued)

Item	ft.-lb.	in.-lb.	N•m
Oil pressure sending unit	–	92-120	11-14
Pipe plug	–	120-144	14-16
Piston oil jet screw	–	20-30	2-3
Rear camshaft sprocket bolt	Refer to text		
Rear footpeg bracket screws	25-30	–	34-41
Rocker arm			
Support bolts	15-18	–	20-24
Housing bolts	–	124-168	14-19
Cover bolts			
1999-2001	10-14	–	14-19
2002	15-18	–	20-24
Shift lever pinch bolt	18-22	–	24-30
Sprocket shaft nut	150-165	–	203-224
Transmission			
Mounting bolts			
Preliminary	15	–	20
Final	30-35	–	41-47
Drain plug	14-21	–	19-29
Voltage regulator flange locknuts	–	90-120	10-14

Table 5 REAR CAMSHAFT SPROCKET SPACERS

Part No.	in.	mm
25722-99	0.230	5.84
25723-99	0.240	6.10
25721-99	0.250	6.35
25719-99	0.260	6.60
25717-99	0.270	6.86

Table 6 CRANKSHAFT LEFT SIDE BEARING SPACER SHIM

Shim part number	in.	mm
9110	0.0905-0.0895	2.299-2.273
9120	0.0925-0.0915	2.350-2.324
9121	0.0945-0.0935	2.400-2.375
9122	0.0965-0.0955	2.451-2.426
9123	0.0985-0.0975	2.502-2.476
9124	0.1005-0.0995	2.553-2.527
9125	0.1025-0.1015	2.602-2.578
9126	0.1045-0.1035	2.654-2.629
9127	0.1065-0.1055	2.705-2.680
9128	0.1085-0.1075	2.756-2.731
9129	0.1105-0.1095	2.807-2.781
9130	0.1125-0.1115	2.858-2.932
9131	0.1145-0.1135	2.908-2.883
9132	0.1165-0.1155	2.959-2.934
9133	0.1185-0.1175	3.010-2.985
9134	0.1205-0.1195	3.061-3.035

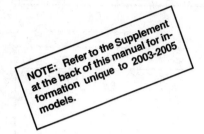
NOTE: Refer to the Supplement at the back of this manual for information unique to 2003-2005 models.

CLUTCH AND PRIMARY DRIVE

This chapter describes service procedures for the clutch and primary drive assemblies.

Specifications are in **Tables 1-3** at the end of this chapter.

PRIMARY CHAINCASE COVER

Removal

Refer to **Figure 1**.

> *NOTE*
> *On models so equipped, always disarm the optional TSSM security system prior to disconnecting the battery or the siren will sound.*

1. Disconnect the negative battery cable as described in Chapter Eight.

> *WARNING*
> *Disconnect the negative battery cable before working on the clutch or any primary drive component to avoid accidentally activating the starter motor.*

2. Remove the front and rear left side footboards as described in Chapter Fourteen.
3. Drain the primary chain oil as described in Chapter Three.

> *NOTE*
> *Note the location of the cover. There are two different length bolts and they must be reinstalled in the correct location.*

4. Remove the bolts and captive washers securing the chaincase cover (**Figure 2**) and remove the chaincase cover.
5. Remove the chaincase cover gasket.
6. Remove the dowel pins, if necessary.

Inspection

1. Remove all gasket residue from the chaincase cover (**Figure 3**) and chaincase housing gasket surfaces.
2. Clean the cover in solvent and dry it with compressed air.
3. Inspect the cover for cracks or damage.
4. Inspect the starter jackshaft bushing (**Figure 4**) for excessive wear or damage. Replace the bushing as follows:
   a. Remove the bushing with a blind bearing removal tool.
   b. Clean the bushing bore in the housing.
   c. Press the new bushing in until its outer surface is flush with the edge of the bushing bore.

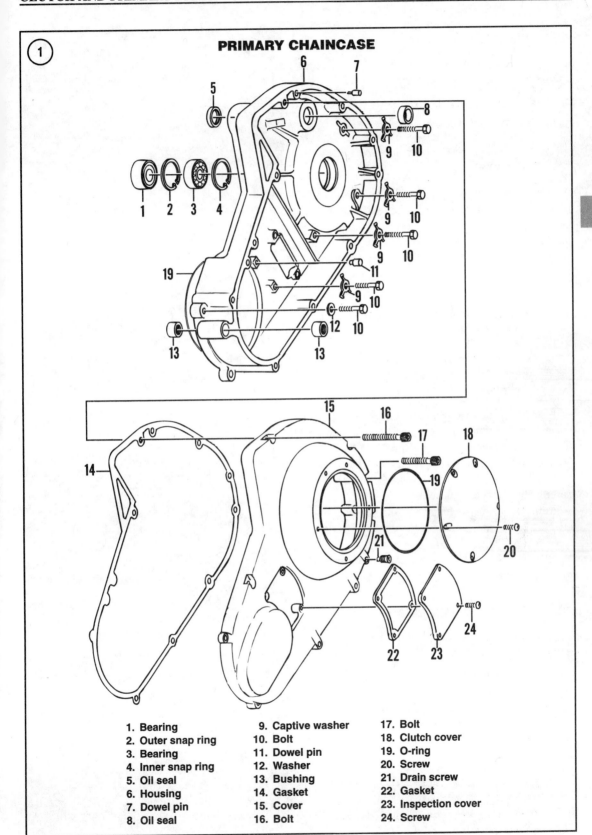

PRIMARY CHAINCASE

1. Bearing
2. Outer snap ring
3. Bearing
4. Inner snap ring
5. Oil seal
6. Housing
7. Dowel pin
8. Oil seal
9. Captive washer
10. Bolt
11. Dowel pin
12. Washer
13. Bushing
14. Gasket
15. Cover
16. Bolt
17. Bolt
18. Clutch cover
19. O-ring
20. Screw
21. Drain screw
22. Gasket
23. Inspection cover
24. Screw

5

Installation

1. If removed, install the dowel pins (**Figure 5** and **Figure 6**) into the chaincase housing.

> *CAUTION*
> *Harley-Davidson specifies that a **new** Print-O-Seal gasket must be installed every time the chaincase outer cover is removed.*

2. Install a *new* gasket (**Figure 7**) over the dowel pins and seat it against the gasket surface of the chaincase housing.

3. Slide the primary cover over the dowel pins and seat it flush against the gasket.

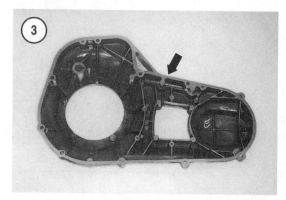

> *NOTE*
> *The gasket sealing surface is very thin and the overall size of the gasket is very large. The gasket may shift prior to the installation of the cover bolts. Make sure the gasket is positioned correctly during installation of the cover bolts in Step 4.*

4. Install the primary cover bolts and captive washers into the locations noted during removal. Tighten the primary cover bolts to the torque in **Table 2**. Make sure the gasket seats flush around the cover.

5. Install the front and rear left side footboards as described in Chapter Fourteen.

6. Refill the primary chaincase with the type and quantity of oil specified under *Primary Chain Lubrication* in Chapter Three.

7. Connect the negative battery cable as described in Chapter Eight.

CLUTCH ASSEMBLY

This section describes removal, inspection and installation of the clutch plates. If the clutch requires additional service, refer to the clutch shell procedures in this chapter.

Refer to **Figure 8**.

Removal

> *NOTE*
> *On models so equipped, always disarm the optional TSSM security system prior to disconnecting the battery or the siren will sound.*

5

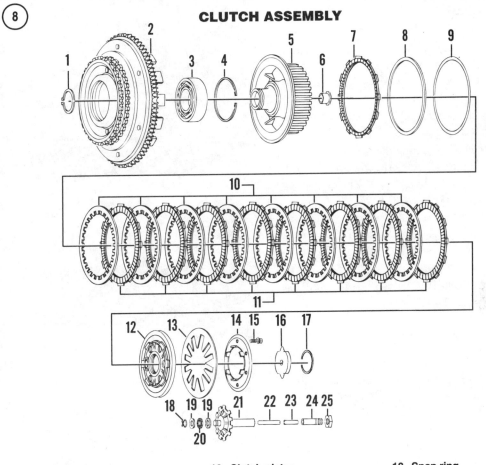

CLUTCH ASSEMBLY

1. Snap ring
2. Clutch shell and sprocket
3. Bearing
4. Snap ring
5. Clutch hub
6. Clutch nut
7. Friction disc B
8. Damper spring seat
9. Damper spring

10. Clutch plates
11. Friction disc A
12. Pressure plate
13. Diaphragm spring
14. Diaphragm spring retainer
15. Bolt
16. Release plate
17. Snap ring

18. Snap ring
19. Thrust washer
20. Radial bearing
21. Oil slinger
22. Pushrod (right side)
23. Pushrod (right side
24. Pushrod (left side)
25. Locknut

1. Disconnect the negative battery cable as described in Chapter Eight.

2. Remove the clutch cover and O-ring (**Figure 9**).

3. At the clutch, loosen the clutch adjusting screw locknut (A, **Figure 10**) and turn the adjusting screw (B) *counterclockwise* to allow slack against the diaphragm spring.

4. Remove the primary chaincase cover as described in this chapter.

5. Loosen the bolts securing the diaphragm spring retainer (A, **Figure 11**) in a crisscross pattern. Remove the bolts and the retainer and diaphragm spring (B, **Figure 11**).

6. Remove the pressure plate.

7. Remove the clutch plates and friction discs from the clutch shell.

8. Remove the damper spring and damper spring seat from the clutch shell. Keep all parts in order as shown in **Figure 12**.

Inspection

When measuring the clutch components, compare the actual measurements to the specifications in **Table 1**. Replace parts that are out of specification or show damage as described in this section.

1. Clean all parts in solvent and thoroughly dry them with compressed air.

2. Inspect the friction discs as follows:

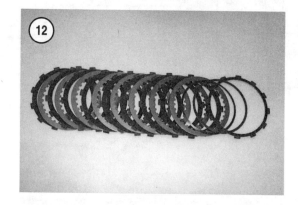

> *NOTE*
> *If any friction disc is damaged or out of specification as described in the following steps, replace **all** of the friction discs as a set. Never replace only one or two discs.*

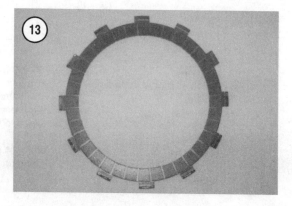

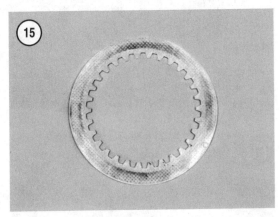

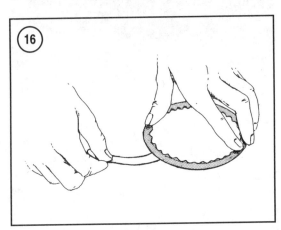

smooth where they contact the clutch shell finger; otherwise, the discs cannot engage and disengage correctly.

NOTE
If the disc tangs are damaged, inspect the clutch shell fingers carefully as described later in this section.

b. Measure the thickness of each friction disc with a vernier caliper (**Figure 14**). Measure at several places around the disc.

3. Inspect the clutch plates (**Figure 15**) as follows:

a. Inspect the clutch plates for cracks, damage or color change. Overheated clutch plates will have a blue discoloration.

b. Check the clutch plates for oil glaze buildup. Remove buildup by lightly sanding both sides of each plate with 400 grit sandpaper placed on a surface plate or piece of glass.

c. Place each clutch plate on a flat surface and check for warp with a feeler gauge (**Figure 16**).

d. The clutch plate inner teeth mesh with the clutch hub splines. Check the clutch plate teeth for roughness or damage. The teeth contact surfaces must be smooth; otherwise, the plates cannot engage and disengage correctly.

NOTE
If the clutch plate teeth are damaged, inspect the clutch hub splines carefully as described later in this section.

4. Inspect the diaphragm spring (**Figure 17**) for cracks or damage.

a. Inspect the friction material (**Figure 13**) for excessive or uneven wear, cracks and other damage. Check the disc tangs for surface damage. The sides of the disc tangs must be

5. Inspect the diaphragm spring retainer for cracks or damage. Also check for bent or damaged tabs (**Figure 18**).

6. Inspect the pressure plate contact surface (**Figure 19**) for cracks or other damage.

7. If necessary, disassemble the pressure plate as follows:

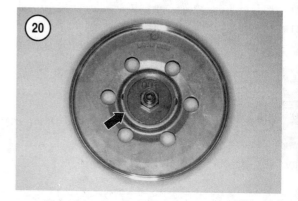

   a. Remove the snap ring (**Figure 20**) and remove the release plate, left side pushrod and locknut from the pressure plate.

   b. Inspect the release plate, left side pushrod and locknut for wear or damage.

   c. Inspect the snap ring groove for damage.

   d. Position the release plate with the OUT mark facing out (**Figure 21**) and install the assembly into the pressure plate.

   e. Install the snap ring and make sure it is correctly seated in the pressure plate groove.

Installation

> *NOTE*
> *The original equipment clutch (**Figure 12**) has nine friction discs, eight steel plates, one damper spring and one damper spring seat. Make sure each part is installed. When installing an aftermarket clutch plate assembly, follow the manufacturer's instructions.*

1. Soak the friction discs and clutch plates in new primary drive oil for approximately 5 minutes before installing them.

> *NOTE*
> *There are two different types of friction discs (**Figure 22**). The wider friction disc A is the normal width disc.*

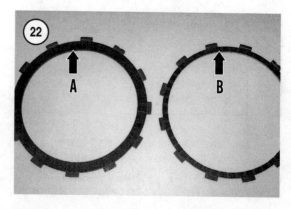

5

The narrow width friction disc B is installed first, as it works in conjunction with the damper spring and damper spring seat.

2. Install friction disc B (**Figure 23**) onto the clutch shell and clutch hub. Push it on until it bottoms within the clutch hub.

3. Install the damper spring seat (**Figure 24**) onto the clutch hub and push it in until it seats within the clutch friction disc B.

4. Position the damper spring with the dished side facing out (**Figure 25**) and install it onto the clutch hub against the damper spring seat (**Figure 26**).

5. Install a clutch plate (**Figure 27**), then a friction disc A (**Figure 28**). Continue to alternately install the clutch plates and friction discs. The last part installed is a friction disc A (**Figure 29**).

6. Make sure the left side pushrod assembly (**Figure 30**) is in place in the pressure plate. Install the pressure plate onto the clutch hub.

7. Position the diaphragm spring with the dished side facing out (**Figure 31**) and install it onto the pressure plate (**Figure 32**). Hold the pressure plate in place.

8. Position the diaphragm spring retainer with the finger side (**Figure 33**) facing in toward the diaphragm spring (B, **Figure 11**). Install the diaphragm spring retainer (A, **Figure 11**) and bolts.

9. Tighten the bolts in a crisscross pattern to the torque specification in **Table 1**.

10. Install the primary chaincase cover as described in this chapter.

11. Install the clutch cover and O-ring.

12. Connect the negative battery cable as described in Chapter Eight.

CLUTCH SHELL, COMPENSATING SPROCKET AND PRIMARY DRIVE CHAIN

Removal

This procedure describes clutch shell (**Figure 8**), primary drive chain and compensating sprocket removal (**Figure 34** or **Figure 35**). These components must be removed as an assembly.

NOTE
On models so equipped, always disarm the optional TSSM security system prior to disconnecting the battery or the siren will sound.

1. Disconnect the negative battery cable as described in Chapter Eight

2. Remove the primary chaincase cover as described in this chapter.

3. If necessary, remove the diaphragm spring, pressure plate, clutch plates and friction discs as described in this chapter.

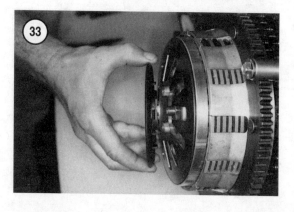

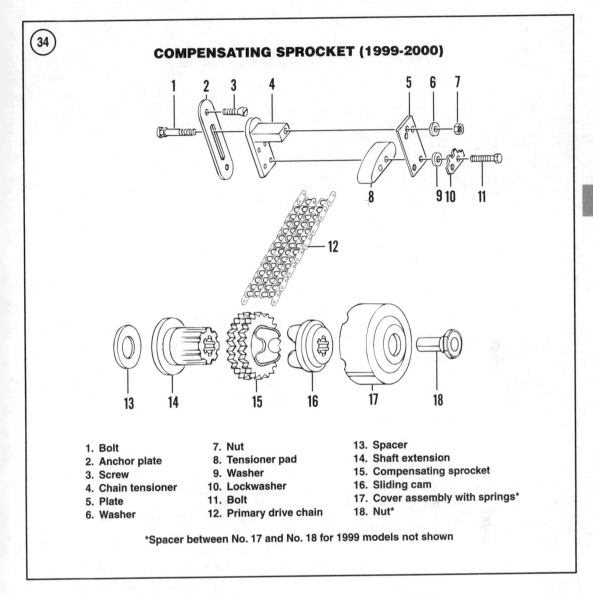

COMPENSATING SPROCKET (1999-2000)

1. Bolt
2. Anchor plate
3. Screw
4. Chain tensioner
5. Plate
6. Washer
7. Nut
8. Tensioner pad
9. Washer
10. Lockwasher
11. Bolt
12. Primary drive chain
13. Spacer
14. Shaft extension
15. Compensating sprocket
16. Sliding cam
17. Cover assembly with springs*
18. Nut*

*Spacer between No. 17 and No. 18 for 1999 models not shown

4A. If a special tool is available, such as a primary drive locking tool (JIMS part No. 2234), place it onto the primary chain next to the clutch housing (**Figure 36**).

4B. If the special tool is not available, shift the transmission into fifth gear. Have an assistant apply the rear brake.

CAUTION
*The clutch nut has **left-hand threads**. Turn the clutch nut **clockwise** to loosen it.*

5. Loosen the clutch hub nut with an impact wrench. Remove the clutch nut (**Figure 37**).

6. Loosen the compensating sprocket nut (**Figure 38**) with an impact wrench.

7. Remove the compensating sprocket nut (**Figure 38**), washer (on 1999 models), cover (**Figure 39**) and sliding cam (**Figure 40**).

8A. On 1999-2000 models, perform the following:
   a. Remove the primary chain tensioner locknut (**Figure 41**).
   b. Remove the compensating sprocket, primary chain, chain tensioner and clutch assembly at the same time (**Figure 42**).

8B. On 2001-on models, perform the following:
   a. Loosen the primary chain tensioner locknut and push the tensioner assembly down to re-

COMPENSATING SPROCKET (2001-ON)

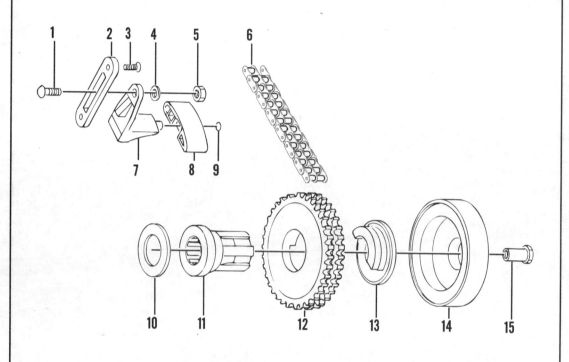

1. Bolt	6. Primary chain	11. Shaft extension
2. Anchor plate	7. Chain tensioner	12. Compensating sprocket
3. Screw	8. Tensioner pad	13. Sliding cam
4. Washer	9. Snap ring	14. Cover assembly with springs*
5. Nut	10. Spacer	15. Nut*

*Spacer between No. 14 and No. 15 not shown

5

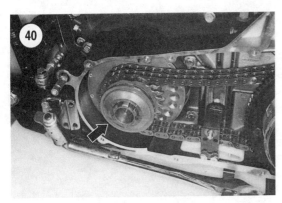

lieve tension on the primary chain. Remove the locknut.

   b. Remove the compensating sprocket (A, **Figure 43**), primary chain and clutch assembly (B) at the same time.

9. Remove the shaft extension (**Figure 44**) and the spacer.

10. Inspect the various components as described in this chapter.

Installation

1. Remove all threadlocking compound residue from the crankshaft and mainshaft threads, and from the compensating sprocket nut and the clutch nut.

2. Remove all gasket residue from the inner primary housing gasket surfaces.

3. Install the spacer and the shaft extension (**Figure 44**) onto the crankshaft.

4A. On 1999-2000 models, perform the following:

   a. Assemble the compensating sprocket, primary chain, chain tensioner and clutch as shown in **Figure 42**.

   b. Install the compensating sprocket, primary chain, chain tensioner and clutch. Insert the chain tensioner bolt through the chain tensioner hole as shown in **Figure 45**.

   c. Install the primary chain tensioner locknut (**Figure 41**) and tighten finger-tight at this time.

4B. On 2001-on models, perform the following:

   a. Assemble the compensating sprocket, primary chain and clutch.

   b. Install the compensating sprocket, primary chain and clutch as shown in **Figure 43**.

5. Install the compensating sprocket (**Figure 40**) and the cover (**Figure 39**).

6. On 1999 models, install the washer.

7. Install the same tool set-up (**Figure 36**) used during removal or shift the transmission into fifth gear to prevent the compensating sprocket and clutch shell from rotating during the following steps.

8. Apply two drops of ThreeBond TB1360 or an equivalent to the compensating sprocket nut threads. Install the nut (**Figure 38**) and tighten it to the specification in **Table 2**.

> *NOTE*
> *The clutch nut has **left-hand threads**. Turn the nut **counterclockwise** to tighten it.*

9. Apply two drops of ThreeBond TB1360 or an equivalent to the clutch hub nut threads. Install the nut (**Figure 37**) and tighten it (**Figure 46**) to the specification in **Table 2**.

10. If used, remove the special tool from the clutch shell.

11. Adjust the primary chain as described in Chapter Three.

12. Install the clutch plates and friction discs, pressure plate, and diaphragm spring as described in this chapter.

13. Install the primary chaincase cover as described in this chapter.

14. Adjust the clutch as described in Chapter Three.

15. Connect the negative battery cable as described in Chapter Eight.

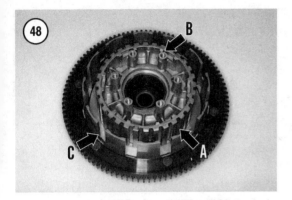

CLUTCH SHELL, CLUTCH HUB
AND SPROCKET

Inspection

The clutch shell is a subassembly consisting of the clutch shell, the clutch hub, the bearing and two snap rings.

1. Remove the clutch shell as described in this chapter.

2. Hold the clutch shell and rotate the clutch hub by hand. The bearing is damaged if the clutch hub binds or turns roughly.

3. Check the sprocket (A, **Figure 47**) and the starter ring gear (B) on the clutch shell for cracks, deep scoring, excessive wear or heat discoloration.

4. If the sprocket or ring gear is worn or damaged, replace the clutch shell. If the primary chain sprocket is worn, also check the primary chain and the compensating sprocket as described in this chapter.

5. Inspect the clutch hub for the following conditions:

   a. The clutch plate teeth slide in the clutch hub splines (A, **Figure 48**). Inspect the splines for

rough spots, grooves or other damage. Repair minor damage with a file or oil stone. If the damage is severe, replace the clutch hub.

   b. Inspect the clutch hub inner splines (**Figure 49**) for galling, severe wear or other damage. Repair minor damage with a fine cut file. If damage is severe, replace the clutch hub.

   c. Inspect the bolt towers and threads (B, **Figure 48**) for thread damage or cracks at the base of the tower. Repair thread damage with the correct size metric tap. If the tower(s) is cracked or damaged, replace the clutch hub.

6. Check the clutch shell. The friction disc tangs slide in the clutch housing grooves (C, **Figure 48**). Inspect the grooves for cracks or galling. Repair minor damage with a file. If the damage is severe, replace the clutch housing.

7. If the clutch hub, clutch shell or bearing is damaged, replace them as described in the following procedure.

Disassembly/Assembly

Do not separate the clutch hub and shell unless either part or the bearing is going to be replaced. If the two parts are separated, the bearing will be damaged. Removal and installation of the bearing requires a hydraulic press.

1. Remove the clutch (**Figure 50**) as described in this chapter. Remove the clutch shell assembly from the primary drive chain.

2. Remove the snap ring (**Figure 51**) from the clutch hub groove.

3. Support the clutch hub and clutch shell in a press with the primary chain sprocket side facing up (**Figure 52**).

4. Place a suitable size arbor in the clutch hub surface and press the clutch hub (A, **Figure 53**) out of the bearing.

5. Remove the clutch shell and sprocket (B, **Figure 53**) from the press.

6. On the inner surface of the clutch shell, remove the bearing retaining snap ring (**Figure 54**) from the groove in the middle of the clutch shell.

CAUTION
Press the bearing out through the primary chain sprocket side of the clutch shell. The bearing bore has a shoulder on the primary chain side.

5

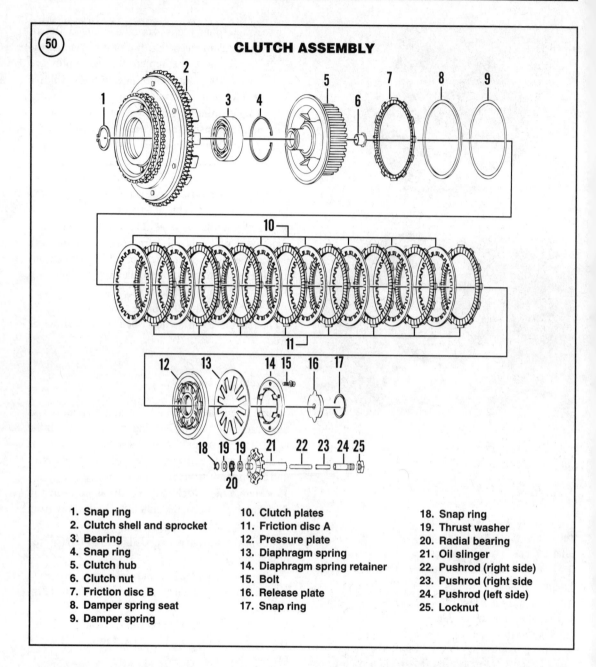

CLUTCH ASSEMBLY

1. Snap ring
2. Clutch shell and sprocket
3. Bearing
4. Snap ring
5. Clutch hub
6. Clutch nut
7. Friction disc B
8. Damper spring seat
9. Damper spring

10. Clutch plates
11. Friction disc A
12. Pressure plate
13. Diaphragm spring
14. Diaphragm spring retainer
15. Bolt
16. Release plate
17. Snap ring

18. Snap ring
19. Thrust washer
20. Radial bearing
21. Oil slinger
22. Pushrod (right side)
23. Pushrod (right side
24. Pushrod (left side)
25. Locknut

7. Support the clutch shell in the press with the primary chain sprocket side *facing up.*

8. Place a suitable size arbor on the bearing inner race and press the bearing out of the clutch shell (**Figure 55**).

9. Thoroughly clean the clutch hub and shell in solvent and dry them with compressed air.

10. Inspect the bearing bore in the clutch shell for damage or burrs. Clean off any burrs that would interfere with new bearing installation.

11. Support the clutch shell in the press with the primary chain sprocket side *facing down.*

12. Apply chaincase lubricant to the clutch shell bearing receptacle and to the outer surface of the bearing.

13. Align the bearing with the clutch shell receptacle.

14. Place a suitable size arbor on the bearing outer race and slowly press the bearing into the clutch shell until it bottoms on the lower shoulder. Press

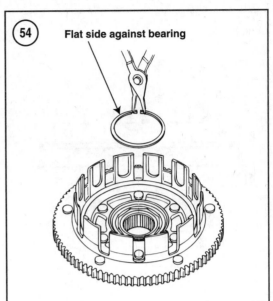

Flat side against bearing

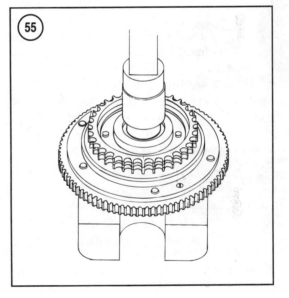

CAUTION
*Failure to support the inner bearing
race properly will cause bearing and
clutch shell damage.*

a. Place the clutch shell in a press. Support the
inner bearing race with a sleeve as shown in
Figure 56.

b. Align the clutch hub with the bearing and
slowly press the clutch hub into the bearing
until the clutch hub shoulder seats against the
bearing inner race.

only on the outer bearing race. Applying force to the
bearing's inner race will damage the bearing. Refer
to *Basic Service Methods* in Chapter One for additional information.

15. Position the *new* snap ring with the flat side
against the bearing and install the snap ring into the
clutch shell groove (**Figure 54**). Make sure the snap
ring is seated correctly in the clutch shell groove.

16. Press the clutch hub into the clutch shell as follows:

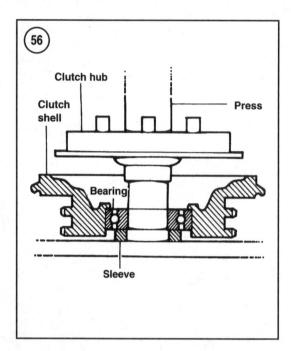

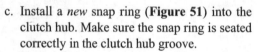

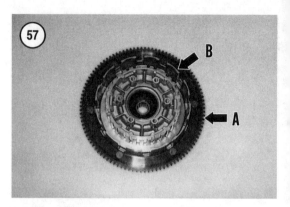

c. Install a *new* snap ring (**Figure 51**) into the clutch hub. Make sure the snap ring is seated correctly in the clutch hub groove.

17. After completing assembly, hold the clutch shell (A, **Figure 57**) and rotate the clutch hub (B) by hand. The shell should turn smoothly with no roughness or binding. If the clutch shell binds or turns roughly, the bearing was installed incorrectly. Repeat this procedure until this problem is corrected.

PRIMARY CHAIN AND GUIDE INSPECTION

1. Remove the primary chain as described under the *Clutch Shell, Compensating Sprocket and Primary Drive Chain* procedure in this chapter.

2. Clean the primary chain in solvent and dry it thoroughly.

3. Inspect the primary chain (**Figure 58**) for excessive wear, cracks or other damage. If the chain is worn or damaged, check both sprockets for wear and damage.

NOTE
*If the primary chain is near the end of its adjustment level or if no more adjustment is available, and the adjusting guide (**Figure 59**) is not worn or*

damaged, the primary chain is excessively worn. Service specifications for chain wear are not available.

4. Inspect the tensioner pad (**Figure 59**) for cracks, severe wear or other damage. Replace the adjusting shoe if necessary.

PRIMARY CHAIN ALIGNMENT

A spacer, installed behind the compensating sprocket, aligns the compensating and clutch shell

5

sprockets. Install the original spacer when reinstalling the compensating sprocket, primary chain and clutch assembly. However, if the primary chain is showing wear on one side, or if new components that could affect alignment have been installed, perform the following steps.

1. Remove the chaincase cover as described in this chapter.

2. Adjust the primary chain tension so the chain is snug against both the compensating sprocket and clutch shell sprocket.

3. Push the primary chain toward the engine and transmission (at both sprockets) as far as it will go.

4. Place a straightedge across the primary chain side plates as close to the compensating sprocket as possible.

5. Close to the compensating sprocket, measure the distance from the chain link side plates to the primary chaincase housing gasket surface (**Figure 60**). Record the measurement.

6. Repeat Steps 4 and 5 with the end of the straightedge as close to the clutch sprocket as possible (**Figure 61**). Record the measurement.

7. The difference between the two measurements should be within 0.030 in. (0.76 mm) of each other. If the difference exceeds this amount, replace the spacer (**Figure 62**) with a suitable size spacer. Refer to **Table 3** for spacer thickness and part numbers.

8. To replace the spacer, refer to *Clutch Shell, Compensating Sprocket and Primary Drive Chain* in this chapter.

9. Install the outer primary cover as described in this chapter.

10. Check and adjust the primary chain tension as described in Chapter Three.

COMPENSATING SPROCKET INSPECTION

Refer to **Figure 34** or **Figure 35**.

1. Remove the compensating sprocket assembly as described in this chapter.

2. Clean all parts in solvent and dry them with compressed air.

3. Check the cam surfaces (**Figure 63**) for cracks, deep scoring or wear.

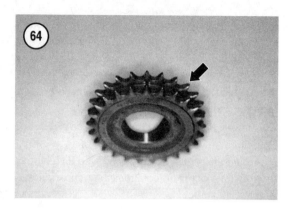

4. Check the compensating sprocket gear teeth (**Figure 64**) for cracks or wear.

> *NOTE*
> *If the compensating sprocket teeth are worn, also check the primary chain and the clutch shell gear teeth for wear.*

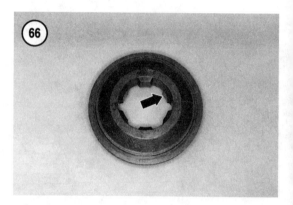

5. Check the compensating sprocket inner bushing (**Figure 65**) for wear.
6. Check the sliding cam inner splines (**Figure 66**) for wear.
7. Check the shaft extension splines for wear or galling.
8. Check the cover (**Figure 67**) for damage.
9. Inspect the inner threads (**Figure 68**) of the nut for damage.
10. If any of these components were replaced, check the primary chain alignment as described in this chapter.

PRIMARY CHAINCASE HOUSING

The primary chaincase housing (**Figure 69**) is bolted to the engine and transmission. It houses the primary drive assembly, flywheel, starter jackshaft, and the mainshaft oil seal and bearing assembly.

Removal

> *NOTE*
> *On models so equipped, always disarm the optional TSSM security system prior to disconnecting the battery or the siren will sound.*

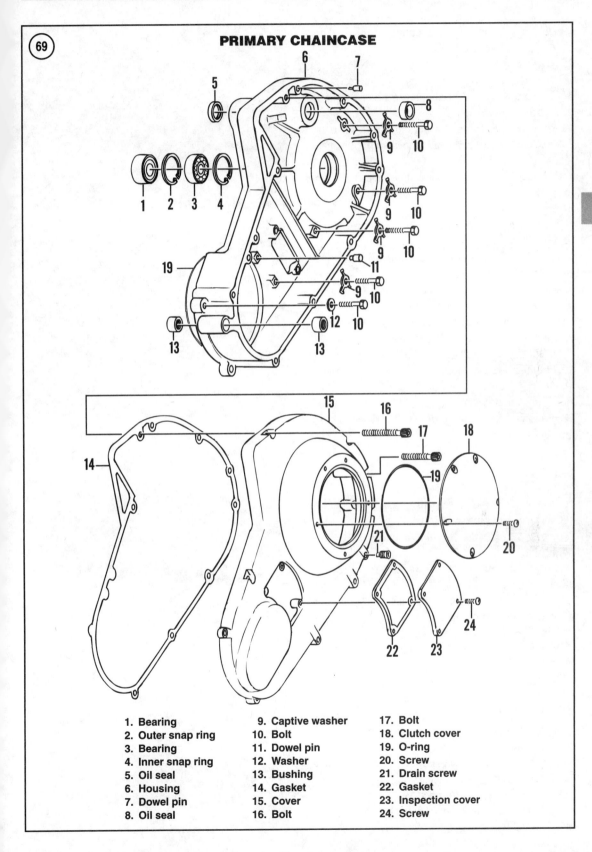

PRIMARY CHAINCASE

1. Bearing
2. Outer snap ring
3. Bearing
4. Inner snap ring
5. Oil seal
6. Housing
7. Dowel pin
8. Oil seal
9. Captive washer
10. Bolt
11. Dowel pin
12. Washer
13. Bushing
14. Gasket
15. Cover
16. Bolt
17. Bolt
18. Clutch cover
19. O-ring
20. Screw
21. Drain screw
22. Gasket
23. Inspection cover
24. Screw

1. Disconnect the negative battery cable as described in Chapter Eight.

2. Remove the shift lever assembly as described under *External Shift Mechanism* in Chapter Six.

3. Remove the primary chaincase outer cover as described in this chapter.

4. Remove the compensating sprocket, primary chain and clutch assembly as described in this chapter.

5. Remove the starter motor as described in Chapter Eight.

6. Pry the lockwasher tabs away from the five inner primary housing bolts (**Figure 70**). Loosen the five bolts.

7. Loosen the front two inner housing bolts with flat washers.

8. Remove all seven bolts securing the inner housing to the engine and the transmission. Discard the five lockwashers as new ones must be installed.

9. Remove the starter jackshaft assembly from the inner housing as described in this chapter.

10. Tap the housing loose.

11. Remove the housing from the engine, transmission and gearshift shaft.

12. Remove the O-ring (**Figure 71**) from the engine crankcase shoulder.

Inspection

1. Remove all gasket residue from the housing gasket surfaces (A, **Figure 72**).

2. Clean the housing in solvent and dry it thoroughly.

3. Check the housing (A, **Figure 73**) for cracks or other damage.

4. Check the starter jackshaft oil seal for excessive wear or damage. If necessary, replace the oil seal, as follows:

   a. Note the direction the oil seal lip faces in the housing.

   b. Pack the new oil seal lips with grease.

   c. Pry the oil seal out of the housing.

   d. Carefully drive the *new* oil seal into the housing until it seats against the housing shoulder.

5. Inspect the starter jackshaft bushing (B, **Figure 72**) for wear, cracks or other damage. If necessary, replace the bushing as follows:

   a. Remove the bushing with a blind bearing removal tool.

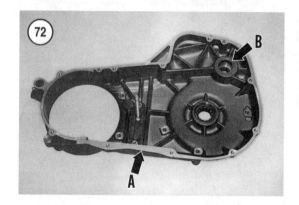

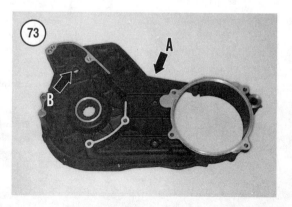

c. Press the new bushing in until its outer surface is flush with the edge of the bushing bore.

d. Repeat substeps a-c for the other bushing.

7. Turn the inner bearing race (**Figure 75**) by hand. Replace the bearing as follows:

a. Remove the oil seal (**Figure 76**) as described in Step 8.

b. Remove the inner and outer bearing snap rings.

c. Support the housing and press the bearing out.

d. Install the outer snap ring (clutch side). Make sure the snap ring is correctly seated in the groove.

CAUTION
When pressing the bearing into the housing, support the outer snap ring. The force required to press the bearing into the housing may force the snap ring out of its groove, damaging the housing.

e. Support the housing and outer snap ring.

f. Press the bearing into the housing until it seats against the snap ring.

g. Install the inner snap ring. Make sure the snap ring is seated correctly in the groove.

h. Install a *new* oil seal as described in Step 8.

8. Inspect the housing oil seal (**Figure 76**) for excessive wear, tearing or other damage. If necessary, replace the oil seal as follows:

a. Remove the oil seal with a wide-blade screwdriver.

b. Clean the oil seal bore.

c. Pack the oil seal lip with a waterproof bearing grease.

d. Position the oil seal with its closed side facing out. Press the *new* oil seal in until its outer surface is flush with the edge of the bearing bore.

9A. On 1999-2000 models, check the primary chain tensioner rack screws (**Figure 77**) for looseness. Tighten the screws if necessary.

9B. On 2001-on models, check the primary chain tensioner rack screws (**Figure 78**) for looseness. Tighten the screws if necessary.

b. Clean the bushing bore in the housing.

c. Press the new bushing in until its outer surface is flush with the edge of the bushing bore.

6. Inspect the shift lever bushings (**Figure 74**) for wear, cracks or other damage. If necessary, replace the bushing as follows:

a. Remove the bushing with a blind bearing removal tool.

b. Clean the bushing bore in the housing.

Installation

1. Thoroughly clean the *outer surface* of the five bolt holes of the inner cover. Apply a light coat of black RTV sealant to the inner surfaces.

2. Install the *new* O-ring (**Figure 71**) onto the engine crankcase shoulder.

3. To prevent the transmission mainshaft splines from damaging the oil seal as it passes over, wrap the mainshaft splines with tape.

4. If removed, install the drive belt prior to installing the housing.

5. Align the housing with the engine and transmission, and install it over the gearshift lever shaft. Push the housing on until it stops.

6. Apply a bead of black RTV sealant to the threads of the five housing bolts that are used with the lockwashers.

7. Install the five housing bolts (**Figure 70**) and *new* lockwashers.

8. Install the front two housing bolts with flat washers (**Figure 79**).

9. Tighten the housing bolts in the following order.

   a. Tighten the four housing-to-engine mounting bolts to the specification in **Table 2**. Bend the lockwasher tabs against the rear two bolt heads.

   b. Tighten the three housing-to-transmission mounting bolts to the specification in **Table 2**. Bend the lockwasher tabs against the three bolt heads.

10. Install the starter jackshaft as described in this chapter.

11. Install the starter motor as described in Chapter Eight.

12. Install the compensating sprocket, primary chain and clutch assembly as described in this chapter.

13. Install the primary chaincase cover as described in this chapter.

14. Connect the negative battery cable as described in Chapter Eight.

STARTER JACKSHAFT

Refer to **Figure 80**.

Removal

NOTE
On models so equipped, always disarm the optional TSSM security system prior to disconnecting the battery or the siren will sound.

1. Disconnect the negative battery cable as described in Chapter Eight.

2. Remove the primary chaincase cover as described in this chapter.

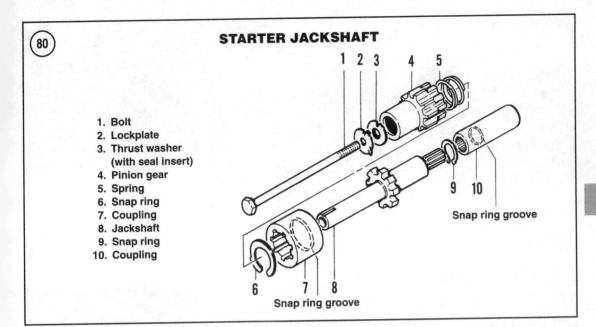

STARTER JACKSHAFT

1. Bolt
2. Lockplate
3. Thrust washer
   (with seal insert)
4. Pinion gear
5. Spring
6. Snap ring
7. Coupling
8. Jackshaft
9. Snap ring
10. Coupling

Snap ring groove

Snap ring groove

NOTE
The pinion gear components (1-5, ***Figure 80****) can be removed with the clutch/primary chain assembly in place. If only these parts require service, do not perform Step 3.*

3. Remove the compensating sprocket, primary chain and clutch assembly as described in this chapter.

4. Straighten the tab on the lockplate (**Figure 81**).

5. Wrap the pinion gear with a cloth to protect the finish, then secure it with pliers (A, **Figure 82**).

6. Loosen and remove the bolt (B, **Figure 82**), lockplate and thrust washer from the starter jackshaft assembly and the end of the starter motor.

7. Remove the pinion gear (**Figure 83**) and spring from the jackshaft.

8. Remove the jackshaft assembly and the coupling from the housing.

Inspection

1. Clean the jackshaft assembly (**Figure 84**) in solvent and dry it with compressed air.

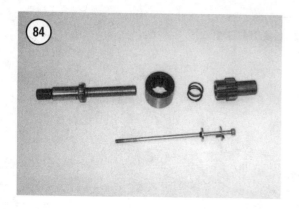

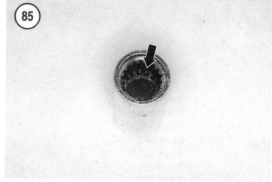

2. Check the snap ring installed in each coupling (**Figure 85** and **Figure 86**). Replace any loose or damaged snap rings.

3. Replace all worn or damaged parts.

Installation

> *NOTE*
> *Before installing the coupling in Step 4, note the snap ring (**Figure 85**) installed inside the coupling. The coupling side with the snap ring closest to its end slides over the jackshaft.*

1. Install the jackshaft (**Figure 87**) into the housing. Push it in until it stops.

2. Position the coupling with its counterbore facing toward the jackshaft and install the coupling (**Figure 88**) into the housing bushing.

3. Install the spring (**Figure 89**) onto the jackshaft.

4. Install the pinion gear (**Figure 90**) onto the jackshaft.

5. Push in on the pinion gear (A, **Figure 91**) and install the bolt, lockplate and thrust washer (B) onto the jackshaft.

6. Push the assembly on until it bottoms.

7. Align the lockplate tab with the thrust washer, then insert the tab into the notch in the end of the jackshaft.

8. Screw the bolt into the starter motor shaft by hand.

9. Wrap the pinion gear with a cloth to protect the finish, then secure it with pliers (A, **Figure 82**).

10. Tighten the bolt (B, **Figure 82**) on the starter motor to the torque specification in **Table 2**. Bend the outer lockplate tab against the bolt head (**Figure 81**).

11. To ensure the components have been installed correctly, perform the following:

    a. Install the clutch shell onto the transmission mainshaft.

    b. With the starter motor not engaged, the pinion gear (A, **Figure 92**) must not engage the clutch shell gear (B).

    c. To check for proper engagement, pull out on the pinion gear and engage it with the clutch shell gear. Then rotate the clutch shell in either direction and make sure the pinion gear rotates with it.

    d. If engagement is incorrect, remove the clutch shell and correct the problem.

    e. Remove the clutch shell.

12. Install the compensating sprocket, primary chain and clutch assembly as described in this chapter.

13. Install the primary chaincase cover as described in this chapter.

14. Connect the negative battery cable as described in Chapter Eight.

CLUTCH CABLE REPLACEMENT

1. Before removing the clutch cable, make a drawing of its routing path from the handlebar to the transmission side door.

2. Disconnect the clutch cable from the clutch release mechanism (**Figure 93**) as described under *Transmission Side Cover* in Chapter Six.

3. Remove the snap ring from the base of the clutch lever pivot pin.

4. Remove the pivot pin (**Figure 94**) and slide the clutch lever out its perch.

5. Remove the plastic anchor pin (**Figure 95**) and disconnect the clutch cable from the lever.

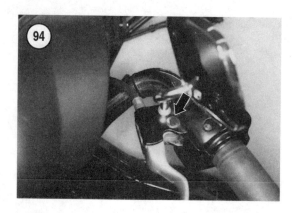

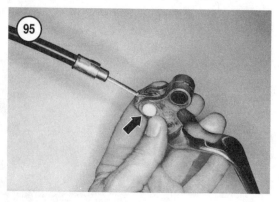

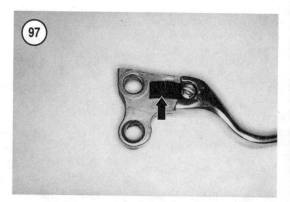

6. Check the clutch lever components (**Figure 96**) for worn or damaged parts.

7. Make sure the antislack spring screw (**Figure 97**) on the bottom of the clutch lever is tight.

8. On all FLHT models, withdraw the clutch cable from the inner fairing rubber grommet (**Figure 98**). Move the clutch cable forward and out of the fairing.

9. Route the new clutch cable from the handlebar to the transmission side cover following the drawing made in Step 1.

10. Fit the clutch cable into its lever and secure it with the plastic anchor pin (**Figure 95**).

11. Slide the clutch lever into the perch and install the pivot pin (**Figure 94**).

12. Secure the pivot pin with the snap ring.

13. Reconnect the clutch cable to the clutch release mechanism as described under *Transmission Side Cover* in Chapter Six.

14. Adjust the clutch as described in Chapter Three.

Table 1 CLUTCH SPECIFICATIONS AND SPROCKET SIZES

Item	Specification
Clutch type	Wet, multiplate disc
Clutch lever free play	1/16-1/8 in. (1.6-3.2 mm)
Clutch friction plate thickness	
Service limit	0.143 in. (3.62 mm)
Clutch plate warp	
Service limit	0.006 in. (0.15 mm)
Compensating sprocket	
Fuel injected models	24 teeth
Carbureted models	25 teeth
Clutch sprocket	
Fuel injected models	37 teeth
Carbureted models	36 teeth
Transmission sprocket	32 teeth
Fuel injected models	32 teeth
Carbureted models	32 teeth

Table 2 CLUTCH AND PRIMARY CHAIN CASE TORQUE SPECIFICATIONS

Item	ft.-lb.	in.-lb.	N•m
Diaphragm spring bolts	–	90-110	10-12
Clutch hub nut	70-80	–	95-108
Compensating sprocket nut	150-165	–	203-224
Primary chaincase cover bolts	–	108-120	12-14
Primary chaincase inspection cover			
Long and short screws	–	84-108	9-12
Primary chain case			
Housing-to-engine and transmission bolts	17-21	–	23-29
Starter jackshaft bolt	–	84-108	9-12

Table 3 SPROCKET ALIGNMENT SPACERS

Spacer part No.	in.	mm
35850-84	0.010	0.25
35851-84	0.020	0.51
35852-84	0.030	0.76
24032-70	0.060	1.52
24033-70	0.090	2.29
24034-70	0.120	3.05
24035-70	0.150	3.81
24036-70	0.180	4.57
24037-70	0.210	5.33

5

NOTE: Refer to the Supplement at the back of this manual for information unique to 2003-2005 models.

CHAPTER SIX

TRANSMISSION

This chapter covers procedures for the transmission, shift linkage and oil pan. Specifications are in **Tables 1-3** at the end of the chapter. Special tool requirements are described in the procedures. All of the special tools used in this manual and their part numbers are listed in **Table 11** of Chapter One.

All models are equipped with a five-speed transmission that is separate from the engine. The transmission shaft and shifter assemblies can be serviced with the transmission mounted in the frame.

and shift arm components. Except for the shift arm assembly, the interal components can be serviced with the transmission side door assembly installed in the frame by removing the top cover.

If a shift problem is encountered, refer to the troubleshooting procedures in Chapter Two and eliminate all clutch and shifter mechanism possibilities *before* considering transmission repairs. Improper clutch adjustment (Chapter Three) is often a cause of poor shifting.

SHIFTER ASSEMBLY

The shifter assembly (**Figure 1** or **Figure 2**) consists of the external shift linkage, internal shift cam

Shift Linkage Adjustment

The shift linkage assembly connects the transmission shift rod lever to the foot-operated shift levers.

The shift linkage does not require adjustment unless it is replaced or the transmission gears do not engage properly.

> *CAUTION*
> *The heel shift lever must never touch the footboard when shifting gears. To ensure proper gear engagement and avoid possible transmission damage, there must be a minimum clearance of 3/8 in. (9.5 mm) between the bottom of the heel shift lever and the top of the footboard. If the clearance is not correct, reposition the heel shift lever as described under* **External Shift Mechanism** *in this chapter.*

> *NOTE*
> *On models so equipped, always disarm the optional TSSM security system prior to disconnecting the battery or the siren will sound.*

1. Disconnect the negative battery cable as described in Chapter Eight.
2. Loosen the two shift linkage rod locknuts (A, **Figure 3**).
3. Remove the acorn nut and washers (B, **Figure 3**) securing the shift linkage rod to the inner shift lever.
4. Turn the shift linkage rod (C, **Figure 3**) as necessary to change the linkage adjustment.
5. Reconnect the shift linkage rod to the shift rod lever and tighten the locknuts to the torque specification in **Table 3**.
6. Recheck the shifting. Readjust if necessary.
7. If this adjustment does not correct the shifting, check the shift linkage for interference problems. Then check the shift linkage assembly for worn or damaged parts. Perform the *Gear Engagement Check/Adjustment* procedure if there are no visible interference problems or damage.

EXTERNAL SHIFT MECHANISM

Removal/Installation

Refer to **Figure 1** and **Figure 2**.

> *NOTE*
> *On models so equipped, always disarm the optional TSSM security system prior to disconnecting the battery or the siren will sound.*

1. Disconnect the battery negative cable as described in Chapter Eight.
2. Remove the front left side footboard as described in Chapter Fourteen.
3. Make an alignment mark on the heal shift lever and the end of the shift lever shaft.
4. Remove the clamp bolt and remove the heal shift lever (**Figure 4**).
5. Make an alignment mark on the toe shift lever that relates to the end of the shift lever shaft.
6. Remove the clamp bolt and remove the toe shift lever (**Figure 5**).
7. Remove the spacer (**Figure 6**) from the shift lever shaft.
8. Remove the primary chaincase assembly as described in Chapter Five.
9. Remove the clamp bolt securing the shift rod lever (**Figure 7**) to the transmission case.
10. Remove the shift rod lever, shift rod, inner shift lever and shift lever shaft (**Figure 8**) as an assembly.
11. Install by reversing these removal steps. Tighten the clamp bolts securely.

Gear Engagement Inspection/Adjustment (1999-2000 Models Only)

If the transmission gears do not engage properly, inspect and adjust gear engagement as follows:
1. Make sure the clutch is working properly. Refer to clutch adjustment in Chapter Three. If the clutch is working properly, continue with Step 2.

> *NOTE*
> *On models so equipped, always disarm the optional TSSM security system prior to disconnecting the battery or the siren will sound.*

2. Disconnect the negative battery cable as described in Chapter Eight.
3. Shift the transmission into third gear. Make sure third gear is fully engaged.
4. Remove the transmission top cover as described in this chapter.
5. Move the shifter shaft lever (**Figure 9**, typical) in both directions to check for free play and spring pressure. Gear engagement is correct if the spring pressure is the same in both directions and there is approximately 0.10 in. (0.25 mm) clearance between the shift pawl arms and the shift cam pins

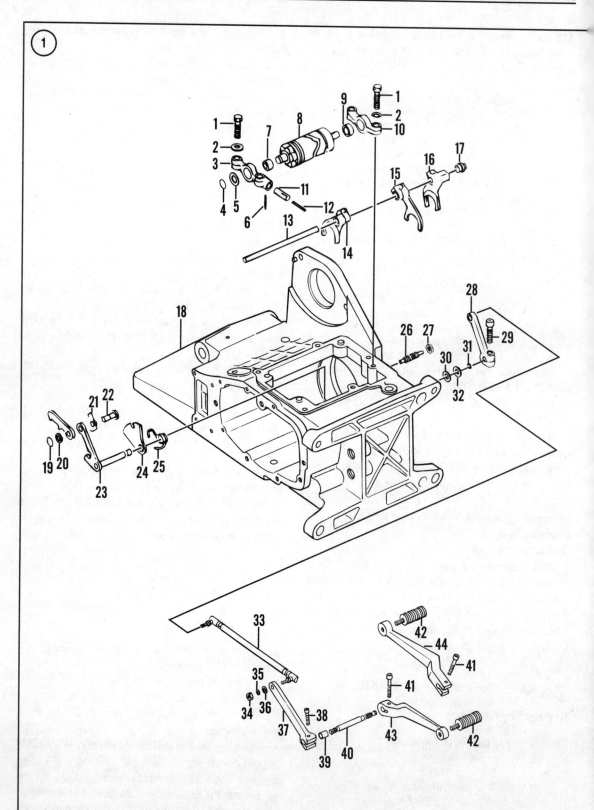

SHIFTER ASSEMBLY
(1999-2000)

1. Bolt
2. Washer
3. Support–right side
4. Snap ring
5. Thrust washer
6. Roll pin
7. Needle bearing
8. Shift cam
9. Needle bearing
10. Support-left side
11. Spring
12. Cam follower
13. Shift fork shaft
14. Sift fork No. 3
15. Shift fork No. 2
16. Shift fork No. 1
17. Set screw
18. Transmission case
19. Snap ring
20. Seal
21. Spring
22. Pivot pin
23. Shift cam pawl
24. Centering plate
25. Spring
26. Adjusting screw
27. Locknut
28. Shift rod lever
29. Bolt
30. Oil seal
31. Washer
32. Snap ring
33. Shift rod
34. Nut
35. Lockwasher
36. Washer
37. Inner shift lever
38. Bolt
39. Bushing
40. Shift lever shaft
41. Bolt
42. Shift peg
43. Shift lever–heel
44. Shift lever–toe

(**Figure 10**). If necessary, adjust gear engagement as described in Step 6.

NOTE
An incorrectly adjusted shift pawl adjuster causes many shifting-related problems.

6. Adjust the gear engagement as follows:
   a. The shift pawl adjuster is mounted on the left side of the transmission case (**Figure 11**) between the transmission case and primary chain housing. **Figure 12** shows the shifter pawl adjusting screw and locknut with the inner primary housing removed for clarity.
   b. Use the transmission pawl adjuster tool (part No. HD-39618) to adjust the shifter pawl adjuster.
   c. Loosen the adjuster screw locknut (**Figure 12**) and turn the shifter pawl adjuster in 1/4 turn or less increments either clockwise or counterclockwise. Turn the screw until the shifter lever travel spring pressure is equal on both sides while maintaining a clearance of 0.010 in. (0.25 mm). Tighten the locknut and recheck the adjustment.
7. Reinstall the transmission top cover as described in this chapter.
8. Reconnect the negative battery cable.

TRANSMISSION TOP COVER

The transmission top cover assembly can be serviced with the transmission installed in the frame.

Removal/Installation

1. Remove the exhaust system as described in Chapter Seven.
2. Disconnect the wire from the neutral indicator switch.
3. Disconnect the vent hose from the top cover or the fittings.
4. Remove the four bolts and washers securing the transmission cover to the transmission case. Remove the top cover and the gasket.
5. Remove the gasket residue from the transmission cover and transmission case gasket surfaces.
6. Install a *new* gasket onto the transmission case.

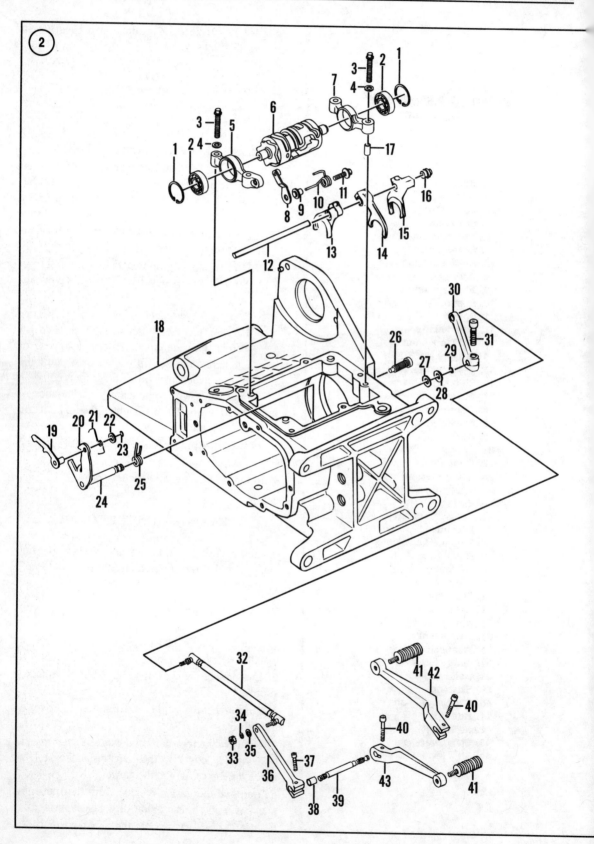

SHIFTER ASSEMBLY
(2001-ON)

1. Snap ring
2. Bearing
3. Bolt
4. Washer
5. Support–right side
6. Shift cam
7. Support–left side
8. Cam follower
9. Sleeve
10. Spring
11. Bolt
12. Shift fork shaft
13. Shift fork No. 1
14. Shift fork No. 2
15. Shift fork No. 3
16. Set screw
17. Locating dowel
18. Transmission case
19. Shift cam pawl
20. Shift cam pawl
21. Spring
22. Washer
23. Snap ring
24. Shift cam pawl shaft
25. Return spring
26. Adjusting screw
27. Oil seal
28. Washer
29. Snap ring
30. Shift rod lever
31. Bolt
32. Shift rod
33. Nut
34. Lockwasher
35. Washer
36. Inner shift lever
37. Bolt
38. Bushing
39. Shift lever shaft
40. Bolt
41. Shift peg
42. Shift lever–heel
43. Shift lever–toe

7. Install the transmission top cover, three bolts and washers. Tighten the bolts in a crisscross pattern to the specification in **Table 3**.

8. Reconnect the vent hose to the fitting and install a *new* hose clamp.

9. Connect the wire to the neutral indicator switch.

10. Install the exhaust system as described in Chapter Seven.

SHIFT CAM (1999-2000)

The shift cam assembly (**Figure 13**) can be serviced with the transmission installed in the frame by removing the transmission top cover.

Removal

1. Remove the transmission top cover as described in this chapter.

2. Remove the shift cam support block mounting bolts and washers.

3. Carefully lift the shift cam assembly up and out of the transmission case.

4. Remove the four dowel pins from the transmission case.

Installation

1. Install the four dowel pins into the transmission case.

2. Measure shift cam end play as follows:
   a. Position the left support block with the numbers facing down toward the transmission case.
   b. Install the shifter cam/support block assembly onto the transmission case. Align the shift fork pins with the shifter cam slots.

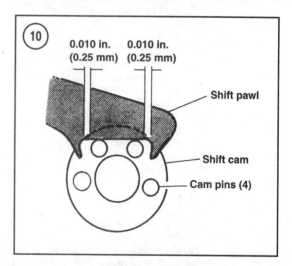

   c. Use a flat feeler gauge (A, **Figure 14**) to measure the clearance between the outer thrust washer and the shift cam (B). The correct shift cam end play is 0.001-0.004 in. (0.025-0.010 mm).

   d. To adjust the end play, replace the outer thrust washer with a suitable thickness thrust washer.

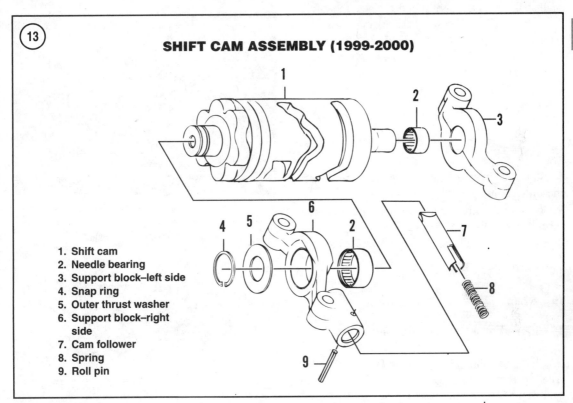

SHIFT CAM ASSEMBLY (1999-2000)

1. Shift cam
2. Needle bearing
3. Support block–left side
4. Snap ring
5. Outer thrust washer
6. Support block–right side
7. Cam follower
8. Spring
9. Roll pin

6

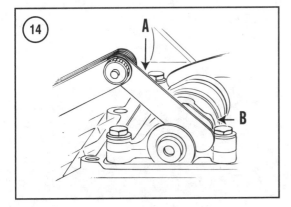

NOTE
Inner and outer thrust washers are available from a Harley-Davidson dealership in the following thicknesses: 0.017, 0.020, 0.022, 0.025, 0.028, 0.031, 0.035 and 0.039 in. (0.43, 0.51, 0.56, 0.63, 0.71, 0.79, 0.89 and 0.99 mm).

e. If necessary, remove the shift cam assembly from the transmission case and install a *new* outer thrust washer.

3. Apply engine oil to the shifter cam bearing surfaces.

4. Align the shift fork pins with the shifter cam slots and install the shift cam into position (**Figure 15**).

5. Engage the shifter pawl with the shifter cam (**Figure 16**).

> *CAUTION*
> *Do not overtighten the shift cam mounting bolts as this can distort the cam follower and cause shifting problems. Do not exceed the torque specification in **Table 3**.*

6. Install the shift cam support block mounting bolts and washers. Tighten the bolts in a crisscross pattern to the specification in **Table 3**.

7. Perform the *Gear Engagement Check/Adjustment* in this chapter.

8. Install the transmission top cover as described in this chapter.

Disassembly

1. Slide the left side support block (**Figure 17**) off the shifter cam.

2. Remove the shift cam snap ring and the outer thrust washer (**Figure 18**).

3. Remove the right side support block (**Figure 19**).

Inspection

1. Clean all parts, except the support block bearings, in solvent and thoroughly dry them.

2. Check the shift cam grooves (**Figure 20**) for wear or roughness. Replace the shift cam if the groove profiles are excessively worn or damaged.

3. Check the shift cam ends where the cam contacts the bearings. If the ends are worn or damaged, replace the shift cam and both support block bearings. Refer to *Support Block Bearing Replacement* in this chapter.

4. Check the support block bearings for excessive wear, cracks or other damage. See **Figure 21** and **Figure 22**. If necessary, refer to *Support Block Bearing Replacement* in this chapter to replace the bearings.

5. Check the support blocks for wear, cracks or other damage. Replace the support blocks if necessary.

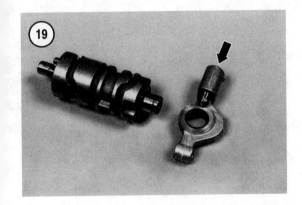

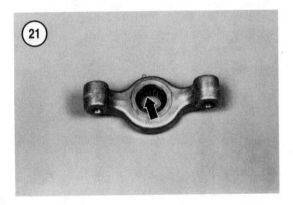

Assembly

1. Coat all bearing and sliding surfaces with assembly oil.

2. Install the right support block (**Figure 19**) on the shifter cam.

3. Install the outer thrust washer (**Figure 18**) and a *new* snap ring. Make sure the snap ring seats in the shift cam groove.

NOTE
After installing the snap ring, make sure the outer thrust washer can be rotated by hand.

4. Install the left support block (**Figure 17**) onto the shift cam.

5. Rotate the support blocks so their numbered sides are facing down.

Support Block Bearing Replacement

Each support block is equipped with a single needle bearing. See **Figure 21** and **Figure 22**. Replace both bearings at the same time. The removal and installation of the bearings requires a press. Refer to *Bearings* in Chapter One. Before removing the bearings, record the direction the bearing manufacturer's marks face for proper installation.

SHIFT CAM (2001-ON)

The shift cam assembly (**Figure 23**) can be serviced with the transmission installed in the frame by removing the transmission top cover.

Removal

1. Remove the transmission top cover as described in this chapter.

2. Remove the shift cam support block mounting bolts and lockwashers.

3. Lift the shift cam pawl off the cam pins to free the assembly.

4. Carefully lift the shift cam assembly up and out of the transmission case.

5. Remove the four dowel pins from the transmission case.

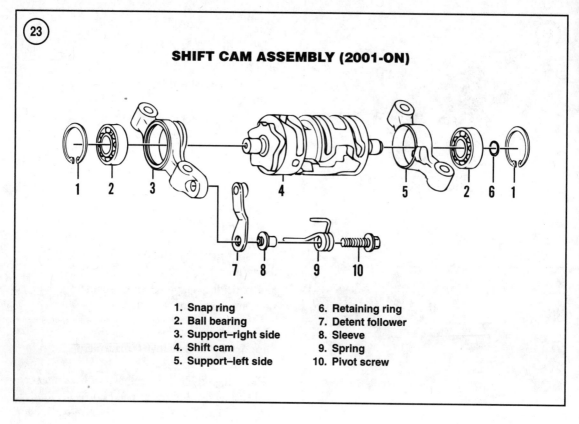

SHIFT CAM ASSEMBLY (2001-ON)

1. Snap ring
2. Ball bearing
3. Support–right side
4. Shift cam
5. Support–left side
6. Retaining ring
7. Detent follower
8. Sleeve
9. Spring
10. Pivot screw

Installation

1. Install the four dowel pins into the transmission case.

2. Lift the shift cam pawl up out of the way.

3. Carefully install the shift cam assembly into the transmission case. Align the shift fork pins with the shift cam slots.

4. Lower the shift cam pawl and engage it with the cam pins.

5. Install the shift cam support block mounting bolts and lockwashers. Tighten the bolts in a criss-cross pattern to the specification in **Table 3**.

6. Install the transmission top cover as described in this chapter.

Disassembly

1. On the right side, perform the following:
   a. Slide the right side support block (A, **Figure 24**) off the shift cam.
   b. Remove the retaining ring (B, **Figure 24**) and withdraw the bearing (C) from the support block.

2. On the left side, perform the following:
   a. Remove the small retaining ring (A, **Figure 25**) from the shifter cam.
   b. Slide the left side support block (B, **Figure 25**) off the shifter cam.
   c. Remove the snap ring (C, **Figure 25**) and withdraw the bearing from the support block.

3. To remove the detent follower, unscrew the pivot bolt (A, **Figure 26**). Remove the spring (B, **Figure 26**), spring sleeve (C) and the detent follower (D).

Inspection

1. Clean all parts, except the support block bearings, in solvent and dry them thoroughly.

2. Check the shift cam grooves (**Figure 20**) for wear or roughness. Replace the shift cam if the groove profiles are excessively worn or damaged.

3. Check the shift cam ends where the cam contacts the bearings. If the ends are worn or damaged, replace the shift cam and both support block bearings. See *Support Block Bearing Replacement* in this chapter.

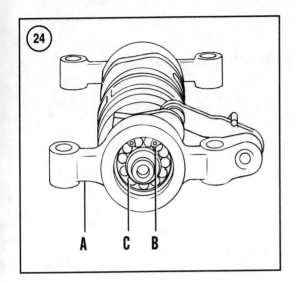

24

A   C   B

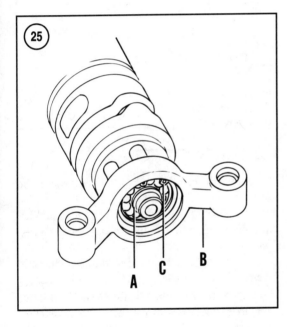

25

C   B
A

4. Check the support block bearings for excessive wear, cracks or other damage. See **Figure 21** and **Figure 22**. If necessary, refer to *Support Block Bearing Replacement* in this chapter to replace the bearings.

5. Check the support blocks for wear, cracks or other damage. Replace the support blocks if necessary.

Assembly

1. Coat all bearing and sliding surfaces with assembly oil.

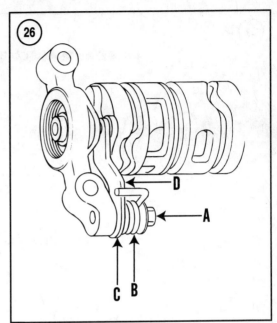

26

D
A
C   B

2. Install the detent follower as follows:
   a. Slide the spring sleeve (C, **Figure 26**) into the spring (B).
   b. Insert the pivot bolt (A, **Figure 26**) through the spring and sleeve.
   c. Correctly position the detent follower onto the bolt and place the spring end over the detent follower.
   d. Install the detent follower assembly onto the right side support and insert the spring's other end into the receptacle in the right side support. Screw the bolt into place and tighten it to the torque specification in **Table 3**.

3. On the left side, perform the following:
   a. Position the bearing with the manufacturer's numbers facing out. Install the bearing into the support block.
   b. Position the *new* snap ring (C, **Figure 25**) so the larger tab will be on the right side when looking at the end of the support block. Install the snap ring.
   c. Make sure the snap ring is correctly seated in the groove.
   d. Slide the left side support block (B, **Figure 25**) onto the shifter cam.
   e. Install a *new* small retaining ring (A, **Figure 25**) onto the shifter cam.
   f. Make sure the small retaining ring is correctly seated in the groove.

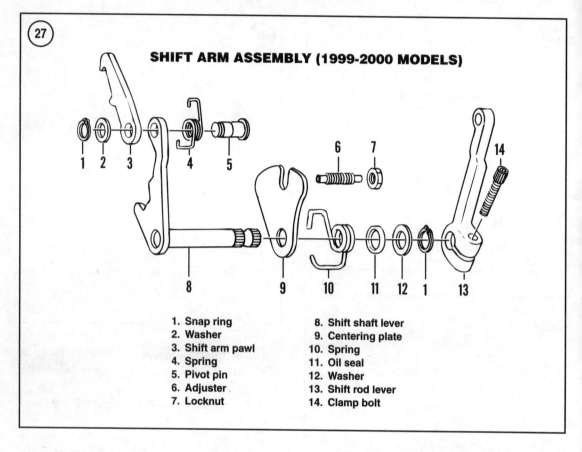

SHIFT ARM ASSEMBLY (1999-2000 MODELS)

1. Snap ring
2. Washer
3. Shift arm pawl
4. Spring
5. Pivot pin
6. Adjuster
7. Locknut
8. Shift shaft lever
9. Centering plate
10. Spring
11. Oil seal
12. Washer
13. Shift rod lever
14. Clamp bolt

4. On the right side, perform the following:
   a. Position the bearing with the manufacturer's numbers facing out. Install the bearing into the support block.
   b. Position the *new* snap ring (B, **Figure 24**) with the beveled side facing out when looking at the end of the support block. Install the snap ring.
   c. Make sure the snap ring is correctly seated in the groove.
   d. Slide the right side support block (A, **Figure 24**) onto the shifter cam.

SHIFT ARM ASSEMBLY

Removal/Disassembly

Refer to **Figure 27** or **Figure 28**.

1. Remove the transmission side door assembly as described in this chapter.
2. Make an alignment mark on the shift rod lever and on the shift arm shaft.

3. Remove the clamp bolt and remove the shift rod lever from the shift shaft lever.
4. On 1999-2000 models, loosen the locknut and back the adjuster out until it clears the centering plate.
5. Remove the snap ring and washer from the shift lever shaft.
6A. On 1999-2000 models, perform the following:
   a. Withdraw the shift shaft lever, centering plate and spring from the inner surface of the transmission case.
   b. Remove the centering plate and spring from the shift shaft lever.
6B. On 2001-on models, withdraw the shift shaft lever, sleeve and spring from the inner surface of the transmission case

NOTE
Proceed with Step 6 only if the components require replacement.

7A. On 1999-2000 models, if necessary, remove the snap ring and washer. Remove the shift cam pawl and spring from the shift shaft lever. The pivot

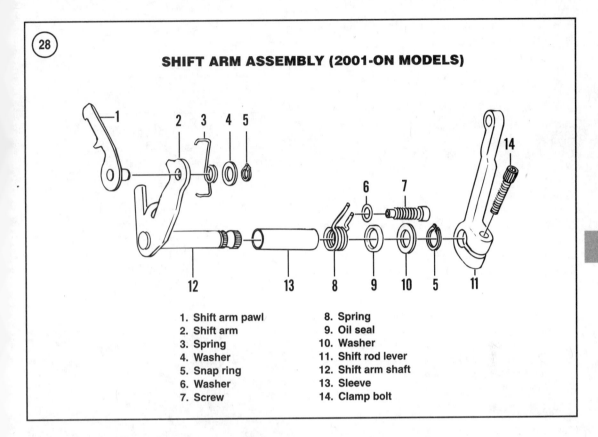

SHIFT ARM ASSEMBLY (2001-ON MODELS)

1. Shift arm pawl
2. Shift arm
3. Spring
4. Washer
5. Snap ring
6. Washer
7. Screw
8. Spring
9. Oil seal
10. Washer
11. Shift rod lever
12. Shift arm shaft
13. Sleeve
14. Clamp bolt

pin is pressed into the shift shaft lever. If removal is necessary, drive it out with a suitable size punch.

7B. On 2001-on models, if necessary, remove the snap ring and washer. Remove the shift cam pawl and spring from the shift shaft lever.

Inspection

1A. On 1999-2000 models, check the shift pawl and centering plate for wear. Replace the pawl if it is damaged. Replace the centering plate if its adjustment slot is elongated.

1B. On 2001-on models, check the shift pawl for wear. Replace the pawl if it is damaged.

2. Check the springs for wear or damage. Assemble the pawl and spring on the shift arm pin. If the spring will not hold the pawl on the cam, replace it.

3. Check the shift shaft lever for wear or damage. Check the end splines for wear or damage.

4. Check the shift rod lever for wear or damage. Check the internal splines for wear or damage.

Assembly/Installation

1A. On 1999-2000 models, install the shift cam pawl and spring onto the shift shaft lever pivot pin if they were disassembled. Secure the shaft lever pivot pin with the washer and a *new* snap ring.

1B. On 2001-on models, install the shift cam pawl and spring onto the shift shaft if they were disassembled. Secure the shift shaft with the washer and a *new* snap ring.

2. On 1999-2000 models, install the centering plate on the shift shaft lever and spring.

3. Install the shift shaft lever assembly into the transmission case.

4A. On 1999-2000 models, align the slot in the centering plate with the adjuster.

4B. On 2001-on models, align the spring with the screw.

5. Refer to the alignment marks made in Step 1 of *Removal/Disassembly* and install the shift rod lever onto the shift shaft lever. Push it on until the bolt hole aligns with the shaft lever groove.

6. Install the clamp bolt and tighten it to the specification in **Table 3**.

7. Install the transmission side door assembly as described in this chapter.

SHIFT FORKS

The shift forks can be serviced with the transmission installed in the frame by removing the transmission top cover.

Refer to **Figure 1** or **Figure 2**.

Removal

1. Remove the shifter cam as described in this chapter.
2. Remove the transmission side cover as described in this chapter.

> *NOTE*
> *Use a waterproof felt-tip pen or scribe to mark the installed position of each shift fork in the transmission (**Figure 29**). All three shift forks are unique and must be reinstalled in the correct position.*

3. Slide the shift shaft (A, **Figure 30**) out of the transmission case and remove the shift forks (**Figure 31**) from the transmission case.

Inspection

1. Inspect each shift fork (**Figure 32**) for excessive wear or damage. Replace worn or damaged shift forks as required.
2. Measure the thickness of each shift fork finger (A, **Figure 33**) where it contacts the sliding gear groove (**Figure 34**). Replace any shift fork with a finger thickness worn to the specification in **Table 2**.
3. Check the shift forks for arc-shaped wear or burn marks (B, **Figure 33**). Replace damaged shift forks.
4. Roll the shift fork shaft on a flat surface and check for bends. Replace the shaft if it is bent.
5. Install each shift fork on the shift shaft. The shift forks must slide smoothly with no binding or roughness.

Assembly

Refer to **Figure 35** to identify the transmission gears.

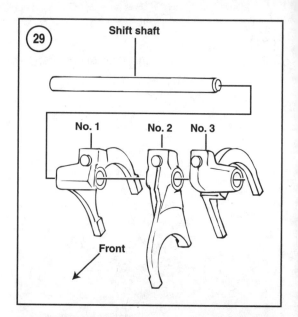

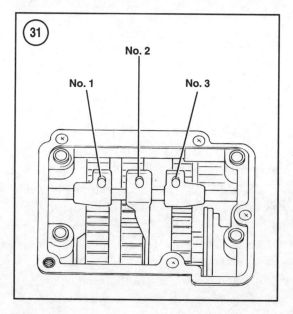

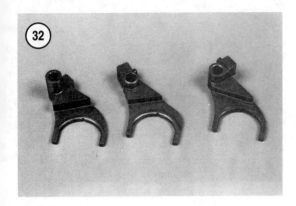

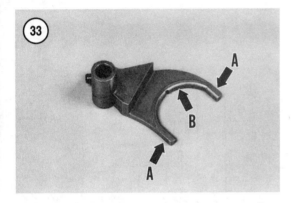

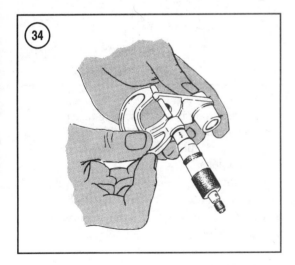

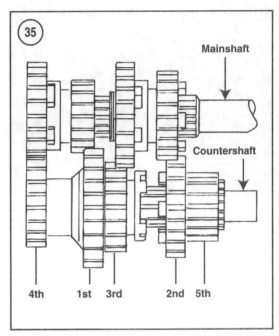

c. Install the No. 3 shift fork into the mainshaft second gear groove.

3. Insert the shift shaft (A, **Figure 30**) through each of the three shift forks and into the transmission case.

4. Install the transmission side door as described in this chapter.

5. Make sure the shift forks move smoothly when shifting the gears by hand.

6. Install the shifter cam as described in this chapter.

TRANSMISSION SIDE DOOR AND TRANSMISSION SHAFT ASSEMBLIES

The transmission side door and transmission shaft assemblies can be serviced with the transmission installed in the frame.

The following special tools are used during disassembly and assembly:

1. Mainshaft bearing race puller and installation tool (JIMS part No. 34902-84).

2. Five-speed door puller (JIMS part No. 2283).

3. Transmission door bearing remover and installer (JIMS part No. 1078).

4. Transmission shaft installers (JIMS part No. 2189).

1. Coat all bearing and sliding surfaces with assembly oil.

2. To install the shift forks and shaft (**Figure 29**), perform the following:

   a. Insert the No. 1 shift fork into the mainshaft first gear groove.

   b. Install the No. 2 shift fork into the countershaft third gear groove.

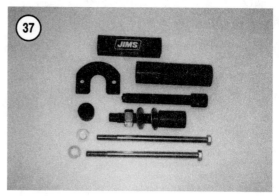

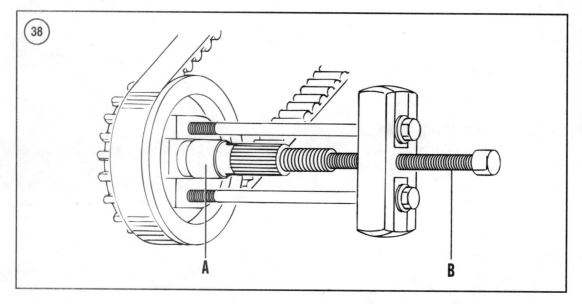

A   B

Removal

Remove the transmission and side door assembly as follows:

1. Remove the exhaust system as described in Chapter Seven.

2. Drain the transmission oil as described in Chapter Three.

3. Remove the primary chaincase cover as described in Chapter Five.

4. Remove the clutch release cover and clutch assembly as described in Chapter Five.

5. Remove the primary chaincase housing as described in Chapter Five.

6. Remove the shift forks as described in this chapter.

7. Remove the bearing inner race (**Figure 36**) from the mainshaft as follows:

a. Attach the mainshaft bearing race puller and installation tool (**Figure 37**) to the inner bearing race following the manufacturer's instructions.

b. Tighten the puller bolt and withdraw the inner race from the mainshaft (**Figure 38**).

8. Remove the pushrod assembly (B, **Figure 30**).

9. Turn the transmission by hand and shift the transmission into two different gears to keep the gears from turning.

NOTE
*The mainshaft and countershaft have left-hand threads. Turn the nuts **clockwise** to loosen them.*

10. If the transmission gear assemblies are going to be removed from the side door, loosen, but do not remove, the countershaft and mainshaft locknuts.

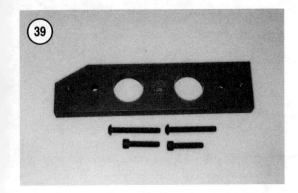

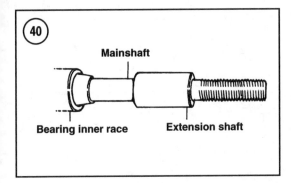

Mainshaft

Bearing inner race   Extension shaft

11. If the main drive gear is going to be removed, remove the drive sprocket as described under *Drive Sprocket* in Chapter Nine.

12. Remove the bolts securing the transmission side door to the transmission case.

CAUTION
When removing the transmission side door in Step 13, do not tap the transmission shafts from the opposite side. This will damage the side door bearings.

13. Tap the transmission side door to loosen its seal with the transmission case.

14. Install the five-speed door puller (**Figure 39**) onto the door following the manufacturer's instructions. Tighten the outside screws one-half turn at a time alternating from side-to-side until the door releases from the transmission case. Remove the special tool.

15. Slowly withdraw the transmission side door and the transmission gear assemblies from the transmission case.

16. Remove the transmission side door gasket. Do not lose the locating pins.

17. If necessary, service the side door and transmission assembly as described in this chapter.

Installation

1. If the main drive gear was removed, install it as described in this chapter.

2. Remove all gasket residue from the side door and transmission case mating surfaces.

3. Install a *new* gasket onto the transmission case. If the locating pins were removed, install them.

4. Install the side door and transmission assembly into the transmission case. Make sure the side door fits flush against the transmission case.

5. Install the transmission side door 5/16 in. and 1/4 in. bolts finger-tight. Tighten the 5/16 in. bolts to the specifications in **Table 3**. Then tighten the 1/4 in. bolts to the specification in **Table 3**.

6. Turn the transmission by hand and shift the transmission into two different gears to keep the gears from turning.

7. Install the bearing inner race (**Figure 36**) onto the mainshaft as follows:

   a. The bearing inner race is 0.950-1.000 in. (24.13-25.40 mm) long. When installing a *new* race, measure it to confirm its length. Race length determines its installation position.

   b. Use the same special tool set-up used for bearing inner race removal.

   c. Apply clean oil to the transmission shaft bearing surface, shaft threads and inner surface of the inner race.

   d. Position the bearing inner race with the chamfered end going on first and slide it onto the mainshaft (**Figure 40**).

   e. Install the extension shaft onto the mainshaft.

   f. Place the pusher tube, and the two flat washers and nut over the extension shaft.

NOTE
*The mainshaft and countershaft nut have left-hand threads. Turn the nut **counterclockwise** to tighten it in substep g.*

CAUTION
Install the inner bearing race to the dimension in substep g. This aligns the race with the bearing outer race installed in the primary chaincase. Installing the wrong race or installing it incorrectly will damage the bearing and race assembly.

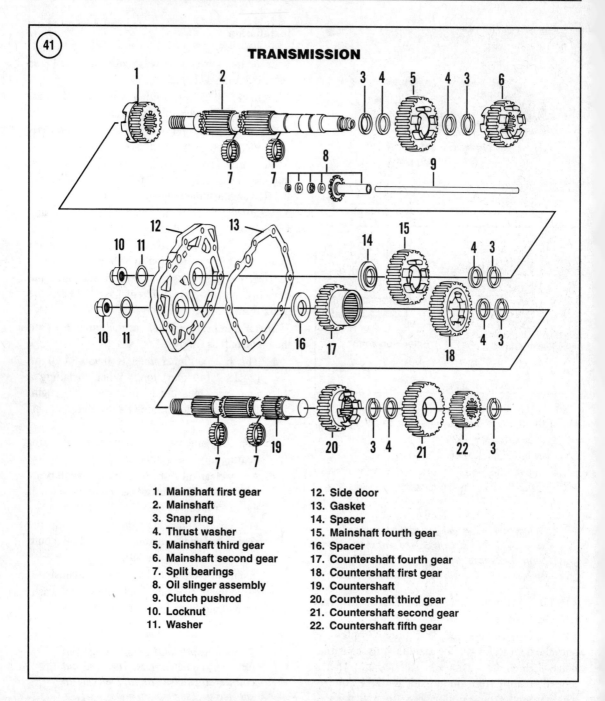

TRANSMISSION

1. Mainshaft first gear
2. Mainshaft
3. Snap ring
4. Thrust washer
5. Mainshaft third gear
6. Mainshaft second gear
7. Split bearings
8. Oil slinger assembly
9. Clutch pushrod
10. Locknut
11. Washer

12. Side door
13. Gasket
14. Spacer
15. Mainshaft fourth gear
16. Spacer
17. Countershaft fourth gear
18. Countershaft first gear
19. Countershaft
20. Countershaft third gear
21. Countershaft second gear
22. Countershaft fifth gear

g. Hold the extension shaft and tighten the nut to press the bearing inner race onto the mainshaft. Install the race so its inside edge is 0.100-0.150 in. (2.540-3.810 mm.) away from the main drive gear.

h. Remove the special tools.

8. Install the pushrod assembly (B, **Figure 30**).

9. Install the shift forks as described in this chapter.

10. Install the primary chaincase housing as described in Chapter Five.

11. Install the clutch assembly and clutch release cover as described in Chapter Five.

12. Install the primary chaincase cover as described in Chapter Five.

13. Install the drain plug and refill the transmission oil as described in Chapter Three.

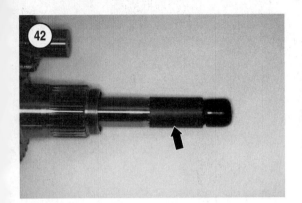

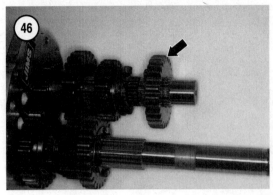

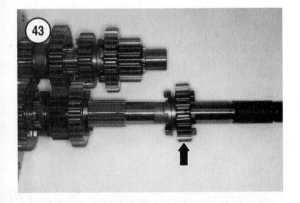

14. Install the exhaust system as described in Chapter Seven.

15. Test-ride the motorcycle slowly and check for proper transmission operation.

TRANSMISSION SHAFTS

This section describes service to the side door and both transmission shaft assemblies.

Disassembly

The transmission shaft assemblies (**Figure 41**) must be partially disassembled prior to removing both shafts from the side door. Do not try to remove the shafts with all of the gears in place.

The snap rings are difficult to loosen and remove even with high quality snap ring pliers. Heavy-duty retaining ring pliers (H-D part No. J-5586), or an equivalent, is recommended for this procedure.

Store all of the transmission gears, snap rings, washers and split bearings in the order of removal.

1. Remove the transmission side door and transmission shaft assemblies as described in this chapter.

2. Protect the splines and threads on the mainshaft with tape or a plastic sleeve (**Figure 42**).

3. Remove the mainshaft second gear (**Figure 43**).

4. Remove the snap ring (**Figure 44**) from the countershaft.

5. Remove the countershaft fifth gear (**Figure 45**).

6. Remove the countershaft second gear (**Figure 46**).

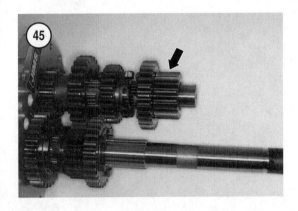

> *CAUTION*
> *Do not expand the split bearings any more than necessary to slide them off the shaft. The bearing carriers are plastic and will fracture if expanded too far.*

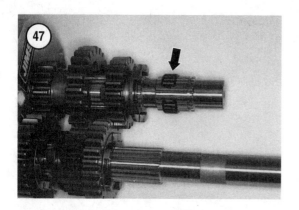

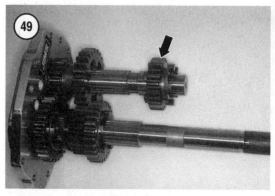

7. Remove the split bearing (**Figure 47**) from the countershaft.

8. Slide off the washer and remove the snap ring (**Figure 48**) from the countershaft.

9. Remove the countershaft third gear (**Figure 49**).

> *NOTE*
> *The snap ring in Step 10 must be released and moved in order to gain access to the snap ring on the other side of the third gear.*

10. Using retaining ring pliers, release the snap ring (**Figure 50**) behind the mainshaft third gear. Slide the snap ring away from the third gear.

11. Slide the third gear toward the side door and remove the snap ring (**Figure 51**) and washer.

12. Remove the mainshaft third gear (**Figure 52**).

13. Remove the washer and snap ring (**Figure 53**).

14. Remove the split bearing (**Figure 54**) from the mainshaft.

15. Place a brass or aluminum washer (**Figure 55**) between the countershaft fourth gear and the mainshaft fourth gear. This locks both transmission shafts from rotation.

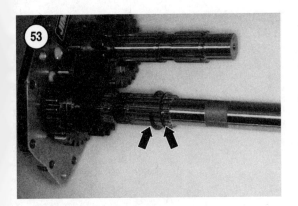

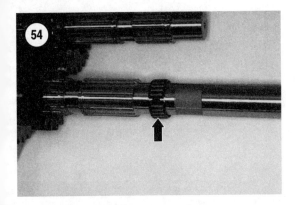

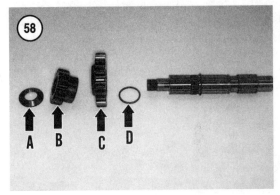

6

16. Loosen and remove the locknuts and washers (**Figure 56**) securing the shaft assemblies to the side door. Remove the brass or aluminum washer. New locknuts must be installed during assembly.

17. Press the countershaft out of its side door bearing as follows:

    a. Support the countershaft first gear in a press with a tube (A, **Figure 57**) so the countershaft can be pressed out without interference. Center the countershaft under the press ram.

    b. Place a mandrel (B, **Figure 57**) on top of the countershaft and press the countershaft out of the side door.

18. Remove the spacer (A, **Figure 58**), fourth gear (B), first gear (C) and washer (D) from the countershaft.

19. Remove the split bearing (A, **Figure 59**) from the countershaft.

20. If necessary, remove the snap ring (B, **Figure 59**) from the countershaft.

21. Remove the first gear (**Figure 60**) from the mainshaft.

22. Remove the snap ring and washer (A, **Figure 61**) from the mainshaft.

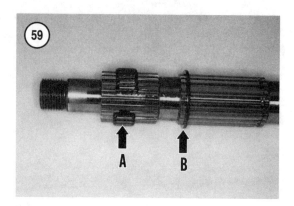

23. Press the mainshaft out of its side door bearing as follows:

   a. Support the mainshaft fourth gear on a tube (A, **Figure 62**) in a press so the mainshaft can be pressed out without interference. Center the mainshaft under the press ram.

   b. Place a mandrel (B, **Figure 62**) on top of the mainshaft and press the mainshaft out of the side door.

24. Remove the fourth gear and spacer (B, **Figure 61**) from the mainshaft.

25. Inspect all parts as described in this section.

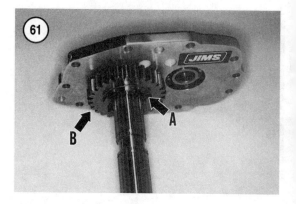

Inspection

Maintain the alignment of the transmission components when cleaning and inspecting the individual parts in the following section. To prevent intermixing parts, work on only one shaft at a time.

Refer to **Table 2** and inspect the service clearance and end play of the indicated gears and shafts. Replace parts that are excessively worn or damaged as described in this section.

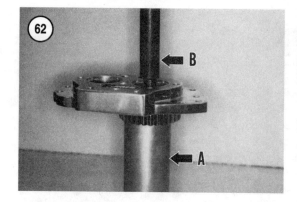

CAUTION
Do not clean the split bearings in solvent. Removing all traces of solvent from the bearing plastic retainers is difficult. Flush the bearings clean with new transmission oil.

1. Clean and dry the shaft assembly.

2. Inspect the mainshaft and countershaft for:

   a. Worn or damages splines (A, **Figure 63**).

   b. Excessively worn or damaged bearing surfaces.

   c. Cracked or rounded-off snap ring grooves (B, **Figure 63**).

   d. Worn or damaged threads (C, **Figure 63**).

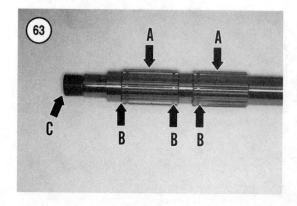

3. Check each gear for excessive wear, burrs, pitting, or chipped or missing teeth. Check the inner splines (**Figure 64**) on sliding gears and the bore on stationary gears for excessive wear or damage.

4. Check the gear bushings (**Figure 65**) for wear, cracks or other damage.

5. To check stationary gears for wear, install them in their original operating positions. If necessary, use the old snap rings to secure them in place. Then spin the gear by hand. The gear should turn smoothly. A rough turning gear indicates heat damage. Check for a dark blue color or galling on the operating surfaces. Rocking indicates excessive wear to the gear and/or shaft.

6. To check the sliding gears, install them in their original operating positions. The gear should slide back and fourth without any binding or excessive play.

7. Check the shift fork slot (**Figure 66**) for wear or damage.

8. Check the dogs on the gears for excessive wear, rounding, cracks or other damage. Refer to **Figure 67**. When wear is noticeable, make sure it is consistent on each gear dog. If one dog is worn more than the others, the others will be overstressed during operation and will eventually crack and fail. Check engaging gears as described in Step 10.

9. Check each gear dog slot for cracks, rounding and other damage. Check engaging gears as described in Step 10.

10. Check engaging gears by installing the two gears on their respective shafts and in their original operating position. Mesh the gears together. Twist one gear against the other and check the dog engagement. Then reverse the thrust load to check the other operating position. Make sure the engagement in both directions is positive and there is no slippage. Make sure there is equal engagement across all of the engagement dogs.

> *NOTE*
> *If there is excessive or uneven wear to the gear engagement dogs, check the shift forks carefully for bends and other damage. Refer to **Shift Assembly** in this chapter.*

> *NOTE*
> *Replace defective gears and their mating gears, though the mating gears may not show as much wear or damage.*

11. Check the spacers (**Figure 68**) for wear or damage.

12. Check the split bearings (**Figure 69**) for excessive wear or damage.

13. Replace all of the snap rings during reassembly. Check the washers for burn marks, scoring or cracks. Replace as necessary.

Side Door Bearings Inspection and Replacement

The side door bearings (**Figure 70**) are pressed into place and secured with a snap ring. They can be removed and installed with a transmission door bearing remover and installer (JIMS part No. 1078) (**Figure 71**). If this special tool set is not available, a press is required.

1. Clean the side door and bearings in solvent, and dry them with compressed air.

2. Turn each bearing inner race (**Figure 72**) by hand. The bearings must turn smoothly. If they need to be replaced, continue to Step 3.

3. Remove both snap rings (**Figure 73**) from the outer surface of the side door.

4A. To remove the bearings with the special tool set, follow the manufacturer's instructions:

4B. Remove the bearings with a press as follows:

a. Support the side door on the press bed with the outer surface facing up.

b. Use a driver or socket to press the bearing out of the backside of the side door.

c. Repeat substeps b for the opposite bearing.

5. Clean the side door in solvent and dry it thoroughly.

6. Inspect the bearing bores in the side cover for cracks or other damage. Replace the side door if it is damaged.

> *NOTE*
> *Both side door bearings have the same part number.*

7A. To install the bearing with the special tool set, follow the manufacturer's instructions.

7B. Install the bearing with a press as follows:

a. Support the side door in a press with the backside facing up.

b. Install bearings with their manufacturer's marks facing out.

c. Use a driver that matches the bearing outer race. Press the bearing into the side door until it bottoms.

d. Repeat substeps b and c for the opposite bearing.

8. Position the beveled snap ring with the sharp side facing toward the bearing outer race and install the snap ring. Make sure the snap ring is correctly seated in the side door groove (**Figure 73**).

Assembly

Refer to **Figure 74**.

> *CAUTION*
> *Install **new** snap rings at every location to ensure proper gear alignment and engagement. Never reinstall a snap ring that has been removed since it is distorted and weakened, and it may fail. Make sure each **new** snap ring is correctly seated in its respective shaft groove.*

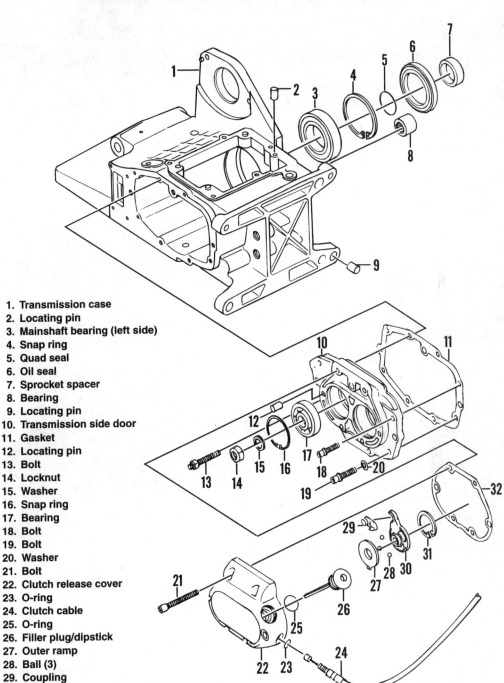

TRANSMISSION CASE BEARINGS AND COVERS

1. Transmission case
2. Locating pin
3. Mainshaft bearing (left side)
4. Snap ring
5. Quad seal
6. Oil seal
7. Sprocket spacer
8. Bearing
9. Locating pin
10. Transmission side door
11. Gasket
12. Locating pin
13. Bolt
14. Locknut
15. Washer
16. Snap ring
17. Bearing
18. Bolt
19. Bolt
20. Washer
21. Bolt
22. Clutch release cover
23. O-ring
24. Clutch cable
25. O-ring
26. Filler plug/dipstick
27. Outer ramp
28. Ball (3)
29. Coupling
30. Inner ramp
31. Snap ring
32. Gasket

1. Apply a light coat of clean transmission oil to all mating gear surfaces and to all split bearing halves before assembly.

2. If removed, install the side door bearings as described in this chapter.

3. Install the following onto the mainshaft:

    a. If the snap ring was removed, install a *new* snap ring (**Figure 75**).

    b. Position the first gear with the shift dog side going on last and install the first gear (**Figure 76**).

    c. Install the snap ring (A, **Figure 77**) and washer (B).

    d. Install the split bearing (**Figure 78**).

    e. Position the fourth gear with the shift dog side going on first and install the fourth gear (**Figure 79**).

    f. Position the spacer with the beveled side facing out (**Figure 80**) and install the spacer.

4. Install the following onto the countershaft:

    a. If the snap ring was removed, install a *new* snap ring (A, **Figure 81**).

    b. Install the washer (B, **Figure 81**) and push it against the snap ring.

    c. Install the split bearing (**Figure 82**).

    d. Position the first gear with the shoulder side (**Figure 83**) going on last and install the first gear onto the split bearing (**Figure 84**).

    e. Position the fourth gear with the wide shoulder (**Figure 85**) going on first and install the fourth gear.

    f. Position the spacer with the beveled side facing out (**Figure 86**) and install the spacer.

5. Apply transmission oil to the inner race of both bearings and to the shoulder of both shaft assemblies. Also apply transmission oil to the inner threads and ends of the special tools used in Step 8.

6. Position the countershaft (A, **Figure 87**) on the left side of the side door. Position the mainshaft (B, **Figure 87**) on the right side of the side door.

7. Mesh the two shaft assemblies together and start them into the side door bearings (**Figure 88**).

8. Attach the shaft installers (JIMS part No. 2189) onto the ends of both shafts.

9. Tighten the shaft installers (**Figure 89**), alternating between both shafts, until both shaft shoulders bottom on the inner race of the side door bearings (**Figure 90**).

10. Unscrew and remove the special tools.

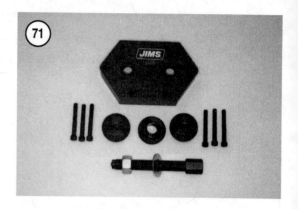

CAUTION
*Always install **new** locknuts. If an old locknut is reinstalled, it may work loose and cause transmission damage.*

11. Install the spacers (A, **Figure 91**) and *new* locknuts (B).

12. Start the *new* locknuts by hand until the locking portion of the nut touches the end of the transmission shaft.

13. Place a brass or aluminum washer between the countershaft fourth gear and the mainshaft fourth gear. This will lock both transmission shafts.

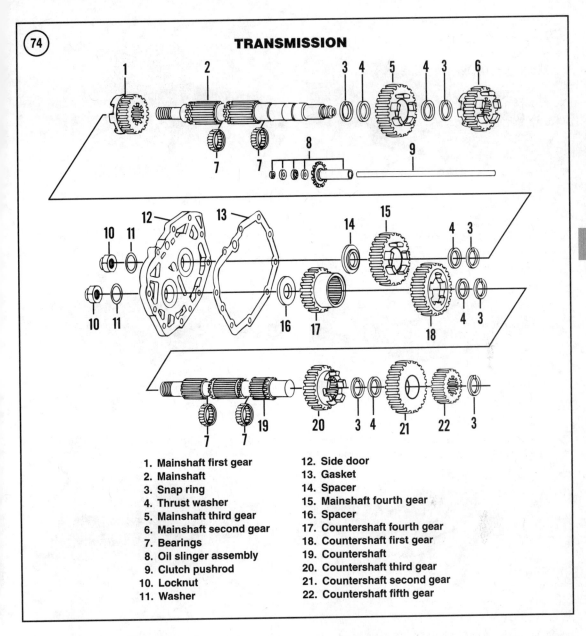

TRANSMISSION

1. Mainshaft first gear
2. Mainshaft
3. Snap ring
4. Thrust washer
5. Mainshaft third gear
6. Mainshaft second gear
7. Bearings
8. Oil slinger assembly
9. Clutch pushrod
10. Locknut
11. Washer

12. Side door
13. Gasket
14. Spacer
15. Mainshaft fourth gear
16. Spacer
17. Countershaft fourth gear
18. Countershaft first gear
19. Countershaft
20. Countershaft third gear
21. Countershaft second gear
22. Countershaft fifth gear

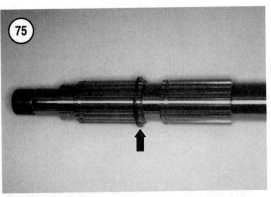

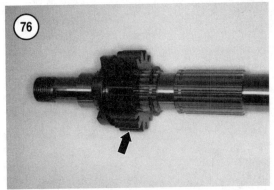

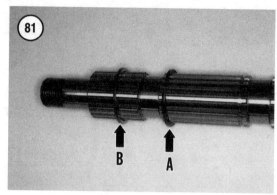

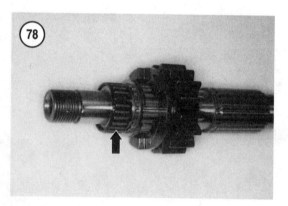

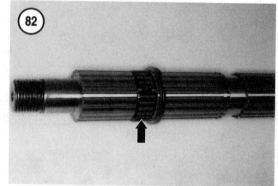

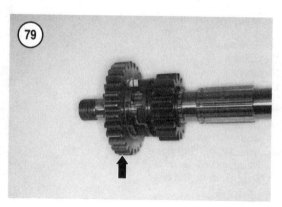

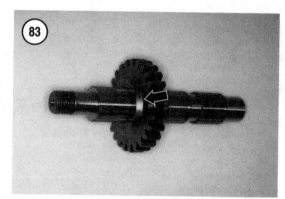

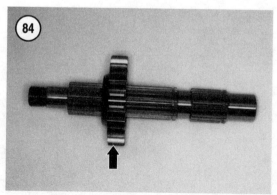

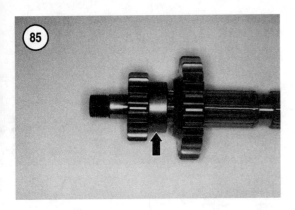

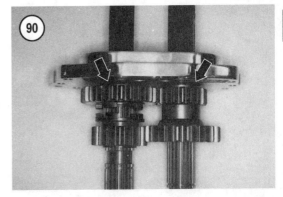

6

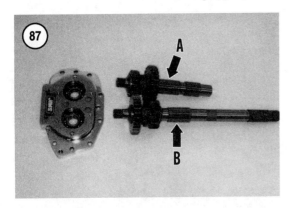

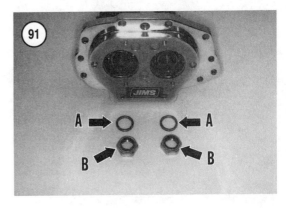

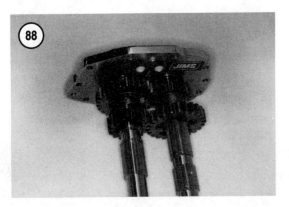

14. Tighten the locknuts (**Figure 92**) to the torque specification in **Table 3**.

15. Install the following onto the mainshaft:

a. Install the split bearing (**Figure 93**).

b. Move the snap ring (A, **Figure 94**) installed in Step 3 out of the groove and toward the first gear.

c. Install the washer (B, **Figure 94**) and slide it against the snap ring (A, **Figure 95**).

d. Position third gear with the shift dogs side (B, **Figure 95**) going on last. Install the third gear onto the split bearing (**Figure 96**).

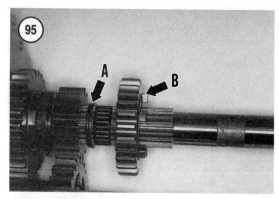

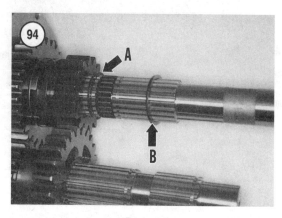

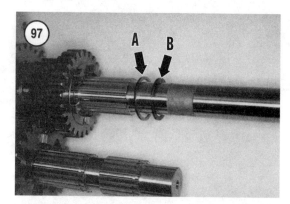

e. Install the washer (A, **Figure 97**) and snap ring (B). Make sure the snap ring is correctly seated in the mainshaft groove.

f. Move third gear away from the first gear, and up against the washer and snap ring installed in sub-step e.

g. Reposition the washer and snap ring (A, **Figure 94**) behind third gear. Make sure the snap ring is correctly seated in the mainshaft goove.

16. Install the following onto the countershaft:

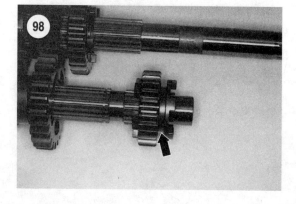

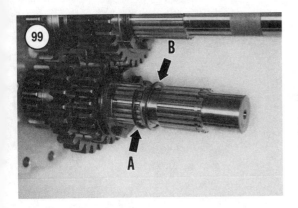

6

a. Position the third gear with the shift fork groove (**Figure 98**) side going on last and install the third gear.

b. Install the snap ring (A, **Figure 99**) and washer (B).

c. Install the split bearing (**Figure 100**).

d. Position the second gear with the shift dog side (**Figure 101**) going on first. Install the second gear onto the split bearing (**Figure 102**).

17. On the mainshaft, position the second gear with the shift fork groove (**Figure 103**) side going on first and install the second gear (**Figure 104**).

18. On the countershaft, install the fifth gear (**Figure 105**), then install the snap ring (**Figure 106**).

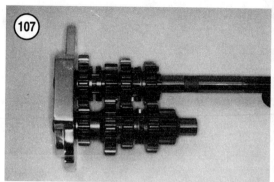

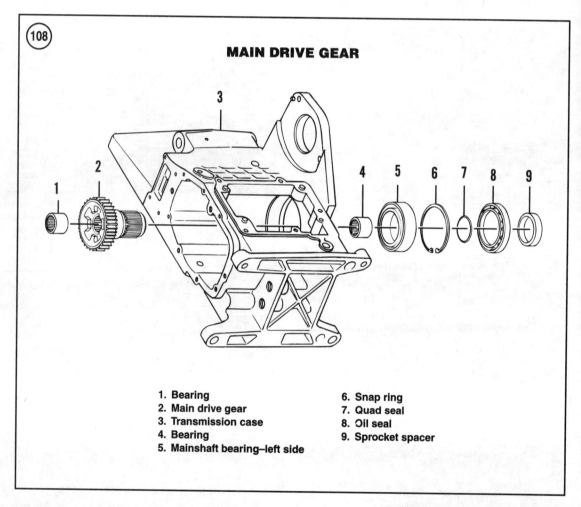

MAIN DRIVE GEAR

1. Bearing
2. Main drive gear
3. Transmission case
4. Bearing
5. Mainshaft bearing–left side
6. Snap ring
7. Quad seal
8. Oil seal
9. Sprocket spacer

Make sure the snap ring is correctly seated in the counter- shaft groove.

19. Refer to **Figure 107** for correct placement of all gears. Also make sure the gears mesh properly to the adjoining gear where applicable. Make sure the gears are correctly assembled before installing the shaft assemblies into the transmission case.

MAIN DRIVE GEAR

The main drive gear (**Figure 108**) and bearing assembly are pressed into the transmission case. If the transmission case is installed in the frame, a special transmission main drive gear tool set (JIMS part No. 35316-80) (**Figure 109**) is required to remove

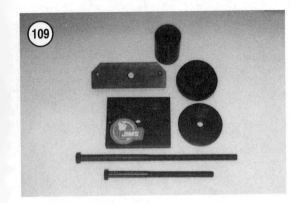

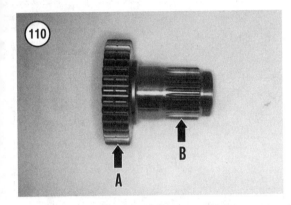

the main drive gear. If the transmission has been removed, use a press to remove and install the main drive gear.

Whenever the main drive gear is removed, the main drive gear bearing must be replaced at the same time.

Removal

1. Remove the transmission shaft assemblies from the transmission case as described in this chapter.
2. Remove the spacer from the main drive gear oil seal.
3. Remove the snap ring behind the bearing.

> *NOTE*
> *If the main drive gear will not loosen from the bearing in Step 4 due to corrosion, remove the special tools and heat the bearing with a heat gun.*

4. Assemble the special tool set onto the main drive gear following the manufacturer's instructions. Then tighten the puller nut slowly to pull the main drive gear from the bearing in the transmission case.
5. Remove the main drive gear bearing from the transmission case as described in this section.

Inspection

1. Clean the main drive gear in solvent and dry it with compressed air, if available.
2. Check each gear tooth (A, **Figure 110**) for excessive wear, burrs, galling and pitting. Check for missing teeth.
3. Check the gear splines (B, **Figure 110**) for excessive wear, galling or other damage.
4. Inspect the two main drive gear needle bearings for excessive wear or damage. Refer to **Figure 111** and **Figure 112**. Insert the mainshaft into the main drive gear to check bearing wear. If necessary, replace the bearings as described in this section.

Needle Bearing Replacement

Both main drive gear needle bearings must be installed to the correct depth within the main drive gear. The correct depth is obtained with a main drive gear bearing tool (JIMS part No. 37842-91).

This tool also installs the oil seal. If this tool is not available, a press is required.

If the special tool is not available, measure the depth of both bearings before removing them.

Replace both main drive gear needle bearings as a set.

> *CAUTION*
> *Never reinstall a main drive gear needle bearing, as it is distorted during removal.*

1. Remove the oil seal (**Figure 113**) from the clutch side of the main drive gear.

2. If the special tool is not used, measure and record the depth of both bearings.

3. Support the main drive gear in a press and press out one needle bearing. Then turn the gear over and press out the opposite bearing.

4. Clean the gear and its bearing bore in solvent and dry them thoroughly.

5. Apply transmission oil to the bearing bore in the main drive gear and to the outer surface of both bearings.

> *NOTE*
> *Install both needle bearings with their manufacturer's name and size code facing out.*

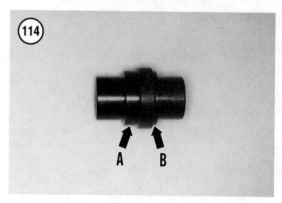

6A. Install the bearings with the special tool as follows:

  a. The special tool has two different length ends. The tool's long side (A, **Figure 114**) is for the clutch side of the main drive gear (**Figure 112**). The tool's short side (B, **Figure 114**) is for the transmission side of the main drive gear (**Figure 111**).

  b. Install the main drive gear in a press with the transmission end facing up. Align the new bearing with the main drive gear and insert the installation tool with the *short side facing down* (**Figure 115**) into the bearing. Operate the press until the tool's shoulder bottoms against the gear.

  c. Turn the main drive gear over so the inner end faces up. Align the *new* bearing with the main drive gear and insert the installation tool with the *long side facing down* into the bearing. Operate the press until the tool's shoulder bottoms against the gear.

6B. If the bearings are being installed without the installation tool, use a suitable mandrel to press in the bearing to the depth recorded in Step 2.

7. Install a *new* oil seal (**Figure 113**) into the clutch side of the main drive gear.

Mainshaft Bearing Replacement

The mainshaft bearing (5, **Figure 108**) is pressed into the transmission case. If the transmission case is installed in the frame, a transmission main bear-

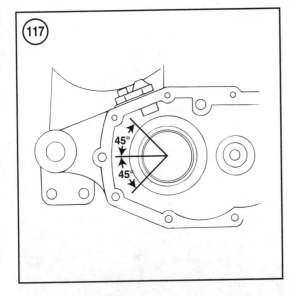

3. Clean the bearing bore and dry it with compressed air. Check the bore for nicks or burrs. Check the snap ring groove for damage.

NOTE
Install the bearing into the transmission case with the bearing manufacturer's name and size code facing out.

4. Apply transmission oil to the bearing bore in the transmission case and to the outer surface of the bearing. Also apply oil to the nut and threaded shaft of the installer tool.

5. Install the bearing onto the installation tool and assemble the installation tool following the manufacturer's instructions.

6. Slowly tighten the puller nut to pull the bearing into the transmission case. Continue until the bearing bottoms in the case.

7. Disassemble and remove the installation tool.

Mainshaft Bearing Installation

1. Remove the mainshaft bearing and oil seal as described in the previous section.

2. Install a *new* snap ring with the flat side facing the bearing.

3. Position the snap ring with the open end facing the rear of the transmission and within a 45° angle to horizontal (**Figure 117**). Make sure it is fully seated in the snap ring groove.

4. Install the *new* oil seal into the case so its closed side faces out.

5. Apply transmission oil to the bearing bore and to the outer surface of the main drive gear. Also apply oil to the nut and threaded shaft of the installer tool.

6. Insert the main drive gear into the mainshaft bearing as far as it will go. Hold it in place and assemble the special tool onto the mainshaft and transmission case following the manufacturer's instructions.

7. Slowly tighten the puller nut to pull the main drive gear into the bearing in the transmission case. Continue until the gear bottoms in the bearings inner race.

8. Disassemble and remove the installation tool.

9. Install the spacer into the main drive gear oil seal.

10. Install the transmission shaft assemblies from the transmission case as described in this chapter.

ing remover set (JIMS part No. 1720) (**Figure 116**), or equivalent, is required to remove the bearing. If the transmission has been removed, use a press to remove the bearing.

Whenever the main drive gear is removed, the mainshaft bearing is damaged and must be replaced at the same time.

CAUTION
Failure to use the correct tools to install the bearing will cause premature failure of the bearing and related parts.

1. Remove the main drive gear from the transmission case as described in this chapter.

2. Assemble the special tool set onto the mainshaft bearing following the manufacturer's instructions. Then tighten the bolt and nut slowly to pull the bearing from the transmission case.

TRANSMISSION CLUTCH RELEASE COVER ASSEMBLY

Removal

1. Remove the exhaust system as described in Chapter Seven.

2. Drain the transmission oil as described in Chapter Three.

> *NOTE*
> *If the cover is difficult to remove, apply the clutch lever after the mounting bolts have been removed. This will usually loosen the cover.*

3. Remove the release cover mounting bolts and remove the cover. Remove the gasket. Do not lose the locating dowels.

4. At the clutch cable in-line adjuster, perform the following:

   a. Slide the rubber boot (**Figure 118**) off the adjuster.

   b. Loosen the adjuster locknut and turn the adjuster to provide as much slack in the cable as possible.

Disassembly

Refer to **Figure 119**.

> *NOTE*
> *Before removing the snap ring in Step 1, note the position of the snap ring opening. The snap ring must be reinstalled with its opening in the same position.*

1. Remove the snap ring (A, **Figure 120**) from the groove in the release cover.

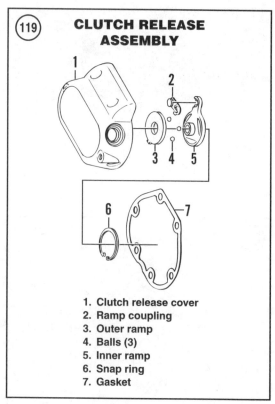

CLUTCH RELEASE ASSEMBLY

1. Clutch release cover
2. Ramp coupling
3. Outer ramp
4. Balls (3)
5. Inner ramp
6. Snap ring
7. Gasket

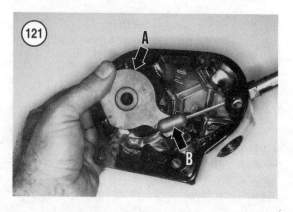

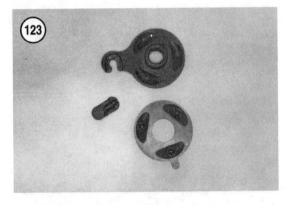

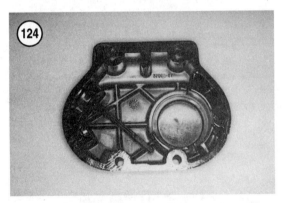

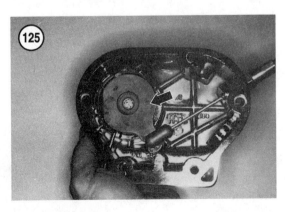

2. Lift the inner ramp (A, **Figure 121**) out of the cover and disconnect it from the ramp coupling (B, **Figure 121**).
3. Remove the ramp coupling (A, **Figure 122**).
4. Remove the inner ramp and balls (B, **Figure 122**).
5. If necessary, remove the clutch cable (B, **Figure 120**) from the release cover.

Inspection

1. Clean the release cover and all components thoroughly in solvent and dry them with compressed air.
2. Check the release mechanism balls and ramp ball sockets (**Figure 123**) for cracks, deep scoring or excessive wear.
3. Check the release cover (**Figure 124**) for cracks or damage. Check the clutch cable threads and the coupling snap ring groove for damage. Check the ramp bore in the release cover for excessive wear, or lips or grooves that could catch the ramps and bind them sideways, causing improper clutch adjustment.
4. Replace the clutch cable O-ring if it is damaged.
5. Replace all worn or damaged parts.

Assembly

1. If removed, screw the clutch cable into the release cover. Do not tighten the cable fitting at this time.
2. Install the inner ramp and balls (B, **Figure 122**). Center a ball into each socket.
3. Install the ramp coupling onto the clutch cable as shown in A, **Figure 122**.
4. Connect the inner ramp (B, **Figure 121**) onto the ramp coupling (A).
5. Align the inner ramp socket with the balls and install the inner ramp as shown in **Figure 125**.
6. Install the snap ring into the release cover groove. Position the snap ring so its opening faces to the right of the outer ramp tang slot as shown in A, **Figure 120**. Make sure the snap ring is seated correctly in the groove.

Installation

1. If removed, install the locating dowels.
2. Install a *new* gasket.

3. Install the release cover and bolts. Tighten the bolts in a crisscross pattern to the torque specification in **Table 3**.

4. Refill the transmission with oil as described in Chapter Three.

5. Install the exhaust system as described in Chapter Seven.

6. Adjust the clutch as described in Chapter Three.

TRANSMISSION DRIVE SPROCKET

Removal/Installation

NOTE
The mainshaft bearing race does not need to be removed for the transmission drive sprocket to be removed.

1. Remove the primary chain case assembly as described in Chapter Five.

2. If necessary, install a sprocket locker tool (JIMS part No. 2260) (**Figure 126**) onto the transmission drive sprocket following the manufacturer's instructions.

3. Remove the Allen bolts and the lock plate (**Figure 127**).

4A. Shift the transmission into gear.

4B. If the drive belt is still in place, have an assistant apply the rear brake.

5. Use a countershaft sprocket nut wrench (JIMS part No. 946600-37A) to install the inner collar (**Figure 128**) onto the mainshaft.

CAUTION
*The sprocket nut has left-hand threads. Turn the tool **clockwise** to loosen it in Step 6.*

6. Install the wrench onto the nut (**Figure 129**) and turn it *clockwise* to loosen the nut.

7. Remove the special tools and the nut from the mainshaft.

8. Carefully remove the transmission drive sprocket from the mainshaft. Do not damage the bearing race.

9. Install by reversing these removal steps. Note the following:

   a. Use the same tool set up used during removal.

   b. Apply Loctite TB1360 or an equivalent to the nut and Allen bolts prior to installation.

   c. Position the nut with the flanged side facing the drive sprocket.

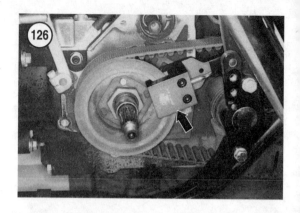

CAUTION
In substep d, do not tighten the nut past an additional 45° to align the lock plate bolt holes or the nut will be damaged.

   d. Tighten the nut *counterclockwise* to the specification in **Table 3**. Then tighten it an additional 30° until the lock plate holes are aligned.

TRANSMISSION CASE

Only remove the transmission case (**Figure 130**) if it requires replacement or to perform extensive frame repair or replace the frame. All internal components can be removed with the case in the frame.

Removal/Installation

1. Drain the transmission oil and primary chain case lubricant as described in Chapter Three.

2. Remove the exhaust system as described in Chapter Seven.

3. Remove the primary chaincase cover as described in Chapter Five.

4. Remove the clutch assembly as described in Chapter Five.

5. Remove the transmission side cover and clutch release assembly as described in this chapter.

6. Remove the primary chaincase housing as described in Chapter Five.

7. Remove the transmission drive sprocket as described in this chapter.

8. Remove the transmission shaft assemblies as described in this chapter.

9. Remove the external shift linkage from the transmission as described in this chapter.

10. Make an alignment mark on the shift rod lever and the end of the shift shaft.

11. Remove the clamp bolt (A, **Figure 131**) securing the shift rod lever (B).

12A. On 1999-2000 models, loosen the locknut (C, **Figure 131**) and back the adjusting screw (D) out until it clears the centering slot in the shift pawl assembly.

12B. On 2001-on models, perform the following:

a. Use a T50 Torx wrench to back the centering screw (A, **Figure 132**) out until it clears the centering slot in the shift pawl assembly.

b. Remove the snap ring (B, **Figure 132**) and flat washer (C) from the shift shaft (D).

13. Remove the starter motor as described in Chapter Eight.

14. Remove the rear wheel as described in Chapter Nine.

15. Remove the oil pan and baffle from the bottom of the transmission case as described in this chapter.

16. Remove the external components of the shift arm assembly as described in the following procedure.

17. Support the swing arm, then remove the swing arm pivot bolt as described in Chapter Eleven.

18. Disconnect the two oil hoses connecting the transmission to the crankcase.

19. Remove the four transmission case-to-engine mounting bolts (**Figure 133**). There are two bolts on each side.

20. Move the transmission case to the rear to clear the two lower locating dowels.

21. Move the transmission toward the right side and remove the transmission case from the frame.

22. Install the transmission case by reversing these removal steps. Note the following:

a. Make sure the two locating dowels are in place on the engine or transmission case (**Figure 134**).

b. Tighten the transmission mounting bolts in a crisscross pattern to the specification in **Table 3**.

OIL PAN

The oil pan mounts to the bottom of the transmission case (**Figure 130**). It can be removed with the transmission mounted in the frame.

Removal

1. Drain the engine oil as described in Chapter Three.

2. Drain the transmission oil as described in Chapter Three.

CAUTION
The dipstick will be damage if it is left
in place during oil pan removal.

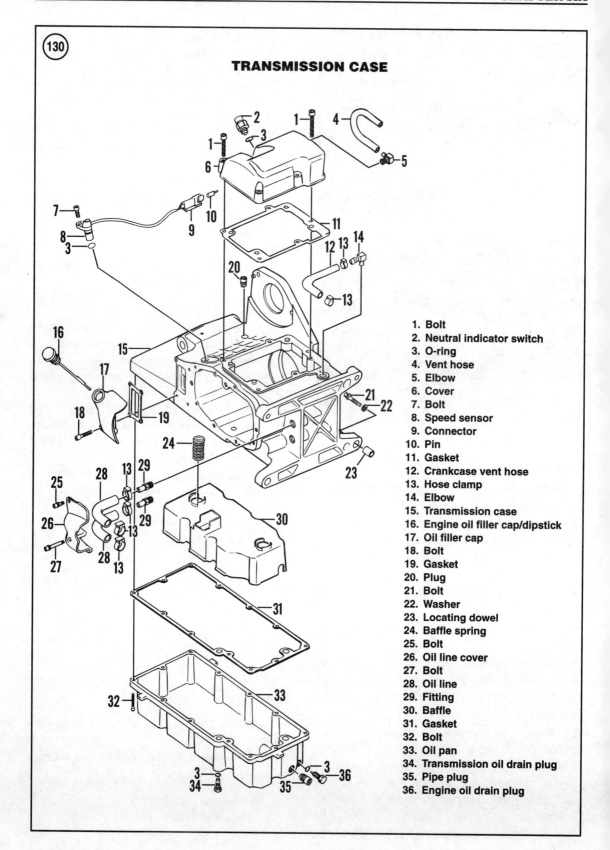

TRANSMISSION CASE

1. Bolt
2. Neutral indicator switch
3. O-ring
4. Vent hose
5. Elbow
6. Cover
7. Bolt
8. Speed sensor
9. Connector
10. Pin
11. Gasket
12. Crankcase vent hose
13. Hose clamp
14. Elbow
15. Transmission case
16. Engine oil filler cap/dipstick
17. Oil filler cap
18. Bolt
19. Gasket
20. Plug
21. Bolt
22. Washer
23. Locating dowel
24. Baffle spring
25. Bolt
26. Oil line cover
27. Bolt
28. Oil line
29. Fitting
30. Baffle
31. Gasket
32. Bolt
33. Oil pan
34. Transmission oil drain plug
35. Pipe plug
36. Engine oil drain plug

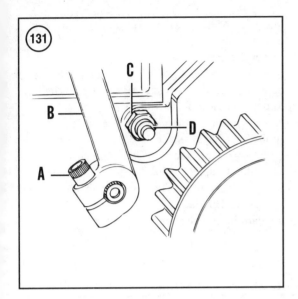

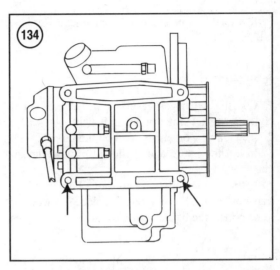

6

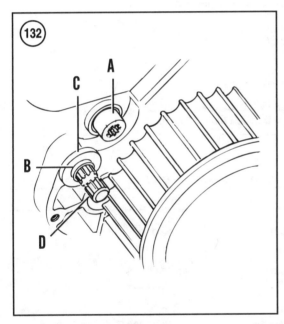

3. Remove the engine oil dipstick (**Figure 135**).

4. Remove the rear wheel as described in Chapter Nine.

NOTE
Access the hidden bolts through the holes in the frame cross member.

5. Remove the twelve Allen bolts securing the oil pan to the transmission case.

6. Lower and slide the oil pan toward the rear. Remove it from the transmission case and the frame. Do not lose the baffle spring.

7. Remove the gasket.

Inspection

1. Clean the oil tank, baffle and spring in solvent and dry them thoroughly.

2. Remove all old gasket residue from the oil tank and transmission case gasket surfaces.

3. Inspect the oil pan for cracks or damage. Replace it if necessary.

Installation

1. Coat the oil pan gasket surface with a thin coat of Hylomar gasket sealer or an equivalent.
2. Install a *new* oil tank gasket on the oil pan.
3. Install the baffle and baffle spring into the oil pan.
4. Partially install the oil pan to the bottom of the transmission case. Use a long flat blade screwdriver to compress the baffle spring as the oil pan moves into place. Make sure the baffle spring is not cocked or distorted as it will hold the oil pan away from the transmission gasket surface.
5. Hold the oil pan in place and install the twelve bolts. Tighten the bolts in a crisscross pattern to the torque specification in **Table 3**.
6. If necessary, replace the engine oil filter as described in Chapter Three.
7. Refill the oil pan with *new* engine oil as described in Chapter Three.
8. Refill the transmission with *new* oil as described in Chapter Three.
9. Start the engine and check for leaks.

Table 1 TRANSMISSION GENERAL SPECIFICATIONS

Transmission type	5-speed, constant mesh
Gear ratios	
First	3.21
Second	2.21
Third	1.57
Fourth	1.23
Fifth	1.00
Transmission fluid capacity	
Oil change	20-24 U.S. oz. (591-709 ml, 19-23 Imp. oz.)
Rebuild (dry)	24 U.S. oz. (709 ml, 23 Imp. oz.)

Table 2 TRANSMISSION SERVICE SPECIFICATIONS

Item	in.	mm
Countershaft		
Runout	0.000-0.003	0.00-0.08
Endplay	None	
First gear		
Clearance	0.003-0.0019	0.008-0.048
End play	0.005-0.0039	0.127-0.099
Second gear		
Clearance	0.003-0.0019	0.008-0.048
End play	0.005-0.044	0.127-1.118
Third gear		
Clearance	0.000-0.008	0.000-0.203
Fourth gear		
Clearance	0.000-0.008	0.000-0.203
End play	0.005-0.039	0.127-0.991
Fifth gear		
Clearance	0.000-0.008	0.000-0.203
End play	0.005-0.004	0.127-0.102
Mainshaft		
Runout	00-0.003	0.00-0.08
Endplay	None	
First gear		
Clearance	0.000-0.008	0.000-0.203
(continued)		

Table 2 TRANSMISSION SERVICE SPECIFICATIONS (continued)

Item	in.	mm
Mainshaft (cont.)		
Second gear		
Clearance	0.000-0.0800	0.000-2.032
Third gear		
Clearance	0.003-0.0019	0.008-0.048
End play	0.005-0.0420	0.127-1.067
Fourth gear		
Clearance	0.0003-0.0019	0.008-0.048
End play	0.005-0.0310	0.127-0.787
Main drive gear (fifth)		
Bearing fit in transmission case	0.0003-0.0017	0.0076-0.043
Fit in bearing		
Tight fit	0.0009	0.023
Loose fit	0.0001	0.0025
Fit on mainshaft	0.0001-0.0009	0.0025-0.023
End play	None	
Shifter cam assembly		
Shift pawl-to-shift cam pins	0.010	0.25
Right edge of middle cam groove		
to right support block distance	1.992-2.002	50.60-50.85
Shifter cam end play	0.001-0.004	0.025-0.10
Shifter forks		
Shifter fork-to-cam groove end play	0.0017-0.0019	0.043-0.048
Shifter fork-to-gear groove end play	0.0010-0.0011	0.025-0.0279
Shift fork finger thickness	0.165	4.19
Side door bearing		
Fit in side door	0.0014-0.0001	0.036-0.0025
Fit on countershaft		
Tight fit	0.0008	0.020
Loose fit	0.0001	0.0025
Fit on mainshaft		
Tight fit	0.0007	0.018
Loose fit	0.0001	0.0025

Table 3 TRANSMISSION TORQUE SPECIFICATIONS

Item	ft.-lb.	in.-lb.	N•m
Clutch cable fitting	–	30-60	3-7
Clutch release cover bolts	–	84-108	9-12
Oil pan bolts	–	84-108	9-12
Shift rod lever clamp bolt	18-22	–	24-30
Shift rod locknuts	20-24	–	27-32
Shift cam support block bolts	–	84-108	9-12
Shift cam detent follower bolt (2001-on)	–	84-108	9-12
Top cover screws	–	84-108	9-12
Transmission main and countershaft			
locknuts at side door	45-55	–	61-75
Transmission case door			
1/4 in. fasteners	–	84-108	9-12
5/16 in. fasteners	13-16	–	18-22
Transmission drain plug	14-21	–	19-28
Transmission mounting bolts	33-38	–	45-52
Transmission drive sprocket			
Mounting nut*	50	–	68
Lockplate bolts	–	84-108	9-12

*Tighten an additional 30°—not to exceed 45°.

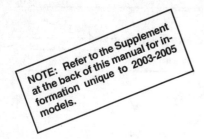

CHAPTER SEVEN

FUEL, EXHAUST AND EMISSION CONTROL SYSTEMS

This chapter includes procedures for all parts of the fuel, exhaust and emission control systems (California Models). Electronic fuel injection (EFI) models are also covered. Specifications and jet sizes are in **Tables 1-3** at the end of the chapter.

> *WARNING*
> *Gasoline is carcinogenic and extremely flammable, and must be handled carefully. Wear latex gloves to avoid skin contact. If gasoline does contact skin, immediately and thoroughly wash the area with soap and warm water.*

AIR FILTER BACKPLATE

Routine air filter maintenance is described in Chapter Three.

Refer to **Figure 1** or **Figure 2**.

Removal

1. Remove the air filter cover screw (A, **Figure 3**) and remove the cover (B).

2. Remove the Torx screws and bracket (**Figure 4**, typical) from the air filter element.

3. Gently pull the air filter element away from the backplate and disconnect the two breather hoses (A, **Figure 5**) from the hollow bolts on the backplate. Remove the air filter element (B, **Figure 5**).

4. Unscrew and remove the breather hollow bolts (A, **Figure 6**) securing the backplate to the cylinder heads.

5A. On California models, pull the backplate (B, **Figure 6**) partially away from the cylinder heads and the carburetor or fuel induction module, then disconnect the evaporation emission control clean air inlet hose (**Figure 7**, typical).

5B. On all other models, pull the backplate (B, **Figure 6**) away from the cylinder heads and remove it.

AIR FILTER
(CARBURETED MODELS)

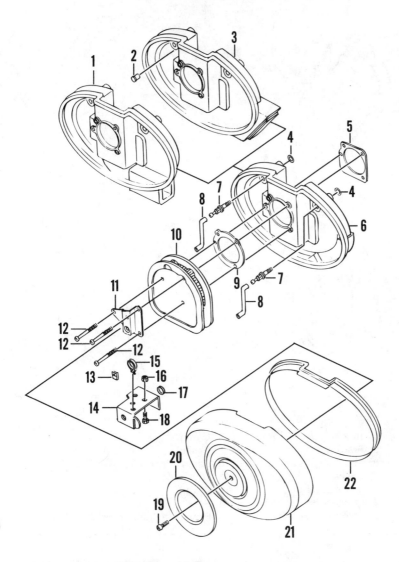

1. Backplate
   (international)
2. Grommet (California)
3. Backplate (California)
4. O-ring
5. Gasket
6. Backplate (49-state)
7. Breather hollow bolt
8. Breather hose
9. Gasket
10. Air filter
11. Mounting bracket
12. Bolts
13. Nut clip
14. Enrichment cable
    bracket
15. Cable strap
16. Nut
17. Grommet
18. Bolt
19. Screw
20. Trim
21. Cover
22. Seal

7

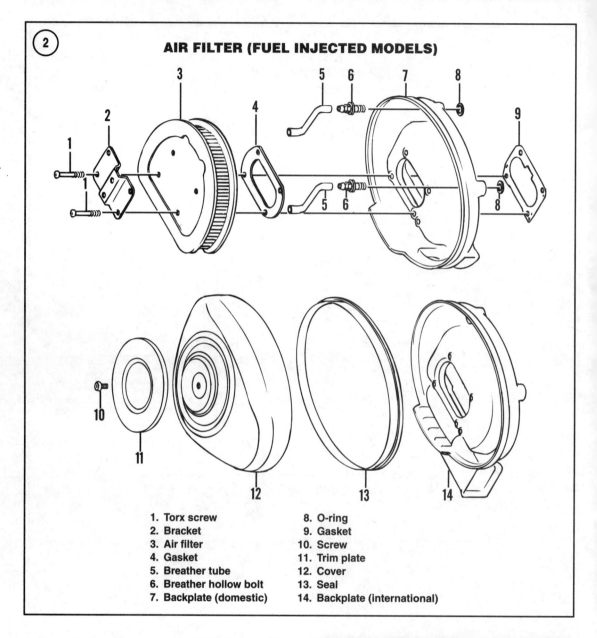

② AIR FILTER (FUEL INJECTED MODELS)

1. Torx screw
2. Bracket
3. Air filter
4. Gasket
5. Breather tube
6. Breather hollow bolt
7. Backplate (domestic)
8. O-ring
9. Gasket
10. Screw
11. Trim plate
12. Cover
13. Seal
14. Backplate (international)

6. Remove the carburetor or fuel injection module gasket from the air filter (**Figure 8**) and from the backing plate (A, **Figure 9**).

Inspection

1. Inspect the backplate (B, **Figure 9**) for damage.
2. On California models, make sure the trap door swings freely (**Figure 10**).
3. Make sure the breather hollow bolts and breather hoses (**Figure 11**) are clear. Clean them out if necessary.

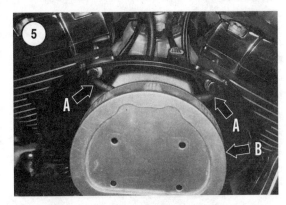

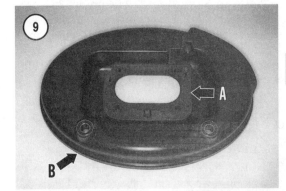

7

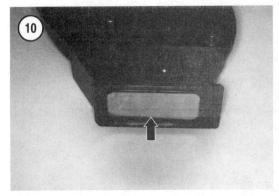

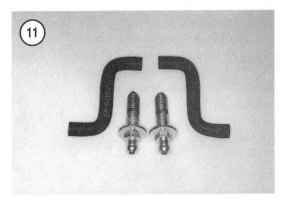

Installation

1. Apply a couple dabs of gasket sealer to the *new* carburetor, or fuel injection module, gasket and attach it to the backside of the backplate (A, **Figure 9**).

2. Move the backplate into position.

3. On California models, move the backplate part way into position. Connect the evaporation emission control clean air inlet hose (**Figure 7**) to the fitting on the backside of the backplate.

4. Position the backplate (B, **Figure 6**) against the carburetor, or fuel induction module, and cylinder heads. Make sure the Torx bolt holes of the gasket and backplate are aligned with the carburetor or fuel induction module. Reposition the gasket if necessary.

5. Install the breather hollow bolts (A, **Figure 6**) securing the backplate to the cylinder heads. Tighten them to the specification in **Table 2**.

6. If the gasket was removed, install a *new* gasket (**Figure 8**) onto the air filter element.

7. Position the element (B, **Figure 5**) with the flat side facing down and attach the breather hoses (A) to the backside of the element.

NOTE
If an aftermarket air filter element is being installed, position it onto the backplate following the manufacturer's instructions.

8. Move the element into position and install the mounting bracket (**Figure 4**) and the Torx screws. Tighten the Torx screws to the specification in **Table 2**.

9. Apply a drop of ThreeBond TB1342 (blue) or an equivalent threadlocking compound to the cover screw prior to installation.

10. Inspect the seal ring (**Figure 12**) on the air filter cover for hardness or deterioration. Replace it if necessary.

11. Install the air filter cover (B, **Figure 3**) and the screw (A). Tighten the screw to the torque specification in **Table 2**

CARBURETOR OPERATION

An understanding of the function of each of the carburetor components and their relation to one an-

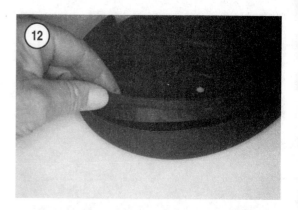

other is a valuable aid for pinpointing the source of carburetor trouble.

The carburetor's purpose is to supply and atomize fuel, and mix it in correct proportions with the air drawn in through the air intake. At the primary throttle opening (idle), a small amount of fuel is siphoned through the pilot jet by the incoming air. As the throttle is opened further, the air stream begins to siphon fuel through the main jet and needle jet. The tapered needle increases the effective flow capacity of the needle jet as it is lifted, and occupies progressively less of the area of the jet. At full throt-

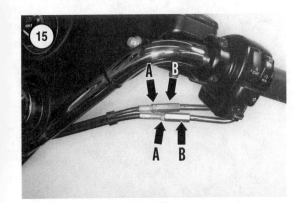

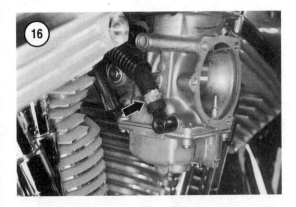

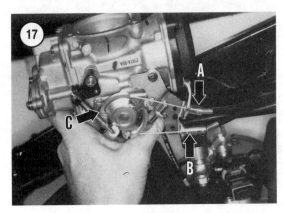

The accelerator pump circuit reduces engine hesitation by injecting a fine spray of fuel into the carburetor intake passage during sudden acceleration.

CARBURETOR

Removal

1. Remove the air filter and backplate as described in this chapter.

2. Remove the fuel tank as described in this chapter.

3. Loosen the locknut (A, **Figure 13**, typical) and disconnect the starting enrichment valve cable from the mounting bracket (B, typical). Move the end of the cable out of the mounting bracket.

4. There are two different throttle cables. Label the two cables at the carburetor before disconnecting them. One is the throttle control cable (A, **Figure 14**) and the other is the idle control cable (B).

5. At the handlebar, loosen both control cable adjuster locknuts (A, **Figure 15**), then turn the cable adjusters (B) *clockwise* as far as possible to increase cable slack.

6. Disconnect the fuel supply hose (**Figure 16**) from the carburetor fitting.

7. Twist and pull the carburetor off the seal ring and intake manifold.

8. Disconnect the vacuum hose from the carburetor fitting.

9. Disconnect the throttle control cable (A, **Figure 17**) and the idle control cable (B) from the carburetor cable guide and the throttle wheel.

10. Drain the gasoline from the carburetor assembly.

11. Inspect the carburetor seal ring on the intake manifold for wear, hardness, cracks or other damage. Replace it if necessary.

12. If necessary, service the intake manifold as described under *Intake Manifold* in this chapter.

13. Cover the intake manifold opening.

Installation

1. If removed, seat the seal ring onto the intake manifold. Make sure it is correctly seated to avoid a vacuum leak.

tle, the carburetor venturi is fully open and the needle is lifted far enough to permit the main jet to flow at full capacity.

The choke circuit is a starting enrichment valve system. The choke knob on the left side of the engine next to the horn opens an enrichment valve; rather than closing a butterfly in the venturi area as on some carburetors. In the open position, the slow jet discharges a stream of fuel into the carburetor venturi to enrich the mixture when the engine is cold.

2. Route the starting enrichment valve cable between the cylinders and toward its mounting bracket on the left side.

3. Connect the idle cable to the carburetor as follows:

   a. The idle cable has the small spring (A, **Figure 18**) on the end of the cable.

   b. Insert the idle cable sheath into the rear cable bracket guide on the carburetor (B, **Figure 18**).

   c. Attach the end of the idle cable to the throttle wheel (C, **Figure 18**).

4. Connect the throttle cable to the carburetor as follows:

   a. Insert the throttle cable sheath into the front cable bracket guide on the carburetor.

   b. Attach the end of the throttle cable to the throttle wheel.

5. Operate the hand throttle a few times. Make sure the throttle wheel operates smoothly with no binding. Also make sure both cable ends are seated squarely in their cable bracket guides and in the throttle wheel.

> *CAUTION*
> *The carburetor must fit squarely onto the intake manifold. If it is misaligned, it may damage the intake manifold seal ring, resulting in a vacuum leak.*

6. Align the carburetor squarely with the intake manifold (**Figure 19**), then push it into the manifold until it bottoms. Position the carburetor so it sits square and vertical with the manifold.

7. Connect the vacuum hose to the carburetor fitting. Make sure it is seated correctly.

8. Slide a *new* hose clamp over the fuel supply hose, then connect the fuel hose to the hose fitting on the carburetor (**Figure 16**).

9. Insert the starting enrichment valve cable into the mounting bracket (B, **Figure 13**), then tighten the locknut (A) securely.

10. Before installing the fuel tank, recheck the idle and throttle cable operation. Open and release the hand throttle. Make sure the carburetor throttle valve opens and closes smoothly. Make sure both cables are routed properly. If necessary, adjust the throttle cables as described in Chapter Three.

11. Install the air filter backplate and air filter as described in this chapter.

12. Install the fuel tank as described in this chapter.

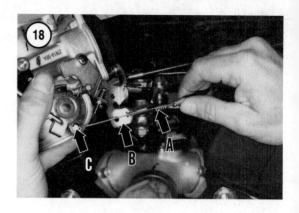

13. Start the engine and allow it to idle. Check for fuel leaks.

14. With the engine idling in NEUTRAL, turn the handlebar from side to side. The idle speed should remain the same. If the idle speed increases while the handlebars are turned, the cables are installed incorrectly or are damaged. Remove the fuel tank and inspect the cables.

Disassembly

Refer to **Figure 20**.

1. Unscrew and remove the starting enrichment valve and cable (**Figure 21**).

2. Remove the screw and washer (A, **Figure 22**) on the side and the top screw (A, **Figure 23**) securing the throttle cable bracket to the carburetor. Remove the bracket (B, **Figure 23**).

3. Remove the collar (**Figure 24**) from the cover.

4. Remove the remaining cover screws (**Figure 25**). Remove the cover and spring (A, **Figure 26**).

5. Remove the vacuum piston (B, **Figure 26**) from the carburetor housing. Do not damage the jet needle extending out of the bottom of the vacuum piston.

6. Remove the float bowl as follows:

   a. Remove the screws (**Figure 27**) securing the float bowl to the carburetor.

   b. Slowly remove the float bowl body and withdraw the pump rod (**Figure 28**) from the boot on the bowl.

   c. Disconnect the pump rod from the lever assembly on the carburetor (**Figure 29**).

> *NOTE*
> *One of the float pin pedestals has an interference fit that holds the float pin in place. An arrow, (Figure 30) cast*

into the carburetor, points to this pedestal. To remove this float pin, tap it in the direction of the arrow.

CAUTION
If the float pin is removed opposite of the arrow, the opposite pedestal may crack or break off. If this occurs, the carburetor must be replaced.

7. Carefully tap the float pin (**Figure 31**) out of the pedestals and remove it.

8. Remove the float (**Figure 32**) and needle valve assembly.

9. Unscrew and remove the pilot jet (**Figure 33**).

10. Unscrew and remove the main jet (**Figure 34**).

11. Unscrew and remove the needle jet holder (**Figure 35**).

12. Remove the needle jet (A, **Figure 36**) from the needle jet bore in the carburetor.

Cleaning and Inspection

Replace worn or damaged parts as described in this section.

CAUTION
The carburetor body is equipped with plastic parts that cannot be removed. Do not dip the carburetor body, O-rings, float assembly, needle valve or vacuum piston in a carburetor cleaner or another harsh solution that can damage these parts. The use of a caustic carburetor cleaning solvent is not recommended. Instead, clean the carburetor and related parts in a petroleum based solvent, or Simple

Green. Then rinse them in clean water.

1. Initially clean all parts in a mild petroleum based cleaning solution. Then clean them in hot, soapy water and rinse with cold water. Blow them dry with compressed air.

CAUTION
*If compressed air is not available, allow the parts to air dry or use a clean, lint-free cloth. Do **not** use a paper towel to dry carburetor parts, as small paper particles may plug openings in the carburetor housing or jets.*

2. Allow the carburetors to dry thoroughly before assembly. Blow out the jets and the needle jet holder with compressed air.

CAUTION
*Do **not** use wire or drill bits to clean jets as minor gouges in the jet can alter the air/fuel mixture.*

3. Inspect the float bowl O-ring gasket (A, **Figure 37**) for hardness or deterioration.

4. Inspect the accelerator pump boot (B, **Figure 37**) for hardness or deterioration.

5. Make sure the accelerator pump cover (**Figure 38**) screws are tight.

6. Inspect the vacuum piston diaphragm (**Figure 39**) for cracks or deterioration. Check the vacuum piston sides (**Figure 40**) for excessive wear. Install the vacuum piston into the carburetor body and move it up and down in the bore. The vacuum piston should move smoothly with no binding or excessive play. If there is excessive play, the vacuum piston slide and/or carburetor body must be replaced.

7. Inspect the needle valve tapered end for steps, uneven wear or other damage (**Figure 41**).

8. Inspect the needle valve seat (B, **Figure 36**) for steps, uneven wear or other damage. Insert the needle valve and slowly move it back and forth to check for smooth operation. If either part is worn or damaged, replace both parts as a pair for maximum performance.

9. Inspect the needle jet holder, pilot jet and main jet (**Figure 42**). Make sure all holes are open and none of the parts are either worn or damaged.

10. Inspect the jet needle, spring and spring seat (**Figure 43**) for deterioration or damage.

7

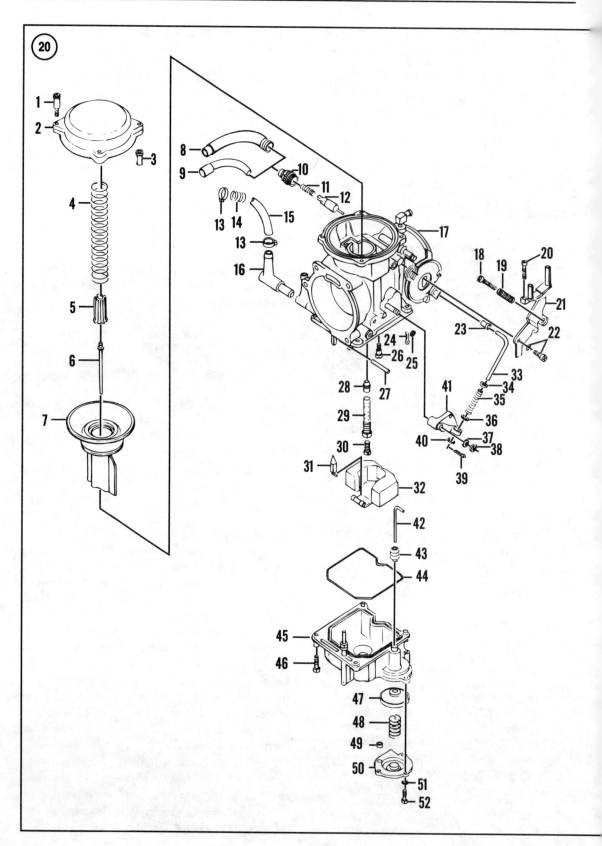

CARBURETOR

1. Screw
2. Cover
3. Collar
4. Spring
5. Spring seat
6. Jet needle
7. Vacuum piston
8. Cable sealing cap
9. Cable guide
10. Starting enrichment cap
11. Spring
12. Starting enrichment valve
13. Hose clamp
14. Spring
15. Hose
16. Fuel inlet fitting
17. Body
18. Screw
19. Spring
20. Screw
21. Throttle cable bracket
22. Screw and washer
23. Collar
24. Pin
25. Washer
26. Pilot jet
27. Float pivot pin
28. Needle jet
29. Main jet holder
30. Main jet
31. Valve
32. Float
33. Rod
34. Washer
35. Spring
36. Collar
37. Washer
38. E-clip
39. Pin
40. Washer
41. Lever
42. Rod
43. Boot
44. O-ring gasket
45. Float bowl
46. Screw
47. Diaphragm
48. Spring
49. O-ring
50. Cover
51. Washer
52. Screw

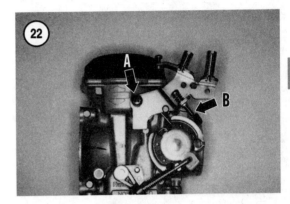

7

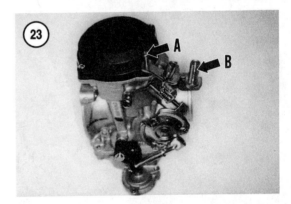

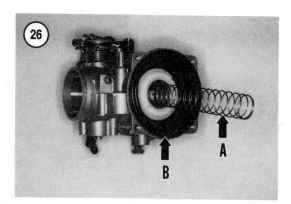

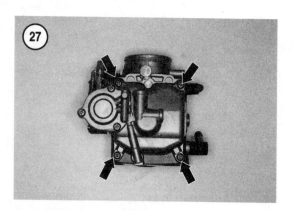

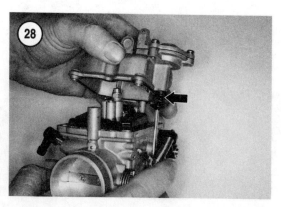

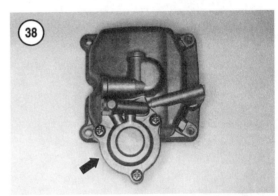

7

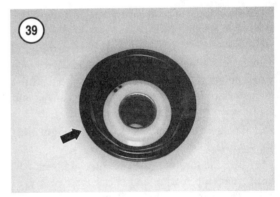

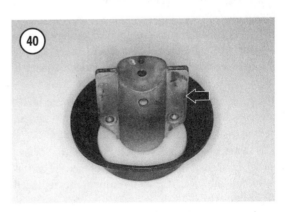

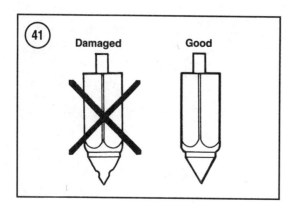

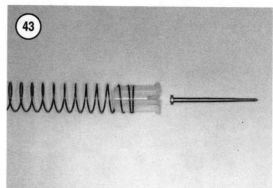

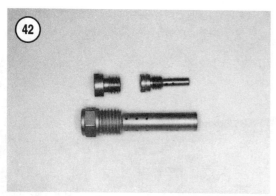

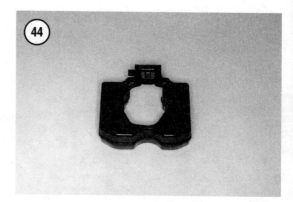

11. Inspect the jet needle tapered end for steps, uneven wear or other damage.

12. Inspect the float (**Figure 44**) for deterioration or damage. If the float is suspected of leakage, place it in a container of water and push it down. If the float sinks or if bubbles appear, there is a leak and the float must be replaced.

13. Make sure the throttle plate screws (**Figure 45**) are tight. Tighten them if necessary.

14. Move the throttle wheel (**Figure 46**) back and forth from stop to stop and check for free movement. The throttle lever should move smoothly and return under spring tension.

15. Check the throttle wheel return spring (**Figure 47**) for free movement. Make sure it rotates the throttle wheel back to the stop position with no hesitation.

16. Make sure all openings in the carburetor housing are clear. Clean them out if they are plugged, then apply compressed air to all openings.

17. Inspect the carburetor body for internal or external damage. If there is damage, replace the carburetor assembly, as the body cannot be replaced separately.

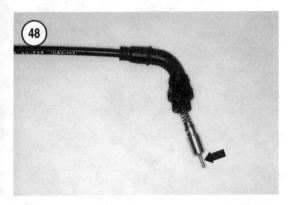

18. Check the top cover for cracks or damage.

19. Check the starting enrichment valve and cable as follows:

    a. Check the end of the valve (**Figure 48**) for damage.

    b. Check the entire length of the cable for bends, chaffing or other damage.

    c. Check the knob, nut and lockwasher for damage. Move the knob and check for ease of movement.

Assembly

NOTE
The needle jet has two different sides and must be installed as described in Step 1.

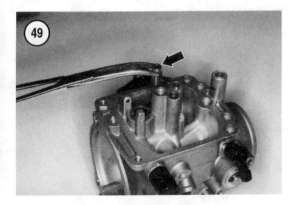

1. Position the needle jet with the long end going in first (**Figure 49**) and install it (A, **Figure 36**).

2. Install the needle jet holder (**Figure 35**) into the main jet passage. Make sure it passes through the opening in the venturi (**Figure 50**), then tighten it securely.

3. Install the main jet and tighten it securely (**Figure 34**).

4. Install the pilot jet and tighten it securely (**Figure 33**).

5. Install the fuel valve (**Figure 51**) onto the float and position the float onto the carburetor so the valve drops into its seat.

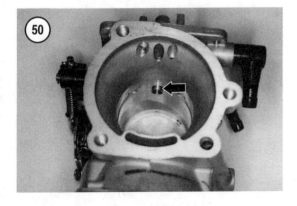

CAUTION
The pedestals that support the float pin are fragile. In the next step, support the pedestal on the arrow side while tapping the float pin into place.

6. Align the float pin with the two pedestals.

7. Install the float pin (A, **Figure 52**) from the side opposite the arrow (B). Support the pedestal and tap the float pin into place in the pedestal.

8. Check the float level as described in this chapter.

9. Install the float bowl as follows:

    a. Make sure the float bowl O-ring seal (A, **Figure 37**) and accelerator rod boot (B) are in place.

    b. Connect the pump rod to the lever assembly on the carburetor (**Figure 53**).

    c. Slowly install the float bowl body and insert the accelerator pump rod through the boot (**Figure 28**) on the float bowl. Engage the rod with the diaphragm while installing the float bowl.

    d. Install the float bowl and screws (**Figure 27**). Tighten the screws securely in a crisscross pattern.

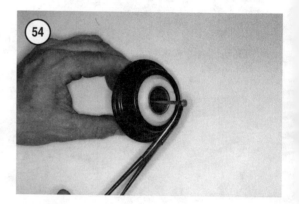

10. Insert the jet needle (**Figure 54**) through the center hole in the vacuum piston.

11. Install the spring seat (A, **Figure 55**) and spring (B) over the top of the needle to secure it in place.

12. Align the slides (A, **Figure 56**) on the vacuum piston with the grooves (B) in the carburetor bore and install the vacuum piston (B, **Figure 26**). The slides on the piston are offset, so the piston can only be installed one way. When installing the vacuum piston, make sure the jet needle drops through the needle jet.

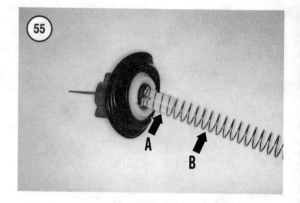

13. Seat the outer edge of the vacuum piston diaphragm into the piston chamber groove (**Figure 57**).

14. Align the free end of the spring with the carburetor top and install the top onto the carburetor.

15. Hold the carburetor top in place and lift the vacuum piston with a finger (**Figure 58**). The piston should move smoothly. If the piston movement is

57

58

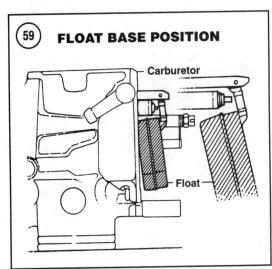

59 FLOAT BASE POSITION

Carburetor

Float

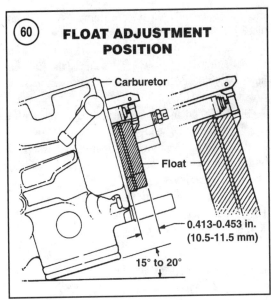

60 **FLOAT ADJUSTMENT POSITION**

Carburetor

Float

0.413-0.453 in.
(10.5-11.5 mm)

15° to 20°

7

screw engages the top of the throttle cam stop (B, **Figure 22**). Hold the bracket in place and install the bracket's side mounting screw and washer (A, **Figure 22**). Tighten the screw securely.

19. Install the top screw (A, **Figure 23**) and tighten it securely.

20. Install the starting enrichment cable and valve into the carburetor body. Tighten the nut securely (**Figure 21**).

Float Adjustment

The carburetor must be removed and partially disassembled for this adjustment.

1. Remove the carburetor as described in this chapter.

2. Remove the float bowl as described in this chapter.

3. Place the engine manifold side of the carburetor on a clean, flat surface as shown in **Figure 59**. This is the base position.

4. Tilt the carburetor upward 15-20° as shown in **Figure 60**. In this position, the float will come to rest without compressing the pin return spring.

NOTE
If the carburetor is tilted less than 15°
or more than 20°, the float measure-
ment will be incorrect.

5. Measure from the carburetor flange surface to the top of the float as shown in **Figure 60**. When

rough or sluggish, the spring is installed incorrectly. Remove the carburetor top and reinstall the spring.

16. Install the carburetor top screws (**Figure 25**) finger-tight.

17. Install the collar (**Figure 24**) into the cover.

18. Install the throttle cable bracket (B, **Figure 23**) onto the carburetor so the end of the idle speed

measuring float level, do not compress the float. The correct float level measurement is 0.413-0.453 in. (10.5-11.5 mm).

6. If the float level is incorrect, remove the float pin and float as described under *Carburetor Disassembly* in this chapter.

7. Slowly bend the float tang (**Figure 61**) with a screwdriver and adjust it to the correct position.

8. Reinstall the float and the float pin as described under *Carburetor Assembly* in this chapter. Recheck the float level.

9. Repeat Steps 4-8 until the float level is correct.

10. Install the float bowl and carburetor as described in this chapter.

INTAKE MANIFOLD (CARBURETED MODELS)

Removal/Installation

Refer to **Figure 62**.

1. Remove the carburetor as described in this chapter.

> *NOTE*
> *The front and rear intake manifold flanges are different. If the flanges are not marked, label them with an F and R so they will be reinstalled in the correct location.*

2. Disconnect the electrical connector from the MAP sensor (A, **Figure 63**) on top of the intake manifold.

> *NOTE*
> *Figure 63 shows only two of the Allen bolts. Remove all four bolts.*

3. Remove the four Allen bolts (B, **Figure 63**) securing the intake manifold to the cylinder heads.

4. Remove the intake manifold, flanges (A, **Figure 64**), manifold seals (B) and seal ring (C).

5. Inspect the intake manifold as described in this section.

6. Install the flanges and manifold seals (A, **Figure 64**) onto the intake manifold.

7. Install the intake manifold onto the cylinder head intake ports.

8. Make sure the front and rear seals seat squarely against the cylinder head mating surfaces.

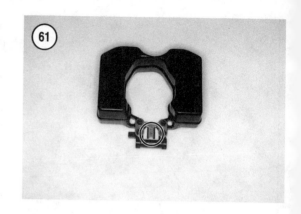

9. Install all four Allen bolts finger-tight at this time.

10. Temporarily install the carburetor (**Figure 65**) into the intake manifold.

> *CAUTION*
> *Do not attempt to align the intake manifold after tightening the bolts. This will damage the manifold seals. If necessary, loosen the bolts, then align the manifold.*

11. Make sure the intake manifold seats squarely against the cylinder heads. Then make sure the carburetor seats squarely in the intake manifold. Remove the carburetor.

> *NOTE*
> *It is very difficult to get an Allen wrench and torque wrench onto the two inboard Allen bolts to tighten them to the torque specification. Tighten the outboard Allen bolts to the specified torque value, then tighten the inboard Allen bolts to the same approximate tightness.*

12. Tighten the intake manifold Allen bolts to the torque specification in **Table 2**.

13. If the MAP sensor was removed, install a *new* seal in the manifold receptacle, then install the MAP sensor.

14. Connect the electrical connector onto the MAP sensor (A, **Figure 63**).

15. Install the carburetor as described in this chapter.

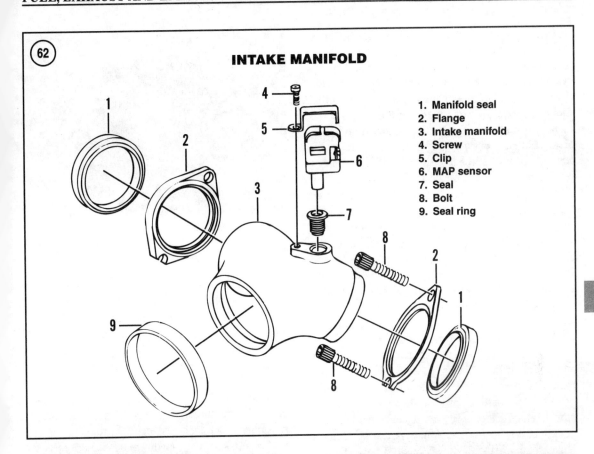

INTAKE MANIFOLD

1. Manifold seal
2. Flange
3. Intake manifold
4. Screw
5. Clip
6. MAP sensor
7. Seal
8. Bolt
9. Seal ring

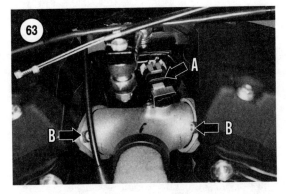

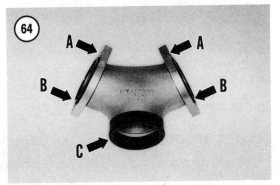

Inspection

1. Check the intake manifold seals (B, **Figure 64**) for wear, deterioration or other damage. Replace the seals as a set if necessary.

2. Check the intake manifold seal ring (C, **Figure 64**) for cracks, flat spots or other damage. Replace it if necessary.

3. If necessary, remove the self-tapping screw and clamp, and remove the MAP sensor.

ELECTRONIC FUEL INJECTION (EFI)

This section describes the components and operation of the sequential port electronic fuel injection (EFI) system. The advantages of a map controlled fuel and ignition system working together are tremendous. It allows for the elimination of an inefficient cold start enrichment devise and allows for accurate control of the idle speed. Without a carburetor there is no need for periodic adjustments and altitude compensation is automatic. Improved torque characteristics are achieved, while at the same time allowing for greater fuel economy and low exhaust emissions due to the matching of the air/fuel ratio and ignition point, dependent upon load conditions. Engine performance modification is possible by simply installing an electronic control module (ECM) with different map characteristics.

Complete service of the system requires a Harley-Davidson Scanalyzer and a number of other specialty tools. However, basic troubleshooting diagnosis is no different on a fuel-injected machine than on a carbureted one. If the check engine light comes on or there is a driveability problem, make sure all electrical connections are clean and secure. A high or erratic idle speed may indicate a vacuum leak. Make sure there is an adequate supply of gasoline. If basic tests fail to reveal the cause of a problem, refer service to a Harley-Davidson dealership. Incorrectly performed diagnostic procedures can damage the fuel injection system.

Electronic Control Module and Sensors

The electronic control module (ECM) (**Figure 66**, typical), mounted under the frame right side cover, determines the optimum injection and ignition timing based on input from six sensors. The sensors (**Figure 67**), their locations and functions are as follows:

1. The throttle position sensor (TP), located on the front of the induction module and attached directly to the throttle shaft, indicates throttle angle. The ECM indicates the air volume entering the engine based on the throttle angle.

2. The crankshaft positions sensor (CKP), located on the forward position of the left crankcase, is an inductive type sensor. The ECM determines the engine speed by how fast the machined teeth on the flywheel pass by the sensor.

NOTE
The 2002 models are not equipped with the camshaft position sensor.

3. The camshaft position (CMP) on 1999-2001 models, located in the camshaft cover, is also an inductive sensor. The ECM determines the camshaft position when the semicircular ridge on the rear cylinder's primary camshaft chain sprocket passes the sensor.

4. The engine temperature sensor (ET) is located on the front cylinder head. The ECM adjusts the injector opening time based on input from this sensor.

5. The intake air temperature sensor (IAT) is located inside the induction module (rear cylinder's intake runner). The ECM determines the air density and adjusts the injector opening time based on input from this sensor.

6. The barometric pressure sensor (BARO) is located on the electrical panel next to the ECM. Barometric pressure varies with altitude; the ECM compensates for altitude changes based on input from this sensor.

7. The bankangle senor (BAS), located under the left side frame cover, interrupts the ignition and shuts off the engine if the motorcycle's lean angle is greater than 55°.

Make sure the ECM is securely mounted on the rubber isolators to prevent damage from vibration. Do not tamper with the ECM; it is sealed to prevent moisture contamination.

Fuel Supply System

Fuel pump and filters

The fuel pump and filter assembly is located inside the fuel tank. This assembly is part of the re-

ENGINE SENSORS

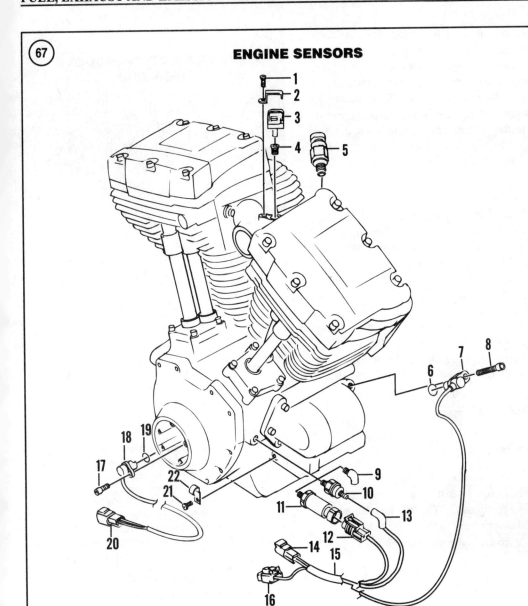

1. Screw
2. Clamp
3. MAP (carbureted models only)
4. Seal
5. Engine temperature sensor
6. O-ring
7. Crankshaft position sensor (CKP)
8. Bolt
9. Elbow (side car only)
10. Oil pressure switch*
11. Oil pressure sensor**
12. Connector (oil pressure sensor**)
13. Connector (oil pressure switch*)
14. Two-pin socket (black)
15. Wiring harness
16. Two-pin socket (black)
17. Screw
18. Camshaft position sensor (CMP)
19. O-ring
20. Three-pin connector (black)
21. Screw
22. Cable clamp

*FLHT, FLHR, FLHRI, FLHRCI models
**FLHTC, FLHTCUI, FLHTCI, FLTR, FLTRI models

movable canopy attached to the top of the fuel tank. The canopy provides easy removal and installation of the attached components without having to work within the fuel tank cavity. An inlet screen on the fuel pump and a secondary fuel filter canister located downstream from the fuel pump provide maximum filtration before the fuel reaches the fuel injectors.

Fuel lines

On 2000-2001 models, quick-disconnect fittings are used on both the high-pressure fuel supply line and the low-pressure fuel line at the base of the fuel tank. The 2002 models are equipped with only one fuel line that is equipped with a quick-disconnect fitting at the base of the fuel tank. On 1999 models, fuel lines are attached to the base of the fuel tank with hex fittings. On 1999-2001 models, the fuel supply line pressure is 43.5 psi (300 kPa) and the return line is 3 psi (21 kPa). On 2002 models, the single fuel supply line pressure is 58 psi (400 kPa).

A check valve is located on the fuel line(s) where it attaches to the fuel tank.

Fuel injectors

The solenoid-actuated constant-stroke pintle-type fuel injectors consist of a solenoid plunger, needle valve and housing. The fuel injector's opening is fixed and fuel pressure is constant.

The ECM controls the time the injectors open.

Induction module

The induction module consists of the two fuel injectors, fuel pressure regulator, throttle position sensor, intake air temperature sensor, idle speed lever, fuel supply and return line fittings, and the idle speed control actuator. Refer to **Figure 68** and **Figure 69**.

DEPRESSURIZING THE FUEL SYSTEM (FUEL INJECTED MODELS)

The fuel system is under pressure at all times, even when the engine is not operating. The system must be depressurized prior to loosening fittings or disconnecting fuel lines within the fuel injection

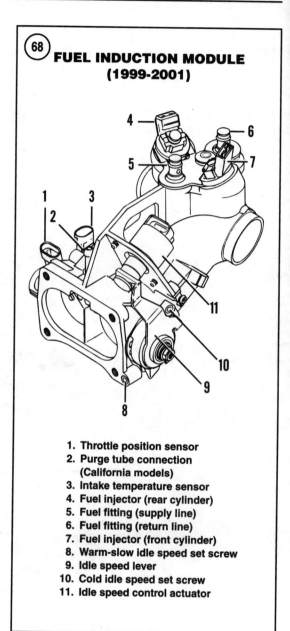

FUEL INDUCTION MODULE (1999-2001)

1. Throttle position sensor
2. Purge tube connection (California models)
3. Intake temperature sensor
4. Fuel injector (rear cylinder)
5. Fuel fitting (supply line)
6. Fuel fitting (return line)
7. Fuel injector (front cylinder)
8. Warm-slow idle speed set screw
9. Idle speed lever
10. Cold idle speed set screw
11. Idle speed control actuator

system. Gasoline will spurt out unless the system is depressurized.

1. Remove the seat as described in Chapter Fourteen.

2. At the rear of fuel tank, disconnect the fuel pump single-pin black electrical connector (**Figure 70**).

3. Start the engine and allow it to idle until it runs out of gasoline.

4. After the engine has stopped, operate the starter for three seconds to eliminate any residual gasoline in the fuel lines.

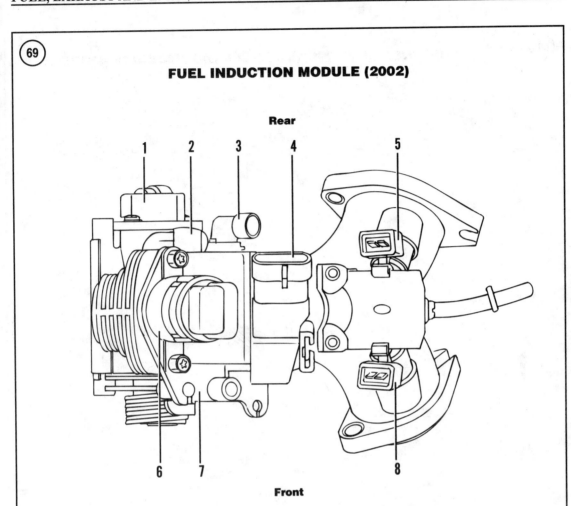

FUEL INDUCTION MODULE (2002)

Rear

Front

1. Throttle position sensor
2. Purge tube fitting
   (California models only)
3. Intake air temperature sensor
4. Manifold absolute pressure sensor
5. Fuel injector (front cylinder)
6. Idle control valve
7. Throttle cable bracket
8. Fuel injector (rear cylinder)

INDUCTION MODULE
(FUEL INJECTED MODELS)

Removal

Refer to **Figure 71** and **Figure 72**.

NOTE
This procedure is shown on a 2001 model.

1. Remove the fuel tank as described in this chapter.

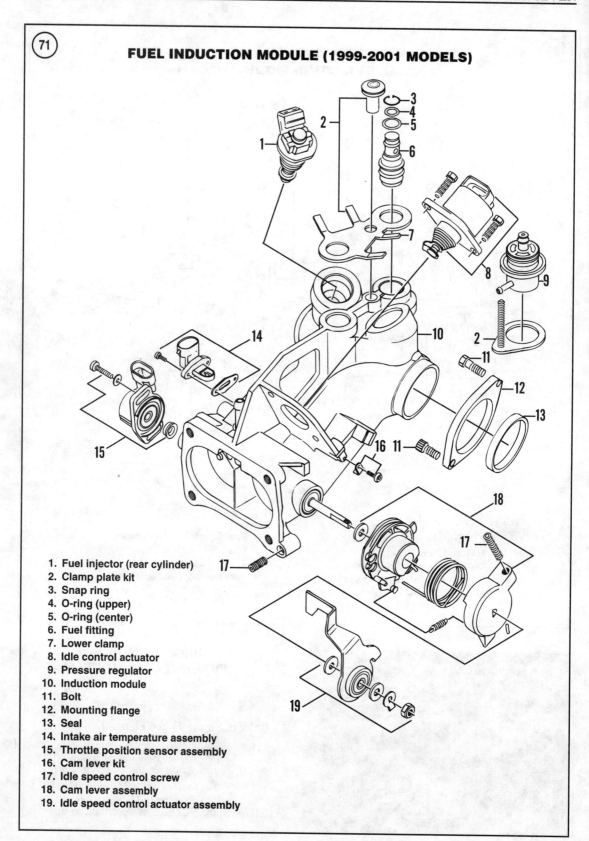

71

FUEL INDUCTION MODULE (1999-2001 MODELS)

1. Fuel injector (rear cylinder)
2. Clamp plate kit
3. Snap ring
4. O-ring (upper)
5. O-ring (center)
6. Fuel fitting
7. Lower clamp
8. Idle control actuator
9. Pressure regulator
10. Induction module
11. Bolt
12. Mounting flange
13. Seal
14. Intake air temperature assembly
15. Throttle position sensor assembly
16. Cam lever kit
17. Idle speed control screw
18. Cam lever assembly
19. Idle speed control actuator assembly

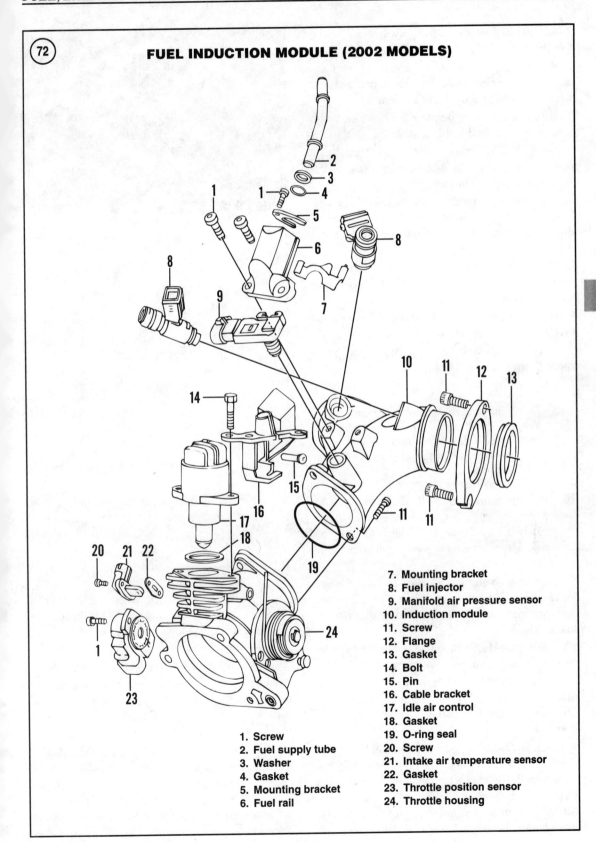

(72)

FUEL INDUCTION MODULE (2002 MODELS)

7. Mounting bracket
8. Fuel injector
9. Manifold air pressure sensor
10. Induction module
11. Screw
12. Flange
13. Gasket
14. Bolt
15. Pin
16. Cable bracket
17. Idle air control
18. Gasket
19. O-ring seal
20. Screw
21. Intake air temperature sensor
22. Gasket
23. Throttle position sensor
24. Throttle housing

1. Screw
2. Fuel supply tube
3. Washer
4. Gasket
5. Mounting bracket
6. Fuel rail

2. Remove the air filter assembly as described in this chapter.

3. Spread the external latch and disconnect the electrical connector from the throttle position sensor and the idle speed control actuator.

4. Disconnect the throttle cables from the induction module as described in this chapter.

5. On FLHTCUI models, disconnect the cruise control cable from the induction module as described in Chapter Thirteen.

6. On California models, disconnect the EVAP hose (A, **Figure 73**) from the port on top of the induction module. Plug the end of the hose to keep out debris.

7. *Carefully* disconnect the electrical connector from each fuel injector by rocking the connector back and forth.

8. Disconnect the electrical connector from the intake air temperature sensor.

9. Disconnect the electrical connector from the idle speed control actuator (B, **Figure 73**).

> *NOTE*
> *The front and rear intake manifold flanges are different. If the flanges are not marked, label them with an F and R so they will be reinstalled in the correct locations.*

10. Working on the right side of the motorcycle, loosen and remove the lower two Allen bolts securing the cylinder head mounting flanges to the cylinder heads. Use a 1/4 inch ball Allen bit with a 4 in. extension.

11. Working on the left side of the motorcycle, loosen, but do not remove, the upper two 1/2 in. hex bolts securing the cylinder head mounting flanges to the cylinder heads.

12. Slide the induction module out of the cylinder head ports past the upper two 1/2 in. hex bolts.

13A. On 1999-2001 models, remove the induction module (C, **Figure 73**) and fuel line assembly. Be careful not to damage the fuel lines as they pass the horn bracket.

13B. On 2002 models, partially remove the induction module and fuel line assembly. Be careful not to damage the fuel line as it passes the horn bracket. Depress the button (A, **Figure 74**) on the fuel line fitting. Disconnect the fuel line and fitting (B, **Figure 74**) from the induction module fitting (C).

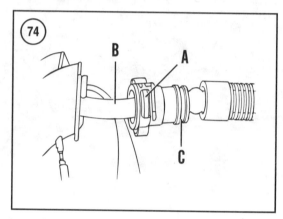

14. Remove the mounting flanges and discard the seals.

15. Inspect the induction module and fuel hoses as described in this section.

Installation

1. Install the flanges onto the correct side of the induction module with the slotted hole at the top. Refer to the marks made during *Removal*. Install *new* seals onto the induction module.

2A. On 1999-2001 models, carefully install the induction module and fuel line assembly past the horn bracket on the cylinder head ports. Slide the induction module into place and onto the upper two 1/2 in. hex bolts.

2B. On 2002 models, partially install the induction module and fuel line assembly. Slide the fuel line connector (B, **Figure 74**) onto the induction module fitting (C) until it clicks. Gently pull on the fuel line to ensure the fitting is locked in place. Slide the induction module on the upper two 1/2 in. hex bolts.

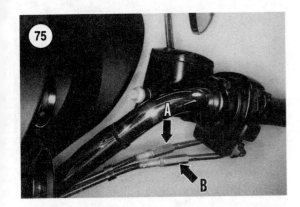

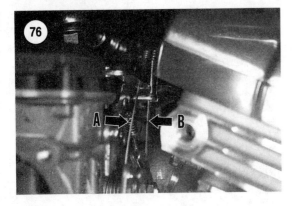

9. Remove the bolts securing the air filter backplate and remove the backplate.

10. Working on the right side of the motorcycle, tighten the lower two Allen bolts to the specification in **Table 2**.

11. Carefully attach the electrical connector to each fuel injector. Align the grooves in the female connector with the tabs in the male space housing. Push the connector halves together until both latches click.

NOTE
In Steps 12 and 13, push the electrical connector halves together until the female latch(es) slot connector is fully engaged with the tab(s) on the male space housing.

12. Attach the electrical connector to the air temperature sensor. Make sure both external latches click into place.

13. Connect the electrical connectors to both the throttle position sensor and the idle speed control actuator (B, **Figure 73**). Make sure the external latch clicks into place.

14. On California models, connect the EVAP hose (A, **Figure 73**) to the port on top of the induction module.

15. Install the air filter assembly as described in this chapter.

16. Install the fuel tank as described in this chapter.

3. On FLHTCUI models, connect the cruise control cable to the induction module as described in Chapter Thirteen.

4. Connect both throttle cables to the induction module as described in this chapter.

5. Align the mounting flanges and install the two lower Allen bolts by hand. Use the same tool set up used to loosen the Allen bolts. Do not tighten the bolts at this time.

6. Ensure correct alignment of the induction module to the cylinder heads as follows:
   a. Install the air filter backplate and two upper breather bolts that secure the backplate to the cylinder heads. Tighten them finger-tight.
   b. Install the T27 Torx screws that secure the backplate to the induction module. Tighten them finger-tight.

7. Working on the right side of the motorcycle, tighten the lower two Allen bolts until snug, do not tighten to the final torque specification at this time. Use the same tool set up used to loosen the Allen bolts.

8. Working on the left side of the motorcycle, tighten the upper two 1/2 in. hex bolts to the specification in **Table 2**.

Inspection

Check the induction module for wear, deterioration or other damage. Replace the seals as a set if necessary.

THROTTLE AND IDLE CABLES (CARBURETED MODELS)

There are two different throttle cables. At the throttle grip, the front cable is the throttle control cable (A, **Figure 75**) and the rear cable is the idle control cable (B). At the carburetor, the outboard cable is the throttle control cable (A, **Figure 76**) and the inboard cable is the idle control cable (B).

Removal

1. Remove the fuel tank as described in this chapter.

2. Remove the air filter and backing plate as described in this chapter.

3. Make a drawing or take a picture of the cable routing from the carburetor through the frame to the right side handlebar.

4. At the right side handlebar, loosen both control cable adjuster locknuts (A, **Figure 77**), then turn the cable adjusters (B) *clockwise* as far as possible to increase cable slack.

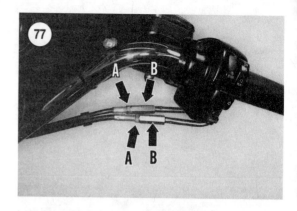

> *CAUTION*
> *Failure to install the spacer in Step 5 will result in damage to the rubber boot and plunger on the front brake switch.*

5. Insert a 5/32 in. (4 mm) thick spacer between the brake lever and lever bracket. Make sure the spacer stays in place during the following steps.

6. Remove the upper and lower T25 Torx screws securing the right side switch assembly together (A, **Figure 78**).

7. Remove the front master cylinder (B, **Figure 78**) as described in Chapter Twelve.

8. Remove the brass ferrules from the notches on the inboard side of the throttle grip (**Figure 79**). Remove the ferrules from the cable end fittings.

9. Remove the friction shoe from the end of the tension adjust screw.

10. Remove the throttle grip from the handlebar.

> *NOTE*
> *Use a rocking motion while pulling on the control cable housings in Step 11. If necessary, place a drop of engine oil on the housings retaining rings to ease removal.*

11. Pull the crimped inserts at the end of the throttle and idle control cable housings from the switch lower housing.

12. Disconnect the throttle control cable and idle control cable from the carburetor cable guide and throttle wheel.

13. On all FLHT models, withdraw the throttle and idle cables from the inner fairing rubber grommet. Move the idle and throttle cables forward and out of the way.

14. Remove all clips and tie-wraps securing the throttle and idle control cables to the frame backbone and ignition coil bracket.

15. Disconnect the cables from the J-clamp on the right side of the frame backbone.

16. If necessary, remove the bolts, washer, P-clamp and locknut securing the cables to the right side of the steering head.

17. Remove the cables from the frame.

18. Clean the throttle grip assembly and dry it thoroughly. Check the throttle slots for cracks or other damage. Replace the throttle if necessary.

19. The friction adjust screw is secured to the lower switch housing with a circlip. If necessary, remove the friction spring, circlip, spring and friction adjust screw. Check these parts for wear or damage. Replace damaged parts and reinstall. Make sure the circlip seats in the friction screw groove completely.

20. Clean the throttle area on the handlebar with solvent.

Installation

1. On all FLHT models, insert the throttle and idle cables through the inner fairing rubber grommet.

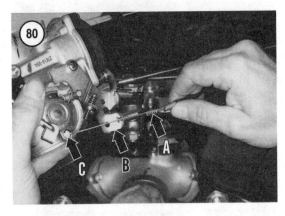

2. Apply a light coat of graphite to the housing inside surfaces and to the handlebar.

3. On the lower switch housing, push the larger diameter silver throttle cable insert into the larger hole in front of the tension adjust screw. Push it in until it snaps into place.

4. Push the smaller diameter gold throttle cable insert into the smaller hole in the rear of the tension adjust screw. Push it in until it snaps into place.

5. Position the friction shoe with the concave side facing up and install it so the pin hole is over the point of the adjuster screw.

6. Install the throttle grip onto the handlebar. Push it on until it stops, then pull it back about 1/8 in. (3.2 mm). Rotate it until the ferrule notches are at the top.

7. Place the lower switch housing below the throttle grip. Install the brass ferrules onto the cables so the end fittings seat in the ferrule recess. Seat ferrules in their respective notches on the throttle control grip. Make sure the cables are captured in the molded grooves in the grip.

8. Install the switch (A, **Figure 78**) and throttle grip assembly. Install the lower switch housing screws and tighten them finger-tight.

9. If it is not in place, insert the 5/32 in. (4 mm) thick spacer between the brake lever and lever bracket. Make sure the spacer stays in place during the following steps.

10. Install the front master cylinder (B, **Figure 78**) onto the handlebar as described in Chapter Twelve.

11. Securely tighten the switch housing screws.

12. Remove the cardboard insert from the front master cylinder.

13. Operate the throttle and make sure both cables move in and out properly.

14. Correctly route the cables from the handlebar to the carburetor. Secure the cables with the clamps and tie-wraps as noted during removal.

15. Connect the idle cable to the carburetor as follows:

   a. The idle cable has the small spring (A, **Figure 80**) on the end of the cable.

   b. Insert the idle cable sheath into the rear cable bracket guide on the carburetor (B, **Figure 80**).

   c. Attach the end of the idle cable into the throttle wheel (C, **Figure 80**).

16. Connect the throttle cable to the carburetor as follows:

   a. Insert the throttle cable sheath into the front cable bracket guide on the carburetor.

   b. Attach the end of the throttle cable to the throttle wheel.

17. At the throttle grip, tighten the cables to keep the cable ends from being disconnected from the throttle wheel.

18. Operate the hand throttle a few times. Make sure the throttle barrel operates smoothly with no binding. Also make sure both cable ends are seated squarely in their cable bracket guides and in the throttle barrel.

19. Adjust the throttle and idle cables as described in Chapter Three.

20. Reinstall the carburetor as described in this chapter.

21. Install the air filter backplate and air filter as described in this chapter.

22. Install the fuel tank as described in this chapter.

23. Start the engine and allow it to idle in NEUTRAL. Then turn the handlebar from side to side. Do not operate the throttle. If the engine speed increases when turning the handlebar assembly, the

7

throttle cables are routed incorrectly or are damaged. Recheck cable routing and adjustment.

WARNING
Do not ride the motorcycle until the throttle cables are properly adjusted. Improper cable routing and adjustment can cause the throttle to stick open. This could cause loss of control.

STARTING ENRICHMENT VALVE (CHOKE) CABLE REPLACEMENT (CARBURETED MODELS)

1. Remove the air filter and backplate as described in Chapter Three.
2. Note the routing of the enrichener cable from its mounting bracket to the carburetor.
3. Loosen the locknut (A, **Figure 81**, typical) and disconnect the starting enrichment valve cable from the mounting bracket (B). Move the end of the cable out of the mounting bracket.
4. Partially remove the carburetor, as described in this chapter, until the starting enrichment valve cable can be disconnected from the backside of the carburetor.
5. Unscrew and remove the starting enrichment valve and cable (**Figure 82**) from the carburetor and remove the cable from the frame.
6. Install by reversing these removal steps. Note the following:
   a. Align the starting enrichment valve needle (A, **Figure 83**) with the needle passage in the carburetor (B) and install the starting enrichment valve. Tighten the valve nut securely.
   b. Position the starting enrichment valve cable into the mounting bracket (B, **Figure 81**), then tighten the locknut (A) securely.

THROTTLE AND IDLE CABLES (FUEL INJECTED MODELS)

There are two different throttle cables. At the throttle grip, the front cable is the throttle control cable (A, **Figure 75**) and the rear cable is the idle control cable (B). At the induction control module, the idle control cable is located at the top of the throttle wheel (A, **Figure 84**) and the throttle control cable (B) is located at the bottom.

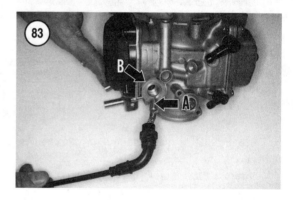

Removal

NOTE
This procedure is shown on a 2001 model.

1. Remove the fuel tank as described in this chapter.
2. Remove the air filter and backing plate as described in this chapter.
3. Make a drawing or take a picture of the cable routing from the induction module through the frame to the right side handlebar.

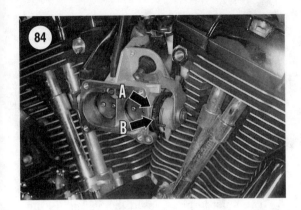

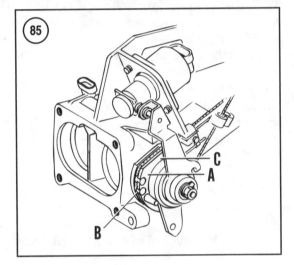

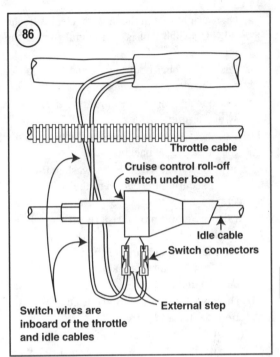

Throttle cable

Cruise control roll-off
switch under boot

Idle cable

Switch connectors

External step

Switch wires are
inboard of the throttle
and idle cables

4. At the right side handlebar, loosen both control cable adjuster locknuts (A, **Figure 77**), then turn the cable adjusters (B) *clockwise* as far as possible to increase cable slack.

5. At the induction module, use needlenose pliers to disconnect the idle cable (A, **Figure 85**) and the throttle cable (B) from the throttle barrel (C).

6. Release the cables from the integral cable guides in the induction module.

CAUTION
Failure to install the spacer in Step 7 will result in damage to the rubber boot and plunger on the front brake switch.

7. Insert a 5/32 in. (4 mm) thick spacer between the brake lever and lever bracket. Make sure the spacer stays in place during the following steps.

8. Remove the upper and lower T25 Torx screws securing the right side switch assembly together (A, **Figure 78**).

9. Remove the front master cylinder (B, **Figure 78**) as described in Chapter Twelve.

10. Remove the brass ferrules from the notches on the inboard side of the throttle grip (**Figure 79**). Remove the ferrules from the cable end fittings.

11. Remove the friction shoe from the end of the tension adjust screw.

12. Remove the throttle grip from the handlebar.

NOTE
Use a rocking motion while pulling on the control cable housings in Step 13. If necessary, place a drop of engine oil on the housings retaining rings to ease removal.

13. Pull the crimped inserts at the end of the throttle and idle control cable housings from the switch lower housing.

14. On all FLHT models, withdraw the throttle and idle cables from the inner fairing rubber grommet. Move the idle and throttle cables forward and out of the way.

15. Remove all clips and tie-wraps securing the throttle and idle control cables to the frame backbone and ignition coil bracket.

16. On models equipped with cruise control, refer to **Figure 86** and perform the following:

a. On the right side of the motorcycle, locate the roll-off switch that is an integral part of the idle cable.

b. Push the rubber boot toward the front to expose the electrical connectors.

c. Disconnect both connectors from the roll-off switch terminals.

17. Disconnect the cables from the J-clamp on the right side of the frame backbone.

18. If necessary, remove the bolts, washer, P-clamp and locknut securing the cables to the right side of the steering head.

19. At the induction module, perform the following:

a. Carefully pull the throttle and idle control cables from the integral cable guides in the induction module.

b. Disconnect the throttle and idle control cables from the throttle barrel.

20. Remove the cables from the frame.

21. Clean the throttle grip assembly and dry it thoroughly. Check the throttle slots for cracks or other damage. Replace the throttle if necessary.

22. The friction adjust screw is secured to the lower switch housing with a circlip. If necessary, remove the friction spring, circlip, spring and friction adjust screw. Check these parts for wear or damage. Replace damaged parts and reinstall. Make sure the circlip seats in the friction screw groove completely.

23. Clean the throttle area on the handlebar with solvent.

Installation

1. Apply a light coat of graphite to the housing inside surfaces and to the handlebar.

2. On the lower switch housing, push the larger diameter silver throttle cable insert into the larger hole in front of the tension adjust screw. Push it in until it snaps into place.

3. Push the smaller diameter gold throttle cable insert into the smaller hole in the rear of the tension adjust screw. Push it in until it snaps into place.

4. Position the friction shoe with the concave side facing up and install it so the pin hole is over the point of the adjuster screw.

5. Install the throttle grip onto the handlebar. Push it on until it stops, then pull it back about 1/8 in. (3.2

mm). Rotate it until the ferrule notches are at the top.

6. Place the lower switch housing below the throttle grip. Install the brass ferrules onto the cables so the end fittings seat in the ferrule recess. Seat the ferrules in their respective notches on the throttle control grip. Make sure the cables are captured in the molded grooves in the grip.

7. Install the switch (A, **Figure 78**) and throttle grip assembly. Install the lower switch housing screws and tighten them finger-tight.

8. If it is not in place, insert the 5/32 in. (4 mm) thick spacer between the brake lever and lever bracket. Make sure the spacer stays in place during the following steps.

9. Install the front master cylinder (B, **Figure 78**) as described in Chapter Twelve.

10. Securely tighten the switch housing screws.

11. Remove the cardboard insert from the front master cylinder.

12. Operate the throttle and make sure both cables move in and out properly.

13. Correctly route the cables from the handlebar to the induction module. Secure the cables with the clamps and tie-wraps as noted during removal.

14. On models equipped with cruise control, refer to **Figure 86** and perform the following:

a. If necessary, straighten the switch terminals.

b. Position the switch terminals so they are parallel to each other and perpendicular to the idle cable.

c. Position the switch wires from the harness so they are located inboard of the throttle and idle cables. Make sure the wires are not tangled and the ends are free.

d. Connect both connectors to the roll-off switch terminals so the external step on the insulators face each other. The connectors can be installed onto either switch terminal. Make sure the connectors are pushed on securely.

e. Slide the rubber boot over the cruise control roll-off switch so the oval cut is located at the electricals connectors.

15. At the induction module, perform the following:

a. Install the idle cable (A, **Figure 85**) ball end over the top of the throttle barrel (C) and install the cable ball end into the upper hole in the throttle barrel. Make sure it is properly seated.

b. Install the throttle cable (B, **Figure 85**) ball end under the bottom of the throttle barrel (C) and install the cable ball ends into the lower hole in the throttle barrel. Make sure they are properly seated.

c. Install the cables into the integral cable guides in the induction module.

16. At the throttle grip, tighten the cables to keep the ball ends from being disconnected from throttle barrel.

17. Operate the hand throttle a few times. Make sure the throttle barrel operates smoothly with no binding. Also make sure both cable ends are seated squarely in their cable bracket guides and in the throttle barrel.

18. Adjust the throttle and idle cables as described in Chapter Three.

19. Install the backing plate and air filter as described in this chapter.

20. Install the fuel tank as described in this chapter.

21. Start the engine and allow it to idle in NEUTRAL. Then turn the handlebar from side to side. Do not operate the throttle. If the engine speed increases when turning the handlebar assembly, the throttle cables are routed incorrectly or are damaged. Recheck cable routing and adjustment.

WARNING
Do not ride the motorcycle until the throttle cables are properly adjusted. Improper cable routing and adjustment can cause the throttle to stick open. This could cause loss of control.

FUEL TANK CONSOLE

Removal/Installation

Refer to **Figure 87** or **Figure 88**.

NOTE
On models so equipped, always disarm the optional TSSM security system prior to disconnecting the battery or the siren will sound.

1. Disconnect the negative battery cable as described in Chapter Eight.
2. Remove the seat as described in Chapter Fourteen.

3. On FLHR models, perform the following:
a. Cut the cable strap securing the fuel level sender wires to the main harness on the left side frame rail.
b. At the rear of the fuel tank, disconnect the fuel level sensor two-pin electrical connector from the main harness.

4A. On FLHT and FLTR models, perform the following:
a. Remove the screw (**Figure 89**) securing the console to the fuel tank.
b. Open the console door.
c. Remove the two front Allen bolts (A, **Figure 90**) securing the console to the fuel tank mounting brackets.
d. Unscrew the fuel filler cap (B, **Figure 90**).

4B. On FLHR models, perform the following:
a. Remove the front acorn nut, rear screw and washer securing the console to the fuel tank.
b. Lift the console partially up off the fuel tank, and disconnect the electrical connector from the ignition switch and the indicator lamp housing.

5. Carefully remove the console and lay it upside down on shop cloths or towels.

6. Reinstall the fuel filler cap (B, **Figure 90**).

7. Install by reversing these removal steps, while noting the following:
a. On FLHT and FLTR models, make sure the rubber boot is in place prior to installation.
b. Carefully route the electrical cables and hose between the console and fuel tank so they will not get pinched.
c. Reposition fuel level sender wires to the main harness on the left side frame rail and install a *new* cable strap.

FUEL TANK
(CARBURETED MODELS)

WARNING
Some fuel may spill from the fuel tank hose during this procedure. Because gasoline is extremely flammable and explosive, perform this procedure away from all open flames, including appliance pilot lights, and sparks. Do not smoke or allow anyone to smoke in the work area, as an explosion and fire may occur. Always work in a

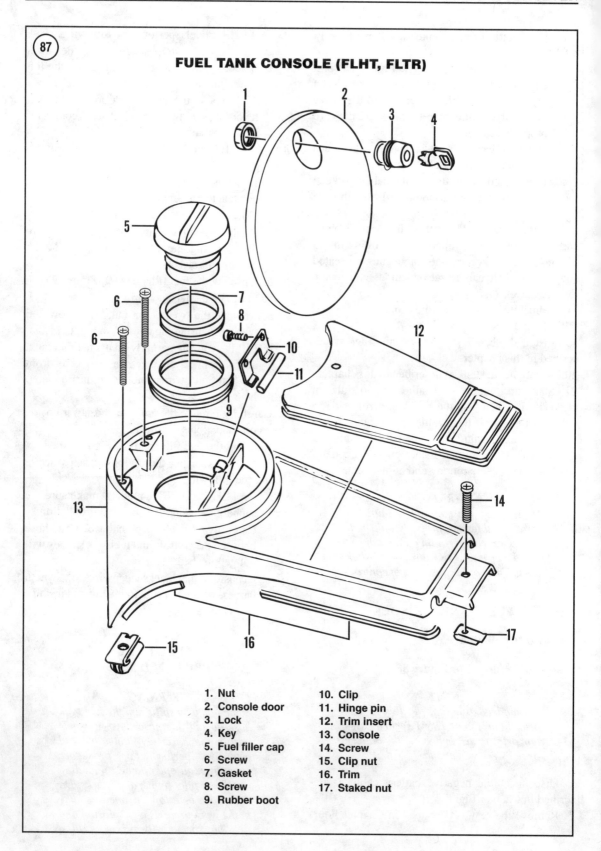

FUEL TANK CONSOLE (FLHT, FLTR)

1. Nut
2. Console door
3. Lock
4. Key
5. Fuel filler cap
6. Screw
7. Gasket
8. Screw
9. Rubber boot
10. Clip
11. Hinge pin
12. Trim insert
13. Console
14. Screw
15. Clip nut
16. Trim
17. Staked nut

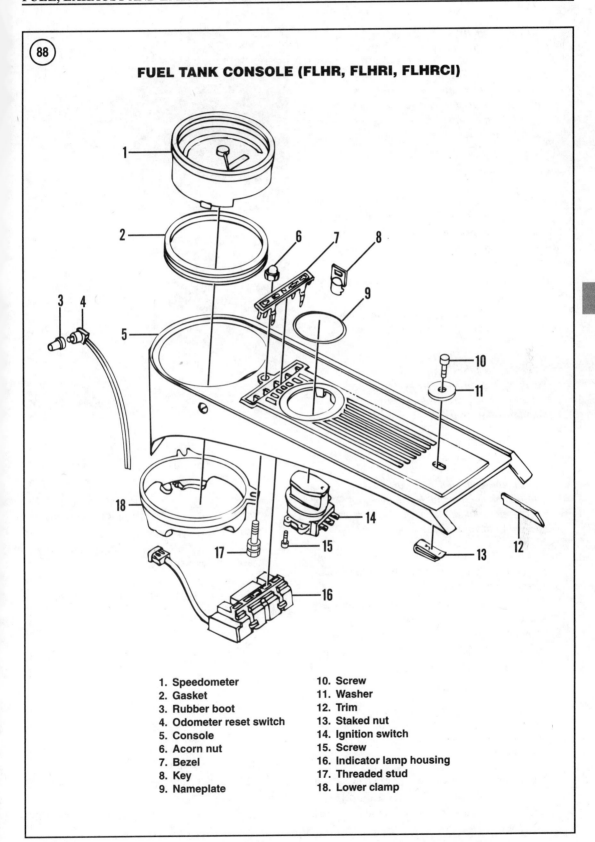

FUEL TANK CONSOLE (FLHR, FLHRI, FLHRCI)

1. Speedometer
2. Gasket
3. Rubber boot
4. Odometer reset switch
5. Console
6. Acorn nut
7. Bezel
8. Key
9. Nameplate
10. Screw
11. Washer
12. Trim
13. Staked nut
14. Ignition switch
15. Screw
16. Indicator lamp housing
17. Threaded stud
18. Lower clamp

well-ventilated area. Wipe up any spills immediately.

WARNING
Route the fuel tank vapor hoses so they cannot contact hot engine or exhaust components. These hoses contain flammable vapors.

Removal/Installation

The fuel hoses are secured to the fuel tank (**Figure 91** or **Figure 92**) with a non-reusable clamp. Purchase *new* ones before servicing the fuel tank.

1. Remove the fuel tank console as described in this chapter.
2. Turn the fuel valve to the OFF position (A, **Figure 93**, typical).
3. Remove the hose clamp and disconnect the fuel hose (B, **Figure 93**) from the valve.

NOTE
A crossover tube connects the two fuel tank compartments. Drain both sides of the tank before removing the tank in the following steps.

4. Drain the fuel tank as follows:

NOTE
A vacuum-operated fuel valve is installed on all carbureted models. A hand-operated vacuum pump is required to drain the fuel tank.

  a. Connect the drain hose to the fuel valve and secure it with a hose clamp. Insert the end of the drain hose into a gas can.
  b. Disconnect the vacuum hose from the fuel valve.
  c. Connect a hand-operated vacuum pump (**Figure 94**) to the fuel valve vacuum hose fitting.
  d. Turn the fuel valve to the RES position.

CAUTION
In the following step, do not apply more than 25 in. (635 mm) Hg of vacuum or the fuel valve diaphragm will be damaged.

  e. Gently operate the vacuum pump handle and apply a *maximum* of 25 in. (635 mm) Hg of vacuum. Once the vacuum is applied, the fuel will start to flow into the gas can.

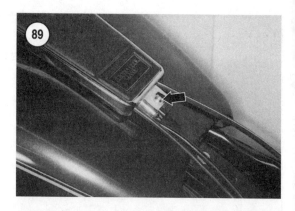

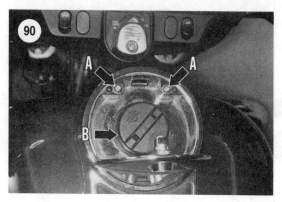

  f. When fuel stops flowing through the hose, turn the fuel valve OFF and release the vacuum. Disconnect the vacuum pump and drain hose.

5. Disconnect the vent hose from the fuel tank.
6. Disconnect the crossover hose from one side of the fuel tank. Plug the tank opening and apply a hemostat to the crossover hose.
7. At the front of the fuel tank, remove the T40 Torx bolt and washer on each side securing the fuel tank to the frame.
8. At the rear of the fuel tank, remove the bolt and washer securing the fuel tank to the frame.
9. Lift and remove the fuel tank.

NOTE
Store the fuel tank in a safe place away from open flames or where it could be damaged.

10. Drain any remaining fuel into a gas can.
11. Installation is the reverse of these steps while noting the following:
  a. Tighten the front and rear bolts and nuts to the specification in **Table 2**.

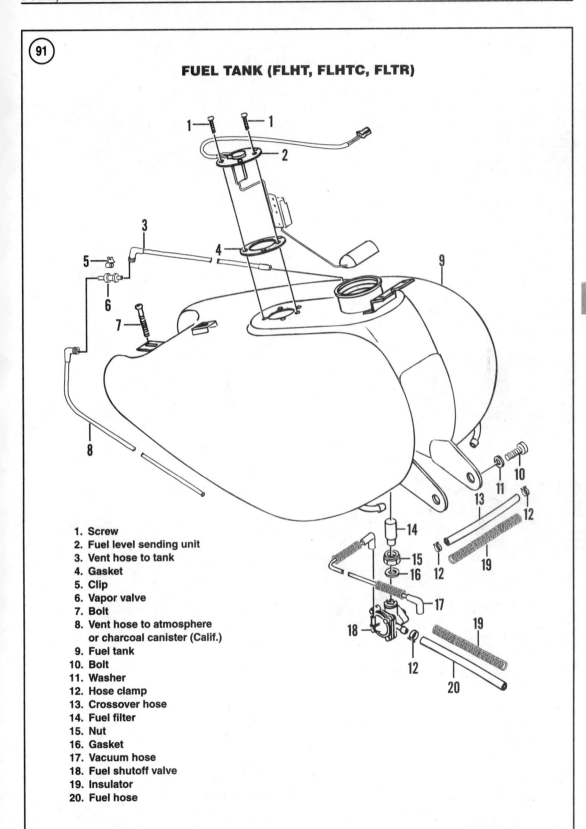

FUEL TANK (FLHT, FLHTC, FLTR)

7

1. Screw
2. Fuel level sending unit
3. Vent hose to tank
4. Gasket
5. Clip
6. Vapor valve
7. Bolt
8. Vent hose to atmosphere
   or charcoal canister (Calif.)
9. Fuel tank
10. Bolt
11. Washer
12. Hose clamp
13. Crossover hose
14. Fuel filter
15. Nut
16. Gasket
17. Vacuum hose
18. Fuel shutoff valve
19. Insulator
20. Fuel hose

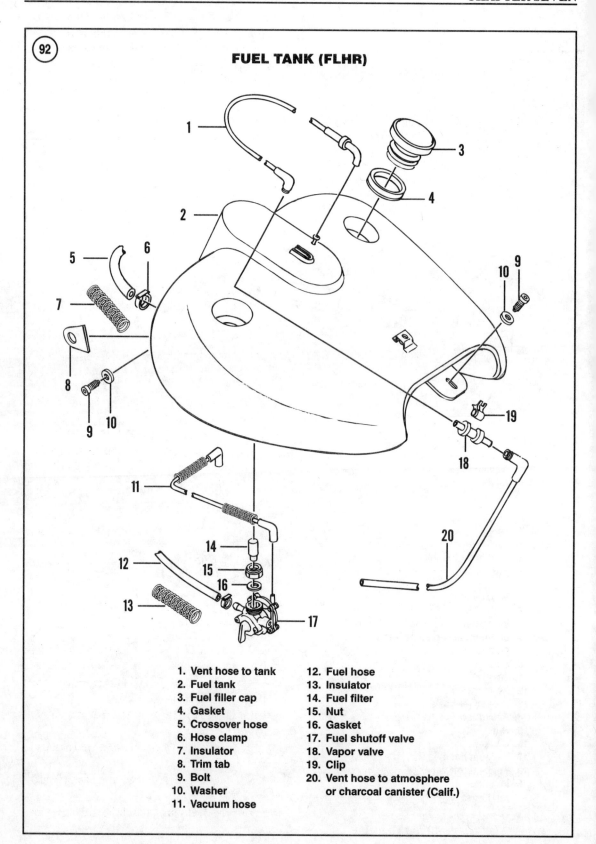

FUEL TANK (FLHR)

1. Vent hose to tank
2. Fuel tank
3. Fuel filler cap
4. Gasket
5. Crossover hose
6. Hose clamp
7. Insulator
8. Trim tab
9. Bolt
10. Washer
11. Vacuum hose
12. Fuel hose
13. Insulator
14. Fuel filter
15. Nut
16. Gasket
17. Fuel shutoff valve
18. Vapor valve
19. Clip
20. Vent hose to atmosphere
    or charcoal canister (Calif.)

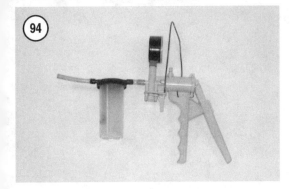

b. Reconnect the fuel hose to the fuel valve and secure it with a *new* hose clamp.

c. Refill the tank and check for leaks.

Inspection

1. Inspect all of the fuel and vent hoses for cracks, deterioration or damage. Replace damaged hoses with the same type and size materials. The fuel line must be flexible and strong enough to withstand engine heat and vibration.

2. Check the fuel line insulator for damage.

3. Check for damaged fuel tank mounting brackets.

4. Remove the filler cap and inspect the tank for rust or contamination. If there is a rust buildup inside the tank, clean and flush the tank as described in this chapter.

5. Inspect the fuel tank for leaks.

FUEL TANK
(FUEL INJECTED MODELS)

WARNING
Some fuel may spill from the fuel tank hose during this procedure. Because

gasoline is extremely flammable and explosive, perform this procedure away from all open flames, including appliance pilot lights, and sparks. Do not smoke or allow anyone to smoke in the work area, as an explosion and fire may occur. Always work in a well-ventilated area. Wipe up any spills immediately.

WARNING
Route the fuel tank vapor hoses so they cannot contact hot engine or exhaust components. These hoses contain flammable vapors.

Fuel Tank Draining

1. Depressurize the fuel system as described in this chapter.

2. Make a drain hose from a 5/16 in. inner diameter hose and plug one end. Make it long enough to go from the fuel tank crossover hose fitting to a gas can.

3. Disconnect the crossover hose from one of the fittings on the fuel tank. Immediately connect the drain hose to the fuel tank fitting.

4. Place the plugged end of the drain hose into the gas can and remove the plug. Drain the fuel from that side of the fuel tank.

5. Disconnect the drain hose and reinstall the plug into the end.

6. Repeat Steps 3-5 for the other side of the fuel tank.

7. Plug the fuel tank crossover fittings to prevent the fuel from draining.

Removal/Installation

The crossover fuel hose is secured to the fuel tank with non-reusable clamps. If the same type of clamps are going to be reinstalled, purchase *new* ones before servicing the fuel tank.

Refer to **Figures 95-98** for fuel tank components and lines.

1. Depressurize the fuel system as described in this chapter.

2. Remove the seat as described in Chapter Fourteen.

3. Remove the fuel tank console as described in this chapter.

7

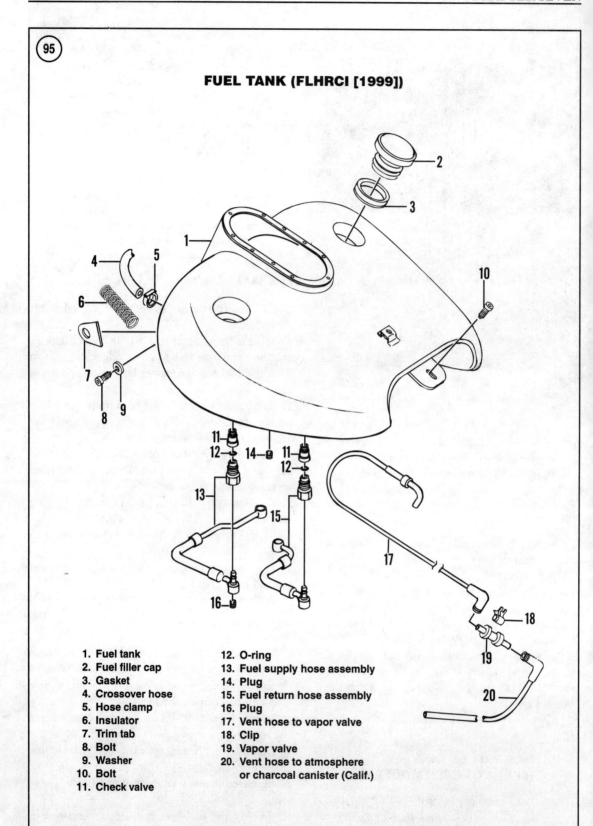

95

FUEL TANK (FLHRCI [1999])

1. Fuel tank
2. Fuel filler cap
3. Gasket
4. Crossover hose
5. Hose clamp
6. Insulator
7. Trim tab
8. Bolt
9. Washer
10. Bolt
11. Check valve
12. O-ring
13. Fuel supply hose assembly
14. Plug
15. Fuel return hose assembly
16. Plug
17. Vent hose to vapor valve
18. Clip
19. Vapor valve
20. Vent hose to atmosphere
    or charcoal canister (Calif.)

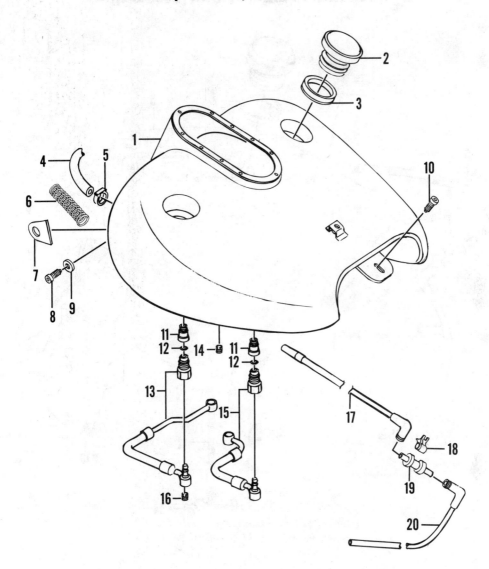

96

FUEL TANK (FLHTCUI, FLHTCI, FHTRI [1999])

1. Fuel tank
2. Fuel filler cap
3. Gasket
4. Crossover hose
5. Hose clamp
6. Insulator
7. Trim tab
8. Bolt
9. Washer
10. Bolt
11. Check valve

12. O-ring
13. Fuel supply hose assembly
14. Plug
15. Fuel return hose assembly
16. Plug
17. Vent hose to vapor valve
18. Clip
19. Vapor valve
20. Vent hose to atmosphere or charcoal canister (Calif.)

7

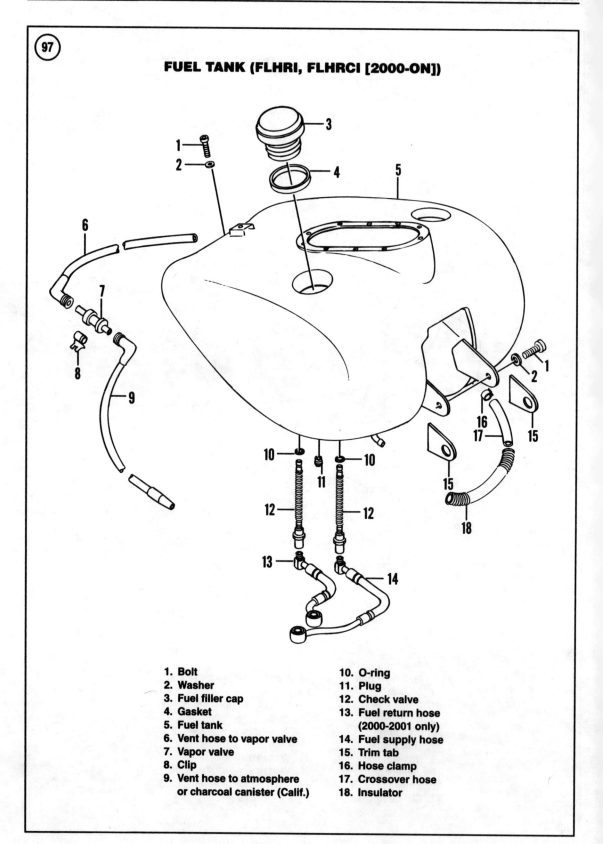

97

FUEL TANK (FLHRI, FLHRCI [2000-ON])

1. Bolt
2. Washer
3. Fuel filler cap
4. Gasket
5. Fuel tank
6. Vent hose to vapor valve
7. Vapor valve
8. Clip
9. Vent hose to atmosphere
   or charcoal canister (Calif.)
10. O-ring
11. Plug
12. Check valve
13. Fuel return hose
    (2000-2001 only)
14. Fuel supply hose
15. Trim tab
16. Hose clamp
17. Crossover hose
18. Insulator

98

FUEL TANK (FLHTCUI, FLHTCI, FLHTRI [2000-ON])

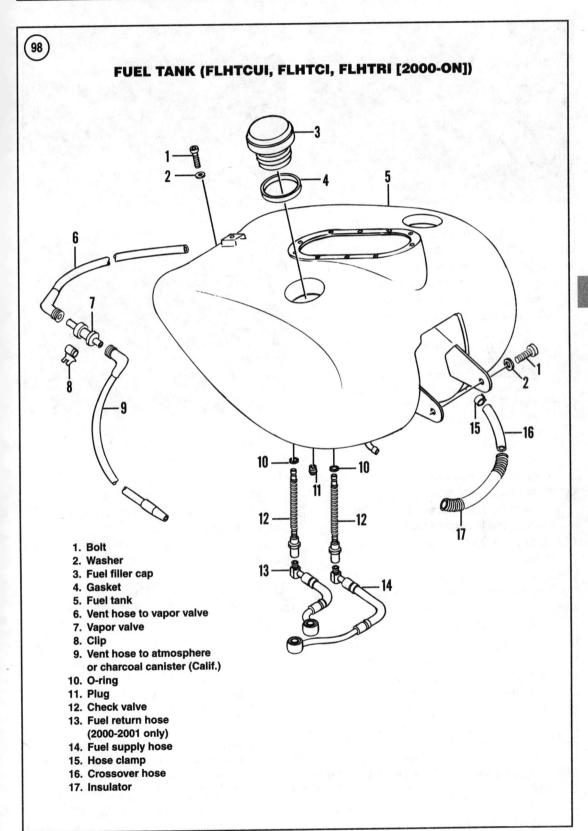

1. **Bolt**
2. **Washer**
3. **Fuel filler cap**
4. **Gasket**
5. **Fuel tank**
6. **Vent hose to vapor valve**
7. **Vapor valve**
8. **Clip**
9. **Vent hose to atmosphere or charcoal canister (Calif.)**
10. **O-ring**
11. **Plug**
12. **Check valve**
13. **Fuel return hose (2000-2001 only)**
14. **Fuel supply hose**
15. **Hose clamp**
16. **Crossover hose**
17. **Insulator**

7

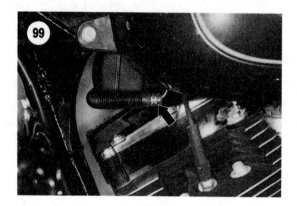

4. Disconnect the crossover hose (**Figure 99**) from one of the fittings on the fuel tank. Drain the fuel tank as described in this chapter.

5. Carefully cut the tie-wraps securing the electrical harness to the left frame tube.

6. Disconnect the vent hose from the fuel tank.

> *WARNING*
> *A small amount of fuel will drain out of the fuel tank when the fuel lines are disconnected from the base of the tank. Place several shop cloths under the fuel line fittings to catch spilled fuel prior to disconnecting them. Discard the shop cloths in a safe manner.*

7A. On 1999 models, disconnect the fuel lines under the fuel tank as follows:

  a. Unscrew the fuel supply line hex nut (front fitting) and disconnect the line.

  b. Unscrew the fuel return line hex nut (rear fitting) and disconnect the line.

  c. Remove the O-ring seal from both fittings.

7B. On 2000-2001 models, disconnect the fuel lines under the fuel tank as follows:

  a. Pull up the chrome sleeve on the supply line quick disconnect fitting (A, **Figure 100**) and disconnect the line.

  b. Repeat sub-step a for the return line (B, **Figure 100**).

7C. On 2002 models, pull up on the chrome sleeve on the quick disconnect fitting and disconnect the fuel line from the fuel tank.

8. On models so equipped, remove the fairing lower cap on each side as described in Chapter Fourteen.

9. Remove the T40 Torx bolt and washer (**Figure 101**) on each side of the fuel tank.

10. Remove the bolt and washer (**Figure 102**) at the rear of the fuel tank.

11. Lift and remove the fuel tank (**Figure 103**).

12. On 2000-on models, inspect the quick-disconnect fitting(s) (**Figure 104**) for signs of leaks. Replace as necessary.

13. Drain any remaining fuel left in the tank into a gas can.

> *WARNING*
> *Store the fuel tank in a safe place away from open flames or where it could be damaged.*

14. Installation is the reverse of these steps while noting the following:

  a. Tighten the front and rear bolts and nuts to the specification in **Table 2**.

  b. On 1999 models, install a *new* O-ring seal onto each fuel line fitting and apply clean engine oil to it. Tighten the hex nut fitting to the specification in **Table 2**.

  c. On 2000-on models, reconnect the fuel line quick disconnect fitting(s) (**Figure 100**) onto the fuel tank until they click into the locked

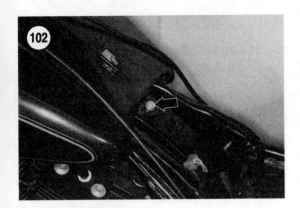

5. Carefully cut the tie-wraps securing the electrical harness to the left frame tube.

6. Disconnect the three individual electrical connectors from the fuel gauge sending unit spade terminals.

7A. On FLHRCI models, perform the following:

    a. Remove the ten T20 Torx bolts securing the top plate to the top of the fuel tank.

    b. Partially lift the top plate away from the fuel tank and disconnect the yellow ground wire from the spade terminal.

    c. Remove the top plate.

7B. On FLHTCUI, FHLTCI and FLTRI models, perform the following:

    a. Remove the ten T20 Torx bolts securing the canopy assembly to the top of the fuel tank.

    b. Partially lift the canopy up away from the fuel tank.

    c. Disconnect the black ground wire from the spade terminal.

    d. Disconnect the yellow wire from the spade terminal.

    e. Carefully pull the canopy assembly straight up and out of the fuel tank. Do not damage the fuel gauge sending unit float during removal.

8. Remove the top plate or canopy gasket. A *new* gasket must be installed.

9. Installation is the reverse of these removal steps while noting the following:

    a. The top plate or canopy gasket is wider at one end. Place the wider end at the front of the fuel tank. Install the gasket and align the bolt holes.

    b. Attach the electrical connector(s) to the spade terminals. The spade terminals are different sizes to eliminate improper connections.

    c. Tighten the T20 Torx bolts securely.

position. Pull down on the fuel lines to make sure they are secured.

    d. Refill the tank and check for leaks.

    e. To synchronize the ECM and the idle speed control actuator, turn the engine stop switch to the RUN position. Then turn the ignition key to the IGNITION position for five seconds and to the OFF position for 10 seconds. Repeat this step once.

FUEL PUMP AND FUEL FILTER (1999 FUEL INJECTED MODELS)

Canopy Assembly
Removal/Installation

Refer to **Figure 105** or **Figure 106**.

1. Depressurize the fuel system as described in this chapter.

2. Remove the seat as described in Chapter Fourteen.

3. Remove the fuel tank console as described in this chapter.

4. Drain the fuel tank as described in this chapter.

FUEL PUMP AND FILTER (FLHRCI [1999])

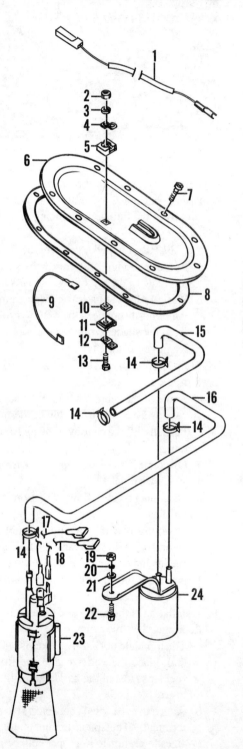

1. Wiring harness
2. Nut
3. Lockwasher
4. Wiring spade terminal
5. Top insulator
6. Top plate
7. Bolt
8. Gasket
9. Ground wire
10. Seal insulator
11. Seal insulator
12. Wiring spade terminal
13. Screw
14. Hose clamp
15. Fuel filter short hose
16. Fuel pump long hose
17. Fuel pump positive wire
18. Fuel pump negative wire
19. Nut
20. Lockwasher
21. Washer
22. Bolt
23. Fuel pump
24. Fuel filter

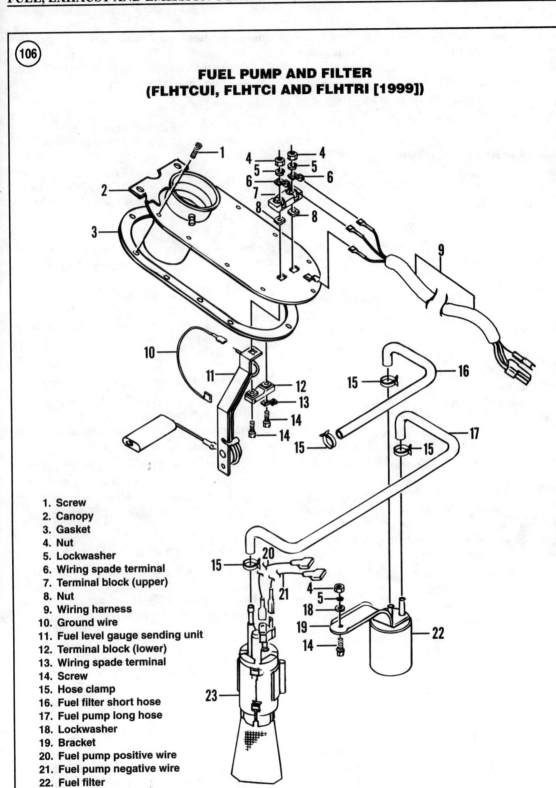

**FUEL PUMP AND FILTER
(FLHTCUI, FLHTCI AND FLHTRI [1999])**

1. Screw
2. Canopy
3. Gasket
4. Nut
5. Lockwasher
6. Wiring spade terminal
7. Terminal block (upper)
8. Nut
9. Wiring harness
10. Ground wire
11. Fuel level gauge sending unit
12. Terminal block (lower)
13. Wiring spade terminal
14. Screw
15. Hose clamp
16. Fuel filter short hose
17. Fuel pump long hose
18. Lockwasher
19. Bracket
20. Fuel pump positive wire
21. Fuel pump negative wire
22. Fuel filter
23. Fuel pump

d. To synchronize the ECM and the idle speed control actuator, turn the engine stop switch to the RUN position. Then turn the ignition key to the IGNITION position for five seconds and to the OFF position for 10 seconds. Repeat this step once.

Fuel Filter Removal/Installation

1. Remove the canopy or top plate assembly as described in this chapter.

WARNING
The fuel tank opening may have some sharp edges. Protect hands accordingly.

2. Use side cutting pliers to cut the hose clamp and remove the short fuel filter hose from the fuel tank inlet supply tube.

CAUTION
Do not drop the nut, lockwasher and washer in the following step as they will fall to the bottom of the fuel tank.

3. Loosen the nut securing the fuel filter mounting bracket to the bolt on top of the fuel tank tunnel. Remove the nut. Then use a magnetic tool to remove the lockwasher and washer from the bolt.
4. Release the fuel filter mounting bracket from the fuel tank tunnel.
5. Partially withdraw the fuel filter and long fuel pump hose from the fuel tank.
6. Use side cutting pliers to cut the hose clamp and remove the long fuel filter hose from the fuel tank outlet supply tube.
7. Use side cutting pliers to cut the remaining hose clamp and remove the short fuel filter hose from the fuel filter inlet supply tube.
8. Remove the fuel filter.
9. Installation is the reverse of removal while noting the following:
   a. Use *new* hose clamps.
   b. Install the short hose onto the *new* fuel filter outlet port so the initial bend runs parallel to the fuel filter bracket. Crimp the hose clamp.
   c. Slide a *new* hose clamp onto the free end of the long hose. Install the hose onto the inlet port so it runs parallel to the short hose. Crimp the clamp.

Fuel Pump Removal/Installation

1. Remove the canopy or top plate assembly as described in this chapter.

WARNING
The fuel tank opening may have some sharp edges. Protect hands accordingly.

2. Lift the fuel pump off the two posts on the left side of the fuel tank. Remove the fuel pump assembly from the fuel tank.
3. Use side cutting pliers to cut the hose clamp on the long hose and disconnect it from the outlet port.
4. Disconnect the wires from the fuel pump.

CAUTION
Do not replace the special Teflon coated wires with ordinary wire as the insulation may deteriorate when exposed to gasoline.

5. Inspect the fuel pump wires and replace them with *new* Teflon coated wires if necessary.
6. Discard the fuel pump.
7. Installation is the reverse of removal while noting the following:
   a. Use *new* hose clamps.
   b. Attach the electrical connectors to the fuel pump terminals. The terminals are different sizes to eliminate improper connections.

FUEL PUMP AND FUEL FILTER (2000-ON FUEL INJECTED MODELS)

Refer to **Figures 107-110** for canopy assembly, fuel pump and fuel filter components.

Canopy Assembly Removal/Installation

1. Depressurize the fuel system as described under in this chapter.
2. Remove the seat as described in Chapter Fourteen.
3. Drain the fuel tank as described in this chapter.
4. Remove the fuel tank and console as described in this chapter.
5. Remove the ten T20 Torx bolts securing the canopy assembly to the top of the fuel tank.

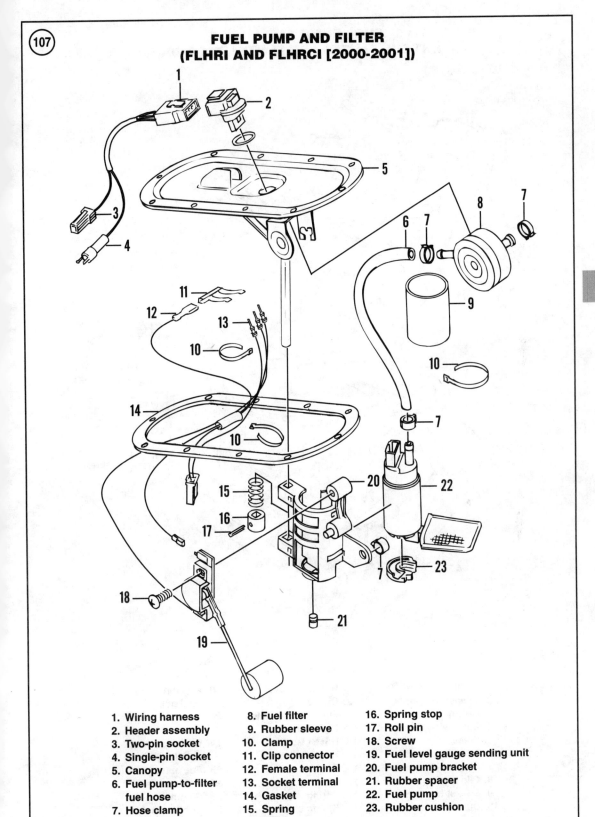

107

FUEL PUMP AND FILTER
(FLHRI AND FLHRCI [2000-2001])

1. Wiring harness
2. Header assembly
3. Two-pin socket
4. Single-pin socket
5. Canopy
6. Fuel pump-to-filter
   fuel hose
7. Hose clamp
8. Fuel filter
9. Rubber sleeve
10. Clamp
11. Clip connector
12. Female terminal
13. Socket terminal
14. Gasket
15. Spring
16. Spring stop
17. Roll pin
18. Screw
19. Fuel level gauge sending unit
20. Fuel pump bracket
21. Rubber spacer
22. Fuel pump
23. Rubber cushion

7

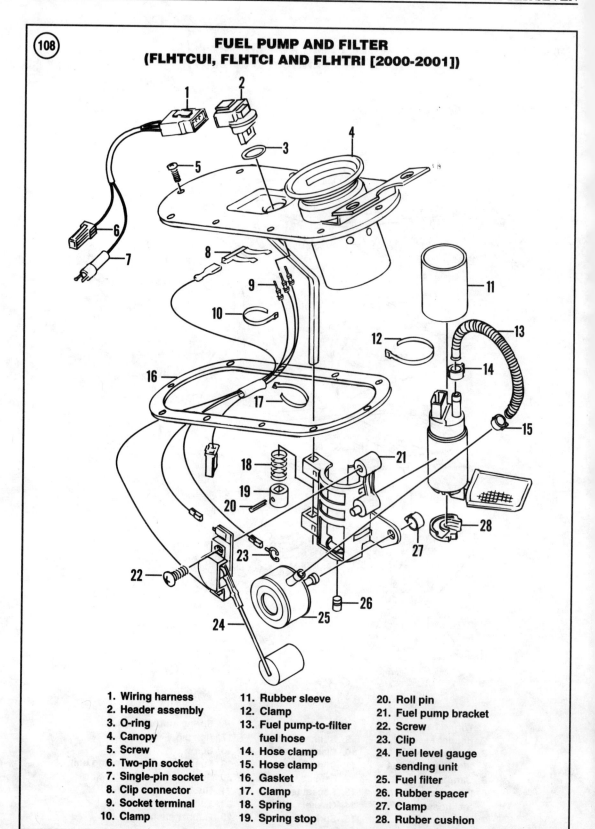

**FUEL PUMP AND FILTER
(FLHTCUI, FLHTCI AND FLHTRI [2000-2001])**

1. Wiring harness
2. Header assembly
3. O-ring
4. Canopy
5. Screw
6. Two-pin socket
7. Single-pin socket
8. Clip connector
9. Socket terminal
10. Clamp
11. Rubber sleeve
12. Clamp
13. Fuel pump-to-filter fuel hose
14. Hose clamp
15. Hose clamp
16. Gasket
17. Clamp
18. Spring
19. Spring stop
20. Roll pin
21. Fuel pump bracket
22. Screw
23. Clip
24. Fuel level gauge sending unit
25. Fuel filter
26. Rubber spacer
27. Clamp
28. Rubber cushion

109

FUEL PUMP AND FILTER
(FLHRI, FLHRCI [2002])

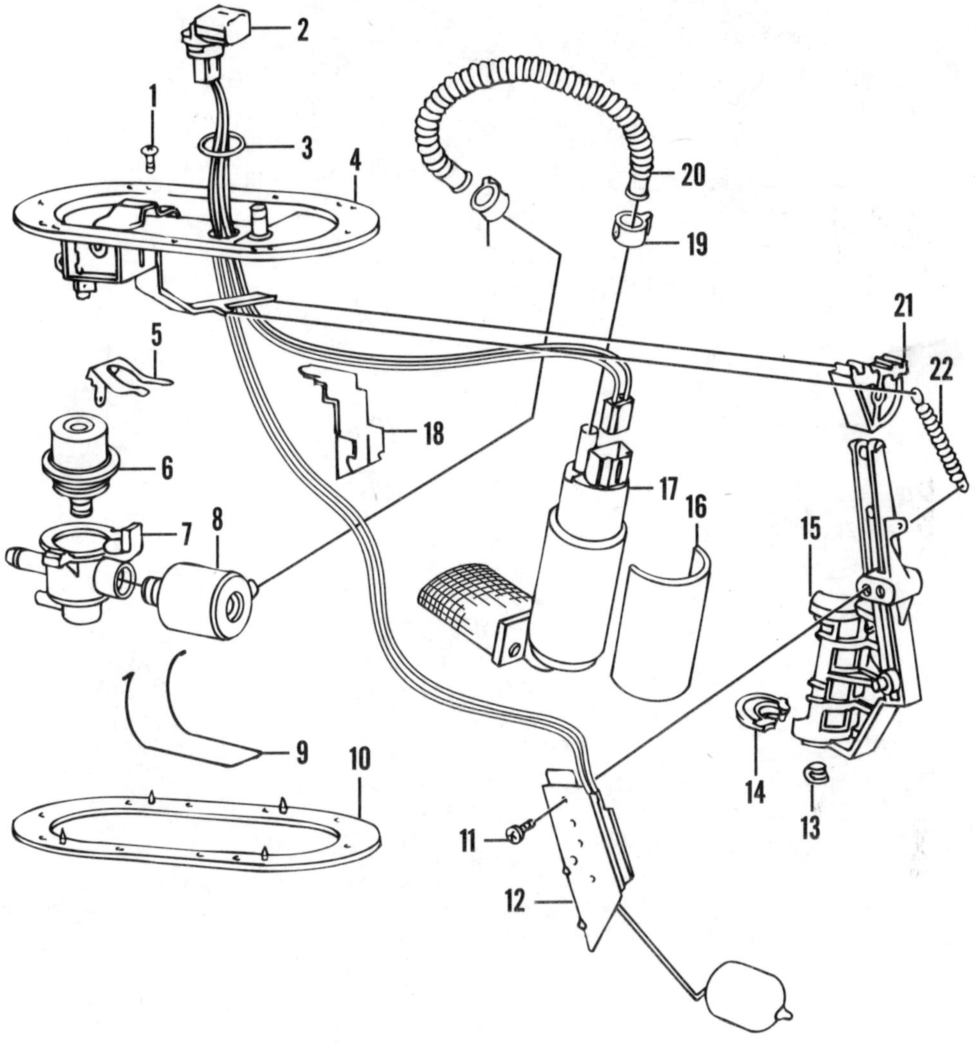

1. Screw
2. 3-way header assembly
3. O-ring
4. Canopy
5. Clip connector
6. Fuel pressure regulator
7. Pressure regulator housing
8. Fuel filter
9. Wire bail
10. Gasket
11. Screw
12. Fuel gauge sending unit
13. Rubber spacer
14. Rubber cushion
15. Fuel pump housing
16. Rubber sleeve
17. Fuel pump
18. Wire bail bracket
19. 8 mm hose clamp
20. Fuel pump-to-filter hose
21. Fuel pump housing end cap
22. Spring

7

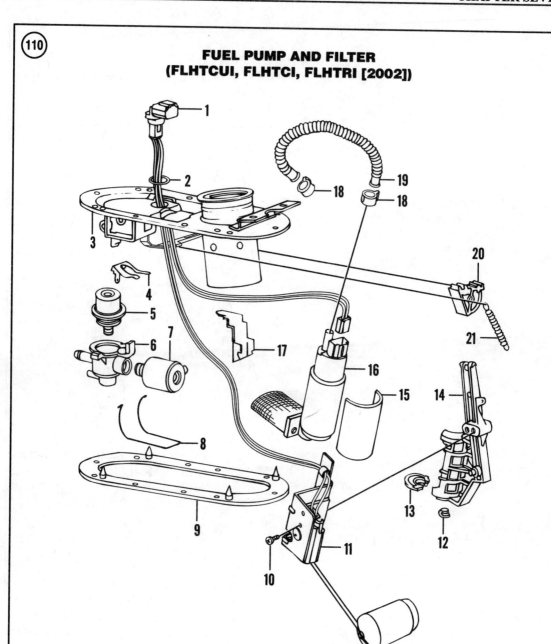

**FUEL PUMP AND FILTER
(FLHTCUI, FLHTCI, FLHTRI [2002])**

1. Three-way header assembly
2. O-ring
3. Canopy
4. Clip connector
5. Fuel pressure regulator
6. Pressure regulator housing
7. Fuel filter
8. Wire bail
9. Gasket
10. Screw
11. Fuel gauge sending unit
12. Rubber spacer
13. Rubber cushion
14. Fuel pump housing
15. Rubber sleeve
16. Fuel pump
17. Wire bail bracket
18. 8 mm hose clamp
19. Fuel pump-to-filter hose
20. Fuel pump housing end cap
21. Spring

7. Partially lift the canopy up away from the fuel tank.

CAUTION
Do not cut the fuel supply hose while cutting the hose clamp in the following step.

8. On the left side of the fuel tank, carefully cut the hose clamp securing the outlet hose to the fuel filter fitting.
9. Carefully pull the canopy assembly straight up and out of the fuel tank. Do not damage the fuel gauge sending unit float during removal.
10. Remove the canopy gasket.
11. Installation is the reverse of these removal steps while noting the following:

   a. Slip a *new* hose clamp onto the outlet hose prior to installing the assembly into the fuel tank.
   b. Install the outlet onto the fuel filter and crimp the hose clamp.
   c. Install a *new* canopy gasket.
   d. Tighten the T20 Torx bolts securely.
   e. To synchronize the ECM and the idle speed control actuator, turn the engine stop switch to the RUN position. Then turn the ignition key to the IGNITION position for five seconds and to the OFF position for 10 seconds. Repeat this step once.

Fuel Filter Removal/Installation (2000-2001 Models)

1. Remove the canopy assembly as previously described.
2. Use side cutting pliers to cut the hose clamp, and remove it and the hose from the fuel pump inlet port.
3A. On FLHTCUI, FLHTCI and FLTRI models, remove the retaining ring from the groove in the fuel filter outlet port. Pull the fuel filter outlet port from the housing and remove the fuel filter.
3B. On FLHRI and FLHRCI models, use a small screwdriver to gently pry the fuel filter from the slotted side of the canopy mounting bracket. Remove the fuel filter from the mounting bracket.
4. Discard the fuel filter.
5. Installation is the reverse of removal. Use *new* hose clamps.

Fuel Filter Removal/Installation (2002 Models)

1. Remove the canopy assembly as previously described.
2. Carefully pull the wire bail from the slots on the fuel filter canister bracket. Move the wire bail out of the way.
3. Pull the canister bracket forward and disengage the tab from the slot on the canopy weldment.
4. Carefully pull the fuel filter out of the pressure regulator housing.
5. Use side cutting pliers to cut the hose clamp and remove it from the fuel pump hose.
6. Disconnect the fuel filter from the fuel pump hose.
7. Discard the fuel pump.
8. Installation is the reverse of removal while noting the following:

   a. Use a *new* hose clamp.
   b. Use a *new* O-ring on the fuel filter.

Fuel Pump Removal/Installation

1. Remove the canopy assembly as described in this chapter.
2. Depress the latch and disconnect the electrical connector from the fuel pump.
3. Remove the T15 Torx screw and remove the fuel sending unit from the fuel pump bracket.
4. Use side cutting pliers to cut the hose clamp, and remove it and the hose from the fuel pump outlet port.
5. On FLHTCUI, FLHTCI and FLTRI models, remove the retaining ring from the groove in the fuel filter outlet port. Pull the fuel filter outlet port from the mounting bracket and remove the fuel filter.
6. Use a 1/8 in. punch to tap the roll pin from the spring stop and the canopy support rod.
7. Slide the fuel pump and bracket assembly, spring and spring stop from the canopy support rod.
8. Discard the fuel pump and bracket assembly.

NOTE
The new fuel pump assembly consists of the fuel pump, mounting bracket, rubber spacer and the rubber cushion.

9. Slide the *new* fuel pump assembly onto the canopy support rod. Before the rod enters the housing's

7

lower square hole, slide the spring and spring stop onto the end of the support rod.

10. Align the spring stop hole with the canopy support rod hole and install the roll pin. Carefully tap the roll pin into place until the end is flush with the spring stop.

11. On FLHTCUI, FLHTCI and FLTRI models, install the fuel filter outlet port through the hole in the mounting bracket and secure it with the retaining ring.

CAUTION
Do not crimp the hose clamp too tight as it may crack the fuel pump plastic outlet port.

12. Install a *new* hose clamp onto the fuel pump outlet hose. Install the hose onto the outlet port and carefully crimp the clamp.

13. Attach the fuel sending unit to the fuel pump bracket and tighten the T15 Torx screws securely.

14. Attach the electrical connector to the top of the fuel pump and push it on until it clicks into the locked position. Pull straight up on the connector to ensure it is locked in place.

15. Install the canopy assembly as previously described.

Fuel Pump Removal/Installation (2002 Models)

NOTE
During the removal procedure, the fuel pump mounting bracket will be damaged and must be replaced along with the fuel pump. Make sure the fuel pump is defective prior to removing it from the bracket.

1. Remove the canopy assembly as previously described.

2. Depress the external latch and disconnect the electrical connector from the fuel pump.

3. Use side cutting pliers to cut the hose clamp, and remove it from the fuel pump hose.

4. Remove the T15 Torx screw and remove the fuel level sending unit from the post on the fuel pump mounting bracket.

5. Disconnect the spring from the hook on the fuel pump mounting bracket.

6. Insert a flat screwdriver tip and crack the webbing at the top of the fuel pump mounting bracket

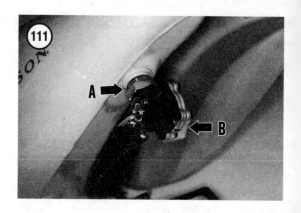

hinge. Remove the hinge from the mounting bracket.

7. Remove the fuel pump and bracket assembly.

8. Installation is the reverse of removal. Install a new fuel pump and fuel pump mounting bracket.

FUEL SHUTOFF VALVE (CARBURETED MODELS)

A three-way vacuum-operated fuel shutoff valve is mounted to the left side of the fuel tank. A replaceable fuel filter is mounted to the top of the fuel shutoff valve.

To troubleshoot this valve, refer to *Vacuum Operated Fuel Shutoff Valve Testing* in Chapter Two.

Removal

WARNING
Gasoline is very volatile and flammable. Work in a well-ventilated area away from any open flames, including pilot lights on household appliances. Do not allow anyone to smoke in the area and have a fire extinguisher rated for gasoline fires on hand.

1. Disconnect the negative battery cable as described in Chapter Eight.

2. Turn the fuel shutoff valve to the OFF position.

3. Drain the fuel tank as described under *Fuel Tank Removal/Installation* in this chapter.

NOTE
*The fuel shutoff valve can be removed with the fuel tank in place. **Figure 111** is shown with the fuel tank removed to better illustrate the step.*

4. Loosen the fuel valve fitting (A, **Figure 111**) and remove the fuel shutoff valve (B) from the fuel tank. Drain residual gasoline still in the tank after the valve is removed.

Cleaning and Inspection

1. Inspect the filter mounted on top of the fuel valve. Remove contamination from the filter. Replace the filter if it is damaged.
2. Install a *new* filter gasket before installing the filter onto the fuel valve.
3. Remove all sealant residue from the fuel tank and fuel valve threads.

Installation

1. Install a *new* filter gasket onto the fuel shutoff valve, then install the filter.
2. Coat the fuel valve threads with Loctite Teflon pipe sealant.
3. Insert the fuel valve into the tank, then start the hex fitting onto the fuel tank threads two turns.
4. Hold the hex fitting and start the fuel valve into the fitting by turning it *counterclockwise* two turns.
5. Hold the fuel valve and tighten the hex fitting to the torque specification in **Table 2**.

WARNING
If the hex fitting is turned more than two turns on the valve, it may bottom out on the valve and cause a fuel leak.

6. Install the insulator tube over the fuel hose.
7. Reconnect the fuel hose to the fuel shutoff valve and secure it with a hose clamp.
8. Refill the fuel tank and check for leaks.

FUEL TANK GAUGE (FLHR)

WARNING
Gasoline is extremely flammable and explosive, perform this procedure away from all open flames, including appliance pilot lights, and sparks. Do not smoke or allow someone to smoke in the work area, as an explosion and fire may occur. Always work in a well-ventilated area. Wipe up any spills immediately.

Removal/Installation

1. Remove the fuel tank as described in this chapter.

NOTE
The fuel gauge electrical wires are routed through a tube in the fuel tank and are secured with a clamp at the bottom of the fuel tank. Loosen the clamp and make sure there is enough slack in the wires to allow the gauge to be pulled up and out of the fuel tank.

2. Pull straight up on the gauge and partially remove it from the tank.
3. Disconnect the electrical connector from the wires in the fuel tank. Do not disconnect the electrical wires from the fuel gauge.
4. Remove the fuel gauge and the gasket.
5. Remove the five screws securing the sending unit to the fuel tank.

CAUTION
Do not bend the float arm during removal of the sending unit. If bent, the gauge will give inaccurate readings.

6. Carefully withdraw the sending unit while moving it back and forth, and while lifting and turning it in either direction.
7. Remove the gasket from the fuel tank.
8. Install by reversing these removal steps while noting the following:
   a. Install *new* gaskets between the fuel gauge and fuel tank.
   b. Install the sending unit *carefully* to avoid damage to the float arm.
   c. Tighten all screws securely.

EXHAUST SYSTEM

Removal

Refer to **Figure 112**.

NOTE
If the system joints are corroded or rusty, spray all connections with WD-40, or an equivalent, and allow the penetrating oil to soak in sufficiently to free the rusted joints.

7

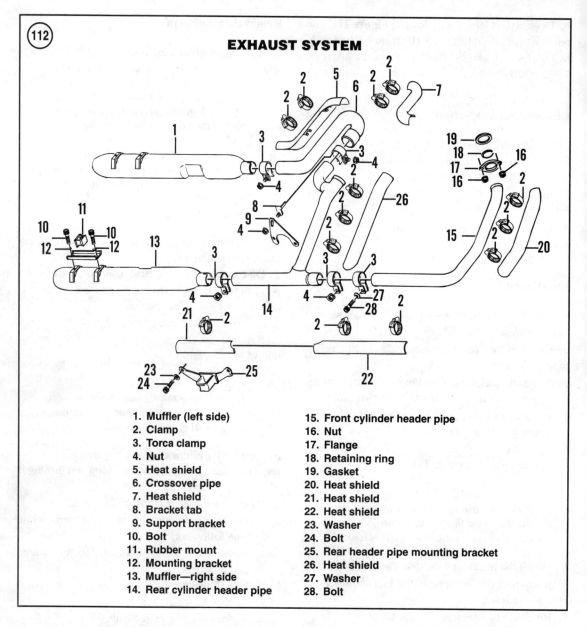

EXHAUST SYSTEM

1. Muffler (left side)
2. Clamp
3. Torca clamp
4. Nut
5. Heat shield
6. Crossover pipe
7. Heat shield
8. Bracket tab
9. Support bracket
10. Bolt
11. Rubber mount
12. Mounting bracket
13. Muffler—right side
14. Rear cylinder header pipe
15. Front cylinder header pipe
16. Nut
17. Flange
18. Retaining ring
19. Gasket
20. Heat shield
21. Heat shield
22. Heat shield
23. Washer
24. Bolt
25. Rear header pipe mounting bracket
26. Heat shield
27. Washer
28. Bolt

1. Support the motorcycle on a work stand. See *Motorcycle Stands* in Chapter Nine.

2. Remove both saddlebags as described in Chapter Fourteen.

3. Remove the footboards as described in Chapter Fourteen.

4. Label the heat shields prior to removal for aid during installation. They look very similar but all have slight differences. Use the numbers assigned to these parts in **Figure 112**.

5. Loosen the clamps and remove the six heat shields.

6. Wrap the left side muffler in a towel, then secure it to the saddlebag mounting bracket with a Bungee cord or rope.

7. At each cylinder head, loosen and remove the two flange nuts securing both the front and rear exhaust pipes to the cylinder heads.

8. Slide the exhaust flange and retaining ring off the cylinder head studs.

9. Loosen the Torca clamps in the following order:
   a. Front header pipe-to-rear header pipe.
   b. Rear header pipe-to-right side muffler.
   c. Rear header pipe-to-crossover pipe.

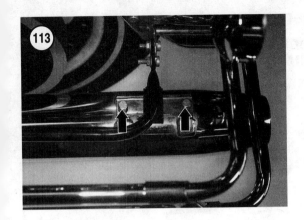

d. Crossover pipe-to-the left side muffler.

10. Remove the bolts and lockwashers securing the right side muffler to the saddlebag lower support rail.

11. Pull the muffler toward the rear and disconnect the right side muffler from the rear header pipe. Remove the muffler. Slightly rotate the muffler during removal.

12. Remove the nut securing the bracket tab to the support bracket.

13. Remove the rear header pipe from the front header pipe, the crossover pipe and the rear cylinder head port studs.

14. Remove the bracket tab from the slot in the Torca clamp.

15. Remove the bolt, washer and lockwasher from the transmission clamp on the front header pipe. Open the clamp and remove the front header pipe from the transmission bracket.

16. Remove the front header pipe from the front cylinder head port studs.

17. Remove the crossover pipe from the left side muffler.

18. Remove the bolts and lockwashers (**Figure 113**) securing the left side muffler to the saddlebag lower support rail.

19. Remove the Bungee cord or rope, and remove the left side muffler.

20. Remove the retaining ring, then remove the exhaust port gaskets.

21. Inspect the exhaust system as described in this chapter.

22. Store the exhaust system components in a safe place until they are reinstalled.

Installation

> *NOTE*
> *New Torca clamps must be installed to ensure correct sealing integrity. The new Torca clamps eliminate the need for graphite or silicone tape during installation of the mufflers.*

> *NOTE*
> *To prevent exhaust leaks, do not tighten any of the mounting bolts and nuts or the Torca clamps until all exhaust components are in place.*

1. Scrape the exhaust port surfaces to remove all carbon residue. Then wipe the port with a rag.

2. Install a *new* exhaust port gasket into each exhaust port with the tapered side facing out. Install the retaining rings to secure the gaskets.

3. If the transmission clamp was removed, install it onto the transmission side cover.

4. Install the front header pipe onto the front cylinder head exhaust port. Install the flange nuts and tighten them finger-tight.

5. Install the front header pipe onto the transmission bracket clamp. Close the clamp and install the bolt, washer and lockwasher, then tighten the bolt finger-tight.

6. Install a *new* Torca clamp onto the end of the front header pipe.

7. Install the rear header pipe onto the rear cylinder head exhaust port. Install the flange nuts and tighten them finger-tight.

8. Move the Torca clamp into position where the front and rear header pipes join.

> *NOTE*
> *The crossover pipe to the rear header pipe Torca clamp is unique since it has a slot for the support bracket tab.*

9. Install a *new* Torca clamp onto each free end of the rear header pipe.

10. Install the right side muffler onto the rear header pipe.

11. Install the bolts and lockwashers securing the right side muffler to the saddlebag lower support rail. Tighten the bolts finger-tight.

12. Move the Torca clamp into position where the muffler and rear header pipe join.

7

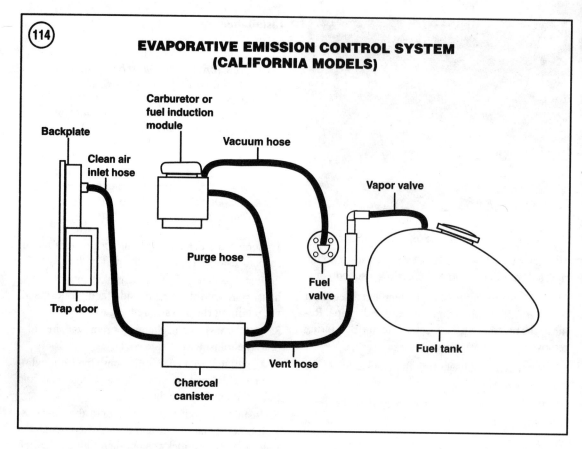

EVAPORATIVE EMISSION CONTROL SYSTEM (CALIFORNIA MODELS)

13. Fit the bracket tab into the slot of the Torca clamp, engaging the stud in the slot of the exhaust pipe bracket. Start the nut and tighten it finger-tight.

14. Install a *new* Torca clamp onto each free end of the crossover pipe.

15. Install the left side muffler onto the crossover pipe.

16. Secure the left side muffler to the saddlebag mounting bracket with a Bungee cord or rope.

17. Move the Torca clamp into position where the muffler and crossover pipe join.

18. Install the bolts and lockwashers securing the left side muffler to the saddlebag lower support rail. Tighten the bolts finger-tight.

19. Check the entire exhaust system to make sure none of the exhaust components are touching the frame. If necessary, make slight adjustments to avoid any contact that would transmit vibrations to the rider through the frame.

20. Check the exhaust assembly alignment, then tighten the mounting bolts and nuts as follows:

   a. Front cylinder head flange nuts. Tighten the upper nut to 9-18 in-lbs. (1-2 N•m), then tighten the lower nut to 120 in-lbs. (14 N•m). Tighten the upper nut to 120 in-lbs. (14 N•m).

   b. Rear cylinder head flange nuts. Tighten the upper nut to 9-18 in-lbs. (1-2 N•m), then tighten the lower nut to 120 in-lbs. (14 N•m). Tighten the upper nut to 120 in-lbs. (14 N•m).

   c. Tighten the transmission clamp bolt securely.

   d. On each side, tighten the muffler-to-saddlebag mounting bracket bolts securely.

21. Tighten the Torca clamps to 45-60 ft. lbs. (61-81 N•m) in the following order:

   a. Crossover pipe-to-left muffler.

   b. Rear header pipe-to-right muffler.

   c. Front header pipe-to-rear header pipe.

   d. Rear header pipe-to-cross over pipe.

22. Tighten the exhaust support bracket nut securely.

23. Open the heat shield clamps completely. Position the clamp so the screw is on the outboard side in the most accessible position. Install the heat shields in the locations marked during removal. Tighten the clamps to 20-40 in-lbs. (2-5 N•m).

24. Check all heat shields to make sure none are touching the frame. If necessary, make slight adjustments to avoid any contact that would transmit vibrations to the rider through the frame.
25. Remove the Bungee cord or rope securing the left side muffler to the saddlebag lower support rail.
26. Start the engine and check for leaks.
27. Install the saddlebags as described in Chapter Fourteen.

Inspection

1. Replace rusted or damaged exhaust system components.
2. Inspect all pipes for rust or corrosion.
3. Remove all rust from exhaust pipes and muffler mating surfaces.
4. The Torca clamps are not reusable.
5. Replace damaged exhaust pipe retaining rings.
6. Replace worn or damaged heat shield clamps as required.
7. Check the mounting bracket bolts and nuts for tightness.

EVAPORATIVE EMISSION CONTROL SYSTEM (CALIFORNIA MODELS)

The evaporative emission control system prevents gasoline vapor from escaping into the atmosphere.

When the engine is not running, the system directs the fuel vapor from the fuel tank through the vapor valve and into the charcoal canister. Also, when the engine is not running, the gravity-operated trap door in the air filter backplate blocks the inlet port of the air filter. This prevents hydrocarbon vapors from the carburetor venturi, or fuel injection induction module, from escaping into the atmosphere.

When the engine is running, these vapors are drawn through a purge hose and into the carburetor, or fuel injection induction module, where they burn in the combustion chambers. The vapor valve also prevents gasoline vapor from escaping from the carbon canister if the motorcycle falls onto its side.

Also, when the engine is running, the engine vacuum pulls the air filter backplate trap door open, allowing air to enter.

Inspection

Refer to **Figure 114** for component placement and hose routing. Before removing the hoses from any of the parts, mark the hose and fitting with a piece of masking tape to identify them.
1. Check all emission control lines and hoses to make sure they are correctly routed and connected.

WARNING
Make sure the fuel tank vapor hoses are routed so they cannot contact hot engine or exhaust components. These hoses contain flammable vapor. If a hose melts from contact with a hot part, leaking vapor may ignite, causing severe motorcycle damage and rider injury.

2. Make sure there are no kinks in the lines or hoses. Also inspect the hoses and lines routed near engine hot spots for excessive wear or burning.
3. Check the physical condition of all lines and hoses in the system. Check for cuts, tears or loose connections. These lines and hoses are subjected to various temperatures and operating conditions, and eventually become brittle and crack. Replace damaged lines and hoses.
4. Check all components in the emission control system for damage, such as broken fittings.

Vapor Valve Replacement

The vapor valve (**Figure 115**) is connected to the vent hose between the fuel tank and carbon canister.
1. Remove the seat as described in Chapter Fourteen.
2. Label the hoses at the vapor valve, then disconnect them.
3. Note that one end of the vapor valve is longer than the other end. The longer end must face up to-

ward the fuel tank. Remove and replace the vapor valve (**Figure 115**).

> *CAUTION*
> *The vapor valve must be installed in the vent hose in a vertical position with the longer end facing up toward the fuel tank.*

4. Install the vapor valve and secure both hoses.

Carbon Canister Replacement

1. Remove the frame right side cover as described in Chapter Fourteen.
2. Move any electrical component surrounding the carbon canister out of the way.
3. Prior to disconnecting any of the hoses, label the hoses and the canister fittings. Plug the open end of each hose to prevent contamination.
4. Disconnect the clean air hose (**Figure 116**) from the right side of the canister.
5. Disconnect the purge hose and the vent hose from the left side of the canister.

6. Using a flat-blade screwdriver, lift the tang on the base of the canister, slide the canister toward the left side and remove the canister from the mounting bracket.

7. Install the carbon canister by reversing these steps while noting the following:

    a. Slide the canister into the mounting bracket until it clicks.

    b. Attach the hoses to the correct fittings as noted during removal.

Table 1 CARBURETOR JET SIZES

Model	Main jet	Pilot jet
49-state	190	45
California	195	45
International	190	45

Table 2 FUEL SYSTEM TORQUE SPECIFICATIONS

Item	ft.-lb.	in.-lb.	N•m
Air filter			
Backplate torx screws	–	17-35	2-4
Cover screw	–	35-62	4-7
Breather hollow bolts	–	124-142	14-16
Fuel line hex fitting at fuel tank (1999)	15-18	–	20-24
Fuel shutoff valve			
Hex fitting	15-20	–	20-27
Diaphragm cover screws	–	18.5	2.1
Fuel tank mounting bolts			
Front	15-18	–	20-24
Rear	–	71	8
Intake manifold bolts	–	71-124	8-14
Induction module bolts (EFI)	–	71-124	8-14

Table 3 EXHAUST SYSTEM TORQUE SPECIFICATIONS

Item	ft.-lb.	in.-lb.	N•m
Exhaust flange nuts	Refer to procedure in text		
Torca clamp nuts	45-60	–	61-81

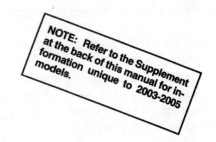

NOTE: Refer to the Supplement at the back of this manual for information unique to 2003-2005 models.

CHAPTER EIGHT

ELECTRICAL SYSTEM

8

This chapter contains service and test procedures for all electrical and ignition system components except the spark plugs. Service information for the spark plugs is in Chapter Three.

The electrical system includes the following systems:

1. Charging system.
2. Ignition system.
3. Starting system.
4. Lighting system.
5. Switches and other electrical components.

Refer to **Tables 1-9** at the end of the chapter for specifications.

BASIC INFORMATION

Wiring and Connectors

Many electrical problems can be traced to damaged wiring, or contaminated or loose connectors.

The locations of the connectors vary by model. Also, if the motorcycle has been serviced previously, the connector may be in a different location.

The electrical system uses three types of connectors. If individual wires or terminals of a particular connector require repair or replacement, refer to *Electrical Connector Service* at the end of this chapter.

Always check the wire colors listed in the procedure or wiring diagrams to verify the location of the components.

Perform the following steps first if an electrical system fault is encountered.

1. Inspect all wiring for fraying, burning and other visual damage.
2. Check the main fuse and make sure it is not blown. Replace it if necessary.
3. Check the individual fuse(s) for each circuit. Make sure it is not blown. Replace it if necessary.
4. Inspect the battery as described in this chapter. Make sure it is fully charged and the battery cables

are clean and securely attached to the battery terminals.

5. Clean connectors with an aerosol electrical contact cleaner. After a thorough cleaning, pack multipin electrical connectors with dialectic grease to seal out moisture.

6. Disconnect electrical connectors in the suspect circuits and check for bent metal pins on the male side of the electrical connector. A bent pin will not connect to the female end of the connector, causing an open circuit.

7. Check each female end of the connector. Make sure the metal connector on the end of each wire is pushed all the way into the plastic connector. If they are not, carefully push them in with a narrow-blade screwdriver.

8. After everything is checked, push the connectors together and make sure they are fully engaged and locked together.

9. Never pull on the electrical wires when disconnecting an electrical connector. Only pull on the connector plastic housing.

10. Test wiring continuity as follows:

    a. Disconnect the negative battery cable as described in this chapter.

> *NOTE*
> *When performing a continuity test, do not disconnect the electrical connector. Instead, insert the test leads into the back of the connectors and check both sides. Because corrosion between the connector contacts may be causing an open circuit, the trouble may be in the connector instead of the wiring.*

    b. When using an analog ohmmeter, always touch the test leads, then zero the needle according to the manufacturer's instructions to assure correct readings.

    c. Attach the test leads to the circuit to be tested.

    d. There should be continuity. If there is no continuity, or infinite resistance, there is an open in the circuit.

Wiring Diagrams

Wiring diagrams are located at the end of this manual.

Electrical Component Resistance Testing

Because the resistance of a component varies with temperature, perform the resistance tests with the component at room temperature (68° F [20° C]). The specifications in this manual are based on tests performed at this temperature.

> *NOTE*
> *When using an analog ohmmeter, always touch the test leads, then adjust the needle to zero to ensure correct readings.*

Electrical Component Replacement

Most motorcycle dealerships and parts suppliers will not accept returns of electrical parts. Avoid purchasing parts unless the cause of the malfunction has been determined. If a thorough diagnosis has not located the exact cause of the electrical system malfunction, have a Harley-Davidson dealership determine the possible cause.

BATTERY

The battery is important to the motorcycle's electrical system, yet most electrical system problems can be traced to battery neglect. Clean and inspect the battery at periodic intervals. Some models are equipped with a maintenance-free sealed battery and the electrolyte level cannot be checked.

On all models in this manual, the negative side is the ground. When removing the battery, disconnect the negative cable first, then the positive cable. This minimizes the chance of a tool shorting to ground when disconnecting the battery positive cable.

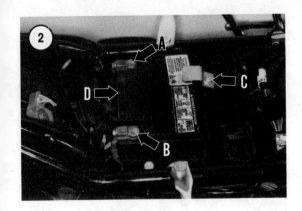

Negative Cable

Some of the component replacement procedures and test procedures in this chapter require disconnecting the negative battery cable as a safety precaution.

NOTE
Always disarm the optional TSSM security system prior to disconnecting the battery or the siren will sound.

1. Remove the seat as described in Chapter Fourteen.
2. Remove the bolt (**Figure 1**) securing the negative battery cable. Move the cable away from the battery to avoid making accidental contact with the battery post.
3. Connect the negative cable to the frame post. Reinstall the nut and tighten it securely.
4. Install the seat.

Battery Cable Service

To ensure good electrical contact between the battery and the electrical cables, the cables must be clean and free of corrosion.
1. If the electrical cable terminals are badly corroded, disconnect them from the motorcycle's electrical system.
2. Thoroughly clean each connector with a wire brush and a baking soda solution. Rinse thoroughly with clean water and wipe dry with a clean cloth.
3. After cleaning, apply a thin layer of dielectric grease to the battery terminals before reattaching the cables.
4. Reconnect the electrical cables to the motorcycle's electrical system if they were disconnected.

5. After connecting the electrical cables, apply a light coat of dielectric grease to the terminals to retard corrosion and decomposition of the terminals.

Battery Removal/Installation

NOTE
Always disarm the optional TSSM security system prior to disconnecting the battery or the siren will sound.

1. Remove the seat as described in Chapter Fourteen.
2. On 1999 models, disconnect the vent tube from the battery. Leave the hose routed through the frame.

NOTE
On 1999 models, do not lose the spacer between the battery cable and the battery terminal. This spacer must be reinstalled when each cable is attached.

3. Remove the bolt and disconnect the negative battery cable (A, **Figure 2**).
4. Remove the bolt and disconnect the positive battery cable (B, **Figure 2**).
5. Remove the T-40 Torx bolt (C, **Figure 2**) securing the battery hold down and remove the hold down.
6. Carefully lift the battery (D, **Figure 2**) up and out of the frame.
7. Inspect the battery tray for corrosion or damage. Replace it if necessary.
8. Position the battery with the negative cable terminal on the left side of the frame.
9. Reinstall the battery onto the battery tray in the frame.
10. Install the battery hold down and tighten the Torx bolt securely.
11. Connect the positive battery cable (B, **Figure 2**). Tighten the bolt securely.
12. Connect the negative battery cable (A, **Figure 2**). Tighten the bolt securely.
13. After connecting the electrical cables, apply a light coat of dielectric grease to the electrical terminals of the battery to retard corrosion and decomposition of the terminals.
14. Install the seat.

8

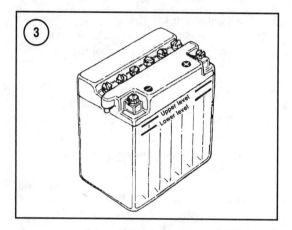

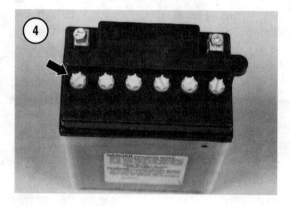

Electrolyte Level Check
(Conventional Battery)

1. Maintain the electrolyte level between the two marks on the battery case (**Figure 3**).

2. To adjust the electrolyte level, remove the battery from the frame as described in this section. Do not add water while the battery is in the frame. If the battery is overfilled, the electrolyte will flow onto the rear frame and cause corrosion.

3. Make sure all cell caps are in place and are tight. Tighten them if necessary.

4. If the electrolyte level is correct, reinstall the battery.

Cleaning, Inspection and Adding Water
(Conventional Battery)

1. Remove the battery as previously described.

2. Inspect the battery tray for contamination or damage. Clean it with a solution of baking soda and water.

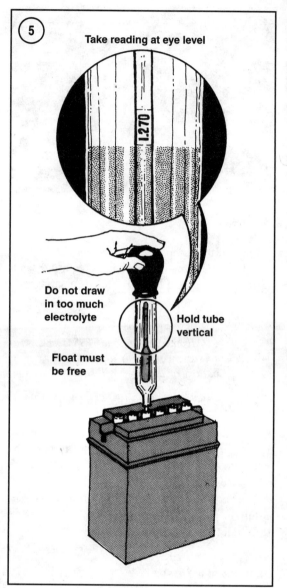

3. Check the entire battery case for cracks or other damage. If the battery case is warped, discolored or has a raised top, the battery has overheated from overcharging.

4. Check the battery terminal bolts, spacers and nuts for corrosion, deterioration or damage. Clean parts thoroughly with a baking soda and water solution. Replace severely corroded or damaged parts.

NOTE
Keep cleaning solution out of the battery cells or the electrolyte level will be seriously weakened.

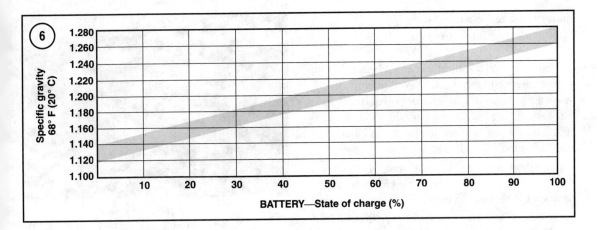

5. Clean the top of the battery with a stiff bristle brush using the baking soda and water solution. Thoroughly rinse off all baking soda residue with freshwater.

6. Check the battery cable clamps for corrosion and damage. If corrosion is minor, clean the battery cable clamps with a stiff wire brush. Replace severely worn or damaged cables.

NOTE
Do not overfill the battery cells in Step 7. The electrolyte expands due to heat from charging and will overflow if the level is above the upper level line.

7. Remove the fill caps (**Figure 4**) from the battery cells and check the electrolyte level in each cell. Add distilled water, if necessary, to bring the level within the upper and lower level lines on the battery case. Install the caps and tighten securely.

CAUTION
Adding water to the cells will dilute the electrolyte. The diluted electrolyte can freeze and destroy the battery during subfreezing temperatures. Therefore, during cold weather, charge the battery after adding water to the cells.

Battery Testing (Conventional Battery)

Check the specific gravity of the battery electrolyte to check the state of charge of the battery. Specific gravity is the density of the electrolyte as compared to pure water. To check the specific gravity, use a hydrometer with numbered graduations from 1.100 to 1.300 rather than one with color-coded bands. To use the hydrometer, squeeze the rubber ball, insert the tip into the cell and release the ball (**Figure 5**).

NOTE
Adding water to the cells will lower the specific gravity (density) of the electrolyte. After adding water, charge the battery for 15-20 minutes at a high rate to mix the water and electrolyte.

Draw enough electrolyte to float the weighted float inside the hydrometer. When using a temperature-compensated hydrometer, release the electrolyte and repeat this process several times to make sure the thermometer has adjusted to the electrolyte temperature before taking the reading.

Hold the hydrometer vertically and note the number in line with the surface of the electrolyte (**Figure 5**). This is the specific gravity for this cell. Return the electrolyte to the cell from which it came. The specific gravity of the electrolyte in each battery cell is an excellent indication of that cell's condition. Refer to **Figure 6**. A fully charged cell will read 1.260-1.280, a cell in good condition reads from 1.230-1.250 and a discharged cell will read below 1.140. Charging is also necessary if the specific gravity varies more than 0.050 from cell to cell. If the specific gravity still varies more than 0.050 after charging, the battery has failed.

NOTE
If a temperature-compensated hydrometer is not used, add 0.004 to the specific gravity reading for every 10° above 80° F (25° C). For every 10° below 80° F (25° C), subtract 0.004.

8

Battery Inspection and Testing (Maintenance-Free Battery)

The battery electrolyte level cannot be serviced in a maintenance-free battery. *Never* attempt to remove the sealing bar cap from the top of the battery. The battery does not require periodic electrolyte inspection or water refilling. Refer to the label (**Figure 7**) on top of the battery.

Even though the battery is sealed, protect eyes, skin and clothing. The corrosive electrolyte may have spilled out and can cause severe chemical skin burns and permanent injury. The battery case may be cracked and leaking electrolyte. If electrolyte is spilled or splashed on clothing or skin, immediately neutralize it with a baking soda and water solution, then flush with an abundance of clean water.

WARNING
Electrolyte is extremely harmful to the eyes. Always wear safety glasses while working with a battery. If electrolyte gets into the eyes, call a physician immediately and force the eyes open and flood them with cool, clean water for approximately 15 minutes.

1. Remove the battery as described in this chapter. Do not clean the battery while it is mounted in the frame.

2. Set the battery on a stack of newspapers or shop cloths to protect the surface of the workbench.

3. Check the entire battery case for cracks or other damage. If the battery case is warped, discolored or has a raised top, the battery has been overcharged and overheated.

4. Check the battery terminal bolts, spacers and nuts for corrosion or damage. Clean parts thoroughly with a baking soda and water solution. Replace corroded or damaged parts.

5. If the top of the battery is corroded, clean it with a stiff bristle brush using the baking soda and water solution.

6. Check the battery cable ends for corrosion and damage. If corrosion is minor, clean the battery cable ends with a stiff wire brush. Replace worn or damaged cables.

7. Connect a digital voltmeter between the battery negative and positive leads (**Figure 8**). Note the following:

a. If the battery voltage is 13.0-13.2 volts (at 20° C [68° F]), or greater, the battery is fully charged

b. If the battery voltage is 12.5 volts (at 20° C [68° F]), or lower, the battery is undercharged and requires charging.

8. If the battery is undercharged, recharge it as described in this chapter. Then test the charging system as described in Chapter Two.

9. Inspect the battery case for contamination or damage. Clean it with a baking soda and water solution.

10. Install the battery as described in this chapter.

Charging (Conventional Battery)

The battery should only self-discharge approximately one percent of its given capacity each day. If a battery not in use, without any loads connected, loses its charge within a week of being fully charged, the battery is defective.

If the motorcycle is not used for long periods of time, an automatic charger with variable voltage and amperage outputs is recommended for optimum battery service life.

CAUTION
Always remove the battery from the motorcycle before connecting the charging equipment.

WARNING
During charging, highly explosive hydrogen gas is released from the battery. Only charge the battery in a well-ventilated area away from open flames, including pilot lights on appliances. Do not allow smoking in the area. Never check the charge of the

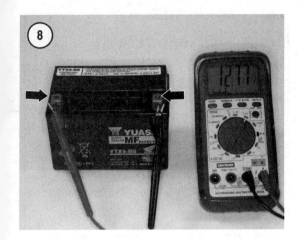

battery by arcing across the terminals; the resulting spark can ignite the hydrogen gas.

1. Remove the battery from the motorcycle as described in this chapter.
2. Set the battery on a stack of newspapers or shop cloths to protect the surface of the workbench.
3. Make sure the battery charger is turned OFF, prior to attaching the charger leads to the battery.
4. Connect the positive charger lead to the positive battery terminal and the negative charger lead to the negative battery terminal.
5. Remove all fill/vent caps (**Figure 4**) from the battery. Set the charger at 12 volts and switch it ON. Normally, a battery should be charged at a slow charge rate of 1/10 its given capacity.

   a. As the battery charges, the electrolyte will begin to bubble (gassing). If one cell does not bubble, it is usually an indication that it is defective. Refer to *Battery Testing* in this chapter.

   b. The charging time depends on the discharged condition of the battery. Normally, a battery should be charged at a slow charge rate of 1/10 its given capacity.

CAUTION
Maintain the electrolyte level at the upper level during the charging cycle. Check and refill with distilled water as necessary.

6. After the battery has been charged for the predetermined time, turn the charger OFF, disconnect the leads and check the specific gravity. It should be

within the limits in **Figure 6**. If it is, and remains stable for one hour, the battery is charged.

Charging (Maintenance-Free Battery)

Refer to *Battery Initialization* in this chapter if the battery is new.

To recharge a maintenance-free battery, a digital voltmeter and a charger with an adjustable amperage output are required. If this equipment is not available, have the battery charged by a shop with the proper equipment. Excessive voltage and amperage from an unregulated charger can damage the battery and shorten service life.

The battery should only self-discharge approximately one percent of its given capacity each day. If a battery not in use, without any loads connected, loses its charge within a week after charging, the battery is defective.

If the motorcycle is not used for long periods of time, an automatic battery charger with variable voltage and amperage outputs is recommended for optimum battery service life.

WARNING
During charging, highly explosive hydrogen gas is released from the battery. Only charge the battery in a well-ventilated area away from open flames, including pilot lights on appliances. Do not allow smoking in the area. Never check the charge of the battery by arcing across the terminals; the resulting spark can ignite the hydrogen gas.

CAUTION
Always disconnect the battery cables from the battery. If the cables are left connected during the charging procedure, the charger may damage the diodes within the voltage regulator/rectifier.

1. Remove the battery from the motorcycle as described in this chapter.
2. Set the battery on a stack of newspapers or shop cloths to protect the surface of the workbench.
3. Make sure the battery charger is turned off prior to attaching the charger leads to the battery.

4. Connect the positive charger lead to the positive battery terminal and the negative charger lead to the negative battery terminal.

5. Set the charger at 12 volts. If the output of the charger is variable, select the low setting.

6. The charging time depends on the discharged condition of the battery. Refer to **Table 3** for the suggested charging time. Normally, a battery should be charged at 1/10th its given capacity.

> *CAUTION*
> *If the battery emits an excessive amount of gas during the charging cycle, decrease the charge rate. If the battery becomes hotter than 110° F (43° C) during the charging cycle, turn the charger off and allow the battery to cool. Then continue with a reduced charging rate and continue to monitor the battery temperature.*

7. Turn the charger to the ON position.

8. After the battery has been charged for the predetermined time, turn the charger off, disconnect the leads and measure the battery voltage. Refer to the following:

  a. If the battery voltage is 13.0 volts (at 20° C [68° F]), or greater, the battery is fully charged

  b. If the battery voltage is 12.5 volts (at 20° C [68° F]), or lower, the battery is undercharged and requires additional charging time.

9. If the battery remains stable for one hour, the battery is charged.

10. Install the battery into the motorcycle as described in this chapter.

Battery Initialization

A new battery must be *fully* charged to a specific gravity of 1.260-1.280 before installation. To bring the battery to a full charge, give it an initial charge. Using a new battery without an initial charge will cause permanent battery damage. The battery will never be able to hold more than an 80% charge. Charging a new battery after it has been used will not bring its charge to 100%. When purchasing a new battery, verify its charge status.

> *NOTE*
> **Recycle the old battery.** *When a new battery is purchased, turn in the old*

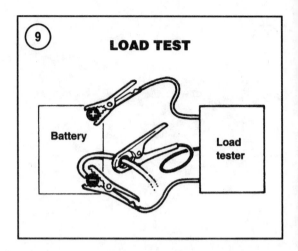

one for recycling. Most motorcycle dealerships will accept the old battery in trade for a new one. Never place an old battery in the household trash since it is illegal, in most states, to place any acid or lead (heavy metal) contents in landfills.

Load Testing

A load test checks the battery's performance under full current load and is the best indication of battery condition.

A battery load tester is required for this procedure. When using a load tester, follow the manufacturer's instructions. **Figure 9** shows a typical load tester and battery arrangement.

1. Remove the battery from the motorcycle as described in this chapter.

> *NOTE*
> *Let the battery stand for at least one hour after charging prior to performing this test.*

2. The battery must be fully charged before beginning this test. If necessary, charge the battery as described in this section.

> *WARNING*
> *The battery load tester must be turned OFF prior to connecting or disconnecting the test cables to the battery. Otherwise, a spark could cause the battery to explode.*

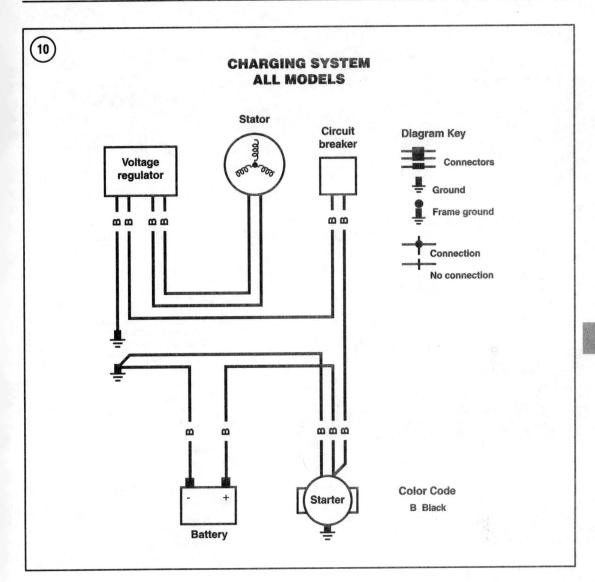

**CHARGING SYSTEM
ALL MODELS**

CAUTION
To prevent battery damage during load testing, do not load test a discharged battery and do not load test the battery for more than 20 seconds. Performing a load test on a discharged battery can cause permanent battery damage.

3. Load test the battery as follows:
   a. Connect the load tester cables to the battery following its manufacturer's instructions.
   b. Load the battery at 50% of the cold cranking amperage (CCA) or 135 amperes.
   c. After 15 seconds, the voltage reading with the load still applied must be 9.6 volts or higher at

70° F (21° C). Now quickly remove the load and turn the tester OFF.

4. If the voltage reading is 9.6 volts or higher, the battery output capacity is good. If the reading is below 9.6 volts, the battery is defective.

5. With the tester OFF, disconnect the cables from the battery.

6. Install the battery as described in this chapter.

CHARGING SYSTEM

The charging system consists of the battery, alternator and a voltage regulator/rectifier (**Figure 10** and **Figure 11**). Alternating current generated by the alternator is rectified to direct current.

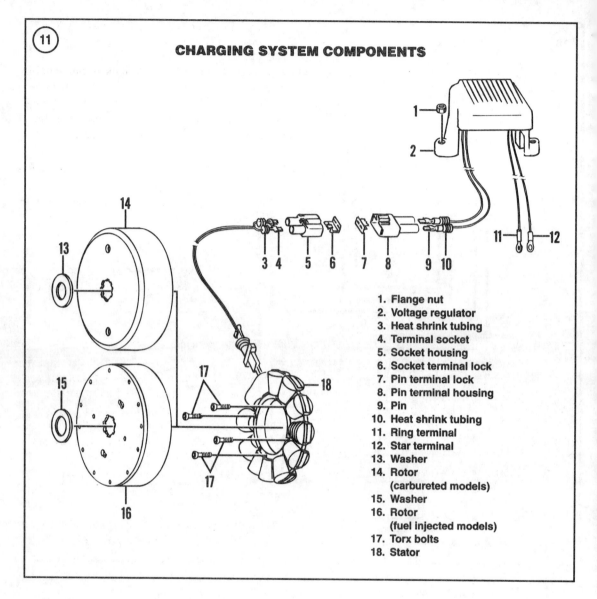

⑪ **CHARGING SYSTEM COMPONENTS**

1. Flange nut
2. Voltage regulator
3. Heat shrink tubing
4. Terminal socket
5. Socket housing
6. Socket terminal lock
7. Pin terminal lock
8. Pin terminal housing
9. Pin
10. Heat shrink tubing
11. Ring terminal
12. Star terminal
13. Washer
14. Rotor
    (carbureted models)
15. Washer
16. Rotor
    (fuel injected models)
17. Torx bolts
18. Stator

The voltage regulator maintains the voltage to the battery and additional electrical loads, such as the lights and ignition system, at a constant voltage regardless of variations in engine speed and load.

A malfunction in the charging system generally causes the battery to remain undercharged. To prevent damage to the alternator and the regulator/rectifier when testing and repairing the charging system, note the following precautions:

1. Always disarm the optional TSSM security system prior to disconnecting the battery or the siren will sound.

2. Always disconnect the negative battery cable, as described in this chapter, before removing a component from the charging system.

3. To charge the battery, remove the battery from the motorcycle and recharge it as described in this chapter.

4. Inspect the battery case. Look for bulges or cracks in the case, leaking electrolyte or corrosion build-up.

5. Check the charging system wiring for signs of chafing, deterioration or other damage.

6. Check the wiring for corroded or loose connections. Clean, tighten or reconnect wiring as required.

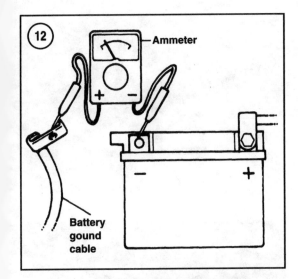

Battery gound cable

Battery Drain

Perform this test prior to performing the output test.

1. Turn the ignition switch OFF.
2. Remove the seat.

NOTE
Always disarm the optional TSSM security system prior to disconnecting the battery or the siren will sound.

3. Disconnect the negative battery cable as described in this chapter.
4. Switch the ammeter from its highest to lowest amperage scale while reading the meter scale.

CAUTION
Before connecting the ammeter to the circuit in Step 4, set the meter to its highest amperage scale. This will prevent a large current flow from damag-

ing the meter or blowing the meter's fuse, if so equipped.

5. Connect the ammeter between the negative battery cable and the negative terminal of the battery (**Figure 12**). If the needle swings the slightest amount when the meter is connected, there is a current draw in the system that could discharge the battery.
6. If the current draw is excessive, the probable causes are:
  a. Loose, dirty or faulty electrical system connectors in the charging system wiring harness.
  b. Short circuit in the system.
  c. Damaged battery.
7. Disconnect the ammeter test leads and reconnect the battery negative lead.

Testing

A malfunction in the charging system generally causes the battery to remain undercharged. Perform the following visual inspection to determine the cause of the problem. If the visual inspection proves satisfactory, test the charging system as described under *Charging System* in Chapter Two.

1. Make sure the battery cables are connected properly (**Figure 13**). If polarity is reversed, check for a damaged voltage regulator/rectifier.
2. Inspect the terminals for loose or corroded connections. Tighten or clean them as required.
3. Inspect the battery case. Look for bulges or cracks in the case, leaking electrolyte or corrosion buildup.
4. Carefully check all connections at the alternator to make sure they are clean and tight.
5. Check the circuit wiring for corroded or loose connections. Clean, tighten or connect wiring as required.

ALTERNATOR

Rotor Removal/Installation

NOTE
Always disarm the optional TSSM security system prior to disconnecting the battery or the siren will sound.

1. Disconnect the negative battery cable as described in this chapter.

2. Remove the primary chain case cover and inner housing as described in Chapter Five.

3. Remove the primary chain, clutch assembly, chain tensioner assembly and compensating sprocket components as an assembly. Refer to Chapter Five.

4. If still in place, remove the shaft extension and washer from the crankshaft.

NOTE
*Fuel injected models have a laminated high-output rotor equipped with **very strong** magnets. Use the Harley-Davidson special tool (part No. HD-41771), or an equivalent puller, for rotor removal.*

5A. On fuel injected models, perform the following:

   a. Use the special tool or a bearing puller and two 5/16 in. × 3 in. course thread bolts (**Figure 14**).

   b. Install the rotor remover over the crankshaft and against the rotor.

   c. Secure the rotor remover to the rotor with the two bolts (**Figure 15**).

   d. Slowly turn the center bolt and withdraw the rotor from the stator coils.

   e. Remove the rotor and special tool. Separate the tool from the rotor.

5B. On carbureted models, slide the rotor off the crankshaft. If necessary, insert two wire hooks into the holes in the face of the rotor. Slide the rotor off.

6. Inspect the rotor magnets (**Figure 16**) for small bolts, washers or other metal debris that may be attached the magnets. Any debris will cause severe damage to the alternator stator assembly.

7. Check the inner splines (**Figure 17**) for wear or damage. Replace the rotor if necessary.

8. Install by reversing these removal steps. Note the following:

WARNING
*Do **not** try to install the rotor without the special tool. The magnets will quickly pull the rotor into place and trap fingers between the rotor and the sharp edge of the crankcase (**Figure 18**).*

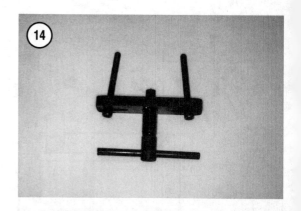

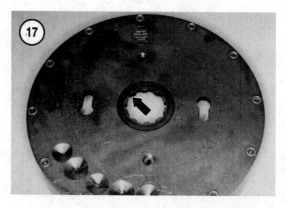

a. On fuel injected models, use the same tool set-up used for removal to install the rotor.

b. Align the rotor splines with the crankshaft splines.

Stator Removal

NOTE
Some of the illustrations in this procedure are shown with the engine removed to better illustrate the steps.

1. Remove the rotor as described in this chapter.

2. On the inboard side of the lower right side frame rail, carefully cut the cable strap securing the stator coil/voltage regulator two-pin electrical connector to the frame.

3. Pull the electrical connector toward the rear to release it from the T-stud on the frame. Remove the clip from the connector.

4A. On 1999-2001 models, depress the external latch, use a rocking motion and separate the socket connector (**Figure 19**).

4B. On 2002 models, perform the following:

    a. Locate the voltage regulator connector attached to the bottom of the voltage regulator.

    b. Slide the connector toward the left side to release the groove on the connector from the bracket ridge.

    c. Raise the external latch and use a rocking motion, separate the connector's pin and socket halves.

5. Insert a small screwdriver between the socket housing side of connector going to the alternator stator and the locking wedge on the socket housing. Gently pivot the screwdriver tip to pop the wedge loose.

6. Lift the terminal latches inside the socket housing and back the sockets through the wire end of the connector.

7. Open the two cable clips on the inboard side of the front lower frame cross member and release the electrical wires from the frame clips. Move the wires to the left side of the frame.

8. Remove the three T27 Torx screws (**Figure 20**) securing the stator assembly to the crankcase. New Torx screws must be used on installation.

NOTE
If necessary, spray electrical contact cleaner or glass cleaner around the wiring harness grommet to help ease it out of the crankcase boss receptacle.

9. Use an awl to carefully lift the capped lip on the grommet (**Figure 21**) from the crankcase and push it into the bore.

10. Carefully push the stator wires and grommet through the crankcase bore (A, **Figure 22**) and remove the stator assembly (B).

11. Inspect the stator mounting surface on the crankcase for oil residue from a damaged oil seal. Clean it off if necessary.

8

12. Inspect the stator wires (A, **Figure 23**) for fraying or damage.

13. Inspect the rubber grommet (B, **Figure 23**) for deterioration or hardness.

14. Check the stator connector pins (**Figure 24**) for looseness or damage.

Stator Installation

1. Apply a light coat of electrical contact cleaner or glass cleaner to the wiring harness grommet to help ease it into the crankcase boss receptacle.

> *NOTE*
> *Figure 25 is shown with the engine removed to better illustrate the step.*

2. Insert the electrical harness and grommet into the crankcase boss receptacle and carefully pull it through until the grommet is correctly seated (**Figure 25**).

> *CAUTION*
> *New T27 Torx screws must be installed. The threadlocking compound originally applied to the Torx screws is for one time use only. If a used Torx screw is installed, it can work loose and cause engine damage.*

3. Move the stator into position on the crankcase and install four *new* T27 Torx screws. Tighten the screws to the torque specifications in **Table 6**.

4. Move the wires to the right side of the motorcycle.

5. Position the wires on the frame clips on the lower frame cross member and secure the wires onto the clips.

6. Apply a light coat of dielectric compound to the electrical connector prior to assembling it. Reassemble the electrical connector socket by reversing Steps 4-6 of *Removal*. Make sure it has locked together securely.

7. Secure the electrical connector to the T-stud on the frame.

8. Position the electrical connector on the inboard side of the lower right side frame rail. Secure it to the frame with a new cable strap.

9. Install the rotor as described in this chapter.

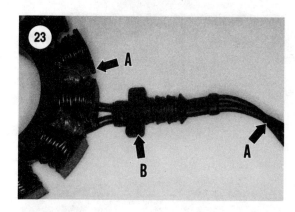

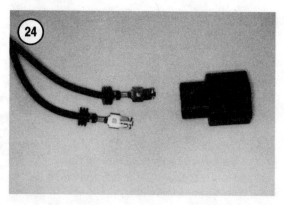

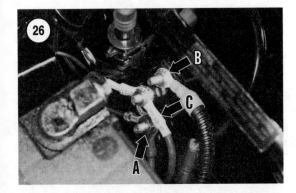

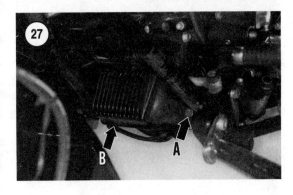

VOLTAGE REGULATOR

Removal/Installation

1. Remove the battery as described in this chapter.
2. Remove the nut (A, **Figure 26**) from the left side ground post in front of the battery box.
3. Remove the internal tooth ring terminal with the black shrink wrap tube (B, **Figure 26**) from the post.
4. Remove the nut securing the silver post on the circuit breaker. Remove the ring terminal with the yellow shrink wrap tube (C, **Figure 26**).
5. On the right side, release the cables from the clip at the front of the battery box.

NOTE
After cutting the five cable straps, leave them in place on the frame as a reference for the path of the wiring during installation.

6. On the right side of the frame side tube, carefully cut the five cable straps and open the three cable clips securing the voltage regulator electrical wires to the frame. Release the wires from the clips.
7. On the inboard side of the lower right side frame rail, carefully cut the cable strap securing the stator coil/voltage regulator two-pin electrical connector to the frame.
8. Pull the electrical connector toward the rear to release it from the T-stud on the frame. Remove the clip from the connector.
9A. On 1999-2001 models, depress the external latch, use a rocking motion and separate the socket connector (**Figure 19**).
9B. On 2002 models, perform the following:
   a. Locate the voltage regulator connector attached to the bottom of the voltage regulator.
   b. Slide the connector toward the left side to release the groove on the connector from the bracket ridge.
   c. Raise the external latch and use a rocking motion to separate the connector's pin and socket halves.
10. Insert a small screwdriver between the socket housing side of connector going to the stator coil/voltage regulator and the locking wedge on the socket housing. Gently pivot the screwdriver tip to pop the wedge loose.
11. Lift the terminal latches inside the socket housing and back the sockets through the wire end of the connector.
12. Remove the flange locknut (A, **Figure 27**) on each side securing the voltage regulator to the lower frame cross member studs.
13. Remove the voltage regulator (B, **Figure 27**) and related wiring from the frame.
14. Install by reversing these removal steps. Note the following:
   a. When installing the voltage regulator onto the lower frame member studs, move the electrical wires away from the studs. Make sure they are not pinched between the frame member and the voltage regulator flange.

8

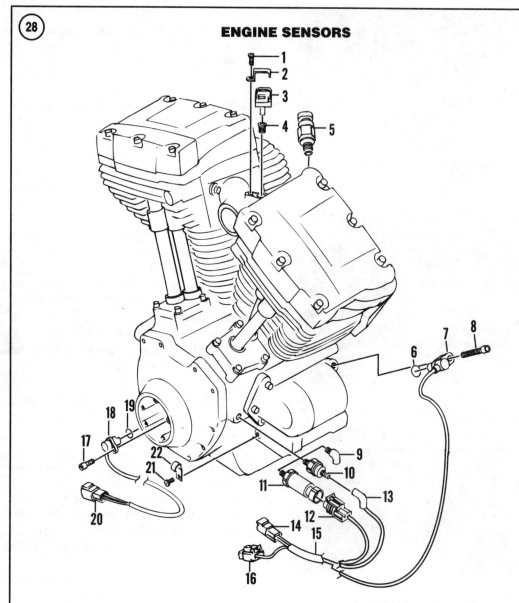

ENGINE SENSORS

1. Screw
2. Clamp
3. MAP sensor
   (carbureted models only)
4. Seal
5. Engine temperature sensor
6. O-ring
7. Crankshaft position sensor (CKP)
8. Bolt
9. Elbow (side car only)
10. Oil pressure switch*
11. Oil pressure sensor**

12. Connector (oil pressure sensor**)
13. Connector (oil pressure switch*)
14. Two-pin socket (black)
15. Wiring harness
16. Two-pin socket (black)
17. Screw
18. Camshaft position sensor (CMP)
    (1999-2001 models only)
19. O-ring
20. Three-pin connector (black)
21. Screw
22. Cable clamp

*FLHT, FLHR, FLHRI, FLHRCI models
**FLHTC, FLHTCUI, FLHTCI, FLTR, FLTRI models

b. Tighten the flange locknuts to the torque specification in **Table 6**.

c. Apply a light coat of dielectric compound to the electrical connectors prior to installing them.

d. Install new cable straps and secure the electrical wires to the three cable clips. The cable clips also secure the engine sensor harness conduit and the rear brake line.

IGNITION SYSTEM

The ignition system consists of an ignition coil, two spark plugs, the ignition module (carbureted models), electronic control module (EFI models), crankshaft position sensor (CKP), manifold absolute pressure sensor (MAP) (carbureted models), barometric pressure sensor (BARO) (fuel injected models), camshaft position sensor (CMP) (1999-2001 models only) and the bank angle sensor (BAS). Refer to **Figure 28** for the locations of the sensors.

The ignition module (carbureted models) or electronic control module (EFI models) is located behind the frame right side panel. It determines the spark advance for correct ignition timing based signals from the CKP, MAP, BARO, BAS and CMP. The ignition system fires the spark plugs near top dead center for starting, then varies the spark advance from 0° to 50° depending on engine speed, crankshaft position and intake manifold pressure. It also regulates the low-voltage circuits between the battery and the ignition coil. The ignition module is not repairable and must be replaced if defective.

On carbureted models, the MAP sensor is located on top of the intake manifold. This sensor monitors the intake manifold vacuum and sends this information to the ignition module. The ignition module adjusts the ignition timing advance curve for maximum performance.

On fuel-injected models, the BARO sensor is located next to the ignition module under the frame right side cover. This monitors atmospheric pressure and allows for altitude compensation.

The rotor and camshaft position sensor (CMP) are located in the camshaft cover on the right side of the crankcase. The raised ridge on the rotor operates at one-half crankshaft speed and it breaks the magnetic field of the Hall-effect device on the camshaft position sensor. The logic-type signal of the Hall-effect device gives accurate timing information to the ignition module.

The bank angle sensor mounts on a frame-mounted panel behind the frame right side cover on 1999-2000 models. On 2001-on models, the bank angle sensor is an integral part of the turn signal/turn signal security module (TSM/TSSM) mounted at the rear of the battery box. The sensor consists of a small magnetic disc that rides within a V-shaped channel. If the motorcycle is tilted at a 55° angle on 1999-2000 models or 45° angle on 2001-on models, for more than one second, the ignition system is shut off. Once the sensor is activated, the motorcycle must be up-righted and the ignition turned OFF then ON. Then, the ignition system is operational and the engine can be restarted.

The basic components of a typical ignition system are shown in **Figure 29**. When servicing the ignition system, refer to the wiring diagrams located at the end of the manual.

Ignition Coil

Performance test

1. Disconnect the plug wire and remove one of the spark plugs as described in Chapter Three.

> *NOTE*
> *A spark tester is useful for testing the ignition system spark output. **Figure 30** shows the Motion Pro Ignition System Tester (part No. 08-0122). This tool is inserted in the spark plug cap and its base is grounded against the cylinder head. The tool's air gap is adjustable and it allows the visual inspection of the spark while testing the intensity of the spark.*

2. Insert a clean shop cloth into the spark plug hole in the cylinder head to reduce gasoline vapors emitting from the hole.

3. Insert the spark plug (**Figure 31**), or spark tester (**Figure 32**), into its cap and touch the spark plug base against the cylinder head to ground it. Position the spark plug so the electrode is visible.

> *NOTE*
> *When not using a spark tester, always use a new spark plug for this test procedure.*

> *WARNING*
> *Mount the spark plug, or tester, away from the spark plug hole in the cylin-*

IGNITION SYSTEM COMPONENTS

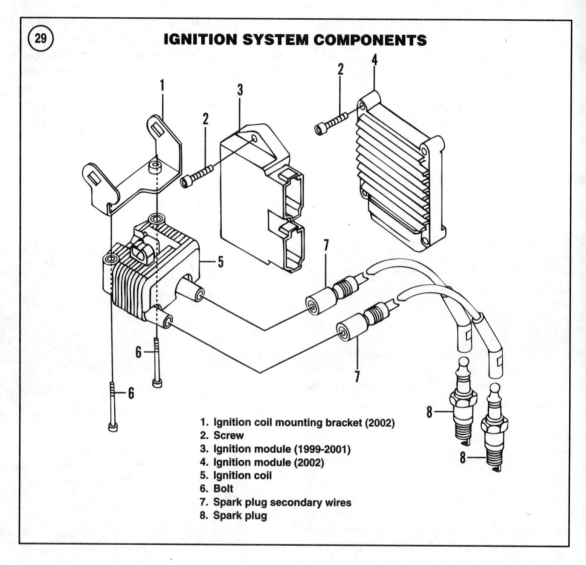

1. Ignition coil mounting bracket (2002)
2. Screw
3. Ignition module (1999-2001)
4. Ignition module (2002)
5. Ignition coil
6. Bolt
7. Spark plug secondary wires
8. Spark plug

der so the spark or tester cannot ignite the gasoline vapors in the cylinder. If the engine is flooded, do not perform this test. The firing of the spark plug can ignite fuel ejected through the spark plug hole.

4. Turn the engine over with the electric starter. A fat blue spark should be evident across the spark plug electrode or spark tester. If there is strong sunlight on the plug, or tester, shade it so the spark is more visible. Repeat for the other cylinder.

WARNING
*If necessary, hold onto the spark plug wire with a pair of insulated pliers. Do **not** hold the spark plug, wire or*

connector or a serious electrical shock could occur.

5. If there is a fat blue spark, the ignition coil is good. If there is not, perform the following resistance test.

Resistance test

NOTE
*Refer to the **Basic Information** section at the beginning of this chapter.*

1. Remove the ignition coil as previously described.
2. Disconnect the secondary wires from the ignition coil.

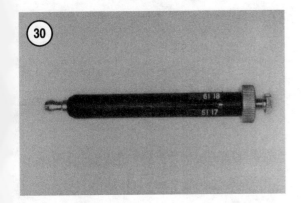

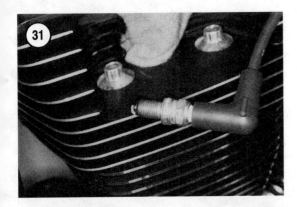

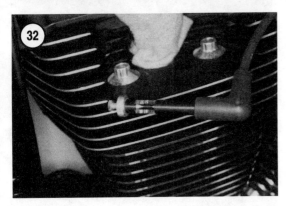

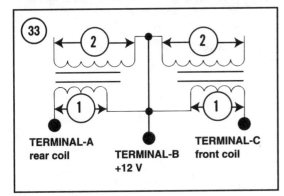

TERMINAL-A
rear coil

TERMINAL-B
+12 V

TERMINAL-C
front coil

3. Use an ohmmeter set at R × 1 to measure the primary coil resistance between terminals A and B, then terminals B and C (**Figure 33**) at the backside of the ignition coil. The specified resistance is in **Table 1**.

4. Use an ohmmeter set at R × 1000 to measure the secondary coil resistance between the spark plug leads of the secondary coil terminals (**Figure 33**). The specified resistance is in **Table 1**.

5. If the resistance is less than specified, there is probably a short in the coil windings. Replace the coil.

6. If the resistance is more than specified, this may indicate corrosion or oxidation of the coil's terminals. Thoroughly clean the terminals, then spray them with an aerosol electrical contact cleaner. Repeat Steps 3 and 4. If the resistance is still high, replace the coil.

7. If the coil resistance does not meet (or come close to) either of these specifications, replace the coil. If the coil is visibly damaged, replace it as described in this chapter.

8. Install the ignition coil as described in this chapter.

Removal/installation (1999-2001 models)

NOTE
Always disarm the optional TSSM security system prior to disconnecting the battery or the siren will sound.

1. Disconnect the negative battery cable as described in this chapter.

2. Remove the fuel tank as described in Chapter Seven.

NOTE
Label all wiring connectors prior to disconnecting them in the following steps.

3. Disconnect the secondary lead (A, **Figure 34**) from each spark plug.

4. Disconnect the front cylinder's secondary lead from the clip on the frame.

5. Disconnect the primary wire connector (B, **Figure 34**) from the front left side of the ignition coil.

6. Remove the bolts and lockwashers (C, **Figure 34**) securing the ignition coil to the frame.

7. Remove the ignition coil.

8. Install the ignition coil by reversing these steps.

Removal/installation (2002 models)

1. Disconnect the negative battery cable as described in this chapter.

2. Remove the fuel tank as described in Chapter Seven.

> *NOTE*
> *Label all wiring connectors prior to disconnecting them in the following steps.*

3. Disconnect the secondary lead from each spark plug.

4. On the left side, disconnect the primary electrical connector (A, **Figure 35**) from the ignition coil.

5. Carefully pull out on the ears (B, **Figure 35**) of the mounting bracket and release the mounting bracket from the frame boss on each side.

6. Remove the ignition coil and secondary leads from the frame.

7. Install the ignition coil assembly by reversing these steps.

Ignition Module (Carbureted Models) Removal/Installation

The ignition module is located behind the frame left side cover. Refer to **Figure 35** for related electrical connectors.

> *NOTE*
> *Always disarm the optional TSSM security system prior to disconnecting the battery or the siren will sound.*

1. Disconnect the negative battery cable as described in this chapter.

2. Remove the seat and the left side saddlebag as described in Chapter Fourteen.

3. Remove the frame left side cover.

4A. On 1999-2001 models, perform the following:

  a. Push the data link (A, **Figure 36**) up and disengage it from the T-stud on the side of the battery box. Move the data link away from the ignition module.

  b. Depress the external latches on the two multipin electrical connectors. Gently pull and disconnect the black and gray electrical connectors (B, **Figure 36**) from the ignition module.

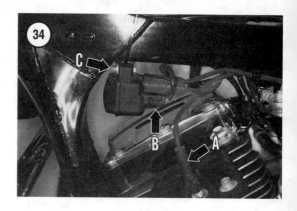

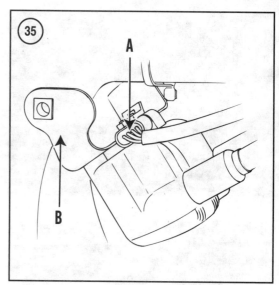

  c. Remove the two Allen screws (C, **Figure 36**) and remove the ignition module from the battery box.

4B. On 2002 models, perform the following:

  a. Depress the external latches on the two multipin electrical connectors. Gently pull and disconnect the black and gray electrical connectors (**Figure 37**) from the ignition module.

  b. Remove the two Allen screws and remove the ignition module from the electrical bracket.

5. Install the ignition module by reversing these steps. Note the following:

  a. Apply a light coat of dielectric compound to the electrical connectors prior to installing them.

  b. Make sure the electrical connectors are pushed tightly onto the ignition module.

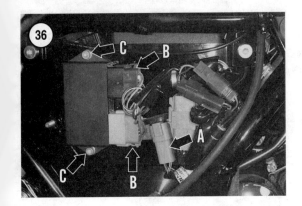

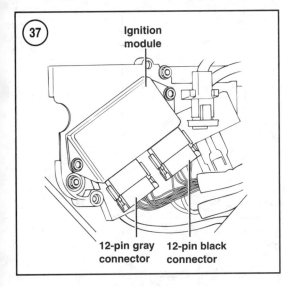

Ignition module

12-pin gray connector   12-pin black connector

**Electronic Control Module
(1999-2001 Fuel-Injected Models)
Removal/Installation**

The ECM is located under the frame right side cover on the electrical bracket. Refer to **Figure 38** for related electrical connectors.

NOTE
Always disarm the optional TSSM security system prior to disconnecting the battery or the siren will sound.

1. Disconnect the negative battery cable as described in this chapter.
2. Remove the seat and the right side saddlebag as described in Chapter Fourteen.
3. Remove the frame right side cover.
4. Open the wiring harness clip, and move the electrical connectors and wiring harness (A, **Figure 39**) out of the way.

5. Push the data link (B, **Figure 39**) up and disengage it from the T-stud on the electrical bracket. Move the data link away from the electrical bracket.
6. Push the EFI fuse holder (C, **Figure 39**) up and disengage it from the T-stud on the electrical bracket. Move the EFI fuse holder away from the electrical bracket.
7. Disconnect any remaining harness connectors from the electrical bracket to gain access to the ECM.
8. Remove the nuts securing the ECM (D, **Figure 39**) and the electrical bracket to the battery box.

CAUTION
Do not disconnect the 35-pin electrical connector from the ECM until it is removed from the battery box. Disconnecting it prior to removal will cause damage to the connector pins.

9. Carefully pull the ECM and electrical bracket away from the battery box and rest it on the passenger footboard.
10. Disconnect the 35-pin electrical connector from the ECM.
11. Install the ECM by reversing these steps. Note the following:
   a. Apply a light coat of dielectric compound to the 35-pin electrical connector prior to installing it.
   b. Make sure all electrical connectors that were moved out of the way are pushed tightly onto the ECM.

**Electronic Control Module
(2002 Fuel-Injected Models)
Removal/Installation**

The ECM is located under the frame right side cover on the electrical bracket.

NOTE
Always disarm the optional TSSM security system prior to disconnecting the battery or the siren will sound.

1. Disconnect the negative battery cable as described in this chapter.
2. Remove the seat and the right side saddlebag as described in Chapter Fourteen.
3. Remove the right side cover.

8

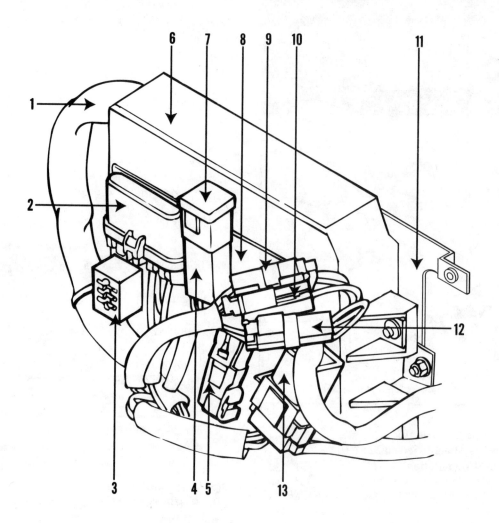

**ELECTRICAL BRACKET ASSEMBLY
(1999-2001 FUEL INJECTED MODELS)**

1. EFI wiring harness
2. EFI fuse holder
3. Spare fuses and holder
4. Data link connector
5. Barometric pressure sensor (BARO)
6. Electronic control module (ECM)
7. Rubber plug
8. Electrical bracket
9. Oil pressure sending unit sensor connector
10. Camshaft position sensor (CMP) connector
11. Battery box
12. Crankshaft position sensor (CKP) connector
13. Main wiring harness connector

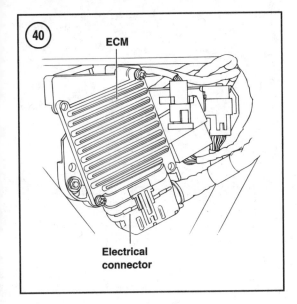

1. Disconnect the negative battery cable as described in this chapter.

2. Remove the fuel tank as described in Chapter Seven.

3. Remove the carburetor as described in Chapter Seven. Place a lint-free shop cloth into the intake manifold opening (A, **Figure 41**) to prevent the entry of debris.

4. Remove the screw and clip (B, **Figure 41**) securing the MAP sensor to the top of the intake manifold.

5. Pull the MAP sensor straight up out of the seal in the intake manifold.

6. Disconnect the electrical connector (C, **Figure 41**) from the MAP sensor and remove the sensor.

7. Install the MAP sensor by reversing these steps. Note the following:

  a. Apply a light coat of dielectric compound to the electrical connector prior to installing it.

  b. Make sure the electrical connector is pushed tightly onto the MAP sensor.

  c. If necessary, replace the seal in the intake manifold.

Barometric Pressure (BARO) Sensor (Fuel-Injected Models) Removal/Installation

The BARO sensor is located next to the electronic control module (ECM) under the frame right side cover.

NOTE
Always disarm the optional TSSM security system prior to disconnecting the battery or the siren will sound.

4. Depress the external latch and use a rocking motion disconnect the 36-pin electrical connector from the ECM (**Figure 40**).

5. Remove the two Allen bolts securing the ECM to the electrical bracket and remove the ECM.

6. Install the ECM by reversing these removal steps while noting the following:

Manifold Absolute Pressure (MAP) Sensor (Carbureted Models) Removal/Installation

The MAP sensor (**Figure 28**) is located on top of the intake manifold.

NOTE
Always disarm the optional TSSM security system prior to disconnecting the battery or the siren will sound.

1. Disconnect the negative battery cable as described in this chapter.

2. Remove the right side saddlebag as described in Chapter Fourteen.

3. Remove the frame right side cover.

4. Open the wiring harness clip, and move the electrical connectors and wiring harness.

5. Push the data link up and disengage it from the T-stud on the electrical bracket. Move the data link (A, **Figure 42**) away from the electrical bracket.

6. Pull the external latch outward and disconnect the electrical connector from the BARO sensor.

7. Carefully pull the BARO sensor (B, **Figure 42**) from the hole in the battery box and remove it.

8. Install the BARO sensor by reversing these steps. Note the following:

    a. Apply a light coat of dielectric compound to the electrical connector prior to installing it.

    b. Make sure the electrical connector is pushed tightly onto the BARO sensor.

Crankshaft Position Sensor (CKP) (1999 Models) Removal/Installation

The crankshaft position sensor (CKP) (**Figure 43**) is mounted on the front left side of the crankcase next to the oil filter.

1. Remove the seat as described in Chapter Fourteen.

NOTE
Always disarm the optional TSSM security system prior to disconnecting the battery or the siren will sound.

2. Disconnect the negative battery cable as described in this chapter.

3. Remove the fuel tank as described in Chapter Seven.

4. Remove the exhaust system as described in Chapter Seven.

5. Locate the engine sensor harness eight-pin Mini-Deutsch electrical connector at the rear left side of the crankcase. Carefully pull the barbed wire anchor from the threaded hole in the crankcase. Depress the external latches and separate the connector halves.

6. Remove the T20 Torx screw, then open the clamp securing the electrical harness to the engine.

7A. On models with an oil pressure warning light, disconnect the single green/yellow wire from the oil pressure switch.

7B. On all other models, disconnect the single brown/green wire from the oil pressure sending unit.

8. Carefully pull the electrical harness and pin side of the Mini-Deutsch connector forward, then up between the rear master reservoir and frame down tube.

9. Use needle nose pliers to remove the secondary locking wedge from the pin side of the electrical connector.

10. Gently depress the terminal latches inside the pin housing and back the pins out through the holes in the wire seal. Remove the black and the red wire pins.

11. On the left side of the motorcycle, remove the Allen screw. Remove the CKP sensor and O-ring from the crankcase.

12. Tie a piece of string to the electrical connector. Tie the other end of the string to the frame cross-member. If necessary, make a drawing of the wire routing through the frame. It is easy to forget the routing path after removing the wire.

13. Carefully pull the sensor and electrical cables through the conduit and under the oil filter mount to the left side of the crankcase. If the wire becomes tight or stuck, do not force it.

14. Untie the string from the wiring harness.

15. Install by reversing these removal steps. Note the following:

    a. Tie the string to the wiring harness and connector(s).

    b. Carefully pull the string and the wiring harness and connector(s) through the right side of the frame into position. Untie and remove the string.

    c. Apply a light coat of dielectric compound to the electrical connector(s) prior to installing them.

    d. Apply clean engine oil to the *new* O-ring on the CKP sensor prior to installation. Install the sensor and tighten the Allen screw to the torque specification in **Table 6**.

Crankshaft Position Sensor (CKP) Sensor (2000-on Models) Removal/Installation

The crankshaft position sensor (CKP) (**Figure 43**) is mounted on the front left side of the crankcase next to the oil filter.

1. Remove the seat as described in Chapter Fourteen.

NOTE
Always disarm the optional TSSM security system prior to disconnecting the battery or the siren will sound.

2. Disconnect the negative battery cable from the battery as described in this chapter.

3. Remove the exhaust system as described in Chapter Seven.

4. Remove the right side frame cover.

5. Release the wiring harness from the clamp (A, **Figure 44**) on the electrical bracket.

6. Disconnect the three engine sensor electrical harness connectors for the oil pressure sending unit, camshaft position sensor and crankshaft position sensor (B, **Figure 44**).

7. Carefully remove the engine sensor electrical connector harness and connectors through the opening between the frame down tube and the bottom corner of the battery box.

8. Carefully cut the cable straps securing the engine sensor electrical connector harness to the down tube and the brake hose clamp.

9. Following the frame down tube, pull the electrical harness and connectors downward to the inboard side of the rear brake light switch. If necessary, remove the rear brake line clamp from the passenger footboard bracket.

10. On the lower frame tube, open the two cable clips and release the electrical harness from the T-studs.

11. Remove the T20 Torx screw, then open the clamp securing the electrical harness to the engine.

12. Disconnect the single green/yellow wire from the oil pressure switch.

13. Carefully pull the electrical harness and connectors forward along the top of the lower frame tube, and then between the rear brake master cylinder reservoir and the frame down tube next to the rear brake pedal.

14. Remove the red and black wire electrical terminals from the CKP two-pin Mini-Deutsch connector.

NOTE
The CKP red and black electrical wires are encased in a conduit containing the wires for the camshaft position sensor and the oil pressure sending unit. In the next step, the red and black wires must be pulled out through the conduit and the new wires must be pulled back through the conduit.

15. Tie a piece of string, or flexible wire, to the red and black electrical connectors. The string, or wire, must be long enough to pull the wires and connectors through the conduit without going into the con-

8

duit. Attach a nut or small object to the loose end of the string so it will not be pulled into the end of the conduit.

16. Slowly pull the wires and connectors through the conduit until they are free of the conduit. Untie the string, or wire, from the old CKP electrical connectors.

17. On the left side of the motorcycle, remove the Allen screw (**Figure 42**) and withdraw the CKP sensor and O-ring from the crankcase.

18. Install by reversing these removal steps. Note the following:

   a. Attach the string to the new CKP red and black electrical connectors.

   b. Slowly pull the wires and connectors back through the conduit until they are completely installed within the conduit. Untie the string, or wire, from the new CKP red and black electrical connectors.

   c. Apply a light coat of dielectric compound to the electrical connector(s) prior to installing them.

   d. Apply clean engine oil to the *new* O-ring on the CKP sensor prior to installation. Install the sensor and tighten the Allen screw to the torque specification in **Table 6**.

Camshaft Position Sensor (CMP) (1999 Models) Removal/Installation

The camshaft position sensor (CMP) is located in the camshaft cover on the right side of the crankcase.

1. Remove the seat as described in Chapter Fourteen.

NOTE
Always disarm the optional TSSM security system prior to disconnecting the battery or the siren will sound.

2. Disconnect the negative battery cable as described in this chapter.

3. Remove the exhaust system as described in Chapter Seven.

4. Locate the engine sensor harness 8-pin Mini-Deutsch electrical connector at the rear left side of the crankcase. Carefully pull the barbed wire anchor from the threaded hole in the crankcase. Depress the external latches and separate the connector halves.

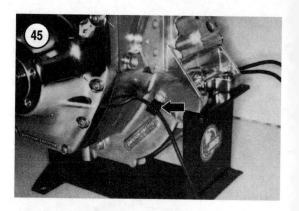

NOTE
Figure 45 is shown with the engine removed from the frame to better illustrate the step.

5. Remove the T20 Torx screw, then open the clamp (**Figure 45**) securing the electrical harness to the engine.

6A. On models with an oil pressure warning light, disconnect the single green/yellow wire from the oil pressure switch.

6B. On all other models, disconnect the single brown/green wire from the oil pressure sending unit.

7. Carefully pull the electrical harness and pin side of the Mini-Deutsch connector forward then up between the rear master reservoir and frame down tube.

8. Use needle nose pliers to remove the secondary locking wedge from the pin side of the electrical connector.

9. Gently depress the terminal latches inside the pin housing and back the pins out through the holes in the wire seal. Remove the red/white, black/white and green/white wires.

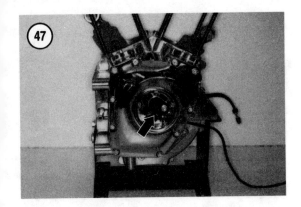

NOTE
Figure 46 and Figure 47 show the engine removed from the frame to better illustrate the steps.

10. Remove the T20 Torx screws securing the inspection cover (**Figure 46**) and remove the cover.

11. Tie a piece of string to the end of the wiring harness.

12. Remove the screw and washer securing the CMP sensor (**Figure 47**) to the camshaft cover. Remove the sensor and O-ring from the cover.

13. Tape a piece of string to the three individual electrical connectors in the CMP harness. Tie the other end of the string to the frame cross-member.

NOTE
Figure 48 shows the camshaft cover removed to better illustrate the step.

14. Carefully pull the electrical harness, with the piece of string, out through both openings in the camshaft cover (**Figure 48**).

15. Install by reversing these removal steps. Note the following:

a. Attach the string to the new CMP electrical connectors.

b. Slowly pull the wires and connectors back through both openings in the camshaft cover. Remove the string.

c. Apply a light coat of dielectric compound to the electrical connector(s) prior to installing them.

d. Apply clean engine oil to the *new* O-ring on the CMP sensor prior to installation. Install the sensor and tighten the Allen screw to the torque specification in **Table 6**.

Camshaft Position Sensor (CMP)
(2000-2001 Models) Removal/Installation

NOTE
The 2002 models are not equipped with the camshaft position sensor.

The camshaft position sensor (CMP) is located in the camshaft cover on the right side of the crankcase.

1. Perform Steps 1-12 of *Crankshaft Position Sensor (CKP) Removal/Installation (2000-On Models)* in this chapter.

NOTE
The CMP red and black electrical wires are encased in a conduit containing the wires for the camshaft position sensor and the oil pressure sending unit. In the next step, the red/white, green/white and black/white wires must be pulled out through the conduit and then the new wires must be pulled back through the conduit.

2. Tie a piece of string, or flexible wire, to the red/white, green/white and black/white wire electrical connectors. The string, or wire, must be long enough to pull the wires and connectors through the conduit without going into the conduit. Attach a nut or small object to the loose end of the string so it will not be pulled into the end of the conduit.

3. Slowly pull the wires and connectors through the conduit until they are free of the conduit. Untie the string, or wire, from the old CMP electrical connectors.

8

NOTE
Figure 46 and *Figure 47* show the engine removed from the frame to better illustrate the steps.

4. Remove the T20 Torx screws securing the inspection cover (**Figure 46**) and remove the cover.

5. Tie a piece of string to the end of the wiring harness.

6. Remove the screw and washer securing the CMP sensor (**Figure 47**) to the camshaft cover. Remove the sensor and O-ring from the cover.

7. Tape a piece of string to the three individual electrical connectors in the CMP harness. Tie the other end of the string to the frame cross-member.

8. Carefully pull the electrical harness, with the piece of string, out through both openings in the camshaft cover.

9. Untie the string and retie it to the new CMP sensor wiring harness.

NOTE
Figure 48 shows the camshaft cover removed to better illustrate the step.

10. Carefully pull the new wiring harness back through the two openings in the camshaft cover (**Figure 48**).

11. Install by reversing these removal steps. Note the following:

   a. Attach the string to the new CMP electrical connectors.

   b. Slowly pull the wires and connectors back through both openings in the camshaft cover. Untie the string.

   c. Apply a light coat of dielectric compound to the electrical connector(s) prior to installing them.

   d. Apply clean engine oil to the *new* O-ring on the CMP sensor prior to installation. Install the sensor and tighten the Allen screw to the torque specification in **Table 6**.

Engine Temperature Sensor Removal/Installation

The engine temperature sensor (**Figure 49**) is located in the rear left side of the front cylinder head.

1. Remove the seat as described in Chapter Fourteen.

NOTE
Always disarm the optional TSSM security system prior to disconnecting the battery or the siren will sound.

2. Disconnect the negative battery cable as described in this chapter.

3. On the left side of the front cylinder head, pull the rubber boot back off the sensor (**Figure 49**).

4. Pull on the external latch and disconnect the electrical connector from the sensor.

5. Use a 3/4 in. deep socket and loosen the sensor. When the socket turns easily, remove the socket and completely unscrew the sensor by hand.

6. Install a new sensor and start it by hand. Use the socket to tighten the sensor to the torque specification in **Table 6**.

7. Apply a light coat of dielectric compound to the electrical connector prior to installing it.

8. Install the electrical connector and push it on until it locks into place.

9. Pull the rubber boot back over the electrical connector.

10. Attach the negative battery cable.

11. Install the seat as described in Chapter Fourteen.

Bank Angle (BAS) Sensor (1999-2000) Removal/Installation

The bank angle sensor mounts to a frame panel on the left side of the motorcycle.

NOTE
*The bank angle sensor is an integral part of the turn signal module/turn signal security module (TSSM) on the 2001-on models. Refer to **Turn Signal Module** in this chapter.*

1. Remove the seat as described in Chapter Fourteen.

NOTE
Always disarm the optional TSSM security system prior to disconnecting the battery or the siren will sound.

2. Disconnect the negative battery cable from the battery as described in this chapter.

3. Remove the left side saddlebag as described in Chapter Fourteen.
4. Remove the frame left side cover.
5. Pull the external latch outward and disconnect the electrical connector from the bank angle sensor.
6. Remove the mounting screw and remove the sensor from the frame panel.
7. Install by reversing these removal steps. Note the following:
   a. Apply a light coat of dielectric compound to the electrical connector prior to installing it.
   b. Tighten the screw securely.

STARTING SYSTEM

When servicing the starting system, refer to the wiring diagrams located at the end of the manual.

CAUTION
Do not operate the starter for more than five seconds at a time. Let it cool approximately 10 seconds before operating it again.

Troubleshooting

Refer to Chapter Two.

Starter Removal

1. Remove the seat as described in Chapter Fourteen.

NOTE
Always disarm the optional TSSM security system prior to disconnecting the battery or the siren will sound.

2. Disconnect the negative battery cable as described in this chapter.
3. Remove the primary drive cover as described in Chapter Five.
4. Straighten the tab on the lockplate (**Figure 50**).
5. Wrap the pinion gear with a cloth to protect the finish, then secure it with pliers (A, **Figure 51**).
6. Loosen and remove the starter jackshaft bolt (B, **Figure 51**), lockplate and thrust washer from the end of the starter motor.
7. Remove the pinion gear (**Figure 52**) and spring from the jackshaft.

8

8. Remove the jackshaft assembly and the coupling from the inner housing.

9. Remove the rear exhaust pipe (A, **Figure 53**) as described in Chapter Seven.

10. Remove the bolt and the cover from the end of the starter motor.

11. Disconnect the solenoid electrical connector (B, **Figure 53**) from the starter motor.

12. Slide back the rubber boot, remove the nut and disconnect the positive cable from the starter motor terminal.

13. Remove the starter motor mounting bolts and washers. Note the location of the negative ground cable under the front bolt and washer.

14. Pull the starter motor straight out of the crankcase and remove it.

15. If necessary, service the starter motor as described in this chapter.

Starter Installation

1. Install the jackshaft (**Figure 54**) into the inner housing if it was removed. Push it in until it stops.

2. Position the coupling with its counterbore facing toward the jackshaft and install the coupling (**Figure 55**) into the inner housing bushing.

3. Install the spring (**Figure 56**) onto the jackshaft.

4. Install the pinion gear (**Figure 57**) onto the jackshaft.

5. Push in on the pinion gear (A, **Figure 58**) and install the bolt, lockplate and thrust washer (B) onto the jackshaft.

6. Push the assembly on until it bottoms.

7. Align the lockplate tab with the thrust washer, then insert the tab into the notch in the end of the jackshaft.

8. Screw the bolt into the starter motor shaft by hand.

9. Wrap the pinion gear with a cloth to protect the finish, then secure it with pliers (A, **Figure 51**).

10. Tighten the starter jackshaft bolt (B, **Figure 51**) to the torque specification in **Table 2**. Bend the lockplate tab (**Figure 50**) against the bolt head.

11. Ensure the components have been installed correctly as follows:

    a. Install the clutch shell onto the transmission mainshaft.

b. With the starter motor not engaged, the pinion gear (A, **Figure 59**) must not engage the clutch shell gear (B).

c. To check for proper engagement, pull out on the pinion gear and engage it with the clutch shell gear. Then rotate the clutch shell in either direction and make sure the pinion gear rotates with it.

d. If the engagement is incorrect, remove the clutch shell and correct the problem.

e. Remove the clutch shell.

12. Tighten the bolt on the starter motor to the specification in **Table 6**. Bend the outer lockplate tab against the bolt head.

13. Install the primary cover as described in Chapter Five.

14. Install the rear exhaust pipe as described in Chapter Seven.

15. Connect the negative battery cable.

16. Install the seat.

Starter Disassembly

> *NOTE*
> *If only the solenoid assembly requires service, refer to **Starter Solenoid** in this chapter.*

1. Clean all grease, dirt and carbon from the exterior of the starter assembly (**Figure 60**).

2. Remove the two throughbolts (**Figure 61**).

3. Remove the two drive housing Phillips screws (**Figure 62**) and lockwashers.

4. Tap the drive housing and remove it from the starter assembly (**Figure 63**).

5. Disconnect the C terminal field wire (A, **Figure 64**) from the solenoid housing.

6. Separate the field coil (B, **Figure 64**) from the solenoid housing (C).

7. Remove the end cap screws, washers and O-rings (A, **Figure 65**). Then remove the end cap (B).

8. Pull the brush holder (A, **Figure 66**) away from the commutator and remove the armature (B) from the field coil assembly.

9. Remove the two field coil brushes from the brush holder (**Figure 67**).

10. Clean all grease, dirt and carbon from the armature, field coil assembly and end covers.

> *CAUTION*
> *Be extremely careful when selecting a solvent to clean the electrical components. Do not immerse any of the wire windings in solvent, because the insulation may be damaged. Wipe the windings with a cloth lightly moistened with solvent, then allow the solution to dry thoroughly.*

11. To service the drive housing assembly, refer to *Drive Housing Disassembly/Inspection/Assembly* in this chapter.

8

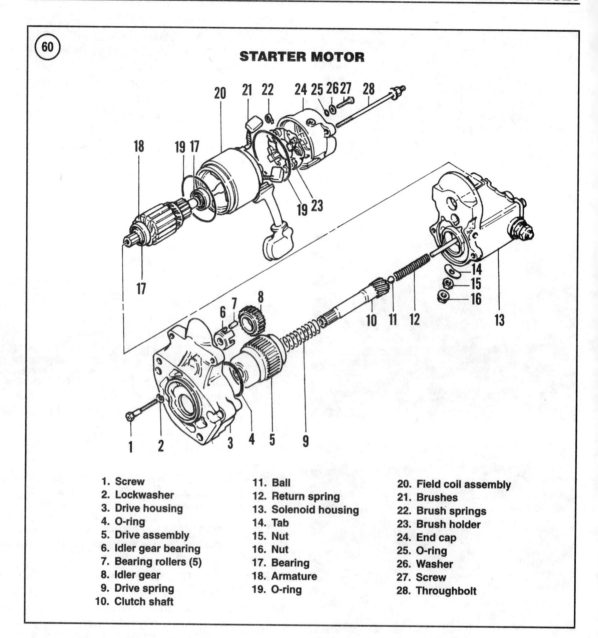

STARTER MOTOR

1. Screw
2. Lockwasher
3. Drive housing
4. O-ring
5. Drive assembly
6. Idler gear bearing
7. Bearing rollers (5)
8. Idler gear
9. Drive spring
10. Clutch shaft
11. Ball
12. Return spring
13. Solenoid housing
14. Tab
15. Nut
16. Nut
17. Bearing
18. Armature
19. O-ring
20. Field coil assembly
21. Brushes
22. Brush springs
23. Brush holder
24. End cap
25. O-ring
26. Washer
27. Screw
28. Throughbolt

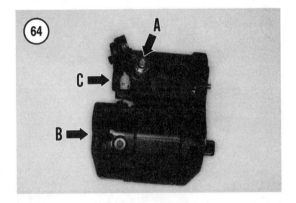

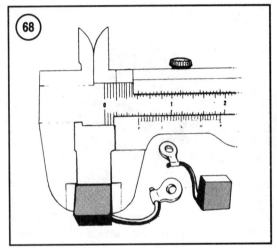

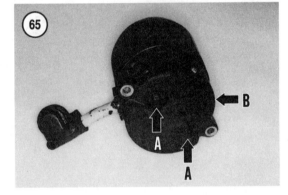

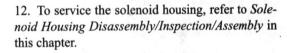

12. To service the solenoid housing, refer to *Solenoid Housing Disassembly/Inspection/Assembly* in this chapter.

Starter Inspection

1. Measure the length of each brush with a vernier caliper (**Figure 68**). If the length is less than the minimum specified in **Table 4**, replace all of the brushes as a set. See **Figure 69** for the field coil and **Figure 70** for the brush holder.

> *NOTE*
> *The field coil brushes (**Figure 69**) are soldered into position. To replace them, unsolder the brushes by heating their joints with a soldering gun, then pull them out with a pair of pliers. Position the new brushes and solder them in place with rosin core solder. Do not use acid core solder.*

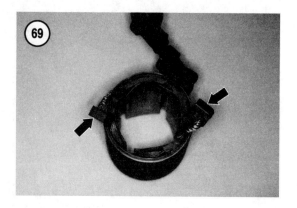

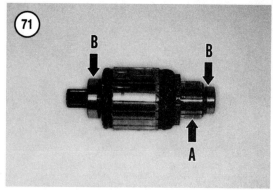

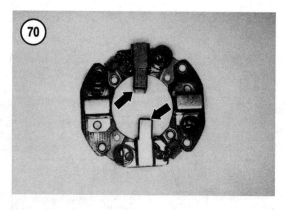

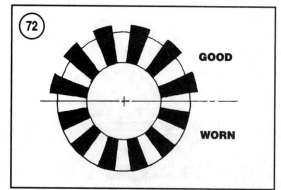

2. Inspect the commutator (A, **Figure 71**). The mica should be below the surface of the copper commutator segments (**Figure 72**). If the commutator bars are worn to the same level as the mica insulation, have the commutator serviced by a dealership or electrical repair shop.

3. Inspect the commutator copper segments for discoloration. If the commutator segments are rough, discolored or worn, have the commutator serviced by a dealership or electrical repair shop.

4. Measure the outer diameter of the commutator with a vernier caliper (**Figure 73**). Replace the armature if it is worn to the service limit in **Table 4**.

5. Use an ohmmeter to perform the following tests.

    a. Check for continuity between the commutator bars (**Figure 74**); there should be continuity between pairs of bars.

    b. Check for continuity between any commutator bar and the shaft (**Figure 75**). There should be no continuity.

    c. If the unit fails either test, replace the armature.

6. Use an ohmmeter to perform the following tests.

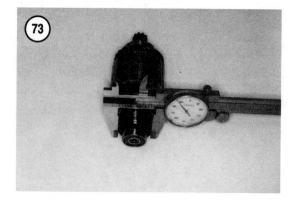

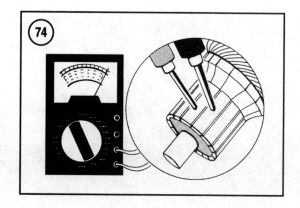

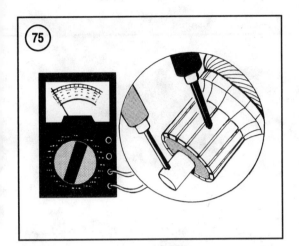

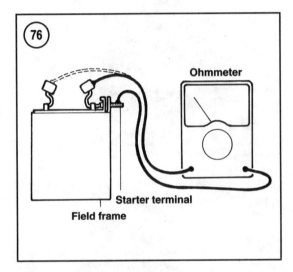

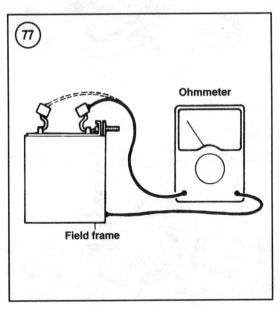

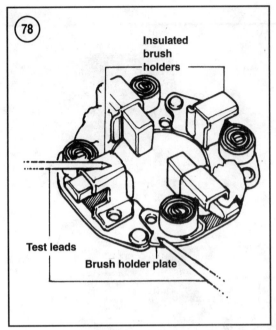

Insulated
brush
holders

Test leads

Brush holder plate

8

a. Check for continuity between the starter cable terminal and each field frame brush (**Figure 76**); there should be continuity.

b. Check for continuity between the field frame housing and each field frame brush (**Figure 77**); there should be no continuity.

c. If the unit fails either test, replace the field frame assembly.

7. Use an ohmmeter to check for continuity between the brush holder plate and each brush holder (**Figure 78**); there should be no continuity. If the unit fails this test, replace the brush holder plate.

8. Service the armature bearings as follows:

a. Check the bearings (B, **Figure 71**) on the armature shaft. Replace worn or damaged bearings.

b. Check the bearing bores in the end cover and solenoid housing. Replace the cover or housing if the area is worn or cracked.

Assembly

1. Assemble the drive housing as described in this chapter if it was serviced.

2. Assemble the solenoid housing as described in this chapter if it was serviced.

3. Lubricate the armature bearings (B, **Figure 71**) with high-temperature grease.

4. Install two *new* O-rings onto the field coil shoulders (**Figure 79**).

5. Install the two field coil brushes into the brush plate holders (**Figure 80**).

6. Install the armature partway through the field coil as shown in **Figure 66**. Then pull the brushes back and push the armature forward, so when released, all of the brushes contact the commutator as shown in **Figure 81** and **Figure 82**.

7. Install the end cap (**Figure 83**) and the two screws, washers and O-rings. Tighten the screws securely.

8. Align the field coil (A, **Figure 84**) with the solenoid housing (B) and assemble both housings. Hold the assembly together while installing the drive housing in Step 9.

9. Align the drive housing (**Figure 85**) with the field coil and solenoid housing assembly, and install it. Install the two drive housing screws and lockwashers (**Figure 62**). Tighten them securely.

10. Install the two throughbolts, washers and O-rings (**Figure 61**). Tighten them securely.

11. Reconnect the C terminal field wire (C, **Figure 84**) at the solenoid housing.

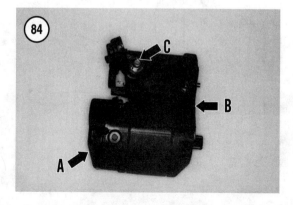

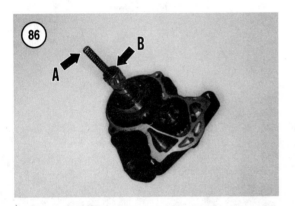

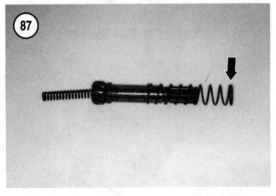

Drive Housing
Disassembly/Inspection/Assembly

The drive housing was removed during starter disassembly.

1. Remove the return spring (A, **Figure 86**), ball, clutch shaft (B) and drive spring (**Figure 87**) from the drive assembly.

2. Remove the idler gear (**Figure 88**) from the drive housing.

3. Remove the idler gear bearing and cage assembly (A, **Figure 89**). There are five individual bearing rollers (**Figure 90**).

4. Remove the drive assembly (B, **Figure 89**).

5. Replace the drive housing O-ring (**Figure 91**) if it is worn or damaged. Lubricate the O-ring with high temperature grease.

6. Inspect the idler gear bearing and cage assembly (**Figure 90**) for worn or damaged parts.

> *CAUTION*
> *The drive assembly (**Figure 92**) is a sealed unit. Do not clean or soak it in any type of solvent.*

8

7. Inspect the drive assembly and its bearings (**Figure 92**) for worn or damaged parts. If the bearings are worn or damaged, replace the drive assembly and bearings as a set.

8. Assemble the drive housing by reversing these steps. Note the following:

9. Lubricate the following components with high temperature grease.

    a. Idler gear bearing and cage assembly (**Figure 90**).

    b. Drive housing O-ring (**Figure 91**) and shaft.

    c. Drive assembly (**Figure 92**).

    d. Clutch shaft, drive spring, return spring and ball.

10. Install the idler gear bearing and cage assembly so the open side of the cage (A, **Figure 89**) faces toward the solenoid housing.

Solenoid Housing
Disassembly/Inspection/Assembly

1. Remove the solenoid housing (**Figure 93**) as described during starter disassembly.

2. Remove the screws, washers and clip securing the end cover to the solenoid housing. Then remove the end cover (**Figure 94**) and the gasket.

3. Remove the plunger assembly (**Figure 95**).

4. Inspect the plunger (**Figure 96**) for scoring, deep wear marks or other damage.

5. Inspect the solenoid housing (**Figure 97**) for wear, cracks or other damage.

6. The solenoid housing is a separate assembly and cannot be serviced. If any part is defective, the solenoid housing must be replaced as an assembly.

7. Assemble the solenoid housing by reversing these steps. Lubricate the solenoid plunger with high temperature grease.

LIGHTING SYSTEM

The lighting system consists of a headlight, passing lamps, taillight/brake light combination and turn signals.

Always use the correct wattage bulb. The use of a larger wattage bulb will give a dim light and a smaller wattage bulb will burn out prematurely. **Table 5** lists replacement bulb specifications.

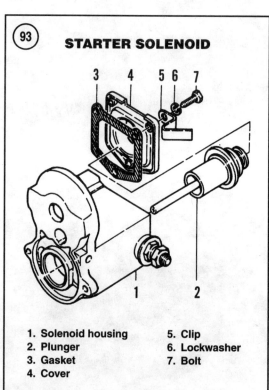

STARTER SOLENOID

1. Solenoid housing
2. Plunger
3. Gasket
4. Cover
5. Clip
6. Lockwasher
7. Bolt

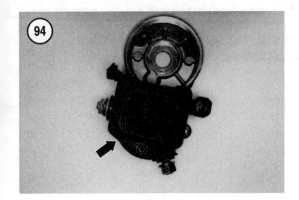

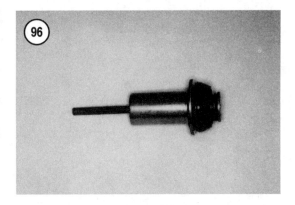

Headlight Bulb Replacement
(FLTR and FLTRI Models)

Refer to **Figure 98**.

CAUTION
All models are equipped with a quartz-halogen bulb. Do not touch the bulb glass. Traces of oil on the bulb will drastically reduce the life of the bulb. Clean all traces of oil from the bulb glass with a cloth moistened in alcohol or lacquer thinner.

WARNING
If the headlight has just burned out or just turned off, it will be hot. To avoid burned fingers, allow the bulb to cool prior to removal.

1. Remove the front fairing and windshield assembly as described in Chapter Fourteen.
2. Place the front fairing on a workbench covered with several towels to protect the finish.
3. Squeeze the two external tabs and pull *straight* out on the electrical connector. Disconnect the electrical connector from the bulb terminals.
4. Remove the rubber cover from the back of the lens assembly. Check the rubber boot for tears or deterioration; replace it if necessary.
5. Rotate the bulb retainer *counterclockwise* and remove it from the lens assembly.
6. Remove and discard the blown bulb.
7. Position the new bulb with the wider tab at the top, then push the bottom of the bulb flange so the lower two tabs fit snugly in the slot of the bulb housing.
8. Place the bulb retainer and carefully rotate it *clockwise* until it is secure in the lens assembly.
9. Install the rubber boot and make sure it is correctly seated against the bulb and the retainer.
10. Correctly align the electrical plug terminals with the bulb and connect the plug. Push it *straight on* until it bottoms on the bulb and the rubber cover.
11. Repeat for the other bulb if necessary.
12. Install the front fairing and windshield assembly as described in Chapter Fourteen.
13. Check headlight operation.
14. Check headlight adjustment as described in this chapter.

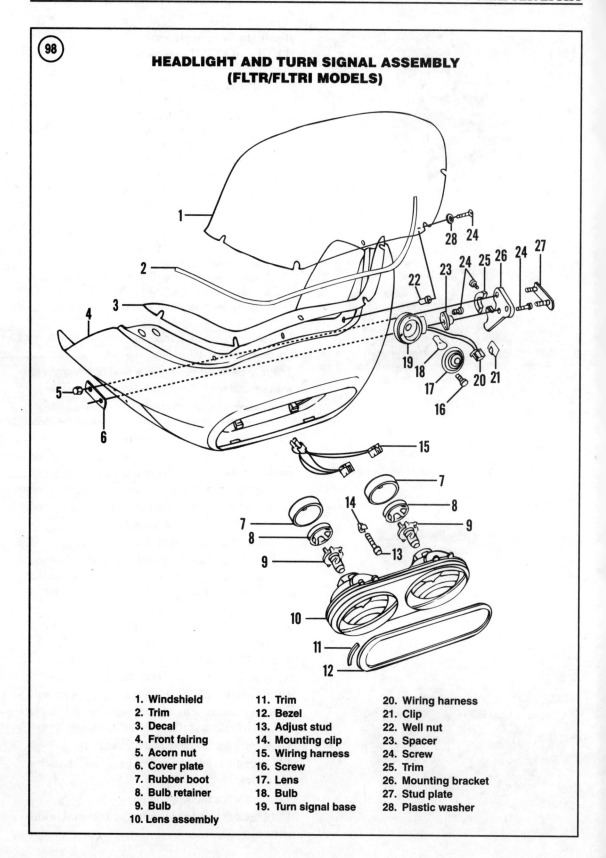

**HEADLIGHT AND TURN SIGNAL ASSEMBLY
(FLTR/FLTRI MODELS)**

1. Windshield
2. Trim
3. Decal
4. Front fairing
5. Acorn nut
6. Cover plate
7. Rubber boot
8. Bulb retainer
9. Bulb
10. Lens assembly
11. Trim
12. Bezel
13. Adjust stud
14. Mounting clip
15. Wiring harness
16. Screw
17. Lens
18. Bulb
19. Turn signal base
20. Wiring harness
21. Clip
22. Well nut
23. Spacer
24. Screw
25. Trim
26. Mounting bracket
27. Stud plate
28. Plastic washer

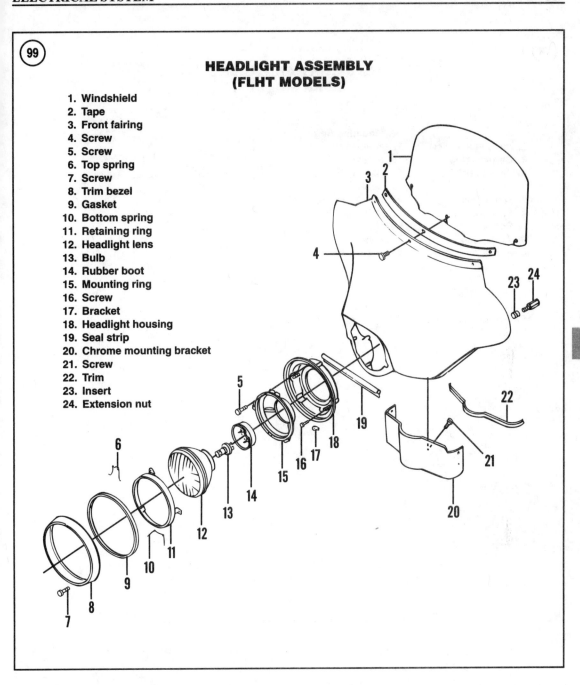

**HEADLIGHT ASSEMBLY
(FLHT MODELS)**

1. Windshield
2. Tape
3. Front fairing
4. Screw
5. Screw
6. Top spring
7. Screw
8. Trim bezel
9. Gasket
10. Bottom spring
11. Retaining ring
12. Headlight lens
13. Bulb
14. Rubber boot
15. Mounting ring
16. Screw
17. Bracket
18. Headlight housing
19. Seal strip
20. Chrome mounting bracket
21. Screw
22. Trim
23. Insert
24. Extension nut

**Headlight Bulb Replacement
(FLHT and FLHR Models)**

Refer to **Figure 99** for FLHT models and **Figure 100** for FLHR models.

*CAUTION
All models are equipped with a quartz-halogen bulb. Do not touch the bulb glass. Traces of oil on the bulb will drastically reduce the life of the bulb. Clean all traces of oil from the bulb glass with a cloth moistened in alcohol or lacquer thinner.*

*WARNING
If the headlight has just burned out or just turned off, it will be hot. To avoid burned fingers, allow the bulb to cool prior to removal.*

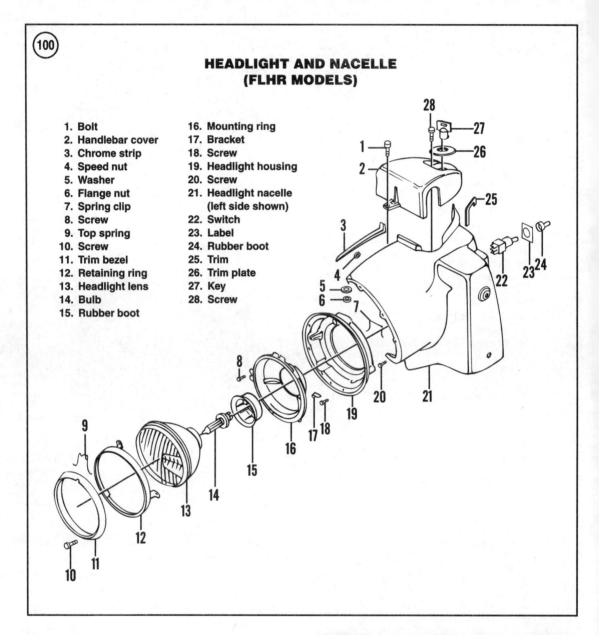

(100)

HEADLIGHT AND NACELLE
(FLHR MODELS)

1. Bolt
2. Handlebar cover
3. Chrome strip
4. Speed nut
5. Washer
6. Flange nut
7. Spring clip
8. Screw
9. Top spring
10. Screw
11. Trim bezel
12. Retaining ring
13. Headlight lens
14. Bulb
15. Rubber boot
16. Mounting ring
17. Bracket
18. Screw
19. Headlight housing
20. Screw
21. Headlight nacelle
    (left side shown)
22. Switch
23. Label
24. Rubber boot
25. Trim
26. Trim plate
27. Key
28. Screw

1. Remove the screw (A, **Figure 101**) at the base of the trim bezel (B) and remove the trim bezel from the headlight lens assembly. Do not lose the two springs on the trim bezel.

2. Remove the three screws securing the retaining ring (**Figure 102**) and remove it while holding the headlight lens assembly in place.

3. Pull the lens assembly (**Figure 103**) out of the front fairing, or headlight nacelle.

4. On models so equipped, squeeze the two external tabs to release the electrical connector from the lens assembly.

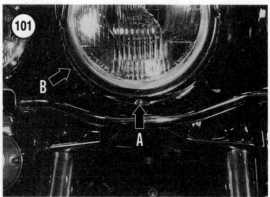

8

5. Pull *straight out* on the electrical connector (**Figure 104**) and disconnect it from the bulb. Remove the headlight assembly.

6. Remove the rubber cover (**Figure 105**) from the back of the headlight lens. Check the rubber boot for tears or deterioration; replace it if necessary.

7. Unhook the light bulb retaining clip (**Figure 106**) and pivot it out of the way.

8. Remove and discard the blown bulb (**Figure 107**).

9. Align the tangs on the new bulb with the notches in the headlight lens and install the bulb.

10. Securely hook the retaining clip onto the bulb (**Figure 106**).

11. Install the rubber boot (**Figure 105**) and make sure it is correctly seated against the bulb and the retainer.

12. Correctly align the electrical plug terminals with the bulb and connect the plug (**Figure 104**). Push it *straight on* until it bottoms on the bulb and the rubber cover.

13. Check headlight operation.

14. Insert the lens (**Figure 103**) into the headlight housing and seat it correctly.

15. Install the retaining ring (**Figure 102**) and three screws. Tighten it securely.

16. Install the square portion of the top spring (**Figure 108**) into the slot in the trim bezel and snap the trim bezel into place. Install the screw and tighten it securely.

17. Check headlight adjustment as described in this chapter.

Headlight Adjustment

1. Park the motorcycle on a level surface approximately 25 ft. (7.6 m) from the wall (**Figure 109**).

2. Check tire inflation pressure. Readjust it if necessary, as described in Chapter Three.

3. Draw a horizontal line on the wall that is 35 in. (0.9 m) above the floor.

4. Have a rider sit on the seat.

5. Aim the headlight at the wall. Switch the headlight to the high beam. Point the wheel straight ahead.

6. Check the headlight beam alignment. The broad, flat pattern of light (main beam of light) must be centered on the horizontal line with an equal area of light above and below line.

7. Turn the key switch to the IGNITION position.

8. Check the headlight beam lateral alignment. With the headlight beam pointed straight ahead, there should be an equal area of light to the left and right of center.

9A. On FLTR models, if the beam is incorrect as described in Step 6 or Step 7, adjust it as follows:

NOTE
The hex-adjusters are located on each side of the lower inner surface of the front fairing.

   a. Use a 4.5 mm socket on a flexible extension to adjust the hex-adjuster.

   b. Refer to **Table 7** for the correct rotation of the adjusters to achieve correct headlight aim.

9B. On all FLHT and FLHR models, if the beam is incorrect as described in Step 6 or Step 7, adjust it as follows.

   a. Turn the top vertical adjuster (A, **Figure 110**) to adjust the headlight vertically

   b. Turn the right side horizontal adjuster (B, **Figure 110**) to adjust the headlight horizontally.

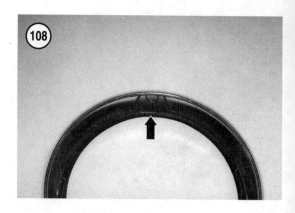

Passing Light and Front Turn Signal Bulb Replacement

Refer to **Figure 111**.

1. Remove the passing light bulb as follows:

   a. Remove the screw (**Figure 112**) at the base of the trim bezel and remove the trim bezel from the passing light housing.

   b. Carefully pull the bulb/lens assembly partially out of the housing.

   c. Loosen the two screws securing the wiring harness (**Figure 113**) to the bulb/lens assembly and remove it.

   d. Connect the wiring harness to the *new* bulb/lens assembly and tighten the screws securely.

   e. Push the bulb/lens assembly into the housing and install the trim bezel

   f. Tighten the screw securely.

2. Remove the front turn signal bulb as follows:

   a. Remove the screws securing the lens (**Figure 114**).

   b. Push in on the bulb, rotate it and remove it (**Figure 115**).

   c. Install a new bulb and lens.

   d. Tighten the screws securely. Do not overtighten the screws as the lens may crack.

Rear Turn Signal Bulb Replacement

1. Remove the screws securing the lens and remove the lens (**Figure 116**).

2. Push in on the bulb (**Figure 117**), rotate it and remove it.

3. Install a new bulb and lens.

4. Install the screws and tighten them securely. Do not overtighten the screws as the lens may crack.

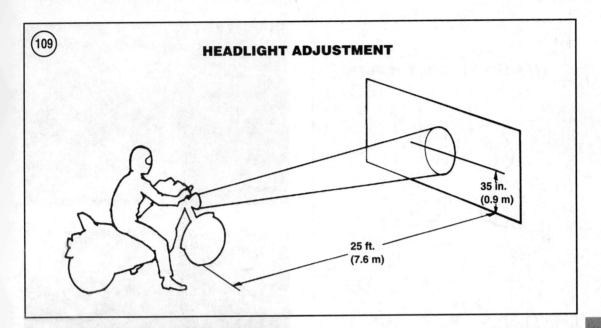

HEADLIGHT ADJUSTMENT

35 in.
(0.9 m)

25 ft.
(7.6 m)

Taillight/Brake Light Replacement

Refer to **Figure 118**.

1. Remove the screws securing the lens (**Figure 119**).

2. Pull the lens off the base (**Figure 120**) and disconnect the electrical connector.

3. Pull the bulb/socket assembly (**Figure 121**) out from the backside of the lens.

4. Rotate the bulb and remove it from the socket assembly (**Figure 122**).

5. Install a new bulb, then install the socket assembly into the lens.

6. Connect the electrical connector (**Figure 120**) and install the lens onto the base.

7. Install the screws and tighten them securely. Do not overtighten the screws as the lens may crack.

8. Replace the base as follows:

a. From underneath the rear fender, disconnect the wiring harness from the backside of the base.

b. Remove the screw securing the printed circuit board and base (**Figure 123**) to the rear fender.

c. Remove the base.

d. Install by reversing these steps.

**Tour-Pak Side Marker
Light Replacement
(FLHT Models)**

1. Open the cover and keep it open.

2. On FLHTCUI models, open the map pocket, and remove the acorn nuts and washers securing the map pocket and molded liner. Remove the molded liner from the lower case.

3. Remove the three T15 Torx screws securing the side marker lens and remove the lens.

4. Remove the bulb from the socket.

5. Install a new bulb and reinstall the side marker lens.

6. On FLHTCUI models, install the map pocket and molded liner into the lower case. Install the acorn nuts and washers, and tighten them securely.

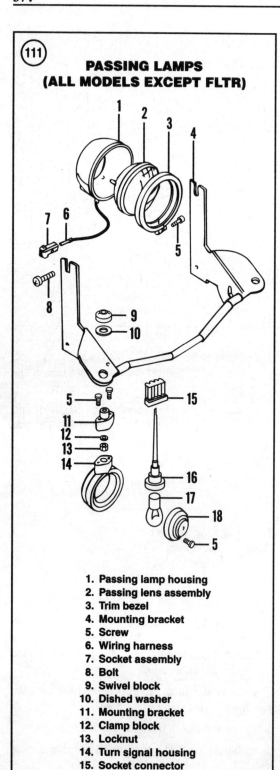

**PASSING LAMPS
(ALL MODELS EXCEPT FLTR)**

1. Passing lamp housing
2. Passing lens assembly
3. Trim bezel
4. Mounting bracket
5. Screw
6. Wiring harness
7. Socket assembly
8. Bolt
9. Swivel block
10. Dished washer
11. Mounting bracket
12. Clamp block
13. Locknut
14. Turn signal housing
15. Socket connector
16. Bulb socket
17. Turn signal bulb
18. Turn signal lens

8

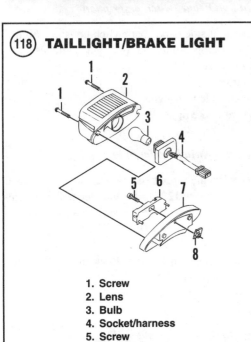

TAILLIGHT/BRAKE LIGHT

1. Screw
2. Lens
3. Bulb
4. Socket/harness
5. Screw
6. Circuit board/cover
   assembly
7. Base
8. Cage nut

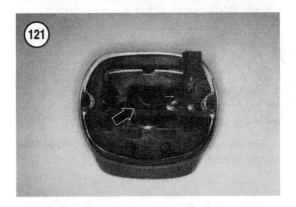

SWITCHES

Testing

Test switches for continuity by using an ohmmeter (see Chapter One) or a self-powered test light at the switch connector plug and operating the switch in each of its operating positions. Compare the results with the wiring diagrams located at the end of the manual.

For example, **Figure 124** shows the continuity diagram for the ignition switch. It shows which terminals should show continuity when the switch is in a given position. When the ignition switch is in the IGNITION position, there should be continuity between the red/black, red and red/gray terminals. Note the line on the continuity diagram. An ohmmeter connected between these three terminals should indicate little or no resistance, or a test light should light. When the ignition switch is OFF, there should be no continuity between the same terminals.

Replace the switch or button if it does not perform properly.

When testing the switches, note the following:

1. Check the battery as described under *Battery* in this chapter. Charge or replace the battery if necessary.

2. Disconnect the negative battery cable as described in this chapter before checking the continuity of any switch.

3. Detach all connectors located between the switch and the electrical circuit.

> *CAUTION*
> *Do not attempt to start the engine with the battery disconnected.*

4. When separating two connectors, pull on the connector housings and not the wires.

5. After locating a defective circuit, check the connectors to make sure they are clean and properly connected. Check all wires going into a connector housing to make sure each wire is positioned properly and the wire end is not loose.

6. To reconnect connectors properly, push them together until they click or snap into place.

Handlebar Switches (All Models Except FLHTC, FLHTCI AND FLHTCUI)

Left handlebar switch description

The left side handlebar switch housing (**Figure 125**) is equipped with the following switches.
1. Headlight HI-LO.
2. Horn.
3. Left side turn signal.

Right handlebar switch description

The right side handlebar switch housing (**Figure 126**) is equipped with the following switches.
1. Engine stop/run.
2. Starter.
3. Right side turn signal.
4. Front brake light.

Handlebar switch replacement

1. Remove the screws securing the left side switch housing (**Figure 127**) to the handlebar. Then carefully separate the switch housing to access the defective switch.
2. Remove the screws securing the right side switch housing (**Figure 128**) to the handlebar. Then carefully separate the switch housing to access the defective switch.

> *NOTE*
> *To service the front brake light switch, refer to **Front Brake Light Switch Replacement** in this chapter.*

3A. On models without splices, remove the screw and bracket.

124

IGNITION SWITCH

Position　Switch	Red/Black	Red	Red/Gray
Off		•	
Acc.		•————————•	
Ignition	•————————•	•————————•	

3B. On models with splices, remove the cable strap.

4. Pull the switch(es) out of the housing.

5. Cut the switch wire(s) from the defective switch(es).

6. Slip a piece of heat shrink tubing over each wire cut in Step 2.

7. Solder the wire end(s) to the new switch. Then shrink the tubing over the wire(s).

8. Install the switch by reversing these steps. Note the following:

a. When clamping the switch housing onto the handlebar, check the wiring harness routing position to make sure it is not pinched between the housing and handlebar.

b. To install the right side switch housing, refer to *Throttle and Idle Cable Replacement* in Chapter Seven.

WARNING
Do not ride the motorcycle until the throttle cables are properly adjusted. Also, the cables must not catch or pull when the handlebars are turned. Improper cable routing and adjustment can cause the throttle to stick open. This could cause loss of control.

Handlebar Switches (FLHTC, FLHTCI AND FLHTCUI Models)

Left handlebar switch description

The left side handlebar switch housing (**Figure 125**) is equipped with the following switches.
1. Headlight HI-LO.
2. Horn.

3. Left side turn signal.

Right handlebar switch description

The right side handlebar switch housing (**Figure 126**) is equipped with the following switches. See **Figure 129** for models without splices, or **Figure 130** for models with splices.
1. Engine stop/run.
2. Starter.
3. Right side turn signal.
4. Front brake light.
5. On FLHT and FLHTCI models, mode select switch UP/DN.
6. On FLHTCUI models, mode select switch UP/DN, cruise control switch.

Handlebar switch replacement

1. Remove the screws securing the left side switch housing (**Figure 127**) to the handlebar. Then carefully separate the switch housing to access the defective switch.

2. Remove the screws securing the right side switch housing (**Figure 128**) to the handlebar. Then carefully separate the switch housing to access the defective switch.

NOTE
*To service the front brake light switch, refer to **Front Brake Light Switch Replacement** in this chapter.*

3A. On models without splices, remove the three screws and brackets.

3B. On models with splices, remove the cable straps.

8

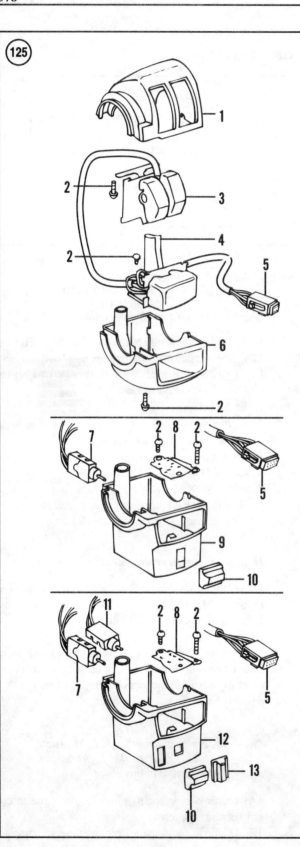

HANDLEBAR SWITCH (LEFT SIDE)

1. Upper housing
2. Screw
3. Headlight HI-LO switch
4. Left turn signal switch
5. Six-pin electrical connector
6. Lower housing (FLHR, FLHRI, FLHRCI)
7. Audio control +/- switch
8. Bracket
9. Lower housing (FLHT, FLHTC, FLHTCI)
10. Audio control +/- knob
11. Cruise control switch
12. Lower housing (FLTR, FLTRI, FLHTCUI)
13. Cruise control knob

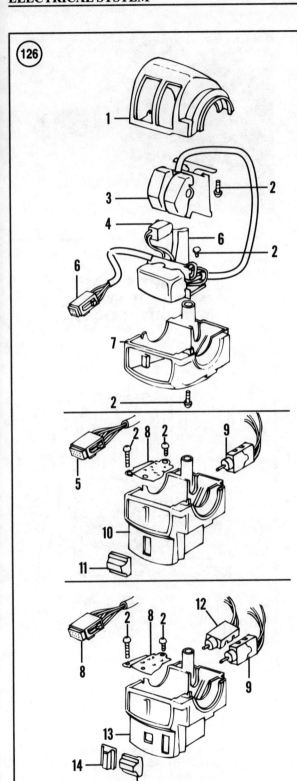

⑫⑥

**HANDLEBAR SWITCH
(RIGHT SIDE)**

1. Upper housing
2. Screw
3. Engine stop/run/start switch
4. Front brake light switch
5. Six-pin electrical connector
6. Right turn signal switch
7. Lower housing
   (FLHR, FLHRI, FLHRCI)
8. Bracket
9. Mode select UP/DN switch
10. Lower housing
    (FLHT, FLHTC, FLHTCI)
11. Mode select UP/DN knob
12. Cruise control set/resume switch
13. Lower housing
    (FLTR, FLTRI, FLHTCUI)
14. Cruise control set/resume knob

8

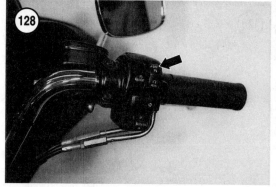

4. Pull the switch(es) out of the housing.

5. Cut the switch wire(s) from the defective switch(es).

6. Slip a piece of heat shrink tubing over each wire cut in Step 2.

7. Solder the wire end(s) to the new switch. Then shrink the tubing over the wire(s).

8. Install the switch by reversing these steps. Note the following:

   a. When clamping the switch housing to the handlebar, check the wiring harness routing position to make sure it is not pinched between the housing and handlebar.

   b. To install the right side switch housing, refer to *Throttle and Idle Cable Replacement* in Chapter Seven.

> *WARNING*
> *Do not ride the motorcycle until the throttle cables are properly adjusted. Also, the cables must not catch or pull when the handlebars are turned. Improper cable routing and adjustment can cause the throttle to stick open. This could cause lose of control. Recheck all work before riding the motorcycle.*

Front Brake Light Switch Replacement

The front brake light switch (**Figure 131**) is mounted in the right side switch lower housing.

1. Separate the right side switch housing as described under *Handlebar Switch Replacement* in this chapter.

2. If the wedge between the switch and the switch housing is still in place, remove it.

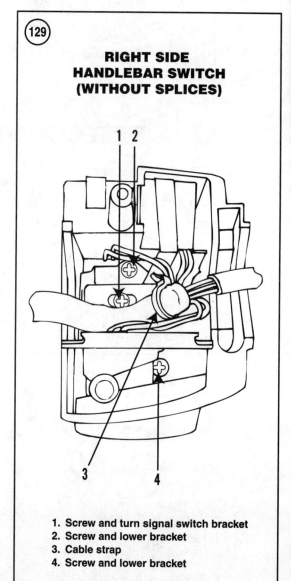

RIGHT SIDE HANDLEBAR SWITCH (WITHOUT SPLICES)

1. Screw and turn signal switch bracket
2. Screw and lower bracket
3. Cable strap
4. Screw and lower bracket

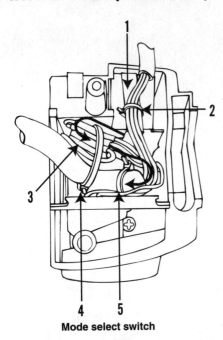

(130) HANDLEBAR SWITCH WITH SPLICES (RIGHT SIDE)

Mode select switch

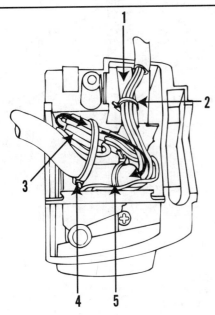

Cruise control switch

1. **Angular arm**
2. **Cable strap**
3. **Splices**
4. **Splices-to-conduit cable strap**
5. **Conduit-to-bracket cable strap**

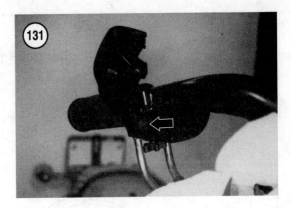

3. While depressing the switch plunger, slowly rotate the switch upward, rocking it slightly, and remove it from the switch housing.

4. Cut the switch wires from the defective switch.

5. Slip a piece of heat shrink tubing over each wire cut in Step 4.

6. Solder the wire ends to the new switch. Then shrink the tubing over the wires.

7. Install the switch by reversing these steps. Note the following steps.

8. When clamping the switch housing onto the handlebar, check the wiring harness routing position to make sure it is not pinched between the housing and handlebar.

9. To install the right side switch housing, refer to *Throttle and Idle Cable Replacement* in Chapter Seven.

WARNING
Do not ride the motorcycle until the throttle cables are properly adjusted. The cables must not catch or pull when the handlebars are turned. Improper cable routing and adjustment can cause the throttle to stick open. This could cause a loss of control. Recheck the work before riding the motorcycle.

Ignition/Light Switch Removal/Installation (FLHR, FLHRI and FLHRCI Models)

Refer to **Figure 132**.

1. Remove the fuel tank console as described under *Fuel Tank Console* in Chapter Seven.

2. Turn the fuel tank console over onto towels on the workbench.

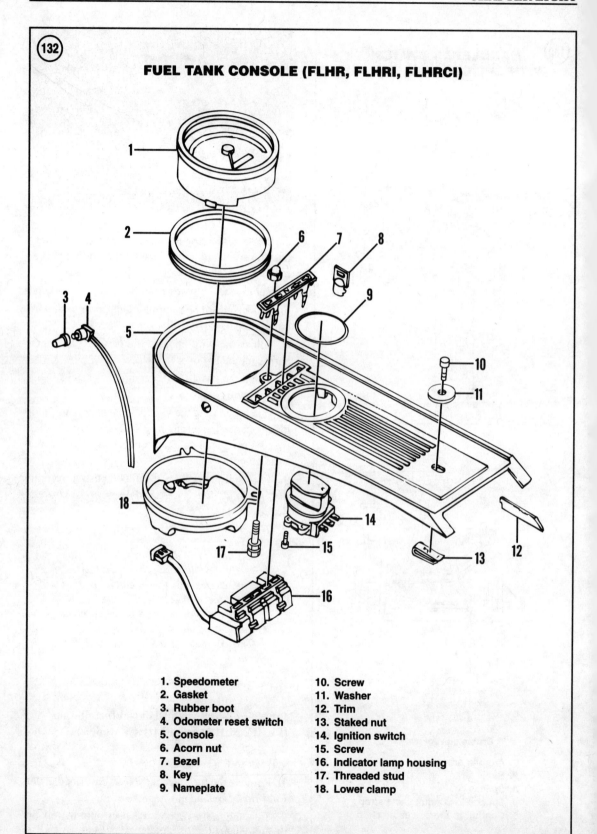

FUEL TANK CONSOLE (FLHR, FLHRI, FLHRCI)

1. Speedometer
2. Gasket
3. Rubber boot
4. Odometer reset switch
5. Console
6. Acorn nut
7. Bezel
8. Key
9. Nameplate
10. Screw
11. Washer
12. Trim
13. Staked nut
14. Ignition switch
15. Screw
16. Indicator lamp housing
17. Threaded stud
18. Lower clamp

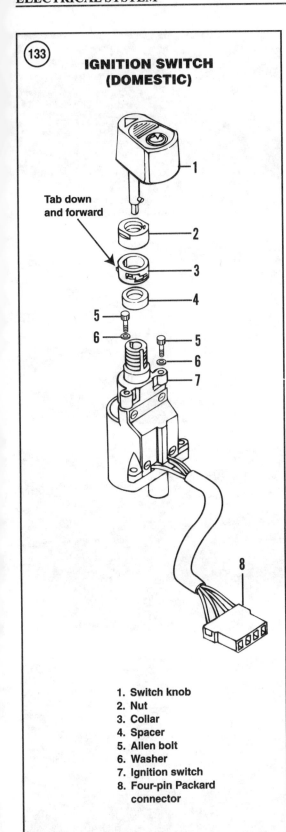

IGNITION SWITCH (DOMESTIC)

Tab down and forward

1. Switch knob
2. Nut
3. Collar
4. Spacer
5. Allen bolt
6. Washer
7. Ignition switch
8. Four-pin Packard connector

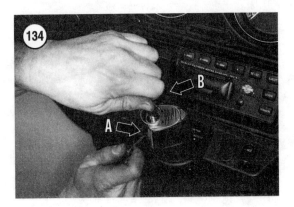

3. Remove the four screws securing the ignition switch to the bottom surface of the fuel tank console.

4. Remove the ignition switch.

5. Install the new ignition switch with the electrical connector terminal facing toward the rear of the fuel console. Tighten the screws securely.

6. Install the fuel tank console as described under *Fuel Tank Console* in Chapter Seven.

Ignition/Light Switch Removal/Installation (FLHT, FLHTC, FLHTCI, FLHTCUI, FLTR and FLTRI Domestic Models)

Refer to **Figure 133**.

1. Remove the outer fairing as described in Chapter Fourteen.

2. Remove the ignition switch knob as follows:

   a. Using the ignition key, turn the ignition switch to the UNLOCK position.

   b. Turn the ignition switch knob to the ACCESS position.

   c. Insert a small flat-bladed screwdriver under the left side of the switch knob (A, **Figure 134**) and depress the release button. Keep it depressed.

   d. Push the ignition key down and turn it 60° *counterclockwise* (B, **Figure 134**), then lift up and remove the switch knob.

3. Use a 7/8 in. open-end wrench to loosen the ignition switch nut (**Figure 135**). Unscrew and remove the nut from the threaded post.

4. Remove the collar and spacer (**Figure 136**) from the threaded post.

5. Pull on the tabs and remove the decal plate (**Figure 137**) from the slots in the fairing cap.

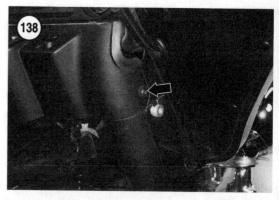

6. Remove the T27 Torx screws and washers (**Figure 138**) securing the fairing cap on each side of the inner fairing.

7. Carefully disengage the fairing cap (**Figure 139**) and pull it down. Disconnect the auxiliary switch electrical connector from the harness (A, **Figure 140**).

8. Carefully remove the auxiliary switch wiring harness (B, **Figure 140**) from the ignition switch and remove the fairing cap from the front fairing inner panel.

9. At the front of the motorcycle, locate the ignition switch black four-pin Packard connector next

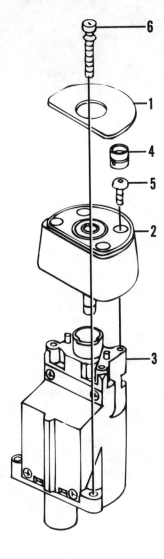

IGNITION SWITCH (INTERNATIONAL)

1. Decal
2. Switch knob
3. Ignition switch
4. Plug
5. Allen screw
6. Break-away screw

to the fork bracket. Disconnect the four-pin connector.

10. Remove the Allen screws and washers (A, **Figure 141**) securing the ignition switch to the upper fork bracket.

11. Carefully remove the ignition switch (B, **Figure 141**) and wiring harness from the inner fairing.

12. Installation is the reverse of removal. Note the following:

   a. Apply a light coat of dielectric compound to the electrical connectors prior to connecting them.

   b. Install the ignition switch to the upper fork bracket and tighten the Allen screws to the torque specification in **Table 6**.

   c. Test the switch in each of its operating positions.

Ignition/Light Switch Removal/Installation (FLHT, FLHTC, FLHTCI, FLHTCUI, FLTR and FLTRI International Models)

Refer to **Figure 142**.

1. Remove the outer fairing as described in Chapter Fourteen.

2. Remove the ignition switch knob as follows:

   a. Remove the decal on top of the ignition switch knob.

   b. Remove the plug above each Allen screw with a screw extractor or Easy-Out. Refer to *Basic Service Methods* in Chapter One.

   c. Remove the four Allen screws securing the knob and remove the knob.

3. Remove the T27 Torx screws and washers (**Figure 138**) securing the fairing cap on each side of the inner fairing.

4. Carefully disengage the fairing cap (**Figure 139**) and pull it down. Disconnect the auxiliary switch electrical connector from the harness (A, **Figure 140**).

5. Carefully remove the auxiliary switch wiring harness (B, **Figure 140**) from the ignition switch and remove the fairing cap from the front fairing inner panel.

6. At the front of the motorcycle, locate the ignition switch black four-pin Packard connector next to the fork bracket. Disconnect the four-pin connector.

7. Carefully working within the inner fairing, use a long shank 3/16 in. drill to drill out the two break-

away screws at the base of the ignition switch that secure the ignition switch to the upper fork bracket.

8. Carefully remove the ignition switch and wiring harness from the inner fairing.

9. Use pliers to remove the remaining portions of the break-away screws from the upper fork bracket.

10. Installation is the reverse of removal. Note the following:

    a. Apply a light coat of dielectric compound to the electrical connectors prior to connecting them.

    b. Install the new ignition switch to the upper fork bracket. Install new break-away screws and tighten them until the heads break off.

    c. Install new plugs over the break-away screws.

    d. Test the switch in each of its operating positions.

Oil Pressure Switch or Sender

Operation

The oil pressure switch, or sender, is located on the front right side of the crankcase.

A pressure-actuated diaphragm-type oil pressure switch, or sender, is used. When the oil pressure is low or when oil is not circulating through a running engine, spring tension inside the switch, or sender, holds the switch contacts closed. This completes the signal light circuit and causes the oil pressure indicator lamp to light.

The oil pressure signal light should turn on when any of the following occurs:

1. The ignition switch is turned on prior to starting the engine.

2. The engine idle speed is below 950-1050 rpm.

3. The engine is operating with low oil pressure.

4. Oil is not circulating through the running engine.

> *NOTE*
> *The oil pressure indicator light may not come on when the ignition switch is turned off then back on immediately. This is due to the oil pressure retained in the oil filter housing. Test the electrical part of the oil pressure switch in the following steps. If the oil pressure switch, indicator lamp and related wiring are in good condition,*

inspect the lubrication system as described in Chapter Two.

Testing/replacement

1A. On FLHT, FLHR, FLHRI and FLHRCI models, remove the rubber boot and disconnect the electrical connector from the switch.

1B. On FLHTC, FLHTCUI, FLHTCI, FLTR and FLTRI models, disconnect the three-pin Packard connector from the sender (**Figure 143**).

2. Turn the ignition switch ON.

3A. On models equipped with a switch, ground the switch wire to the engine.

3B. On models equipped with a sender, ground the green/yellow terminal in the Packard connector.

4. The oil pressure indicator lamp on the instrument panel should light.

5. If the indicator lamp does not light, check for a defective indicator lamp, and inspect all wiring between the switch, or sender, and the indicator lamp.

6A. If the oil pressure warning light operates properly, attach the electrical connector to the pressure switch. Make sure the connection is tight and free of oil. On models with a switch, slide the rubber boot back into position.

6B. If the warning light remains ON when the engine is running, shut the engine OFF. Check the engine lubrication system as described in Chapter Two.

7A. To replace the switch, perform the following:

    a. Use a 1 1/16 in. open-end crow foot wrench to unscrew the switch from the engine.

    b. Apply Teflon Loctite pipe sealant to the switch threads prior to installation.

    c. Install the switch and tighten it to the torque specification in **Table 6**.

d. Test the new switch as described in Steps 2-6.

7B. To replace the sending unit, perform the following:

    a. Use a 15/16 in. open-end crow foot wrench to unscrew the sending unit from the engine.

    b. Apply Loctite pipe sealant with Teflon to the switch threads prior to installation.

    c. Install the switch and tighten it to the torque specification in **Table 6**.

    d. Test the new switch as described in Steps 2-6.

Neutral Indicator Switch Replacement

The neutral indicator switch is located on the transmission top cover. The neutral indicator light on the instrument panel should light when the ignition is turned ON and the transmission is in NEUTRAL.

1. Disconnect the electrical connector from the neutral indicator switch.

2. Turn the ignition switch ON.

3. Ground the neutral indicator switch wire to the transmission case.

4. If the neutral indicator lamp now lights, the neutral switch is defective. Replace the neutral indicator switch and retest.

5. If the neutral indicator lamp does not light, check for a defective indicator lamp, faulty wiring or a loose or corroded connection.

NOTE
The electrical connector can be attached to either stud on the switch.

6A. If the neutral switch operates correctly, attach the electrical connector to the neutral switch. Make sure the connection is tight and free of oil.

6B. If the neutral switch is defective, replace the neutral indicator switch.

7. To replace the switch, perform the following:

    a. Shift the transmission into NEUTRAL.

    b. Unscrew and remove the switch and O-ring from the transmission top cover.

    c. Apply clean transmission oil to a *new* O-ring seal.

    d. Install the new switch and tighten it to the specification in **Table 6**.

Rear Brake Light Switch Testing/Replacement

A hydraulic, normally-open rear brake light switch is used on all models. The rear brake light is attached to the rear brake caliper brake hose assembly. When the rear brake pedal is applied, hydraulic pressure closes the switch contacts, providing a ground path so the rear brake lamp comes on. If the rear brake lamp does not come on, perform the following:

NOTE
Removal of the exhaust system is not necessary, but it provides additional work room if necessary for this procedure.

1. If necessary, remove the exhaust system from the right side as described in Chapter Seven.

2. Turn the ignition switch OFF.

3. Disconnect the electrical connector from the switch.

4. Connect an ohmmeter between the switch terminals. Check the following:

    a. Apply the rear brake pedal. There should be continuity.

    b. Release the rear brake pedal. There should be no continuity.

    c. If the switch fails either of these tests, replace the switch.

5. Place a drip pan under the switch, as some brake fluid will drain out when the switch is removed.

6. Loosen and remove the switch from the fitting on the rear brake line.

7. Thread the new switch into the fitting and tighten it securely.

8. Reconnect the switch electrical connectors.

9. Bleed the rear brake as described in Chapter Twelve.

10. Check the rear brake light with the ignition switch turned ON and the rear brake applied.

HORN

The horn is mounted on the frame boss on the left side of the frame.

Testing

1. Remove the seat.

2. Disconnect the yellow/black electrical connector from the backside of the horn.

3. Connect a positive voltmeter test lead to the yellow/black electrical connector and the negative test lead to ground.

4. Turn the ignition switch to the ON position.

5. Press the horn button. If battery voltage is present, the horn is faulty or is not grounded properly. If there is no battery voltage, either the horn switch or the horn wiring is faulty.

6. Connect an ohmmeter across both horn terminals. Replace the horn if the resistance is not within 45-66 ohms.

7. Replace the horn or horn switch as necessary.

Replacement

1. Remove the seat as described in Chapter Fourteen.

2. Disconnect the negative battery cable as described in this chapter.

3. Remove the long acorn nut securing the horn assembly bracket to the frame post.

4. Move the horn assembly to the frame and engine, and disconnect the electrical connectors from the horn spade terminals.

5. Remove the screw and nut securing the horn to the mounting bracket, and remove the horn.

6. Install the horn by reversing these removal steps. Note the following.

   a. Make sure the electrical connectors and horn spade terminals are free of corrosion.

   b. Connect the wires to the horn's top spade terminals.

   c. Make sure the horn operates correctly.

TURN SIGNAL MODULE
(1999-2000 MODELS)

The turn signal module (TSM) is an electronic microprocessor that controls the turn signals and the four-way hazard flasher. The turn signal module receives its information from the speedometer and turn signal switches.

The turn signal module is located under the seat within the cavity in the frame backbone.

If the following tests do not locate the problem, refer TSM testing to a Harley-Davidson dealership.

Operation

Refer to **Figure 144**.

1. When the left turn signal switch is pressed, a momentary 12 VDC pulse is sent to Pin No. 8 (input) on the TSM module. The module responds to this signal by sending a series of 12 VDC pulses to Pin No. 4 (output) to flash the left front and rear turn signal lamps.

2. The TSM module then monitors the number of motorcycle sensor pulses sent from the speedometer sending unit to Pin No. 5. These pulses indicate the distance the motorcycle has traveled. When the number of speedometer pulses is equal to the quantity preset in the module program, the turn signal is cancelled.

NOTE
If the turn signal switch is pressed and held in, the turn signal will flash indefinitely until the switch is released.

3. When the right turn signal switch is pressed, a momentary 12 VDC pulse is sent to Pin No. 7 (input) on the TSM module and an output signal at Pin No. 3 (output). The remaining signal process is identical to the left turn signal operation.

Preliminary Troubleshooting

If one of the turn signals does not flash, perform the following:

1. Remove the lens and check for a defective bulb(s). Replace the bulb(s) if necessary.

2. If the bulb(s) is good, check for one of the following problems.

   a. Check the bulb socket contacts for corrosion. Clean the contacts and recheck them. If there is a problem with corrosion building on the contacts, wipe the contacts with a dielectric grease before reinstalling the bulb.

   b. Check for a broken wire in the circuit. Repair the wire(s) or connector(s).

   c. Check for a loose bulb socket where it is staked to the housing. If the bulb socket is loose, replace the light assembly.

   d. Check for a poor ground connection. If the ground is poor, clean the ground mounting area or replace damaged ground wire(s) as required.

   e. Check for a stuck turn signal button.

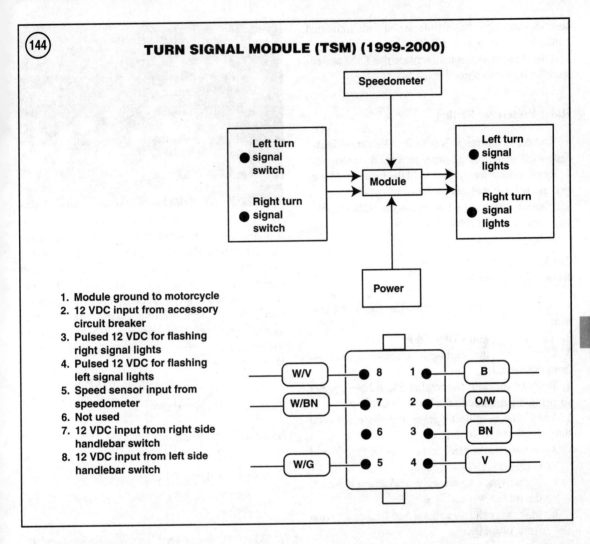

(144)

TURN SIGNAL MODULE (TSM) (1999-2000)

Speedometer

Left turn signal switch

Right turn signal switch

Module

Left turn signal lights

Right turn signal lights

Power

1. Module ground to motorcycle
2. 12 VDC input from accessory circuit breaker
3. Pulsed 12 VDC for flashing right signal lights
4. Pulsed 12 VDC for flashing left signal lights
5. Speed sensor input from speedometer
6. Not used
7. 12 VDC input from right side handlebar switch
8. 12 VDC input from left side handlebar switch

W/V	8	1	B
W/BN	7	2	O/W
	6	3	BN
W/G	5	4	V

8

3. Remove the TSM or TSSM as described in this chapter.

4. Disconnect the electrical connector from the TSM or TSSM.

5. Check the electrical connectors in the TSM or TSSM and in the wiring harness for corrosion. Clean the connectors off if necessary.

Distance Test

The turn signal module (TSM) recognizes four different speed ranges and uses these to activate the cancellation action at a predetermined distance. Refer to the speed/distance ranges in **Table 8**.

1. Ride the motorcycle at the midpoint of speed range No. 1.

2. Press and release the right turn button. Check the motorcycle speed and the odometer when the button is released and the turn signal is cancelled.

3. Repeat Step 1 and Step 2 for right and left turns at the midpoint of speed ranges No. 2 through No. 4.

4. If the distances observed in Steps 1-3 are not correct, check for the following:

    a. Check the TSM ground connection and module pin connections for corrosion.

    b. Check all lamps and lamp connections.

    c. Check the motorcycle speed sensor connections and ground for corrosion.

Time Test

This is an alternate to the speed/distance test, to test if the TSM module is operating correctly. Measure the turn signal ON time at the four indicated constant speeds in **Table 9**.

If the TSM fails this test, replace the TSM and repeat the test with a good module.

Rider Preference Setting

To make the turn signals flash for a longer or shorter distance than the pre-set time, perform the following:
1. Longer distance cycle—hold the turn signal longer and release it closer to the turning point.
2. Shorter distance cycle—press the button a second time to cancel the turn signals.

Turn Signal Module (TSM) Removal/Installation

1. Remove the seat as described in Chapter Fourteen.
2. Turn the ignition switch OFF.
3. Disconnect the eight-pin Deutsch connector from the module.
4. Remove the bolt, flat washer and rubber washer securing the module to the frame backbone.
5. Install the module by reversing these removal steps. Note the following:
   a. Make sure the electrical connectors are free of corrosion.
   b. Tighten the bolt securely. Make sure to install the rubber washer.
   c. Make sure the turn signal and flasher systems work properly.

TURN SIGNAL MODULE (2001-ON MODELS) AND TURN SIGNAL/SECURITY MODULE (2001-ON MODELS)

The turn signal module (TSM) is an electronic microprocessor that controls the turn signals and four-way hazard flasher. The turn signal module receives its information from the speedometer and turn signal switches. On models equipped with a security system (TSSM), it is incorporated into the TSM module. The bank angle sensor (BAS) provides motorcycle movement signals to the module. TSM and TSSM modules are not interchangeable.

The turn signal module, TSM or TSSM, is located under the seat within the frame backbone cavity at the rear of the battery box.

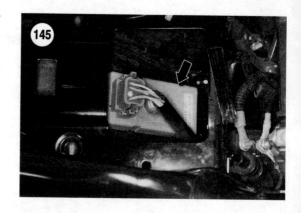

When there is a problem with either system, a diagnostic fault code(s) is set. The TSM or TSSM can only be tested for fault codes with Harley-Davidson diagnostic equipment. However, first make sure that the bulbs and all connections are in good condition. The following information describes how the systems are designed to operate. If any portion of the module is inoperative, refer testing to a Harley-Davidson dealership.

Turn Signal Operation

Automatic cancellation

> *NOTE*
> *The TSM/TSSM will not cancel the signal before the turn is actually completed.*

1. When the turn signal button is pressed and released, the system begins a 20 count. As long as the motorcycle is moving above 7 MPH (11 KPH) and the ISM does not receive any additional input, the turn signals will cancel after 20 bulb flashes.
2. If the motorcycle's speed drops to 7 MPH (11 KPH) or less, the turn signals will continue to flash. The count resumes when the motorcycle reaches 8 MPH (13 KPH) and the turn signal will cancel when the total count equals 20 bulb flashes.
3. The turn signals will cancel two seconds after a turn of 45° or more is completed.

Manual cancellation

1. After the turn signal button is pressed and released, the system begins a 20 count. To cancel the turn signal, press the turn signal button a second time.

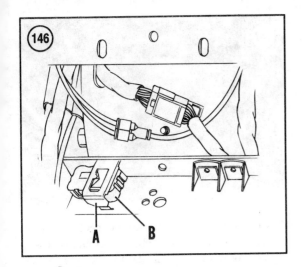

2. If the turn direction is changed, press the opposite turn signal button. The primary signal is cancelled and the opposite turn signal will flash.

Four-way flashing

1. Turn the ignition key to the ON position. On models so equipped, disarm the security system. Press the right and left turn signal buttons at the same time. All four turn signals will flash at the same time.
2. On models with the security system, the system can be armed so all four signals flash for up to two hours. Turn the ignition key to the OFF position and arm the security system. Press both the right and left turn signal buttons at the same time.
3. To cancel the four-way flashing, disarm the security system, on models so equipped, and press both the right and left turn signal buttons at the same time.

Bank angle sensor

The bank angle sensor automatically shuts off the engine if the motorcycle tilts more than 45° for longer than one second. The shutoff will occur even at a very slow speed.

To restart the motorcycle, return the motorcycle to vertical. Turn the ignition key from OFF to ON, then restart the engine.

Security System (TSSM) Operation

If a theft attempt is detected and the TSSM is in operation, it immobilizes the starting and ignition systems. It also flashes the right and left turn signals alternately and sounds the siren, if so equipped. The following conditions activate the armed security system.

1. Small motorcycle movement—the turn signals flash three times and the optional siren chirps once. If the motorcycle is not returned to its original position, the warnings will reactivate after four seconds. This cycle will repeat a maximum of 255 times.

2. Large motorcycle movement—the system will activate for 30 seconds, then turn off. If the motorcycle is not returned to its original position, the warnings will reactivate after ten seconds. This cycle may repeat a maximum of ten times.

3. Tampering of the security lamp circuit—system activates for 30 seconds. The cycle will repeat for each tampering incident.

4. A battery ground or ground disconnect has occurred while the system is armed—the siren will sound, if so equipped, but the turn signals will not flash.

NOTE
Always disarm the optional TSSM prior to disconnecting the battery or the siren will sound. If the TSSM is in auto-alarming mode, disarm the system with two clicks of the key fob, and disconnect the battery or remove the TSSM fuse before the 30-second arming period expires.

Turn Signal Security Module (TSSM) Removal/Installation

1. Remove the seat as described in Chapter Fourteen.
2. Turn the ignition switch OFF.
3A. On 2001 models, perform the following:
   a. Depress the clip and lift it to release the module's legs from the hole in the frame.
   b. Remove the TSSM module (**Figure 145**) from the frame and disconnect the eight-pin electrical Deutsch connector from the module.
3B. On 2002 models, perform the following:
   a. Depress the tab in front of the spring clip (A, **Figure 146**), then lift up and release the legs from the hole in the cross member.

8

b. Remove the TSSM module (B, **Figure 146**) from the frame and disconnect the 12-pin electrical Deutsch connector from the module.

4. Install the module by reversing these removal steps. Note the following:

a. Make sure the electrical connectors are free of moisture.

b. Make sure the module is secure in the frame hole.

c. Make sure the turn signal and flasher systems work properly.

SPEEDOMETER SPEED SENSOR

All models are equipped with an electronic speedometer assembly that consists of the speedometer, speed sensor and function switch.

The speed sensor mounts on top of the transmission housing, directly over fourth gear.

Performance Check

The Harley-Davidson Speedometer Tester is required to check the performance of the speedometer.

> *NOTE*
> *This test cannot be used to verify the calibration of the speedometer and will not verify the speedometer's function for legal proceedings. The test verifies speedometer function for service diagnosis or repair, and verifies if the speedometer requires replacement.*

Speedometer Speed Sensor Removal/Installation

The speedometer speed sensor mounts on top of the transmission case.

1. Remove the seat as described in Chapter Fourteen.

2. Disconnect the negative battery cable as described in this chapter.

3. Remove the Allen screw and remove the speed sensor from the transmission case.

4. Disconnect the three-pin Mini-Deutsch connector containing one red, one black and one white wire in front of the battery box.

5. Carefully pull the electrical connector out from under the frame crossmember. Disconnect the secondary locks on the Mini-Deutsch connector and disconnect the connector.

6. Tie a piece of string to the electrical connector. Tie the other end of the string to the frame crossmember.

7. Carefully pull the wiring harness and connector out of the frame on the right side. If the wire is tight or stuck, do not force it. If necessary, make a drawing of the wire routing through the frame. It is easy to forget the routing path after removing the wire.

8. Untie the string from the wiring harness.

9. Installation is the reverse of removal. Note the following:

a. Tie the string to the wiring harness and connector.

b. Carefully pull the string and the wiring harness and connector through the right side of the frame into position under the seat. Untie and remove the string.

c. Apply a light coat of dielectric compound to the electrical connector(s) prior to installing them.

d. Apply clean engine oil to the *new* O-ring on the speedometer sensor prior to installation. Install the sensor and tighten the Allen screw to the specification in **Table 6**.

STARTER RELAY SWITCH REPLACEMENT

The starter relay switch is mounted under the fuse cover on the left side of the frame.

1. Remove the seat as described in Chapter Fourteen.

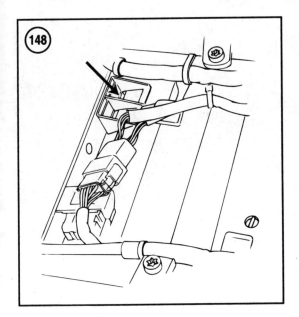

2. Disconnect the negative battery cable as described in this chapter.

3. Remove the left side saddlebag and frame left side cover as described in Chapter Fourteen.

4A. On 1999-2001 and 2002 FLHR and FLHRI models, perform the following:

   a. Remove the left side saddlebag and frame left side cover as described in Chapter Fourteen.

   b. Depress the latches and remove the fuse block cover (**Figure 147**).

   c. Unplug and remove the starter relay switch from the rear fuse block.

4B. On 2002 models, except FLHR and FLHRCI models, perform the following.

   a. Remove the seat as described in Chapter Fourteen.

   b. Pull up and disconnect the starter relay switch (**Figure 148**) from the relay holder.

5. Install by reversing these steps.

INSTRUMENTS

Removal/Installation
(All FLHT Models)

Refer to **Figure 149**.

1. Remove the seat.

NOTE
Always disarm the optional TSSM security system prior to disconnecting the battery or the siren will sound.

2. Disconnect the negative battery cable as described in this chapter.

3. Remove the outer front fairing as described in Chapter Fourteen.

4. Disconnect the electrical connector from the instrument to be removed.

5. Remove the screws, or nuts, securing the instrument to the mounting bracket.

6A. Carefully push the speedometer and tachometer out through the gasket and the front of the inner front fairing.

6B. Carefully push the other gauges out through the front of the inner front fairing.

7. Store the meters in a safe place.

8. Install the gasket onto the speedometer and tachometer mounting brackets if it was removed.

9. Installation is the reverse of removal. Note the following:

NOTE
If necessary, apply alcohol or glass cleaner to the gasket surfaces to ease installation of the meters.

   a. Install the instruments into the mounting brackets. Press firmly until the instrument is correctly seated and secure with the screws or nuts.

   b. Connect the negative battery cable as described in this chapter.

Removal/Installation (All FLTR Models)

Refer to **Figure 150**.

1. Remove the seat.

NOTE
Always disarm the optional TSSM security system prior to disconnecting the battery or the siren will sound.

2. Disconnect the negative battery cable as described in this chapter.

3. Remove the T25 Torx screw on each side of the instrument bezel.

4. Carefully push the rear of the bezel and release it from the slot above the ignition switch.

5. Raise the loose side of the bezel until the tabs at the front of the instrument housing are disengaged from the slot at the front of the bezel.

6. Disconnect the twelve-pin Packard connector from the speedometer.

8

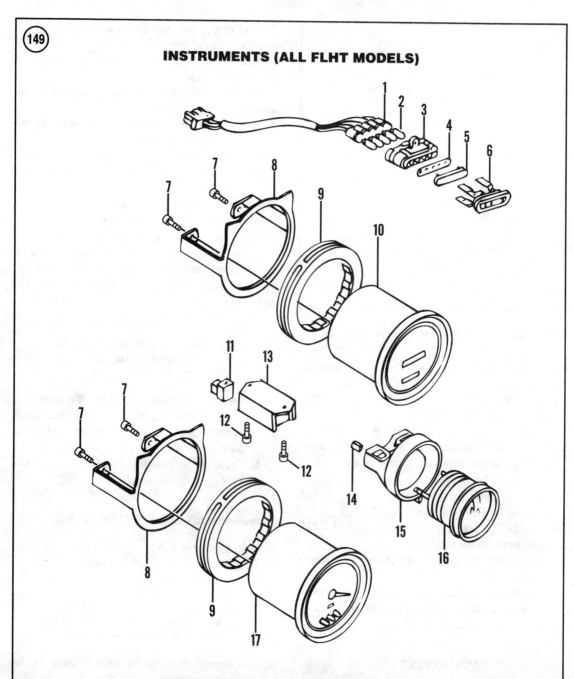

INSTRUMENTS (ALL FLHT MODELS)

1. Indicator lamp socket
2. Indicator lamps
3. Indicator lamp housing
4. Indicator lamp jewel
5. Indicator lamp lens
6. Indicator lamp bezel
7. Screw
8. Mounting bracket
9. Gasket
10. Speedometer
11. Air temperature sensor
12. Screw
13. Low fuel warning module
14. Nut
15. Gauge mounting bracket
16. Voltmeter
17. Tachometer

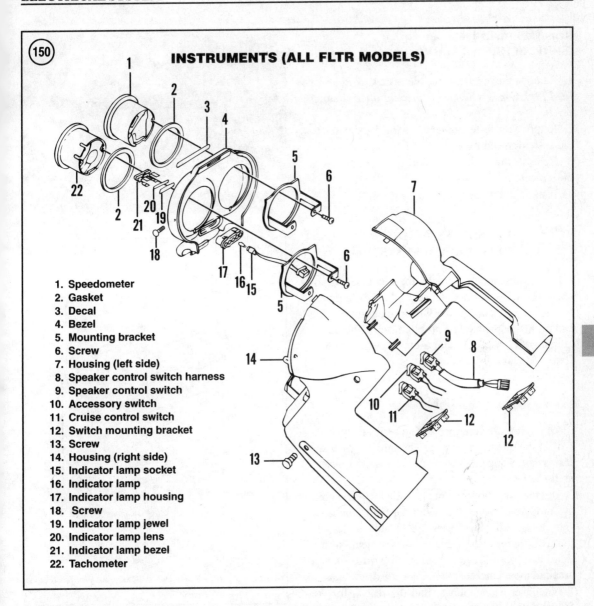

(150) **INSTRUMENTS (ALL FLTR MODELS)**

1. Speedometer
2. Gasket
3. Decal
4. Bezel
5. Mounting bracket
6. Screw
7. Housing (left side)
8. Speaker control switch harness
9. Speaker control switch
10. Accessory switch
11. Cruise control switch
12. Switch mounting bracket
13. Screw
14. Housing (right side)
15. Indicator lamp socket
16. Indicator lamp
17. Indicator lamp housing
18. Screw
19. Indicator lamp jewel
20. Indicator lamp lens
21. Indicator lamp bezel
22. Tachometer

7. Disconnect the six-pin Packard connector from the tachometer.

8. Carefully cut the cable strap between the speedometer and tachometer brackets.

9. Disconnect the ten-pin Multi-lock connector from the indicator lamp housing.

10. Remove the bezel from the instrument housing.

11. Remove the screws securing the instrument to the mounting bracket.

12. Carefully push the speedometer and tachometer out through the gasket and the front of the bezel.

13. Store the meters in a safe place.

14. Install the gasket onto the speedometer and tachometer if it was removed.

15. Installation is the reverse of removal. Note the following:

NOTE
If necessary, apply alcohol or glass cleaner to the gasket surfaces to ease installation of the meters.

a. Install the instruments into the mounting brackets. Press firmly until the instrument is correctly seated and secure with the screws.

b. Connect the negative battery cable as described in this chapter.

Removal/Installation
(FLHR, FLHRI and FLHRCI)

1. Remove the fuel tank console as described under *Fuel Tank Console Removal/Installation* in Chapter Seven.
2. Remove the fasteners securing the back clamp to the base of the console.
3. Remove the back clamp and speedometer from the console.
4. Installation is the reverse of removal.

PREMIUM SOUND, CB
AND INTERCOM SYSTEMS

If a malfunction occurs with the sound, CB or intercom systems, check the fuses and wiring connectors while referring to the wiring diagrams at the end of this manual. If the problem cannot be determined with basic electrical tests, refer service to a Harley-Davidson dealership.

FUSES

All models are equipped with a series of fuses to protect the electrical system. The number of fuses varies depending on the model. The fuse ratings are in **Table 1**.

The fuel injection fuel pump and electronic control module fuses are located under the frame right side cover. All other fuses are located under the frame left side cover. If there is an electrical failure, first check for a blown fuse. A blown fuse has a break in the element.

Whenever a fuse blows, find the reason for the failure before replacing the fuse. Usually, the trouble is a short circuit in the wiring. This may be caused by worn-through insulation or a disconnected wire shorted to ground. Check the circuit that the fuse protects.

Fuse Replacement

1. Remove the seat as described in Chapter Fourteen.

NOTE
Always disarm the optional TSSM security system prior to disconnecting the battery or the siren will sound.

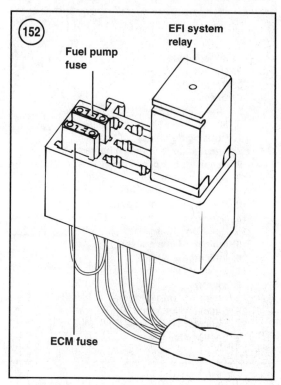

2. Disconnect the negative battery cable as described in this chapter.
3. Remove the right or left side saddlebag and frame right or left side cover as described in Chapter Fourteen.
4A. On 1999-2001 fuel injected models, depress the latch and remove the fuse block cover (**Figure 151**). Remove the fuse for the ECM and/or fuel pump.
4B. On 2002 fuel injected models, perform the following:
   a. Unhook the data link connector from the clip and move it out of the way.

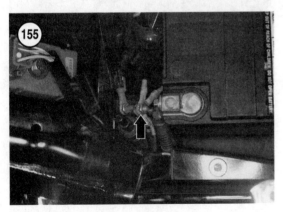

b. Carefully pull the fuse block out from the cover on the electrical bracket.

c. Remove the fuse for the ECM and/or fuel pump (**Figure 152**).

4C. On all other models, depress the latches and remove the fuse block cover (**Figure 153**).

5. Locate the blown fuse (**Figure 154**) and install a new fuse with the *same* amperage.

NOTE
Always carry spare fuses.

CIRCUIT BREAKER

All models use a single circuit breaker with a 40 amp rating to protect the electrical circuits.

Whenever a failure occurs in any part of the electrical system, the circuit breaker is self-resetting and will automatically return power to the circuit when the electrical fault is found and corrected.

CAUTION
If the electrical fault is not found and corrected, the circuit breaker will cycle on and off continuously. This will cause the motorcycle to run erratically.

Usually the problem causing a short circuit is in the wiring connected to the circuit breaker.

Determine the circuits protected by the circuit breaker by following the wiring diagrams at the end of the manual.

Do not consider a tripped circuit breaker a minor annoyance; it indicates something is wrong in the electrical system and must be corrected immediately.

Replacement

The circuit breaker is located under the seat.
1. Remove the seat as described in Chapter Fourteen.

NOTE
Always disarm the optional TSSM security system prior to disconnecting the battery or the siren will sound.

2. Disconnect the negative battery cable as described in this chapter.

NOTE
Record the wires colors and the terminal to which they are connected. The wires must be reinstalled onto the correct terminal.

3. Remove the nuts and wire connections at the circuit breaker (**Figure 155**).
4. Remove the circuit breaker from the mounting bracket on the inner panel.
5. Install the circuit breaker by reversing these steps.

8

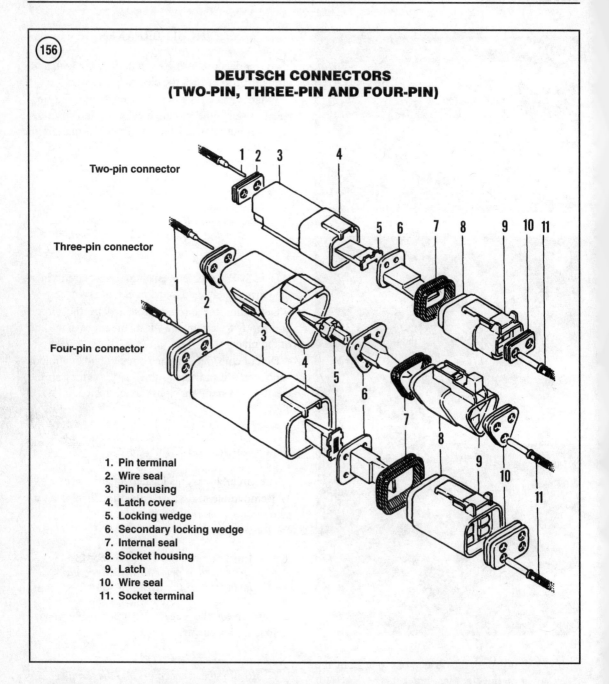

**DEUTSCH CONNECTORS
(TWO-PIN, THREE-PIN AND FOUR-PIN)**

Two-pin connector

Three-pin connector

Four-pin connector

1. Pin terminal
2. Wire seal
3. Pin housing
4. Latch cover
5. Locking wedge
6. Secondary locking wedge
7. Internal seal
8. Socket housing
9. Latch
10. Wire seal
11. Socket terminal

ELECTRICAL CONNECTOR SERVICE

A variety of electrical connectors are used throughout the electrical system. The following procedures are for disassembly of the connector in order to replace an individual electrical wire in the connector.

These connectors are designed for a superior seal to prevent dirt and moisture from entering the connector and damaging a pin connector.

Deutsch Electrical Connectors
Socket Terminal Removal/Installation

This procedure shows how to remove and install the socket terminals from the socket housing connector half (**Figure 156** and **Figure 157**). The procedure refers to a 12-pin Duetsch connector and is similar for two-, three-, four- and six-pin Duetsch connectors.

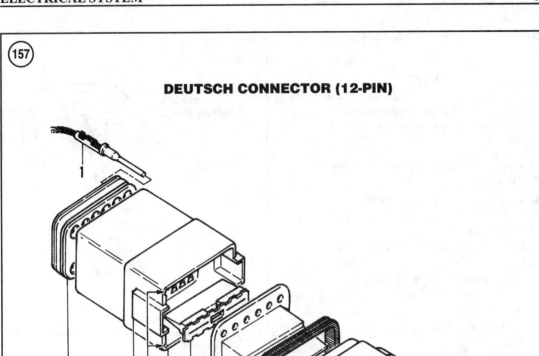

DEUTSCH CONNECTOR (12-PIN)

1. Pin terminal
2. Wire seal
3. Pin housing
4. Latch cover
5. Alignment grooves
6. Locking wedge
7. Secondary locking wedge
8. Internal seal
9. Alignment tabs
10. External latch
11. Socket
12. Wire seal
13. Seal pin
14. Socket terminal

8

1. Remove the seat as described in Chapter Fourteen.

NOTE
Always disarm the optional TSSM security system prior to disconnecting the battery or the siren will sound.

2. Disconnect the negative battery cable as described in this chapter.
3. Disconnect the connector housing.
4. Remove the secondary locking wedge (7, **Figure 157**) as follows:
   a. Locate the secondary locking wedge.
   b. Insert a wide-blade screwdriver between the socket housing and the locking wedge. Turn the screwdriver 90° to force the wedge up (**Figure 158**).
   c. Remove the secondary locking wedge (7, **Figure 157**).
5. Lightly press the terminal latches inside the socket housing and remove the socket terminal (14, **Figure 157**) through the holes in the rear wire seal.
6. Repeat Step 5 for each socket terminal.
7. If necessary, remove the wire seal (12, **Figure 157**).
8. Install the wire seal (12, **Figure 157**) into the socket housing if it was removed.
9. Hold onto the socket housing and insert the socket terminals (14, **Figure 157**) through the holes in the wire seal so they enter their correct chamber hole. Continue until the socket terminal locks into place. Then lightly tug on the wire to make sure it is locked into place.
10. Set the internal seal (8, **Figure 157**) onto the socket housing if it was removed.

NOTE
With the exception of the three-pin Duetsch connector, all of the secondary locking wedges are symmetrical. When assembling the three-pin connector, install the connector so the arrow on the secondary locking wedge is pointing toward the external latch as shown in Figure 159.

NOTE
If the secondary locking wedge does not slide into position easily, one or more of the socket terminals are not

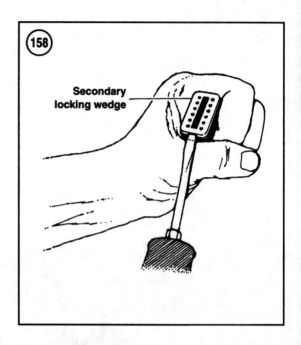

installed correctly. Correct the problem at this time.

11. Install the secondary locking wedge into the socket housing as shown in **Figure 156** or **Figure 157**. Press the secondary locking wedge down until it locks into place.

Deutsch Electrical Connectors Pin Terminal Removal/Installation

This procedure shows how to remove and install the pin terminals from the pin housing connector half (**Figure 156** and **Figure 157**). The procedure refers to a 12-pin Duetsch connector and is similar for Duetsch connectors (two-, three-, four- and six-pin).

1. Remove the seat as described in Chapter Fourteen.

NOTE
Always disarm the optional TSSM security system prior to disconnecting the battery or the siren will sound.

2. Disconnect the negative battery cable as described in this chapter.
3. Disconnect the connector housing.
4. Use needlenose pliers to remove the locking wedge (6, **Figure 157**).

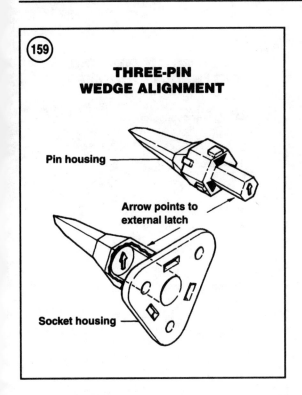

THREE-PIN WEDGE ALIGNMENT

Pin housing

Arrow points to external latch

Socket housing

5. Lightly press the terminal latches inside the pin housing and remove the pin terminal(s) (1, **Figure 157**) through the holes in the rear wire seal.

6. Repeat Step 5 for each pin terminal.

7. If necessary, remove the wire seal (2, **Figure 157**).

8. Install the wire seal (2, **Figure 157**) into the socket housing if it was removed.

9. Hold onto the pin housing and insert the pin terminals (1, **Figure 157**) through the holes in the wire seal so they enter their correct chamber hole. Continue until the pin terminal locks into place. Then lightly tug on the wire to make sure it is locked into place.

10. Set the internal seal (8, **Figure 157**) onto the socket housing if it was removed.

NOTE
*With the exception of the three-pin Duetsch connector, all of the locking wedges are symmetrical. When assembling the three-pin connector, install the connector so the arrow on the locking wedge is pointing toward the external latch as shown in **Figure 159**.*

NOTE
If the secondary locking wedge does not slide into position easily, one or more of the terminals are not installed correctly. Correct the problem at this time.

11. Install the locking wedge into the pin housing as shown in **Figure 156** or **Figure 157**. Press the locking wedge down until it locks into place. When properly installed, the wedge will fit into the pin housing center groove.

Packard Electrical Connectors
External Latch-Type
Removal/Installation

This procedure shows how to remove and install the electrical terminals from external latch-type connectors with pull-to-seat terminals (**Figure 160**).

1. Remove the seat as described in Chapter Fourteen.

NOTE
Always disarm the optional TSSM security system prior to disconnecting the battery or the siren will sound.

2. Disconnect the negative battery cable as described in this chapter.

3. Bend back the external latch(es) slightly and separate the connector.

4. Look into the mating end of the connector and locate the locking tang (1, **Figure 161**) in the middle chamber and on the external latch side of connector. On locking ear connectors, the tang is on the side opposite the ear.

5. Insert the point of a one-inch safety pin about 1/8 in. into the middle chamber (2, **Figure 161**). Pivot the end of the safety pin up toward the terminal body until a click is heard. Repeat this step several times. The click is the tang returning to the locked position as it slips from the point of the safety pin. Continue to pick at the tang until the clicking stops and the safety pin seems to slide in at a slightly greater depth indicating the tang has been depressed.

6. Remove the safety pin, push the wire end of the lead and remove the lead from the connector (3, **Figure 161**). If additional slack is necessary, pull back on the harness conduit and remove the wire seal at the back of the connector.

8

7. To install the terminal and wire back into the connector, use a thin flat blade of an X-Acto knife to carefully bend the tang away from the terminal (4, **Figure 161**).

8. Carefully pull the lead and terminal into the connector until a click is heard indicating the terminal is seated correctly within the connector. Gently push on the lead to ensure the terminal is correctly seated.

9. If necessary, install the wire seal and push the harness conduit back into position on the backside of the connector.

10. Push the socket halves together until the latch(es) are locked together.

Packard Electrical Connectors
Wire Form Type
Removal/Installation

This procedure shows how to remove and install the electrical terminals from wire form type connectors with pull-to-seat terminals (**Figure 162**).

1. Remove the seat as described in Chapter Fourteen.

NOTE
Always disarm the optional TSSM security system prior to disconnecting the battery or the siren will sound.

2. Disconnect the negative battery cable as described in this chapter.

3. Depress the wire form and separate the connector.

4. Hold the connector so the wire form is facing down.

5. Look into the mating end of the connector and locate the plastic rib that separates the wire terminals. The terminal is on each side of the rib with the tang at the rear.

6. Use the thin flat blade of an X-Acto knife to depress the tang. Tilt the blade at an angle and place the tip at the inboard edge of the terminal. Push down slightly until the spring tension is relieved and a click is heard. Repeat this step several times. The click represents the tang returning to the locked position as it slips from the point of the knife blade. Continue to push down until the clicking stops indicating the tang has been depressed.

7. Remove the knife blade, push the wire end of the lead and remove the lead from the connector. If ad-

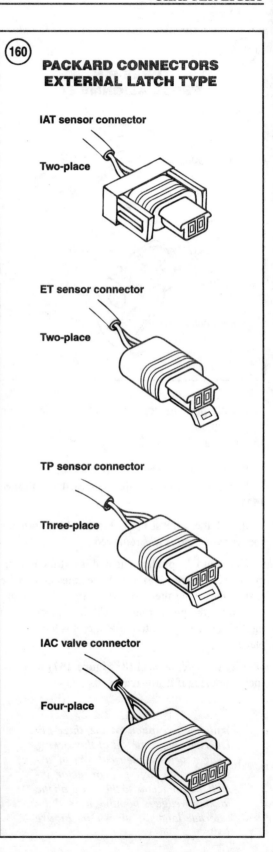

PACKARD CONNECTORS EXTERNAL LATCH TYPE

IAT sensor connector

Two-place

ET sensor connector

Two-place

TP sensor connector

Three-place

IAC valve connector

Four-place

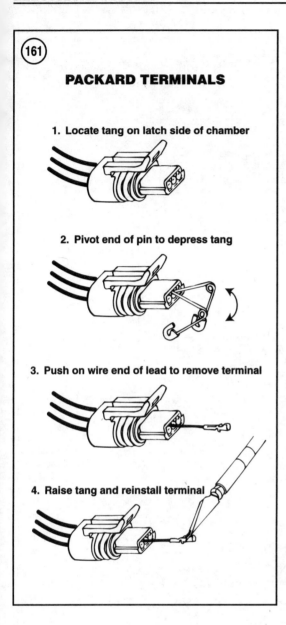

(161)

PACKARD TERMINALS

1. Locate tang on latch side of chamber

2. Pivot end of pin to depress tang

3. Push on wire end of lead to remove terminal

4. Raise tang and reinstall terminal

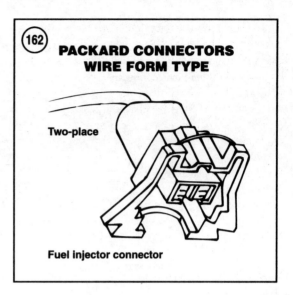

(162)

PACKARD CONNECTORS
WIRE FORM TYPE

Two-place

Fuel injector connector

11. Push the socket halves together until the latch(es) are locked together.

Amp Electrical Connectors Socket and Pin Terminals Removal/Installation

This procedure shows how to remove and install the socket and pin terminals from the pin and socket housing connector. This procedure relates to all three-, six- and ten-pin Amp connectors.

Refer to **Figure 163**.

1. Remove the seat as described in Chapter Fourteen.

NOTE
Always disarm the optional TSSM security system prior to disconnecting the battery or the siren will sound.

2. Disconnect the negative battery cable as described in this chapter.

3. Press the button on the socket on the terminal side and pull the connector apart.

4. Slightly bend the latch back and free one side of the secondary lock. Repeat this step for the other side.

5. Rotate the secondary lock (1, **Figure 164**) out on the hinge to access the terminals within the connector.

NOTE
Do not pull too hard on the wire until the tang is released or the terminal will be difficult to remove.

ditional slack is necessary, pull back on the harness conduit and remove the wire seal at the back of the connector.

8. To install the terminal and wire back into the connector, use a thin flat blade of an X-Acto knife to carefully bend the tang away from the terminal.

9. Carefully pull the lead and terminal into the connector until a click is heard indicating the terminal is seated correctly within the connector. Gently pull on the lead to ensure the terminal is correctly seated.

10. If necessary, install the wire seal and push the harness conduit back into position on the backside of the connector.

8

163

AMP MULTILOCK CONNECTORS

Three-place connector

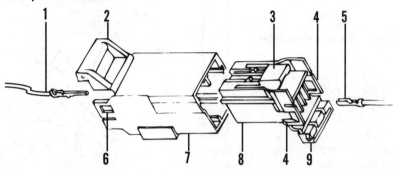

Six-place connector

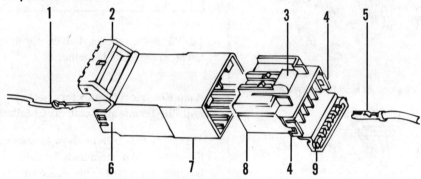

Ten-place connector

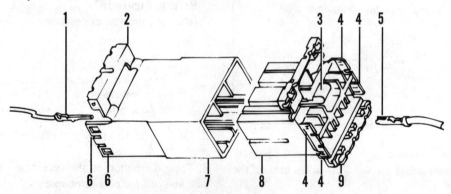

1. Pin terminal
2. Secondary lock
3. Button
4. Latch
5. Socket terminal
6. Latch
7. Pin housing
8. Socket housing
9. Secondary lock

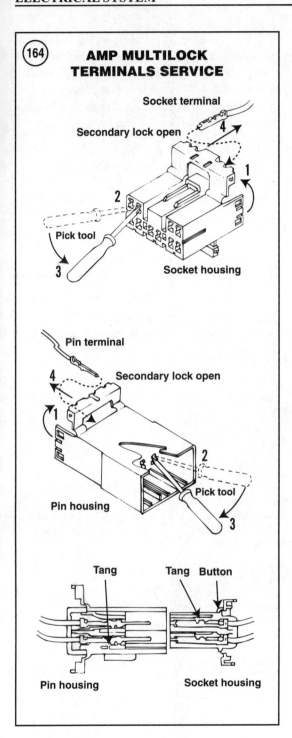

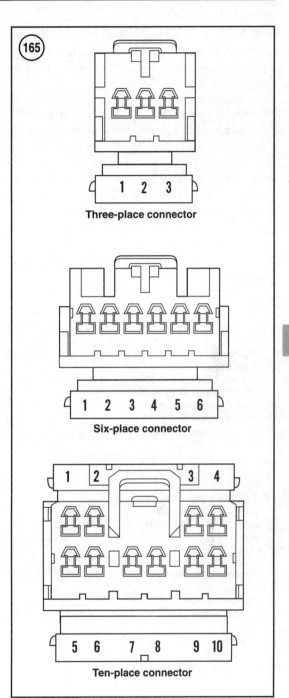

6. Insert a pick tool (2, **Figure 164**) into the flat edge of the terminal cavity until it stops. Pivot the pick tool away (3) from the terminal and gently pull on the wire to pull the terminal (4) from the terminal cavity. Note the wire location number on the connector (**Figure 165**).

NOTE
The release button used to separate the connectors is at the top of the connector.

7. The tang in the chamber engages the pin terminal slot to lock the terminal into position. The tangs (**Figure 164**) are located as follows:

a. Pin housing side—the tangs are located at the bottom of each chamber. The pin terminal slot, on the side opposite the crimp tails, must face downward.

b. Socket housing side—the tangs are located at the top of each chamber. The pin terminal slot, on the same side as the crimp tails, must face upward.

8. On the secondary lock side of the connector, push the wire and terminal into the correct location until it snaps into place. Gently pull on the lead to ensure the terminal is correctly seated.

9. Rotate the hinged secondary lock down and inward until the tabs are fully engaged with the latches on both sides of the connector. Pull upward to make sure the tabs are locked in place.

10. Insert the socket housing into the pin housing and push it in until it locks into place.

WIRING DIAGRAMS

Wiring diagrams are located at the end of this manual.

Table 1 ELECTRICAL SPECIFICATIONS

Item	Specification
Battery capacity	
1999	12 volts, 30 amp hour @ 10 hour rate
2000-on	12 volts, 28 amp hour @ 20 hour rate
Alternator	
AC voltage output	14.3-14.7 @ 3600 rpm
Amperes	
FLHR, FLHRI, FLHRCI, FLHT, FLHTC, FLTR	38 amps
FLHTCI, FLHTCUI, FLLTRI	45 amps
Stator coil resistance	NA
Voltage regulator	
Voltage output @ 3600 rpm	14.3-14.7 @ 75° F (24° C)
Amps @ 3000 rpm	
FLHR, FLHRI, FLHRCI, FLHT, FLHTC, FLTR	34-40 amps
FLHTCI, FLHTCUI, FLLTRI	41-48 amps
Ignition coil	
Primary resistance	0.5-0.7 ohm
Secondary resistance	5500-7500 ohms
Spark plug cable resistance	5000-11,666 ohms
Circuit breaker	40 amp
Fuses	
P & A	10 amp
Brakes/cruise control	15 amp
Radio power	10 amp
Radio memory	15 amp
Instruments	15 amp
Ignition	15 amp
Lights	15 amp
Accessory	15 amp
Fuel pump (EFI)	15 amp
Electronic control module (EFI)	5 amp

Table 2 BATTERY STATE OF CHARGE

1.110-1.130	Discharged
1.140-1.160	Almost discharged
1.170-1.190	1/4 charged
1.200-1.220	1/2 charged
1.230-1.250	3/4 charged
1.260-1.280	Fully charged

Table 3 BATTERY CHARGING RATES/TIMES (APPROXIMATE)

Voltage	% of charge	3 amp charger	6 amp charger	10 amp charger	20 amp charger
12.8	100%	–	–	–	–
12.6	75%	1.75 hours	50 minutes	30 minutes	15 minutes
12.3	50%	3.5 hours	1.75 hours	1 hour	30 minutes
12.0	25%	5 hours	2.5 hours	1.5 hours	45 minutes
11.8	0%	6 hours and 40 minutes	3 hours and 20 minutes	2 hours	1 hour

Table 4 STARTER MOTOR SPECIFICATIONS

Minimum no-load speed @ 11.5 volts	3000 rpm
Maximum no-load current @ 11.5 volts	90 amps
Current draw	
Normal	160-180 amps
Maximum	200 amps
Brush length (minimum)	0.433 in. (11.0 mm)
Commutator diameter (minimum)	1.141 in. (28.981 mm)

Table 5 REPLACEMENT BULBS

Item	Size (all 12-volt) × quantity
Headlamp	
FLTR	55/60 × 2
All models except FLTR	55/60
Position lamp[1]	3.9
Passing lamps	30
Passing lamps[1]	35
Instrument panel/gauge lamps	
(FLHR, FLHRI, FLHRC modelsl)	
High beam[2]	2.7
Oil pressure[2]	2.7
Neutral[2]	2.7
Turn signal[2]	2.7
Fuel gauge	2.7
Speedometer[2]	2.7
Odometer[2]	2.7
Engine check[2]	2.7
Instrument panel lamps	
(except FLHR, FLHRI, FLHRCI models)	
High beam	2.1
Oil pressure	2.1
Neutral	2.1
Turn signal	2.1
Gauge lamps	
(except FLHR, FLHRI, FLHRCI models)	
Speedometer[2]	3.4
Tachometer[2]	3.4
Voltmeter	3.4
Oil pressure gauge	3.4
Air temperature gauge	3.4
Fuel gauge	3.4
Engine check[2]	3.4
Tail lamp	7
Tail lamp[1]	5
Stop lamp	27
Stop lamp[1]	21

(continued)

8

Table 5 REPLACEMENT BULBS (continued)

Item	Size (all 12 volt) × quantity
License plate lamp[1]	5.2
Front turn signal/running light	27/7 × 2
Front turn signal[1]	21 × 2
Rear turn signal	27 × 2
Rear turn signal[1]	21 × 2
Tour-pack lamps[3]	3.7 × 4
Fender tip lamps[3]	3.7 × 2

1. Indicates bulb specification for HD International models.
2. Indicates LED illuminated. LEDs are not repairable and the assembly must be replaced.
3. Indicates domestic bulb specification—not applicable for Harley-Davidson International models

Table 6 ELECTRICAL SYSTEM TORQUE SPECIFICATIONS

Item	ft.-lb.	in.-lb.	N•m
Alternator stator Torx screws	–	30-40	3-5
Camshaft position sensor (CMP)			
Mounting screw	–	50-80	6-9
Crankshaft position sensor (CKP)			
Allen screw	–	90-120	10-14
Engine temperature sensor	10-12	–	14-16
Fuel gauge sending unit			
Plate screws (FLHR)	–	17	2
Handlebar switch housing screws			
Right side	–	35-45	4-5
Left side	–	60-80	7-9
Horn mounting nut	–	110	12
Ignition coil bolts	–	65-120	7-14
Ignition module screw	–	15-21	2-3
Ignition switch Allen bolts	–	40-50	5-6
Inspection cover screws	–	20-30	2-3
Jackshaft lockplate bolt	–	84-108	9-12
Neutral switch	–	120-180	14-20
Oil pressure switch	–	96-120	11-14
Speedometer sensor	–	84-108	9-12
Starter			
Mounting bolts	13-20	–	18-27
Positive terminal nut	–	65-80	7-9
Starter jackshaft bolt	–	84-108	9-12
Stop light switch	–	96-120	11-14
Tail/brake light			
Base screws	–	40-48	5-6
Lens screws	–	20-24	2-3
Voltage regulator locknuts	–	90-120	10-14

Table 7 HEADLIGHT AIM ADJUSTMENTS (FLTR MODELS)

Hex adjuster	Rotation	Beam movement
Left bulb	Clockwise	To the right
Right bulb	Counterclockwise	To the right
Left bulb	Counterclockwise	To the left
Right bulb	Clockwise	To the left
Left and right bulb equally	Clockwise	Upward
Left and right bulb equally	Counterclockwise	Downward

Table 8 TURN SIGNAL SPEED/DISTANCE TEST

Range	1	2	3	4
MPH	0-34	35-44	45-60	61+
KMH	0-56	56-71	72-97	98+
Feet	221	339	680	1051
Miles	0.04	0.06	0.13	0.20
Meters	67	103	207	320

Table 9 TURN SIGNAL SPEED/TIME TEST

Constant speed		
MPH	KMH	Turn signal ON time in seconds
25	40	5-7
38	61	5-7
52	84	8-10
65	105	10-12

8

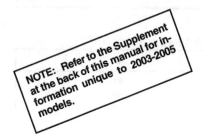

CHAPTER NINE

WHEELS, HUBS AND TIRES

This chapter includes procedures for disassembly and repair of the front and rear wheels, and hubs and tire service. For routine maintenance, see Chapter Three.

Tables 1-4 are at the end of the chapter.

MOTORCYCLE STANDS

Many procedures in this chapter require the front or rear wheel to be lifted off the ground. A quality motorcycle front end stand (**Figure 1**), swing arm stand or suitable size jack is required. Before purchasing or using a stand, check the manufacturer's instructions to make sure the stand will work with the specific model being worked on. If any adjustments or accessories are required, perform the necessary adjustments and install the correct parts before lifting the motorcycle. When using the stand, have an assistant standing by to help. Some means to tie down one end of the motorcycle may also be required. Make sure the motorcycle is properly supported on the stand.

FRONT WHEEL

Removal

1. Support the motorcycle with the front wheel off the ground. See *Motorcycle Stands* in this chapter.

2. On the left side, loosen the axle nut (**Figure 2**).

3A. On 1999 models, remove the caliper mounting bolts (**Figure 3**) and remove both calipers as described in Chapter Twelve.

3B. On 2000-on models, remove the caliper mounting bolts (**Figure 4**) and remove both calipers as described in Chapter Twelve.

> *NOTE*
> *Place a plastic or wooden spacer between the brake pads in place of the disc. Then, if the brake lever is inadvertently applied, the pistons will not be forced out of the calipers. If the pistons are forced out, disassemble the caliper to reseat the pistons.*

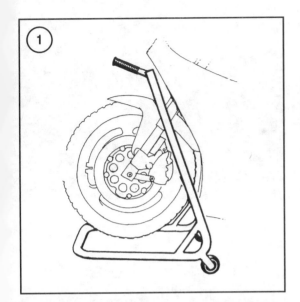

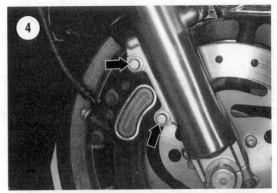

4. On 1999 models so equipped, disconnect the speedometer cable (A, **Figure 5**) from the drive unit.

5. On the right side, insert a drift or screwdriver through the front axle hole to prevent it from rotating in the next step.

6. On the left side, remove the axle nut (**Figure 2**), lockwasher and flat washer.

7. On the right side, loosen the fork cap nuts (**Figure 6**).

8. Prior to removing the front axle, note the location of the right side spacer and left side spacer. The spacers must be reinstalled on the correct sides during installation.

9. Use the tool inserted in Step 5 to withdraw the front axle from the fork sliders and front wheel. Remove the tool from the axle.

10. Pull the wheel away from the fork sliders and remove it.

NOTE
The wheel spacers are different. Label the spacers before removing them. Models equipped with a speedometer have only one spacer which is on the right side.

11A. On 1999 models so equipped, remove the speedometer drive unit and felt seal from the left side, and remove the spacer from the right side.

11B. On all other models, remove the spacers from the right and the left side of the wheel.

CAUTION
Do not set the wheel down on the brake disc surface, as it may be damaged.

12. Inspect the front wheel assembly as described in this chapter.

Installation (1999 Models)

1. Clean the axle in solvent and dry it thoroughly. Make sure the axle bearing surfaces on both fork sliders and the axle are free of burrs and nicks.

2. Apply an antiseize lubricant to the axle shaft prior to installation.

3. If the oil seals or bearings were replaced, check front axle spacer alignment as described under *Front Hub* in this chapter.

4A. On models so equipped, install the speedometer drive unit and felt seal onto the left side, and install the spacer onto the right side.

4B. On all other models, install the spacer onto the right and the left side of the wheel.

5. Install the wheel between the fork sliders and install the axle from the right side. Push the front axle through the left side fork and through the hub until the axle shoulder contacts the right side spacer.

6A. On models so equipped, align the speedometer tang with the notch in the brake disc.

6B. On models without a speedometer drive unit, make sure axle spacers are installed correctly.

7. Install the flat washer, lockwasher and axle nut (B, **Figure 5**) finger-tight. Make sure axle spacers are installed correctly.

8. Insert a drift or screwdriver into the hole in the end of the front axle to keep it from rotating.

9. Tighten the front axle nut (B, **Figure 5**) to the specification in **Table 2**.

10. Remove the tool used in Step 8 from the front axle.

11. On the right side fork slider, tighten the fork cap nut (**Figure 7**) to the torque specification in **Table 2**.

12. Make sure the front wheel is centered between the fork sliders. If it is not, check the position of the left and right axle spacers or speedometer drive unit.

13. Perform the *Front Wheel Bearing End Play Check* in this chapter.

14. Install both front brake calipers as described in Chapter Twelve.

15. With the front wheel off the ground, rotate it several times and apply the front brake to seat the brake pads against the discs.

16. Remove the stand and lower the front wheel to the ground.

Installation (2000-on Models)

1. Clean the axle in solvent and dry it thoroughly. Make sure the axle bearing surfaces on both fork sliders and the axle are free of burrs and nicks.

2. Apply an antiseize lubricant to the axle shaft prior to installation.

3. If the oil seals or bearings were replaced, check front axle spacer alignment as described under *Front Hub* in this chapter.

4. Install the spacer onto the right and the left side of the wheel. Refer to **Figure 8** for the right side and to **Figure 9** for the left side.

5. Install the wheel between the fork sliders and install the axle from the right side.

6. Make sure axle spacers are still positioned correctly.

7. Install the flat washer, lockwasher and axle nut (**Figure 2**) finger-tight. Make sure the axle spacers are installed correctly.

8. Insert a drift or screwdriver into the hole in the end of the front axle to keep it from rotating.

9. Tighten the front axle nut (**Figure 2**) to the specification in **Table 2**.

10. Remove the tool used in Step 8 from the front axle.

11. Insert a 7/16 in. drill bit into the hole in the front axle. Pull the fork leg up against the drill bit and hold it there. Tighten the fork cap nuts (**Figure 6**) to the torque specification in **Table 2**.

12. Remove the drill bit from the hole in the front axle.

13. Install the front brake calipers as described in Chapter Twelve.

14. With the front wheel off the ground, rotate it several times and apply the front brake to seat the brake pads against the discs.

15. Remove the stand and lower the front wheel to the ground.

Inspection

Replace worn or damaged parts as described in this section.

1. On 1999 models, inspect the seals (**Figure 10**) for excessive wear, hardness, cracks or other damage. If necessary, replace the seals as described under *Front and Rear Hubs* in this chapter.

2. Turn each bearing inner race by hand. The bearing should turn smoothly. Some axial play (end play) is normal, but radial play (side play) should be negligible. See **Figure 11**. If one bearing is damaged, replace both bearings as a set. Refer to *Front and Rear Hubs* in this chapter.

3. Clean the axle and axle spacers in solvent to remove all grease and dirt. Make sure the axle contact surfaces are clean and free of dirt and old grease.

4. Check the axle runout with a set of V-blocks and a dial indicator (**Figure 12**).

5. Check the spacers for wear, burrs and damage. Replace as necessary.

6. Check the brake disc bolts (**Figure 13**) for tightness. To service the brake disc, refer to Chapter Twelve.

7. Check wheel runout and spoke tension as described in this chapter.

REAR WHEEL

Removal

1. Remove the saddlebags as described in Chapter Fourteen.

9

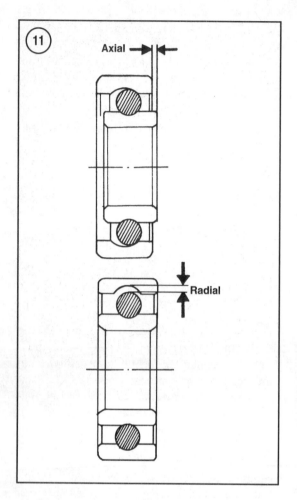

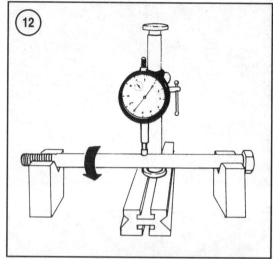

2. Remove both mufflers as described in Chapter Seven.

3. Support the motorcycle with an appropriate size jack with the rear wheel off the ground.

4. Remove the bolts securing the drive belt debris deflector and remove the deflector.

NOTE
The rear wheel is heavy and can be difficult to remove. Check the tire-to-ground clearance before removing the rear axle. If necessary, have an assistant help in the removal.

5A. On 1999-2001 models, perform the following:

a. Remove the spring clip and loosen the rear axle nut.

b. Loosen and remove the axle nut (**Figure 14**) and washer.

c. From the right side, withdraw the rear axle (A, **Figure 15**) while holding onto

the rear wheel. Lower the wheel to the ground.

5B. On 2002 models, perform the following:

a. On the right side, remove the E-clip (A, **Figure 16**) from the rear axle groove.

b. Loosen and remove the rear axle nut and the adjuster cam (B, **Figure 16**).

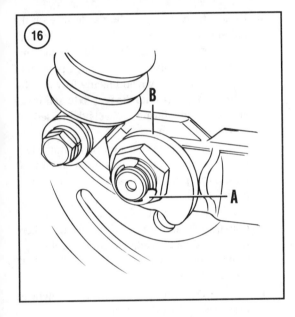

9

c. Using a soft faced mallet, gently tap the rear axle toward the right side.

d. From the left side, withdraw the rear axle (**Figure 17**) while hold onto the rear wheel. Lower the wheel to the ground.

6. Remove the rear brake caliper (B, **Figure 15**) from the swing arm and tie it to the frame with a bungee cord or wire.

7. Lift the drive belt off the driven sprocket and remove the rear wheel.

8. Remove the right side (**Figure 18**) and left side (**Figure 19**) spacers from the wheel hub.

NOTE
Place a plastic or wooden spacer between the brake pads in place of the disc. Then, if the brake pedal is inadvertently depressed, the pistons will not be forced out of the caliper. If the pistons are forced out, disassemble the caliper to reseat the pistons.

CAUTION
Do not set the wheel down on the brake disc surface, as it may be damaged.

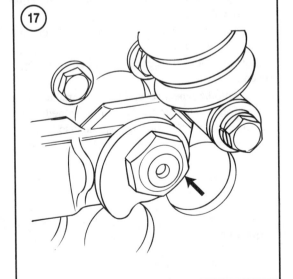

9. Inspect the rear wheel as described in this chapter.

Installation

1. Clean the axle in solvent and dry it thoroughly. Make sure the bearing surfaces on the axle are free of burrs and nicks.
2. Apply an antiseize lubricant to the axle shaft prior to installation.
3. On 1999 models, slide the rear brake caliper onto the locating post on the swing arm.
4. Position the rear wheel between the swing arm sides and place the drive belt on the sprocket.
5. Install the right side (**Figure 18**) and left side (**Figure 19**) spacers into the rear wheel seals or bearings.
6. Remove the spacer block from between the brake pads.

> *CAUTION*
> *When installing the rear wheel in the following steps, carefully insert the brake disc between the brake pads in the caliper assembly. Do not force the brake disc as it can damage the leading edge of both brake pads.*

7. On 2002 models, move the rear brake caliper (B, **Figure 15**) into position on the swing arm.
8. Lift the rear wheel and install the rear axle from the right side (A, **Figure 15**). Install the axle through the swing arm, the rear brake caliper mounting bracket and the other side of the swing arm.
9. After the rear axle is installed, make sure both axle spacers are still in place.
10A. On 1999-2001 models, perform the following:
   a. Install the washer and axle nut (**Figure 14**). Tighten the axle nut finger tight at this time
   b. On 1999 models, perform the *Front and Rear Axle End Play Check* in this chapter. When the rear axle end play is correct, continue with substep c.
   c. Check drive belt tension and adjustment as described in Chapter Three.
   d. If necessary, tighten the rear axle nut to align the spring clip hole with the nut slot. Then install the spring clip and snap it into place.
10B. On 2002 models, perform the following:

   a. Rotate the rear axle so the flat surface on the left side faces up and make sure the cam adjuster contacts the raised tab on the swing arm.
   b. Position the adjuster with the large portion of the cam facing down and facing forward. Install the adjuster onto the rear axle and make sure the cam adjuster contacts the raised tab on the swing arm.
   c. Make sure that the cam adjuster on both sides contacts the raised tab on the swing arm. If necessary, push the rear wheel forward to achieve this.
   d. Apply a light coat of anti-seize compound onto the inboard surface of the axle nut where it contacts the cam adjuster and install it.
   e. Tighten the axle nut to 15-20 ft.-lb. (2-27 N•m) at this time.
   f. Check drive belt tension and adjustment as described in Chapter Three.
   g. Tighten the rear axle nut to the specification in **Table 2**.
11. Install the drive belt debris deflector and tighten the bolts securely
12. Install both mufflers as described in Chapter Seven.
13. Rotate the wheel several times to make sure it rotates freely. Then apply the rear brake pedal several times to seat the pads against the disc.
14. Remove the stand and lower the rear wheel to the ground.
15. Install the saddlebags as described in Chapter Fourteen.

Inspection

Replace worn or damaged parts as described in this section.

1. On 1999 models, inspect the seals (**Figure 10**, typical) for excessive wear, hardness, cracks or other damage. If necessary, replace the seals as described under *Front and Rear Hubs* in this chapter.

2. Turn each bearing inner race by hand. The bearing should turn smoothly. Some axial play (end play) is normal, but radial play (side play) should be negligible. See **Figure 11**. If one bearing is damaged, replace both bearings as a set. Refer to *Front and Rear Hubs* in this chapter.

3. Clean the axle and axle spacers in solvent to remove all grease and dirt. Make sure the axle contact surfaces are free of dirt and old grease.

4. Check the axle runout with a set of V-blocks and a dial indicator (**Figure 12**).

5. Check the spacers for wear, burrs and damage. Replace as necessary.

6. Check the brake disc bolts (**Figure 20**) for tightness. To service the brake disc, refer to Chapter Twelve.

7. Check the driven sprocket bolts (**Figure 21**) for tightness. Driven sprocket service is covered in this chapter.

8. Check wheel runout and spoke tension as described in this chapter.

FRONT AND REAR HUBS (1999)

Non-sealed tapered roller bearings are installed on each side of the hub. Seals are installed on the outside of each bearing to protect them from dirt and other contaminants.

The bearing outer races are pressed into the hub. Do not remove the bearing races unless they require replacement.

Preliminary Inspection

Inspect each wheel bearing prior to removing it from the wheel hub.

CAUTION
Do not remove the wheel bearing outer races for inspection as they will be damaged during the removal process. Remove wheel bearings only if they are to be replaced.

1. Perform Steps 1-4 of *Disassembly* the procedure.

2. Turn each bearing by hand. The bearings should turn smoothly with no roughness.

3. Inspect the play of the inner race of each wheel bearing. Check for excessive axial play and radial play. Replace the bearing if free play is excessive.

4. Check the balls for wear, pitting or bluish tint (excessive heat). Replace the bearings if necessary; always replace them as a complete set. When replacing the bearings, make sure the replacement bearings match the old bearings.

Disassembly

This procedure applies to both the front and rear wheel and hub assemblies. Differences between the hubs are identified. Refer to **Figure 22** and **Figure 23**.

NOTE
The bearings and races are matched pairs. Label all parts so they will be returned to their original positions.

1A. Remove the front wheel as described in this chapter.

1B. Remove the rear wheel as described in this chapter.

2. If necessary, remove the brake disc as described in Chapter Twelve.

3. Remove the axle spacers from the hub if they are still in place.

4. Pry one of the seals out of the hub (**Figure 24**), and remove the bearing (**Figure 25**) and spacer sleeve (**Figure 26**). Turn the wheel over and remove the opposite seal and bearing. Remove the washer and spacer shim.

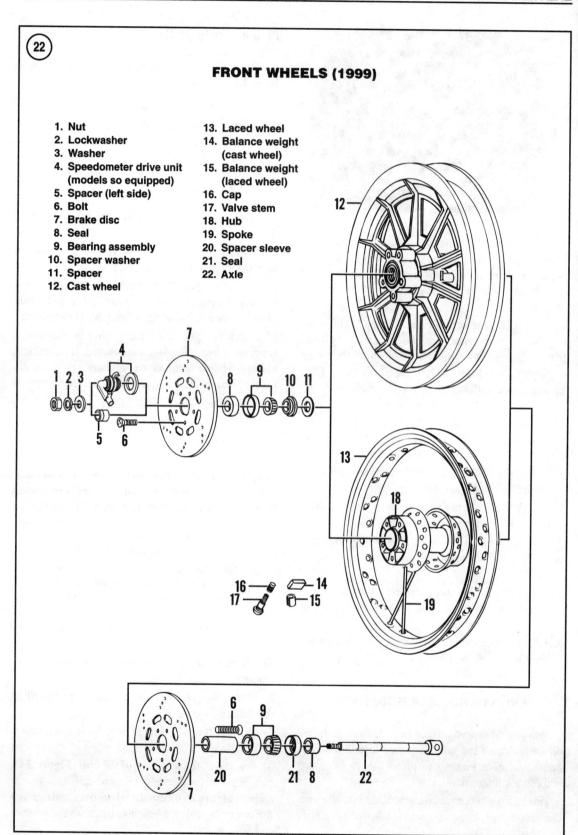

FRONT WHEELS (1999)

1. Nut
2. Lockwasher
3. Washer
4. Speedometer drive unit (models so equipped)
5. Spacer (left side)
6. Bolt
7. Brake disc
8. Seal
9. Bearing assembly
10. Spacer washer
11. Spacer
12. Cast wheel
13. Laced wheel
14. Balance weight (cast wheel)
15. Balance weight (laced wheel)
16. Cap
17. Valve stem
18. Hub
19. Spoke
20. Spacer sleeve
21. Seal
22. Axle

REAR WHEEL (1999)

1. Cast wheel
2. Bolt
3. Axle
4. Spacer (right side)
5. Brake disc
6. Seal
7. Bearing outer race
8. Bearing
9. Spacer washer
10. Washer
11. Balance weight
   (cast wheel)
12. Cap
13. Valve stem
14. Balance weight
   (laced wheel)

15. Hub
16. Spoke
17. Spacer sleeve
18. Bearing outer race
19. Bearing
20. Seal
21. Spacer
22. Driven sprocket
23. Spacer (left side)
24. Washer
25. Spring clip
26. Nut
27. Washer
28. Bolt

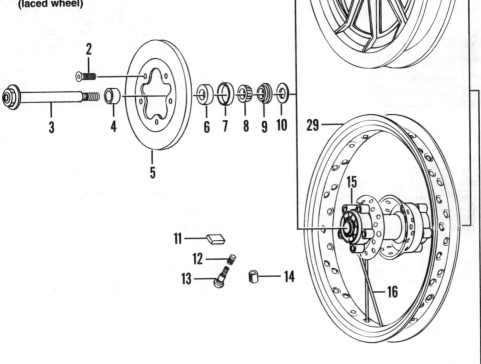

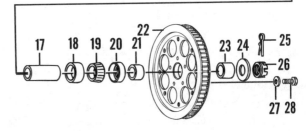

9

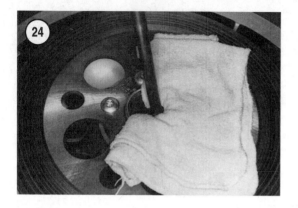

5. Wash the bearings in clean solvent and dry it with compressed air. Wipe the bearing races with a clean rag dipped in solvent.

6. Check the bearings and races (**Figure 27**) for wear, pitting or excessive bluish tint. If a bearing requires replacement, replace the bearings and races as a complete set. Perform Step 7 to replace the bearing races. If the bearings and races do not require replacement, go to Step 8. If original bearings are to be reused, pack the bearings with grease and wrap them in a clean lint-free cloth until assembly. Apply a film of grease across the bearing race (**Figure 27**).

> *NOTE*
> *A wheel bearing race remover and installer tool (JIMS part No. 33461-80) (Figure 28) is available.*

7A. To remove the right and left side wheel bearing outer races (**Figure 27**) using special tools, perform the following:

    a. Install the special tool into the hub against the bearing race following the manufacturer's instructions.

    b. Tap the bearing race out of one side of the hub.

    c. Reposition the special tool and tap the other bearing race out of other side of the hub.

    d. Remove the special tool.

7B. To remove the right and left side wheel bearing outer races (**Figure 27**) without using special tools, perform the following:

    a. Insert a drift punch through the hub and drive the bearing outer race out of the hub. Tap on alternate sides of the race to drive it squarely out of the hub. If the race binds in the hub

bore, level it by tapping it from its opposite side.

    b. Repeat substep a for the outer race on the other side of the hub.

8. Clean the hub with solvent. Dry it with compressed air.

Installation

1. Wipe the outside of the new race and the hub receptacle with oil and align the new race with its bore in the hub.

> *NOTE*
> *When installing the race, stop and check the work often, to make sure the race is square with the hub bore. Do not allow the race to bind during installation or the race bore in the hub will be damaged.*

2A. To install the right and left side wheel bearing outer races (**Figure 27**) using special tools, perform the following:

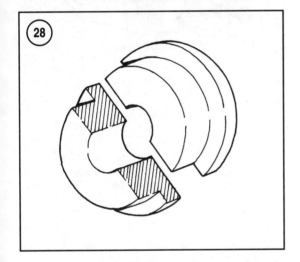

a. Install the special tool into the bearing outer race and the hub following the manufacturer's instructions.

b. Tap the bearing race straight into one side of the hub until it bottoms on the hub shoulder.

c. Reposition the special tool and tap the other bearing race into the other side of the hub.

d. Remove the special tool.

2B. To install the right and left side wheel bearing outer races (**Figure 27**) without using special tools, perform the following:

a. Select a driver with an outside diameter slightly smaller than the bearing race's outside diameter.

b. Drive the bearing outer race squarely into the hub bore until it bottoms on the hub shoulder.

c. Repeat substep b for the outer race on the other side of the hub.

3. Pack the bearings with grease and install them in their original positions as noted during removal.

4. Pack each seal lip with grease and install them with a bearing driver or socket with an outer diameter smaller than the oil seal.

5A. On cast wheels, assemble the front hub in the order shown in **Figure 22** or **Figure 23**. Note the following:

a. Apply grease to both ends of the spacer sleeve.

b. Install the spacer washer with its shoulder (smaller diameter) facing toward its adjacent bearing.

> *CAUTION*
> *If the spacer washer is installed with its larger diameter side toward the bearing, the spacer washer could contact the bearing cage and damage it.*

c. After installing the bearings, pack the area between the bearings and seals with grease.

d. Install the seals until they are flush with the hub or recessed 0.04 in. (1.0 mm) below the hub surface (**Figure 10**).

e. Install the spacer so its large chamfered end faces toward the bearing on the valve stem hole side of the wheel.

5B. On laced wheels, assemble the front hub in the order shown in **Figure 22** or **Figure 23**. Note the following:

a. Apply grease to both ends of the spacer sleeve.

b. Install the spacer washer with its shoulder (smaller diameter) facing toward its adjacent bearing.

> *CAUTION*
> *If the spacer washer is installed with its larger diameter side toward the bearing, the spacer washer could contact the bearing cage and damage it.*

c. After installing the bearings, pack the area between the bearings and seals with grease.

d. Install the seals until they are flush with the hub or recessed 0.02 in. (0.51 mm) below the hub surface (**Figure 10**).

e. Install the spacer so its large chamfered end faces toward the bearing on the valve stem hole side of the wheel.

9

6. Install the brake disc as described in Chapter Twelve if it was removed.

7. After the wheel is installed and the axle nut is tightened, check bearing end play as described in this chapter.

FRONT AND REAR WHEEL BEARING END PLAY CHECK (1999 MODELS)

Front and rear wheel bearing end play establishes the amount of axial (lengthwise) movement between the left and right bearings. **Table 1** lists the correct end play specifications. Excessive end play can cause bearing side loading. If the end play is too tight, bearing seizure could occur. Check end play each time the rear wheel is installed.

The thickness of the spacer shim (**Table 3**) controls end play between the spacer sleeve and spacer washer.

1. Support the motorcycle on a stand with the front or rear wheel off the ground.

2. On the rear wheel, remove the spring pin from the rear axle nut.

3. Tighten the front or rear axle to the specifications in **Table 2**.

4. Mount a dial indicator securely on the brake disc and center its stem against the end of the axle (**Figure 29**). Then zero the dial gauge. Grasp the tire and move it with the axle in and out along the axle center line and note the indicator reading. The total indicator reading is axle end play.

5. If there is not enough end play, install a thinner spacer shim.

6. If the end play is excessive, install a thicker spacer shim.

7. To replace a spacer shim, disassemble the front or rear hub as described in this chapter.

FRONT AND REAR HUBS (2000-ON)

Sealed ball bearings are installed on each side of the hub. Do not remove the bearing assemblies unless they require replacement.

Preliminary Inspection

Inspect each wheel bearing prior to removing it from the wheel hub.

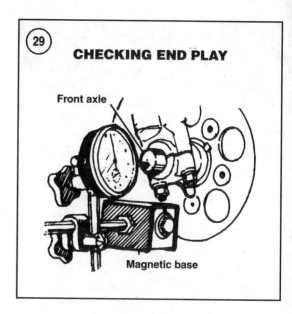

CHECKING END PLAY

Front axle

Magnetic base

CAUTION
Do not remove the wheel bearings for inspection as they will be damaged during the removal process. Remove wheel bearings only if they are to be replaced.

1. Perform Steps 1-3 of *Disassembly* in the following procedure.

2. Turn each bearing by hand. The bearings should turn smoothly with no roughness.

3. Inspect the play of the inner race of each wheel bearing. Check for excessive axial play and radial play (**Figure 11**). Replace the bearing if free play is excessive.

Disassembly

This procedure applies to both the front and rear wheel and hub assemblies. Differences between the different hubs are identified. Refer to **Figure 30-32**.

1A. Remove the front wheel as described in this chapter.

1B. Remove the rear wheel as described in this chapter.

2. Remove the axle spacers from each side of the hub if they are still in place.

3. If necessary, remove the bolts securing the brake disc and remove the disc.

4. Before proceeding, inspect the wheel bearings as described in this chapter. If they must be replaced, proceed as follows.

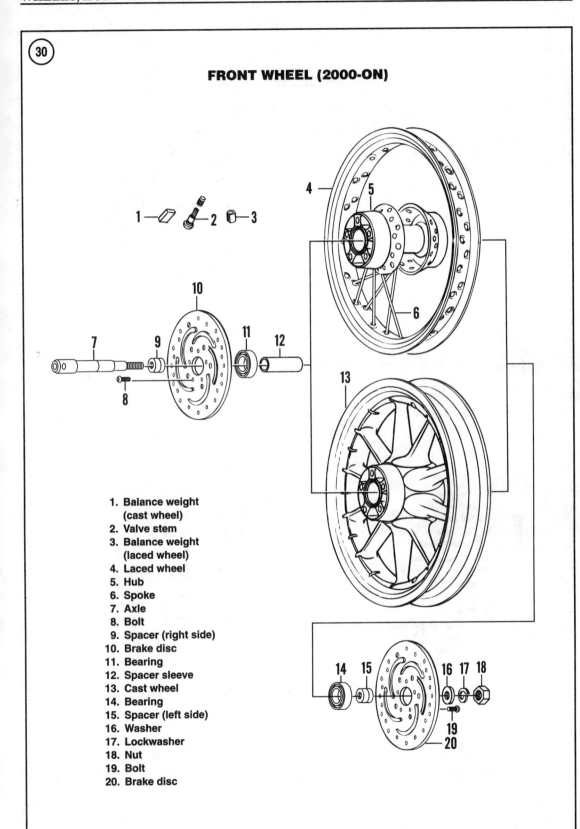

FRONT WHEEL (2000-ON)

1. Balance weight (cast wheel)
2. Valve stem
3. Balance weight (laced wheel)
4. Laced wheel
5. Hub
6. Spoke
7. Axle
8. Bolt
9. Spacer (right side)
10. Brake disc
11. Bearing
12. Spacer sleeve
13. Cast wheel
14. Bearing
15. Spacer (left side)
16. Washer
17. Lockwasher
18. Nut
19. Bolt
20. Brake disc

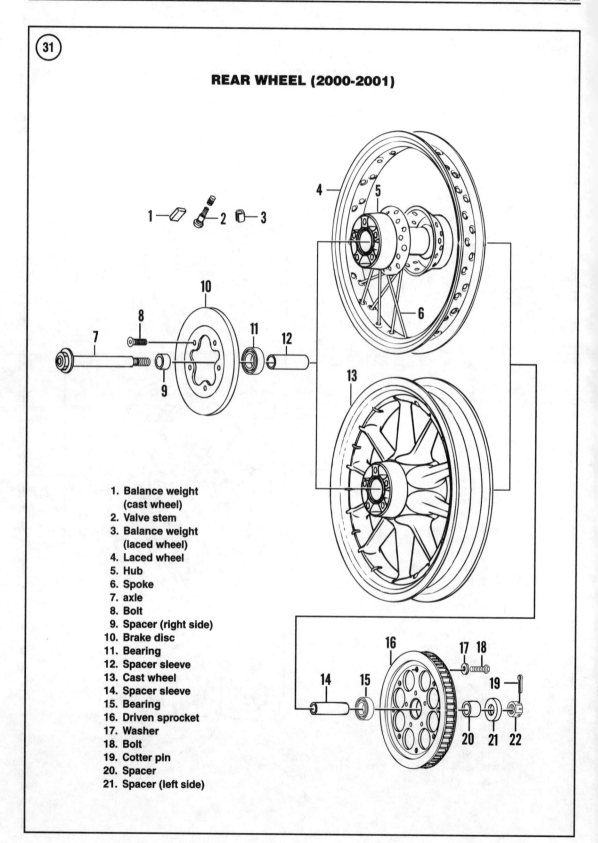

REAR WHEEL (2000-2001)

1. Balance weight
   (cast wheel)
2. Valve stem
3. Balance weight
   (laced wheel)
4. Laced wheel
5. Hub
6. Spoke
7. axle
8. Bolt
9. Spacer (right side)
10. Brake disc
11. Bearing
12. Spacer sleeve
13. Cast wheel
14. Spacer sleeve
15. Bearing
16. Driven sprocket
17. Washer
18. Bolt
19. Cotter pin
20. Spacer
21. Spacer (left side)

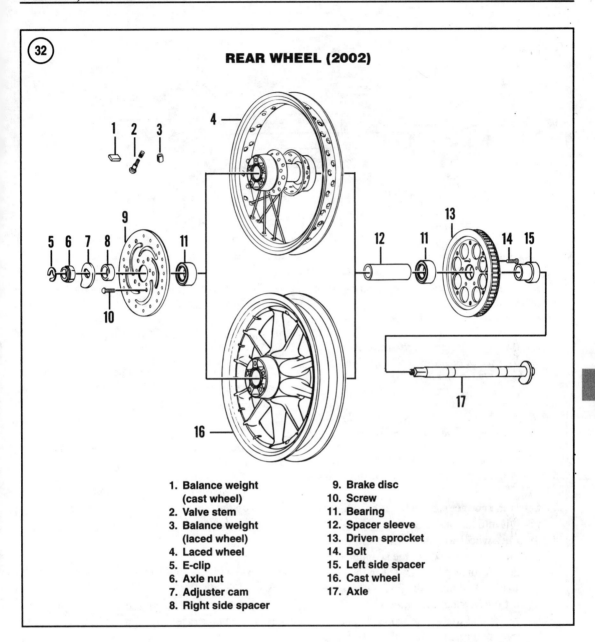

REAR WHEEL (2002)

1. Balance weight
   (cast wheel)
2. Valve stem
3. Balance weight
   (laced wheel)
4. Laced wheel
5. E-clip
6. Axle nut
7. Adjuster cam
8. Right side spacer
9. Brake disc
10. Screw
11. Bearing
12. Spacer sleeve
13. Driven sprocket
14. Bolt
15. Left side spacer
16. Cast wheel
17. Axle

9

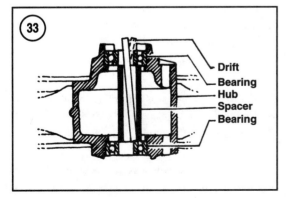

5A. If the special tools are not used, perform the following:

  a. To remove the right and left bearings and
    spacer collar, insert a soft aluminum or brass
    drift into one side of the hub.

  b. Push the spacer collar over to one side and
    place the drift on the inner race of the lower
    bearing.

  c. Tap the bearing out of the hub with a hammer,
    working around the perimeter of the inner
    race (**Figure 33**). Remove the bearing and
    distance collar.

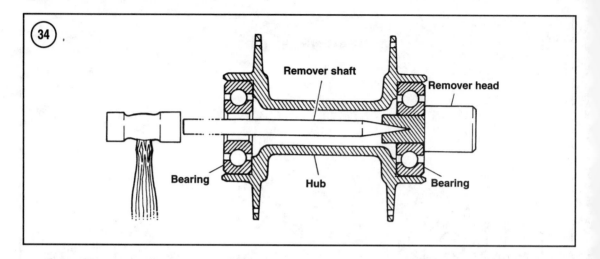

34

Remover shaft

Remover head

Bearing

Hub

Bearing

d. Repeat substeps b and c for the bearing on the other side.

> *NOTE*
> *The Kowa Seiki Wheel Bearing Remover set can be ordered through a K & L Supply Co. dealer.*

> *WARNING*
> *Be sure to wear safety glasses while using the wheel bearing remover set.*

5B. To remove the bearings with the Kowa Seiki Wheel Bearing Remover set, perform the following:

a. Select the correct size remover head tool and insert it into the bearing.

b. Turn the wheel over and insert the remover shaft into the backside of the adapter. Tap the wedge and force it into the slit in the adapter (**Figure 34**). This will force the adapter against the bearing inner race.

c. Tap the end of the wedge bar with a hammer to drive the bearing out of the hub. Remove the bearing and the distance collar.

d. Repeat substeps a-c for the bearing on the other side.

6. Clean the inside and the outside of the hub with solvent. Dry it with compressed air.

Assembly

> *CAUTION*
> *The removal process will generally damage the bearings. Replace the wheel bearings in pairs. **Never** rein-*

*stall bearings after they are removed. Always install **new** bearings.*

1. Blow any debris out of the hub prior to installing the new bearings.

2. Apply a light coat of wheel bearing grease to the bearing seating areas of the hub. This will make bearing installation easier.

> *CAUTION*
> *Install non-sealed bearings with the single sealed side facing outward. Tap the bearings squarely into place and tap on the outer race only. Do not tap on the inner race or the bearing might be damaged. Make sure the bearings are completely seated.*

3. Select a driver with an outside diameter slightly smaller than the bearing's outside diameter.

4. Tap the right side bearing squarely into place and tap on the outer race only. Tap the bearing into the hub bore until it bottoms. Make sure the bearing is completely seated.

5. Turn the wheel over (right side up) on the workbench and install the spacer collar.

6. Use the same tool set-up to drive in the left side bearing.

7. If the brake disc was removed, install it as described in Chapter Twelve.

8A. Install the front wheel as described in this chapter.

8B. Install the rear wheel as described in this chapter.

DRIVEN SPROCKET ASSEMBLY

Inspection

Inspect the sprocket teeth. If the teeth are visibly worn, replace the drive belt and both sprockets.

Removal/Installation

1. Remove the rear wheel as described in this chapter.
2. Remove the bolts, washers and nuts (**Figure 21**), if so equipped, securing the driven sprocket to the hub, and remove the sprocket.
3. Position the driven sprocket onto the rear hub.
4. Apply a light coat of ThreeBond TB1360, or an equivalent, to the bolts prior to installation.
5. Install the bolts, washers and nuts, if so equipped, and tighten the bolts to specifications in **Table 2**.

DRIVE SPROCKET

The drive sprocket is covered in Chapter Six under *Transmission Drive Sprocket*.

DRIVE BELT

CAUTION
When handling a new or used drive belt, never wrap the belt in a loop smaller than 5 in. (130 mm) or bend it sharply. This will weaken or break the belt fibers and cause premature belt failure.

Removal/Installation

1. Remove the compensating sprocket and clutch as described in Chapter Five.
2. Remove the primary chain inner and outer housings as described in Chapter Five.

WARNING
Make sure the motorcycle is securely supported before removing the rear wheel.

3. Support the motorcycle with the rear wheel off the ground.
4. Remove the rear wheel as described in this chapter.
5. Remove both passenger footboards as described in Chapter Fourteen.

NOTE
If the existing drive belt is being reinstalled, install it so it travels in the same direction. Before removing the belt, draw an arrow on the top surface of the belt facing forward.

6. Refer to *Rear Swing Arm* in Chapter Eleven and perform the following:
   a. Leave both shock absorbers in place on the frame and rear swing arm.
   b. Remove the screws securing the drive belt debris deflector if they are still in place, and remove the drive belt debris deflector.
   c. On the right side, place a 11/16 in. socket onto the pivot shaft to keep it from rotating in the following step.
   d. On the left side, use a 3/4 in. socket to loosen the locknut. Remove the locknut and the cup washer from the pivot shaft.
   e. Support the swing arm and tap on the left side of the pivot shaft with a drift. Drive the pivot shaft out through the right side and remove it.
   f. Pivot the front of the rear swing arm down enough to slip the drive belt past the pivot area of the frame.
   g. If the drive belt is going to remain off for a period of time, move the swing arm up into position and reinstall the pivot bolt and nut, or bolt.
7. Remove the drive belt (**Figure 35**) from the drive sprocket.
8. Installation is the reverse of these steps. Note the following:

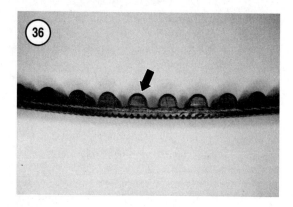

a. Tighten the swing arm pivot shaft nut as described in Chapter Eleven.

b. Adjust the drive belt tension as described in Chapter Three.

Inspection

Do not apply any type of lubricant to the drive belt. Inspect the drive belt and teeth (**Figure 36**) for severe wear, damage or oil contamination.

Refer to **Figure 37** for various types of drive belt wear or damage. Replace the drive belt if it is worn or damaged.

WHEEL RUNOUT

1. Remove the front or rear wheel as described in this chapter.

2. Install the wheel in a wheel truing stand and check the wheel for excessive wobble or runout.

3. If the wheel is not running true, remove the tire from the rim as described in this chapter. Then remount the wheel into the truing stand, and measure axial and lateral runout (**Figure 38**) with a pointer or dial indicator. Compare actual runout readings with the service limit specification in **Table 1**. Note the following:

a. *Cast wheels*—if the runout meets or exceeds the service limit in **Table 1**, check the wheel bearings as described under *Front and Rear Hub* in this chapter. If the wheel bearings are acceptable, replace the cast wheel as it cannot be serviced. Inspect the wheel for cracks, fractures, dents or bends. Replace a damaged wheel.

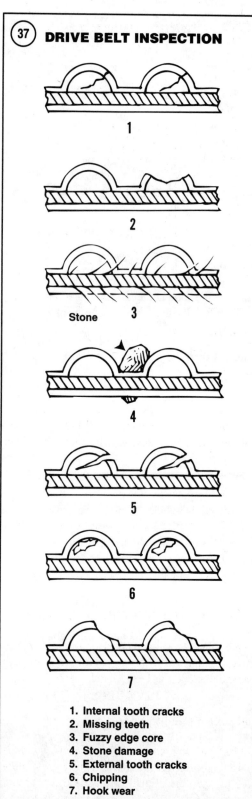

DRIVE BELT INSPECTION

Stone

1. Internal tooth cracks
2. Missing teeth
3. Fuzzy edge core
4. Stone damage
5. External tooth cracks
6. Chipping
7. Hook wear

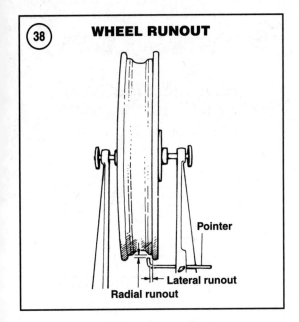

WHEEL RUNOUT

Pointer

Lateral runout

Radial runout

WARNING
*Do not try to repair damage to a cast
wheel as it will result in an unsafe riding condition.*

b. *Laced wheels*—if the wheel bearings, spokes,
hub and rim assembly are not damaged, the
runout can be corrected by truing the wheel.
Refer to *Spoke Adjustment* in this chapter. If
the rim is dented or damaged, replace the rim
and rebuild the wheel.
4. While the wheel is off, perform the following:
a. Check the brake disc mounting bolts for tightness as described in Chapter Twelve.
b. On the rear wheel, check the driven sprocket
bolts for tightness as described in this chapter.

RIM AND LACED WHEEL SERVICE

The laced wheel assembly consists of a rim,
spokes, nipples and hub containing the bearings,
spacer collar and, on 1999 models, seals.

Component Condition

Wheels are subjected to a significant amount of
punishment. Inspect the wheel regularly for lateral
(side-to-side) and radial (up-and-down) runout,
even spoke tension and visible rim damage. When a
wheel has a noticeable wobble, it is out of true. This
is usually caused by loose spokes, but it can be
caused by an impact-damaged rim.

Truing a wheel corrects the lateral and radial runout to bring the wheel back into specification.

The condition of the individual wheel components will effect the ability to successfully true the
wheel. Note the following:
1. *Spoke condition*—Do not attempt to true a wheel
with bent or damaged spokes. Doing so places an
excessive amount of tension on the spoke and rim.
The spoke may break and/or pull through the spoke
nipple hole in the rim. Inspect the spokes carefully
and replace any spokes that are damaged.
2. *Nipple condition*—When truing the wheels, the
nipples should turn freely on the spoke. It is common for the spoke threads to become corroded and
make turning the nipple difficult. Spray a penetrating liquid onto the nipple and allow sufficient time
for it to penetrate before trying to force the nipple
loose. Work the spoke wrench in both directions
and continue to apply penetrating liquid. If the
spoke wrench rounds off the nipple, remove the tire
from the rim and cut the spoke(s) out of the wheel.
3. *Rim condition*—Minor rim damage can be corrected by truing the wheel; however, trying to correct excessive runout caused by impact damage
causes hub and rim damage due to spoke
overtightening. Inspect the rims for cracks, flat
spots or dents. Check the spoke holes for cracks or
enlargement. Replace rims with excessive damage.

Wheel Truing Preliminaries

Before checking runout and truing the wheel,
note the following:
1. Make sure the wheel bearings are in good condition. Refer to *Front and Rear Hubs* in this chapter.
2. A small amount of wheel runout is acceptable,
do not try to true the wheel to a perfect zero reading.
Doing so causes excessive spoke tension and possible rim and hub damage. **Table 1** lists the lateral
(side-to-side) and radial (up-and-down) runout
limit specifications.
3. The runout can be checked on the motorcycle by
mounting a pointer against the fork or swing arm
and slowly rotating the wheel.
4. Perform major wheel truing with the tire removed and the wheel mounted in a truing stand
(**Figure 38**). If a stand is not available, mount the

9

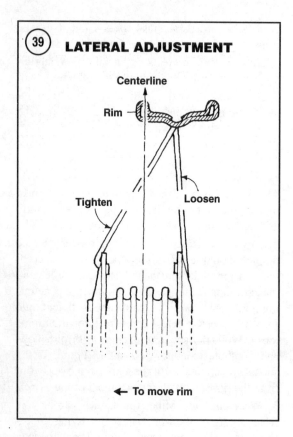

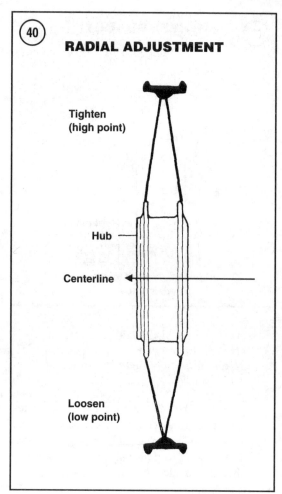

wheel on the motorcycle with spacers on each side of the wheel to prevent it from sliding on the axle.

5. Use a spoke nipple wrench of the correct size. Using the wrong type of tool or one that is the incorrect size will round off the spoke nipples, making adjustment difficult. Quality spoke wrenches have openings that grip the nipple on four corners to prevent nipple damage.

6. Refer to the spoke nipple torque specifications in **Table 2** when using a torque wrench.

Wheel Truing Procedure

1. Position a pointer facing toward the rim (**Figure 38**). Then spin the wheel slowly and check the lateral and radial runout. If the rim is out of adjustment, continue with Step 2.

> *NOTE*
> *If there is a large number of loose spokes, make sure the hub is centered in the rim. This must be done visually as there are no hub and rim centering specifications for these models.*

> *NOTE*
> *The number of spokes to loosen and tighten in Steps 2 and 3 depends on how far the runout is out of adjustment. As a minimum, always loosen two or three spokes, then tighten the opposite two or three spokes. If the runout is excessive and affects a greater area along the rim, a greater number of spokes will require adjustment.*

2. If the lateral (side-to-side) runout is out of specification, adjust the wheel by using **Figure 39** as an example. Always loosen and tighten the spokes an equal number of turns.

3. If the radial (up and down) runout is out of specification, the hub is not centered in the rim. Draw the high point of the rim toward the centerline of the wheel by tightening the spokes in the area of the

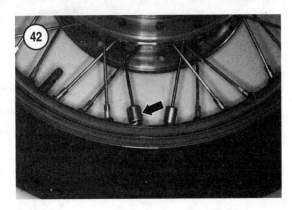

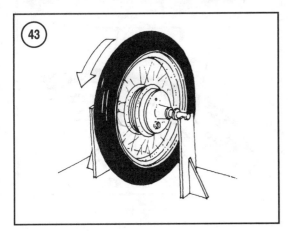

high point, and loosening the spokes on the side opposite the high point (**Figure 40**). Tighten spokes in equal amounts to prevent distortion.

4. After truing the wheel, seat each spoke in the hub by tapping it with a flat nose punch and hammer. Then recheck the spoke tension and wheel runout. Readjust if necessary.

5. Check the ends of the spokes where they are threaded in the nipples. Grind off ends that protrude through the nipples.

CAST WHEELS

Cast wheels consist of a single assembly equipped with bearings, a spacer sleeve and, on 1999 models, seals.

While these wheels are virtually maintenance free, they must be checked for damage at the maintenance intervals in Chapter Three. Wheel bearing service is described in this chapter.

To check these wheels, refer to *Inspection* under *Wheel Runout* in this chapter.

WARNING
Do not try to repair any damage to a cast wheel as it will result in an unsafe riding condition.

WHEEL BALANCE

An unbalanced wheel is unsafe. Depending on the degree of unbalance and the speed of the motorcycle, the rider may experience anything from a mild vibration to a violent shimmy that may cause loss of control.

On alloy wheels, weights are attached to the flat surface on the rim (**Figure 41**). On laced wheels, the weights are attached to the spoke nipples (**Figure 42**).

Before attempting to balance the wheel, make sure the wheel bearings are in good condition and properly lubricated. The wheel must rotate freely.

1A. Remove the front wheel as described in this chapter.

1B. Remove the rear wheel as described in this chapter.

2. Mount the wheel on a fixture (**Figure 43**) so it can rotate freely.

3. Spin the wheel and let it coast to a stop. Mark the tire at the lowest point.

4. Spin the wheel several more times. If the wheel keeps coming to rest at the same point, it is out of balance.

5A. On alloy wheels, tape a test weight to the upper or light side of the wheel (**Figure 41**).

5B. On laced wheels, attach a weight to the spoke (**Figure 42**) on the upper or light side of the wheel.

6. Experiment with different weights until the wheel comes to a stop at a different position each time it is spun.

7. On cast wheels, remove the test weight and install the correct size weight.

9

a. Attach the weights to the flat surface on the rim (**Figure 41**). Clean the rim of all road residue before installing the weights; otherwise, the weights may fall off.

b. Add weights in 1/4 oz. (7g) increments. If 1 oz. (28 g) or more must be added to one location, apply half the amount to each side of the rim.

c. To apply Harley-Davidson wheel weights, remove the paper backing from the weight and apply three drops of Loctite 420 Superbonder to the bottom of the weight. Position the weight on the rim, press it down and hold in position for 10 seconds. To allow the adhesive to cure properly, do not use the wheel for 8 hours.

8. When fitting weights on laced wheels for the final time, crimp the weights onto the spoke with slip-joint pliers.

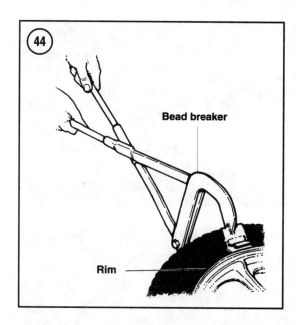

TIRES

Tire Safety

Maintain the tire inflation pressure at the specification in **Table 4**. If a different brand of tire is used, follow the inflation recommendation provided by the tire manufacturer. Tire inflation specifications are cold inflation specifications. Do not check/adjust tire pressure after riding the motorcycle.

Always allow the tires to warm up by riding before subjecting them to high cornering loads. Warm tires provide more adhesion.

New tires provide significantly less adhesion until they are broken in. Do not subject new tires to high speed or high cornering forces for at least 60 mile (100 km). Be especially careful when encountering wet conditions with new tires.

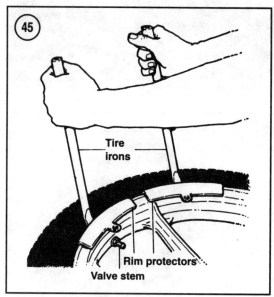

TUBELESS TIRE CHANGING

The cast alloy wheels can easily be damaged during tire removal. Take special care with tire irons when changing a tire to avoid scratches and gouges to the outer rim surface. Insert scraps of leather between the tire iron and the rim to protect the rim from damage. All original equipment laced and cast wheels are designed for use with tubeless tires only.

When removing a tubeless tire, take care not to damage the tire beads, inner liner of the tire or the wheel rim flange. Use tire levers or flat handle tire irons with rounded heads

Tire Removal

CAUTION
To avoid damage when removing the tire, support the wheel on two wooden blocks, so the brake discs or the driven sprocket does not contact the floor.

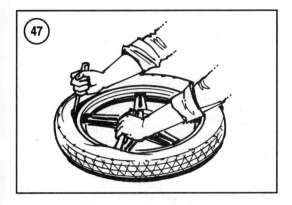

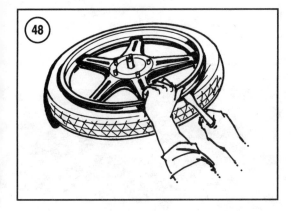

NOTE
To make tire removal easier, warm the tire to make it softer and more pliable. Place the wheel and tire assembly in the sun. If possible, place the wheel assembly and the new tire in a completely closed motorcycle.

1A. Remove the front wheel as described in this chapter.

1B. Remove the rear wheel as described in this chapter.

2. If not already marked by the tire manufacturer, mark the valve stem location on the tire, so the tire can be installed in the same location for easier balancing.

3. Remove the valve core from the valve stem and deflate the tire.

NOTE
*Removal of tubeless tires from their rims can be difficult because of the exceptionally tight tire bead-to-rim seal. Breaking the bead seal may require a special tool (**Figure 44**). If unable to break the seal loose, take the wheel to a motorcycle dealership or tire repair shop, and have them break it loose on a tire changing machine.*

CAUTION
The inner rim and tire bead area are the sealing surfaces on the tubeless tire. Do not scratch the inside of the rim or damage the tire bead.

4. Press the entire bead on both sides of the tire away from the rim and into the center of the rim.

5. Lubricate both beads with soapy water.

CAUTION
*Use rim protectors (**Figure 45**) or insert scraps of leather between the tire iron and the rim to protect the rim from damage.*

NOTE
Use only quality tire irons without sharp edges. If necessary, file the ends of the tire irons to remove rough edges.

6. Insert a tire iron under the top bead next to the valve stem (**Figure 46**). Force the bead on the opposite side of the tire into the center of the rim and pry the bead over the rim with the tire iron.

7. Insert a second tire iron next to the first iron to hold the bead over the rim. Then work around the tire with the first tire iron, prying the bead over the rim (**Figure 47**).

8. Stand the wheel upright. Insert a tire iron between the back bead and the side of the rim that the top bead was pried over (**Figure 48**). Force the bead on the opposite side from the tire iron into the center of the rim. Work around the tire and pry the back bead off the rim.

9

9. Inspect the valve stem seal. Because rubber deteriorates with age, replace the valve stem when replacing the tire.

10. Remove the old valve stem and discard it. Inspect the valve stem hole (**Figure 49**) in the rim. Remove any dirt or corrosion from the hole and wipe it dry with a clean cloth. Install a new valve stem and make sure it is properly seated in the rim.

11. Carefully inspect the tire and wheel rim for damage as described in the following section.

Tire and Wheel Rim Inspection

1. Wipe off the inner surfaces of the wheel rim. Clean off any rubber residue or oxidation.

> *WARNING*
> *Carefully consider whether a tire should be replaced. If there is any doubt about the quality of the existing tire, replace it with a new one. Do not take a chance on a tire failure at any speed.*

2. If any of the following conditions are observed, replace the tire.
   a. A puncture or split whose total length or diameter exceeds 1/4 in. (11 mm).
   b. A scratch or split on the side wall.
   c. Any type of ply separation.
   d. Tread separation or excessive abnormal wear pattern.
   e. Tread depth of less than 1/16 in. (1.6 mm) on original equipment tires. Tread depth minimum may vary on aftermarket tires
   f. Scratches on either sealing bead.
   g. The cord is cut in any place.
   h. Flat spots in the tread from skidding.
   i. Any abnormality in the inner liner.

Tire Installation

1. Inspect the valve stem core rubber seal for hardness or deterioration. Replace the valve core if necessary.

2. A new tire may have balancing rubbers inside. These are not patches. Do not remove them.

3. Lubricate both beads of the tire with soapy water.

4. When installing the tire on the rim, make sure the correct tire (either front or rear) is installed on

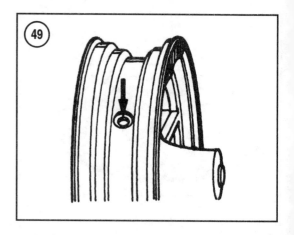

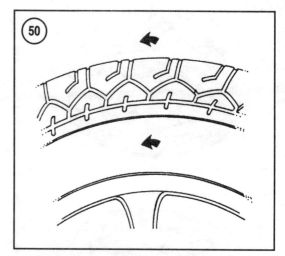

the correct wheel and make sure the direction arrow faces the direction of wheel rotation (**Figure 50**).

5. When remounting the old tire, align the mark made in Step 2 of *Removal* with the valve stem (**Figure 51**). If a new tire is being installed, align the col-

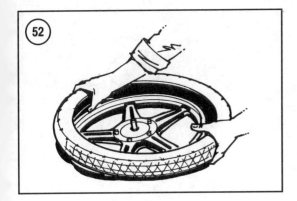

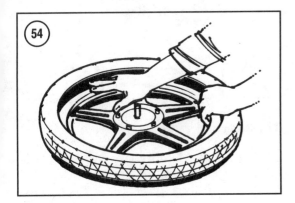

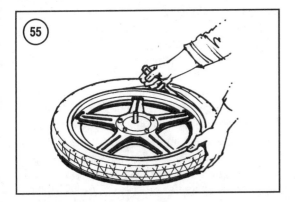

ored spot near the bead, which indicates the lightest point of the tire, with the valve stem.

6. Align the tire with the rim, then place the backside of the tire into the center of the rim. The lower bead should go into the center of the rim with the upper bead inside the rim. Work around the tire in both directions (**Figure 52**) using a tire iron for the last few inches of bead (**Figure 53**).

7. Press the upper bead into the rim opposite the valve stem (**Figure 54**). Pry the bead with both hands into the rim on both sides of the initial point and work around the rim to the valve stem (**Figure 55**). If the tire pulls up on one side, use either a tire iron or one knee to hold the tire in place. The last few inches are usually the toughest to install. Continue to push the tire into the rim by hand. Relubricate the bead if necessary. If the tire bead pulls out from under the rim, use both knees to hold the tire in place. If necessary, use a tire iron for the last few inches.

8. Bounce the wheel several times, rotating it each time. This will force the tire bead against the rim flanges. After the tire beads are in contact with the rim, inflate the tire to seat the beads.

9. Place an inflatable band around the circumference of the tire. Slowly inflate the band until the tire beads are pressed against the rim. Inflate the tire enough to make it seat, deflate the band and remove it.

WARNING
In the next step, never exceed 40 psi (276 kPa) inflation pressure as the tire could burst, causing severe injury. Never stand directly over a tire while inflating it.

10. After inflating the tire, make sure the beads are fully seated and the rim lines are the same distance from the rim all the way around the tire. If the beads will not seat, deflate the tire and lubricate the rim and beads with soapy water.

11. Reinflate the tire to the pressure in **Table 4**. Install the valve stem cap.

12. Balance the wheel as described in this chapter.

13A. Install the front wheel as described in this chapter.

13B. Install the rear wheel as described in this chapter.

9

TIRE REPAIRS

NOTE
Changing or patching on the road is
very difficult. A can of pressurized tire
inflator and sealer can inflate the tire
and seal the hole, but this is only a
temporary fix.

WARNING
Do not install an inner tube inside a
tubeless tire. The tube will cause an
abnormal heat buildup in the tire.

Tubeless tires have the TUBELESS molded into the sidewall and the rims have SUITABLE FOR TUBELESS TIRES or equivalent stamped or cast on them.

If the tire is punctured, remove it from the rim to inspect the inside of the tire and apply a combination plug/patch from inside the tire (**Figure 56**). Never attempt to repair a tubeless motorcycle tire using a plug or cord patch applied from outside the tire.

After repairing a tubeless tire, do not exceed 50 mph (80 km/h).

As soon as possible, replace the patched tire with a new one.

Repair

Do not rely on a plug or cord patch applied from outside the tire. Use a combination plug/patch applied from inside the tire (**Figure 56**).

1. Remove the tire from the wheel rim as described in this chapter.

2. Inspect the rim inner flange. Smooth scratches on the sealing surface with emery cloth. If a scratch is deeper than 0.020 in. (0.5 mm), replace the wheel.

3. Inspect the inside and outside of the tire. Replace a tire if any of the following conditions are found.

   a. A puncture larger than 1/8 in. (3 mm) diameter.

   b. A punctured or damaged side wall.

   c. More than two punctures in the tire.

4. Apply the plug/patch following the manufacturer's instructions with the patch kit.

5. As soon as possible, replace the patched tire with a new one.

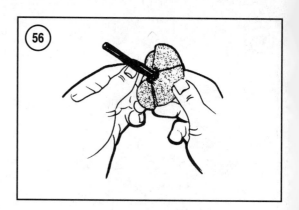

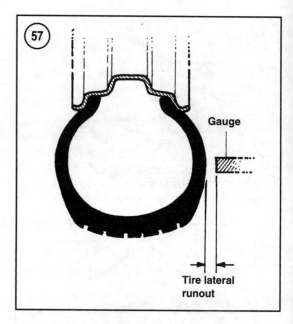

Gauge

Tire lateral runout

Tire Runout

Check the tires for excessive lateral and radial runout after a wheel has been mounted or if the motorcycle developed a wobble that cannot be traced to another component. Mount the wheels on their axles when making the following checks.

1. *Lateral runout*—Check the tire for excessive side-to-side play as follows:

   a. Position a fixed pointer next to the tire sidewall as shown in **Figure 57**. Position the pointer tip so it is not directly in line with the molded tire logo or any other raised surface.

   b. Rotate the tire and measure lateral runout.

   c. The lateral runout should not exceed 0.080 in. (2.03 mm). If runout is excessive, remove the tire from the wheel and recheck the wheel's lateral runout as described in this chapter. If

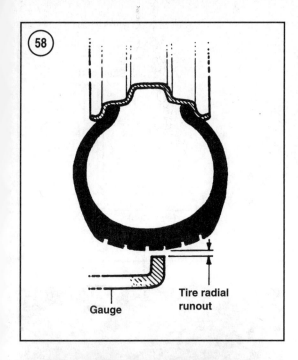

Tire radial runout

Gauge

the runout is excessive, the wheel must be trued (laced wheels) or replaced (alloy wheels). If wheel runout is correct, the tire runout is excessive and the tire must be replaced.

2. *Radial runout*—Check the tire for excessive up-and-down play as follows:

  a. Position a fixed pointer at the center bottom of the tire tread as shown in **Figure 58**.

  b. Rotate the tire and measure the amount of radial runout.

  c. The radial runout should not exceed 0.090 in. (2.29 mm). If runout is excessive, remove the tire from the wheel and recheck the wheel's radial runout as described in this chapter. If the runout is excessive, true or replace the

wheel. If wheel runout is correct, the tire runout is excessive and the tire must be replaced.

MOTORCYCLE ALIGNMENT

Proper suspension and engine alignment is necessary to ensure good motorcycle performance and drivability. The following procedures describe how to check the engine stabilizers and rear axle-to-swing arm pivot shaft alignment.

Preliminary Inspection

Check the following area for problems caused by normal wear. Adjust, repair or replace any component as required.

1. Check the top (**Figure 59**) and bottom (**Figure 60**) engine stabilizers for loose or damaged parts. Refer to *Engine* in Chapter Four to remove and install the stabilizers. To adjust the stabilizers, refer to *Alignment* in this chapter.

2. Check the steering head bearing adjustment as described under *Steering Play Adjustment* in Chapter Ten.

3. Check the runout of each wheel as described in this chapter.

Alignment

Each alignment check and adjustment affects the next one. Work carefully and accurately when performing the following steps.

1. Perform all of the checks listed under *Preliminary Inspection* in this section. When all components are within specifications, continue with Step 2. If the motorcycle has been involved in an accident, refer frame alignment inspection to a

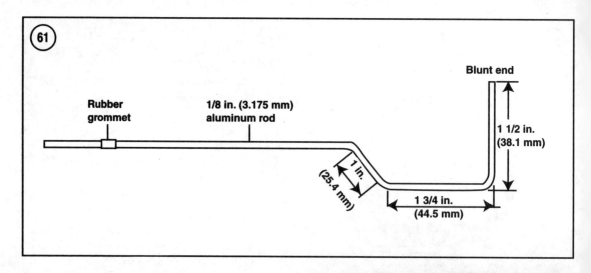

Harley-Davidson dealership or motorcycle frame alignment specialist.

> *NOTE*
> *On models so equipped, always disarm the optional TSSM security system prior to disconnecting the battery or the siren will sound.*

2. Disconnect the negative battery cable as described in Chapter Eight.

3. Remove both saddlebags as described in Chapter Fourteen.

4. Remove the fuel tank as described in Chapter Seven.

5. Remove the mufflers as described in Chapter Seven.

6. Remove both passenger footboards as described in Chapter Fourteen.

7. Remove the chrome trim cap from the swing arm passenger footrest brackets.

8. Insert the blunt end of the alignment tool (**Figure 61**) into the center of the swing arm pivot shaft (**Figure 62**). Slide the rubber grommet down the length of the tool until it is aligned with the center of the rear axle.

9. Remove the tool without disturbing the position of the grommet and insert the tool into the opposite side of the swing arm. Compare the axle center point with the position of the grommet. Axle alignment is correct if the position of the grommet is the same on both sides.

10. If the alignment is incorrect, perform the *Final Drive Belt Deflection and Alignment* procedure in

Chapter Three. When the adjustment is correct, continue with Step 11.

> *NOTE*
> *The following steps must be performed with the rear wheel off the ground.*

11. Support the motorcycle with the rear wheel off the ground.

12. At the top stabilizer on the left side of the motorcycle, remove the bolt securing the stabilizer link to the top engine mounting bracket (**Figure 63**).

13. Remove the flange locknuts securing the voltage regulator to the frame. Remove the voltage regulator from the mounting studs and move it out of the way. Suspend it with a piece of wire. Do not suspend it with the electrical harness.

14. On the lower engine mount, refer to **Figure 64** and perform the following:

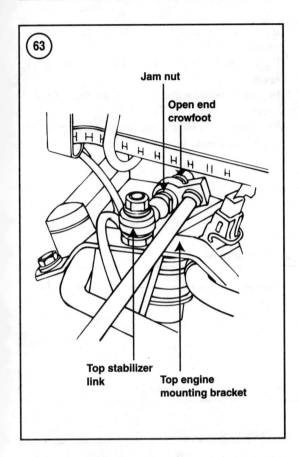

63

Jam nut

Open end
crowfoot

Top stabilizer
link

Top engine
mounting bracket

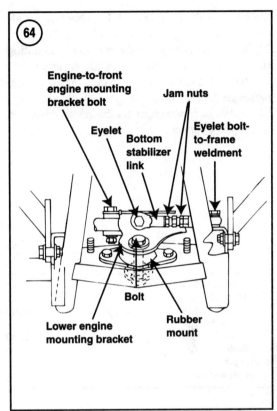

64

Engine-to-front
engine mounting
bracket bolt

Jam nuts

Eyelet

Bottom
stabilizer
link

Eyelet bolt-
to-frame
weldment

Bolt

Lower engine
mounting bracket

Rubber
mount

9

a. Loosen the lower engine mounting bracket-to-rubber mount bolt.

b. Loosen the lower engine mounting bracket-to-the frame bolts.

15. Make sure the front and rear wheels are aligned as follows:

a. Place a straightedge along each side of the rear wheel and make sure the front wheel is centered between the two straightedges.

b. If alignment is incorrect, use an open-end crowfoot wrench to loosen the two jam nuts on the bottom stabilizer link (**Figure 64**).

c. Use an open-end crowfoot wrench to loosen the two jam nuts on the top stabilizer link (**Figure 63**).

d. Adjust the top stabilizer until the bolt removed in Step 12 can be reinstalled without pushing the engine either to the left or right. Install the bolt and washer, and tighten the bolt securely.

16. Tighten the jam nuts on both the top and bottom stabilizer links.

17. With the engine weight on the rubber mount, make sure the two lower engine mounting bracket-to-rubber mount bolts are loose.

18. Push the rubber mount plate from side to side until the rubber bulge, below the frame cross member, is centered with the plate and is equally compressed from side to side. Tighten the two rubber mount-to-frame mount bolts to the torque specification in **Table 2**.

19. Remove the lower engine mounting bracket-to-rubber mount bolt, washer and nut (**Figure 64**).

20. With the engine weight on the front rubber mount, push the rubber mount plate forward and rearward until the rubber bulge, below the frame cross member, is centered with the plate and is equally compressed forward and rear ward.

21. With the rubber mount centered, install the lower engine mounting bracket-to-rubber mount bolt, washer and nut. Make sure the bolt does not bind when inserted through the rubber mount and the front engine mount.

22. Tighten the lower engine mounting bracket-to-rubber mount bolt to the torque specification in **Ta-**

ble 2. Check the alignment of the rubber mount after the bolts are tightened in Step 18 and Step 22.

23. Install the voltage regulator onto the mounting studs and tighten the flange locknuts securely.

24. Install the chrome trim cap onto the swing arm passenger footrest brackets.

25. Install both passenger footboards as described in Chapter Fourteen.

26. Install the mufflers as described in Chapter Seven.

27. Install the fuel tank as described in Chapter Seven.

28. Install both saddlebags as described in Chapter Fourteen.

29. Connect the negative battery cable as described in Chapter Eight.

Table 1 WHEEL SPECIFICATIONS

	in.	mm
Wheel runout (maximum)		
Laced wheels		
Lateral and radial	0.031	0.79
Cast wheels		
Lateral	0.047	1.19
Radial	0.031	0.79
End play (1999)		
Front and rear	0.002-0.006	0.05-0.15

Table 2 WHEEL TORQUE SPECIFICATIONS

Item	ft.-lb.	in.-lb.	N•m
Brake disc bolts			
Front wheel	16-24	–	22-32
Rear wheel	30-45	–	41-61
Driven sprocket bolts	55-60	–	75-81
Front axle nut	50-55	–	68-75
Front fork cap nuts	–	62-132	7-15
Front brake caliper mounting bolt	28-38	–	38-51
Lower engine mounting bracket			
Rubber mount-to-frame bolts	33-38	–	45-51
Rubber mount-to-engine			
mounting bracket	35-45	–	47-61
Rear axle nut			
1999-2001	60-65	–	81-88
2002	95-105	–	129-142
Spoke nipples	–	40-50	4-6
Valve stem nut	–	12-15	1-2

Table 3 FRONT AND REAR WHEEL BEARING SPACER SHIMS (1999)

Part No.	Thickness in. (mm)
43290-82	0.030-0.033 (0.76-0.84)
43291-82	0.015-0.017 (0.38-0.43)
43292-82	0.0075-0.0085 (0.190-0.216)
43293-82	0.0035-0.0045 (0.089-0.114)
43294-82	0.0015-0.0025 (0.038-0.064)

Table 4 TIRE INFLATION PRESSURE (COLD)*

Model	kPa	PSI
Front wheels		
Rider only	248	36
Rider and passenger	248	36
Rear wheels		
Rider only	248	36
Rider and passenger	275	40

*Tire pressure for original equipment tires. Aftermarket tires may require different inflation pressure.

9

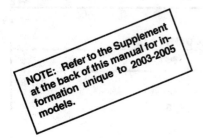

NOTE: Refer to the Supplement at the back of this manual for information unique to 2003-2005 models.

CHAPTER TEN

FRONT SUSPENSION AND STEERING

This chapter covers the handlebar, steering head and front fork assemblies.

Tables 1-3 at the end of the chapter list specifications.

HANDLEBAR

Removal/Installation

Refer to **Figure 1**.

1A. On all FLHT models, refer to Chapter Fourteen and perform the following:

  a. Remove the outer fairing.

  b. Partially remove the inner fairing (A, **Figure 2**) until the handlebar forward mounting bolts are accessible. It is not necessary to completely remove the inner fairing.

1B. On all FLHR models, remove the headlight nacelle as described in Chapter Eight.

2. Support the motorcycle with the front wheel off the ground. See *Motorcycle Stands* in Chapter Nine.

NOTE
Cover the fuel tank with a heavy cloth or plastic tarp to protect it from accidental scratches or dents when removing the handlebar.

NOTE
Before removing the handlebar, make a drawing of the clutch and throttle cable routing from the handlebar through the frame. This information will help when reinstalling the handlebar and connecting the cables.

3. On the right side of the handlebar, perform the following:

  a. Unscrew and remove the mirror (A, **Figure 3**).

  b. Remove the screws securing the master cylinder (B, **Figure 3**). Do not disconnect the hydraulic brake line.

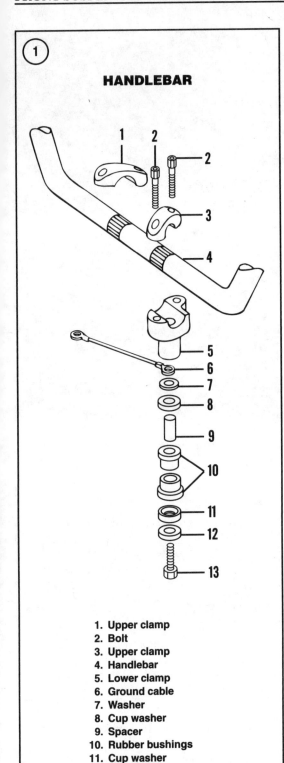

HANDLEBAR

1. Upper clamp
2. Bolt
3. Upper clamp
4. Handlebar
5. Lower clamp
6. Ground cable
7. Washer
8. Cup washer
9. Spacer
10. Rubber bushings
11. Cup washer
12. Washer (right side only)
13. Bolt

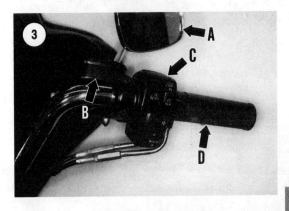

10

c. Remove the screws securing the right side switch assembly (C, **Figure 3**) and separate the housing halves.

d. Slide the throttle housing assembly (D, **Figure 3**) off the handlebar.

4. On the left side of the handlebar, perform the following:

a. Unscrew and remove the mirror (A, **Figure 4**).

b. Remove the screws securing the left side switch assembly (B, **Figure 4**) and separate the housing halves.

c. Remove the clutch lever clamp (C, **Figure 4**) mounting screws and washers, and separate the clamp halves.

5. Disconnect or remove any wiring harness clamps at the handlebar.

6. Remove the two front handlebar clamp bolts, then the rear clamp bolts (B, **Figure 2**). Remove the holders and handlebar.

7. Install the handlebar by reversing these steps. Note the following:

a. Check the knurled rings on the handlebar for galling and bits of aluminum. Clean the knurled section with a wire brush.

b. Check the handlebar for cracks, bends or other damage. Replace the handlebar if necessary. Do not attempt to repair it.

c. Thoroughly clean the clamp halves of all residue.

d. After installing the handlebar, reposition the handlebar while sitting on the motorcycle.

e. Tighten the handlebar clamp bolts securely.

f. Adjust the mirrors.

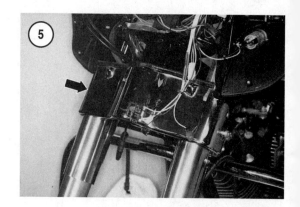

FRONT FORK—NON-CARTRIDGE TYPE (ALL 1999-2001 MODELS AND 2002 FLHR, FLHRI AND FLHRCI RIGHT SIDE ONLY)

NOTE
The right side fork on 2002 FLHR, FLHRI, FLHRCI models is covered in this section. On these models, the left side fork is a cartridge type and is covered in the following procedure.

Front Fork Service

Before assuming a fork is malfunctioning, drain the front fork oil and refill with the proper type and quantity fork oil as described in Chapter Three. If there is still a problem, such as poor damping, a tendency to bottom or top out, or leakage around the oil seals, follow the service procedures in this section.

To simplify fork service and to prevent the mixing of parts, remove, service and install the fork legs individually.

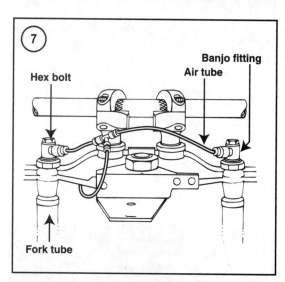

Removal (Fork Not To Be Serviced)

1A. On all FLHT models, remove the outer fairing. On FLHTC models, also remove the storage box. Refer to Chapter Fourteen.

1B. On all FLHR models, remove the headlight nacelle as described in Chapter Eight.

2. Remove the passing lamp assembly as described in Chapter Eight.

3. Support the motorcycle with the front wheel off the ground. See *Motorcycle Stands* in Chapter Nine.

4. Remove the front fender and front wheel as described in Chapter Nine.

5. Remove the screws securing the chrome mounting bracket (**Figure 5**) and remove the bracket.

6. If both fork tube assemblies are going to be removed, mark them with an R (right side) and L (left side) so the assemblies will be reinstalled on the correct side.

7. Remove the right side saddlebag as described in Chapter Fourteen.

> *WARNING*
> *Be careful when releasing the air from the front fork air valve. Moisture and fork oil may spurt out when the air pressure is released. Protect eyes accordingly.*

8. Cover the rear brake assembly and wheel prior to releasing the compressed air from the rear air valve. If necessary, wipe up oil residue that may have been ejected from the air valve.

9. On 1999-2001 models, remove the cap from the front fork air valve (**Figure 6**), then slowly depress the air valve to release the air from the front fork air pipe system. Unscrew and remove the core from the air valve. Place the air valve core and cap in a reclosable plastic bag to avoid misplacing them.

10. Refer to **Figure 7**. Unscrew and remove the hex bolts (**Figure 8**) securing the banjo bolt on top of each fork tube. Move the air tube assembly away from the fork assemblies.

11. Remove the fork cap bolt (**Figure 9**) from the top of the fork tube.

12. Working at the base of the steering stem, loosen the pinch bolt (**Figure 10**).

13. Slide the fork tube out of the upper fork bracket. Remove the rubber stop (**Figure 11**) from the fork tube.

14. Continue to slide the fork tube out of the lower fork bracket. It may be necessary to rotate the fork tube slightly while pulling it down and out. Remove the fork assembly and take it to the workbench for service. If the fork is not going to be serviced, wrap it in a bath towel or blanket to protect the surface from damage.

15. Repeat Steps 8-14 for the other fork assembly.

10

Installation (Fork Was Not Serviced)

1. Install a fork tube through the lower fork bracket and install the rubber fork stop (**Figure 11**).

2. Continue to push the fork tube up through the top fork bracket until it bottoms against the upper fork bracket.

3. Tighten the pinch bolt (**Figure 10**) to the specification in **Table 1**.

4. Install the fork cap bolt (**Figure 9**) onto the top of the fork tube and tighten it securely.

5. Install a *new* O-ring onto each hex bolt (**Figure 12**) and apply a light coat of clean engine oil to them.

6. Install the air tube assembly onto the top of the fork assemblies and install the hex bolts through the banjo bolts. Tighten the hex bolts to the specification in **Table 1**.

7. Install the right side saddlebag as described in Chapter Fourteen.

8. Install the front fender and front wheel as described in Chapter Nine.

9A. On all FLHT models, install the outer fairing. On FLHTC models, also install the storage box. Refer to Chapter Fourteen.

9B. On all FLHR models, install the headlight nacelle as described in Chapter Eight.

10. Apply the front brake and pump the front fork several times to seat the fork tubes and front wheel.

11. On 1999-2001 models, adjust the front fork air pressure as described in this chapter.

Removal (Fork To Be Serviced)

1A. On all FLHT models, remove the outer fairing. On FLHTC models, also remove the storage box. Refer to Chapter Fourteen.

1B. On all FLHR models, remove the headlight nacelle as described in Chapter Eight.

2. Remove the passing lamp assembly as described in Chapter Eight.

3. Support the motorcycle with the front wheel off the ground. See *Motorcycle Stands* in Chapter Nine.

4. Remove the front fender and front wheel as described in Chapter Nine.

5. Remove the screws securing the chrome mounting bracket (**Figure 5**) and remove the bracket.

6. If both fork tube assemblies are going to be removed, mark them with an R (right side) and L (left

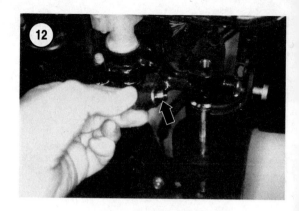

side) so the assemblies will be reinstalled on the correct side.

7. Remove the right side saddlebag as described in Chapter Fourteen.

> *WARNING*
> *Be careful when releasing the air from the front fork air valve. Moisture and fork oil may spurt out when the air pressure is released. Protect eyes accordingly.*

8. On 1999-2001 models, cover the rear brake assembly and wheel prior to releasing the compressed air from the air valve. If necessary, wipe up oil residue that may have been ejected from the air valve.

9. On 1999-2001 models, remove the cap from the front fork air valve (**Figure 6**), then slowly depress the air valve to release the air from the front fork air pipe system. Unscrew and remove the core from the air valve. Place the air valve core and cap in a reclosable plastic bag to avoid misplacing them.

10. Refer to **Figure 7**. Unscrew and remove the hex bolts (**Figure 8**) securing the banjo bolt on top of each fork tube. Move the air tube assembly away from the fork assemblies.

11. Remove the fork cap bolt (**Figure 9**) from the top of the fork tube.

12. Working at the base of the steering stem, loosen the pinch bolt (**Figure 10**).

13. Slide the fork assembly part way down and retighten the pinch bolt (**Figure 13**).

14. Place a drain pan under the fork slider to catch the fork oil.

15. Use an 8 mm Allen wrench and impact driver to loosen the damper rod cartridge bolt at the base of the slider.

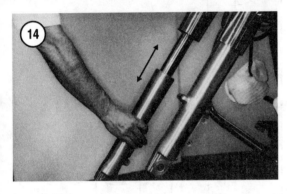

16. Remove the Allen bolt and drain the fork oil. Pump the slider several times to expel most of the fork oil. Reinstall the Allen bolt to keep residual oil in the fork.

17. Remove the stopper ring from the fork slider.

18. Lower the fork slider on the fork tube.

NOTE
It may be necessary to slightly heat the area on the slider around the oil seal prior to removal. Use a rag soaked in hot water; do not apply a flame directly to the fork slider.

19. There is an interference fit between the bushing in the fork slider and the bushing on the fork tube. Remove the fork tube from the slider, pull hard on the fork tube using quick in and out strokes (**Figure 14**). This will withdraw the bushing and the oil seal from the slider.

20. Remove the slider from the fork tube. Remove the oil lock piece from the damper rod if it is still in place.

21. Loosen the pinch bolt (**Figure 13**). Slide the fork tube out of the lower fork bracket and remove the rubber stop (**Figure 11**) from the fork tube. It may be necessary to rotate the fork tube slightly

while pulling it down and out. Remove the fork assembly and take it to the workbench for service.

22. Repeat Steps 11-21 for the other fork assembly.

Installation (Fork Was Serviced)

1. Assemble the fork as described in this chapter.

2. Install a fork tube through the lower fork bracket and install the rubber fork stop (**Figure 11**).

3. Continue to push the fork tube up through the top fork bracket until it bottoms against the upper fork bracket.

4. Tighten the pinch bolt (**Figure 10**) to the specification in **Table 1**.

5. Install the fork cap bolt (**Figure 9**) onto the top of the fork tube and tighten it securely.

6. Install a *new* O-ring onto each hex bolt (**Figure 12**) and apply a light coat of clean engine oil to them.

7. Install the air tube assembly onto the top of the fork assemblies and install the hex bolts through the banjo bolts. Tighten the hex bolts to the specification in **Table 1**.

8. Install the right side saddlebag as described in Chapter Fourteen.

9. Install the front fender and front wheel as described in Chapter Nine.

10A. On all FLHT models, install the outer fairing. On FLHTC models, also install the storage box. Refer to Chapter Fourteen.

10B. On all FLHR models, install the headlight nacelle as described in Chapter Eight.

11. On 1999-2001 models, apply the front brake and pump the front fork several times to seat the fork legs and front wheel.

12. On 1999-2001 models, adjust the front fork air pressure as described in this chapter.

Disassembly

Refer to **Figure 15**.

NOTE
A special fork holding tool is required to disassemble and assemble the fork assembly. The fork spring cannot be compressed enough by hand to loosen and remove the fork tube plug. This special tool is available from motorcycle dealerships or motorcycle parts suppliers houses.

10

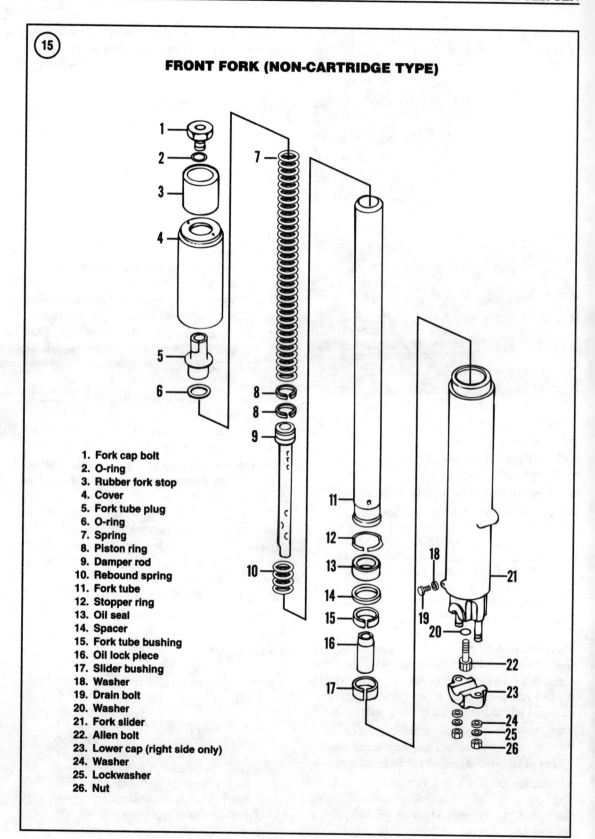

⑮

FRONT FORK (NON-CARTRIDGE TYPE)

1. Fork cap bolt
2. O-ring
3. Rubber fork stop
4. Cover
5. Fork tube plug
6. O-ring
7. Spring
8. Piston ring
9. Damper rod
10. Rebound spring
11. Fork tube
12. Stopper ring
13. Oil seal
14. Spacer
15. Fork tube bushing
16. Oil lock piece
17. Slider bushing
18. Washer
19. Drain bolt
20. Washer
21. Fork slider
22. Allen bolt
23. Lower cap (right side only)
24. Washer
25. Lockwasher
26. Nut

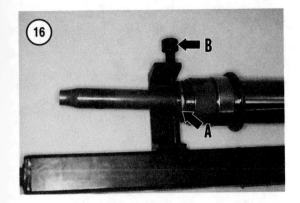

1. To protect the fork tube, place a steel washer (A, **Figure 16**) over the fork damper rod and up against the base of the fork tube.

2. Tighten the bolt (B, **Figure 16**) so it is seated below the steel washer. Do not over tighten the bolt as the damper rod will be damaged. Make sure the tool is indexed properly against the steel washer.

3. Install the special tool's upper bolt into the hole in the fork tube plug (A, **Figure 17**) following the manufacturer's instructions. Make sure the tool is indexed properly in the hole in the fork tube plug.

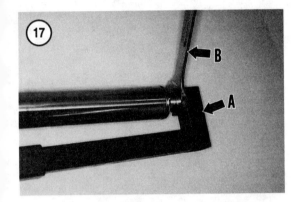

WARNING
Be careful when removing the fork top plug as the spring is under pressure. Protect eyes and face accordingly.

4. Hold onto the fork tube and loosen the fork tube plug (B, **Figure 17**). Slowly loosen the special tool while unscrewing the fork tube plug.

5. When the fork tube plug is completely unscrewed from the fork tube, loosen and remove the special tool from the fork assembly.

6. Remove the fork tube plug and fork spring, and drain any residual fork oil. Dispose of the fork oil properly.

7. Turn the fork tube upside down, and remove the damper rod and rebound spring.

10

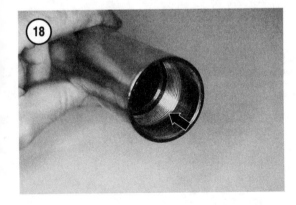

Inspection

Replace worn or damaged parts.

1. Thoroughly clean all parts in solvent and dry them. Check the fork tube for signs of wear or scratches.

2. Check the fork tube for bending, nicks, rust or other damage. Place the fork tube on a set of V-blocks and check runout with a dial indicator. If the special tools are not available, roll the fork tube on a large plate glass or another flat surface. Harley-Davidson does not provide service specifications for runout.

3. Check the internal threads in the top of the slider (**Figure 18**) for stripping, cross-threading or sealer residue. Use a tap to true the threads and to remove sealer deposits.

4. Check the external threads on the fork top plug (A, **Figure 19**) for stripping, cross-threading or sealer residue. Use a die to true the threads and to remove sealer deposits.

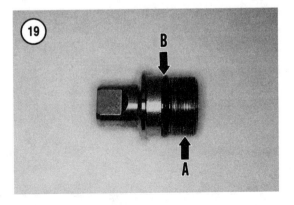

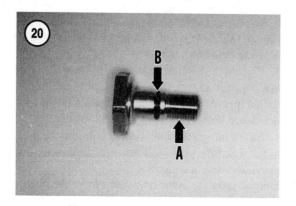

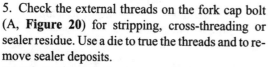

5. Check the external threads on the fork cap bolt (A, **Figure 20**) for stripping, cross-threading or sealer residue. Use a die to true the threads and to remove sealer deposits.

6. Check the slider for dents or other exterior damage. Check the retaining ring groove (**Figure 21**) in the top of the slider for cracks or other damage.

7. Check the threaded studs (**Figure 22**) at the base of the slider for damage. Repair them if necessary.

8. Check the front caliper mounting bosses (**Figure 23**) for cracks or damage.

9. Check the slider and fork tube bushings for excessive wear, cracks or damage.

10. Remove the fork tube bushing as follows:
    a. Expand the bushing slit (**Figure 24**) with a screwdriver and slide the bushing off the fork tube.
    b. Coat the new bushing with new fork oil.
    c. Install the new bushing by expanding the slit with a screwdriver.
    d. Seat the new bushing into the fork tube groove.

11. Check the damper rod piston ring(s) (A, **Figure 25**) for excessive wear, cracks or other damage. If necessary, replace both rings as a set.

12. Check the damper rod (B, **Figure 25**) for straightness with a set of V-blocks and a dial indicator (**Figure 26**), or by rolling it on a piece of plate glass. Specifications for runout are not available. If the damper rod is not straight, replace it.

13. Make sure the oil passage hole in the damper rod (C, **Figure 25**) is open. If it is clogged, flush it with solvent and dry it with compressed air.

14. Check the internal threads in the bottom of the damper rod for stripping, cross-threading or sealer residue. Use a tap to true the threads and to remove sealer deposits.

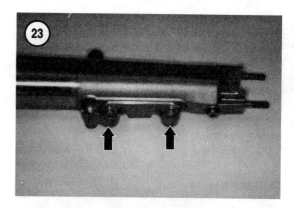

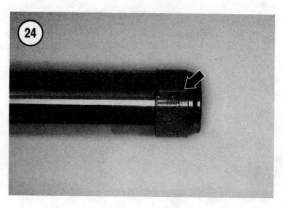

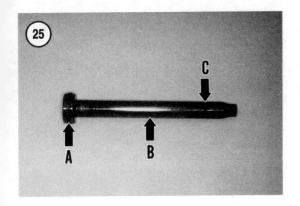

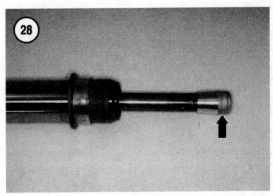

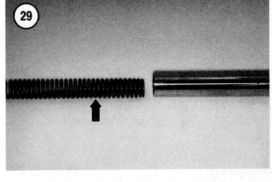

15. Check the damper rod rebound spring and the fork spring for wear or damage. Service limit specifications for spring free length are not available.

16. Replace the oil seal whenever it is removed. Always replace both oil seals as a set.

Assembly

1. Install a *new* O-ring onto the fork top plug (B, **Figure 19**).

2. Install a *new* O-ring onto the fork cap bolt (B, **Figure 20**).

3. Coat all parts with Harley-Davidson Type E Fork Oil, or an equivalent, before assembly.

4. Install the rebound spring (A, **Figure 27**) onto the damper rod and slide the damper rod (B) into the fork tube until it extends out the end of the fork tube.

5. Install the oil lock piece (**Figure 28**) onto the end of the damper rod.

6. Position the fork spring with the closer wound coils going in first (**Figure 29**) and install the fork spring into the fork tube.

7. To protect the fork tube, place a steel washer (A, **Figure 16**) over the fork damper rod and up against the base of the fork tube.

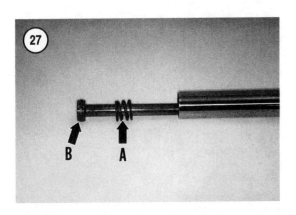

10

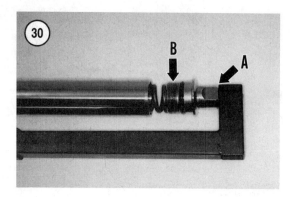

8. Tighten the bolt (B, **Figure 16**) so it is seated below the steel washer. Do not over tighten the bolt as the damper rod will be damaged. Make sure the tool is indexed properly against the steel washer.

9. Position the fork tube plug onto the top of the fork spring.

10. Install the special tool's upper bolt into the hole in the fork tube plug (A, **Figure 30**) following the manufacturer's instructions. Make sure the tool is indexed properly in the hole in the fork tube plug.

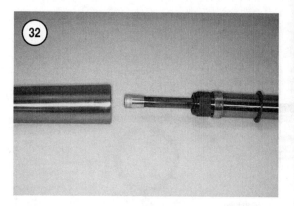

CAUTION
While tightening the special tool, do not jamb the fork tube plug into the threaded portion of the fork tube. This will damage the threads on both parts.

11. Hold onto the fork tube plug and slowly tighten the special tool while guiding the fork tube plug into the top of the fork tube (B, **Figure 30**).

12. Place a wrench on the fork tube plug (B, **Figure 17**) and screw the fork tube plug into the fork tube while tightening the special tool. Once the fork tube plug has started to thread into the fork tube, loosen the special tool and remove it from the fork assembly.

13. Place the slider in a vise with soft jaws and tighten the fork top plug (**Figure 31**) securely.

14. Push the fork slider and damper rod (**Figure 32**) into the fork slider. Insert a Phillips screwdriver through the opening in the bottom of the fork tube and guide the damper rod end into the receptacle in the base of the slider. Remove the screwdriver.

15. Install a new washer onto the damper rod Allen bolt.

16. Apply a non-permanent threadlocking compound to the damper rod Allen bolt threads prior to installation. Insert the Allen bolt (**Figure 33**) through the lower end of the slider and thread it into the damper rod. Tighten the bolt securely.

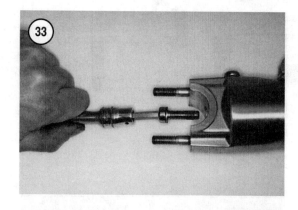

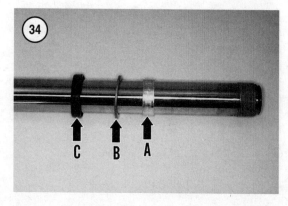

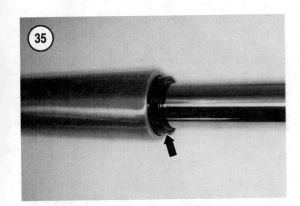

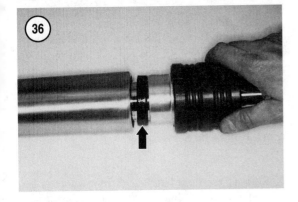

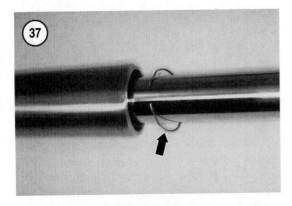

NOTE
To protect the oil seal lips, place a thin plastic bag on top of the fork tube. Before installing the seal in the following steps, lightly coat the bag and the seal lips with fork oil.

17. Slide the fork slider bushing (A, **Figure 34**), oil seal spacer (B) and oil seal (C) (with the letters facing up) down into the fork tube receptacle (**Figure 35**).

NOTE
A fork seal driver is required to install the fork tube bushing and seal into the fork tube. A number of different aftermarket fork seal drivers (JIMS part No. 2046) are available. Another method is to use a piece of pipe or a metal collar with the correct dimensions to slide over the fork tube and seat against the seal. Select or fabricate a driver tool that has sufficient weight to drive the bushing and oil seal into the fork tube.

18. Slide the fork seal driver down the fork tube and seat it against the oil seal (**Figure 36**).

19. Operate the driver and drive the fork slider bushing and new seal into the fork tube. Continue to operate the driver until the stopper ring groove in the tube is visible above the fork seal. Remove the fork seal driver tool.

20. Install the stopper ring (**Figure 37**) into the slider groove. Make sure the retaining ring seats in the groove (**Figure 38**).

21. Install the fork leg as described in this chapter.

22. Insert a clear plastic tube into the fork cap bolt opening (**Figure 39**). Attach a funnel to the plastic tube and refill each fork leg with the correct viscos-

10

ity and quantity of fork oil as indicated in **Table 2**. Remove the small funnel and plastic tube.

FRONT FORK AIR PRESSURE ADJUSTMENT (1999-2001 MODELS)

WARNING
Be careful when releasing the air from the front fork and the front fork air valve. Moisture and/or fork oil may spurt out when the air pressure is released. Protect eyes accordingly.

NOTE
The air chambers in the front fork legs are small and fill rapidly. Do not use compressed air. Only use a small hand-held or foot-operated air pump.

1. Place the motorcycle on the jiffy stand.
2. Remove the right side saddlebag as described in Chapter Fourteen.
3. Remove the front air valve cap (**Figure 40**).
4. Use a no-loss air gauge to check air pressure. Refer to the recommended air pressure in **Table 3**.
5. Increase or decrease air pressure to achieve the desired ride and control.
6. At the same time, check and adjust, if necessary, the air pressure in the rear shock absorbers.
7. Install the air valve cap(s) and the saddlebag.

FRONT FORK—CARTRIDGE TYPE (2002 MODELS EXCEPT 2002 FLHR, FLHRI AND FLHRCI RIGHT SIDE)

NOTE
The right side fork on 2002 FLHR, FLHRI, FLHRCI models is covered in the previous procedure.

Front Fork Service

Before assuming a fork is malfunctioning, drain the front fork oil and refill with the proper type and quantity fork oil as described in Chapter Three. If there is still a problem, such as poor damping, a tendency to bottom or top out, or leakage around the oil seals, follow the service procedures in this section.

To simplify fork service and to prevent the mixing of parts, remove, service and install the fork legs individually.

Removal/Installation (Fork Not To Be Serviced)

1. Remove the front fender and front wheel as described in Chapter Nine.

2. Loosen and remove the fork cap bolt.

3. Loosen the fork bracket pinch bolts.

4. If both fork tube assemblies are going to be removed, mark them with an R (right side) and L (left side) so the assemblies can be reinstalled on the correct side.

5. Carefully lower the fork assembly out of the upper and lower fork brackets. It may be necessary to rotate the fork tube slightly while pulling it down and out. Remove the fork assembly and take it to a workbench for service. If the fork is not going to be serviced, wrap it in a bath towel or blanket to protect the surface from damage.

6. Slowly install the fork tube through the lower fork bracket until the for cap plug contacts the upper fork bracket.

7. With the fork assembly in position, tighten the fork cap bolt and the fork bracket pinch bolt to the torque specification in **Table 1**.

8. Install the front wheel and front fender as described in Chapter Nine.

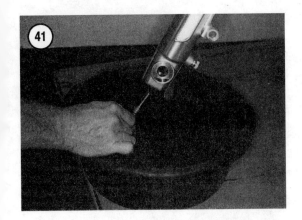

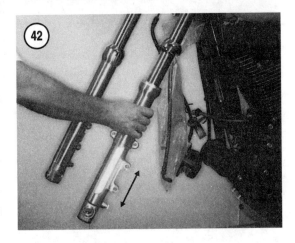

Removal/Installation
(Fork To Be Serviced)

1. Remove the front fender and front wheel as described in Chapter Nine.

2. Remove the fork cap bolt and quad sealing ring from the top of the fork tube.

3. If both fork tube assemblies are going to be removed, mark them with an R (right side) and L (left side) so the assemblies can be reinstalled on the correct side.

4. Place a drain pan under the fork slider.

5. Use an 6 mm Allen wrench and impact driver, loosen the damper rod cartridge Allen bolt at the base of the slider.

6. Remove the Allen bolt and washer (**Figure 41**) and drain the fork oil. Pump the slider several times to expel most of the fork oil. Reinstall the Allen bolt and washer to keep residual oil in the fork.

7. Remove the stopper ring from the fork slider.

8. Lower the fork slider on the fork tube.

NOTE
It may be necessary to slightly heat the area on the slider around the oil seal prior to removal. Use a rag soaked in hot water; do not apply a flame directly to the fork slider.

9. There is an interference fit between the bushing in the fork slider and the bushing on the fork tube. To remove the fork tube from the slider, pull hard on the fork tube using quick in-and-out strokes (**Figure 42**). This will withdraw the bushing and the oil seal from the slider.

10. Loosen the fork bracket pinch bolts.

11. Carefully lower the fork assembly out of the upper and lower and upper brackets. It may be necessary to rotate the fork tube slightly while pulling it down.

12. Lower the fork tube between the upper and the lower bracket, and tighten the lower bracket pinch bolt.

13. Loosen the fork cap plug.

14. Loosen the lower bracket pinch bolt and remove the fork from the lower bracket.

15. Service the fork assembly as described in this chapter.

16. Slowly install the fork tube through the lower fork bracket until the for cap plug contacts the upper fork bracket.

17. With the fork assembly in position, tighten the fork cap bolt and the fork bracket pinch bolt to the specification in **Table 1**.

18. Install the front wheel and front fender as described in Chapter Nine.

Disassembly

Refer to **Figure 43**.

NOTE
A special fork holding tool is required to disassemble and assemble the fork assembly. The fork spring cannot be compressed enough by hand to gain access to the locknut on top of the damper rod cartridge. This special tool is available from motorcycle dealerships or motorcycle parts suppliers.

1. If still in place, unscrew the fork cap bolt and O-ring from the fork cap.

10

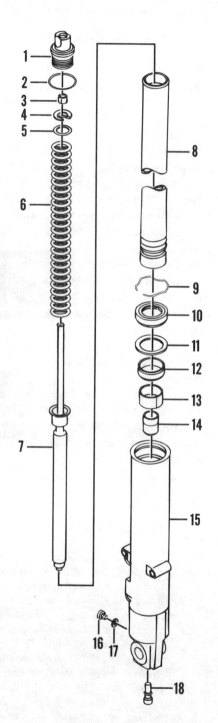

**FRONT FORK—CARTRIDGE TYPE
(2002 MODELS EXCEPT FLHR, FLHRI, FLHRCI RIGHT SIDE)**

1. Fork cap plug
2. O-ring
3. Locknut
4. Spring seat
5. Washer
6. Fork spring
7. Damper rod cartridge
8. Fork tube
9. Stopper ring
10. Oil seal
11. Spacer
12. Fork tube bushing
13. Slider bushing
14. Oil lock piece
15. Fork slider
16. Drain screw
17. Washer
18. Allen bolt and washer

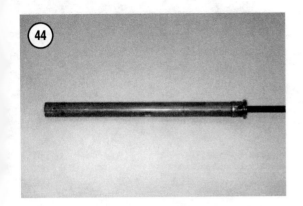

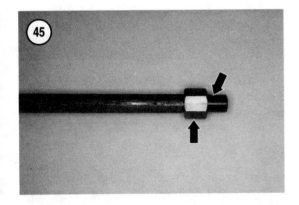

9. Install the special tool's upper bolt between the springs forth and fifth coils. Make sure the tool is indexed properly between the two coils and tighten the upper bolt securely.

10. Slowly tighten the special tool and compress the fork assembly until the fork spring is no longer pressing against the washer and spring seat.

11. Unscrew the locknut from the damper rod cartridge, and remove the spring seat and washer.

12. Slowly loosen the special tool and release the spring pressure within the fork assembly.

13. Remove the fork assembly from the special tool.

14. Remove the fork spring and damper rod cartridge from the fork tube. Do not lose the oil lock piece at the base of the damper rod cartridge.

15. Slide the slider bushing, spacer and oil seal from the fork tube. Keep them in the order of removal.

NOTE
Do not remove the fork tube bushing
unless it is going to be replaced. In-
spect it as described in this chapter.

16. Inspect the components as described in this chapter.

Inspection

Replace any damaged or excessively worn components. True damaged threads with an appropriate size metric tap or die. Simply cleaning and reinstalling unserviceable components will not improve performance of the front suspension.

1. Thoroughly clean all parts in solvent and dry them. Check the fork tube for signs of wear or scratches.

2. Check the damper rod cartridge (**Figure 44**) for straightness and damage.

3. Check the threads and nut (**Figure 45**) at the top of the damper rod cartridge for damage.

4. Make sure the oil hole (A, **Figure 46**) in the damper rod cartridge is clear.

5. Inspect the damper rod cartridge threads for the Allen bolt (B, **Figure 46**) for wear or damage.

6. Inspect the fork cap plug threads for wear or damage.

7. Install a *new* O-ring on the fork cap plug.

8. Check the fork tube (A, **Figure 47**) for straightness.

2. Hold the fork in a vertical position and completely unscrew the fork cap plug from the fork tube. The fork cap plug cannot be removed at this time as it is still attached to the damper rod cartridge.

3. Turn the fork assembly upside down and drain the residual fork oil into a suitable container. Pump the fork several times by hand to expel most of the oil. Dispose of the fork oil properly.

4. Slide the fork tube down into the fork slider to expose the upper end of the cartridge and the locknut.

5. Install an open end wrench on the damper rod cartridge nut, and another one on the flats of the fork cap plug.

6. Hold onto the fork cap plug and loosen the damper rod cartridge locknut.

7. Completely unscrew the fork cap plug from the damper rod cartridge.

8. Install the lower end of the fork assembly in the fork holding tool following the manufacturer's instructions. Make sure the tool is indexed properly in the lower hole in the slider.

10

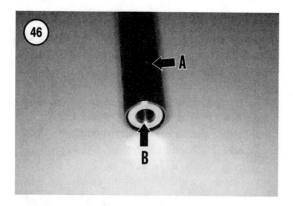

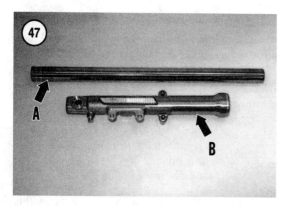

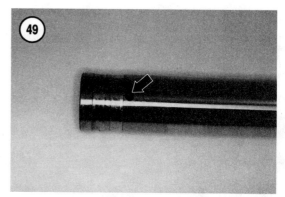

9. Inspect the fork cap plug threads in the fork tube (**Figure 48**) for wear or damage.

10. Make sure the oil hole (**Figure 49**) in the fork tube is clear.

11. Check the slider (B, **Figure 47**) for dents or exterior damage that may cause the upper fork tube to stick.

12. Inspect the brake caliper mounting bosses on the slider for cracks or other damage.

13. Check the front axle bore in the slider for burrs or damage.

14. Inspect the oil seal seating area (**Figure 50**) in the slider for damage or burrs.

15. Inspect the slider bushing (A, **Figure 51**) and fork tube (B). If either is scratched or scored they must be replaced.

16. Measure the uncompressed length of the fork spring as shown in **Figure 52**. Replace the spring if it has sagged to service limit in **Table 3**.

Assembly

1. Coat all parts with H-D Type E fork oil prior to installation.

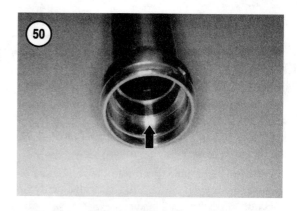

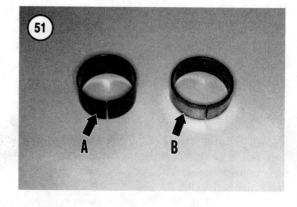

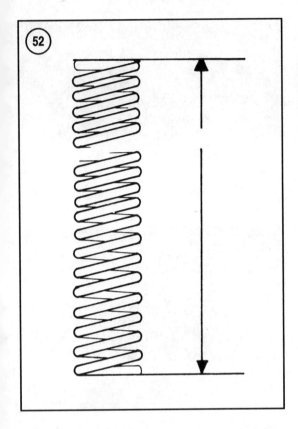

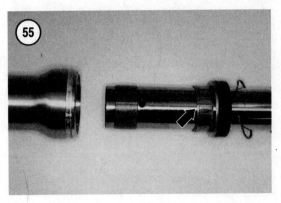

2. If removed, install a new bushing (**Figure 53**) onto the fork tube.

> *NOTE*
> *Place a clinging-type plastic wrap over the end of the slider and coat it with fork oil to avoid damaging the oil seal lips.*

3. Coat the new seal with clean fork oil.

> *NOTE*
> *Position the new oil seal with the open groove facing upward.*

4. Slide the fork slider bushing, spacer and oil seal down into the fork tube.

5. Insert the damper rod cartridge into the fork tube (**Figure 54**).

> *NOTE*
> *The slider bushing opening must be positioned to either side of the slider after the fork tube has been installed. Orientate the opening in relation to the front fender mounting bosses. If the opening is positioned toward either the front or rear of the slider, it will wear prematurely.*

6. Position the slider bushing with the opening (**Figure 55**) toward either side of the slider.

7. Insert the fork tube into the slider until the slider bushing reaches the slider.

8. Recheck the slider bushing opening (A, **Figure 56**). Make sure it is correctly located in relation to the fender bosses (B). Readjust if necessary.

> *NOTE*
> *A fork seal driver is required to install the fork tube bushing and seal into the*

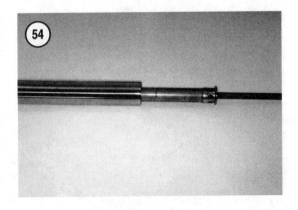

10

fork tube. A number of different after-market fork seal drivers (JIMS part No. 2044) are available. Another method is to use a piece of pipe or a metal collar with correct dimensions to slide over the fork tube and seat against the seal. Select or fabricate a driver tool that has sufficient weight to drive the bushing and oil seal into the fork tube.

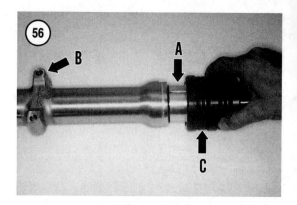

9. Slide the fork seal driver down the fork tube and seat it against the oil seal (C, **Figure 56**).

10. Operate the driver and drive the fork slider bushing, spacer and new seal into the fork tube. Continue until the fork tube stopper ring groove is visible above the fork seal (**Figure 57**). Remove the driver tool.

11. Slide the stopper ring down the fork tube.

12. Install the stopper ring and make sure it is completely seated in the groove in the fork slider (**Figure 58**).

13. If removed, install the oil lock piece onto the end of the damper rod cartridge.

14. Insert the damper rod cartridge (**Figure 59**) into the fork tube.

> *NOTE*
> *The lower end of the damper rod cartridge must be guided into the lower stop in the base of the slider. If not aligned correctly, the Allen bolt can not be installed in Step 16.*

15. Insert a scribe or thin screwdriver into the hole in the base of the slider to guide the lower end of the damper rod cartridge and oil lock piece into the base of the slider.

> *NOTE*
> *If the damper rod cartridge rotates while tightening the Allen bolt, temporarily install the fork spring and the fork cap plug to hold it stationary.*

16. Install a *new* washer on the *new* 6 mm Allen bolt (**Figure 60**). Install it in the fork slider and tighten to the specification in **Table 1**. If installed, remove the fork cap plug and fork spring.

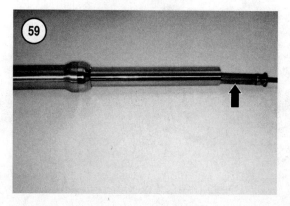

> *NOTE*
> *The following special tool is usually part of the fork holding tool. If not so equipped, one can be fabricated that*

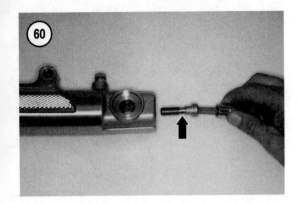

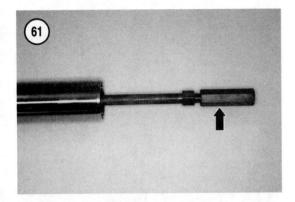

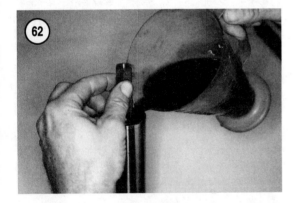

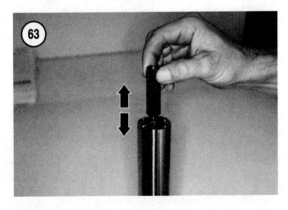

is approximately 2 inches long with an inner metric thread of 12 × 1.0. This tool is to extend the length of the damper rod for the fork bleeding process.

17. If removed, install the locknut onto the top of the damper rod cartridge.

18. Install the special tool extension (**Figure 61**) onto the damper rod cartridge.

19. Secure the fork assembly in a vertical position.

NOTE
To measure the correct amount of fluid, use a plastic baby bottle with milliliters (ml) measurements.

20. Completely compress the fork tube into the slider.

21. Add one-half of the recommended amount (**Table 2**) of H-D Type E fork oil to the fork assembly (**Figure 62**).

NOTE
During the bleeding procedure, maintain the fork oil level above the sliding portion of the damper rod cartridge. If the oil level drops below this level, air may enter the cartridge nullifying the bleeding procedure.

22. Bleed air from the damper rod cartridge as follows:

  a. Hold the fork assembly in a vertical position and hold it this way during this step.

  b. Hold onto the special tool extension installed in Step 18 and *slowly* move the damper rod cartridge up and down (**Figure 63**) using full travel strokes.

  c. Repeat 10 times or more, or until the fork oil is free of bubbles.

  d. If necessary, add additional fork oil until the oil is almost level with the top of the compressed fork tube.

  e. Slowly move the fork tube up and down several stokes or until bubbles do not come from the oil.

  f. Secure the fork assembly in this vertical position for 5-10 minutes to allow any additional trapped air to escape. Tap on the side of the fork assembly to break away any bubbles adhering to the side of the fork.

10

g. Add the remaining amount of the fork oil.

NOTE
Harley-Davidson recommends that the fork oil level be measured, if possible, to ensure a more accurate filling.

23. Adjust the fork oil level as follows:
    a. Hold the fork assembly vertical and fully compress the fork tube.
    b. Use an accurate ruler or the Motion Pro oil gauge (part No. 08-0121) (**Figure 64**), or an equivalent, to achieve the oil level in **Table 2**.
    c. Allow the oil to settle completely and recheck the oil level measurement. Adjust the oil level if necessary.
    d. Remove the special tools including the extension.

24. Fully extend the fork tube.

25. Position the fork spring with the closer wound coils (**Figure 65**) going in first and install the fork spring.

26. Keep the fork assembly upright so the fork oil will not drain out and slightly compress the fork so the top of the damper rod is extended up through the top of the spring.

27. Install the lower end of the fork assembly in the fork holding tool following the manufacturer's instructions. Make sure the tool is indexed properly in the lower hole in the slider.

28. Install the special tool's upper bolt between the springs fourth and fifth coil. Make sure the tool is indexed properly between these two coils.

29. Slowly tighten the special tool and compress the fork assembly until the fork spring is below the locknut on the damper rod cartridge. If necessary, pull up on the damper rod cartridge.

30. Position the washer with the rounded side facing up and install it onto the top of the spring (**Figure 66**).

31. Position the spring seat with the concave side facing up and install it onto the washer.

32. If necessary, thread the locknut down until it contacts the shoulder on the damper rod cartridge.

33. Install a *new* O-ring seal on the fork cap plug and install the fork cap plug onto the damper rod cartridge. Screw it on until it bottoms.

34. Screw the locknut up against the fork cap plug. Tighten the locknut against the fork cap plug to the specification in **Table 1**.

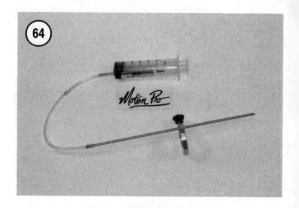

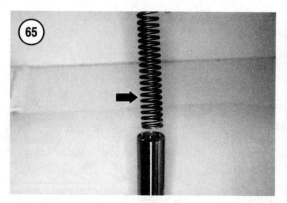

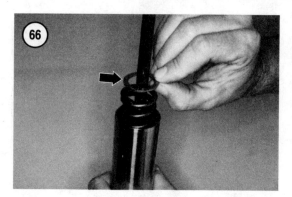

35. Slowly loosen the special tool making sure the spring is positioned correctly against the washer and spring seat. Disconnect the upper portion of the tool from the spring coils.

36. Remove the fork assembly from the special tool.

37. Pull the fork tube up against the fork cap plug and screw the fork cap plug into the fork tube and tighten securely. Do not try to tighten to the torque specification at this time.

38. Install the fork assemblies as described in this chapter and tighten the fork cap plug to the torque specification in **Table 1**.

STEERING STEM

1. Bolt
2. Steering stem nut
3. Locking plate
4. Roll pin
5. Upper fork bracket
6. Harness guide
7. Bearing adjuster
8. Dust shield
9. Upper roller bearing assembly
10. Lower roller bearing assembly
11. Dust shield
12. Steering stem/lower fork bracket
13. Washer

STEERING HEAD AND STEM

Removal

Refer to **Figure 67**.

1. On models so equipped, remove the front fairing as described in Chapter Fourteen.

2. Remove the fuel tank as described in Chapter Seven.

3. Remove the front fender and front wheel as described in Chapter Nine.

4. Remove both front fork legs as described in this chapter.

5. Remove the handlebar as described in this chapter.

6. Remove the passing lamp bracket assembly as described in Chapter Eight.

7. Remove the bolt securing the front brake hose assembly to the bottom of the lower fork bracket. Do not disconnect any brake hose connections.

8. Pry the tabs on the locking plate away from the steering stem nut.

9. Loosen and remove the steering stem nut.

10. Remove the upper fork bracket.

> *CAUTION*
> *Hold or secure the steering stem to keep it from falling after removal of the bearing adjuster in Step 11.*

11. Loosen and remove the bearing adjuster, then slide the steering stem out of the steering head.

12. Remove the upper dust shield and bearing.

13. Inspect the steering stem and bearing assembly as described under *Inspection* in this section.

Installation

1. If the steering head bearing races were replaced, make sure they are seated in the frame.

2. Wipe the bearing races with a clean lint-free cloth. Then lubricate each race with bearing grease.

3. Pack the upper and lower bearings with bearing grease.

4. If removed, install the lower bearing and lower dust shield on the steering stem as described in this chapter.

5. Insert the steering stem into the frame steering head and hold it firmly in place.

10

6. Install the upper bearing over the fork stem and seat it into to the upper race. Install the upper dust shield.

7. Install the bearing adjuster and tighten it to remove all bearing play within the steering head.

8. Install the upper fork bracket over the steering stem.

9. Install a new locking plate, then install the steering stem nut. Only tighten the nut hand-tight at this time.

10. Install the front fork legs as described in this chapter.

CAUTION
Do not overtighten the steering stem bolt in Step 11 or damage will occur to the bearings and races. Final adjustment of the fork stem will take place after the front wheel is installed.

11. Tighten the steering stem nut until the steering stem can be turned from side to side with no axial or lateral play. When the play feels correct, tighten the steering stem nut to the specification in **Table 1**.

12. Bend the tabs on the locking plate up against the flats on the steering stem nut.

13. Install the handlebar as described in this chapter.

14. Install the front brake hose assembly onto the bottom of the lower fork bracket. Tighten the bolt securely.

15. Install the passing lamp bracket assembly as described in Chapter Eight.

16. Install the front fender and front wheel as described in Chapter Nine.

17. Install the fuel tank as described in Chapter Seven.

18. Adjust the steering play as described under *Steering Play Adjustment* in this chapter.

19. On models so equipped, install the front fairing as described in Chapter Fourteen.

Inspection

The bearing outer races are pressed into the steering head. Do not remove them unless they are going to be replaced.

1. Wipe the bearing races with a solvent soaked rag and dry them with compressed air or a lint-free cloth. Check the races in the steering head for pitting, scratches, galling or excessive wear. If any of

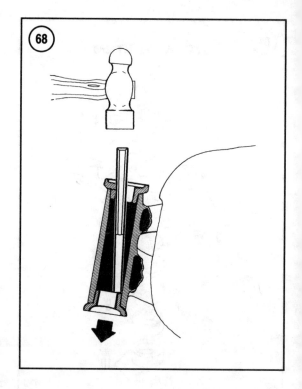

these conditions exist, replace the races as described in this chapter. If the races are in good condition, wipe each race with grease.

2. Clean the bearings in solvent to remove all of the old grease. Blow the bearing dry with compressed air, making sure not to allow the air jet to spin the bearing. Do not remove the lower bearing from the fork stem unless it is to be replaced. Clean the bearing while it is installed in the steering stem.

3. After the bearings are dry, hold the inner race with one hand and turn the outer race with the other hand. Turn the bearing slowly. The bearing should turn smoothly with no roughness. Visually check the bearing for pitting, scratches or visible damage. If the bearings are worn, check the dust covers for wear or damage, or for improper bearing lubrication. Replace the bearing if necessary. If a bearing is going to be reused, pack it with grease and wrap it with wax paper or some other lint-free material until it is reinstalled. Do not store the bearings for any length of time without lubricating them to prevent rust.

4. Check the steering stem for cracks or damage. Check the threads at the top of the stem for damage. Check the steering stem nut for damage. Thread it into the steering stem. Make sure the nut threads easily with no roughness.

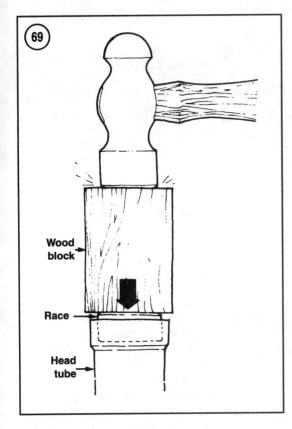

Wood block

Race

Head tube

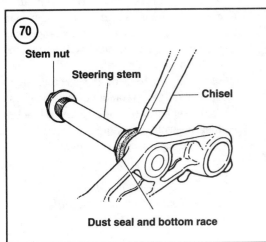

Stem nut

Steering stem

Chisel

Dust seal and bottom race

5. Replace all worn or damaged parts. Replace bearing races as described in this chapter.

6. Replace the lower steering stem bearing and the dust shield as described in this chapter.

7. Check for broken welds on the frame around the steering head. If any are found, have them repaired by a competent frame shop or welding service familiar with motorcycle frame repair.

STEERING HEAD BEARING RACE REPLACEMENT

The upper and lower bearing outer races are pressed into the frame. Do not remove the bearing races unless replacement is necessary. If they are removed, replace both the outer race and bearing at the same time. Never reinstall an outer race that has been removed as it is no longer true and will damage the bearing.

1. Remove the steering stem as described in this chapter.

2. To remove a race, insert an aluminum or brass rod into the steering head and carefully tap the race out from the inside (**Figure 68**). Tap all around the race so neither the race nor the steering head is bent.

3. Clean the steering head with solvent and dry it thoroughly.

4A. Install the bearing races with the steering head bearing race installer tool (JIMS part No. 1725) following the manufacturer's instructions.

4B. If the special tools are not available, install the bearing races as follows:

    a. Clean the race thoroughly before installing it.

    b. Align the upper race with the frame steering head and tap it slowly and squarely in place. Do not contact the bearing race surfaces. See **Figure 69**. Drive the race into the steering head until it bottoms on the bore shoulder.

    c. Repeat substeps a-b to install the lower race into the steering head.

5. Apply bearing grease to the face of each race.

Fork Stem Lower Bearing Replacement

Do not remove the steering stem lower bearing and seal unless they are going to be replaced. The lower bearing can be difficult to remove. If the lower bearing cannot be removed as described in this procedure, take the steering stem to a Harley-Davidson dealership.

Never reinstall a lower bearing that has been removed as it is no longer true and will damage the bearing assembly.

1. Install the steering stem bolt onto the top of the steering stem to protect the threads.

2. Remove the lower bearing from the shoulder at the base of the steering stem with a chisel as shown in **Figure 70**. Slide the lower bearing and grease seal off the steering stem.

10

3. Clean the steering stem with solvent and dry it thoroughly.

4. Position the new lower dust seal with the flange side facing up.

5. Slide a new grease seal and the lower bearing onto the steering stem until the bearing stops on the raised shoulder.

6. Align the lower bearing with the machined shoulder on the steering stem. Press or drive the lower bearing onto the steering stem until it bottoms (**Figure 71**).

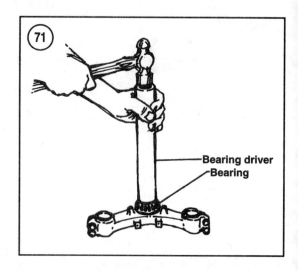

Bearing driver
Bearing

STEERING PLAY ADJUSTMENT

If aftermarket accessories have been installed on the steering assembly, they must be removed before attempting to adjust the steering play.

1. Use a floor jack centrally located under the frame. Support the motorcycle with both the front and rear wheels the same distance off the ground. If necessary, place a wooden block(s) under the rear wheel until the motorcycle is level.

2A. On FLHTC, FLHTCI and FLHTCUI models, remove the outer fairing (Chapter Fourteen) and radio (Chapter Eight). On FLHTC models, also remove the storage box.

2B. On FLHR, FLHRI and FLHRCI models, remove the headlight nacelle as described in Chapter Eight.

3A. On FLHTC, FLHTCI and FLHTCUI models, disconnect the clutch cable from the handlebar and fairing as described in Chapter Five.

3B. On FLHR, FLHRI and FLHRCI models, disconnect the clutch cable from the handlebar and passing lamp bracket.

4. Pry the tabs on the locking plate away from the steering stem nut.

5. Make sure the steering stem nut is tightened to the torque specification in **Table 1**. Tighten or loosen it if necessary.

NOTE
In Step 6, the components must be reinstalled to add their weight. It is not necessary to tighten all fasteners at this time as they will be removed again.

6A. On FLHTC, FLHTCI and FLHTCUI models, loosely install the outer fairing and radio. On FLHTC models, also install the storage box.

6B. On FLHR, FLHRI and FLHRCI models, loosely install the headlight nacelle.

7. Turn the front wheel full left and let go.

8. The front wheel should swing to the right, then to the left and stop. The wheel does not need to face straight ahead, but it should face slightly to the right from the straight-ahead position.

9. If the front wheel does not move as indicated, perform the following:

   a. On FLHTC, FLHTCI and FLHTCUI models, remove the outer fairing and radio. On FLHTC models, also remove the storage box.

   b. On FLHR, FLHRI and FLHRCI models, remove the headlight nacelle.

   c. Working at the base of the steering stem, loosen the pinch bolt on the fork assemblies.

   d. Slide the rubber fork stops up several inches on their respective fork tubes.

   e. Loosen the steering stem hex nut.

NOTE
Turning the bearing adjuster one notch will make a noticeable difference in the swing pattern.

   f. Working under the upper fork bracket, loosen the steering stem bearing adjuster with a drift or piece of drill rod. Tighten the bearing adjuster to decrease the front wheel swing pattern or loosen the bearing adjuster to increase the pattern.

   g. Tighten the steering stem hex nut to the specification in **Table 1**.

   h. Tighten the pinch bolt on both fork assemblies to the specification in **Table 1**.

i. Slide the rubber fork stop back down into position.

j. On FLHTC, FLHTCI and FLHTCUI models, loosely install the outer fairing and radio. On FLHTC models, also install the storage box.

k. On FLHR, FLHRI and FLHRCI models, loosely install the headlight nacelle.

l. Recheck the front wheel swing pattern, and readjust it if necessary.

10. On FLHTC, FLHTCI and FLHTCUI models, remove the outer fairing and radio. On FLHTC models, also remove the storage box.

11. On FLHR, FLHRI and FLHRCI models, remove the headlight nacelle.

12. Make sure the steering stem nut is tightened to the torque specification in **Table 1**. Tighten it if necessary.

13. Bend the tabs on the locking plate up against the flats on the steering stem nut.

14A. On FLHTC, FLHTCI and FLHTCUI models, install the outer fairing and radio. On FLHTC models, also install the storage box.

14B. On FLHR, FLHRI and FLHRCI models, install the headlight nacelle.

15. Lower the motorcycle to the ground.

10

Table 1 FRONT SUSPENSION TORQUE SPECIFICATIONS

Item	ft.-lb.	in.-lb.	N•m
Front fork (non-cartridge type)			
Drain plug	–	72-96	8-11
Air tube assembly hex bolt	8-12	–	11-16
Fork cap bolt	50-55	–	68-75
Fork cap plug	22-58	–	30-79
Front fork (cartridge type)			
Allen bolt	11-18	–	15-24
Fork cap bolt	50-55	–	68-75
Fork plug	22-58	–	30-79
Damper rod cartridge locknut	13-20	–	18-27
Fork bracket pinch bolts	40	–	54
Steering stem nut	50-65	–	68-88
Brake hose bracket bolt	–	132	15
Front fender bolts	14-18	–	19-24

Table 2 FRONT FORK OIL CAPACITY/OIL LEVEL

Model	Capacity/level (each fork leg)
Fork oil capacity	
Non-cartridge type	
1999-2001 models	9.7 U.S. oz. (287 ml, 8.08 Imp. oz.)
2002-2005 models	11.1 U.S. oz. (328 ml, 9.24 Imp. oz.)
Cartridge type	11.1 U.S. oz. (328 ml, 9.24 Imp. oz.)[1]
Fork oil level (cartridge type)	
2002 models	4.4 in. (111.8 mm)[2]
2003-2005 models	4.21 in. (107 mm)[2]

1. The fork oil capacity is approximately this amount. The fork oil level must be at the specified level.
2. From the top surface of the fork tube

Table 3 AIR SUSPENSION ADJUSTMENTS (1999-2001 MODELS)

Load	Recommended pressure PSI (kPa)	
	Front fork*	Rear shock absorbers
Rider weight		
Up to 150 lbs (68 kg) add:	–	–
For each additional		
25 lbs (11 kg)	1.0 (7)	1.0 (7)
Passenger weight for each		
additional 50 lbs (23 kg)	–	1.5 (10)
Luggage weight for each		
additional 10 lbs (6 kg)	1.0 (7)	3.0 (21)
Maximum pressure	25 (172)	25 (172)

*The front fork on 2002 models is not equipped with air suspension.

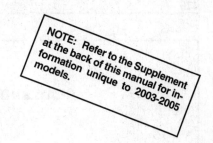

NOTE: Refer to the Supplement at the back of this manual for information unique to 2003-2005 models.

REAR SUSPENSION

This chapter includes repair and replacement procedures for the rear suspension components. **Table 1** and **Table 2** are located at the end of this chapter.

> *WARNING*
> *All nuts and bolts used on the rear suspension must be replaced with parts of the same type. Do not use a replacement part of lesser quality or substitute design. It may affect the performance of the rear suspension or fail, leading to loss of control of the motorcycle. Use the torque specifications in* **Table 1** *during installation to ensure proper retention of these components.*

SHOCK ABSORBERS

All models are equipped with an air-adjustable suspension. The amount of air pressure in the rear shock absorbers can be varied to suit personal comfort. The lower the air pressure, the softer the ride. The higher the air pressure, the firmer the ride. The front fork on 1999-2001 models is also air assisted and both systems must work in unison to provide the best possible ride and control. Refer to **Table 2** for the recommended air pressure for both the front fork and the rear shock absorbers.

Removal/Installation

Refer to **Figure 1**.

When servicing the rear shocks, remove one shock at a time. If it is necessary to remove both shocks, support the motorcycle with the rear wheel off the ground on a suitable floor jack.

1. Support the motorcycle with the rear wheel off the ground. See *Motorcycle Stands* in Chapter Nine.

2. Place wooden blocks under the rear wheel to place the rear wheel in a neutral position with no strain on the shock absorber mounting hardware.

①

REAR SHOCK ABSORBERS AND AIR LINES

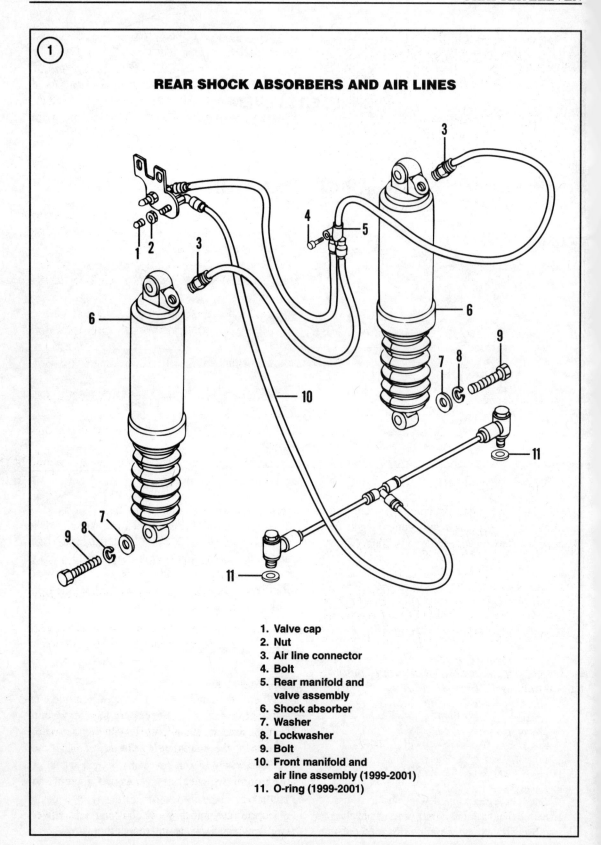

1. Valve cap
2. Nut
3. Air line connector
4. Bolt
5. Rear manifold and
   valve assembly
6. Shock absorber
7. Washer
8. Lockwasher
9. Bolt
10. Front manifold and
    air line assembly (1999-2001)
11. O-ring (1999-2001)

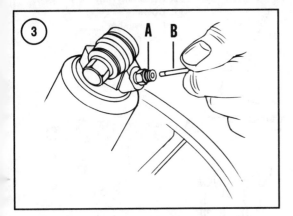

3. Remove the saddlebag(s) as described in Chapter Fourteen.

WARNING
Be careful when releasing the air from the shock absorber air valve. Moisture may spurt out when the air pressure is released. Protect eyes accordingly.

4. Cover the rear brake assembly and wheel prior to releasing the shock absorber air valve. If necessary,

wipe up oil residue that may have been ejected from the air valve.

5. Remove the cap from the rear shock absorber air valve (**Figure 2**), then slowly depress the air valve to release the air from the front fork air pipe system. Unscrew and remove the core from the air valve. Place the air valve core and cap in a reclosable plastic bag to avoid misplacing them.

6. Depress the collar (A, **Figure 3**) on the fitting with your thumb and carefully pull the air hose (B) from the fitting.

7. Loosen both the upper (A, **Figure 4**) and lower (B) mounting bolts securing the shock absorber to the frame and to the swing arm.

8. Remove the lower bolt, lockwasher and washer (B, **Figure 4**) securing the shock absorber to the swing arm.

9. Remove the upper bolt, lockwasher and washer (A, **Figure 4**) securing the shock absorber to the frame.

10. Remove the shock absorber from the motorcycle.

11. Repeat Steps 6-10 for the other shock absorber if necessary.

12. Inspect the shock absorber as described in this chapter.

13. Install the shocks by reversing these removal steps. Note the following:

    a. Apply a few drops of ThreeBond TB1342, or an equivalent, to the shock mounting bolt threads.

    b. Install the washers, the lockwashers and bolts, and tighten the bolts to the specification in **Table 1**.

    c. Adjust the shock absorbers air pressure as described in this chapter.

    d. Lower the motorcycle and test ride it to make sure the rear suspension is working properly.

Inspection

There are no shock replacement parts available for these models. If any part requires replacement, other than the mounting hardware, replace the shock assembly.

1. Remove the shock absorber as described in this chapter.

2. Inspect the upper shock bushing and lower shock bushing for wear and deterioration.

11

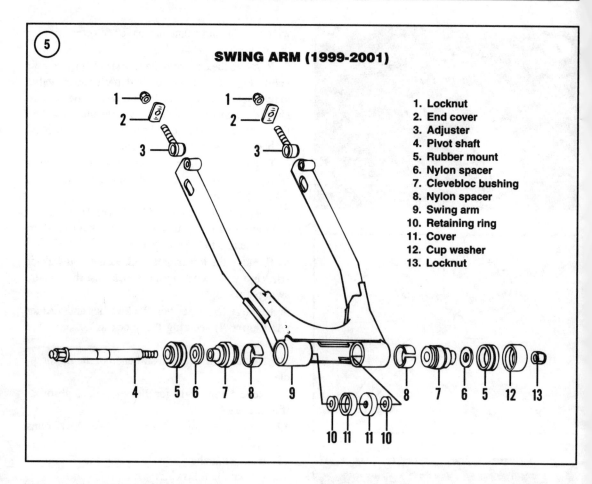

SWING ARM (1999-2001)

1. Locknut
2. End cover
3. Adjuster
4. Pivot shaft
5. Rubber mount
6. Nylon spacer
7. Clevebloc bushing
8. Nylon spacer
9. Swing arm
10. Retaining ring
11. Cover
12. Cup washer
13. Locknut

3. Inspect the shock absorber. If the rubber boot portion is cracked or deteriorated, replace the shock absorber.

SHOCK AIR PRESSURE ADJUSTMENT

WARNING
Be careful when releasing the air from the rear shock absorber and the front fork air valve (1999-2001 models). Moisture and/or fork oil may spurt out when the air pressure is released. Protect eyes accordingly.

NOTE
The air chambers in the rear shock are small and fill rapidly. Do not use compressed air. Only use a small hand-held or foot-operated air pump.

1. Place the motorcycle on the jiffy stand.

2. Remove the right side saddlebag as described in Chapter Fourteen.

3. Remove the rear shock absorber air valve cap (**Figure 2**).

4. Use a no-loss air gauge to check air pressure. Refer to the recommended air pressure in **Table 2**.

5. Increase or decrease air pressure to achieve the desired ride and control.

6. At the same time, check and adjust, if necessary, the air pressure in the front fork.

7. Install the air valve cap(s) and the saddlebag.

REAR SWING ARM (1999-2001 MODELS)

Refer to **Figure 5**.

Rear Swing Arm Bearing Check

The swing arm clevebloc bushings wear over time and require replacement. Worn or damaged

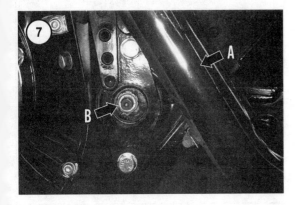

clevebloc bushings can produce erratic and dangerous handling. Common symptoms are wheel hop,
pulling to one side during acceleration and pulling
to the other side during braking.

1. Remove the rear wheel (A, **Figure 6**) as described in Chapter Nine.

2. Remove the bolt, lockwasher and washer securing both shock absorbers (B, **Figure 6**) to the swing
arm. Move them up away from the swing arm.

3. Make sure the swing arm pivot shaft nut is tight.

4. Have an assistant hold the motorcycle securely.

5. Grasp the back of the swing arm and try to move
it from side to side. Any play between the swing
arm and the frame, or the swing arm and transmission, may indicate worn or damaged swing arm
clevebloc bushings. If there is any play, remove the
swing arm and inspect the clevebloc bushing assemblies.

6. Install all components removed.

Removal

1. Remove both saddlebags as described in Chapter Fourteen.

2. Remove the exhaust system (A, **Figure 7**) as described in Chapter Seven.

3. Place wooden blocks or a floor jack under the
transmission and engine assembly to support it after
the swing arm pivot shaft is removed.

4. Remove the rear wheel as described in Chapter
Nine.

5. Remove the chrome trim caps from both frame
brackets.

6. Remove both passenger footboards as described
in Chapter Fourteen.

7. On the right side, place a 11/16 in. socket onto
the pivot shaft to keep it from rotating in the following step.

8. On the left side, use a 3/4 in socket to loosen the
locknut (B, **Figure 7**). Remove the locknut and the
cup washer from the pivot shaft.

9. Support the swing arm and tap on the left side of
the pivot shaft with a drift. Drive the pivot shaft out
through the right side and remove it.

10. Remove the rubber mount and nylon spacer
from the pivot area on each side of the frame.

11. Remove the swing arm from the frame and
transmission case.

12. Clean and lubricate the swing arm assembly as
described in the following procedure.

13. Temporarily install the pivot shaft.

Inspection

1. Wash the exterior of the swing arm in solvent
and thoroughly dry it with compressed air.

2. Inspect the welded sections on the swing arm for
cracks or fractures.

3. Inspect the rubber mounts removed in Step 10 of
Removal. Replace the mounts as a pair if either one
is starting to deteriorate or harden.

4. Inspect the pivot shaft for surface cracks, deep
scoring, wear or heat distortion. Replace it if necessary.

5. The clevebloc bushings are filled with silicone.
Replace the bushings as a pair if either is leaking or
damaged.

11

Clevebloc Bushing Replacement
(With Harley-Davidson Special Tool
and Hydraulic Press)

Replacement of the clevebloc requires the Harley-Davidson Swing Arm Assembly tool (part No. HD-96200-80).

1. Remove the rubber mounts and nylon washers from the outside surface on each side of the swing arms pivot point if they are still in place.

2. Pry out the cover and retaining ring from the inside surface on each side of the swing arm.

CAUTION
Do not apply pressure against the swing arm without supporting the lower pivot point as described in Step 3. If it is not properly supported, the swing arm will become distorted and require replacement.

3. Support the swing arm on the press bed with both pivots aligned with the press ram. Place the support block (**Figure 8**) under the lower pivot.

4. Install a long extension and the press collar adapter, or 1 1/4 in. socket, onto the swing arm and onto the outside diameter of the clevebloc (**Figure 8**).

5. Support the swing arm and slowly press out the clevebloc bushing from the lower pivot.

6. Remove the swing arm from the press. Repeat Steps 3-5 to remove the clevebloc bushing from the opposite side of the swing arm.

7. Thoroughly clean the pivot areas with solvent and dry them with compressed air.

8. Inspect the pivot areas for burrs or other internal damage. Clean them out if necessary.

9. Install the new nylon spacer onto the new clevebloc bushing. These two parts are installed at the same time.

10. Support the swing arm on the press bed with both pivots aligned with the press ram.

11. Center the clevebloc bushing on the swing arm pivot and start it in by hand.

12. Place the press plug onto the outside diameter of the clevebloc bushing.

13. Support the swing arm and slowly press the clevebloc bushing into the pivot (**Figure 9**).

14. Press the clevebloc bushing into the swing arm until the outer diameter shoulder is flush with the swing arm outer surface (**Figure 10**).

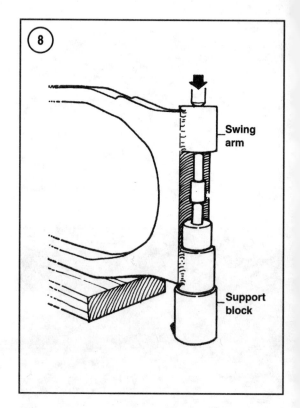

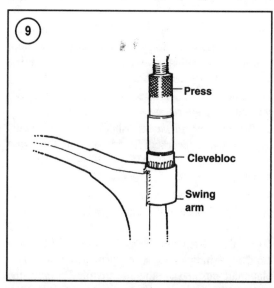

15. Remove the swing arm from the press and repeat Steps 9-14 to install the clevebloc bushing into the opposite side of the swing arm.

16. Install a new cover and retaining ring onto the inside surface of the swing arm pivots.

17. Install the nylon washer and the rubber mounts onto the outside surface of the swing arm pivots.

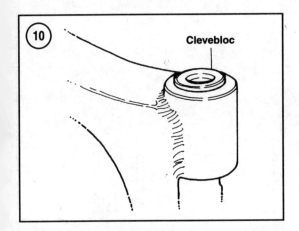

Clevebloc

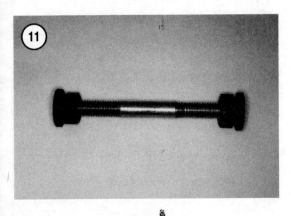

Clevebloc Bushing Replacement (With JIMS Special Tools— No Hydraulic Press Required)

Replacement of the clevebloc requires the use of clevebloc bushing assembly rear swing arm assembly tool (JIMS part No. 1743) (**Figure 11**). This special tool does not require the use of a hydraulic press.

1. Remove the rubber mounts and nylon washers from the outside surface on each side of the swing arm if they are still in place.

2. Pry out the cover and retaining ring from the inside surface of the swing arm pivot.

3. Install the tool assembly onto the swing arm following the manufacturer's instructions.

4. Remove the clevebloc bushing from each side of the swing arm.

5. Thoroughly clean the pivot areas with solvent and dry them with compressed air.

6. Inspect the pivot areas for burrs or other internal damage. Clean them out if necessary.

7. Install the new nylon spacer onto the new clevebloc bushing. These two parts are installed at the same time.

8. Install the tool assembly onto the swing arm following the manufacturer's instructions.

9. Install the clevebloc bushing into each side of the swing arm until the outer diameter shoulder is flush with the swing arm outer surface (**Figure 10**).

10. Install a new cover and retaining ring onto the inside surface of the swing arm pivots.

11. Install the nylon washer and the rubber mounts onto the outside surface of the swing arm pivots.

Rear Swing Arm Installation

Refer to **Figure 12**.

1. Withdraw the pivot shaft and lubricate it with Loctite antiseize, or an appropriate grease.

2. Position the swing arm on the pivot area of the transmission case.

3. If the swing arm will not fit onto the transmission case, slightly spread the clevebloc bushings apart as follows:

   a. Remove the swing arm from the transmission case.

   b. Install the clevebloc spreading tool (JIMS part No. 1707) onto the swing arm following the manufacturer's instructions as shown in **Figure 13**.

   c. Slowly tighten the nuts and press the clevebloc bushings into the swing arm until there is approximately 4.56 in. (115.9 mm) clearance between them.

   d. Remove the special tool and check the swing arm fit into the transmission case.

   e. If necessary, repeat this step until the swing arm fits correctly into the transmission case.

4. Position the swing arm on the pivot area of the transmission case and support it in this position.

5. Install the following parts onto the pivot shaft.

   a. Position the right side rubber mount with the smaller diameter boss facing outward. Slide the rubber mount onto the pivot shaft and rotate it so the pinhole is at the top. This must align with the pin located on the passenger footboard bracket.

11

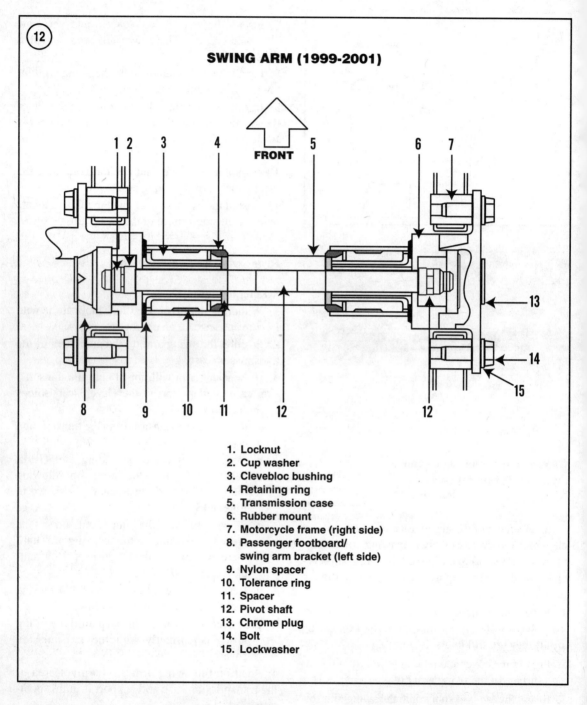

SWING ARM (1999-2001)

FRONT

1. Locknut
2. Cup washer
3. Clevebloc bushing
4. Retaining ring
5. Transmission case
6. Rubber mount
7. Motorcycle frame (right side)
8. Passenger footboard/
   swing arm bracket (left side)
9. Nylon spacer
10. Tolerance ring
11. Spacer
12. Pivot shaft
13. Chrome plug
14. Bolt
15. Lockwasher

b. Position the nylon spacer with the smaller diameter end facing inside toward the swing arm and slide it into place against the rubber mount.

NOTE
It may be necessary to slightly reposition the swing arm to accept the pivot

shaft. Also, it may be necessary to adjust the jack under the transmission and engine assembly.

6. Make sure the pivot shaft holes in both sides of the frame, the swing arm and the transmission case are correctly aligned prior to inserting the pivot shaft. Insert a long drift punch into one side of the

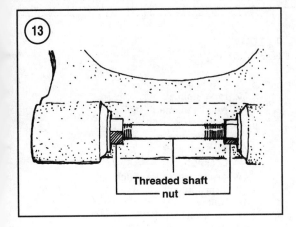

13

Threaded shaft
nut

frame to align the parts on that side. Insert another drift punch into the other side and align those parts. Remove both drift punches.

7. From the right side, insert the pivot shaft assembly into the frame and transmission case. Push the pivot shaft in until it bottoms. Make sure the pinhole in the rubber mount is located at the top. Reposition it if necessary.

8. On the left side of the pivot shaft:

    a. Position the nylon spacer with the smaller diameter end facing inside toward the swing arm and slide it into place against the swing arm.

    b. Position the left side rubber mount with the smaller diameter boss facing outward. Slide the rubber mount onto the pivot shaft and rotate it so the pinhole is at the top. This pinhole must align with the pin located on the passenger footboard bracket.

    c. Install the cup washer and locknut onto the pivot shaft.

9. Install the passenger footboards as described in Chapter Fourteen.

10. On the right side, place a 11/16 in. socket onto the pivot shaft to keep it from rotating in the following step.

11. On the left side, use a 3/4 in. socket to tighten the locknut (B, **Figure 7**) to the specification in **Table 1**.

12. Install the chrome trim caps onto both frame brackets. Press them on until they bottom.

13. Install the rear wheel as described in Chapter Nine.

14. Remove the wooden blocks or floor jack from under the transmission and engine assembly.

15. Have an assistant sit on the seat. Push down on the rear to make sure the swing arm is moving freely with no interference.

16. Install the exhaust system as described in Chapter Seven.

17. Install both saddlebags as described in Chapter Fourteen.

REAR SWING ARM
(2002 MODELS)

Refer to **Figure 14**.

Rear Swing Arm Bearing Check

The swing arm needle bearings wear over time and require replacement. Worn or damaged needle bearings can produce erratic and dangerous handling. Common symptoms are wheel hop, pulling to one side during acceleration and pulling to the other side during braking.

1. Remove the rear wheel (A, **Figure 6**) as described in Chapter Nine.

2. Remove the bolt, lockwasher and washer securing both shock absorbers (B, **Figure 6**) to the swing arm. Move them up away from the swing arm.

3. Make sure both nuts on the swing arm pivot shaft are tight.

4. Have an assistant hold the motorcycle securely.

5. Grasp the back of the swing arm and try to move it from side to side. Any play between the swing arm and the frame, or the swing and transmission, may indicate worn or damaged swing arm needle bearings. If there is any play, remove the swing arm and inspect the needle bearing assemblies.

6. Install all components removed.

Removal

1. Remove both saddlebags as described in Chapter Fourteen.

2. Remove both passenger footboards as described in Chapter Fourteen.

3. Remove the exhaust system (A, **Figure 7**) as described in Chapter Seven.

4. Remove the bolts securing the drive belt guard and remove the guard.

5. Place wooden blocks or a floor jack under the transmission and engine assembly to support it after the swing arm pivot shaft is removed.

11

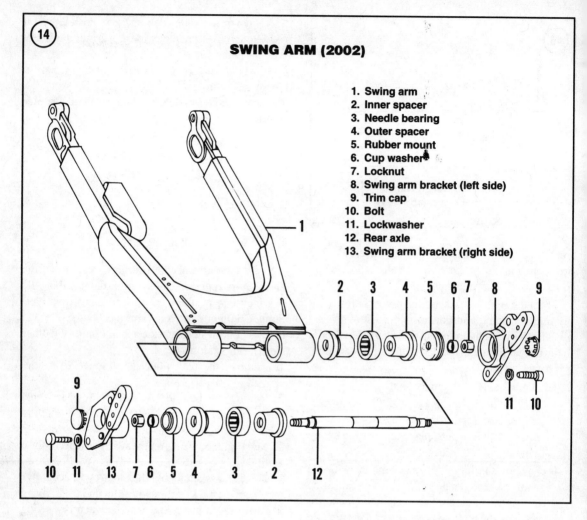

SWING ARM (2002)

1. Swing arm
2. Inner spacer
3. Needle bearing
4. Outer spacer
5. Rubber mount
6. Cup washer
7. Locknut
8. Swing arm bracket (left side)
9. Trim cap
10. Bolt
11. Lockwasher
12. Rear axle
13. Swing arm bracket (right side)

6. Remove the rear wheel (A, **Figure 6**) as described in Chapter Nine.

7. Unhook the rear brake caliper hose from the clips on the right side of the swing arm.

8. Remove the bolt, lockwasher and washer securing both shock absorbers (B, **Figure 6**) to the swing arm. Move them up away from the swing arm.

9. Remove the chrome trim caps from both swing arm brackets.

10. On the left side, remove the two bolts and lock washers securing the left swing arm bracket. Pull straight out and remove the bracket.

11. On the left side, secure the nut on the pivot shaft to keep it from rotating in the following step.

12. On the right side, loosen and remove the locknut and cup washer.

13. Support the swing arm and tap on the right side of the pivot shaft with a drift. Drive the pivot shaft out through the left side.

14. Remove the pivot shaft assembly (pivot shaft, locknut, cup washer, rubber mount and outer spacer) from the frame and transmission case.

15. Remove the swing arm from the frame and transmission case.

16. Remove the outer spacer from the right side of the swing arm pivot point.

17. Remove the rubber mount from behind the right side swing arm bracket.

18. Inspect the swing arm as described in this chapter.

Inspection

1. Wash the exterior of the swing arm in solvent and thoroughly dry it with compressed air.

2. Inspect the welded sections on the swing arm for cracks or fractures.

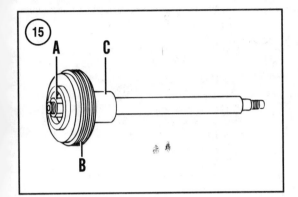

15

A   C

B

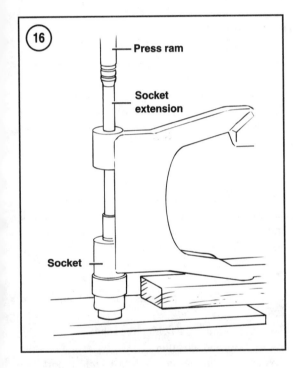

16

Press ram

Socket
extension

Socket

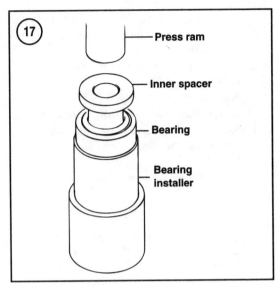

17

Press ram

Inner spacer

Bearing

Bearing
installer

Needle Bearing and Inner Spacer Replacement

Remove and install the needle bearings only if the bearings must be replaced. Never install a needle bearing that has been removed. Both the needle bearings and the inner spacers must be replaced as set.

A hydraulic press and several H-D special tools are required for bearing and inner spacer replacement.

1. Place the swing arm on the press bed so the left side faces down (**Figure 16**). Place a wooden block on the press bed to protect the swing arm finish.

2. Place a socket with an inner diameter larger than the needle bearing under the left side pivot point.

3. Place a long socket extension with another socket that matches the outer diameter of the needle bearing down through the right side pivot point and place it on the needle left side bearing.

4. Make sure the swing arm pivot areas are square with the press bed.

5. Hold the swing arm vertical and square, then slowly apply press pressure on the long extension and drive the needle bearing and inner spacer out of the left side pivot bore.

6. Release the pressure and remove the tools from the swing arm.

7. Turn the swing arm over, repeat Steps 1-6 and remove the remaining needle bearing.

8. Clean out the swing arm bearing bores with solvent and dry with compressed air.

9. Refer to **Figure 17** and install the inner spacer into the new needle bearing as follows:

3. Inspect the right side rubber mount and the left side rubber mount on the pivot shaft. If the left side replacement is necessary, hold onto the pivot shaft. Remove the locknut (A, **Figure 15**), the rubber mount (B) and inner spacer (C) from the pivot shaft. Replace the rubber mounts as a pair if either one is starting to deteriorate or harden.

4. Inspect the pivot shaft for surface cracks, deep scoring, wear or heat distortion. Replace if necessary.

5. Turn the needle bearings with a finger. The bearing should turn smoothly with no sign of roughness or damage. If necessary, replace the needle bearings as described in the following procedure. Replace the needle bearings as a pair if either is damaged.

11

a. Place one of the bearing installers (H-D part No. 45327) on the press bed with the nose of the installer facing up.

b. Place the new needle bearing onto the bearing installer.

c. Position the inner collar with the flange side facing up and place it onto the needle bearing.

d. Slowly apply pressure and press the inner spacer into the needle bearing until it bottoms.

e. Repeat for the other needle bearing and inner spacer.

NOTE
There are two H-D bearing installers, one for the right side (Brake Side) and one for the left side (Drive Side). The longer installer is to be used on the left side.

10. Place the swing arm on the press bed so the right side faces up (**Figure 18**). Place a wooden block on the press bed to protect the swing arm finish.

11. Make sure the swing arm pivot areas are square with the press bed.

12. Place the needle bearing and inner spacer onto the right side bearing bore. Place the *Brake Side* installer onto the bearing and inner spacer.

13. Make sure the swing arm pivot areas are square with the press bed.

14. Hold the swing arm so it is vertical and square, then slowly apply press pressure on the installer, and drive the needle bearing and inner spacer into the right side pivot bore. Press the bearing into the swing arm until the shoulder on the installer tool makes contact with the swing arm.

15. Release the pressure and remove the installer from the swing arm.

CAUTION
*The Drive Side installer shoulder **will not** make contact with the swing arm on the left side. In Step 16, only press the needle bearing into the pivot bore until the bearing bottoms—do not press it in until the installer shoulder contacts the swing arm as the swing arm will be damaged.*

16. Turn the swing arm over, repeat Steps 10-15 and install the remaining needle bearing and inner spacer into the left side of the swing arm. Use the

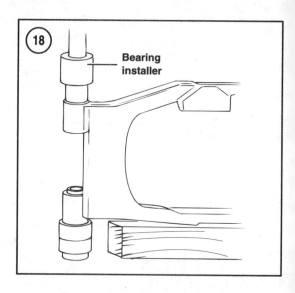

18   Bearing installer

Drive Side installer to install the left side bearing and inner collar. Press the bearing and inner collar into the swing arm until the bearing bottoms.

Installation

1. On the right side, position the pin hole in the rubber mount at the 11 o'clock position and install it into the backside of the swing arm bracket. Make sure the pin on the inboard side of the bracket engages the pin hole in the rubber mount. Reposition if necessary.

2. Install the outer spacer into the right side of the swing arm pivot point

3. Position the drive belt on the inboard side of the swing arm and position the swing arm onto the pivot area of the transmission case and support it in this position. If necessary, use a soft faced mallet and tap the swing arm into position.

4. Install the pivot shaft as follows:

   a. Coat the pivot shaft with Loctite antiseize, or an appropriate type of grease.

   b. From the left side, install the pivot shaft assembly (pivot shaft, locknut, cup washer, rubber mount and outer spacer) through the left side of the frame and the swing arm. Guide the pivot shaft through the holes in the right side rubber mount and the frame.

   c. On the right side, position the cup washer with the concave side going in first and install it onto the pivot shaft.

   d. Install the locknut onto the pivot shaft.

e. Secure the left side locknut and tighten the right side locknut to the specification in **Table 1**.

f. Secure the right side locknut and tighten the left side locknut to the specification in **Table 1**.

5. Slowly raise and lower the swing arm to ensure ease of movement. If binding occurs, repeat Step 4 and correct the problem.

6. On the left side, position the pin hole in the rubber mount at the 11 o'clock position.

7. Install the left swing arm bracket and fit the pin into the rubber mount hole. Reposition the rubber mount if necessary to ensure correct alignment.

8. Install the two bolts and lockwashers securing the left swing arm bracket. Tighten the bolts to the specification in **Table 1**.

9. Install the chrome trim caps on both swing arm brackets.

10. Move the shock absorbers into position and install the bolt, lockwasher and washer securing both shock absorbers (B, **Figure 6**) to the swing arm. Tighten the bolts to the specification in **Table 1**.

11. Position the rear brake caliper hose into the clips on the right side of the swing arm.

12. Install the rear wheel (A, **Figure 6**) as described in Chapter Nine.

13. Remove the wooden blocks or floor jack from under the transmission and engine assembly.

14. Install the drive belt guard and tighten the bolts securely.

15. Install the exhaust system (A, **Figure 7**) as described in Chapter Seven.

16. Install both passenger footboards as described in Chapter Fourteen.

17. Install both saddlebags as described in Chapter Fourteen.

Table 1 REAR SUSPENSION TORQUE SPECIFICATIONS

Item	ft.-lb.	in.-lb.	N•m
Passenger footboard			
bracket bolts	34-42	–	45-57
Shock absorber			
Upper bolt	33-35	–	45-47
Lower bolt	35-40	–	47-54
Swing arm			
1999-2001			
Pivot shaft locknut	40-45	–	54-61
2002			
Pivot shaft locknuts	40-45	–	54-61
Swing arm bracket bolt (left side)	34-42	–	46-57

Table 2 AIR SUSPENSION ADJUSTMENTS

Load	Recommended pressure PSI (kPa)	
	Front fork	Rear shock absorbers
Rider weight		
Up to 150 lbs (68 kg) add:	–	–
For each additional		
25 lbs (11kg)	1.0 (7)	1.0 (7)
Passenger weight for each		
Additional 50 lbs (23 kg)	–	1.5 (10)
Luggage weight for each		
Additional 10 lbs (6 kg)	1.0 (7)	3.0 (21)
Maximum pressure	25 (172)	25 (172)

11

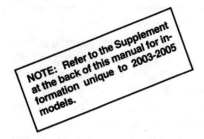

NOTE: Refer to the Supplement at the back of this manual for information unique to 2003-2005 models.

CHAPTER TWELVE

BRAKES

This chapter includes repair and replacement procedures for all brake system components.

Refer to **Table 1** and **Table 2** located at the end of this chapter for brake system specifications.

BRAKE SERVICE

> *WARNING*
> *Do not use brake fluid labeled **DOT 5.1**. This is a glycol based fluid that is **not compatible** with silicone based DOT 5. DOT 5 brake fluid is purple while DOT 5.1 is amber/clear. Do not intermix these two different types of brake fluid. It will lead to brake component damage and possible brake failure.*

> *WARNING*
> *Do not intermix DOT 3, DOT 4, or DOT 5.1 brake fluids as they are not silicone-based. Using non-silicone brake fluid in these models can cause brake failure.*

> *WARNING*
> *When working on the brake system, do **not** inhale brake dust. It may con-*

*tain asbestos, which is a know carcinogen. Do **not** use compressed air to blow off brake dust. Use an aerosol brake cleaner. Wear a facemask and wash thoroughly after completing the work.*

The disc brake system transmits hydraulic pressure from the master cylinders to the brake calipers. This pressure is transmitted from the caliper(s) to the brake pads, which grip both sides of the brake disc(s) and slow the motorcycle. As the pads wear, the pistons move out of the caliper bores to automatically compensate for wear. As this occurs, the fluid level in the master cylinder reservoir goes down. Compensate for this by occasionally adding fluid.

The proper operation of this system depends on a supply of clean brake fluid (DOT 5) and a clean work environment when any service is being performed. Any particle of debris that enters the system can damage the components and cause poor brake performance.

Brake fluid is hygroscopic (easily absorbs moisture) and moisture in the system reduces brake performance. Purchase brake fluid in small containers and properly discard small quantities that remain.

Small quantities of fluid will quickly absorb the moisture in the container. Only use fluid clearly marked DOT 5. If possible, use the same brand of fluid. Do not replace the fluid with a non-silicone fluid. It is not possible to remove all of the old fluid. Other types are not compatible with DOT 5. Do not reuse drained fluid. Discard old fluid properly. Do not combine brake fluid with fluids for recycling.

When adding fluid, punch a small hole into the edge of the fluid container's seal to help control the fluid flow. This is especially important to prevent spills while adding fluid to the small reservoirs.

Perform service procedures carefully. Do not use sharp tools inside the master cylinders or calipers or on the pistons. Damage to these components could cause a loss in the system's ability to maintain hydraulic pressure. If there is any doubt about the ability to correctly and safely service the brake system, have a professional technician perform the task.

Consider the following when servicing the brake system:

1. The hydraulic components rarely require disassembly. Make sure disassembly is necessary.

2. Keep the reservoir covers in place to prevent the entry of moisture and debris.

3. Clean parts with an aerosol brake part cleaner or isopropyl alcohol. Never use petroleum-based solvents on internal brake system components. They will cause seals to swell and distort.

4. Do not allow brake fluid to contact plastic, painted or plated parts. It will damage the surface.

5. Dispose of brake fluid properly.

6. If the hydraulic system, not including the reservoir cover, has been opened bleed the system to remove air from the system. Refer to *Bleeding the System* in this chapter.

7. The manufacturer does not provide wear limit specifications for the caliper and master cylinder assemblies. Use good judgment when inspecting these components or consult a professional technician for advice.

FRONT BRAKE PAD REPLACEMENT (1999 MODELS)

There is no recommended mileage interval for changing the friction pads in the disc brakes. Pad wear depends on riding habits and conditions. Frequently check the brake pads for wear. Increase the inspection interval when the wear indicator reaches the edge of the brake disc. After removal, measure the thickness of each brake pad with a vernier caliper or ruler, and compare measurements to the dimensions in **Table 1**.

Always replace both pads in the caliper at the same time to maintain even brake pressure on the disc. Also, replace both brake pads in *both calipers* at the same time. Do not disconnect the hydraulic brake hose from the brake caliper for brake pad replacement. Only disconnect the hose if the caliper assembly is going to be removed.

CAUTION
Check the pads more frequently when the lining approaches the pad metal backing plate. If pad wear is uneven for some reason, the backing plate may come in contact with the disc and cause damage.

1. Read the information under *Brake Service* in this chapter.
2. Park the motorcycle on a level surface.
3. To prevent the front brake lever from being applied, place a spacer between the brake lever and the throttle grip and secure it in place. Then if the brake lever is inadvertently squeezed, the piston will not be forced out of the cylinder.
4. Loosen the brake caliper upper mounting bolt (A, **Figure 1**) and the lower mounting pin (B). Remove the upper mounting bolt, washer and the lower mounting pin.
5. Slide the brake caliper off the brake disc.

NOTE
If the brake pads are going to be reused, mark them so they can be reinstalled into their original locations.

12

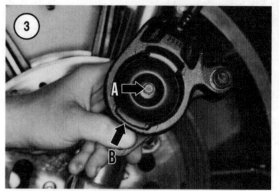

6. Remove the outboard pad, pad holder and spring clip as an assembly (**Figure 2**).

7. Remove the bolt (A, **Figure 3**) and the pad retainer (B) securing the inner pad to the caliper.

8. Remove the inboard pad (**Figure 4**).

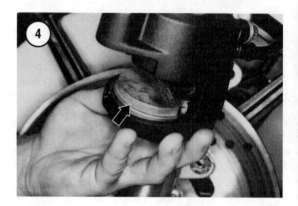

9. Push the outboard pad (A, **Figure 5**) free of the spring clip (B) and remove it.

10. Check the brake pads (**Figure 6**) for wear or damage. Measure the thickness of the brake pad friction material (**Figure 7**). Replace the brake pads if they are worn to the service limit in **Table 1**. Replace the pad sets in both calipers at the same time.

11. Check the friction surface of the new pads for any debris or manufacturing residue. If necessary, clean them off with an aerosol brake cleaner.

> *NOTE*
> *When purchasing new pads, check with the dealership to make sure the friction compound of the new pad is compatible with the disc material. Remove roughness from the backs of the new pads with a fine-cut file, then thoroughly clean them off with brake cleaner.*

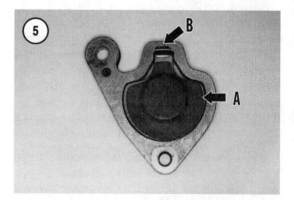

12. Inspect the upper mounting bolt and the lower mounting pin. Replace them if they are damaged or badly corroded.

13. Replace the pad retainer (**Figure 8**) if it is damaged.

14. Check the piston dust boot (**Figure 9**) in the caliper. Remove and overhaul the caliper if the boot is swollen or damaged, or if brake fluid is leaking from the caliper. Refer to *Front Brake Caliper (1999 Models)* in this chapter.

15. Remove all corrosion from the pad holder.

16. Replace the spring clip if it is damaged or badly corroded.

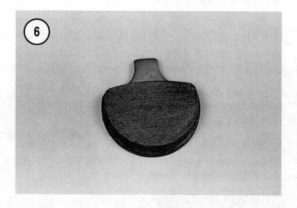

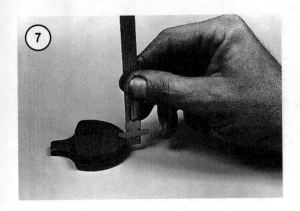

17. Check the brake disc for wear as described under *Brake Disc* in this chapter. Service the brake disc if necessary.

18. Assemble the pad holder, spring clip and outboard brake pad as follows:

    a. Lay the pad holder on a workbench so the upper mounting bolt hole is positioned at the upper right as shown in A, **Figure 10**.

    b. Install the spring clip (B, **Figure 10**) at the top of the pad holder so the spring loop faces in the direction shown in **Figure 11**.

    c. The outboard brake pad has an insulator pad mounted on its backside (A, **Figure 5**).

    d. Center the outboard brake pad into the pad holder so the lower end of the pad rests inside the pad holder. Push the upper end of the brake pad past the spring clip and into the holder (**Figure 10**).

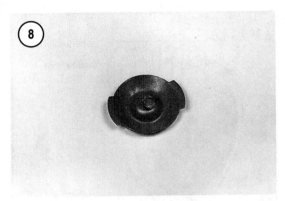

19. After the installation of new brake pads, the caliper piston must be relocated into the caliper before the caliper is installed over the brake disc. This will force brake fluid back up into the reservoir. To prevent the reservoir from overflowing, perform the following:

    a. Remove the screws securing the cover (**Figure 12**) and remove the cover and diaphragm.

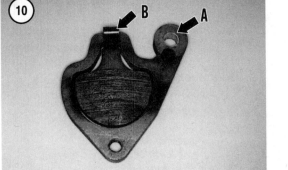

12

b. Use a shop syringe and remove about 50 percent of the brake fluid from the reservoir. Do *not* drain more than 50 percent of the brake fluid or air will enter the system. Discard the brake fluid properly.

> *CAUTION*
> *Do not allow the master cylinder to overflow during this step. Wash brake fluid off any painted, plated, or plastic surfaces immediately as it will damage most surfaces it contacts. Use soapy water and rinse completely.*

c. Install the old outer brake pad into the caliper and against the piston.

d. Slowly push the outer brake pad and piston back into the caliper. Watch the brake fluid level in the master cylinder reservoir. If necessary, siphon off fluid before it overflows.

e. Remove the old brake pad.

f. Temporarily install the diaphragm and cover. Install the screws finger-tight at this time.

20. Install the inner brake pad into the caliper (**Figure 4**) from the inside surface. Push the pad into place.

21. Install the pad retainer onto the backside of the caliper (B, **Figure 3**), indexing the tabs into the caliper recesses.

22. Install the bolt through the pad retainer and into the backside of the inner brake pad. Tighten the screw to the specification in **Table 2**.

> *WARNING*
> *The bushings on the fork tube (**Figure 13**) locate the brake caliper on the fork tube in relation to the brake disc. The bushings must be in place as noted in Step 23. If they are not installed, the brake may lock up when applied and cause a loss of motorcycle control.*

23. Install the caliper bushings into the fork tube lugs (**Figure 13**) if they were removed.

24. Install the outer brake pad/pad holder assembly (**Figure 2**) as follows:

> *WARNING*
> *The spring clip loop and the brake pad friction material (**Figure 14**) must face away from the piston when the pad holder is installed in the cali-*

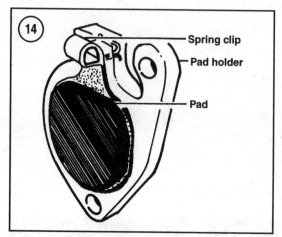

Spring clip
Pad holder
Pad

per. *Brake failure will occur if this assembly is installed incorrectly.*

a. Insert the outer brake pad/pad holder assembly into the caliper so the brake pad insulator backing faces against the piston.

> *CAUTION*
> *The brake caliper threaded bushing shoulder (**Figure 15**) must be posi-*

mounting lug. Tighten the mounting pin finger-tight at this time.

30. First tighten the lower mounting pin, then the upper mounting bolt, to the specification in **Table 2**.

31. Repeat this procedure for the other caliper assembly.

32. Refill the master cylinder reservoir with DOT 5 brake fluid, if necessary, to maintain the correct fluid level. Install the diaphragm, top cover (**Figure 12**) and tighten the screws to the specification in **Table 2**.

33. Apply the front brake lever several times to seat the pads against the disc.

> *WARNING*
> *Do not ride the motorcycle until the front brakes operate correctly with full hydraulic advantage. If necessary, bleed the brakes as described in this chapter.*

FRONT BRAKE PAD REPLACEMENT (2000-ON MODELS)

There is no recommended mileage interval for changing the friction pads in the disc brakes. Pad wear depends on riding habits and conditions. Frequently check the brake pads for wear. Increase the inspection interval when the wear indicator reaches the edge of the brake disc. After removal, measure the thickness of each brake pad with a vernier caliper or ruler, and compare measurements to the dimensions in **Table 1**.

Always replace both pads in the caliper at the same time to maintain even brake pressure on the discs. Also, replace both brake pads in *both calipers* at the same time. Do not disconnect the hydraulic brake hose from the brake caliper for brake pad replacement. Only disconnect the hose if the caliper assembly is going to be removed.

> *CAUTION*
> *Check the pads more frequently when the lining approaches the pad metal backing plate. If pad wear is uneven for some reason, the backing plate may come in contact with the disc and cause damage.*

tioned as described in substep b. Otherwise, the pad holder rivet and bushing will be damaged when the caliper mounting bolt and pin are tightened.

    b. Position the threaded bushing flange (**Figure 15**) with its shoulder between the pad holder and the rivet head. Position the bushing so one notch engages the rivet (**Figure 16**).

25. Carefully install the caliper over the brake disc, making sure the friction surface on each pad faces against the disc.

26. Coat the lower mounting pin shoulder (**Figure 17**) and O-ring with Dow Corning Moly 44 grease or an equivalent prior to installation.

27. Align the caliper two mounting holes with the fork tube mounting lugs.

28. Install the brake caliper upper mounting bolt and washer (A, **Figure 1**) through the fork slider mounting lug, and thread it into the caliper bushing. Tighten the bolt finger-tight at this time.

29. Insert the lower mounting pin (B, **Figure 1**) through the caliper and thread it into the slider

1. Read the information under *Brakes Service* in this chapter.

2. Park the motorcycle on level ground.

12

3. Place a spacer between the brake lever and the throttle grip, and secure it in place. If the brake lever is inadvertently squeezed, this will prevent the pistons from being forced out of the cylinders.

4. Clean the top of the master cylinder of all dirt and debris.

5. Remove the screws securing the cover (**Figure 12**), and remove the cover and diaphragm.

6. Use a shop syringe and remove about 50 percent of the brake fluid from the reservoir. This will prevent the master cylinder from overflowing when the pistons are compressed for reinstallation. Do *not* drain more than 50 percent of the brake fluid or air will enter the system. Discard the brake fluid properly.

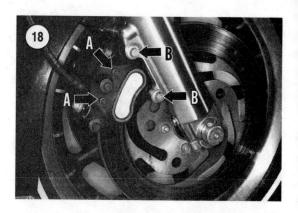

CAUTION
Do not allow the master cylinder to overflow during Step 7. Wash brake fluid off any painted, plated, or plastic surfaces immediately as it will damage most surfaces it contacts. Use soapy water and rinse completely.

7. Loosen the pad pin bolts (A, **Figure 18**).

CAUTION
The brake disc is thin in order to dissipate heat and may bend easily. When pushing against the disc in the following step, support the disc adjacent to the caliper to prevent damage to the disc.

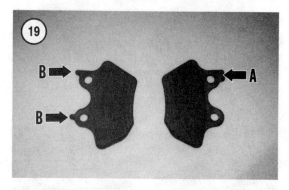

8. Hold the caliper body from the outside and push it toward the brake disc. This will push the outer pistons into the caliper bores to make room for the new brake pads. Constantly check the reservoir to make sure brake fluid does not overflow. Remove fluid, if necessary, before it overflows. Install the diaphragm and cover. Tighten the screws finger-tight.

9. Remove the caliper mounting bolts (B, **Figure 18**).

10. Remove the pad pin bolts (A, **Figure 18**).

11. Remove the inboard and outboard brake pads from the caliper.

12. Check the brake pads for wear or damage. Measure the thickness of the brake pad friction material. Replace the brake pads if they are worn to the service limit in **Table 1**.

13. Carefully remove rust or corrosion from the disc.

14. Thoroughly clean the pad pin bolts of corrosion or road dirt.

15. Check the friction surface of the new pads for debris or manufacturing residue. If necessary, clean them off with an aerosol brake cleaner.

NOTE
When purchasing new pads, check with the dealership to make sure the friction compound of the new pad is compatible with the disc material. Remove roughness from the backs of the new pads with a fine-cut file, then thoroughly clean them off.

NOTE
The brake pads are not symmetrical. The pad with one tab (A, Figure 19) must be installed on the inboard side of the left side caliper and on the outboard side of the right side caliper. The pad with two tabs (B) must be installed on the outboard side of the left side caliper and on the inboard side of the right side caliper.

16. Install the inboard pad (A, **Figure 20**) and the outboard pad (B) into the caliper.

17. Hold the pads in place against the antirattle spring and install one of the pad pin bolts (**Figure**

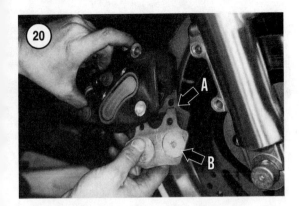

21) through the caliper and both brake pads. Install the remaining pad pin bolt (**Figure 22**).

18. Install the caliper onto the brake disc and install the mounting bolts (B, **Figure 18**). Tighten the bolts to the specification in **Table 2**.

19. Tighten the pad pins (A, **Figure 18**) to the specification in **Table 2**.

20. Repeat Steps 7-19 to replace the brake pads in the other caliper assembly.

21. Remove the spacer from the front brake lever.

22. Make sure there is sufficient brake fluid in the master cylinder reservoir. Top it off if necessary.

23. Pump the front brake lever several times to reposition the brake pads against the brake disc.

24. Refill the master cylinder reservoir, if necessary, to maintain the correct fluid level as indicated on the side of the reservoir. Install the diaphragm and the top cover. Tighten the screws to the specification in **Table 2**.

WARNING
Do not ride the motorcycle until the front brakes operate correctly with full hydraulic advantage. If necessary, bleed the brake as described in this chapter.

FRONT BRAKE CALIPER
(1999 MODELS)

Removal (Caliper Will Not Be Disassembled)

To remove the brake caliper (**Figure 23**) without disassembling it, perform this procedure. To disassemble the brake caliper, refer to *Caliper Removal/Piston Removal* in this chapter.

1A. To remove the brake caliper from the motorcycle, perform the following:

  a. Loosen the banjo bolt (A, **Figure 24**) at the caliper. Remove the banjo bolt and the two washers.

  b. Remove the upper mounting bolt and washer (B, **Figure 24**), and the lower mounting pin (C).

  c. Lift the brake caliper off the brake disc and remove it.

1B. To partially remove the brake caliper from the motorcycle without disconnecting the brake hose, perform the following:

  a. Remove the upper mounting screw and washer (B, **Figure 24**), and the lower mounting pin (C).

  b. Lift the brake caliper off the brake disc.

  c. Insert a wooden or plastic spacer block between the brake pads in the caliper.

NOTE
Squeezing the brake lever with the caliper removed from the brake disc will force the piston out of its bore. Using the spacer block can prevent this.

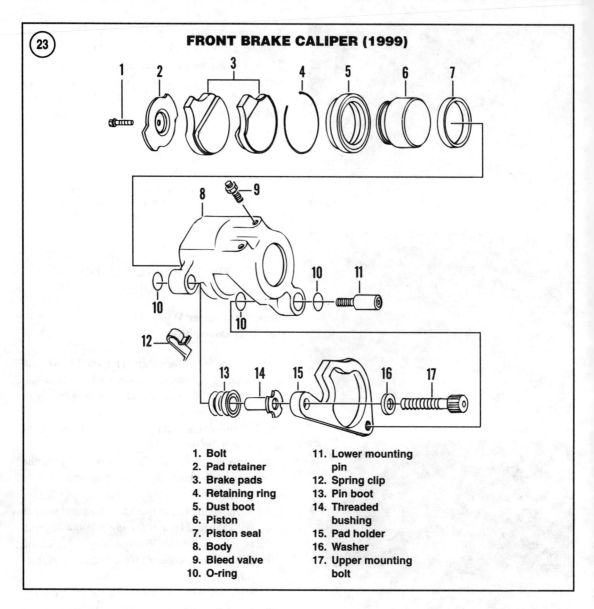

FRONT BRAKE CALIPER (1999)

1. Bolt
2. Pad retainer
3. Brake pads
4. Retaining ring
5. Dust boot
6. Piston
7. Piston seal
8. Body
9. Bleed valve
10. O-ring
11. Lower mounting pin
12. Spring clip
13. Pin boot
14. Threaded bushing
15. Pad holder
16. Washer
17. Upper mounting bolt

d. Secure the caliper to the frame with a bungee cord or piece of heavy wire.

2. If the front caliper is not going to be serviced, place it in a reclosable plastic bag to keep it clean.

Installation (Caliper Was Not Disassembled)

WARNING
The bushings on the fork tube (Figure 13) locate the brake caliper on the fork tube in relation to the brake disc. The bushings must be in place as noted in Step 1. If they are not in-stalled, the brake may lock up when applied and cause loss of control.

1. Install the caliper bushings into the fork tube lugs (**Figure 13**) if they were removed.

2. Install the brake pads as described in this chapter if they were removed.

3. Carefully install the caliper over the brake disc, making sure the friction surface on each pad faces against the disc.

4. Coat the lower mounting pin shoulder (**Figure 13**) and O-ring with Dow Corning Moly 44 grease or an equivalent prior to installation.

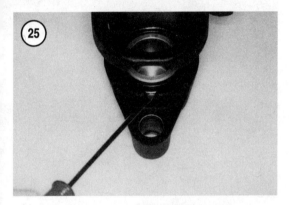

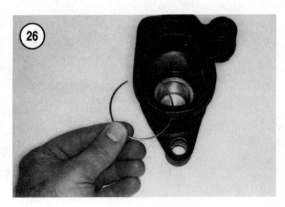

5. Align the caliper's two mounting holes with the fork tube mounting lugs.

6. Install the brake caliper upper mounting bolt and washer (B, **Figure 24**) through the fork slider mounting lug, and thread it into the caliper bushing. Tighten the bolt finger-tight at this time.

7. Insert the lower mounting pin (C, **Figure 24**) through the caliper and thread it into the slider mounting lug. Tighten the mounting pin finger-tight at this time.

8. First tighten the lower mounting pin, then the upper mounting bolt, to the specification in **Table 2**.

NOTE
Install new steel/rubber banjo bolt washers in Step 9.

9. If the brake line was removed, install it onto the caliper with a *new* washer on both sides of the brake line fitting, then secure the fitting to the caliper with the banjo bolt (A, **Figure 24**). Tighten the banjo bolt to the specification in **Table 2**. Make sure the fitting seats against the caliper as shown in A, **Figure 24**.

10. Repeat this procedure for the other caliper assembly.

11. Refill the master cylinder reservoir with DOT 5 brake fluid, if necessary, to maintain the correct fluid level. Install the diaphragm, top cover and tighten the screws to the torque specification in **Table 2**.

12. Apply the front brake lever several times to seat the pads against the disc.

WARNING
Do not ride the motorcycle until the front brakes operate correctly with full hydraulic advantage. If necessary, bleed the brakes as described in this chapter.

Caliper Removal/Piston Removal
(Caliper Will Be Disassembled)

Force is required to remove the piston from the caliper. This procedure describes how to remove the piston with the caliper connected to the brake hose.

1. Remove the brake pads as described in this chapter.

2. Insert a small screwdriver into the notched groove machined in the bottom of the piston bore (**Figure 25**). Then pry the retaining ring (**Figure 26**) out of the caliper body.

3. Wrap a large cloth around the brake caliper.

4. Hold the caliper by hand away from the piston/brake pad area.

5. Operate the front brake lever to force the piston part way out of the caliper. Do not completely remove the piston until necessary for disassembly. Leaving the piston partially in the bore prevents brake fluid from spilling out.

NOTE
*If the piston did not come out, remove it as described under **Disassembly** in this section.*

12

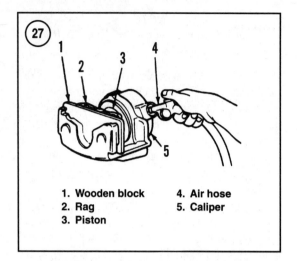

1. Wooden block   4. Air hose
2. Rag   5. Caliper
3. Piston

6. Remove the caliper banjo bolt (A, **Figure 24**) and washers. Seal the brake hose to prevent brake fluid from dripping out.

7. Place the caliper on a workbench for disassembly.

Disassembly

1. Partially remove the piston from the caliper (**Figure 23**) as described under *Caliper Removal/Piston Removal (Caliper Will Be Disassembled)* in this chapter.

> *WARNING*
> *Compressed air will force the piston out of the caliper under considerable force. Do not block the piston by hand as injury will occur.*

2. If the piston did not come partially out of the caliper bore, perform the following:
   a. Place a rag and a piece of wood in the caliper (**Figure 27**). Keep fingers out of the way of the piston.
   b. Apply compressed air through the brake hose port and force the piston out of the caliper.

3. Remove the piston and dust boot assembly (**Figure 28**).

4. Remove the piston seal (**Figure 29**) from the groove in the caliper body.

5. Pull the threaded bushing (A, **Figure 30**) out of the caliper, then remove the pin boot (B).

6. Remove the three O-rings from the caliper body (10, **Figure 23** and **Figure 31**).

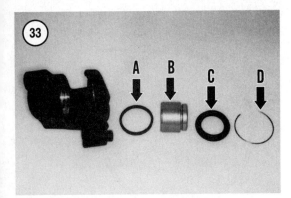

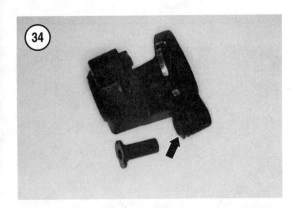

Inspection

Service specifications for the front caliper components are not available. Replace worn, damaged or questionable parts.

1. Clean the caliper body and piston in clean DOT 5 brake fluid or isopropyl alcohol, and dry them with compressed air.

2. Make sure the fluid passageway in the base of the piston bore is clear. Apply compressed air to the opening to make sure it is clear. Clean it out, if necessary, with clean brake fluid.

3. Inspect the piston seal groove in the caliper body for damage. If it is damaged or corroded, replace the caliper assembly.

4. Inspect the banjo bolt threaded hole in the caliper body. If it is worn or damaged, clean it out with a metric thread tap or replace the caliper assembly.

5. Inspect the bleed valve threaded hole in the caliper body. If it is worn or damaged, clean it out with a metric thread tap or replace the caliper assembly.

6. Inspect the bleed valve. Apply compressed air to the opening and make sure it is clear. Clean it out, if necessary, with clean brake fluid. Install the bleed valve and tighten it to the specification in **Table 2**.

7. Inspect the caliper body for damage.

8. Inspect the cylinder wall and piston (**Figure 32**) for scratches, scoring or other damage.

Assembly

1. A Harley-Davidson factory rebuild kit (part No. 44020-83) includes a piston seal (A, **Figure 33**), piston (B), dust boot (C) and retaining ring (D).

> *WARNING*
> *Never reuse an old dust boot or piston seal. Very minor damage or age deterioration can make the boot and seal ineffective.*

2. Soak the new dust and piston seal in clean DOT 5 brake fluid.

3. Carefully install the *new* piston seal into the groove. Make sure the seal is properly seated in its groove.

4. Install *new* O-rings into the caliper grooves.

5. Wipe the inside of the pin boot with Dow Corning MOLY 44 grease. Then insert the boot into the bushing bore with the flange end seating in the bore groove (**Figure 34**).

6. Insert the threaded bushing into the boot (**Figure 35**).

12

7. Install the piston dust boot on the piston before the piston is installed in the caliper bore. Perform the following:

  a. Place the piston on the workbench with its open side facing up.

  b. Align the piston dust boot with the piston so the shoulder on the dust boot faces up.

  c. Slide the piston dust boot onto the piston until the inner lip on the dust boot seats in the piston groove (**Figure 28**).

8. Coat the piston and the caliper bore with DOT 5 brake fluid.

9. Align the piston with the caliper bore so its open end faces out (**Figure 28**). Then push the piston in until it bottoms.

10. Seat the piston dust boot (**Figure 36**) into the caliper bore.

11. Locate the retaining ring groove in the top end of the caliper bore. Align the retaining ring so its gap (**Figure 37**) is at the top of the caliper bore and install the ring into the ring groove. Make sure the retaining ring is correctly seated in the groove.

12. Apply a light coat of Dow Corning MOLY 44 grease to the caliper mounting lug bores.

13. If the bleed valve assembly was removed, install it and tighten it to the torque specification in **Table 2**.

14. Install the caliper and brake pads as described in this chapter.

15. Bleed the brakes as described under *Bleeding the System* in this chapter.

FRONT BRAKE CALIPER
(2000-ON MODELS)

Removal/Installation

> *CAUTION*
> *Do not spill brake fluid on the front fork or front wheel. Wash brake fluid off any painted, plated, or plastic surfaces immediately as it will destroy most surfaces it contacts. Use soapy water and rinse completely.*

1. If the caliper assembly is going to be disassembled for service, perform the following:

> *NOTE*
> *By performing Steps 1b and 1c, compressed air may not be necessary for*

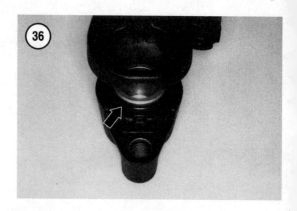

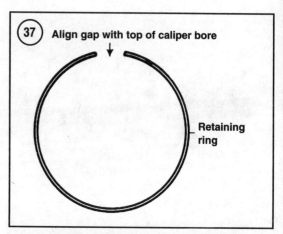

Align gap with top of caliper bore

Retaining ring

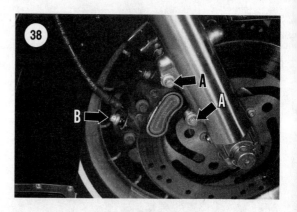

piston removal during caliper disassembly.

  a. Remove the brake pads as described in this chapter.

> *CAUTION*
> *Do not allow the pistons to travel out far enough to come in contact with the brake disc. If this happens the pistons*

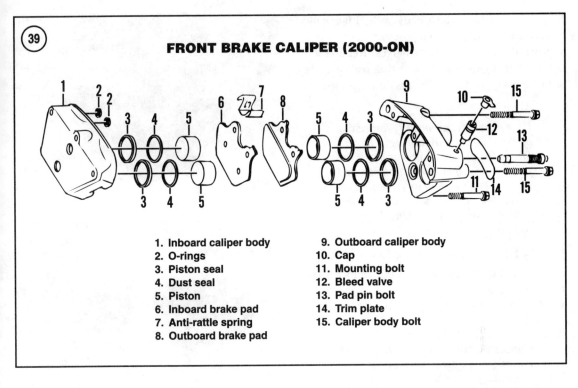

FRONT BRAKE CALIPER (2000-ON)

1. Inboard caliper body
2. O-rings
3. Piston seal
4. Dust seal
5. Piston
6. Inboard brake pad
7. Anti-rattle spring
8. Outboard brake pad
9. Outboard caliper body
10. Cap
11. Mounting bolt
12. Bleed valve
13. Pad pin bolt
14. Trim plate
15. Caliper body bolt

may scratch or gouge the disc during caliper removal.

b. Slowly apply the brake lever to push the pistons part way out of the caliper assembly for ease of removal during caliper service.

c. Loosen the two caliper body mounting bolts (A, **Figure 38**).

d. Loosen the brake hose banjo bolt (B, **Figure 38**).

2. Remove the banjo bolt and sealing washers attaching the brake hose to the caliper assembly. Do not lose the sealing washer on each side of the hose fittings.

3. Place the loose end of the brake hose in a reclosable plastic bag to prevent the entry of debris and to prevent residual brake fluid from leaking out.

4. Remove the bolts (A, **Figure 38**) securing the brake caliper assembly to the front fork and remove the caliper.

5. If necessary, disassemble and service the caliper assembly as described in this chapter. If the front caliper is not going to be serviced, place it in a reclosable plastic bag to keep it clean.

6. Install by reversing these removal steps. Note the following:

a. Install the caliper assembly onto the disc, being careful not to damage the leading edge of the brake pads.

b. Install the bolts (A, **Figure 38**) securing the brake caliper assembly to the front fork and tighten them to the specifications in **Table 2**.

c. Apply clean DOT 5 brake fluid to the rubber portions of the new sealing washers prior to installation.

d. Install a *new* sealing washer on each side of the brake hose fitting and install the banjo bolt (B, **Figure 38**). Tighten the banjo bolt to the torque specification in **Table 2**.

e. Bleed the brakes as described under *Bleeding the System* in this chapter.

WARNING
Do not ride the motorcycle until the front brakes operate correctly with full hydraulic advantage. If necessary, bleed the brakes as described in this chapter.

Disassembly

1. Remove the caliper and brake pads (**Figure 39**) as described in this chapter.

12

2. Remove the two caliper body bolts (**Figure 40**) loosened during the removal procedure.

3. Separate the caliper body halves. Remove the O-ring seals (**Figure 41**). *New* O-ring seals must be installed every time the caliper is disassembled.

> *NOTE*
> *If the pistons were partially forced out of the caliper body during removal, Steps 4-6 may not be necessary. If the pistons or caliper bores are corroded or very dirty, a small amount of compressed air may be necessary to completely remove the pistons from the body bores.*

4. Place a piece of soft wood or a folded shop cloth over the end of the pistons and the caliper body. Turn the assembly over and place it on the workbench with the pistons facing down.

> *WARNING*
> *Compressed air will force the pistons out of the caliper bodies under considerable force. Do no block the piston by hand as injury will occur.*

5. Apply the air pressure in short spurts to the hydraulic fluid passageway to force out the pistons. Repeat this for the other caliper body half. Use a service station air hose if compressed air is not available.

> *CAUTION*
> *In Step 6, do not use a sharp tool to remove the dust and piston seals from the caliper cylinders. Do not damage the cylinder surface.*

6. Use a piece of wood or a plastic scraper to carefully push the dust seal and the piston seal (**Figure 42**) in toward the caliper cylinder and out of their grooves. Remove the dust and piston seals.

7. If necessary, unscrew and remove the bleed valve (A, **Figure 43**).

8. Inspect the caliper assembly as described in this section.

Inspection

1. Clean both caliper body halves and pistons in clean DOT 5 brake fluid or isopropyl alcohol, and dry them with compressed air.

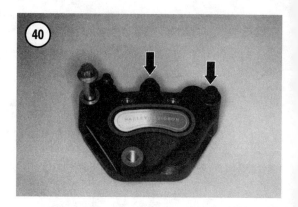
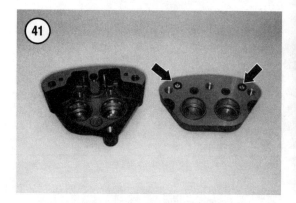
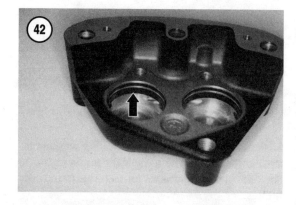
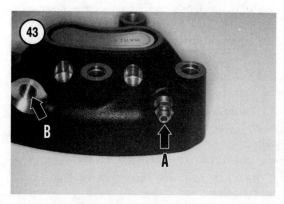

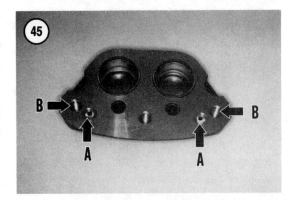

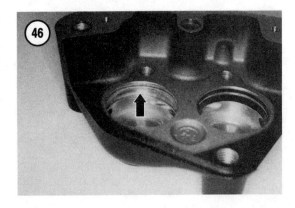

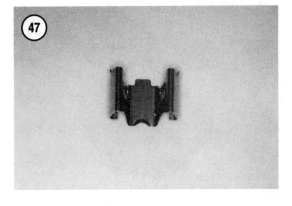

2. Make sure the fluid passageways (**Figure 44**) in the piston bores are clear. Apply compressed air to the openings to make sure they are clear. Clean them out, if necessary, with clean brake fluid.

3. Make sure the fluid passageways (A, **Figure 45**) in both caliper body halves are clear. Apply compressed air to the openings to make sure they are clear. Clean them out, if necessary, with clean brake fluid.

4. Inspect the piston and dust seal grooves (**Figure 46**) in both caliper bodies for damage. If they are damaged or corroded, replace the caliper assembly.

5. Inspect the banjo bolt threaded hole (B, **Figure 43**) in the outboard caliper body. If it is worn or damaged, clean it out with a metric thread tap or replace the caliper assembly.

6. Inspect the bleed valve threaded hole in the caliper body. If it is worn or damaged, clean it out with a metric thread tap or replace the caliper assembly.

7. Inspect the bleed valve. Apply compressed air to the opening and make sure it is clear. Clean it out, if necessary, with clean brake fluid. Install the bleed valve and tighten it to the specification in **Table 2**.

8. Inspect both caliper bodies for damage. Check the inboard caliper mounting bolt hole threads (B, **Figure 45**) for wear or damage. Clean the threads with an appropriately sized metric tap or replace the caliper assembly.

9. Inspect the cylinder walls and pistons for scratches, scoring or other damage.

10. Check the antirattle spring (**Figure 47**) for wear or damage.

12

Assembly

> *NOTE*
> *Never reuse old dust seals or piston seals. Very minor damage or age deterioration can make the seals ineffective.*

1. Soak the new dust and piston seals in clean DOT 5 brake fluid.

2. Coat the piston bores and pistons with clean DOT 5 brake fluid.

3. Carefully install the new piston seals into the lower grooves. Make sure the seals are properly seated in their respective grooves.

4. Carefully install the new dust seals into the upper grooves. Make sure all seals are properly seated in their respective grooves (**Figure 48**).

5. Repeat Step 3 and Step 4 for the other caliper body half.

6. Position the pistons with the open end facing out and install the pistons into the caliper cylinders (A, **Figure 49**). Push the pistons in until they bottom (B, **Figure 49**).

7. Repeat Step 6 for the other caliper body half. Make sure all pistons are installed correctly.

8. Coat the *new* O-ring seals in DOT 5 brake fluid and install the O-rings (**Figure 41**) into the inboard caliper half.

9. Install the antirattle spring (**Figure 50**) onto the boss on the outboard caliper half.

10. Make sure the O-rings are still in place and assemble the caliper body halves.

11. Install one of the caliper mounting bolts through the upper hole (A, **Figure 51**) to correctly align the caliper halves.

12. Install the two caliper body bolts (B, **Figure 51**) and tighten them securely. Tighten them to the specification after the caliper is installed on the front fork.

13. If the bleed valve assembly was removed, install it and tighten it to the specification in **Table 2**.

14. Install the caliper and brake pads as described in this chapter.

15. Tighten the two caliper body bolts (A, **Figure 38**) to the specification in **Table 2**.

16. Bleed the brakes as described under *Bleeding the System* in this chapter.

FRONT MASTER CYLINDER

Removal

> *CAUTION*
> *Cover the fuel tank and front fairing with a heavy cloth or plastic tarp to protect them from accidental brake fluid spills. Wash brake fluid off painted, plated, or plastic surfaces immediately as it will destroy most surfaces it contacts. Use soapy water and rinse completely.*

1. Clean the top of the master cylinder of all dirt and debris.

> *CAUTION*
> *Failure to install the spacer in Step 2 will result in damage to the rubber*

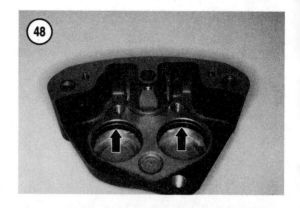

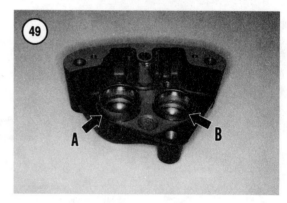

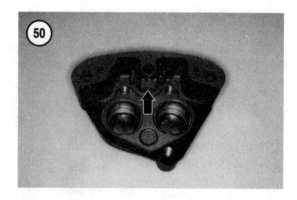

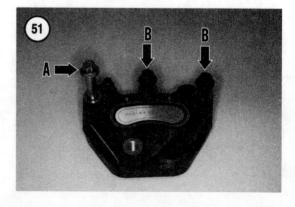

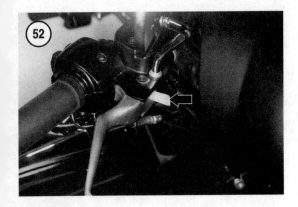

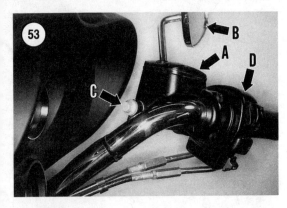

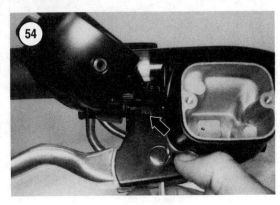

boot and plunger on the front brake switch.

2. Insert a 5/32 in. (4 mm) thick spacer (**Figure 52**) between the brake lever and lever bracket. Make sure the spacer stays in place during the following steps.

3. Remove the screws securing the top cover.

4. Remove the top cover (A, **Figure 53**) and diaphragm from the master cylinder reservoir.

5. Use a shop syringe to draw all of the brake fluid out of the master cylinder reservoir. Temporarily re-

install the diaphragm and the cover. Tighten the screws finger-tight.

6. On models so equipped, remove the windshield or front fairing.

7. Loosen and remove the mirror (B, **Figure 53**) from the master cylinder.

8. Remove the banjo bolt and sealing washers (C, **Figure 53**) securing the brake hose to the master cylinder.

9. Place the loose end of the brake hose in a reclosable plastic bag to prevent the entry of moisture and debris. Tie the loose end of the hose to the handlebar.

10. Remove the screw securing the right side switch together and separate the switch (D, **Figure 53**).

11. Remove the T27 Torx bolts and washers securing the clamp and master cylinder to the handlebar.

12. Remove the master cylinder assembly from the handlebar.

13. Drain any residual brake fluid from the master cylinder and dispose of it properly.

14. If the master cylinder assembly is not going to be serviced, reinstall the clamp and Torx bolts to the master cylinder. Place the assembly in a reclosable plastic bag to protect it from debris.

Installation

1. Insert the 5/32 in. (4 mm) thick spacer (**Figure 52**) between the brake lever and lever bracket if not in place. Make sure the spacer stays in place during the following steps.

2. Position the front master cylinder onto the handlebar. Align the master cylinder notch (**Figure 54**) with the locating tab on the lower portion of the right side switch.

CAUTION
*Do not damage the front brake light switch and rubber boot (**Figure 55**, typical) when installing the master cylinder in Step 3.*

3. Push the master cylinder all the way onto the handlebar (A, **Figure 56**). Hold it in this position and install the upper portion of the right side switch (B, **Figure 56**). Install the switch's clamping screw and tighten it securely.

4. Position the clamp and install the Torx bolts and washers. Tighten the upper mounting bolt, then the

12

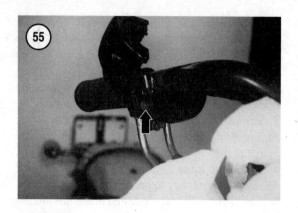

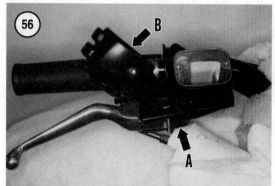

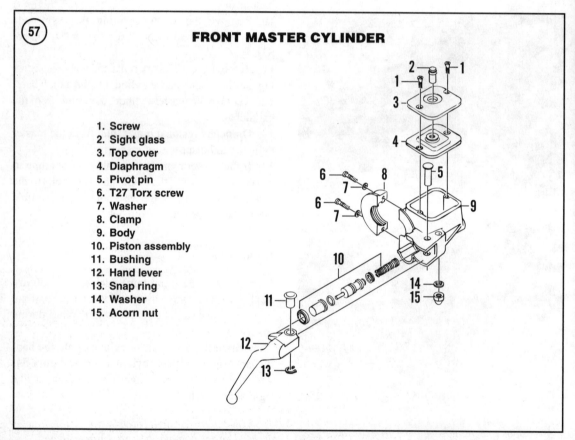

FRONT MASTER CYLINDER

1. Screw
2. Sight glass
3. Top cover
4. Diaphragm
5. Pivot pin
6. T27 Torx screw
7. Washer
8. Clamp
9. Body
10. Piston assembly
11. Bushing
12. Hand lever
13. Snap ring
14. Washer
15. Acorn nut

lower bolt. Tighten the bolts to the specification in **Table 2**.

5. Apply clean DOT 5 brake fluid to the rubber portions of the new sealing washers prior to installation.

6. Install *new* sealing washers and the banjo bolt (C, **Figure 53**) securing the brake hose to the master cylinder. Tighten the banjo bolt to the specification in **Table 2**.

7. Remove the spacer (**Figure 52**) from the brake lever.

8. Install the mirror (B, **Figure 53**) onto the master cylinder.

9. On models so equipped, install the windshield or front fairing.

10. Temporarily install the diaphragm and top cover (A, **Figure 53**) onto the reservoir. Tighten the screws finger-tight at this time.

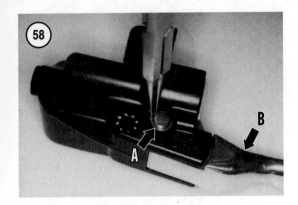

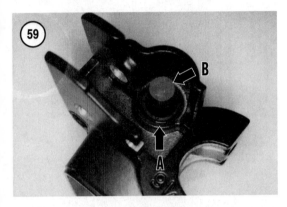

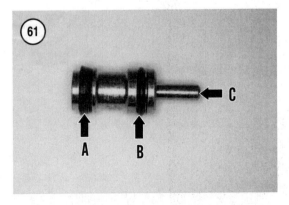

11. Refill the master cylinder reservoir and bleed the brake system as described under *Bleeding the System* in this chapter.

12. On models so equipped, install the windshield or front fairing.

Disassembly

1. Store the master cylinder components (**Figure 57**) in a divided container, such as a restaurant-size egg carton, to help maintain their correct alignment positions.

2. Remove the screws securing the top cover if they are still in place. Remove the top cover and the diaphragm from the master cylinder.

3. Remove the master cylinder assembly as described in this chapter.

4. Remove the snap ring (A, **Figure 58**) and pivot pin securing the hand lever to the master cylinder. Remove the hand lever (B, **Figure 58**).

5. Remove the retainer (A, **Figure 59**) and the rubber boot (B, **Figure 59**) from the area where the hand lever actuates the piston assembly.

6. Remove the piston assembly (**Figure 60**) and the spring.

7. Inspect all parts as described in this section.

Inspection

Replace worn or damage parts as described in this section. It is recommended that a new piston kit assembly be installed every time the master cylinder is disassembled.

1. Clean all parts in isopropyl alcohol or clean DOT 5 brake fluid. Inspect the body cylinder bore surface for signs of wear and damage. If it is less than perfect, replace the master cylinder assembly. The body cannot be replaced separately.

2. Inspect the piston cup (A, **Figure 61**) and O-ring (B) for signs of wear and damage.

3. Check the end of the piston (C, **Figure 61**) for wear caused by the hand lever.

4. Make sure the fluid passage (**Figure 62**) in the bottom of the master cylinder reservoir is clear. Clean it out if necessary.

5. Inspect the piston contact surface for signs of wear and damage.

6. Check the hand lever pivot lugs in the master cylinder body for cracks or elongation.

12

7. Inspect the hand lever pivot hole and bushing (A, **Figure 63**), and the pivot pin (B) for wear, cracks or elongation.

8. Inspect the piston cap and retainer (**Figure 64**) for wear or damage.

9. Inspect the threads in the bore for the banjo bolt. If they are worn or damaged, clean them out with a thread tap or replace the master cylinder assembly.

10. Check the top cover and diaphragm for damage or deterioration.

11. If necessary, separate the cover from the diaphragm as follows:
    a. Pull straight up on the sight glass (**Figure 65**) and remove it from the cover and diaphragm.
    b. Separate the diaphragm from the cover.
    c. The trim plate may separate from the cover.

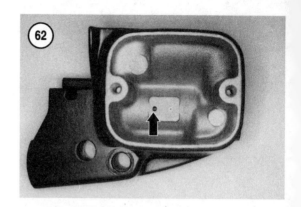

Assembly

> *NOTE*
> *When installing a new piston assembly, coat all parts with the lubricant provided with the Harley-Davidson parts kit. When installing existing parts, coat them with DOT 5 brake fluid.*

> *NOTE*
> *Make sure the new piston kit is for a dual front disc motorcycle.*

> *CAUTION*
> *The cover and diaphragm must be assembled as described. If the sight glass is not installed correctly through the cover and diaphragm neck, brake fluid will leak past these components.*

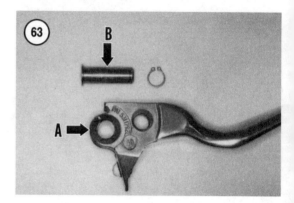

1. If the cover and the diaphragm were disassembled, assemble them as follows:
    a. Install the trim plate (**Figure 66**) onto the cover if it was removed.
    b. Insert the neck of the diaphragm into the cover. Press it in until it seats correctly and the outer edges are aligned with the cover.
    c. Push the sight glass (**Figure 65**) straight down through the cover and the neck of the diaphragm (**Figure 67**) until it snaps into place. The sight glass must lock these two parts together to avoid a brake fluid leak.

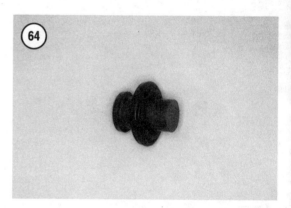

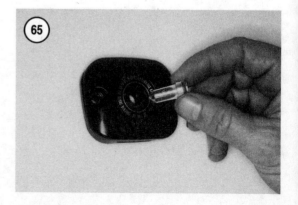

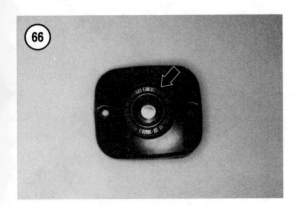

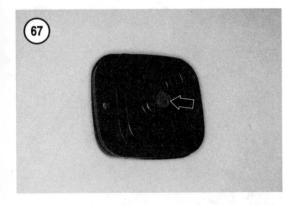

2. Soak the *new* cup, O-ring and piston assembly in clean DOT 5 brake fluid for 15 minutes to make them pliable. Coat the inside of the cylinder bore with clean brake fluid prior to the assembly of parts.

> *CAUTION*
> *When installing the piston assembly, do not allow the cup to turn inside out as it will be damaged and allow brake fluid leaks within the cylinder bore.*

3A. On 1999 and 2000 models, position the flared end of the spring so it enters the master cylinder first.

3B. On 2001-on models, position the metal tab end of the spring (**Figure 68**) so it enters the master cylinder first.

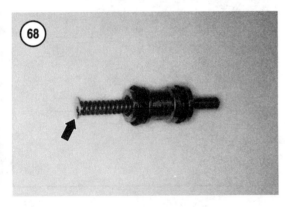

4. Install the spring and piston assembly into the cylinder (**Figure 69**). Push them in until they bottom in the cylinder (**Figure 60**).

5. Position the retainer with the flat side going on first, and install the piston cap and retainer onto the piston end.

6. Push down on the piston cap (**Figure 70**). Hold it in place and press the retainer down until it correctly seats in the cylinder groove (A, **Figure 59**).

7. Make sure the bushing is in place in the hand lever pivot area.

8. Install the hand lever (B, **Figure 58**) into the master cylinder. Install the pivot pin and secure it with the snap ring. Make sure the snap ring is correctly seated in the pivot pin groove (A, **Figure 58**).

9. Slowly apply the lever to make sure it pivots freely.

10. Install the master cylinder as described in this chapter.

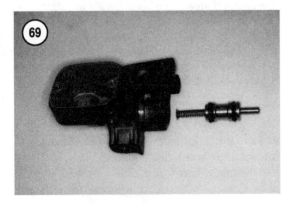

12

REAR BRAKE PAD REPLACEMENT
(1999 MODELS)

There is no recommended mileage interval for changing the brake pads. Pad wear depends on riding habits and conditions. Frequently check the pads for wear. Increase the inspection interval when the wear indicator reaches the edge of the brake disc. After removal, measure the thickness of each brake pad with a vernier caliper or ruler, and compare measurements to the dimensions in **Table 1**.

Always replace both pads in the caliper at the same time to maintain even brake pressure on the disc. Do not disconnect the hydraulic brake hose from the brake caliper for brake pad replacement. Only disconnect the hose if the caliper assembly is going to be removed.

CAUTION
Check the pads more frequently when the lining approaches the pad metal backing plate. If pad wear is uneven for some reason, the backing plate may come in contact with the disc and cause damage.

1. Read *Brake Service* in this chapter.
2. Park the motorcycle on level ground.
3. Tie the end of the brake pedal up to the frame. If the brake pedal is inadvertently applied, this will prevent the piston from being forced out of the cylinder.
4. Remove the right side saddlebag as described in Chapter Fourteen.
5. Clean the top of the master cylinder of all dirt and debris.
6. Remove the screws securing the cover (**Figure 71**), and remove the cover and diaphragm.
7. Use a shop syringe to remove about 50 percent of the brake fluid from the reservoir. This will prevent the master cylinder from overflowing when the pistons are compressed for reinstallation. Do *not* drain more than 50 percent of the brake fluid or air will enter the system. Discard the brake fluid properly.

CAUTION
Do not allow the master cylinder to overflow during Step 7. Wash brake fluid off painted, plated, or plastic surfaces immediately, as it will destroy most surfaces it contacts. Use soapy water and rinse completely.

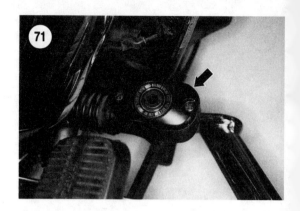

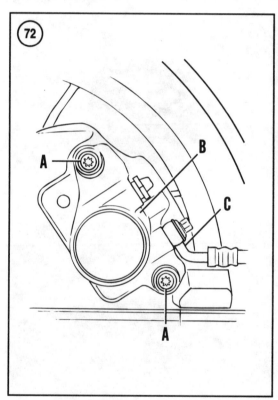

8. Loosen both pad pin bolts (A, **Figure 72**).

CAUTION
The brake disc is thin and easily damaged. When pushing against the disc in the following step, support the disc adjacent to the caliper to prevent damage.

9. Hold the caliper body from the outside and push it toward the brake disc. This will push the piston into the caliper bore to make room for the new brake pads. Constantly check the reservoir to make sure

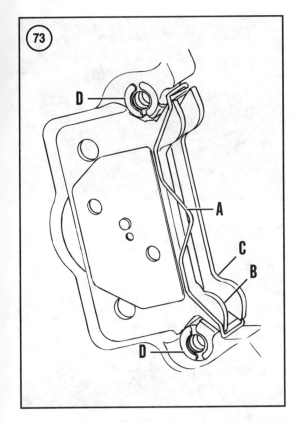

brake fluid does not overflow. Remove fluid, if necessary, before it overflows. Install the diaphragm and cover. Tighten the screws finger-tight.

10. Remove the two caliper pin bolts (A, **Figure 72**) and lift the caliper (B) off the mounting bracket. Do not disconnect the brake hose (C, **Figure 72**) from the caliper. Support the caliper with a Bungee cord or piece of heavy wire.

11. Lift, then pull the retainer clip (A, **Figure 73**) over the mounting bracket and remove it.

NOTE
If the pads are to be reused, mark them so they will be reinstalled in their original locations.

12. Slide the outboard brake pad (B, **Figure 73**) off the mounting bracket.

13. Slide the inboard brake pad (C, **Figure 73**) toward the wheel and off the mounting bracket.

14. Remove both pad shims (D, **Figure 73**) from the mounting bracket.

15. Check the brake pads for wear or damage. Measure the thickness of the brake pad friction material. Replace the brake pads if they are worn to the service limit in **Table 1**. Replace both pads as a set.

16. Clean the pad shims and check for cracks or damage.

17. Clean the pad shim mounting areas on the mounting bracket.

18. Check the retainer clip for rust, cracks or other damage.

19. Inspect the caliper pin bolts for cracks, corrosion or other damage. Replace as necessary.

20. Check the piston dust boot (**Figure 74**) for damage. Remove and overhaul the caliper if the boot is swollen or damaged, or if brake fluid is leaking from the caliper. Refer to *Rear Brake Caliper (1999 Models)* in this chapter.

21. Check the brake disc for wear.

22. Install the pad shims so their retaining loops face against the outer caliper mounting bracket rails.

23. Slide the outboard brake pad (**Figure 75**) over the pad shims and against the outer brake disc surface.

24. Slide the inboard brake pad (**Figure 76**) over the pad shims and against the inner brake disc surface.

25. Make sure the pad shims (D, **Figure 73**) did not move out of position.

26. Insert the retainer clip into the two large holes in the backside of the caliper mounting bracket. Then swing the retainer clip over the top of the

12

brake pads and snap it in place against the outer
brake pad (A, **Figure 73**).

> *CAUTION*
> *The brake pads must seat against both
> pad shims evenly. If they do not, the
> rear brake will drag, causing uneven
> pad wear and caliper bracket dam-
> age.*

> *NOTE*
> *When installing the caliper over the
> brake pads, do not dislodge the brake
> pads and pad shims.*

27. Slide the caliper (B, **Figure 72**) over the brake
pads. Install the two pad pin bolts (A, **Figure 72**)
and tighten them to the specification in **Table 2**.

28. Make sure there is sufficient brake fluid in the
master cylinder reservoir. Top it off if necessary.

29. Untie the brake pedal from the frame and pump
the rear brake pedal to reposition the brake pads
against the brake disc. Roll the motorcycle back and
forth, and continue to pump the brake pedal as many
times as it takes to refill the cylinder in the caliper
and correctly locate the brake pads against the disc.

30. Refill the master cylinder reservoir, if necessary, to maintain the correct fluid level as indicated
on the side of the reservoir. Install the diaphragm
and the top cover. Tighten the screws to the torque
specification in **Table 2**.

> *WARNING*
> *Do not ride the motorcycle until the
> rear brake is operating correctly with
> full hydraulic advantage. If neces-
> sary, bleed the brakes as described in
> this chapter.*

31. On models so equipped, install the right side
saddlebag.

REAR BRAKE PAD REPLACEMENT
(2000-ON MODELS)

There is no recommended mileage interval for
changing the friction pads. Pad wear depends on
riding habits and conditions. Frequently check the
pads for wear. Increase the inspection interval when
the wear indicator reaches the edge of the brake
disc. After removal, measure the thickness of each
brake pad with a vernier caliper or ruler, and compare measurements to the dimensions in **Table 1**.

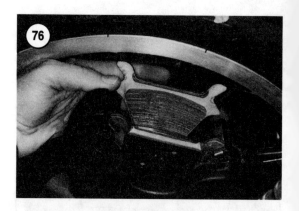

Always replace both pads in the caliper at the
same time to maintain even brake pressure on the
disc. Do not disconnect the hydraulic brake hose
from the brake caliper for brake pad replacement.
Only disconnect the hose if the caliper assembly is
going to be removed.

> *CAUTION*
> *Check the pads more frequently when
> the lining approaches the pad metal
> backing plate. If pad wear is uneven
> for some reason, the backing plate
> may come in contact with the disc and
> cause damage.*

1. Read *Brake Service* in this chapter.

2. Park the motorcycle on level ground.

3. Tie the end of the brake pedal to the frame. If the
brake pedal is inadvertently applied, this will prevent the piston from being forced out of the cylinder.

4. Remove the right side saddlebag as described in
Chapter Fourteen.

5. Clean the top of the rear master cylinder of all
dirt and debris.

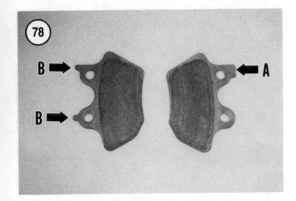

tons into the caliper bores to make room for the new brake pads. Constantly check the reservoir to make sure brake fluid does not overflow. Remove fluid, if necessary, before it overflows. Install the diaphragm and cover. Tighten the screws finger-tight.

10. Remove the pad pin bolts (**Figure 77**).

11. Remove the inboard and outboard brake pads from the caliper.

12. Check the brake pads for wear or damage. Measure the thickness of the brake pad friction material. Replace the brake pads if they are worn to the service limit in **Table 1**.

13. Carefully remove any rust or corrosion from the disc.

14. Thoroughly clean the pad pins of any corrosion or debris.

15. Check the friction surface of the new pads for debris or manufacturing residue. If necessary, clean them off with an aerosol brake cleaner.

NOTE
When purchasing new pads, check with the dealership to make sure the friction compound of the new pad is compatible with the disc material. Remove roughness from the backs of the new pads with a fine-cut file then thoroughly clean them off.

NOTE
The brake pads are not symmetrical. The pad with one tab (A, Figure 78) must be installed on the outboard side. The pad with two tabs (B) must be installed on the inboard side of the caliper

16. Install the outboard pad (**Figure 79**) into the caliper.

17. Hold the pad in place and install the pad pin bolts (**Figure 80**) part way in to hold the outboard pad in place.

18. Install the inboard pad (**Figure 81**) into the caliper.

19. Push the pad pin bolts through the inboard pad (**Figure 77**) and tighten them to the specification in **Table 2**.

20. Make sure there is sufficient brake fluid in the master cylinder reservoir. Top it off if necessary.

21. Untie the brake pedal from the frame and pump the rear brake pedal to reposition the brake pads

6. Remove the screws securing the cover, and remove the cover (**Figure 71**) and diaphragm.

7. Use a shop syringe to remove about 50 percent of the brake fluid from the reservoir. This will prevent the master cylinder from overflowing when the pistons are compressed for reinstallation. Do *not* drain more than 50 percent of the brake fluid or air will enter the system. Discard the brake fluid.

8. Loosen the pad pin bolts (**Figure 77**).

CAUTION
Do not allow the master cylinder to overflow during Step 9. Wash brake fluid off painted, plated, or plastic surfaces immediately as it will destroy most surfaces it contacts. Use soapy water and rinse completely.

CAUTION
The brake disc is thin and easily damaged. When pushing against the disc in the following step, support the disc adjacent to the caliper to prevent damage.

9. Hold the caliper body from the outside and push it toward the brake disc. This will push the outer pis-

12

against the brake disc. Roll the motorcycle back and forth. Continue to pump the brake pedal as many times as it takes to refill the cylinders in the caliper and correctly position the brake pads against the disc.

22. Refill the master cylinder reservoir, if necessary, to maintain the correct fluid level as indicated on the side of the reservoir. Install the diaphragm and the top cover. Tighten the screws to the specification in **Table 2**.

> *WARNING*
> *Do not ride the motorcycle until the rear brake is operating correctly with full hydraulic advantage. If necessary, bleed the brakes as described in this chapter.*

REAR BRAKE CALIPER
(1999 MODELS)

Removal/Installation

1. If the caliper assembly is going to be disassembled for service, perform the following:

> *NOTE*
> *By performing Steps 1a-1e, compressed air may not be necessary for piston removal during caliper disassembly.*

a. Remove the caliper pad pin bolts (A, **Figure 72**) and remove the caliper from the caliper mounting bracket and the brake disc.

b. Insert a small screwdriver into the notched groove machined in the bottom of the piston bore (A, **Figure 82**). Then pry the retaining ring (**Figure 83**) out of the caliper body.

c. Wrap a large cloth around the brake caliper.

d. Hold the caliper away from the piston/brake pad area.

e. Operate the rear brake pedal to force the piston part way out of the caliper. Do not completely remove the piston until it is removed for disassembly. Leaving the piston partially in the bore helps prevent brake fluid from spilling out.

> *NOTE*
> *If the piston did not come out, remove it as described under **Disassembly** in this section.*

2. Remove the banjo bolt and sealing washers attaching the brake hose (C, **Figure 72**) to the caliper assembly. Remove the caliper assembly.

3. To remove the rear caliper mounting bracket, refer to *Rear Wheel Removal* in Chapter Eleven.

4. If the rear caliper is not going to be serviced, place it in a reclosable plastic bag to keep it clean.

5. Installation is the reverse of removal. Note the following:

a. Install the piston assembly as described in this chapter if it was removed.

b. Install the brake pads as described in this chapter if they were removed.

c. Carefully install the caliper assembly onto the brake pads.

d. Install the bolts securing the brake caliper assembly and tighten them to the specifications in **Table 2**.

e. Apply clean DOT 5 brake fluid to the rubber portions of the new sealing washers prior to installation.

f. Install a *new* sealing washer on each side of the brake hose fitting (C, **Figure 72**) and install the banjo bolt. Tighten the banjo bolt to the specification in **Table 2**.

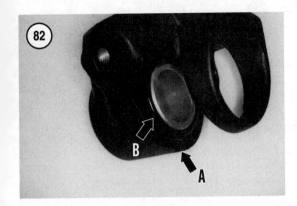

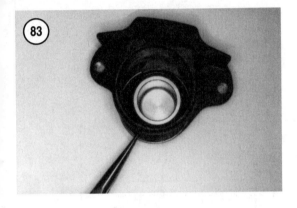

g. Bleed the brakes as described under *Bleeding the System* in this chapter.

> ### WARNING
> *Do not ride the motorcycle until the rear brake is operating correctly with full hydraulic advantage. If necessary, bleed the brakes as described in this chapter.*

Disassembly

1. Remove the brake caliper (**Figure 84**) as described in this chapter.

> ### NOTE
> *If the piston was partially forced out of the caliper body during removal, Steps 2-4 may not be necessary. If the piston or caliper bore is corroded or very dirty, a small amount of compressed air may be necessary to completely remove the piston from the body bore.*

2. Insert a screwdriver into the retaining ring groove (A, **Figure 82**) and pry the retaining ring out of the groove (**Figure 83**).

3. Place a piece of soft wood or a folded shop cloth over the end of the piston and the caliper body (**Figure 85**). Turn the assembly over with the piston facing down.

> ### WARNING
> *Compressed air will force the piston out of the caliper bodies under considerable force. Do not block the piston by hand, as injury will occur.*

4. Apply the air pressure in short spurts to the hydraulic fluid passageway to force out the piston. Use a service station air hose if compressed air is not available.

5. Remove the piston and dust boot assembly (**Figure 86**).

6. Remove the piston seal (**Figure 87**) from the groove in the caliper body.

Inspection

Service specifications for the caliper components are not available. Replace any worn, damaged or questionable parts.

1. Clean the caliper body and piston in clean DOT 5 brake fluid or isopropyl alcohol and dry them with compressed air.

2. Inspect the hydraulic fluid passageway in the cylinder bore. Make sure it is clean and open. Clean it with compressed air.

3. Inspect the piston and cylinder bore wall for scratches, scoring or other damage.

4. Make sure the hole in the bleed valve screw is clean and open. Clean it with compressed air.

5. Check the pin bolts for wear or damage.

6. Replace the pad shims if they are corroded or damaged.

7. Check the brake pads for excessive wear or damage. Measure the thickness of the brake pad friction material. Replace the brake pads if they are worn to the service limit dimension in **Table 1**.

8. Check all of the rubber parts for cracks, wear or deterioration.

12

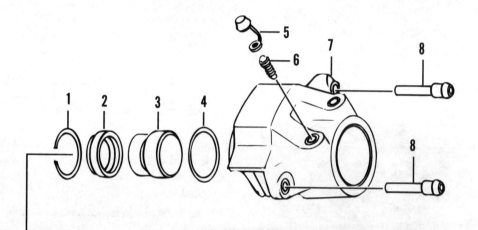

REAR BRAKE CALIPER (1999)

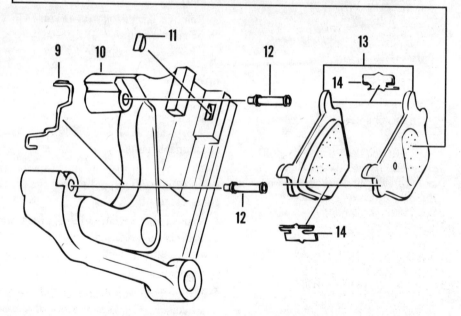

1. Retaining ring
2. Dust boot
3. Piston
4. Piston seal
5. Cap
6. Bleed valve
7. Body
8. Pad pin bolt
9. Retaining clip
10. Mounting bracket
11. Bumper
12. Rubber boot
13. Brake pads
14. Shim

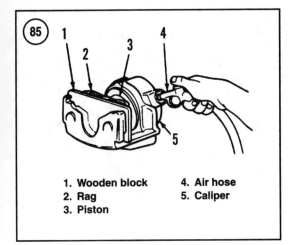

85
1. Wooden block   4. Air hose
2. Rag   5. Caliper
3. Piston

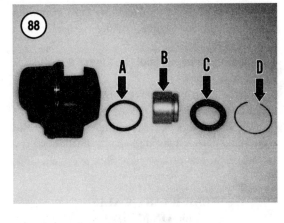

88

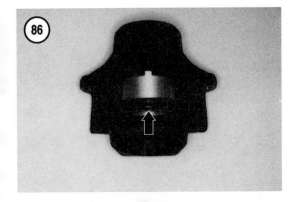

86

89

rioration can make the boot and seal ineffective.

2. Soak the new dust and piston seal in clean DOT 5 brake fluid.

3. Make sure the retaining ring, piston and caliper bore are thoroughly clean.

4. Install the piston seal (**Figure 87**) into the caliper body groove.

5. Install the piston dust boot (**Figure 89**) on the piston before installing the piston in the caliper bore. Perform the following:

   a. Place the piston on the workbench with its open side facing up.

   b. Align the piston dust boot with the piston so the shoulder on the dust boot faces up.

   c. Slide the dust boot over the piston until the inner lip on the dust boot seats in the piston groove.

6. Coat the piston and caliper bore with DOT 5 brake fluid.

Assembly

1. A Harley-Davidson rebuild kit (part No. 43946-86) includes a piston seal (A, **Figure 88**), piston (B), dust boot (C) and retaining ring (D).

NOTE
Never reuse an old dust boot or piston seal. Very minor damage or age dete-

12

7. Align the piston with the caliper bore so that its open end faces out (**Figure 90**), then push the piston in until it bottoms.

8. Seat the piston dust boot (B, **Figure 82**) into the caliper bore.

9. Install the retaining ring (**Figure 83**) so the gap in the ring (**Figure 90**) is at the top of the caliper bore (**Figure 91**). Make sure the retaining ring seats in the groove and pushes against the piston dust boot.

10. Install the brake pads as described in this chapter.

REAR BRAKE CALIPER (2000-ON MODELS)

Removal/Installation

CAUTION
Do not spill brake fluid on the swing arm or rear wheel. Wash brake fluid off any painted, plated, or plastic surfaces immediately as it will damage most surfaces it contacts. Use soapy water and rinse completely.

1. If the caliper assembly is going to be disassembled for service, perform the following:

NOTE
By performing Steps 1b and 1c, compressed air may not be necessary for piston removal during caliper disassembly.

   a. Remove the brake pads as described in this chapter.

CAUTION
Do not allow the pistons to travel out far enough to come in contact with the brake disc. If this happens, the pistons may scratch or gouge the disc during caliper removal.

   b. Slowly apply the brake lever to push the pistons part way out of the caliper assembly for ease of removal during caliper service.
   c. Loosen the brake hose banjo bolt (A, **Figure 92**).
   d. Loosen the three caliper body bolts (B, **Figure 92**).

2. Remove the banjo bolt and sealing washers (A, **Figure 92**) attaching the brake hose to the caliper assembly.

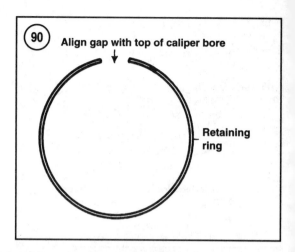

90 Align gap with top of caliper bore

Retaining ring

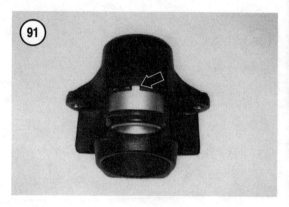

91

3. Place the loose end of the brake hose in a reclosable plastic bag to prevent the entry of debris and to prevent residual brake fluid from leading out.

4. Refer to *Rear Wheel Removal/Installation* in Chapter Nine and follow the procedure until the rear axle is removed sufficiently (A, **Figure 93**) to allow removal of the rear caliper assembly (B). After removal of the caliper assembly, push the rear axle back into place and install the nut on the other side.

5. If necessary, disassemble and service the caliper assembly as described in this chapter.

6. If the rear caliper is not going to be serviced, place it in a reclosable plastic bag to keep it clean.

7. Installation is the reverse of removal. Note the following:

   a. Install the caliper assembly onto the disc, being careful not to damage the leading edge of the brake pads.

   b. Refer to Chapter Nine to complete the installation of the rear axle.

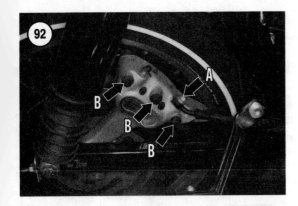

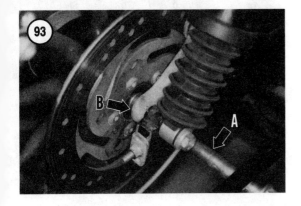

c. Apply clean DOT 5 brake fluid to the rubber portions of the *new* sealing washers prior to installation.

d. Install a *new* sealing washer on each side of the brake hose fitting and install the banjo bolt (A, **Figure 92**). Tighten the banjo bolt to the specification in **Table 2**.

e. If disassembled, tighten the three caliper body bolts (B, **Figure 92**) to the specification in **Table 2**.

f. Bleed the brakes as described under *Bleeding the System* in this chapter.

> *WARNING*
> *Do not ride the motorcycle until the rear brake is operating correctly with full hydraulic advantage. If necessary, bleed the brakes as described in this chapter.*

Disassembly

1. Remove the caliper and brake pads (**Figure 94**) as described in this chapter.

2. Remove the three caliper body bolts (**Figure 95**) loosened during the removal procedure.

3. Separate the caliper body halves. Remove the O-ring seals (**Figure 96**). New O-ring seals must be installed every time the caliper is disassembled.

> *NOTE*
> *If the pistons were partially forced out of the caliper body during removal, Steps 4-6 may not be necessary. If the pistons or caliper bores are corroded or very dirty, a small amount of compressed air may be necessary to completely remove the pistons from the body bores.*

4. Place a piece of soft wood or a folded shop cloth over the end of the pistons and the caliper body. Turn the assembly over and place it on the workbench with the pistons facing down.

> *WARNING*
> *Compressed air will force the pistons out of the caliper bodies under considerable force. Do not block the piston by hand as injury will occur.*

5. Apply the air pressure in short spurts to the hydraulic fluid passageway to force out the pistons. Repeat this for the other caliper body half. Use a service station air hose if compressed air is unavailable.

> *CAUTION*
> *In Step 7, do not use a sharp tool to remove the dust and piston seals from the caliper cylinders. Do not damage the cylinder surface.*

6. Use a piece of wood or a plastic scraper to carefully push the dust seal and the piston seal in toward the caliper cylinder and out of their grooves. Remove the dust and piston seals.

7. If necessary, unscrew and remove the bleed valve (**Figure 97**).

8. Inspect the caliper assembly as described in this section.

Inspection

1. Clean both caliper body halves and pistons in clean DOT 5 brake fluid or isopropyl alcohol, and dry them with compressed air.

12

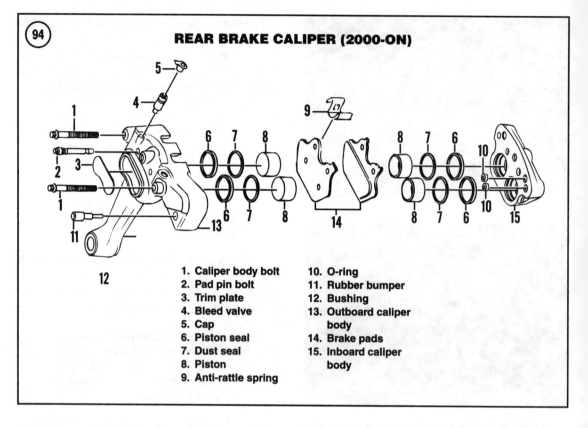

REAR BRAKE CALIPER (2000-ON)

1. Caliper body bolt
2. Pad pin bolt
3. Trim plate
4. Bleed valve
5. Cap
6. Piston seal
7. Dust seal
8. Piston
9. Anti-rattle spring
10. O-ring
11. Rubber bumper
12. Bushing
13. Outboard caliper body
14. Brake pads
15. Inboard caliper body

2. Make sure the fluid passageways (**Figure 98**) in the piston bores are clear by applying compressed air to the openings. Clean them out, if necessary, with clean brake fluid.

3. Make sure the fluid passageways (**Figure 99**) in both caliper body halves are clear by applying compressed air to the openings. Clean them out, if necessary, with clean brake fluid.

4. Inspect the piston and dust seal grooves in both caliper bodies for damage. If they are damaged or corroded, replace the caliper assembly.

5. Inspect the banjo bolt threaded hole in the outboard caliper body. If it is worn or damaged, clean it out with a metric thread tap or replace the caliper assembly.

6. Inspect the bleed valve threaded hole in the caliper body. If it is worn or damaged, clean it out with a metric thread tap or replace the caliper assembly.

7. Inspect the bleed valve. Apply compressed air to the opening and make sure it is clear. Clean it out if necessary with clean brake fluid. Install the bleed valve and tighten it to the specification in **Table 2**.

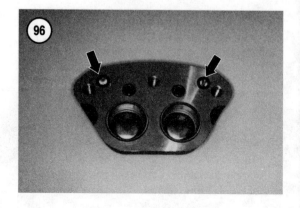

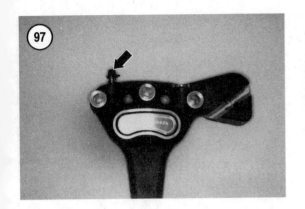

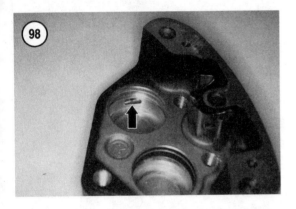

8. Inspect both caliper bodies for damage. Check the inboard caliper mounting bolt hole threads (**Figure 100**) for wear or damage. Clean them with an appropriate size metric tap or replace the caliper assembly.

9. Inspect the cylinder walls and pistons for scratches, scoring or other damage.

10. Check the antirattle spring for wear or damage.

Assembly

> *NOTE*
> *Never reuse old dust seals or piston seals. Very minor damage or age deterioration can make the seals ineffective.*

1. Soak the new dust and piston seals in clean DOT 5 brake fluid.

2. Coat the piston bores and pistons with clean DOT 5 brake fluid.

3. Carefully install the new piston seals into the lower grooves. Make sure the seals are properly seated in their respective grooves.

4. Carefully install the new dust seals into the upper grooves. Make sure all seals are properly seated in their respective grooves.

5. Repeat Step 3 and Step 4 for the other caliper body half.

6. Position the pistons with the open end facing out and install the pistons into the caliper cylinders. Push the pistons in until they bottom.

7. Repeat Step 6 for the other caliper body half. Make sure all pistons are installed correctly.

8. Coat the *new* O-ring seals in DOT 5 brake fluid and install the O-rings (**Figure 96**) into the inboard caliper half.

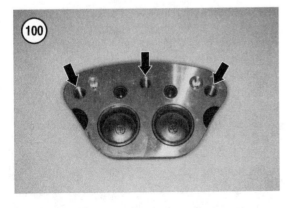

9. Install the antirattle spring (**Figure 101**) onto the boss on the outboard caliper half.

12

10. Make sure the O-rings are still in place and assemble the caliper body halves.

11. Install the three caliper body bolts (**Figure 95**) and tighten them securely. Tighten them to the specified torque after the caliper is installed on the rear disc.

12. Install the rubber bumper (**Figure 102**) if it was removed.

13. Install the bleed valve (**Figure 97**) if it was removed and tighten it to the torque specification in **Table 2**.

14. Install the caliper and brake pads as described in this chapter.

15. Tighten the three caliper body bolts to the specification in **Table 2**.

16. Bleed the brakes as described under *Bleeding the System* in this chapter.

REAR MASTER CYLINDER AND REAR BRAKE PEDAL

Removal

1. Remove the exhaust system as described in Chapter Seven.

2. Refer to Chapter Fourteen and perform the following:

    a. On models so equipped, remove the right side lower fairing.

    b. Remove the right side saddlebag.

    c. Remove the right side rider footboard.

3. At the rear brake caliper, perform the following:

    a. Insert a hose onto the end of the bleed valve (**Figure 103**). Insert the open end of the hose into a container.

    b. Open the bleed valve and operate the rear brake pedal to drain the brake fluid. Remove the hose and close the bleed valve after draining the assembly. Discard the brake fluid properly.

4. Remove the screws securing the cover, and remove the cover (A, **Figure 104**) and diaphragm.

5. Remove the banjo bolt (B, **Figure 104**) and sealing washers securing the brake hose to the front of the master cylinder cartridge body.

6. Remove and/or release clips or tie-wraps securing the rear brake line to the chassis until there is only enough slack in the brake line to allow the removal of the brake line from the front of the master cylinder fitting.

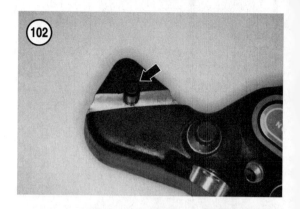

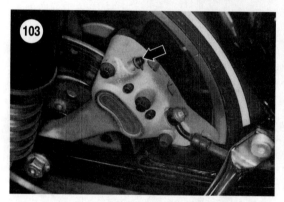

7. Disconnect the rear brake line from the front of the master cylinder. Place the loose end of the brake hose in a reclosable plastic bag to prevent the entry of debris and to prevent any residual brake fluid from leaking out.

8. Using an 1 1/8 in. open-end wench, remove the hex nut (A, **Figure 105**) securing the front of the master cylinder cartridge assembly to the frame boss. Pull the master cylinder free from the square hole in the frame boss.

9. Remove the locknut and washer (B, **Figure 105**) securing the master cylinder and rear brake pedal

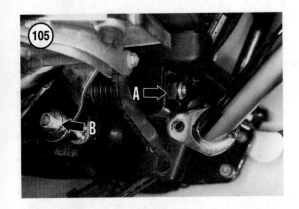

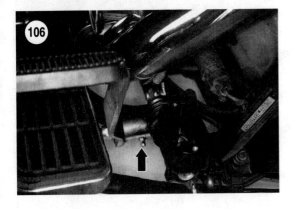

assembly to the frame pivot post. Remove the assembly from the frame.

10. If necessary, disconnect the rear brake pedal from the master cylinder as follows:

    a. Remove the cotter pin and washer from the clevis pin. Discard the cotter pin.

    b. Support the assembly in a vise. Use a brass drift to carefully tap out the clevis pin from both parts.

11. If necessary, service the master cylinder as described in this chapter. If the master cylinder is not going to be serviced, place it in a reclosable plastic bag to keep it clean.

Installation

1. If the brake pedal was disconnected from the master cylinder, perform the following:

    a. Reposition the rear brake pedal onto the rear master cylinder.

    b. Support the assembly in a vise and tap the clevis pin into both parts. Tap it in until it bottoms.

    c. Install the washer and a *new* cotter pin. Bend the ends over completely.

2. Install the master cylinder and rear brake pedal assembly to the frame pivot post.

3. Install the washer and a *new* locknut (B, **Figure 105**). Tighten the locknut to the specification in **Table 2**.

4. Using a grease gun, apply grease to the grease fitting (**Figure 106**) until the grease is visible around the edges of the brake pedal lever. Wipe off excess grease.

5. Carefully insert the master cylinder cartridge body into the square hole in the frame boss.

6. Apply ThreeBond TB1342 or an equivalent threadlocking compound to the hex nut threads prior to installation. Install the hex nut (A, **Figure 105**) and tighten it to the specification in **Table 2**.

7. Connect the rear brake line to the front of the master cylinder cartridge body.

8. Install a *new* steel/rubber washer on each side of the brake hose banjo fitting. Insert the banjo bolt (B, **Figure 104**) through the washers and banjo fitting, and thread it into the cartridge body. Then tighten the banjo bolt to the torque specification in **Table 2**.

9. Secure the rear brake line to the chassis using tie-wraps or new clips.

10. Bleed the brakes as described under *Bleeding the System* in this chapter.

11. Refer to Chapter Fourteen and perform the following:

    a. Install the right side rider footboard.

    b. Install the right side saddlebag.

    c. On models so equipped, install the right side lower fairing.

12. Install the exhaust system as described in Chapter Seven.

> *WARNING*
> *Do not ride the motorcycle until the rear brake is operating correctly with full hydraulic advantage.*

Disassembly

Refer to **Figure 107**.

1. Clean the exterior master cylinder housing with clean DOT 5 brake fluid or isopropyl alcohol and dry it.

2. Store the master cylinder components in a divided container, such as a restaurant-size egg car-

12

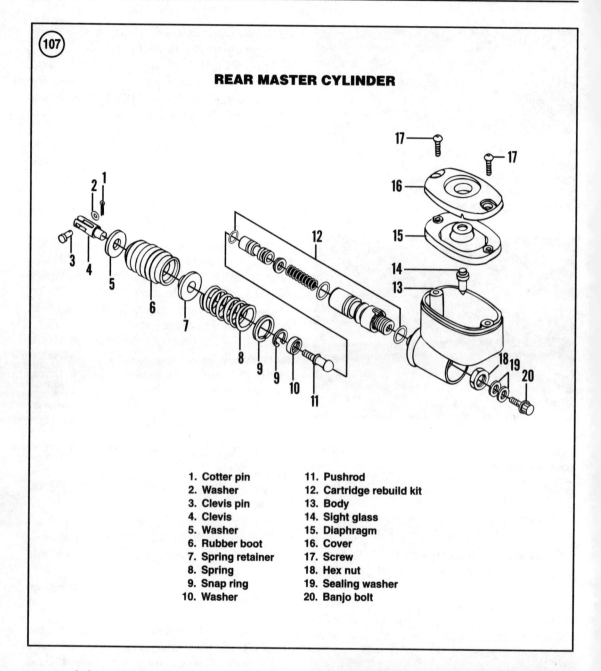

REAR MASTER CYLINDER

1. Cotter pin
2. Washer
3. Clevis pin
4. Clevis
5. Washer
6. Rubber boot
7. Spring retainer
8. Spring
9. Snap ring
10. Washer
11. Pushrod
12. Cartridge rebuild kit
13. Body
14. Sight glass
15. Diaphragm
16. Cover
17. Screw
18. Hex nut
19. Sealing washer
20. Banjo bolt

ton, to help maintain their correct alignment positions.

3. Remove the master cylinder cover and diaphragm if it is still installed.

4. Compress the spring, rubber boot and washer.

5. Carefully tap out the roll pin (A, **Figure 108**) securing the clevis to the pushrod.

6. Unscrew the clevis (B, **Figure 108**) and remove it from the pushrod.

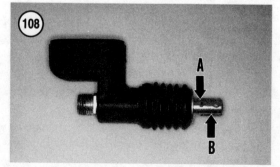

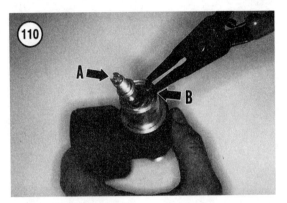

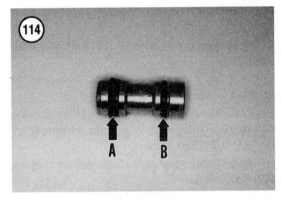

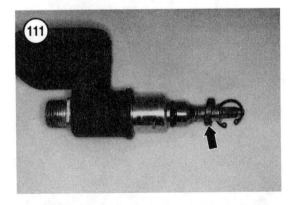

7. Remove the washer, rubber boot, spring retainer and spring (**Figure 109**).

8. Depress the pushrod (A, **Figure 110**) and remove the snap ring (B).

9. Remove the pushrod (**Figure 111**).

10. Remove the piston assembly (A, **Figure 112**) and spring (B) from the cartridge.

12

Inspection

1. Clean all parts in clean DOT 5 brake fluid or isopropyl alcohol and dry them with compressed air. Replace worn or damage parts as described in this section. It is recommended that a new cartridge rebuild kit assembly be installed every time the master cylinder is disassembled.

2. Inspect the cartridge body cylinder bore surface (**Figure 113**) for signs of wear and damage. Do not hone the cartridge bore to clean or repair it. If it is less than perfect, replace the cartridge and/or the master cylinder reservoir.

3. Check the piston primary cup (A, **Figure 114**) and the O-ring (B) for deterioration or damage.

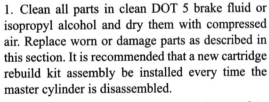

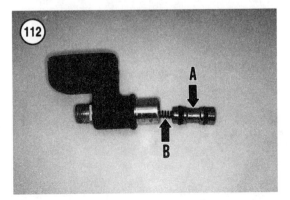

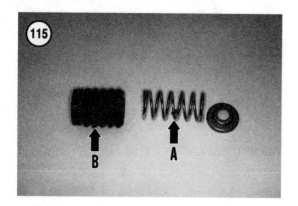

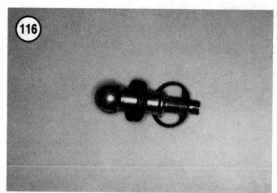

4. Check the spring (A, **Figure 115**) for bending, unequally spaced coils or corrosion.

5. Inspect the boot (B, **Figure 115**) for tears or deterioration.

6. Check the pushrod, washer and snap ring (**Figure 116**) for bending, wear or damage.

7. Check the reservoir body (**Figure 117**) for corrosion or other damage. Make sure the opening (**Figure 118**) in the base is clear.

8. Check the reservoir cap and diaphragm (**Figure 119**) for damage.

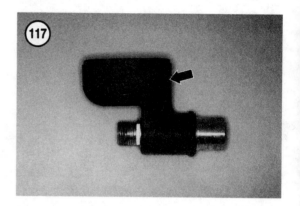

Assembly

1. Coat all parts with clean DOT 5 brake fluid.

2. Soak the primary cup, O-ring and piston assembly in clean DOT 5 brake fluid for 15 minutes to make them pliable. Coat the inside of the cartridge bore with clean brake fluid prior to the assembling the parts.

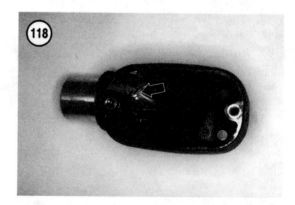

> *CAUTION*
> *When installing the piston assembly, do not allow the primary cup to turn inside out as it will be damaged and allow brake fluid leaks in the cartridge cylinder bore.*

3. Install the spring (B, **Figure 112**) into the cartridge.

4. Position the piston assembly with the primary cup (A, **Figure 112**) end going in first. Make sure the piston cup does not tear as it passes through the bore entrance.

5. Turn the reservoir on its end on a shop cloth. Carefully push the piston assembly into the cartridge with a Phillips screwdriver. Push the piston

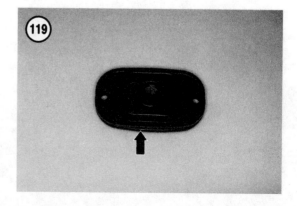

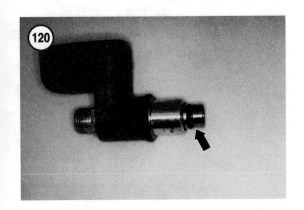

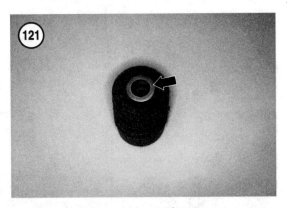

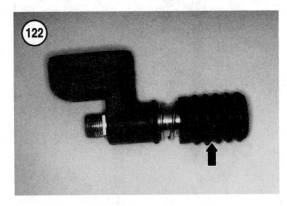

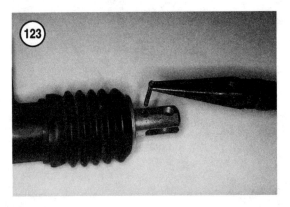

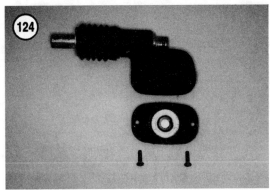

assembly in, then let it move out, several times to check for ease of movement.

6. Position the pushrod onto the end of the piston (**Figure 111**) and push the piston (**Figure 120**) into the cartridge. Hold the push rod in place (A, **Figure 110**) and install the snap ring (B). Make sure the snap ring is correctly seated in the cartridge groove.

7. Install the spring and spring seat (**Figure 109**) onto the pushrod and cartridge.

8. Install the washer into the boot and push it all the way to the end (**Figure 121**).

9. Install the boot (**Figure 122**) onto the pushrod and cartridge.

10. Install the clevis and tighten it against the pushrod until the roll pin holes are aligned.

11. Install the roll pin (**Figure 123**) and tap it into place until it is flush.

12. Install the diaphragm and reservoir cover (**Figure 124**).

12

BRAKE HOSE AND LINE REPLACEMENT

A combination of steel and flexible brake lines connect the master cylinder to the brake calipers. Banjo fittings and bolts connect brake hoses to the master cylinder and brake calipers. Steel/rubber washers seal the banjo fittings.

Replace a hose if the flexible portion is swelling, cracking or damaged. Replace the brake hose if the metal portion leaks or if there are dents or cracks.

Front Brake Hose Removal/Installation

A combination steel/flexible brake hose (**Figure 125**) connects the front master cylinder to the front brake caliper. When purchasing a new hose, compare it to the old hose to make sure the length and angle of the steel hose portion are correct. Install new banjo bolt washers at both ends.

> *CAUTION*
> *Do not spill brake fluid on the front fork or front wheel. Wash brake fluid off painted, plated, or plastic surfaces immediately as it will damage most surfaces it contacts. Use soapy water and rinse completely.*

1. On models so equipped, refer to Chapter Fourteen and remove all fairing panels necessary to gain access to the front brake line where it attaches to the lower steering stem.
2. Drain the front brake system as follows:
   a. Connect a hose over the bleed valve (A, **Figure 126**).
   b. Insert the loose end of the hose into a container to catch the brake fluid.
   c. Open the bleed valve and apply the front brake lever to pump the fluid out of the master cylinder and brake line. Continue until the fluid is removed.
   d. Close the bleed valve and disconnect the hose.
   e. Repeat this step for the opposite side.
   f. Dispose of the brake fluid. Never reuse brake fluid. Contaminated brake fluid will cause brake failure.
3. Before removing the brake line assembly, note the brake line routing from the master cylinder to the calipers. Note the number and position of metal hose clamps and/or plastic ties used to hold the brake lines in place.
4. Remove any metal clamp or cut any plastic ties.
5. Remove the bolt securing the brake hose mounting plate (**Figure 127**) to the lower steering stem. On models so equipped, do not lose the guide plate between the hose mounting plate and the steering stem.
6. Remove the screw or nut securing the metal clamps around the brake line. Spread the clamp and remove it from the brake line.
7. Remove the banjo bolt (B, **Figure 126**) and washers securing the hose to the brake calipers.
8. Remove the banjo bolt (**Figure 128**) and washers securing the hose to the front master cylinder.

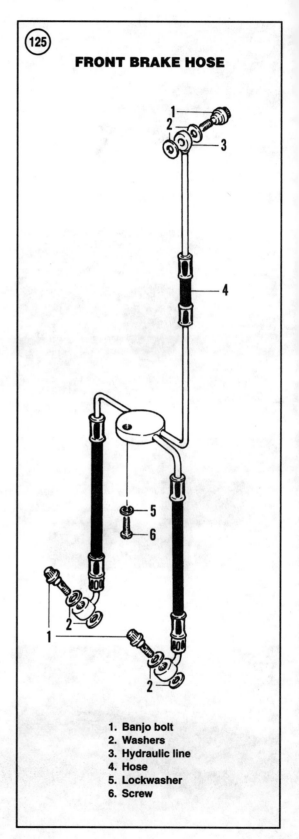

(125)

FRONT BRAKE HOSE

1. Banjo bolt
2. Washers
3. Hydraulic line
4. Hose
5. Lockwasher
6. Screw

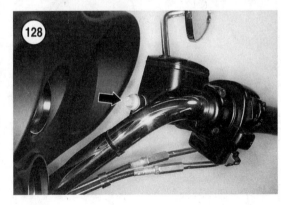

c. If wear or damage is found, replace the brake hose assembly.

12. Install the brake hose, washers and banjo bolts (**Figure 125**) in the reverse order of removal. Note the following:

    a. Install *new* sealing washers against the side of each hose fitting.

    b. Carefully install the clips and guides to hold the brake hose in place.

    c. Tighten the banjo bolts to the torque specification in **Table 2**.

    d. Refill the front master cylinder with clean brake fluid clearly marked DOT 5. Bleed the front brake system as described in this chapter.

> *WARNING*
> *Do not ride the motorcycle until the front brakes operate correctly with full hydraulic advantage.*

Rear Brake Hose
Removal/Installation

A single combination steel and rubber brake hose (**Figure 129**) connects the rear master cylinder to the rear brake caliper. The rear brake switch is installed in the rear brake hose. When buying a new hose, compare it to the old hose. Make sure the length and angle of the steel hose portion are correct. Install new banjo bolt washers at both hose ends.

> *CAUTION*
> *Do not spill brake fluid on the swing arm, frame or rear wheel. Wash brake fluid off any painted, plated or plastic surfaces immediately as it will damage most surfaces it contacts. Use soapy water and rinse completely.*

1. Remove the exhaust system as described in Chapter Seven.

2. On models so equipped, remove the right side saddlebag as described in Chapter Fourteen.

3. Drain the hydraulic brake fluid from the rear brake system as follows:

    a. Connect a hose to the rear caliper bleed valve. Refer to A, **Figure 130**, typical.

    b. Insert the loose end of the hose in a container to catch the brake fluid.

9. Cover the ends of the brake hoses to prevent brake fluid from leaking out.

10. Remove the brake hose assembly from the motorcycle.

11. If the existing brake hose assembly is going to be reinstalled, inspect it as follows:

    a. Check the metal pipes where they enter and exit at the flexible hoses. Check the crimped clamp for looseness or damage.

    b. Check the flexible hose portions for swelling, cracks or other damage.

12

c. Open the caliper bleed valve and operate the rear brake pedal to pump the fluid out of the master cylinder and brake line. Continue until all of the fluid is removed.

d. Close the bleed valve and disconnect the hose.

e. Dispose of the brake fluid. Never reuse brake fluid. Contaminated brake fluid will cause brake failure.

4. Before removing the brake line, note the brake line routing from the master cylinder to the caliper. Note the number and position of the metal hose clamps, plastic clips and plastic ties used to hold the brake line in place. The metal clamp and plastic clips can be reused.

NOTE
To open the cable clips, insert a small screwdriver into the gap at the side of the clip and carefully rotate the screwdriver.

5. Open the two cable clips on the lower frame tube T-studs.

6. At the rear brake light switch, cut the plastic tie securing the rear brake light switch wires, voltage regulator wires and the engine sensor harness to the frame lower tube.

7. Cut the plastic tie securing the voltage regulator wires and the engine sensor harness to the brake hose.

8. Remove the bolt and clamp securing the brake hose to the rear swing arm.

9. Open the two cable clips on the rear swing arm T-studs and release the brake hose from the clips.

10. Disconnect the electrical connector from the rear brake switch.

11. Remove the screw securing the brake light switch to the frame bracket.

12. Remove the banjo bolt (B, **Figure 130**) and washers securing the hose to the brake caliper.

13. Remove the banjo bolt (**Figure 131**) and washers securing the hose to the master cylinder.

14. Carefully move the rear brake line assembly forward and away from the rear swing arm bracket. Remove the brake hose from the motorcycle.

15. If the existing brake hose assembly is going to be reinstalled, inspect it as follows:

a. Check the metal pipe where it enters and exits the flexible hose. Check the crimped clamp for looseness or damage.

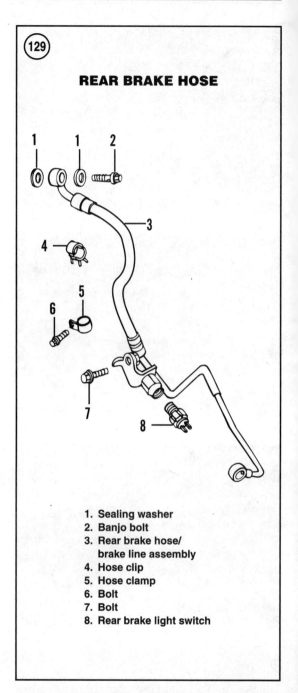

REAR BRAKE HOSE

1. Sealing washer
2. Banjo bolt
3. Rear brake hose/ brake line assembly
4. Hose clip
5. Hose clamp
6. Bolt
7. Bolt
8. Rear brake light switch

b. Check the flexible hose portion for swelling, cracks or other damage.

c. If wear or damage is found, replace the brake hose.

16. If replacement is necessary, remove the stoplight switch from the rear brake hose fitting.

17. Installation is the reverse of removal. Note the following:

12

WARNING
Do not ride the motorcycle until the rear brake is operating correctly with full hydraulic advantage.

BRAKE DISC

The brake discs are separate from the wheel hubs and can be removed once the wheel is removed from the motorcycle.

Inspection

It is not necessary to remove the disc from the wheel to inspect it. Small nicks and marks on the disc are not important, but radial scratches deep enough to snag a fingernail reduce braking effectiveness and increase brake pad wear. If these grooves are present, and the brake pads are wearing rapidly, replace the disc.

Each disc is marked with the minimum (MIN) thickness. If the disc is worn to this thickness, replace the disc.

When servicing the brake discs, do not have the discs surfaced to compensate for warp. The discs are thin, and grinding will only reduce their thickness, causing them to warp rapidly. A warped disc may be caused by the brake pads dragging on the disc, due to a faulty caliper, and overheating the disc. Overheating can also be caused by unequal pad pressure on the disc.

Three main causes of unequal brake pad pressure are:

1. The brake caliper piston seals are worn or damaged.

2. The small master cylinder relief port is plugged.

3. The primary cup on the master cylinder piston is worn or damaged.

NOTE
It is not necessary to remove the wheel to measure the disc thickness. The measurement can be performed with the wheel installed or removed from the motorcycle.

4. Measure the thickness of the disc at several locations around the disc with a vernier caliper or a micrometer (**Figure 132**). Replace the disc if the thickness in any area is less than that specified on the marked MIN dimension on the disc.

a. Install and tighten the stoplight switch securely.

b. Install *new* sealing washers against the side of each hose fitting.

c. Carefully install the clips and guides to hold the brake hose in place.

d. Tighten the banjo bolts to the torque specification in **Table 2**.

e. Refill the master cylinder with clean brake fluid clearly marked DOT 5. Bleed the rear brake system as described in this chapter.

5. Make sure the disc mounting bolts are tight prior to running this check. Check the disc runout with a dial indicator as shown in **Figure 133**.

> *NOTE*
> *When checking the front disc, turn the handlebar all the way to one side, then to the other side.*

6. Slowly rotate the wheel and watch the dial indicator. If the runout exceeds the specification in **Table 1**, replace the disc(s).

7. Clean the disc of any rust or corrosion and wipe it clean with brake cleaner. Never use an oil-based solvent that may leave an oil residue on the disc.

Removal/Installation

1. Remove the front or rear wheel as described in Chapter Nine.

> *NOTE*
> *On the front wheels on some models, the disc is marked with a LEFT or RIGHT. If the disc is not marked, mark it prior to removal. The disc must be reinstalled on the correct side of the wheel.*

2. Remove the Torx bolts (**Figure 134**) securing the brake disc to the hub and remove the disc.

3. Check the brake disc bolts for thread damage. Replace worn or damaged fasteners.

4. Check the threaded bolt holes for the brake disc in the wheel hub for thread damage. True them with a tap if necessary.

5. Clean the disc and the disc mounting surface thoroughly with brake cleaner. Allow the surfaces to dry before installation.

6A. On 1999 models, install the front brake discs as follows:

  a. Install the disc onto the correct side of the wheel hub, aligning the notch in the brake disc with the 1/4 in. (6.3 mm) blind hole in the hub (**Figure 135**).

  b. Apply a drop of ThreeBond TB1342 or an equivalent to the threads of the *new* Torx bolts prior to installation.

  c. Install the bolts and tighten them to the specification in **Table 2**.

  d. Repeat substeps a-c for the other disc.

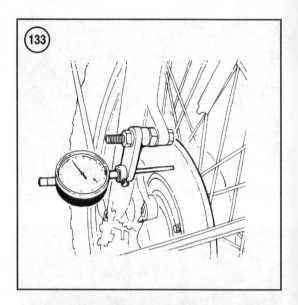

6B. On 2000-on models, install the front brake discs as follows:

  a. Install the disc onto the correct side of the wheel hub.

  b. Apply a drop of ThreeBond TB1342 or an equivalent to the threads of *new* Torx bolts prior to installation.

  c. Install the bolts and tighten them to the specification in **Table 2**.

  d. Repeat substeps a-c for the other disc.

7. Install the rear brake disc as follows:

  a. Apply a drop of ThreeBond TB1342 or an equivalent to the threads of *new* Torx bolts prior to installation.

  b. Install the bolts and tighten them to the specification in **Table 2**.

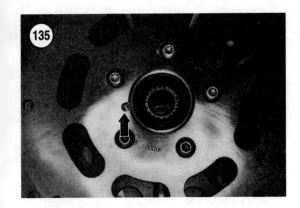

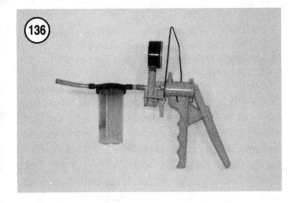

BLEEDING THE SYSTEM

If air enters the brake system, the brake will feel soft or spongy and braking pressure will be reduced. Bleed the system to remove the air. Air can enter the system if there is a leak in the system, the brake fluid level in a master cylinder runs low, a brake line is opened or the brake fluid is replaced.

The brakes can be bled with a brake bleeder or manually. This section includes procedures for both.

Before bleeding the brake system:

1. Check the brake lines to make sure all fittings are tight.

2. Make sure the caliper piston does not stick or bind in its bore.

3. Check piston movement in each master cylinder. Operate the lever or brake pedal, making sure there is no binding or other abnormal conditions.

Brake Bleeder Process

This procedure uses the Mityvac hydraulic brake bleeding kit (**Figure 136**) available from automo-

tive or motorcycle supply stores and mail order outlets.

NOTE
This procedure is shown on the rear wheel and relates to the front wheel as well.

1. Remove the dust cap from the caliper bleed valve.

2. Place a clean shop cloth over the caliper to protect it from accidental brake fluid spills.

3. Open the bleed screw approximately a half turn.

4. Assemble the brake bleeder according to its manufacturer's instructions. Secure it to the caliper bleed valve.

5. Clean the top of the master cylinder of all dirt and debris.

6. Remove the screws securing the master cylinder top cover, and remove the cover and rubber diaphragm.

7. Fill the reservoir almost to the top with DOT 5 brake fluid, and reinstall the diaphragm and cover. Leave the cover in place during this procedure to prevent the entry of dirt.

WARNING
Do not intermix DOT 3, DOT 4, or DOT 5.1 brake fluids as they are not silicone-based. Non-silicone brake fluid used in these models can cause brake failure.

8. Operate the pump several times to create a vacuum in the line. Brake fluid will quickly flow from the caliper into the pump's reservoir. Tighten the caliper bleed valve before the fluid stops flowing through the hose. To prevent air from being drawn through the master cylinder, add fluid to maintain the level at the top of the reservoir.

NOTE
Do not allow the master cylinder reservoir to empty during the bleeding operation or more air will enter the system. If this occurs, the procedure must be repeated.

9. Continue the bleeding process until the fluid drawn from the caliper is bubble free. If bubbles are in the brake fluid, more air is trapped in the line. Repeat Step 8, making sure to refill the master cylinder to prevent air from being drawn into the system.

12

10. When the brake fluid is free of bubbles, tighten the bleed valve and remove the brake bleeder assembly. Reinstall the bleed valve dust cap.

NOTE
Dispose of the brake fluid expelled during the bleeding process. Do not reuse the brake fluid.

11. If necessary, add fluid to correct the level in the master cylinder reservoir. When topping off the front master cylinder, turn the handlebar until the reservoir is level. Add fluid until it is level with the reservoir gasket surface. The fluid level in the rear master cylinder must be slightly below the upper gasket surface.

12. On models with a dual-disc front brake, repeat Steps 1-11 for the other caliper.

13. Reinstall the reservoir diaphragm and cover. Install the screws and tighten securely.

14. Test the feel of the brake lever or pedal. It should be firm and offer the same resistance each time it is operated. If it feels spongy, there is probably still air in the system. Bleed the system again. After bleeding the system, check for leaks and tighten all fittings and connections as necessary.

WARNING
Do not ride the motorcycle until the front and/or rear brakes are operating correctly with full hydraulic advantage.

15. Test ride the motorcycle slowly at first to make sure the brakes are operating properly.

Without a Brake Bleeder

NOTE
Before bleeding the brakes, make sure all brake hoses and lines are tight.

1. Connect a length of clear tubing to the bleed valve on the caliper. Place the other end of the tube into a clean container. Fill the container with enough clean DOT 5 brake fluid to keep the end of the tube submerged. The tube must be long enough so a loop can be made higher than the bleeder valve to prevent air from being drawn into the caliper during bleeding.

2. Clean the top of the master cylinder of all debris.

3. Remove the screws securing the master cylinder top cover, and remove the cover and diaphragm.

4. Fill the reservoir almost to the top with DOT 5 brake fluid, and reinstall the diaphragm and cover. Leave the cover in place during this procedure to prevent the entry of dirt.

WARNING
Do not intermix DOT 3, DOT 4, or DOT 5.1 brake fluids as they are not silicone-based. Non-silicone brake fluid used in these models can cause brake failure.

NOTE
During this procedure, check the fluid level in the master cylinder reservoir often. If the reservoir runs dry, air will enter the system.

5. Slowly apply the brake lever several times. Hold the lever in the applied position and open the bleed valve about a half turn. Allow the lever to travel to its limit. When the limit is reached, tighten the bleed valve, then release the brake lever. As the brake fluid enters the system, the level will drop in the master cylinder reservoir. Maintain the level at the top of the reservoir to prevent air from being drawn into the system.

6. Continue the bleeding process until the fluid emerging from the hose is completely free of air bubbles. If the fluid is being replaced, continue until the fluid emerging from the hose is clean.

NOTE
If bleeding is difficult, allow the fluid to stabilize for a few hours. Repeat the bleeding procedure when the bubbles in the system dissipate.

7. Hold the lever in the applied position and tighten the bleed valve. Remove the bleed tube and install the bleed valve dust cap.

NOTE
Dispose of the brake fluid expelled during the bleeding process. Do not reuse the brake fluid.

8. If necessary, add fluid to correct the level in the master cylinder reservoir. When topping off the front master cylinder, turn the handlebar until the reservoir is level. Add fluid until it is level with the reservoir gasket surface. The fluid level in the rear

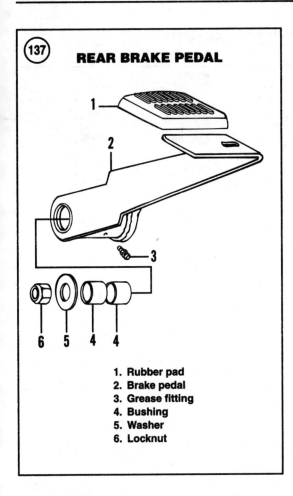

REAR BRAKE PEDAL

1. Rubber pad
2. Brake pedal
3. Grease fitting
4. Bushing
5. Washer
6. Locknut

master cylinder must be slightly below the upper gasket surface.

9. On models with a dual-disc front brake, repeat Steps 1-9 for the other caliper.

10. Install the diaphragm and top cover, and tighten the screws securely.

11. Test the feel of the brake lever or pedal. It should be firm and offer the same resistance each time it is operated. If it feels spongy, there is probably still air in the system and it must be bled again. After bleeding the system, check for leaks and tighten all fittings and connections as necessary.

WARNING
Do not ride the motorcycle until the front and/or rear brakes are operating correctly with full hydraulic advantage.

12. Test ride the motorcycle slowly at first to make sure the brakes are operating properly.

REAR BRAKE PEDAL

Removal/Installation

NOTE
The rear brake pedal is removed along with the rear master cylinder as an assembly.

1. Remove the rear brake pedal (**Figure 137**) as described under *Rear Master Cylinder* and *Rear Brake Pedal Removal* in this chapter.
2. If the rear brake pedal is still connected to the master cylinder, perform the following:
   a. Remove the cotter pin and washer from the clevis pin. Discard the cotter pin.
   b. Support the assembly in a vise. Use a brass drift to carefully tap out the clevis pin from both parts.
   c. Separate the rear brake pedal from the master cylinder.
3. Inspect the brake pedal bushings for fractures or damage, and replace it if necessary.
4. Install the pedal by reversing these removal steps.
5. Connect the brake pedal onto the master cylinder as follows:
   a. Reposition the rear brake pedal onto the rear master cylinder.
   b. Support the assembly in a vise and tap the clevis pin into both parts. Tap it in until it bottoms.
   c. Install the washer and a new cotter pin. Bend the ends over completely.

12

Table 1 BRAKE SYSTEM SPECIFICATIONS

Brake fluid	DOT 5 silicone base
Brake pad minimum thickness	
1999	1/16 in. (1.6 mm)
2000-on	0.04 in. (1.02 mm)
Brake disc thickness	Stamped on disc
Brake disc runout	.008 in. (0.20 mm)

Table 2 BRAKE SYSTEM TORQUE SPECIFICATIONS

Item	ft.-lb.	in.-lb.	N•m
Bleed valves	–	80-100	9-11
Brake disc bolts			
Front wheel	16-24	–	22-32
Rear wheel	30-45	–	41-61
Brake pad pins (2000-on)			
Front and rear calipers	15-17	180-200	20-23
Front brake caliper (1999)			
Inner brake pad retainer bolt	–	40-50	5-6
Upper mounting bolt	25-30	–	34-41
Lower mounting pin	25-30	–	34-41
Front brake caliper (2000-on)			
Caliper body bolts	28-38	–	38-51
Mounting bolt	28-38	–	38-52
Front master cylinder			
Clamp screw	–	70-80	8-9
Cover screws	–	6-8	1
Rear brake caliper (1999)			
Brake pad pin bolt	15-20	–	20-27
Caliper body bolts	28-38	–	38-51
Rear master cylinder			
Cartridge hex nut	50	–	68
Cover screws	–	6-8	1
Rear brake pedal locknut	15-18	–	20-24
Brake line banjo bolts	17-22	–	23-30

CHAPTER THIRTEEN

CRUISE CONTROL

This chapter covers service procedures for the mechanical and electrical components of the cruise control system.

The cruise control system is equipped with an on-board diagnostic system that displays codes if a problem with the system has occurred. Refer to *Cruise Control System Diagnostic Codes* in Chapter Two.

During normal operation, the cruise engagement light *C* is illuminated only when the cruise is in operation

SYSTEM COMPONENTS AND OPERATION

The cruise control system consists of a cruise control module containing the stepper motor, switches and the related wiring. The stepper motor actuates the cruise control cable through a gear train and ribbon reel.

The cruise control module receives command signals from the cruise control SET/RESUME switch on the right side handlebar switch. The cruise control module receives information on operating conditions from the speedometer output signal.

The cruise control system will automatically maintain any speed between 30-85 mph (48-137 km/h). To set the cruise control, turn the front fairing cap cruise ON/OFF switch to the ON position. Power is supplied to the cruise control module through the 15 amp fuse in the fuse block under the frame left side cover.

After reaching the desired speed, momentarily push the cruise SET/RESUME switch to the SET position. The cruise control module receives a signal input from the speedometer. The cruise control module then sends a signal to the steeper motor to open or close the throttle via the cruise control cable. The cruise control module monitors both the engine speed and the speedometer output signal to control the steeper motor and maintain the desired speed.

13

The cruise control is automatically disengaged whenever the cruise control module receives one of the following inputs.

1. The front or rear brake is applied.

2. The throttle is rolled back or closed.

3. The clutch is disengaged.

4. The cruise ON/OFF switch is moved to the OFF position.

5. The engine stop switch is moved to the OFF position.

6. The handlebar cruise SET/RESUME switch is moved to the SET position and held in that position until the motorcycle speed drops below 30 mph (48 km/h).

CONTROL CABLES

Throttle and Idle Cables

The throttle and idle cable adjustment must be performed by a Harley-Davidson dealership equipped with a Scanalyzer tool. The engine must be at a specific temperature during this procedure and must be monitored to assure correct adjustment.

Cruise Control Cable

The cruise control cable only requires adjustment if the cruise control module or cruise control cable are removed or replaced. If necessary, adjust the cruise control cable using the *Cable Lash Initialization* procedure in this chapter.

Removal

1. Remove the fuel tank as described in Chapter Seven.

2. Remove the left side saddlebag as described in Chapter Fourteen.

3. Remove the frame left side cover.

4. Remove the air filter and backing plate as described in this chapter.

5. Remove the E-clip and release the cable housing from the induction module.

6. At the outboard side of the pin wheel (A, **Figure 1**), push on the plastic end fitting (B) and remove it from the pin wheel.

7. Remove the cruise cable (A, **Figure 2**) from the cable clip (B) on the frame.

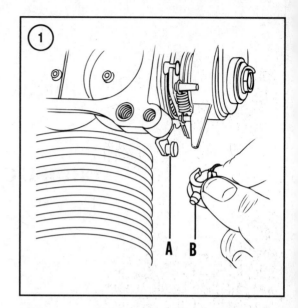

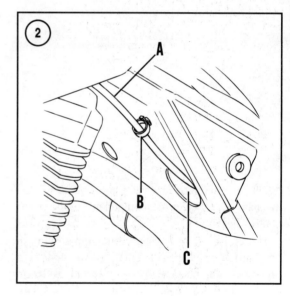

8. Make a drawing or take a picture of the cable routing from the cruise control module to the induction module.

9. Carefully remove the cruise cable from under the fuel tank.

10. Rotate the cruise cable connector in a counterclockwise direction and detach it from the cruise control module.

11. Pull the cable out of the connector and remove the cable end bead from the ribbon end eyelet.

12. Pull the cruise control cable and connector from the hole (C, **Figure 2**) in the frame cross member and remove it from the frame.

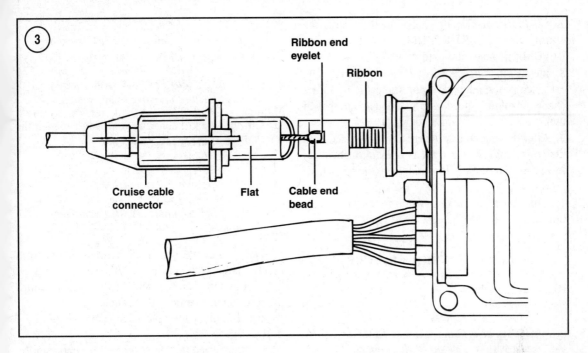

Ribbon end eyelet

Ribbon

Cruise cable connector

Flat

Cable end bead

③

Installation

1. On the left side, route the new cruise control cable forward, over the top of the top engine stabilizer, then down between the cylinder heads to the induction module.

2. On the right side, position the new cruise control cable housing into the cable guide. Install a *new* E-clip on the cable housing and lock the cable into place.

3. Route the cruise control cable through the hole in the frame (C, **Figure 2**).

4. Position the hole in the ribbon end eyelet flat on the cable connector facing outward. Insert the cable end bead into the ribbon end eyelet (**Figure 3**). Make sure it is secure in the eyelet.

5. Make sure the cable end bead, the eyelet and the ribbon are aligned correctly. At the induction end of the cable, gently pull on the end fitting to remove cable slack.

6. Insert the cruise control connector into the cruise control module. Rotate it clockwise until the connector tabs are fully engaged with the detents in the cruise control module. Carefully pull on the connector to make sure it is secure.

7. Attach the cruise cable (A, **Figure 2**) to the frame with a *new* cable clip (B).

8. Adjust the throttle and idle cables as described in this chapter.

9. Hold onto the cam lever assembly to prevent it from rotating. Install the cruise control cable and plastic end fitting (B, **Figure 1**) on the pin wheel (A). Push the end fitting on until it locks into place.

10. Install the backing plate and the air filter as described in this chapter.

11. Install the frame left side cover.

12. Install the left side saddlebag.

13. Install the fuel tank as described in this chapter.

Cable Lash Initialization

This is not a routine adjustment and is only necessary if the cruise control module or cruise control cable are removed or replaced.

1. Start the engine and allow it to reach normal operating temperature. Shut off the engine.

2. On the right side handlebar switch, push the cruise control SET/RESUME switch to the RESUME position and hold it on.

3. On the front fairing cap, turn the cruise control ON/OFF switch to the ON position.

4. Turn the ignition/key switch to the ON position.

5. Start the engine and allow it to idle. The cruise engagement light *C* on the tachometer face will illuminate. Wait for three seconds for the lamp to go off.

6. Release the SET/RESUME switch from the RESUME position.

13

7. On the right side handlebar switch, push the cruise control SET/RESUME switch to the RESUME position and hold it on.

8. Increase engine speed and return to idle. The cruise control module will pull the cable in until a change in engine speed is detected. The number of motor steps is stored in the memory.

9. After the engine has returned to idle speed, and the cruise engagement light *C* is extinguished, release the SET/RESUME switch from the RESUME position.

10. Turn the ignition/key switch to the OFF position.

CRUISE CONTROL MODULE

Removal/Installation

NOTE
Always disarm the optional TSSM security system prior to disconnecting the battery or the siren will sound.

1. Remove the battery as described in Chapter Eight

2. Disconnect the cruise control cable from the module as described in this chapter.

3. Disconnect the cruise control electrical connector from the module.

4. Working within the battery box, remove the three locknuts from the cruise control mounting studs.

5. Carefully remove the cruise control module from the outer surface of the battery box. Do not lose the rubber grommet on each mounting stud.

6. Installation is the reverse of removal. Note the following:

  a. Install the rubber grommet onto each mounting stud.

  b. Tighten the mounting locknuts securely.

CRUISE CONTROL SWITCHES

ON/OFF Switch Replacement

1. Remove the inner fairing cap as described in Chapter Fourteen.

NOTE
The cruise control ON/OFF switch black/green wire is connected to the speaker switch. This wire is permanently attached to both switches and must be cut to remove either switch.

2. Cut the black/green wire half way between the ON/OFF and the speaker switches.

NOTE
Note the switch terminals to which the following wires are connected. They must be reconnected to the same terminals.

3. Disconnect the wire terminal connectors from the backside of the switch.

4. Remove the screws securing the switch mounting bracket and remove the switch.

5. Installation is the reverse of removal. Note the following:

  a. Butt splice the black/green wire between the ON/OFF and the speaker switches.

  b. Make sure the other wires are connected to the correct switch terminals and pushed on securely.

SET/RESUME Switch Replacement

1. Disassemble the right side switch assembly as described under *Handlebar Switch Replacement* in Chapter Eight.

2. Locate the switch and partially remove it from the switch housing.

3. Cut the wires approximately 1 1/2 in. (40 mm) from the old SET/RESUME switch.

NOTE
The wires on a new replacement switch are 2 in. (50 mm) long and the insulation is partially stripped.

4. Slide a one-inch piece of dual wall heat shrink tubing, supplied with the new switch, over the wire.

5. Securely splice the new switch onto the existing wires and solder the connection.

6. Cover the splice with the dual wall heat shrink tubing.

7. Assemble the right side switch.

CHAPTER FOURTEEN

BODY

This chapter provides procedures for the removal and installation of the body components. Most of these components are fragile and must be handled carefully. Protect the finish when handling them. If a component is going to be left off for a period of time, wrap it with a blanket or towels and place it in a safe location.

SEAT

Removal/Installation

1. Place the motorcycle on level ground on the jiffy stand.

2A. On all FLHT models, remove the screw (**Figure 1**) securing the rider's seat bracket to the top of the rear fender.

2B. On all FLHTC and FLHTCU models, pull up on the lower portion of the backrest pad. Remove the bolt securing (**Figure 2**) the seat bracket to the top of the rear fender.

2C. On all FLHR models, remove the screw securing the back or the passenger seat to the top of the rear fender. Slightly lift up on the rear of the passenger seat, slide it towards the rear and remove it. Remove the two hex nuts securing the rear of the rider's seat bracket to the mounting studs.

2D. On all FLTR models, perform the following:

   a. Remove the right side saddlebag.

   b. Remove the bolt securing the seat strap to the frame mounting bracket. Pull the seat strap from the slots in the seat.

   c. Remove the screw securing the seat bracket to the top of the rear fender.

3. On all models, slide the rider's seat towards the rear and disengage the front bracket from the slot in the frame backbone.

4. Remove the rider's seat.

5. Inspect the seat front mounting tab (**Figure 3**) and bracket (**Figure 4**). Replace if necessary.

6. On all FLHR models, install the passengers seat onto the frame. Push it forward and engage the front

bracket into the slot in the frame backbone. Push the seat down and install the screw securing the back or the passenger seat to the top of the rear fender.

7. On all models, install the rider's seat onto the frame. Push it forward and engage the front bracket into the slot in the frame backbone.

8. On all models, install the screw or hex nuts securing the rear of the rider's seat to the top of the rear fender.

9. On all FLTR models, perform the following:
   a. Insert the seat strap back through the seat slots and secure it to the frame mounting bracket.
   b. Install the right side saddlebag.

10. On all models, pull up on the front of the seat (**Figure 5**) to ensure the seat front hook is secured in the frame backbone slot.

FRONT FENDER

Removal/Installation

1. Place the motorcycle on level ground on the jiffy stand.

2A. On all FLHT models, perform the following:
   a. Remove the outer portion of the front fairing as described in this chapter.
   b. On the left side of the inner front fairing, locate and disconnect the front fender tip lamp two-pin electrical connector (one black and one orange/white wire).
   c. Carefully pull the electrical connector from the inner front fairing.

2B. On all FLHR models, perform the following:
   a. Remove the headlight unit as described in Chapter Eight.
   b. Within the headlight case, locate and disconnect the front fender tip lamp two-pin electrical connector (one black and one orange/white wire).
   c. Carefully pull the electrical connector from the headlight case.

3. Carefully cut the cable strap securing the fender tip lamp wire to the front brake line.

4. Remove the front wheel as described in Chapter Nine.

5. Straighten the locking tabs away from the front fender mounting bolts (**Figure 6**).

6. Remove the mounting bolts and lock plates securing the front fender to the fork sliders.

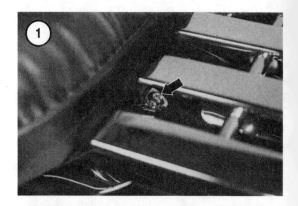

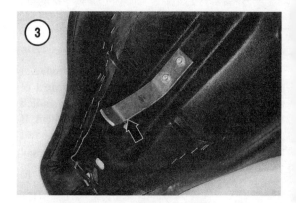

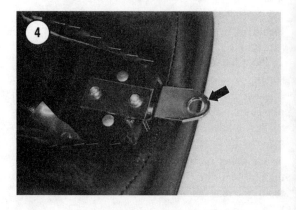

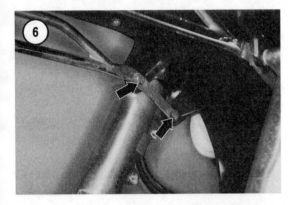

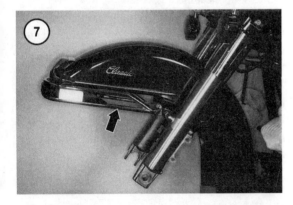

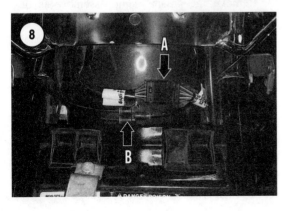

7. Remove the front fender (**Figure 7**) from the fork sliders. Be careful not scratch the paint.

8. Installation is the reverse of removal. Note the following:

  a. Install the lock plates and tighten the bolts securely.

  b. Bend the locking tabs up against the bolt heads.

REAR FENDER

Removal/Installation

> *CAUTION*
> *Elevate the rear of the motorcycle sufficiently to allow the rear fender to roll back and over the rear wheel, and clear the frame rear cross member*

1. Raise the motorcycle on a center lift with the rear wheel off the ground. Secure the motorcycle in the raised position.

2. Remove the seat as described in this chapter.

3. Disconnect the rear fender lights electrical connector (A, **Figure 8**) from the top of the rear fender.

4. Release the rear shock absorber air inlet tee fitting (B, **Figure 8**) from the top of the rear fender.

5. Remove both saddlebags as described in this chapter.

6. Remove both frame side covers.

7. Remove the two bolts and lockwashers securing the muffler clamp to the saddlebag lower support rail. Carefully pull the muffler toward the outboard side of the support rail. Repeat this step for the other side.

8. Remove the shock absorber lower mounting bolt, lockwasher and washer securing the shock absorber to the swing arm. Repeat this step for the other side.

9. On the left side, remove the T40 Torx bolt securing the rear fender to the battery box.

10. At the rear, remove the inside bolt and flange nut securing the rear bumper support rail to the saddlebag support bracket and saddlebag support rail. Repeat this step for the other side.

11. Working under the rear bumper, remove the nut with the flat washer and release the bumper bracket from the fender weld nut. Remove the rear bumper and rear bumper cushion.

14

12. Remove the T40 Torx bolt securing the fender side mounting bolt adjacent to the frame side cover rubber grommet. Repeat this step for the other side.

13. Remove the T40 Torx upper *rear bolt* securing the saddlebag support to the frame support. Repeat this step for the other side.

CAUTION
Hold onto the rear fender as it will drop down slightly when the following front bolt is removed.

14. Hold onto the rear fender and remove the T40 Torx upper *front bolt* securing the saddlebag support to the frame support.

15. Be careful not to scratch the fender paint on any of the surrounding brackets. Have an assistant spread the saddlebag supports outward. Slowly roll the rear fender back and off the rear wheel, staying away from the saddlebag supports and mufflers.

16. Installation is the reverse of removal. Tighten all bolts and nuts securely.

WINDSHIELD AND HEADLIGHT NACELLE (FLHR MODELS)

Windshield Only Removal/Installation

1. Place the motorcycle on level ground on the jiffy stand.

2. Use a finger to lift up on the wire form latch spring on each side of the windshield next to the headlight nacelle.

3. Straddle the front wheel and hold onto the windshield. Gently pull straight up on the top of the windshield until the upper notches on the side brackets are free of the upper grommets on the passing lamp support.

4. Continue to raise the windshield until the side brackets lower notches are free from the lower grommets and remove the windshield.

5. Installation is the reverse of removal. Note the following:
   a. Lower the windshield down until the latches are seated on the grommets.
   b. Push down on the wire form latch springs until they overhang the upper grommets.
   c. Make sure the windshield is securely in place prior to riding.

Headlight Nacelle Removal/Installation

Refer to **Figure 9**.

1. Place the motorcycle on level ground on the jiffy stand.

2. Remove the seat.

NOTE
Always disarm the optional TSSM security system prior to disconnecting the battery or the siren will sound.

3. Disconnect the negative battery cable as described in Chapter Eight

4. Remove the windshield as described in this chapter.

5. Remove the screw securing the trim bezel and remove the bezel.

6. Remove the seven screws securing the headlight assembly to the nacelle.

7. Partially remove the headlight assembly from the nacelle, then disconnect the electrical connector from the backside of the headlight lens assembly. Remove the headlight assembly.

8. Working within the headlight nacelle, remove the speed nut and washer securing the center chrome strip. Remove the chrome strip.

9. Carefully pry off the fork lock trim plate.

10. Loosen, but do not remove, the screw on the handlebar cover front mounting tab.

11. Remove the two acorn nuts on each side securing the right and left side headlight nacelles to the fork tube studs.

12. Cover the front fender with towels or a blanket to protect the painted finish.

13. Remove the passing lamp assembly as described in Chapter Eight.

14. Remove the rubber grommets and clutch cable clamp from both fork tubes.

15. Slightly raise the handlebar cover. Carefully spread the rear of the nacelle halves from the fork tube studs.

16. Disconnect the accessory switch and passing lamp switch connectors.

17. Remove the nacelle halves from the fork tubes and store them in safe place.

18. Installation is the reverse of removal.

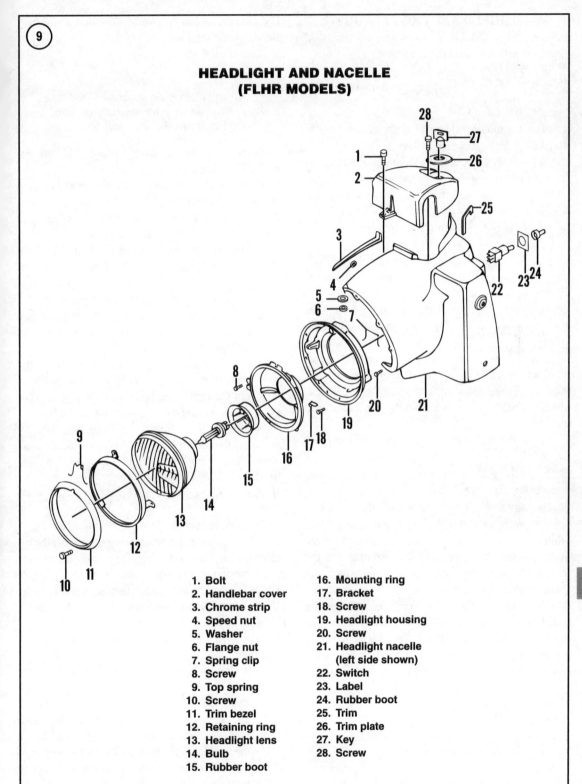

HEADLIGHT AND NACELLE
(FLHR MODELS)

1. Bolt
2. Handlebar cover
3. Chrome strip
4. Speed nut
5. Washer
6. Flange nut
7. Spring clip
8. Screw
9. Top spring
10. Screw
11. Trim bezel
12. Retaining ring
13. Headlight lens
14. Bulb
15. Rubber boot
16. Mounting ring
17. Bracket
18. Screw
19. Headlight housing
20. Screw
21. Headlight nacelle
    (left side shown)
22. Switch
23. Label
24. Rubber boot
25. Trim
26. Trim plate
27. Key
28. Screw

14

WINDSHIELD AND FRONT FAIRING
(FLTR MODELS)

Windshield Only
Removal/Installation

Refer to **Figure 10**.
1. Place the motorcycle on level ground on the jiffy stand.
2. At the front surface of the front outer fairing, locate the five screws securing the windshield to the outer fairing. Use an alternating pattern to loosen and remove the five screws and the plastic washers.
3. Carefully pull the windshield and trim from the outer fairing.
4. Carefully remove the well-nuts straight out from the outer faring. Do not push them into the inner fairing during removal.
5. Inspect the well-nuts in the front outer fairing for wear, cuts or damage. Replace them as a set if necessary.
6. If installing a new windshield, carefully poke holes for the screws in the decal from the inside surface. If they are poked from the outside surface, the decal will be broken loose from the windshield and may tear.
7. Install the flat plastic washer onto the mounting screw.
8. Insert the screws through the windshield slots and the decal.
9. Partially screw the well-nuts onto the screws.
10. At the front surface of the front outer fairing, align the five well-nuts with the openings in the outer fairing. Carefully push the well-nuts into the fairing openings. Push the windshield onto the outer fairing until it is flush.
11. Starting with the center screw and alternating from side to side, tighten the five screws securely. Do not overtighten them as the area around the screw may fracture.

Outer Front Fairing
Removal/Installation

Refer to **Figure 10**.

NOTE
It is not necessary to remove the windshield when removing the outer fairing.

1. Place the motorcycle on level ground on the jiffy stand.
2. Remove the seat.

NOTE
Always disarm the optional TSSM security system prior to disconnecting the battery or the siren will sound.

3. Disconnect the negative battery cable as described in Chapter Eight
4. Cover the front fender with towels or a blanket to protect the painted finish.
5. Remove the screws securing the outer fairing to the inner fairing in the following order.
    a. On the left side, remove the long T25 Torx screw just below the left side glove box.
    b. On the left side, remove the screw at the edge of the fairing next to the left speaker.
    c. Loosen, but do not remove, the top left and right side screws outboard of the fuel and voltmeter gauges.
    d. On the right side, remove the screw at the edge of the fairing next to the right speaker.
    e. On the right side, remove the long T25 Torx screw just below the right side glove box.
6. Next to the front turn signal lamp assembly, remove the two acorn nuts and washers from the stud plate. Push on both studs and release the stud plate from the left side fairing support.
7. Repeat Step 6 for the stud plate on the opposite side.
8. Remove the screws loosened in Step 3c.
9. Carefully raise the outer faring up and off the radio mounting bracket hooks. Rest it on the protective covering on the front fender.
10. Working inside the outer fairing, disconnect the electrical connector from the backside of each headlight assembly.
11. Remove the front outer fairing and store it in a safe place.
12. Installation is the reverse of removal. Note the following:
    a. Place the outer fairing onto the inner fairing and engage the two slots with the radio mounting bracket on the inner fairing. Move the wiring harness and individual wires out of the way so they will not get pinched during installation.
    b. The alignment tabs on the inner fairing must be positioned outside of those on the outer

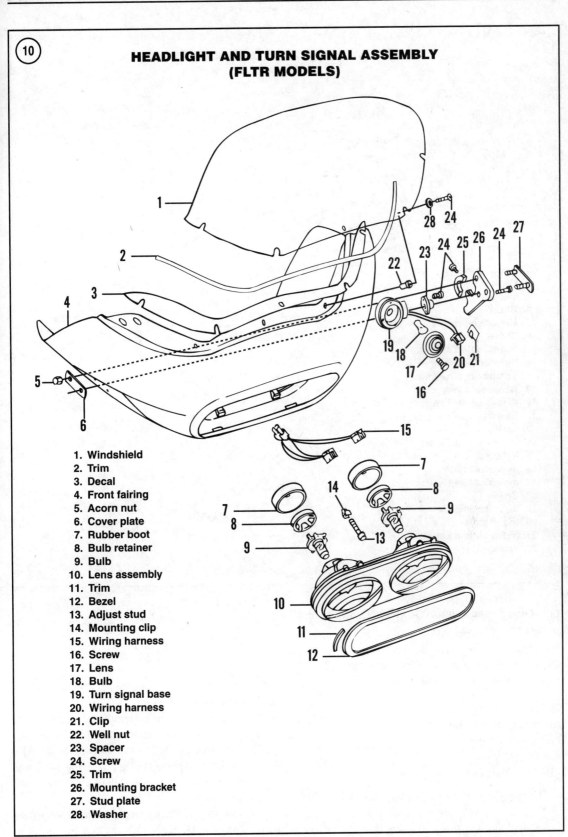

**HEADLIGHT AND TURN SIGNAL ASSEMBLY
(FLTR MODELS)**

1. Windshield
2. Trim
3. Decal
4. Front fairing
5. Acorn nut
6. Cover plate
7. Rubber boot
8. Bulb retainer
9. Bulb
10. Lens assembly
11. Trim
12. Bezel
13. Adjust stud
14. Mounting clip
15. Wiring harness
16. Screw
17. Lens
18. Bulb
19. Turn signal base
20. Wiring harness
21. Clip
22. Well nut
23. Spacer
24. Screw
25. Trim
26. Mounting bracket
27. Stud plate
28. Washer

14

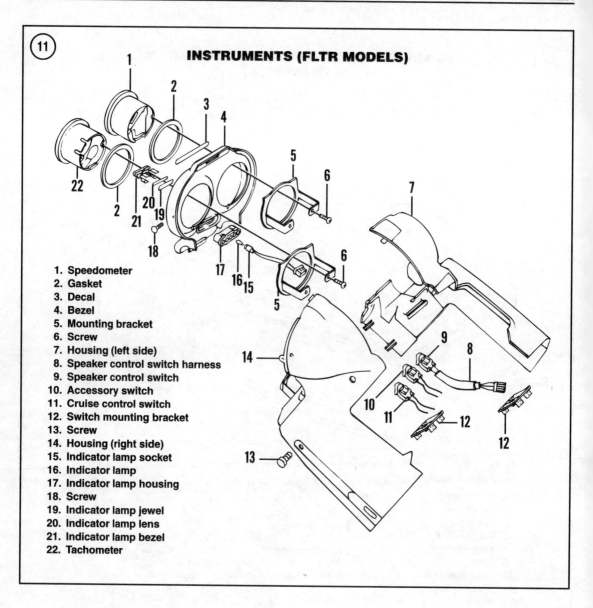

INSTRUMENTS (FLTR MODELS)

1. Speedometer
2. Gasket
3. Decal
4. Bezel
5. Mounting bracket
6. Screw
7. Housing (left side)
8. Speaker control switch harness
9. Speaker control switch
10. Accessory switch
11. Cruise control switch
12. Switch mounting bracket
13. Screw
14. Housing (right side)
15. Indicator lamp socket
16. Indicator lamp
17. Indicator lamp housing
18. Screw
19. Indicator lamp jewel
20. Indicator lamp lens
21. Indicator lamp bezel
22. Tachometer

fairing. Check the tabs on both sides of the fairing.

c. Tighten the screws securely. Do not overtighten them as the plastic around the screw hole may fracture.

Instrument Bezel Housing Removal/Installation

Refer to **Figure 11**.

1. Place the motorcycle on level ground on the jiffy stand.

2. Remove the seat as described in this chapter.

NOTE
Always disarm the optional TSSM security system prior to disconnecting the battery or the siren will sound.

3. Disconnect the negative battery cable as described in Chapter Eight.

4. Remove the instruments and bezel as described under *Instruments Removal/Installation* (FLTR and FLTRI) in Chapter Eight.

5. On the lower right side of the housing, unscrew the rubber boot and remove the odometer reset switch from the housing.

6. Remove the throttle cable clip for the hole on the upper right side housing.

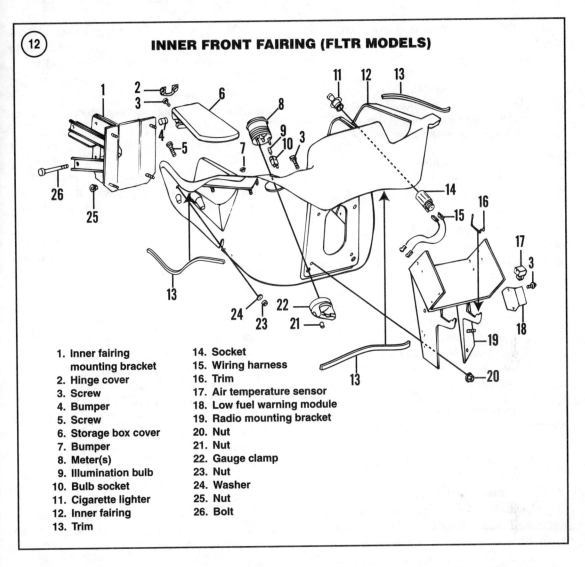

INNER FRONT FAIRING (FLTR MODELS)

1. Inner fairing mounting bracket
2. Hinge cover
3. Screw
4. Bumper
5. Screw
6. Storage box cover
7. Bumper
8. Meter(s)
9. Illumination bulb
10. Bulb socket
11. Cigarette lighter
12. Inner fairing
13. Trim
14. Socket
15. Wiring harness
16. Trim
17. Air temperature sensor
18. Low fuel warning module
19. Radio mounting bracket
20. Nut
21. Nut
22. Gauge clamp
23. Nut
24. Washer
25. Nut
26. Bolt

7. Remove the ignition switch knob, nut, collar and washer as described under *Switches* in Chapter Eight.

8. Disconnect the speaker switch from the wiring harness.

9. Remove the two T40 Torx bolts and washers securing the left side housing to the fork assembly. Carefully remove the left side housing from the frame and store it in a safe place.

10. Remove the outer front fairing as described in this chapter.

11. Carefully pull the electrical wire bundles and conduit from the funnel of the fairing bracket and allow them to hang down. If necessary, cut the cable strap securing the interconnect harness to the front corners of the radio mounting bracket.

12. At the front portion of the bezel housing, disconnect the ten-pin electrical connector for the indicator lamps and the 12-pin electrical connector for the instrument nacelle.

13. Remove the two T40 Torx bolts and washers securing the right side housing to the front fork.

14. Pull the free end of the jumper cable harness through the tunnel of the faring bracket and remove the right side housing from the frame. Store it in a safe place.

15. Install by reversing these removal steps.

Inner Front Fairing Removal/Installation

Refer to **Figure 12**.

14

1. Place the motorcycle on level ground on the jiffy stand.

2. Remove the seat.

NOTE
Always disarm the optional TSSM security system prior to disconnecting the battery or the siren will sound.

3. Disconnect the negative battery cable as described in Chapter Eight.

4. Cover the front fender with towels or a blanket to protect the painted finish.

5. Remove the instrument bezel housing as described in this chapter.

6. Remove the outer front fairing as previously described.

NOTE
Due to the number of electrical connectors to be disconnected in the following steps, be sure to identify each mating half of the connectors for installation.

7. Disconnect the following connectors to separate the main harness from the interconnect harness:

   a. The interconnect 12-pin Deutsch black electrical connector below the radio on the right side.

   b. The main-to-interconnect harness 12-pin Deutsch gray electrical connector secured to the T-stud on the radio right side bracket.

   c. The main power two-pin Packard black electrical connector on the back, left side of the radio.

   d. The radio antenna cable connector on the left side of radio.

8. Disconnect the ignition switch four-pin Packard black connector from the main harness at the inside surface of the left side fairing bracket.

9. On FLHTCUI models, disconnect the 12-pin Duetsch black overlay harness from the interconnect harness secured to the T-stud on the radio left side bracket.

10. Disconnect the following connectors to separate the handlebar switch controls and radio ground from the interconnect harness:

   a. The left side handlebar switch 12-pin Deutsch gray electrical connector secured to the T-stud on the radio left side bracket.

   b. The right side handlebar switch 12-pin Deutsch black electrical connector secured to the T-stud on the radio right side bracket.

   c. The front turn signal six-pin connector below the right side of radio.

   d. The radio ground single spade and socket terminal.

11. Make sure all electrical connectors have been disconnected.

12. Unhook the turn signal conduit from the flexible clips on both sides of the inner fairing. Carefully pull the conduit downward to free it from the slots at the bottom of the inner fairing.

13. Release the jumper harness, main harness, and on FLHTCUI models, the overlay harness and handlebar switch control conduit from the interconnect harness. Carefully cut and remove any cable straps if necessary.

14. Carefully pull all of the disconnected harnesses and electrical connectors forward and away from the front opening in the inner fairing. Wrap the harnesses tightly with shop cloths and secure them with tape or string. This bundle of wires must pass through the front opening in the inner fairing.

15. Hold onto the front inner fairing and remove the four locknuts securing the front inner fairing and radio mounting bracket to the fairing mounting bracket. Remove the front inner fairing and radio mounting bracket from the frame. Store them in a safe place.

16. Installation is the reverse of removal. Correctly reconnect all electrical connectors. Refer to the numbered marks made in the NOTE before Step 7.

FRONT FAIRING (FLHT MODELS)

Front Outer Fairing
Removal/Installation

Refer to **Figure 13**.

1. Place the motorcycle on level ground on the jiffy stand.

2. Remove the seat.

NOTE
Always disarm the optional TSSM security system prior to disconnecting the battery or the siren will sound.

3. Disconnect the negative battery cable as described in Chapter Eight.

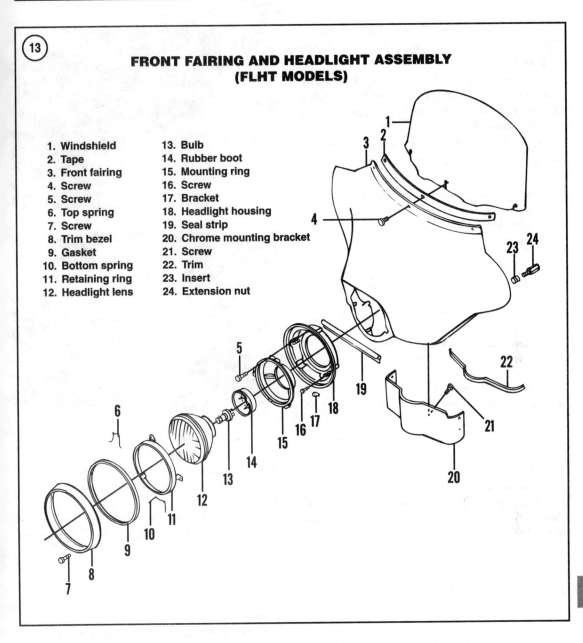

13

**FRONT FAIRING AND HEADLIGHT ASSEMBLY
(FLHT MODELS)**

1. Windshield
2. Tape
3. Front fairing
4. Screw
5. Screw
6. Top spring
7. Screw
8. Trim bezel
9. Gasket
10. Bottom spring
11. Retaining ring
12. Headlight lens
13. Bulb
14. Rubber boot
15. Mounting ring
16. Screw
17. Bracket
18. Headlight housing
19. Seal strip
20. Chrome mounting bracket
21. Screw
22. Trim
23. Insert
24. Extension nut

14

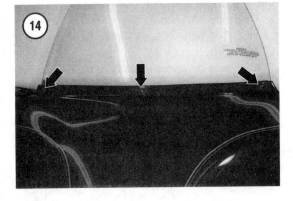

14

4. Cover the front fender with towels or a blanket to protect the painted finish.

NOTE
The windshield will stay with the front outer fairing.

5. At the front of the front outer fairing, locate the three T27 Torx screws (**Figure 14**) securing the windshield and the outer fairing to the inner fairing. Use an alternating pattern to loosen and remove the three screws.

6. Working on the inner fairing side, remove the T25 Torx screw on each side of the inner fairing (**Figure 15**).

7. Turn the front wheel all the way to the left. Working below the fairing cap, remove the screw (**Figure 16**) securing the front outer fairing to the mounting bracket.

8. Have an assistant hold onto the front outer fairing as it will be loose after removal of the fasteners in Step 9.

9. Turn the front wheel all the way to the right. Working below the fairing cap, remove the other screw securing the front outer fairing to the mounting bracket.

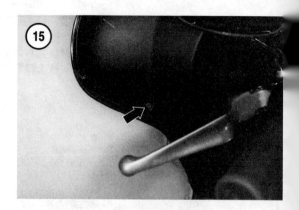

> ### CAUTION
> *The windshield is **not** mechanically attached to the front outer fairing and may fall off during fairing removal. The windshield may remain attached to the fairing with the cushion tape securing it to outer front fairing.*

10. Pull the front outer fairing forward and disconnect the electrical connector from the headlight assembly.

11. Remove the front outer fairing and windshield, and store them in a safe place. If necessary, remove the windshield from the front outer fairing.

12. Installation is the reverse of removal. Starting with the center screw and alternating from side to side, tighten the three screws securely. Do not overtighten them as the plastic around the screw may fracture.

Front Inner Fairing Cap
Removal/Installation

The inner fairing cap is removed when the ignition switch is removed. Refer to *Ignition/Light Switch Removal/Installation (FLHT, FLHTC, FLHTCI, FLHTCUI, FLTR and FLTRI Domestic Models)* in Chapter Eight.

Front Inner Fairing
Removal/Installation

Refer to **Figure 17**.

1. Place the motorcycle on level ground on the jiffy stand.

2. Remove the front outer fairing and windshield as previously described.

3. On the left side of the inner fairing, unscrew the rubber boot and remove the odometer reset switch from the housing.

4. On the lower left side, disconnect the six-pin electrical connector (A, **Figure 18**) for the turn signal lamps.

5. Remove the passing lamp assembly as described in Chapter Eight.

6. Remove the inner fairing cap as described in Chapter Eight.

7. Remove the screws securing the chrome mounting skirt (**Figure 19**) and remove it.

8. Disconnect the clutch cable from the clutch lever as described under *Clutch Cable Replacement* in Chapter Five.

9. Withdraw the clutch cable from the inner fairing rubber grommet (**Figure 20**). Move the clutch cable forward and out of the way. Remove the rubber grommet.

10. Remove the front brake master cylinder from the handlebar as described in Chapter Twelve.

11. Separate the right side switch housing as described in Chapter Eight.

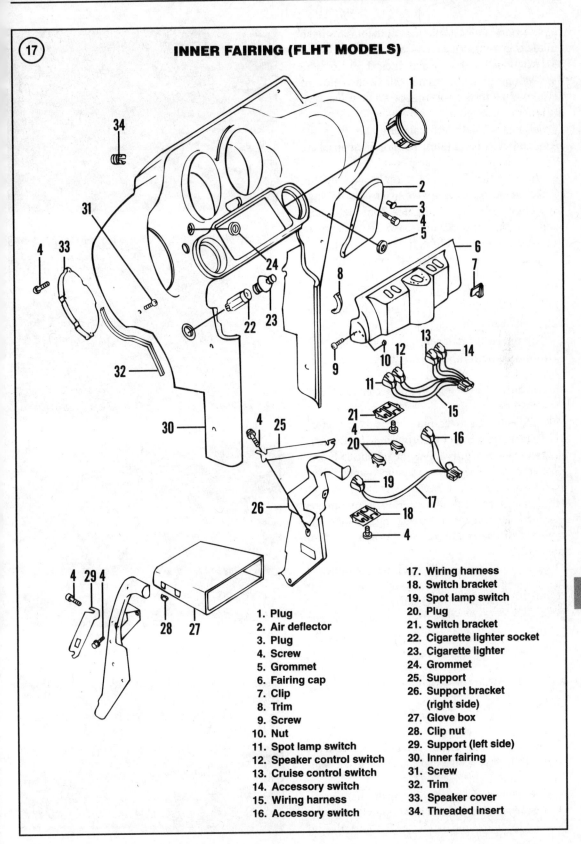

INNER FAIRING (FLHT MODELS)

1. Plug
2. Air deflector
3. Plug
4. Screw
5. Grommet
6. Fairing cap
7. Clip
8. Trim
9. Screw
10. Nut
11. Spot lamp switch
12. Speaker control switch
13. Cruise control switch
14. Accessory switch
15. Wiring harness
16. Accessory switch
17. Wiring harness
18. Switch bracket
19. Spot lamp switch
20. Plug
21. Switch bracket
22. Cigarette lighter socket
23. Cigarette lighter
24. Grommet
25. Support
26. Support bracket
    (right side)
27. Glove box
28. Clip nut
29. Support (left side)
30. Inner fairing
31. Screw
32. Trim
33. Speaker cover
34. Threaded insert

14

12. Disconnect the throttle and idle cables from the throttle grip as described in Chapter Seven.

13. Withdraw the throttle and idle cables from the inner fairing rubber grommet. Move the idle and throttle cables forward and out of the way. Remove the rubber grommet.

14. Disconnect the electrical terminals from the cigarette lighter (B, **Figure 18**) and both speakers (C).

15. Remove the T25 Torx screws securing the speaker adapters (D, **Figure 18**) to the inner fairing.

16. Remove the cigarette lighter from the socket. Hold onto the socket and unscrew the outer shell. Remove the outer shell from the inner fairing.

17. Disconnect the electrical terminals from the voltmeter and the fuel gauge.

18. Carefully cut the cable strap securing the indicator lamp connector between the speedometer and tachometer brackets.

19. Disconnect the following electrical connectors:

   a. Speedometer 12-pin Packard electrical connector.

   b. Tachometer six-pin Packard electrical connector.

   c. Indicator lamps ten-pin electrical connector.

20. Remove the screws securing the speedometer and tachometer (**Figure 21**) to the mounting brackets. Remove the speedometer and tachometer from the inner fairing.

21. Remove the hex nuts securing the voltmeter and fuel level gauges to the mounting brackets. Remove the voltmeter and fuel level gauges from the inner fairing.

22. Release the four paddles and free the indicator bulb housing from the lens assembly. Remove the lens assembly from the inner fairing.

23. Spread the lower legs of the inner fairing and the support brackets outward, and disengage the lower legs from the locating dowels on the lower fork brace. Raise the lower fairing and support brackets high enough to gain access to the lower row of gauges.

24. On FLHTC, FLHTCI and FLHTCUI models, perform the following:

   a. Disconnect the electrical connectors from the oil pressure gauge and the ambient air temperature gauge.

   b. Remove the hex nuts securing the oil pressure gauge and the ambient air temperature gauges to the mounting brackets. Remove the oil

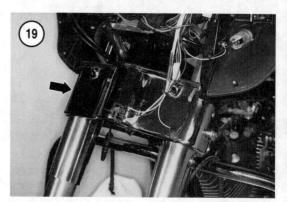

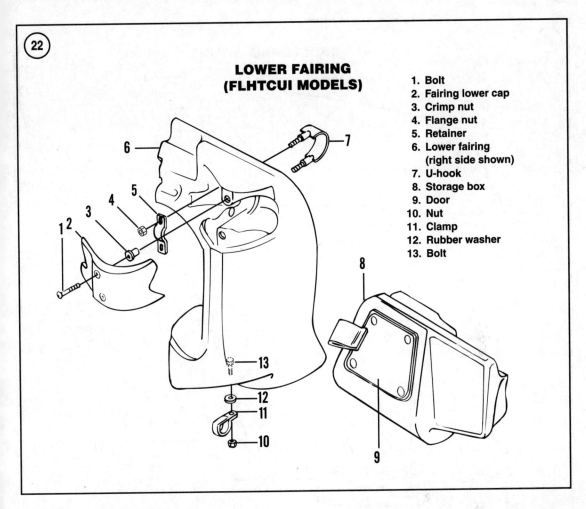

**LOWER FAIRING
(FLHTCUI MODELS)**

1. Bolt
2. Fairing lower cap
3. Crimp nut
4. Flange nut
5. Retainer
6. Lower fairing
   (right side shown)
7. U-hook
8. Storage box
9. Door
10. Nut
11. Clamp
12. Rubber washer
13. Bolt

pressure gauge and the ambient air temperature gauges from the inner fairing.

25. Remove the four Allen bolts securing the inner fairing to the fairing mounting bracket.

26. Raise the inner fairing and the support brackets further up, tilt the inner fairing toward the rear of the motorcycle and free the fairing from the radio nose seal.

27. Remove the front inner fairing from the mounting bracket. The radio and the interconnecting harness will remain with the frame.

28. Installation is the reverse of removal.

**Lower Fairing and Glove Boxes
(FLHTCUI Models)
Removal/Installation**

Refer to **Figure 22**.

1. Place the motorcycle on level ground on the jiffy stand.

2. Remove the two screws securing the lower cap on the right side. Remove the lower cap.

3. Secure the locknut on the base of the lower fairing. Unscrew the T40 Torx screw from the clamp and locknut. Remove the clamp and rubber washer.

4. Have an assistant hold onto the lower fairing.

5. Remove the two locknuts securing the U-bolt and retainer to the engine guard. Remove the U-bolt and retainer. Remove the lower fairing and storage box from the frame.

6. Repeat Steps 4-5 for the other side if necessary.

7. Installation is the reverse of removal.

SADDLEBAGS AND GUARDS

Saddlebags Removal/Installation

Refer to **Figure 23**.

14

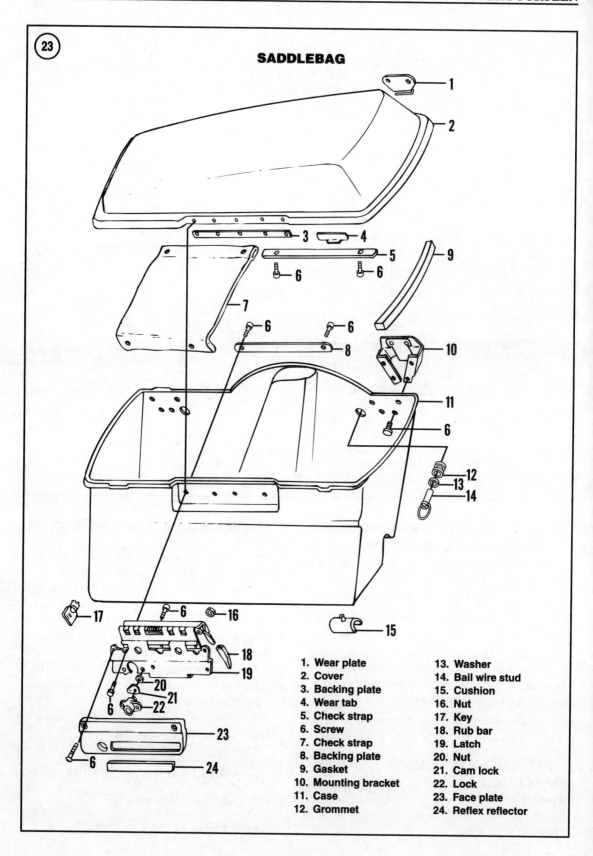

SADDLEBAG

1. Wear plate
2. Cover
3. Backing plate
4. Wear tab
5. Check strap
6. Screw
7. Check strap
8. Backing plate
9. Gasket
10. Mounting bracket
11. Case
12. Grommet
13. Washer
14. Bail wire stud
15. Cushion
16. Nut
17. Key
18. Rub bar
19. Latch
20. Nut
21. Cam lock
22. Lock
23. Face plate
24. Reflex reflector

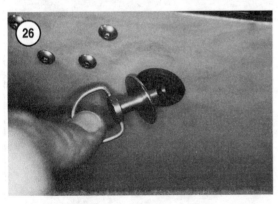

1. Place the motorcycle on level ground on the jiffy stand.

2A. On FLHRCI models, perform the following:
   a. Lift up on the decorative buckle, press in on the tabs and release the catch from the receptacle.
   b. Rotate the hinge on the outboard side of the saddlebag and open the lid.

2B. On models other than FLHRCI, perform the following:
   a. Unlock the handle latch.
   b. Pull out on the bottom of latch (**Figure 24**) and open the lid.

3. Within the saddlebag case, grasp the latch bail wire (**Figure 25**), rotate the latch stud a fourth turn counterclockwise and release the stud from the mounting bracket (**Figure 26**).

4. Repeat Step 3 for the other latch stud.

5. Carefully pull the saddlebag up and out of the bracket or guards.

6. Inspect the latch mounting brackets (**Figure 27**) for damage.

7. Installation is the reverse of removal. Make sure the saddlebag is locked into place.

Saddlebag Guards
Removal/Installation

Refer to **Figure 28**.

1. Place the motorcycle on level ground on the jiffy stand.

2. Remove the saddlebag.

3. Remove the front lower bolt and locknut (**Figure 29**) securing the front guard to the frame bracket.

4. Remove the bolts and lockwashers (A, **Figure 30**) securing the muffler to the lower support. Remove the support bracket and rubber cushion.

5. Remove one of the bolts (B, **Figure 30**) securing the rear support bracket to the frame bracket. Loosen the other bolt at this time, but leave it in place.

6. Hold onto the saddlebag support and remove the front upper bolt (**Figure 31**) securing the front guard to the frame.

7. Remove the other bolt (B, **Figure 30**) securing the rear support bracket to the frame bracket.

8. Remove the saddlebag guard assembly (**Figure 32**) from the frame.

9. Support the rear of the muffler to the frame with a Bungee cord or rope.

14

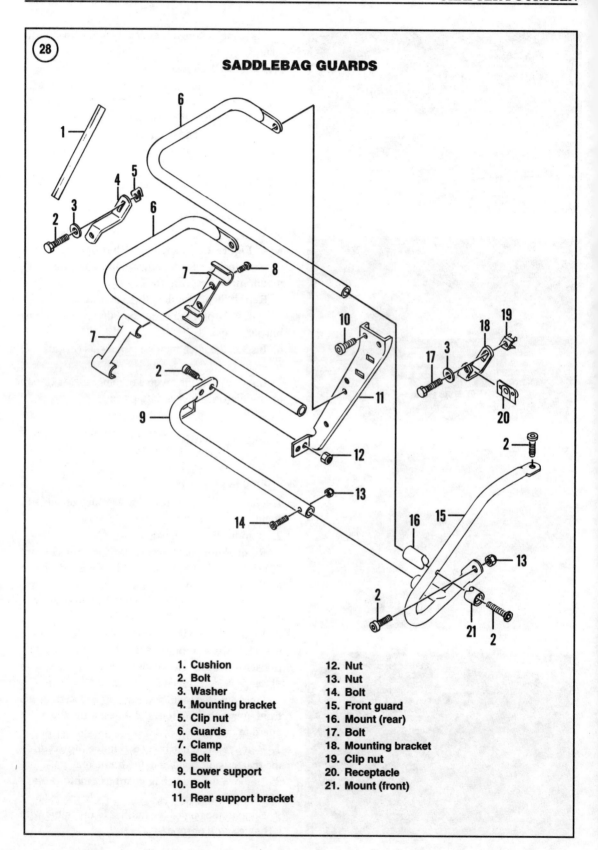

SADDLEBAG GUARDS

1. Cushion
2. Bolt
3. Washer
4. Mounting bracket
5. Clip nut
6. Guards
7. Clamp
8. Bolt
9. Lower support
10. Bolt
11. Rear support bracket
12. Nut
13. Nut
14. Bolt
15. Front guard
16. Mount (rear)
17. Bolt
18. Mounting bracket
19. Clip nut
20. Receptacle
21. Mount (front)

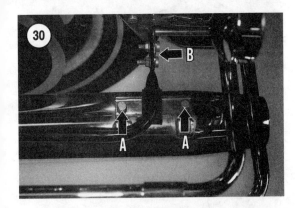

10. Installation is the reverse of removal steps. Tighten all bolts and nuts securely.

TOUR-PAK (FLHT MODELS)

Removal/Installation

Refer to **Figure 33**.

1. Place the motorcycle on level ground on the jiffy stand.

2. Remove the seat.

> *NOTE*
> *Always disarm the optional TSSM security system prior to disconnecting the battery or the siren will sound.*

3. Disconnect the negative battery cable as described in Chapter Eight

4. Remove both saddlebags.

5. Open the cover and remove the rubber mat. Leave the cover open for the remainder of this procedure.

6. On FLHTCUI models, perform the following:

   a. Open the map pocket and remove the acorn nuts and flat washers securing the molded inner liner to the lower case. Remove the molded liner.

   b. Depress the latch, rotate the housing and release the bulb socket from the left side of the lower case.

7. Rotate the knurled locking ring counterclockwise and disconnect the radio antenna cable connector.

8. Separate the three-pin electrical connector for the Tour-Pak light harness. Pull the grommet into the lower case and remove it from the wire harness.

9. Feed the harness down and through the opening in the bottom of the lower case.

10. On FLHTCUI models, perform the following:

   a. Release the headrest receptacle from the bottom of the left side speaker box.

   b. Remove the trim ring and carefully pull the wire harness out of the left side speaker box. Disconnect the six-pin mini-Deutsch connector.

   c. On the right side, disconnect the CB antenna cable connector and release the cable from the two clips on the bottom of the lower case.

14

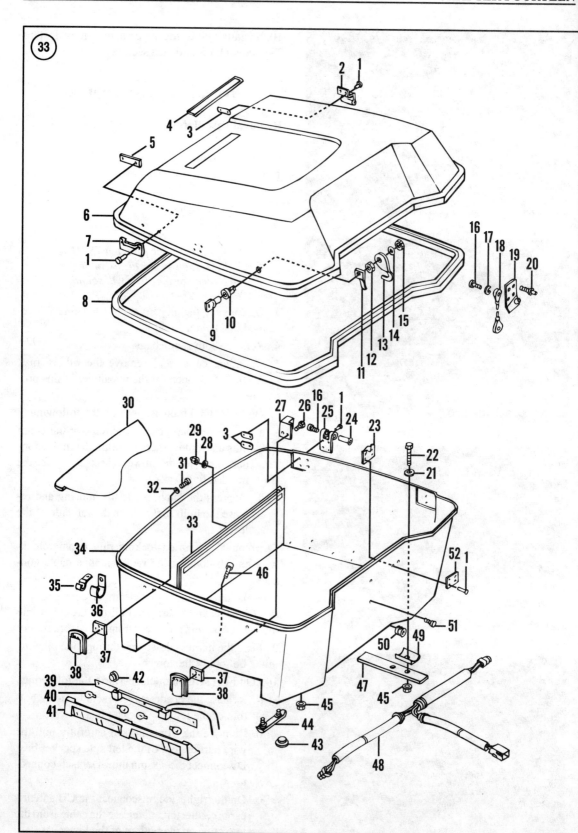

TOUR-PACK (FLHT MODELS)

1. Rivet
2. Hinge
3. Backing plate
4. Nameplate
5. Backing plate
6. Cover
7. Upper catch
8. Gasket
9. Key
10. Lock
11. Lock guide
12. Nut
13. Cam hook
14. Lockwasher
15. Nut
16. Screw
17. Spring washer
18. Cable brace
19. Bracket
20. Nylon rivet
21. Washer
22. Screw
23. Bracket
24. Hinge pin
25. Hinge
26. Screw
27. Lower catch
28. Washer
29. Nut
30. Rubber mat
31. Screw
32. Washer
33. Pouch
34. Lower case
35. Antenna cable clip
36. Clamp
37. Spacer
38. Catch body
39. Mounting bracket
40. Bulb
41. Side marker lens
42. Eyelet
43. Grommet
44. Bumper
45. Nut
46. Screw
47. Gasket
48. Wiring harness
49. Spacer
50. Grommet
51. Screw
52. Backing plate

d. Pull the grommet surrounding the CB antenna cable into the lower case and remove it from the cable.

e. Feed the CB antenna down and through the opening in the bottom of the lower case.

f. Remove the trim ring and carefully pull the wire harness out of the right side speaker box. Disconnect the six-pin mini-Deutsch connector.

11. Have an assistant hold onto the Tour-Pak during bolt and nut removal. The Tour-Pak is top heavy on the left side with the cover open.

12. Secure the locknut below each mounting bolt and remove the five bolts and nuts securing the Tour-Pak lower case to the luggage rack. Remove the Tour-Pak from the luggage rack.

13. Remove the five spacers and three spacers from the luggage rack and place them in a plastic bag.

14. Installation is the reverse of removal. Tighten the bolts and nuts securely.

FOOTBOARDS

Refer to **Figure 34**.

Driver Footboard Removal/Installation

1. Place the motorcycle on level ground on the jiffy stand.

2A. On the right side, perform the following:

a. Working on the inner side of the frame side rail, loosen and remove the Allen bolt, lockwasher and washer securing the front mounting bracket to the frame.

b. Working on the inner side of the frame side rail, loosen and remove the upper hex bolt, lockwasher and washer, and the lower hex bolt and lockwasher securing the rear mounting bracket to the frame.

2B. On the left side, working on the inner side of the frame side rail, loosen and remove the Allen bolts, lockwashers and washers securing the front (A, **Figure 35**) and rear mounting brackets (B) to the frame.

3. Remove the footboard assembly from the frame.

4. If necessary, remove the rubber pad (**Figure 36**) from the footboard and install a new one. Push the locating pins all the way through the footboard to secure the rubber pad in place.

14

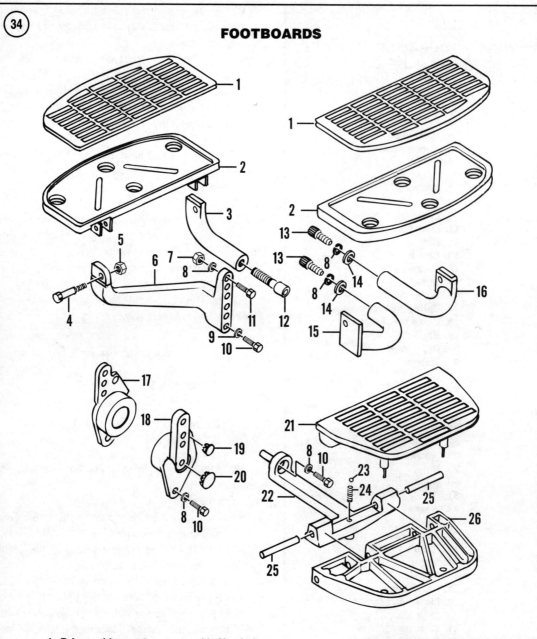

FOOTBOARDS

1. Driver rubber mat
2. Driver footboard
3. Front bracket (left side)
4. Pivot bolt
5. Nut
6. Rear bracket (left side)
7. Nut
8. Lockwasher
9. Lockwasher
10. Hex bolt
11. Hex bolt
12. Allen bolt
13. Allen bolt
14. Washer
15. Rear mounting bracket (right side)
16. Front mounting bracket (right side)
17. Bracket (left side)
18. Bracket (right side)
19. Plug
20. Plug
21. Passenger rubber pad*
22. Mounting bracket*
23. Steel ball*
24. Spring*
25. Pivot pin*
26. Passenger footboard*

*Items shown are for right side. Left side is identical.

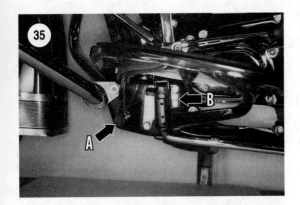

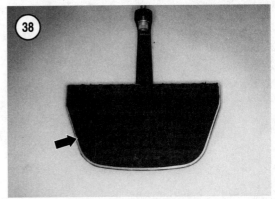

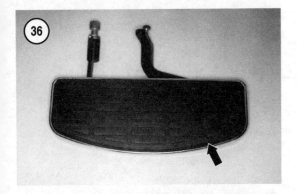

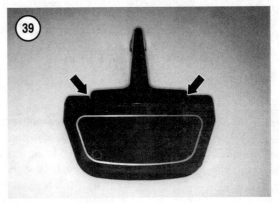

**Passenger Footboard
Removal/Installation**

1. Place the motorcycle on level ground on the jiffy stand.

2. Remove the upper hex bolt and lockwasher (**Figure 37**), and the lower hex bolt and lockwasher securing the passenger footpeg to the frame and remove it.

3. Repeat Step 2 for the other side if necessary.

4. If necessary, remove the rubber pad (**Figure 38**) from the footboard and install a new one. Push the locating pins all the way through the footboard to secure the rubber pad in place.

5. Inspect the pivot pins (**Figure 39**) for looseness. Replace them if necessary.

6. Install the footboard onto the frame and tighten the hex bolt securely.

14

5. Inspect the pivot bolts and nuts for looseness. Replace them if necessary.

6. Inspect the footboard and the mounting brackets for damage and fractures. Replace as necessary.

7. Install the footboard onto the frame, and tighten the Allen and hex bolts securely.

SUPPLEMENT

2003-2005 MODEL SERVICE INFORMATION

This Supplement contains all procedures and specifications unique to the 2003-2005 models, including the Screamin' Eagle models. If a specific procedure is not included, refer to the procedure in the prior chapter in the main body of this manual. Refer to **Table 1** in this Supplement to cross-reference 2005 models to their equivalent base models. **Tables 1-16** are located at the end of the appropriate sections.

This Supplement is divided into sections that corresprond to those in the other chapters of this manual.

CHAPTER ONE

GENERAL INFORMATION

Table 1 MODEL DESIGNATION

FLHRCI* Road King Classic (2005)
  Base model FLHRI Road King
FLHTCSE2** Screamin' Electra Glide 2 (2005)
  Base model FLHTC/FLHTCI Electra Glide Classic

* The I designation indicates models equipped with fuel injection. ** The FLHTCSE2 model is fuel injected but does not have the "I" designation.

Table 2 MOTORCYCLE DIMENSIONS

Wheel base—all models	64.5 in. (1638.3 mm)
Overall length	
FLHT	93.7 in. (2380.0 mm)
FLHTC/FLHTCI	97.5 in. (2476.5 mm)
FLHTCUI ULTRA	98.3 in. (2496.82 mm)
FLHTCSE2	96.9 in. (2461.26 mm)
FLHR/FLHRI	93.7 in. (2380.0 mm)
FLHRCI	93.7 in. (2380.0 mm)
FLHRS/FLHRSI	93.7 in. (2380.0 mm)
FLTR/FLTRI	93.7 in. (2380.0 mm)
Overall width	
FLHT	39.0 in. (990.6 mm)
FLHTC/FLHTCI	39.0 in. (990.6 mm)
FLHTCUI ULTRA	39.0 in. (990.6 mm)
FLHTCSE2	38.5 in. (977.9 mm)
FLHR/FLHRI	34.45 in. (875.0 mm)
FLHRCI	34.45 in. (875.0 mm)
FLHRS/FLHRSI	39.40 in. (1000.8 mm)
FLTR/FLTRI	35.75 in. (908.1 mm)
Road clearance	
FLHT	5.12 in. (130.0 mm)
FLHTC/FLHTCI	5.12 in. (130.0 mm)
FLHTCUI ULTRA	5.12 in. (130.0 mm)
FLHTCSE2	4.12 in. (104.7 mm)
FLHR/FLHRI	5.12 in. (130.0 mm)
FLHRCI	5.12 in. (130.0 mm)
FLHRS/FLHRSI	5.12 in. (130.0 mm)
FLTR/FLTRI	5.12 in. (130.0 mm)
Overall height	
FLHT	61.0 in. (1549.4 mm)
FLHTC/FLHTCI	61.0 in. (1549.4 mm)
FLHTCUI ULTRA	61.0 in. (1549.4 mm)
FLHTCSE2	53.27 in. (1353.1 mm)
FLHR/FLHRI	55.06 in. (1398.5 mm)
	(continued)

15

Table 2 MOTORCYCLE DIMENSIONS (continued)

Overall height (continued)
  FLHRCI   55.06 in. (1398.5 mm)
  FLHRS/FLHRSI   55.0 in. (1397 mm)
  FLTR/FLTRI   55.0 in. (1397 mm)
Saddle height
  FLHT   27.25 in. (692.15 mm)
  FLHTC/FLHTCI   27.25 in. (692.15 mm)
  FLHTCUI ULTRA   27.25 in. (692.15 mm)
  FLHTCSE2   26.29 in. (667.76 mm)
  FLHR/FLHRI   27.25 in. (692.15 mm)
  FLHRCI   26.94 in. (684.27 mm)
  FLHRS/FLHRSI   26.10 in. (662.94 mm)
  FLTR/FLTRI   26.94 in. (684.27 mm)

Table 3 MOTORCYCLE WEIGHT (DRY)

Model	lbs.	kg
FLHT	742	337
FLHTC/FLHTCI	760	345
FLHTCUI ULTRA	772	350
FLHTCSE2	808	367
FLHR/FLHRI	707	321
FLHRCI	694	315
FLHRS/FLHRSI	721	327
FLTR/FLTRI	715	324

Table 4 GROSS VEHICLE WEIGHT RATINGS

Model	lbs.	kg
Gross vehicle weight rating (GVWR)*	1259	571
Gross axle weight rating (GAWR)		
Front axle	500	227
Rear axle	827	375

*GVWR is the maximum allowable vehicle weight. This includes combined motorcycle, rider(s) and accessory weight.

CHAPTER THREE

LUBRICATION, MAINTENANCE AND TUNE-UP

ROUTINE SAFETY CHECKS

On FLHTCSE2 models, check the clutch fluid level and condition in the master cylinder. If necessary, add fluid as described in this section.

PERIODIC LUBRICATION

Engine, Transmission and Primary Chaincase Oil Recommendations (FLHTCSE2 Models)

The motorcycle comes equipped with Harley-Davidson Screamin' Eagle SYN3 synthetic motorcycle lubricant. If additional oil must be added to correct oil level, and the SYN3 oil is not available, *temporarily add* Harley-Davidson HD-360 motor oil. Although both types of lubricant are compatible, it is suggested that the lubricant be changed as soon as possible since they should not be combined for any long duration. If the Screamin' Eagle SYN3 is not going to be used permanently, drain the engine, or transmission or primary chaincase oil and use the recommended oil listed in **Table 3**, Chapter Three.

Engine Oil and Filter Change (FLHTCSE2 Models)

The engine oil filter change procedure is the same as on previous models with the exception of the front fairing lower panels. To gain access to the oil filter, remove the left side front fairing lower panel assembly as described in the *Body* section of this Supplement.

Primary Chaincase Oil Level Check (All 2005 Models)

The primary chaincase oil level check is identical to prior to years with the exception of the seal on the clutch inspection cover. The O-ring has been replaced with a large gasket. Install the *new* large gasket as follows:

1. Position the *new* gasket with the rubber molding and the words *Toward Engine* facing the chaincase cover.
2. Align the triangular shaped hole in the *new* gasket with the top hole in the clutch inspection cover.

CAUTION
Do not push the screw through the triangular shaped hole in the new gasket as the sealing qualities of the gasket will be damaged.

3. Insert the screw, with the captive washer, through the clutch inspection cover and carefully *thread it* it all the way through the triangular shaped hole in the new gasket.
4. Install the clutch inspection cover and new gasket onto the chaincase cover and thread the top screw part way in.
5. Make sure the clutch inspection cover is correctly aligned with the chaincase cover and install the remaining four screws with captive washers.
6. Use a T27 Torx driver and tighten the screws in a crisscross pattern to 84-108 in.-lb. (10-12 N•m).

Primary Chaincase Oil Change (2004-2005 Models)

The primary chaincase oil change is the same as on previous models with the exception of the additional O-ring seal on the drain plug (**Figure 1**). The

15

drain plug is now equipped with an O-ring seal that must be replaced every time the drain plug is removed. Install a *new* O-ring onto the drain plug, install it and tighten to 33-60 in.-lb (3.7-6.8 N•m).

Refer to the preceding procedure regarding the installation of the new clutch cover gasket.

Clutch Lever Pivot Pin Lubrication (FLHTCSE2 Models)

Inspect the clutch lever pivot pin at the interval in Chapter Three, **Table 1**. Lubricate the pivot pin with silicone brake grease. To service the pivot pin, refer to *Clutch Master Cylinder* in the Chapter Five section of this Supplement.

PERIODIC MAINTENANCE

Final Drive Belt Defection and Alignment

2003 models

The final drive belt deflection is the same as on previous models with the exception of the amount of deflection.

Apply a force of 10 lbs. (4.5 kg) to the middle of the lower belt run and measure as follows:
1. Motorcycle on ground without rider or luggage: 5/16-3/8 (7.9-9.5 mm).
2. Motorcycle upright on ground with rider: 1/4 -5/16 in. (6.4-7.9 mm).

2004-2005 models

The final drive belt deflection is the same as on previous models with the exception of the amount of deflection.

Apply a force of 10 lbs. (4.5 kg) to the middle of the lower belt run and measure as follows:
1. Motorcycle on Jiffy stand without rider or luggage: 1/4-5/16 in. (6.4-7.9 mm).
2. Motorcycle upright with rear wheel off the ground: 3/16-1/4 in. (4.8-6.4 mm).

Clutch Hoses and Seals (FLHTCSE2 Models)

Replace the clutch hose every four years and the seals in the master cylinder and release cylinder every two years.

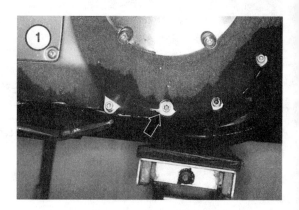

Check the clutch hose between the master cylinder and the release cylinder. If there is any leak, tighten the connections and bleed the clutch as described in this supplement. If this does not stop the leak or if a line is obviously damaged, cracked, or chafed, replace the hose and/or the master cylinder or release cylinder(s), then bleed the clutch as described in the *Clutch* section of this Supplement.

Clutch Fluid Change (FLHTCSE2 Models)

A small amount of dirt and moisture enters the clutch fluid each time the reservoir cap is removed. The same thing happens if a leak occurs or when any part of the hydraulic system is loosened or disconnected. Dirt can clog the system and cause unnecessary wear.

To change the clutch brake fluid, drain the fluid from the clutch system as described in the *Clutch* section of this supplement. Add new fluid to the master cylinder, and bleed the clutch at the release cylinder until the fluid leaving the release cylinder is clean and free of contaminants and air bubbles.

Checking Clutch Fluid Level (FLHTCSE2 Models)

1. Turn the handlebar straight ahead so the master cylinder is level.

2. Observe the brake fluid level by looking at the sight glass on the master cylinder reservoir top cover. If the fluid level is correct, the sight glass will be dark purple. If the level is low, the sight glass will have a lightened, clear appearance.

WARNING
Do not use brake fluid labeled DOT 5.1. This is a glycol-based fluid that is not compatible with silicone based DOT 5. DOT 5 brake fluid is purple while DOT 5.1 is an amber/clear color

CAUTION
Be careful when handling brake fluid. Do not spill it on painted or plastic surfaces, as it damages them. Wash the area immediately with soap and water, and thoroughly rinse it.

3. If the clutch fluid level is low, perform the following:

a. Clean any dirt from the master cylinder cover prior to removing it.

b. Remove the top cover and lift the diaphragm out of the reservoir.

c. Add fresh DOT 5 brake fluid to the FILL LEVEL mark at the top of the ledge on the rear inside wall of the reservoir.

d. Reinstall the diaphragm and top cover. Tighten the screws securely.

e. If the clutch fluid level is low enough to allow air in the hydraulic system, bleed the clutch system.

Table 5 MAINTENANCE AND TUNE-UP TORQUE SPECIFICATIONS

Item	ft.-lb.	in.-lb.	N•m
Clutch inspection cover screws	–	84-108	10-12
Primary chaincase drain plug	–	33-60	3.7-6.8

CHAPTER FOUR

ENGINE

Refer to **Tables 6-9** for engine specifications unique to 2003-2005 models.

ENGINE

Removal/Installation (FLHTCSE2 Models)

Engine removal and installation is the same as on previous models with the exception of the oil cooler. Remove the oil cooler as described in this section of this Supplement.

ROCKER ARMS AND PUSHRODS

Removal/Installation

The removal procedure is the same as on prior years.

The installation procedure is the same as on prior years with the exception of the breather assembly components. The 1999-2002 models were equipped with a breather assembly consisting of the cover, filter element, breather baffle and gaskets. On the 2003 models the breather assembly was combined into a one-piece unit along with the filter element and gasket. The 2004-2005 models once again use the components equipped on the 1999-2002 models.

15

CYLINDER HEAD

Installation

On 2003-2005 models, refer to **Figure 2** for the front and rear cylinder head bolt tightening sequence. Tighten the cylinder head bolts as follows:

1. Starting with bolt No. 1, tighten each bolt in order to 120-144 in.-lb. (13.6-16.3 N•m).
2. Starting with bolt No. 1, tighten each bolt in order to 15-17 ft.-lb. (20.3-23.1 N•m).
3. Make a vertical mark with a permanent marker on each bolt head (A, **Figure 3**). Make another mark on the cylinder head (B, **Figure 3**) at a 90° angle, or 1/4 turn from the mark on the head bolt.
4. Use the marks as a guide and tighten each bolt head 90°, or 1/4 turn, clockwise until the marks are aligned (**Figure 4**).

On 2005 models, the two O-rings (**Figure 5**) are no longer used in junction with the cylinder head dowel pins.

VALVE AND VALVE COMPONENTS (2005 MODELS—EXCEPT FLHTCSE2 MODELS)

Complete valve service requires a number of special tools, including a valve spring compressor, to remove and install the valves. The following procedures describe how to check for valve component wear and to determine what type of service is required.

Refer to **Figure 6**.

Valve Removal

1. Remove the cylinder head as described in Chapter Four.
2. Install the valve spring compressor (**Figure 7**) squarely over the valve spring upper retainer (**Figure 8**) and against the valve head.

CAUTION
To avoid loss of spring tension, compress the spring only enough to remove the valve keepers.

3. Tighten the valve spring compressor until the valve keepers separate from the valve stem. Lift the valve keepers out through the valve spring compressor with a magnet or needlenose pliers.

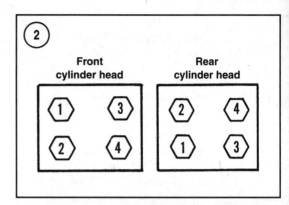

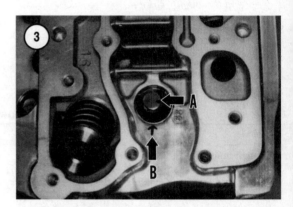

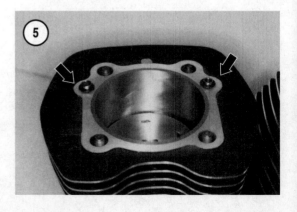

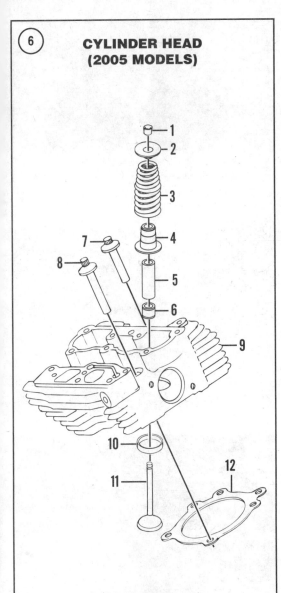

CYLINDER HEAD (2005 MODELS)

1. Valve keeper
2. Upper retainer
3. Spring
4. Valve stem seal/
   spring seat assembly
5. Valve guide
6. Valve guide collar
   (exhaust valve only)
7. Bolt–short
8. Bolt–long
9. Cylinder head
10. Valve seat
11. Valve
12. Gasket

4. Gradually loosen the valve spring compressor and remove it from the cylinder head.

5. Remove the spring upper retainer and the valve spring.

CAUTION
*Remove any burrs from the valve stem groove before removing the valve (**Figure 9**); otherwise the valve guide will be damaged as the valve stem passes through it.*

6. Remove the valve from the cylinder head while rotating it slightly.

7. Using needlenose pliers, carefully twist and remove the valve stem seal/spring seat assembly from the valve guide. Discard the valve stem seal/spring seat assembly.

CAUTION
Keep the components of each valve assembly together by placing each set in a divided carton, or into separate small boxes or small reclosable plastic bags. Identify the components as either intake or exhaust. If both cylin-

15

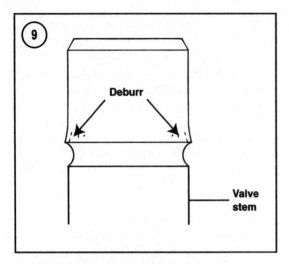

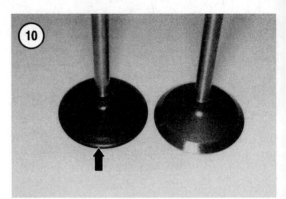

ders are disassembled, also label the components as front and rear. Do not intermix components from the valves or excessive wear may result.

8. Repeat Steps 2-7 to remove the remaining valve.

Valve Inspection

When measuring the valves and valve components in this section, compare the actual measurements to the new and service limit specifications in **Table 7** and **Table 8**. Replace parts that are out of specification or are damaged as described in this section.

1. Clean valves in solvent. Do not gouge or damage the valve seating surface.

2. Inspect the valve face. Minor roughness and pitting (**Figure 10**) can be removed by lapping the valve as described in this Supplement. Excessive unevenness to the contact surface indicates the valve is not serviceable.

3. Inspect the valve stem for wear and roughness. Then measure the valve stem outside diameter with a micrometer (**Figure 11**).

4. Remove all carbon and varnish from the valve guides with a stiff spiral wire brush before measuring wear.

5. Measure the valve guide inside diameter with a small hole gauge (**Figure 12**) at the top, center and bottom locations. Then measure the small hole gauge.

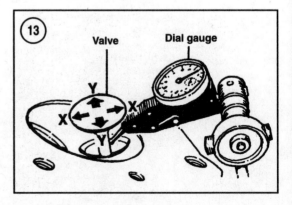

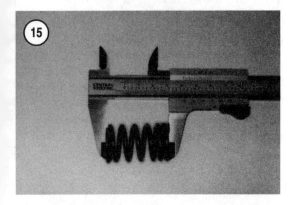

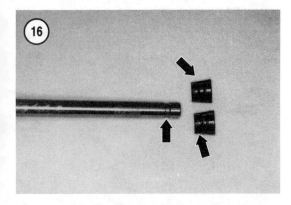

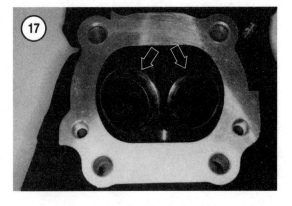

6. Determine the valve stem-to-valve guide clearance by subtracting the valve stem outside diameter from the valve guide inner diameter.

7. If a small hole gauge is not available, insert each valve into its guide. Attach a dial indicator to the valve stem next to the head (**Figure 13**). Hold the valve slightly off its seat and rock it sideways in both directions 90° to each other. If the valve rocks more than slightly, the guide is probably worn. Take the cylinder head to a Harley-Davidson dealership or machine shop and have the valve guides measured.

8. Check the valve spring as follows:
    a. Inspect the valve spring for visual damage.
    b. Use a square to visually check the spring for distortion or tilt (**Figure 14**).
    c. Measure the valve spring free length with a vernier caliper (**Figure 15**) and compare it to the specifications.
    d. Repeat sub-steps a-c for each valve spring.
    e. Replace the defective spring(s).

9. Check the valve spring upper retainer seats for cracks or other damage.

10. Check the valve keepers fit on the valve stem end (**Figure 16**). They should index tightly into the valve stem groove.

11. Inspect the valve seats (**Figure 17**) in the cylinder head. If they are worn or burned, they can be reconditioned as described in Chapter Four. Seats and valves in near-perfect condition can be reconditioned by lapping with fine Carborundum paste.
    a. Clean the valve seat and corresponding valve mating areas with contact cleaner.
    b. Coat the valve seat with layout fluid.
    c. Install the valve into its guide and tap it against its seat. Do not rotate the valve.
    d. Lift the valve out of the guide and measure the seat width at various points around the seat with a vernier caliper.
    e. Compare the seat width with the specifications. If the seat width is less than specified or uneven, resurface the seats as described in Chapter Four.
    f. Remove all layout fluid residue from the seats and valves.

Valve Installation

1. Clean the end of the valve guide.

15

2. Assemble the valve stem seal/spring seat assembly as follows:

    a. Apply engine oil to the oil seal (A, **Figure 18**) and the spring seat (B).

    b. Position the oil seal with the spring end going in last (C, **Figure 18**) and insert it into the spring seat.

    c. Press the oil seal down until it seats completely within the spring seat (D, **Figure 18**).

3. Coat a valve stem with Torco MPZ, molybdenum disulfide paste or equivalent. Install the valve part way into the guide. Then slowly turn the valve as it enters the oil seal and continue turning it until the valve is installed all the way.

4. Work the valve back and forth in the valve guide to ensure the lubricant is distributed evenly within the valve guide.

5. Withdraw the valve and apply an additional coat of the lubricant.

6. Reinstall the valve into the valve guide but do not push the valve past the top of the valve guide.

7. Push the valve all the way into the cylinder head until it bottoms (A, **Figure 19**).

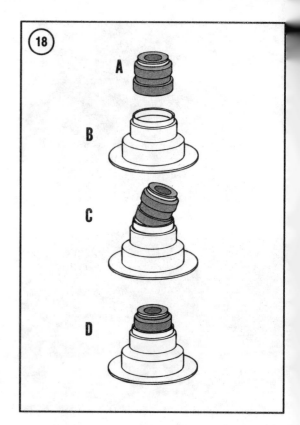

> *CAUTION*
> *The oil seal will be torn as it passes the valve stem keeper groove if the plastic capsule is not installed in Step 8. The capsule is included in the top end gasket set.*

8. Hold the valve in place and install the plastic capsule (B, **Figure 19**) onto the end of the valve stem. Apply a light coat of clean engine oil to the outer surface of the capsule.

9. With the valve held in place, slowly slide the valve stem seal/spring seat assembly onto the valve stem. Push the assembly down until it bottoms on the machined surface of the cylinder head.

10. Remove the plastic capsule from the valve stem. Keep the capsule as it will be used on the remaining valves.

11. Position the valve spring with tapered end going on last and install the valve spring (A, **Figure 20**). Make sure it is properly seated on the spring seat.

12. Install the upper spring retainer (B, **Figure 20**) on top of the valve spring.

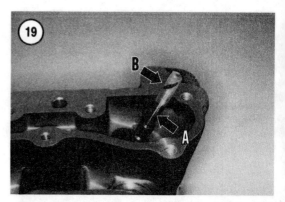

> *CAUTION*
> *To avoid loss of spring tension, only compress the springs enough to install the valve keepers.*

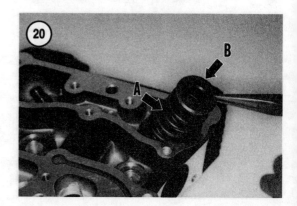

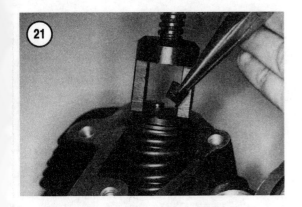

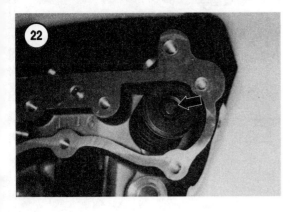

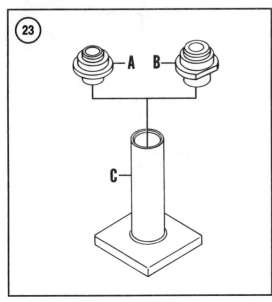

13. Compress the valve spring with a valve spring compressor (**Figure 7**) and install the valve keepers (**Figure 21**).

14. Make sure both keepers are seated around the valve stem prior to releasing the compressor.

15. Slowly release tension from the compressor and remove it. After removing the compressor, inspect the valve keepers to make sure they are properly seated (**Figure 22**). Tap the end of the valve stem with a *soft-faced* hammer to ensure the keepers are properly seated.

16. Repeat Steps 1-15 for the remaining valves.

17. Install the cylinder head as described in this Supplement.

Valve Guide Replacement

Tools

The following tools or their equivalents are required to replace the valve guides.

1. Cylinder head stand (HD-39782-A).
2. Intake valve seat adapter (HD-39782A-3).
3. Exhaust valve seat adapter (HD-39782A-4).
4. Valve guide driver (B-45524-1)
5. Valve guide installer sleeve (B-45524-2A).
6. Valve guide brush (HD-34751-A).
7. Valve guide reamer (B-45523) and T-handle (HD-39847).
8. Valve guide reamer honing lubricant (HD-39964).
9. Valve guide hone (B-45525).
10. Hydraulic press.

Procedure

> *CAUTION*
> *The valve guides must be removed and installed using the following special tools to avoid damage to the cylinder head. Use the correct size valve guide removal tool to remove the valve guides or the tool may expand the end of the guide. An expanded guide will widen and damage the guide bore in the cylinder head as it passes through it.*

1. Remove the old valve guide as follows:
   a. Install the intake (A, **Figure 23**) or exhaust (B) valve seat adapter into the tube at the top of the support stand (C).
   b. Install the support stand on the hydraulic press table.
   c. Install the cylinder head (A, **Figure 24**) onto the support stand (B) *centering* the cylinder head valve seat onto the seat adapter.

15

d. Insert the valve guide driver (C, **Figure 24**) into the valve guide bore until it stops on the valve guide shoulder.

e. Center the valve guide driver under the press ram and make sure the driver is perpendicular to the press table.

f. Support the cylinder head, slowly apply pressure and drive valve guide out through the combustion chamber side. Discard the valve guide.

g. Remove the cylinder head and special tools from the press bed.

h. Repeat sub-steps a-g for the remaining valve guides.

2. Clean the valve guide bores in the cylinder head.

3. Because the valve guide bores in the cylinder head may have enlarged during removal of the old guides, measure each valve guide bore prior to purchasing the new guides. Then purchase the new valve guides to match their respective bore diameters. Determine the bore diameter as follows:

a. Measure the valve guide bore diameter in the cylinder head with a bore gauge or snap gauge. Record the bore diameter.

b. The *new* valve guide outside diameter must be 0.0020-0.0033 in. (0.050-0.083 mm) larger than the guide bore in the cylinder head. When purchasing new valve guides, measure the new guide's outside diameter with a micrometer. If the new guide's outside diameter is not within this specification, install oversize valve guide(s). See a Harley-Davidson dealership for available sizes and part numbers.

NOTE
The intake valves are not equipped with the valve guide collar. On exhaust valves, the collar must be installed onto the valve guide, see Step 4.

4. On *exhaust valve guides*, install the collar onto the valve guide as follows:

a. Insert the valve guide collar (A, **Figure 25**) onto the installer sleeve (B) and center it squarely onto the counter bore of the installer sleeve.

b. Install the *new* valve guide (C, **Figure 25**) into the installer sleeve (B) until it contacts the valve guide collar.

c. Install the installer sleeve and valve guide onto the press table and center it.

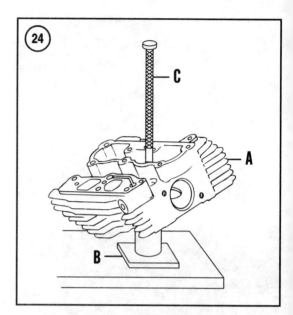

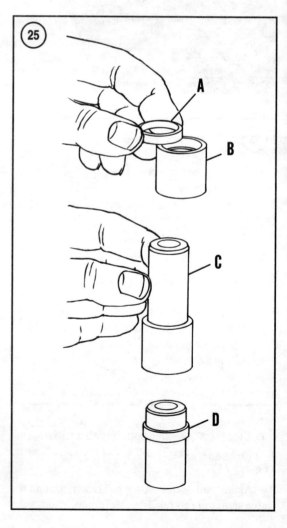

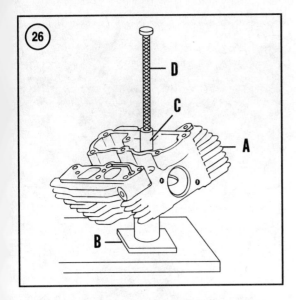

d. Slowly apply pressure and drive valve guide onto the collar until the valve guide bottoms in the installer sleeve.

e. Remove the valve guide/collar assembly (D, **Figure 25**) from the installer sleeve.

5. Apply a thin coat of Vaseline to the entire outer surface of the valve guide before installing it in the cylinder head.

CAUTION
When installing oversize valve guides, make sure to match each guide to its respective bore in the cylinder head.

6. Install the *new* valve guide as follows:

a. Install the intake (A, **Figure 23**) or exhaust (B) valve seat adapter into the tube at the top of the support stand (C).

b. Install the support stand on the hydraulic press table.

c. Install the cylinder head (A, **Figure 26**) onto the support stand (B) *centering* the cylinder head valve seat onto the seat adapter.

d. On exhaust valves, position the valve guide with the collar end going in last. The intake valve guides are non-directional, either end can go in first.

e. Install the valve guide onto the cylinder head receptacle.

f. Install the valve guide installer sleeve (C, **Figure 26**) over the valve guide, and insert the tapered end of the valve guide driver (D) into the installer sleeve.

g. Center the valve guide driver under the press ram and make sure the driver is perpendicular to the press table.

f. Support the cylinder head, slowly apply pressure and slowly start to drive the valve guide into the cylinder head receptacle. Stop and back off the press ram to allow the valve guide to center itself.

g. Verify that the support stand (B, **Figure 26**) and valve guide driver (D) are square with the press table.

h. Once again apply press pressure and continue to drive the valve guide part way into the cylinder head receptacle. Once again, stop and back off the press ram to allow the valve guide to center itself.

i. Again apply press pressure and continue to drive the valve guide into the cylinder head receptacle until the installer sleeve (C, **Figure 26**) contacts the machined surface of the cylinder head.

j. Remove the cylinder head and special tools from the press bed.

k. Repeat sub-steps a-j for the remaining valve guides.

7. Replacement valve guides are sold with a smaller inside diameter than the valve stem. Ream the guide to fit the valve stem as follows:

a. Apply a liberal amount of reamer lubricant to the ream bit and to the valve guide bore.

b. Start the reamer straight into the valve guide bore.

CAUTION
Only apply pressure to the end of the drive socket. If pressure is applied to the T-handle, the bore will be uneven, rough cut and tapered.

c. Apply thumb pressure to the end of the drive socket portion of the T-handle while rotating the T-handle *clockwise*. Only *light* pressure is required. Apply additional lubricant to the reamer and into the valve guide while rotating the reamer.

d. Continue to rotate the reamer until the entire bit has traveled through the valve guide and the shank of the reamer rotates freely.

CAUTION
Never back the reamer out through the valve guide as the guide will be damaged.

15

e. Remove the T-handle from the reamer. Remove the reamer from the combustion chamber side of the cylinder head.

f. Apply low-pressure compressed air to remove the small shavings from the valve guide bore. Then clean the valve guide bore with the small spiral brush.

8. Hone the valve guide as follows:

a. Install the valve guide hone into a high-speed electric drill.

b. Lubricate the valve guide bore and hone stones with the reamer lubricant—*do not use motor oil.*

c. Carefully insert the hone stones into the valve guide bore.

d. Start the drill and move the hone back and forth in the valve guide bore for 10 to 12 complete strokes to obtain a 60° crosshatch pattern.

9. Repeat Steps 7 and 8 for each valve guide.

10. Soak the cylinder head in a container filled with hot, soapy water. Then clean the valve guides with a valve guide brush or an equivalent bristle brush. Do *not* use a steel brush. Do not use cleaning solvent, kerosene or gasoline as these chemicals will not remove all of the abrasive particles produced during the honing operation. Repeat this step until all of the valve guides are thoroughly cleaned. Then rinse the cylinder head and valve guides in clear, cold water and dry them with compressed air.

11. After cleaning and drying the valve guides, apply clean engine oil to the guides to prevent rust.

12. Resurface the valve seats as described in *Valve Seat Reconditioning* in Chapter Four.

PISTONS AND PISTON RINGS

Piston Clearance

Late 2003 and all 2004-2005 models have a small oval-shaped opening on the piston skirt coating. This opening is used to locate the micrometer for an accurate outer diameter measurement. This small oval-shaped opening is too small for the standard flat anvil micrometer to obtain an accurate measurement. Use a 3-4 in. blade or ball anvil style micrometer, or a 4-5 in. micrometer with spherical ball adapters to achieve a correct measurement.

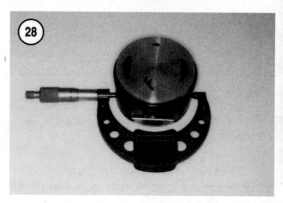

1. Make sure the piston skirt and cylinder bore is clean and dry.

2. Measure the cylinder bore with a bore gauge (**Figure 27**) as described under *Cylinder, Inspection* in Chapter Four.

NOTE
Some early 2003 models were not equipped with the bare aluminum spots on the piston skirt coating.

3A. On early 2003 models, measure the piston diameter with a micrometer as follows:

a. Hold the micrometer at the bottom of the piston skirt at a right angle to the piston pin bore (**Figure 28**). Adjust the micrometer so the spindle and anvil just touch the skirt.

b. Start below the bottom ring and slowly move the micrometer toward the bottom of the skirt.

c. The micrometer will be loose, then tight at about 0.5 in. (12.7 mm) from the bottom and then loose again.

d. Measure the piston skirt at the tightest point.

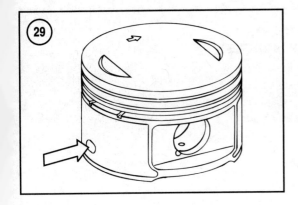

3B. On late 2003 and 2004-2005 models, measure the piston diameter with a micrometer as follows:
  a. Use the previously described special micrometer and correctly position it on the bare aluminum spot on each side of the piston as shown in **Figure 29**.
  b. Measure the piston at this location only.
4. Subtract the piston diameter from the largest bore diameter; the difference is piston-to-cylinder clearance. If the clearance exceeds the specification in **Table 7** and **Table 8**, the pistons should be replaced and the cylinders bored oversize and then honed. Purchase the new pistons first. Measure their diameter and add the specified clearance to determine the proper cylinder bore diameter.

OIL COOLER, OIL FILTER MOUNT AND THERMOSTAT (FLHTCSE2 MODELS)

The oil cooler and oil filter are mounted on the front of the crankcase and can be removed with the engine in the frame.

NOTE
The original equipment hose clamps are destroyed when removed. A quality screw-type hose clamp can be used instead or new original equipment hose clamps must be installed using the Harley-Davidson hose clamp pliers (part No. HD-41137).

Oil Cooler and Cover
Removal/Installation

Refer to **Figure 30**.
1. Place the motorcycle on level ground.
2. Cover the front fender to protect the finish.

3. Remove the front cylinder's exhaust pipe as described in Chapter Seven.
4. Remove the left side front fairing lower panel assembly as described in the *Body* section of this Supplement.
5. Place a drain pan under the oil cooler assembly.
6. Remove the locknuts and washers securing the oil cooler and cover assembly to the mounting bracket.
7. Carefully move the assembly forward, use side cutting pliers to cut the tie-warps securing the assembly to both oil hoses.
8. Remove the hose clamps and disconnect the hoses form the oil cooler.
9. Remove the oil cooler and cover assembly and drain residual oil from the oil cooler.
10. Plug the ends of the oil lines to prevent the entry of debris.
11. If necessary, carefully separate the cover from the oil cooler. The cover is held in place with adhesive tape.
12. Install by reversing these removal steps. Note the following:
  a. Connect the oil filter mount rear hose to the lower fitting on the oil cooler and the front hose to the upper hose fitting.
  b. Install *new* hose clamps securing the oil hoses to the oil cooler.
  c. Tighten the oil cooler mounting locknuts to 80-110 in.-lb. (9.0-12.4 N•m).
  d. Check engine oil level and add additional oil to the correct level as described in Chapter Three.
  e. Start the engine and check for oil leaks.

Oil Filter Mount and Hoses

Removal

1. Remove the oil cooler and cover assembly as described in this section.
2. Remove the oil filter as described under *Engine Oil and Filter Change* in Chapter Three.
3. Remove the rubber boot and disconnect the electrical connector from the oil pressure switch.
4. Use a 1 1/16 in. open-end crow foot wrench and unscrew the switch from the engine.
5. If the oil filter adapter is going to be replaced, unscrew it from the mount at this time.

15

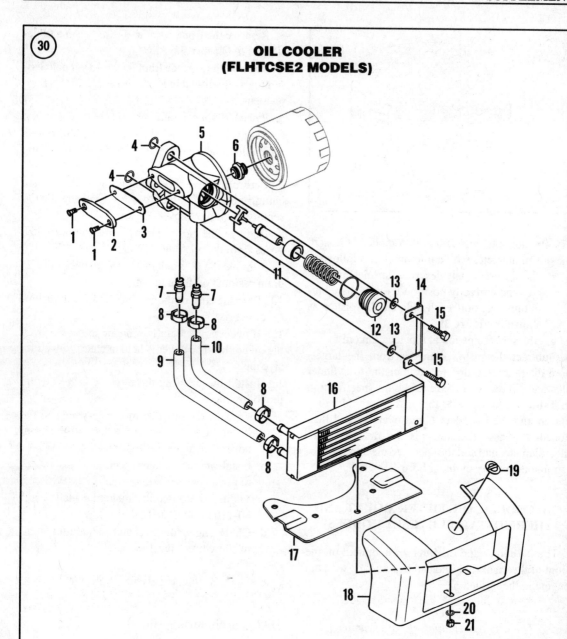

30

OIL COOLER
(FLHTCSE2 MODELS)

1. Screw
2. Transfer passage cover
3. Gasket
4. O-ring
5. Oil filter mount
6. Adapter
7. Straight barbed fitting
8. Hose clamp
9. Lower oil hose
10. Upper oil hose
11. Thermostat assembly
12. Plug
13. Washer
14. Lock plate
15. Bolt
16. Oil cooler
17. Mounting bracket
18. Cover
19. Decal
20. Washer
21. Locknut

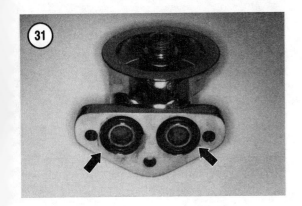

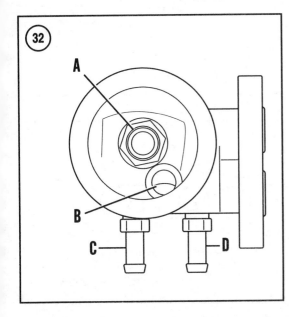

6. Use side cutting pliers cut the tie-wraps securing both oil hoses to the oil filter mount. Remove both hoses.

7. If necessary, loosen but do not remove the thermostat plug.

8. Bend the locking tabs away from the mounting bolts.

9. Remove the two mounting bolts, lock plate and washers securing the oil filter mount to the crankcase.

10. Remove the center mounting bolt and washer and remove the oil filter mount. Remove the O-rings from oil filter mount and discard them.

Installation

1. Apply a medium strength threadlocking compound to all mounting bolt threads.

2. Install *new* O-rings into the grooves in the oil filter mount (**Figure 31**).

3. Install the oil filter mount onto the crankcase and align the mounting bolt holes.

4. Install the washers into the recesses in the top and bottom holes in the mount.

5. Install the two mounting bolts and lock plate securing the oil filter mount to the crankcase. Make sure the washers are still in place in the recesses. Tighten both bolts finger-tight.

6. Install the center bolt and washer and tighten finger-tight.

7. Starting with the top bolt, alternately tighten the three bolts to 130-150 in.-lb. (14.7-17.0 N•m).

8. Bend the locking tabs against the top and bottom mounting bolts.

9. If the oil filter adapter (A, **Figure 32**) was removed, install it as follows:

    a. Remove all old threadlocking reside from the adapter and the mount.

    b. Apply a medium strength threadlocking compound to the adapter.

    c. Thread it into the mount and tighten to 144-192 ft.-lb. (16.3-21.7 N•m).

10. Install the oil hoses onto the oil filter mount and *new* hose clamps. Tighten the hose clamps securely.

11. Apply Loctite Thread sealant to the oil pressure switch and install the switch. Use a 1 1/16 in. open-end crow foot wench and tighten the switch to 96-144 in.-lb. (10.9-16.3 N•m).

12. Install the electrical connector onto the oil pressure switch and rubber boot.

13. Install the oil filter as described under *Engine Oil and Filter Change* in Chapter Three.

14. Install the oil cooler and cover assembly as described in this section

Inspection

1. If still in place, remove the O-rings from the oil filter mount.

2. Remove the screws securing the transfer passage cover. Remove the cover and gasket from the mount.

3. Thoroughly clean the oil filter mount in solvent and dry with compressed air.

4. Inspect the oil passageway to the oil filter (B, **Figure 32**), from the oil filter (A, **Figure 33**) and to the

15

oil cooler (B, **Figure 33**). Make sure there is no residual oil sludge, especially in the thermostat area.

5. If necessary, unscrew the supply oil hose (C, **Figure 32**) and return oil hose (D) straight barbed fittings from the mount.

6. Install a *new* gasket on the transfer passage cover. Install the cover and screws and tighten the screws to 90-120 in.-lb. (10.2-13.6 N•m).

7. Apply pipe sealant or Teflon tape to the oil hose straight barbed fittings. Install the fittings and tighten securely.

Thermostat Test Procedure

When the engine is cool, the thermostat is in its closed position as shown in **Figure 34**. The spring holds the piston over the return passageway from the oil cooler blocking off the oil flow to the crankcase.

When the engine warms, the thermostat moves to the open position as shown in **Figure 35**. This allows the oil to flow from the oil cooler to the crankcase.

> *NOTE*
> *This test procedure requires the use of an infrared thermometer in order to test the oil temperature at both the oil pan and the oil cooler while the engine is operating.*

1. Place the motorcycle on level ground.
2. Remove the side front fairing lower panel assembly as described in the *Body* section of this Supplement.
3. Ride the motorcycle a short distance to achieve normal operating temperature. Let the engine run at idle speed.
4. With the engine running at idle speed, aim the thermometer at the engine oil pan and note the reading.
5. Aim the thermometer at the oil cooler and note the reading.
6. Shut off the engine.
7. If the oil cooler temperature is the same as the oil pan temperature below 180° F (82° C), then the thermostat may be stuck open.
8. If the oil cooler temperature is lower than the oil pan temperature below 180° F (82° C), but above 180° F (82° C), then the thermostat is operating correctly.

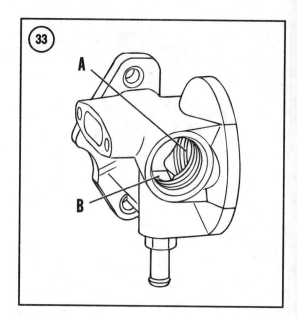

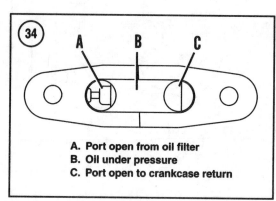

A. Port open from oil filter
B. Oil under pressure
C. Port open to crankcase return

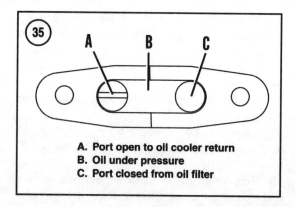

A. Port open to oil cooler return
B. Oil under pressure
C. Port closed from oil filter

9. If the oil pan temperature exceeds 210° F (99° C) and the oil cooler is cooler, then the thermostat is stuck closed.

10. If the temperatures are incorrect in either Step 7 or Step 8, proceed to Step 11.

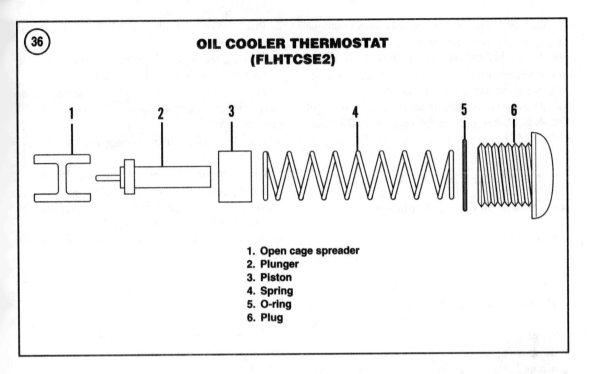

(36)

OIL COOLER THERMOSTAT
(FLHTCSE2)

1. Open cage spreader
2. Plunger
3. Piston
4. Spring
5. O-ring
6. Plug

11. Allow the engine to cool to room temperature, and remove the thermostat assembly from the oil filter mount as described in the following procedure.

12. Test the plunger operation as follows:

NOTE
Do not allow the thermometer or the plunger to touch the sides or bottom of the pan, or a false reading will result.

a. Suspend the plunger in a container of water and place the thermometer in the pan of water. Use a thermometer that is rated higher than the test temperature.

b. With the water at room temperature, verify that the plunger is not extended.

c. Gradually heat the water and continue to gently stir the water until it reaches the *Start To Open* temperature of 180° F (82° C). Verify that the plunger starts to extend.

d. Continue to heat the water past the *Start To Open* temperature to the *Full Open* temperature of 210° F (99° C). Verify that the plunger is fully extended.

e. If the plunger does not extend as specified; replace the thermostat assembly as described in this section.

13. Install the left side front fairing lower panel assembly as described in the *Body* section of this Supplement.

Thermostat Replacement

Refer to **Figure 36**.
1. Place the motorcycle on level ground.
2. Remove the side front fairing lower panel assembly as described in the *Body* section of this Supplement.
3. The engine must be at room temperature.
4. Place several old shop cloths under the thermostat plug as some engine oil will drain out in the next step.
5. Use a ball Allen wrench and remove the plug from the thermostat.
6. Use needlenose pliers and remove the spring and the plunger assembly from the receptacle in the oil filter mount.
7. Use a pick and remove the open cage spreader from the receptacle.
8. Clean the thermostat housing receptacle in the oil filter mount with a lint-free shop cloth and solvent, and wipe dry.
9. Insert the open cage spreader part way into the receptacle.
10. Install the plunger into piston.

15

11. Position the pointed end of the plunger onto the open cage spreader and slowly push the plunger/piston assembly and the spreader into the receptacle until they bottom.

12. Install the spring onto the piston.

13. Install a *new* O-ring onto the plug and install the plug. Slowly tighten the plug to 15-20 ft.-lb. (20.4-27.1 N•m).

CRANKCASE AND CRANKSHAFT

Right Side Main Bearing Replacement

Refer to **Figure 37**.

Tools

The following tools or their equivalents are required to remove and install the right side main bearing:

1. Hydraulic press.
2. Crankshaft bearing support tube (HD-42720-5).
3. Pilot/driver (B-45655).

Removal

NOTE
The H-D support tube is marked with either A or B.

1. Place the support tube with the *A* side facing up on the press bed.
2. Position the right side crankcase with the outer surface facing up and position the bearing directly over the support tube on the press bed.
3. Install the pilot shaft through the bearing and into the support tube.
4. Center the press driver over the pilot shaft.
5. Hold the crankcase half parallel to the press bed and have an assistant slowly apply pressure on the pilot shaft until the bearing is free from the case half.
6. Remove the case half and tools from the press bed.

Installation

1. Apply a light coat of clean engine oil to the outer surface of the bearing and to the crankcase receptacle.

2. Place the support tube with the *B* side facing up on the press bed.
3. Position the right side crankcase with the outer surface facing up on the press bed.
4. Position the new bearing with the manufacturer's marks facing up and place it over the crankcase receptacle.
5. Install the pilot/driver through the bearing and into the support tube.
6. Center the press driver over the pilot driver.
7. Slowly apply press pressure on the pilot driver, pressing the bearing into the crankcase. Apply pressure until resistance is felt and the bearing bottoms in the support tube. This will correctly locate the bearing within the crankcase. Remove the pilot driver.
8. Remove the crankcase and the support tube from the press bed.
9. Check on each side of the crankcase to make sure the bearing is centered within the receptacle. If not, reposition the bearing until it is centered correctly.
10. Spin the bearing to make sure it rotates smoothly with no binding.

Left Side Main Bearing Assembly Replacement

Refer to **Figure 37**.

Tools

The following tools or their equivalents are required to remove and install the right side main bearing:

1. Hydraulic press.
2. Crankshaft bearing support tube (HD-42720-5).
3. Pilot/driver (B-45655).

Bearing removal

1. Place the crankcase on the workbench with the inboard surface facing up.
2. If still in place, remove the crankshaft spacer from the bearing bore.
3. Carefully pull the thrust washer from the outer surface of the crankcase past the oil seal.
4. Place the support tube on the workbench with the *A* side facing up.

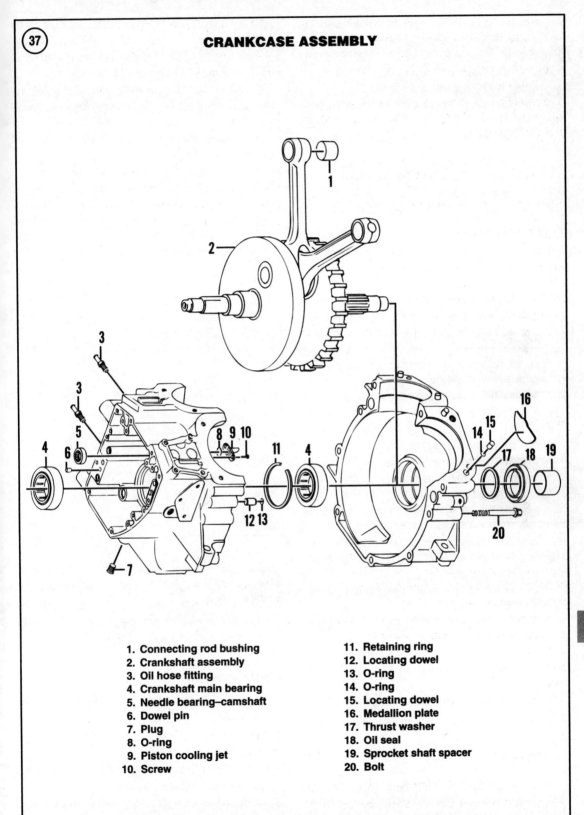

(37)

CRANKCASE ASSEMBLY

1. Connecting rod bushing
2. Crankshaft assembly
3. Oil hose fitting
4. Crankshaft main bearing
5. Needle bearing–camshaft
6. Dowel pin
7. Plug
8. O-ring
9. Piston cooling jet
10. Screw
11. Retaining ring
12. Locating dowel
13. O-ring
14. O-ring
15. Locating dowel
16. Medallion plate
17. Thrust washer
18. Oil seal
19. Sprocket shaft spacer
20. Bolt

15

5. Position the crankcase with the inner surface facing up and place the bearing bore over the support tube.

6. Use a suitable size drift and tap the oil seal out of the bearing bore. Discard the oil seal.

7. Turn the crankcase over with the inner surface facing up.

CAUTION
Do not damage the crankcase retaining ring groove with the screwdriver. The groove must remain sharp to correctly seat the retaining ring.

8. The roller bearing (A, **Figure 38**) is secured in the crankcase with a retaining ring (B) on the inner surface of the bearing bore. Remove the retaining ring (C, **Figure 38**) as follows:

   a. Use a flat tip screwdriver and place it under the retaining ring. Carefully lift the edge of the retaining ring up and out of the crankcase groove.

   b. Slide the tip of the screwdriver around the edge of the bearing and continue to lift the retaining ring out of the crankcase groove.

   c. Remove the retaining ring.

9. Position the support tube (A, **Figure 39**) on the press bed with the *A* side facing up.

10. Position the crankcase half with the outer side facing up and position the crankshaft's bearing bore over the support tube. Correctly align the two parts.

11. Slide the pilot/driver (B, **Figure 39**) through the crankcase bearing and into the support.

12. Center the press ram (C, **Figure 39**) directly over the pilot/driver (B) and slowly press the bearing out of the crankcase.

13. Remove the crankcase and special tools from the press bed.

14. Clean the crankcase half in solvent and dry it with compressed air.

Bearing installation

1. Apply clean engine oil, or press lube, to the bearing receptacle in the crankcase and to the outer race of the *new* bearing.

2. Position the support tube (A, **Figure 40**) on the press bed with the *A* side facing up.

3. Position the crankcase half with the inner side facing up and position the crankshaft's bearing bore over the support tube. Correctly align the two parts.

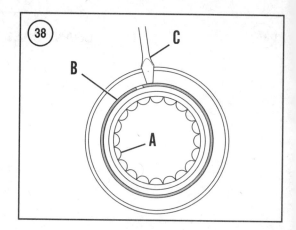

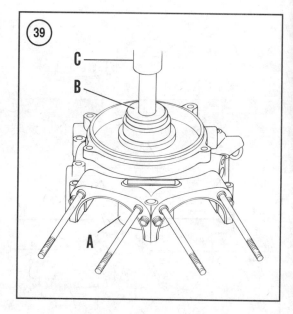

4. Correctly position the *new* bearing (B, **Figure 40**) over the crankcase bore with the manufacturer's marks facing down.

5. Slide the pilot/driver (C, **Figure 40**) through the new bearing and the crankcase and into the support.

6. Center the press ram (D, **Figure 40**) directly over the pilot/driver (C) and slowly press the bearing into the crankcase until it *lightly* bottoms in the crankshaft bearing bore.

7. Remove the crankcase and special tools from the press.

8. Make sure the bearing has been pressed in past the retaining ring groove. If the groove is not visible above the bearing, repeat Steps 2-6 until the groove is visible.

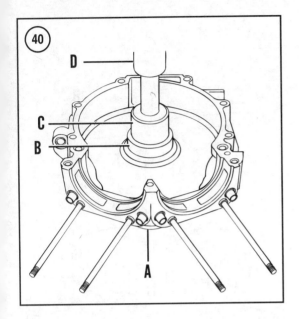

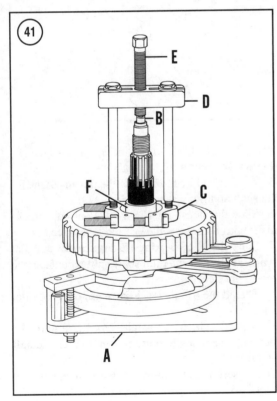

9. Position the crankcase on the workbench with the inner surface facing up.

CAUTION
Do not damage the crankcase retaining ring groove with the screwdriver.

The groove must remain sharp to correctly seat the retaining ring.

NOTE
If the retaining ring will not correctly seat in the crankcase groove, the bearing is not correctly seated in the crankcase bore. Repeat Steps 2-6

10. Install the bearing's *new* retainer ring as follows:

     a. Work the retaining ring into the crankcase groove being careful not to damage the crankcase groove.

     b. Use a flat tip screwdriver and push the retaining ring. Continue to push the retaining ring into the crankcase groove and make sure it is correctly seated in the groove.

Crankshaft End Play Inspection

NOTE
All 2003-2005 models are equipped with assembled roller bearings and this procedure is no longer necessary.

Crankshaft Left Side Main Bearing Assembly Inner Race Replacement

Removal

1. Support the crankshaft in a support fixture (HD-44358), or an equivalent, with the bearing side facing up (A, **Figure 41**).

2. Place a hardened plug (B, **Figure 41**) between the bearing puller and the end of the crankshaft.

3. Install the bearing splitter under the bearing inner race (C, **Figure 41**).

4. Apply graphite lubricant to the bearing puller center screw, and attach a bearing puller (D, **Figure 41**) to the splitter.

WARNING
*In Step 5, **never** use the heat gun in conjunction with the penetrating oil. The heat from the gun may ignite the oil resulting in a fire.*

5A. Use an industrial heat gun and apply heat uniformly to the bearing inner race for approximately 30 seconds.

15

5B. If a heat gun is not available, apply penetrating oil to the inner race and crankshaft and allow the oil to penetrate for 30 minutes.

6. Make sure the bearing puller is square to the crankshaft so the bearing inner race is not out of alignment with the crankshaft shoulder.

7. Slowly tighten the center screw (E, **Figure 41**) and withdraw the bearing inner race (F) from the crankshaft shoulder.

8. Remove the bearing puller, splitter and bearing inner race from the crankshaft.

9. Remove the thrust washer from the crankshaft. Discard the thrust washer, it cannot be re-used.

10. Clean the sprocket shaft with contact cleaner. Check the sprocket shaft for cracks or other damage. If it is damaged, refer service to a Harley-Davidson dealership.

Installation

The sprocket shaft bearing cone installer (HD-997225-55B) is required to install the sprocket shaft bearing inner race.

1. Support the crankshaft in a support fixture (HD-44358), or an equivalent, with the bearing side facing up (A, **Figure 42**).

2. Thread the pilot shaft (B, **Figure 42**) onto the crankshaft until it contacts the crankshaft

3. Slide the *new* thrust washer (C, **Figure 42**) over the sprocket shaft.

> **WARNING**
> In Step 4, **never** use the heat gun in conjunction with the penetrating oil. The heat from the gun may ignite the oil resulting in a fire.

4A. Place the *new* bearing race on the workbench. Use heat gun and uniformly heat the bearing race for approximately 60 seconds. Wear heavy duty gloves and install the *new* inner race (D, **Figure 42**) onto the crankshaft

4B. If a heat gun is not available, apply penetrating oil to the inner surface of the bearing race and to the

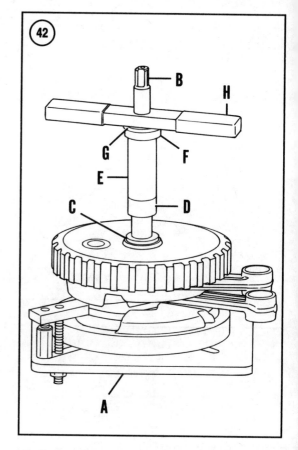

crankshaft shoulder. Install the *new* inner race (D, **Figure 42**) onto the crankshaft.

5. Apply graphite lubricant to the threads of the pilot shaft and flat washer

6. Slide the sleeve (E, **Figure 42**) onto the crankshaft until it contacts the bearing inner race.

7. Slide the Nice bearing (F, **Figure 42**) and flat washer (G) over the pilot shaft until it contacts the top of the sleeve.

8. Thread the handle (H, **Figure 42**) onto the pilot shaft (B).

9. Slowly tighten the handle *clockwise* until the bearing inner race bottoms on the crankshaft shoulder.

10. Unscrew and remove all parts of the special tool.

Table 6 GENERAL ENGINE SPECIFICATIONS

Item	Specification
Engine type	Four-stroke, 45° OHV V twin Twin Cam 88 and 103
Bore and Stroke	
88 models	3.75 × 4.00 in. (95.25 × 101.6 mm)
103 models	3.875 × 4.375 in. (98.425 × 111.125 mm)
Displacement	
88 models	88 cubic inch (1450 cc)
103 models	103 cubic inch (1690 cc)
Compression ratio	9.0 to 1
Torque	
88 models	85 ft. lb. (115.2 N•m) @ 3000 rpm
103 models	100 ft. lb. (136 N•m) @ 3500 rpm
Maximum sustained engine speed	
88 engine	5500 rpm
103 engine	5800 rpm
Engine and transmission weight	165 lbs. (74.8 kg)
Cooling system	Air cooled

Table 7 ENGINE SERVICE SPECIFICATIONS (88 ENGINE)

Item	New in. (mm)	Service limit in. (mm)
Cylinder bore		
Standard	–	3.752 (95.301)
Oversize 0.005 in.	–	3.757 (95.428)
Oversize 0.010 in.	–	3.762 (95.555)
Piston-to-cylinder clearance		
Early style piston	0.0006-0.0017 (0.015-0.043)	0.003 (0.076)
Late style piston	0.0014-0.0025 (0.036-0.064)	0.003 (0.076)
Piston pin fit in piston	0.0002-0.0005 (0.005-0.013)	0.002 (0.051)
Valve stem-to-guide clearance (2005 models)		
Intake	0.001-0.003 (0.0254-0.0762)	0.0038 (0.0965)
Exhaust	0.001-0.003 (0.0254-0.0762)	0.0038 (0.0965)
Valve seat width (2005 models)		
Intake and exhaust	0.040-0.062 (1.02-1.58)	–
Valve stem protrusion (2005 models)		
Intake and exhaust	2.005-2.039 (50.93-51.79)	–
Valve spring free length (2005 models)		
Intake and exhaust	2.325 (59.1)	–
Camshaft support plate		
Camshaft chain tensioner		
shoe	–	0.090 (2.29)*
Camshaft bushing fit	–	0.0008 (0.0203)
Camshaft bushing		
inside diameter	–	0.8545 (21.704)
Valve lifters		
Roller fit	–	0.015 (0.38)
Roller end clearance	–	0.015 (0.38)

* 1/2 thickness of shoe.

15

Table 8 ENGINE SERVICE SPECIFICATIONS (103 ENGINE)

Item	New in. (mm)	Service limit in. (mm)
Cylinder bore		
Standard	–	3.877 (98.48)
Oversize 0.005 in.	–	3.882 (98.60)
Oversize 0.010 in.	–	3.887 (98.73)
Piston-to-cylinder clearance	0.0014-0.0025 (0.036-0.064)	0.003 (0.076)
Piston pin clearance in piston	–	0.0008 (0.020)
Piston rings		
Compression ring end gap		
Top ring	0.010-0.020 (0.254 0-0.508)	0.030 (0.762)
Second ring	0.014-0.024 (0.356-0.609)	0.034 (0.863)
Oil control ring end gap	0.010-0.050 (0.254-1.270)	0.050 (1.270)
Compression ring side clearance		
Top ring	0.0012-0.0037 (0.030-0.094)	0.0045 (0.114)
Second ring	0.0012-0.0037 (0.030-0.094)	0.0045 (0.114)
Oil control ring end gap	0.0031-0.0091 (0.079-0.231)	0.010 (0.254)

Table 9 ENGINE TORQUE SPECIFICATIONS

Item	ft.-lb.	in.-lb.	N•m
Oil cooler mounting locknuts	–	80-110	9.0-12.4
Oil filter mounting bolts	–	130-150	14.7-17.0
Oil filter adapter	–	144-192	16.3-21.7
Oil pressure switch	–	96-144	10.9-16.3
Transfer passage cover	–	90-120	10.2-13.6
Thermostat plug	15-20	–	20.4-27.1
Cylinder head bolts	See text		

CHAPTER FIVE

CLUTCH AND PRIMARY DRIVE

CLUTCH ASSEMBLY
(ALL 2005 MODELS)

The clutch assembly is identical to prior years with the exception of the seal on the clutch inspection cover. The O-ring has been replaced with a large gasket. Install the *new* gasket as follows:

1. Position the *new* gasket with the rubber molding and the words *Toward Engine* facing the chaincase cover.

2. Align the triangular shaped hole in the *new* gasket with the top hole in the clutch inspection cover.

CAUTION
Do not push the screw through the triangular shaped hole in the new gasket as the sealing qualities of the gasket will be damaged.

3. Insert the screw, with the captive washer, though the clutch inspection cover and *carefully* thread it all

the way through the triangular shaped hole in the new gasket.

4. Install the clutch inspection cover and new gasket onto the chaincase cover and thread the top screw part way in.

5. Make sure the clutch inspection cover is correctly aligned with the chaincase cover and install the remaining four screws with captive washers.

6. Use a T27 Torx driver and tighten the screws in a crisscross pattern to 84-108 in.-lb. (10-12 N•m).

CLUTCH ASSEMBLY (FLHTCSE2 MODELS)

The clutch assembly is identical to prior to years with the exception of the release mechanism. The clutch release mechanism is now hydraulically operated instead of with a clutch cable. The release mechanism consists of a clutch master cylinder on the left side handlebar and a release cylinder on the right side of the transmission case.

CLUTCH RELEASE BEARING AND PUSHROD (FLHTCSE2 MODELS)

The hydraulic clutch release bearing assembly shown in **Figure 43** is the only major difference from the bearing assembly on cable operated models. On the hydraulic clutch models, it is not necessary to perform any procedure to allow slack on the diaphragm spring during the clutch assembly removal procedure.

Removal/Installation

NOTE
On models so equipped, always disarm the optional TSSM security system prior to disconnecting the battery or the siren will sound.

NOTE
The clutch release bearing and pushrod can be removed without first removing the primary chaincase outer cover.

1. Disconnect the battery negative cable as described in Chapter Eight.

2. Remove the clutch mechanism inspection cover and gasket.

CAUTION
*Harley-Davidson specifies that a **new** gasket must be installed every time the chaincase outer cover is removed.*

3. Remove the screws securing the clutch cover. Remove the cover and the gasket.

4. Remove the outer large snap ring (A, **Figure 44**) securing the release bearing plate.

5. Remove the release bearing plate (B, **Figure 44**) and the pushrod (C) as an assembly.

6. If necessary, remove the small snap ring (D, **Figure 44**) and remove the pushrod from the release bearing plate.

7. Measure the pushrod and release plate movement as described in the following procedure.

8. Install by reversing the removal steps. Note the following:

   a. Make sure the snap rings seat correctly into their respective grooves.

   b. Install a *new* clutch cover gasket as described under *Clutch Assembly (All 2005 Models)* in this Supplement.

   c. Install the inspection cover and tighten the screws to 84-108 in.-lb. (10-12 N•m).

Pushrod and Release Plate Movement Inspection

CAUTION
Transmission gear changing will be difficult or impossible if the correct amount of release movement is not maintained.

1. If still in place, remove the clutch mechanism inspection cover and gasket.

2. Mount a dial indicator onto the crankcase outer cover, or onto a suitable stationary stand.

3. Position the dial indicator anvil against the end of the pushrod (C, **Figure 44**).

4. Fully apply the clutch hand lever and note the pushrod movement.

5. The pushrod must move a minimum of 0.065 in. (1.65 mm) to guarantee complete clutch disengagement.

NOTE
Correct clutch fluid level and proper bleeding will result in pushrod movement greater than 0.065 in. (1.65 mm).

15

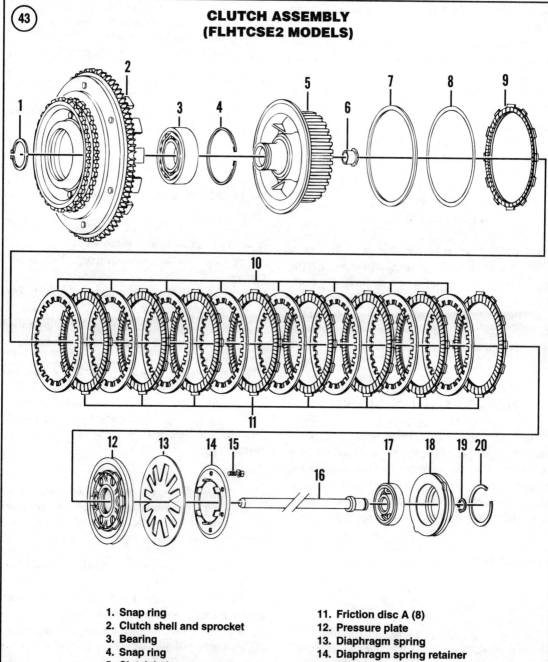

CLUTCH ASSEMBLY
(FLHTCSE2 MODELS)

1. Snap ring
2. Clutch shell and sprocket
3. Bearing
4. Snap ring
5. Clutch hub
6. Clutch nut
7. Diaphragm spring seat
8. Diaphragm spring
9. Friction disc B
10. Clutch plates (8)
11. Friction disc A (8)
12. Pressure plate
13. Diaphragm spring
14. Diaphragm spring retainer
15. Bolt
16. Pushrod
17. Bearing
18. Release plate
19. Snap ring–small
20. Snap ring–large

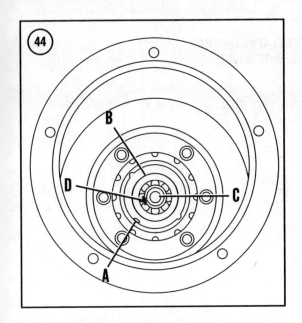

6. If the pushrod movement is less than specified, the clutch fluid level is low and/or the clutch system must be bled as described in this section.

7. Bleed the clutch as described under *Clutch System Bleeding* in this section.

CLUTCH SERVICE
(FLHTCSE2 MODELS)

The hydraulic clutch system transmits hydraulic pressure from the master cylinder to the clutch release mechanism on the transmission case. As the clutch components wear, the clutch release piston moves out. As this occurs, the fluid level in the master cylinder reservoir goes down. This must be compensated for by occasionally adding fluid.

The proper operation of this system depends on a supply of clean brake fluid (DOT 5) and a clean work environment when any service is being performed. Any tiny particle of debris that enters the system can damage the components and cause poor clutch performance.

Brake fluid is hygroscopic (easily absorbs moisture) and moisture in the system will reduce clutch performance. Purchase brake fluid in small containers and properly discard any small quantities that remain. Small quantities of fluid will quickly absorb the moisture in the container. Use only fluid clearly marked DOT 5. If possible, use the same brand of fluid. It is not possible to remove all of the old fluid. DOT 5 is not compatible with other types

of brake fluid. Do not reuse drained fluid and discard old fluid properly. Do not combine brake fluid with fluids for recycling.

Perform clutch service procedures carefully. Do not use any sharp tools inside the master cylinder or release mechanism piston. Damage of these components could cause a loss in the system's ability to maintain hydraulic pressure. If there is any doubt about the ability to correctly and safely service the clutch system, have a professional technician perform the task.

Consider the following when service the clutch system:

1. The hydraulic components rarely require disassembly. Make sure it is necessary.

2. Keep the reservoir cover in place to prevent the entry of moisture and debris.

3. Clean parts with an aerosol brake part cleaner or isopropyl alcohol. Never use petroleum-based solvents on internal clutch system components. They will cause seals to swell and distort.

4. Do not allow brake fluid to contact plastic, painted or plated parts. It will damage the surface.

5. Dispose of brake fluid properly.

6. If the hydraulic system, not including the reservoir cover, has been opened bleed the system to remove air from the system. Refer to *Clutch System Bleeding* in this Supplement.

CLUTCH MASTER CYLINDER
(FLHTCSE2 MODELS)

Read the information listed under *Clutch Service* in this section before servicing the clutch master cylinder.

Removal/Installation

1. Support the motorcycle on level ground on a swing arm stand.

2. Block the front wheel so the motorcycle will not roll in either direction while on the swing arm stand.

3. Cover the fuel tank and front fender with a heavy cloth or plastic tarp to protect them from accidental brake fluid spills.

CAUTION
Wash brake fluid off any surface immediately, as it damages the finish.

15

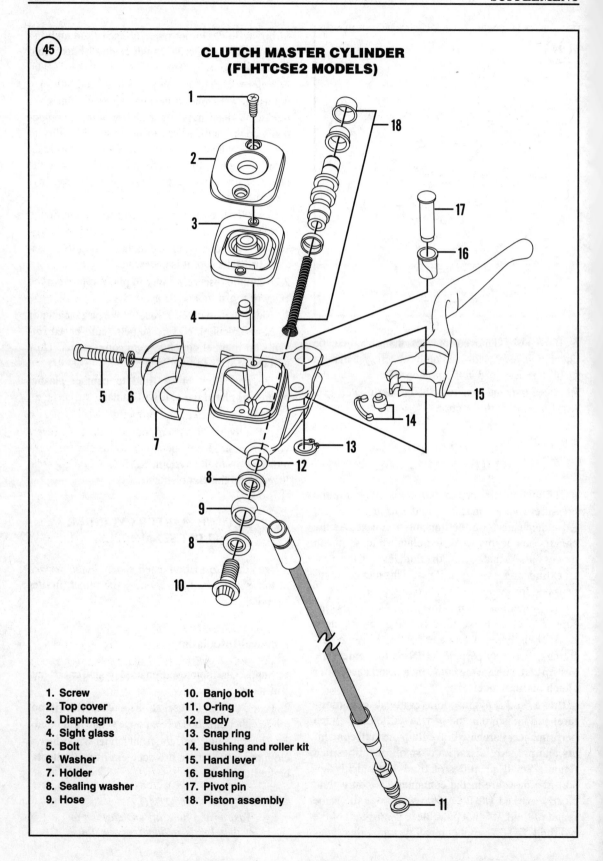

45

CLUTCH MASTER CYLINDER
(FLHTCSE2 MODELS)

1. Screw
2. Top cover
3. Diaphragm
4. Sight glass
5. Bolt
6. Washer
7. Holder
8. Sealing washer
9. Hose
10. Banjo bolt
11. O-ring
12. Body
13. Snap ring
14. Bushing and roller kit
15. Hand lever
16. Bushing
17. Pivot pin
18. Piston assembly

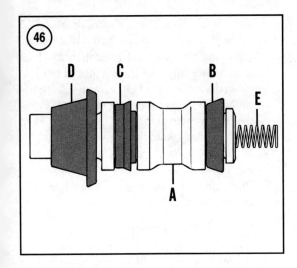

Use soapy water and rinse completely.

4. Drain the front clutch lever line as described under *Clutch Fluid Draining* in this Supplement.

5. Remove the banjo bolt and washers securing the clutch hose to the master cylinder. Plug the clutch hose to prevent brake fluid from dripping out. Tie the loose end of the hose to the handlebar to prevent it from dripping brake fluid.

6. Plug the bolt opening in the master cylinder to prevent leakage when removing the master cylinder in the following steps.

7. Remove the clutch master cylinder holder mounting bolts, washers and the holder, and remove the clutch master cylinder from the handlebar.

8. If necessary, service the master cylinder as described in this section.

9. Clean the handlebar, master cylinder and clamp mating surfaces.

10. Mount the master cylinder onto the handlebar and position it to rider's preference.

11. Install the master cylinder holder and its mounting bolts and washers.

12. Tighten the upper master cylinder clamp bolt first, then the lower bolt. Tighten both bolts to 60-80 in.-lb. (7-9 N•m).

NOTE
When the master cylinder clamp is correctly installed, the upper edge of the clamp touches the master cylinder, leaving a gap at the bottom.

13. Secure the clutch hose to the master cylinder with the banjo bolt and two *new* washers on each side of the clutch hose. Tighten the banjo bolt to 17-22 ft.-lb. (23-30 N•m).

14. Bleed the clutch as described under *Clutch System Bleeding* in this Supplement.

15. Test ride the motorcycle to ensure the clutch is operating correctly.

Disassembly

Refer to **Figure 45**
1. Remove the master cylinder as described in this section.
2. If still in place, remove the master cylinder cover and diaphragm. Pour out any remaining brake fluid and discard it.
3. Remove the snap ring from hand lever pivot pin.
4. Slightly apply hand lever pressure to remove some of the spring pressure on the pivot pin.
5. Withdraw the pivot pin from the body and remove the clutch lever. Do not lose the bushing and roller kit from the lever.
6. Remove the rubber boot from the groove in the body at the end of the piston.
7. Remove the piston assembly and spring from the master cylinder bore. Do not remove the primary and secondary cups from the piston.

NOTE
If brake fluid is leaking from the piston bore, the piston cups are worn or damaged. Replace the piston assembly.

Assembly

1. If installing a new piston assembly, assemble it as described under *Inspection* in this section.
2. Lubricate the piston (A, **Figure 46**), primary cup (B), secondary cup (C), rubber boot (D) and cylinder bore with DOT 5 brake fluid.
3. Position the spring (E, **Figure 46**) with the flange end going in last and install the spring onto the piston.

CAUTION
Do not allow the piston cups to tear or turn inside out when installing the piston into the master cylinder bore. Both cups are larger than the bore. To

15

*ease installation, lubricate the cups
and piston with DOT 5 brake fluid.*

4. Insert the spring and piston assembly into the master cylinder bore. Push in on the piston and completely compress the spring until it is flush with the end of the body.

5. Hold the piston in place and carefully install the rubber boot into the groove in the body. Make sure the entire perimeter of the boot is correctly seated around the groove.

CAUTION
The rubber boot must seat in the master cylinder groove completely. Slowly push and release the piston a few times to make sure it moves smoothly and that the rubber boot does not pop out.

6. Lubricate the pivot pin with silicone brake grease.

7. If removed, install the bushing and roller kit into the end of the hand lever.

8. Install the hand lever onto the body and install the pivot pin part way in from the top.

9. Slightly apply the hand lever pressure to compress the spring and push the piston in all the way.

10. Install a *new* snap ring into the pivot pin and make sure it is correctly seated in the groove.

11. Check that the hand lever moves freely. If there is any binding or roughness, remove the pivot pin and hand lever and inspect the parts.

12. Temporarily install the diaphragm and cover. Install the screws and tighten finger tight. Do not tighten the screws, as brake fluid will be added later.

13. Install the master cylinder as described in this section.

Inspection

The manufacturer does not provide specifications for the clutch master cylinder. Replace visually worn or damaged parts as described in this section.

1. Clean and dry the master cylinder assembly as follows:

a. Handle the clutch components carefully when servicing them.

b. Use only DOT 5 brake fluid or isopropyl alcohol to wash rubber parts (rubber boot and piston assembly) in the clutch system. Never allow any petroleum-based cleaner to contact

the rubber parts. These chemicals cause the rubber to swell, requiring their replacement.

c. Clean the master cylinder piston rubber boot groove carefully. Use a small pick or brush to clean the groove. If a hard varnish residue has built up in the groove, soak the master cylinder in solvent to help soften the residue. Then wash in soapy water and rinse completely.

d. Blow the master cylinder dry with compressed air.

e. Place cleaned parts on a clean lint-free cloth until assembly.

CAUTION
Do not get any oil or grease onto any of the master cylinder components. These chemicals cause the rubber parts in the brake system to swell, permanently damaging them.

CAUTION
Do not remove the primary and secondary cups from the piston assembly for cleaning or inspection purposes.

2. Check the piston assembly for the following defects:

a. Check the piston (A, **Figure 47**) for scratches and/or corrosion.

b. Worn, cracked, damaged or swollen primary (B, **Figure 47**) and secondary cups (C).

c. Worn or damaged rubber boot (D, **Figure 47**).

d. Broken, distorted or collapsed piston return spring (E, **Figure 47**).

e. Corroded, weak or damaged snap ring.

If any of these parts are worn or damaged, replace the piston assembly.

3. To assemble a *new* piston assembly, perform the following:

a. If replacing the piston, install the new primary and secondary cups onto the piston. Use the original piston assembly as a reference when installing the new cups onto the piston.

b. Before installing the new piston cups, lubricate them with DOT 5 brake fluid.

c. Clean the new piston (A, **Figure 47**) in brake fluid.

d. Install the primary cup (B, **Figure 47**) onto the spring and then the secondary cup (C) onto the piston.

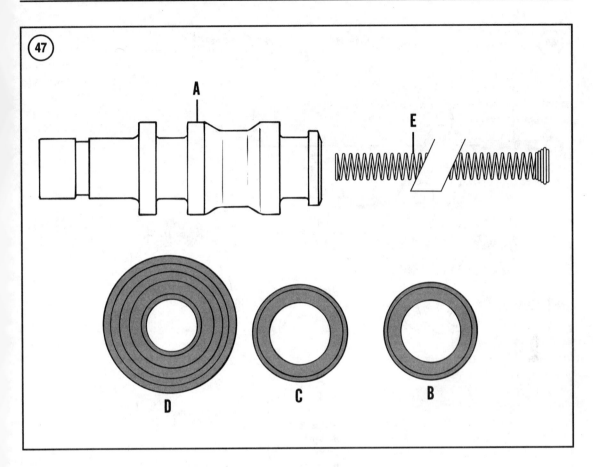

4. Inspect the master cylinder bore. Replace the master cylinder if its bore is corroded, cracked or damaged in any way. Do not hone the master cylinder bore to remove scratches or other damage.

5. Make sure the fluid passageway in the base of the body is clear. Clean out with compressed air if necessary.

6. Check the banjo bolt threads for damage.

7. Inspect the diaphragm and cover for deterioration and other damage.

8. Check the hand lever assembly for the following defects:

    a. Damaged hand lever.

    b. Excessively worn or damaged pivot bolt.

    c. Worn or damaged bushing.

CLUTCH RELEASE MECHANISM (FLHTCSE2 MODELS)

Release Mechanism Cover

Refer to **Figure 48**.

Removal

1. Support the motorcycle on level ground on a swing arm stand.

2. Block the front wheel so the motorcycle will not roll in either direction while on the swing arm stand.

3. Remove the front cylinder exhaust pipe as described in Chapter Seven.

4. Drain the transmission oil as described in Chapter Three.

5. Cover the frame under the transmission case with a heavy cloth or plastic tarp to protect it from accidental brake fluid spills.

CAUTION
Wash brake fluid off any surface immediately, as it damages the finish. Use soapy water and rinse completely.

6. Remove the transmission oil level dipstick.

7. Slightly loosen the bolts securing the cover and apply the clutch lever. This will break the cover loose from the transmission case.

15

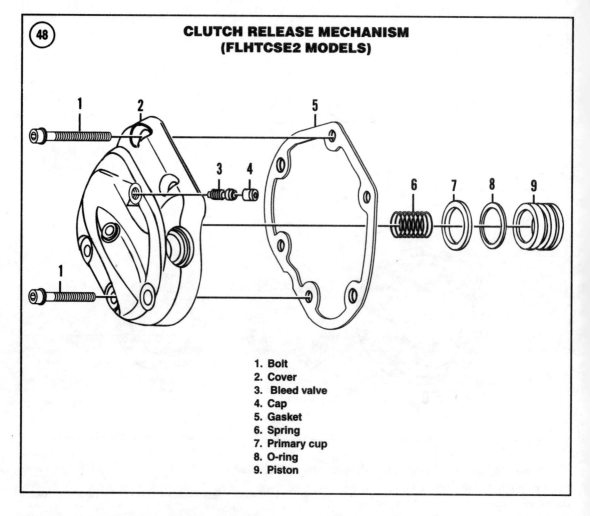

**CLUTCH RELEASE MECHANISM
(FLHTCSE2 MODELS)**

1. Bolt
2. Cover
3. Bleed valve
4. Cap
5. Gasket
6. Spring
7. Primary cup
8. O-ring
9. Piston

8. Drain the front clutch lever line as described under *Clutch Fluid Draining* in this section.

9. Carefully loosen the flare nut (A, **Figure 49**) securing the clutch hose to the cover. Do not scratch the chrome cover.

10. Disconnect the clutch hose (B, **Figure 49**) from the cover and place the end into a reclosable plastic bag. Remove the O-ring (**Figure 50**) from the end of the clutch hose, or if necessary, remove the O-ring from within the cover threaded outlet.

NOTE
There are two different length cover bolts, note the location during removal.

11. Remove the bolts loosened in Step 7 securing the clutch cover. Remove the cover and gasket from the transmission case.

12. Remove the locating dowels if loose.

Installation

1. If removed, install the locating dowels.

2. Install a *new* gasket over the locating dowels.

3. Install the cover and the bolts in the correct location as noted during removal. Tighten the bolts in a crisscross pattern to 120-144 in.-lb. (14-16 N•m).

4. Install a *new* O-ring (**Figure 50**) onto the end of the clutch hose.

5. Connect the clutch hose (B, **Figure 49**) onto the cover. Thread the flare nut all the way into the cover by hand until it bottoms. Do not cross-thread it and tighten to 80-115 in.-lb. (9-13 N•m). Do not scratch the cover.

6. Install the transmission oil level dipstick.

7. Refill the transmission oil as described in Chapter Three.

8. Install the front cylinder exhaust pipe as described in Chapter Seven.

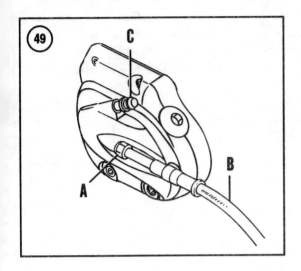

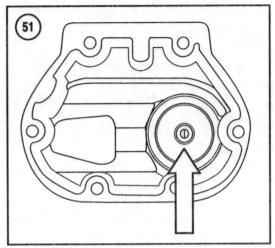

9. Refill the clutch master cylinder and bleed the system as described under *Clutch System Bleeding* in this Supplement.

10. Start the engine and check for proper clutch operation, then test ride the motorcycle.

Release Cylinder

Removal/installation

1. Remove the release mechanism cover as described in this section.

2. If removed, install the bleed valve and tighten securely.

3. To remove the piston, perform the following:

   a. Place a piece of soft wood on the work bench.

   b. Position the release cover with the piston side facing toward the work bench.

   c. Apply compressed air through the clutch hose hole in the cover and force the piston part way out of the cover receptacle.

4. Withdraw the piston assembly (**Figure 51**) and spring from the cover receptacle.

5. If the primary cup was removed from the piston, install the cup with the raised leading edge lip positioned toward the spring receptacle end.

6. Apply DOT 5 brake fluid to the *new* primary cup, O-ring and piston. Also apply DOT 5 brake fluid to the piston receptacle in the cover.

7. Install the spring into the piston and install the assembly into the cover receptacle. Guide the primary cup into the receptacle to prevent the lips from turning over.

8. Push the piston and spring in until they bottom. Push in on the piston and check that the spring pushes it back out part way. The piston must move freely within the receptacle.

9. Install the release mechanism cover as described in this section.

Inspection

Replacement parts are not available for the piston assembly. If any part is worn or damaged, replace the piston and spring as an assembly. Refer to **Figure 52**.

15

1. Clean the cover receptacle and piston in DOT 5 brake fluid and dry with compressed air.

2. Inspect the spring for fractures or sagging.

3. Check the O-ring and primary cup for hardness or deterioration.

4. Check the piston and receptacle for scratches, scoring or other damage.

5. Check the piston O-ring and primary cup grooves for damage.

6. Inspect the flare nut threaded hole in the cover. If it is worn or damaged, clean it out with a thread tap or replace the cover.

7. Inspect the bleed valve threaded hole in the cover. If it is worn or damaged, clean it out with a thread tap or replace the cover.

8. Inspect the bleed screw. Apply compressed air to the opening and make sure it is clear. Clean it out, if necessary, with brake fluid. Install the bleed screw and tighten securely.

CLUTCH HYDRAULIC HOSE REPLACEMENT (FLHTCSE2 MODELS)

1. Support the motorcycle on level ground on a swing arm stand.

2. Block the front wheel so the motorcycle will not roll in either direction while on the swing arm stand.

3. Remove the front cylinder exhaust pipe as described in Chapter Seven.

4. Cover the frame under the transmission case with a heavy cloth or plastic tarp to protect it from accidental brake fluid spills.

> *CAUTION*
> *Wash brake fluid off any surface immediately, as it damages the finish. Use soapy water and rinse completely.*

5. Drain the front clutch lever line as described under *Clutch System Flushing* in this section.

6. Carefully loosen the flare nut (A, **Figure 49**) securing the clutch hose to the cover. Do not scratch the chrome cover.

7. Disconnect the clutch hose (B, **Figure 49**) from the cover and place the end into a reclosable plastic bag.

8. Remove the O-ring (**Figure 50**) from the end of the clutch hose, or if necessary, remove the O-ring within the cover threaded outlet.

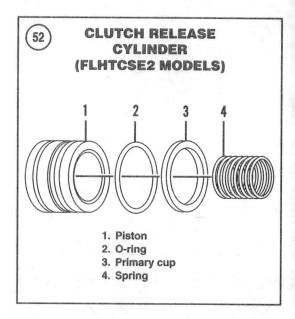

CLUTCH RELEASE CYLINDER (FLHTCSE2 MODELS)

1. Piston
2. O-ring
3. Primary cup
4. Spring

9. Remove the banjo bolt and washers securing the clutch hose to the master cylinder. Plug the clutch hose to prevent brake fluid from dripping out.

10. Plug the bolt opening in the master cylinder to prevent leakage and the entry of debris.

11. Note the routing of the clutch hose. On the left side frame down tube, remove the bracket securing the clutch hose to the frame.

12. Remove the clutch hose from the frame and out from behind the voltage regulator/rectifier and from the eyelet on the right side of the crankcase behind the rear brake master cylinder.

13. Install the *new* clutch hose through the frame following the same path noted during removal.

14. Secure the clutch hose to the master cylinder with the banjo bolt and two *new* washers on each side of the clutch hose. Tighten the banjo bolt to 17-22 ft.-lb. (23-30 N•m).

15. Install a *new* O-ring (**Figure 50**) onto the end of the clutch hose.

16. Connect the clutch hose (B, **Figure 49**) onto the cover. Thread the flare nut all the way into the cover by hand until it bottoms. Do not cross-thread it and tighten to 80-115 in.-lb. (9-13 N•m). Do not scratch the cover.

17. Bleed the clutch as described under *Clutch System Bleeding* in this Supplement.

18. Test ride the motorcycle to ensure the clutch is operating correctly.

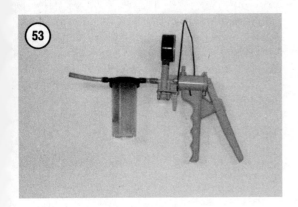

CLUTCH SYSTEM FLUSHING
(FLHTCSE2 MODELS)

When flushing the clutch system, use DOT 5 brake fluid as a flushing fluid. Flushing consists of pulling new brake fluid through the clutch system until the new fluid appears at the release cover bleed valve without the presence of any air bubbles. To flush the clutch system, follow one of the bleeding procedures described under *Clutch System Bleeding* in this section.

CAUTION
Never reuse old brake fluid. Properly discard all brake fluid flushed from the system.

CLUTCH SYSTEM BLEEDING
(FLHTCSE2 MODELS)

Brake Bleeder Process

This procedure uses the Mityvac hydraulic brake bleeding kit (**Figure 53**) that is available from automotive or motorcycle supply stores.

1. Remove the dust cap from the bleed valve (C, **Figure 49**) from the release cover.

2. Place a clean shop cloth over the exhaust pipe and frame to protect it from accidental brake fluid spills.

3. Assemble the Mityvac tool according to its manufacturer's instructions. Secure it to the bleed valve.

4. Open the bleed screw approximately a half turn.

5. Clean the top of the master cylinder of all dirt and foreign matter.

6. Turn the handlebars to level the clutch master cylinder and remove the screws, reservoir cover and diaphragm.

7. Fill the reservoir almost to the top with DOT 5 brake fluid and reinstall the diaphragm and cover. Leave the cover in place during this procedure to prevent the entry of dirt.

8. Operate the pump several times to create a vacuum in the line. Brake fluid will quickly draw from the release cylinder into the pump's reservoir. Tighten the bleed valve before the fluid stops flowing through the hose. To prevent air from being drawn through the master cylinder, add fluid to maintain its level at the top of the reservoir.

NOTE
Do not allow the master cylinder reservoir to empty during the bleeding operation or more air will enter the system. If this occurs, the procedure must be repeated.

9. Continue the bleeding process until the fluid drawn from the release cylinder is bubble free. If bubbles are withdrawn with the brake fluid, more air is trapped in the line. Repeat Step 8, making sure to refill the master cylinder to prevent air from being drawn into the system.

10. When the brake fluid is free of bubbles, tighten the bleed valve and remove the brake bleeder assembly. Reinstall the bleed valve dust cap.

NOTE
Dispose of the brake fluid expelled during the bleeding process. Do not reuse the brake fluid.

11. If necessary, add fluid to correct the level in the master cylinder reservoir. When topping off the clutch master cylinder, turn the handlebar until the reservoir is level; add fluid to the fill level mark in the reservoir.

12. Reinstall the reservoir diaphragm and cover. Install the screws and tighten securely.

13. Test the feel of the clutch lever. It must be firm and offer the same resistance each time it's operated. If it feels spongy, it is likely that there is still air in the system and it must be bleed again. After bleeding the system, check for leaks and tighten all fittings and connections as necessary.

WARNING
Do not ride the motorcycle until the clutch lever is operating correctly with full hydraulic advantage.

15

14. Test ride the motorcycle slowly at first to make sure that the clutch is operating properly.

Without a Brake Bleeder

NOTE
Before bleeding the clutch, check that all hoses and lines are tight.

1. Remove the dust cap from the bleed valve (C, **Figure 49**) from the release cover.
2. Connect a length of clear tubing to the bleed valve on the release cover. Place the other end of the tube into a clean container. Fill the container with enough fresh DOT 5 brake fluid to keep the end of the tube submerged. The tube must be long enough so that a loop can be made higher than the bleeder valve to prevent air from being drawn into the release cylinder during bleeding.
3. Clean the top of the clutch master cylinder of all dirt and debris.
4. Remove the screws securing the master cylinder top cover and remove the cover and the diaphragm.
5. Fill the reservoir almost to the top with DOT 5 brake fluid and reinstall the diaphragm and cover. Leave the cover in place during this procedure to prevent the entry of dirt.

NOTE
During this procedure, it is important to check the fluid level in the master cylinder reservoir often. If the reservoir runs dry, more air will enter the system.

6. Slowly apply the clutch lever several times. Hold the lever in the applied position and open the bleed valve about 1/2 turn. Allow the lever to travel to its limit. When the limit is reached, tighten the bleed valve, then release the clutch lever. As the brake fluid enters the system, the level will drop in the master cyl-

inder reservoir. Maintain the level at the top of the reservoir to prevent air from being drawn into the system.
7. Continue the bleeding process until the fluid emerging from the hose is completely free of air bubbles. If the fluid is being replaced, continue until the fluid emerging from the hose is clean.

NOTE
If bleeding is difficult, allowing the fluid to stabilize for a few hours. Repeat the bleeding procedure when the tiny bubbles in the system settle out.

8. Hold the lever in the applied position and tighten the bleed valve. Remove the bleed tube and install the bleed valve dust cap.

NOTE
Dispose of the brake fluid expelled during the bleeding process. Do not reuse the brake fluid.

9. If necessary, add fluid to correct the level in the master cylinder reservoir. When topping off the front master cylinder, turn the handlebar until the reservoir is level; add fluid until it is level with the reservoir gasket surface.
10. Install the diaphragm and the top cover and tighten the screws securely.
11. Test the feel of the clutch lever. It must be firm and offer the same resistance each time it's operated. If it feels spongy, it is likely that there is still air in the system and it must be bled again. After bleeding the system check for leaks and tighten all fittings and connections as necessary.

WARNING
Do not ride the motorcycle until the clutch is operating correctly with full hydraulic advantage.

12. Test ride the motorcycle slowly at first to make sure that the clutch is operating properly.

Table 10 CLUTCH TORQUE SPECIFICATIONS

Item	ft.-lb.	in.-lb.	N•m
Clutch inspection cover	–	84-108	10-12
Master cylinder clamp bolts	–	60-80	7-9
Master cylinder banjo bolts	17-22	–	23-30
Clutch release mechanism cover	–	120-144	14-16
Clutch hose-to-cover	–	80-115	9-13

CHAPTER SIX

TRANSMISSION

SHIFTER ASSEMBLY
(FLHTCSE2 MODELS)

The shifter assembly (**Figure 54**) consists of the external shift linkage and internal shift cam and shift arm components. The internal components can be serviced with the transmission case installed in the frame by removing the top cover.

If a shift problem is encountered, refer to the troubleshooting procedures in Chapter Two and eliminate all clutch and shifter mechanism possibilities *before* considering transmission repairs. Improper clutch adjustment (Chapter Three) is often a cause of poor shifting.

EXTERNAL SHIFT MECHANISM
(FLHTCSE2 MODELS)

Removal/Installation

Refer to **Figure 54**.

> *NOTE*
> *On models so equipped, always disarm the optional TSSM security system prior to disconnecting the battery or the siren will sound.*

1. Disconnect the negative battery cable as described in Chapter Eight.

2. Support the motorcycle with the front wheel off the ground. See *Motorcycle Stands* in Chapter Nine.

3. Make an alignment mark on the heel shift lever and the end of the shift shaft lever.

4. Remove the clamp bolt and remove the heel shift lever.

5. Make an alignment mark on the toe shift lever and the end of the shift shaft lever.

6. Remove the clamp bolt and remove the toe shift lever.

7. Remove the spacer from the shift lever shaft.

8. Remove the Acorn nut and washers securing the shift linkage rod to the outer shift lever.

9. Remove the bolt securing the shift linkage to the inner shift lever.

10. Remove the jiffy stand and mounting bracket assembly.

11. Remove the primary chaincase assembly as described in Chapter Five.

12. Remove the clamp bolt securing the inner shift shaft lever to the transmission case.

13. Remove the shift rod, inner and outer shift lever as an assembly.

14. Install by reversing these removal steps. Tighten the clamp bolts securely.

SHIFT ARM ASSEMBLY
(ALL MODELS)

Removal/Disassembly

Refer to **Figure 55**.

1. Remove the transmission side door assembly as described in Chapter Six.

2. Make an alignment mark on the shift rod lever and the end of the shift shaft lever/pawl.

3. Remove the clamp bolt and remove the shift rod lever from the shift shaft lever/pawl.

4. Remove the snap ring and washer from the shift lever shaft.

5. Withdraw the shift shaft lever/pawl, sleeve and spring from the inner surface of the transmission case

15

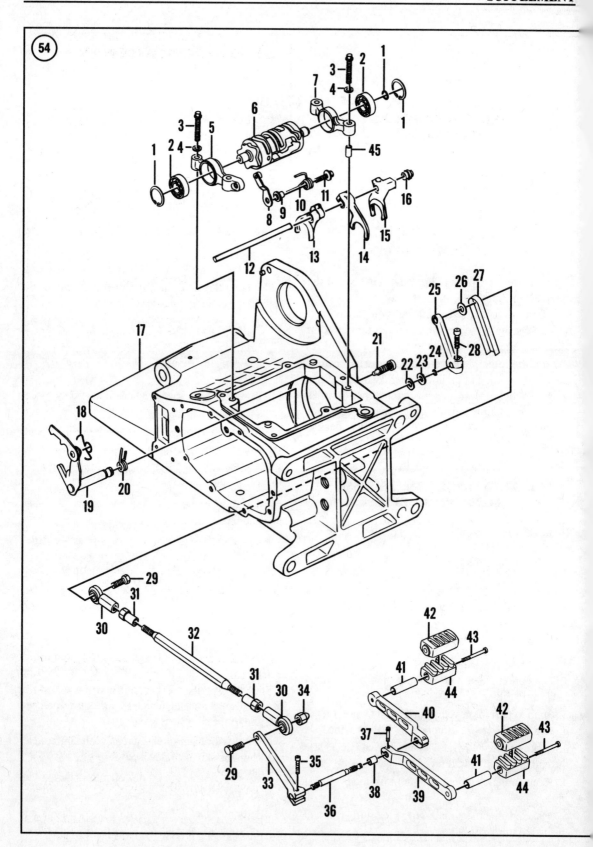

SHIFT ASSEMBLY (FLHTCSE2)

1. Snap ring
2. Bearing
3. Bolt
4. Washer
5. Support–right side
6. Shift cam
7. Support–left side
8. Cam follower
9. Sleeve
10. Spring
11. Bolt
12. Shift fork shaft
13. Shift fork No. 1
14. Shift fork No. 2
15. Shift fork No. 3
16. Set screw
17. Transmission case
18. Spring
19. Shift shaft lever/pawl
20. Return spring
21. Adjusting screw
22. Seal
23. Washer
24. Snap ring
25. Shift rod lever–inner
26. Spacer
27. Cover
28. Bolt
29. Bolt
30. Rod end
31. Nut
32. Shift rod
33. Shift rod lever–outer
34. Acorn nut
35. Bolt
36. Shaft
37. Bolt
38. Spacer
39. Shift lever–toe
40. Shift lever–heel
41. Spacer
42. Shifter pedal peg
43. Bolt
44. Shifter pedal pad
45. Locating dowel

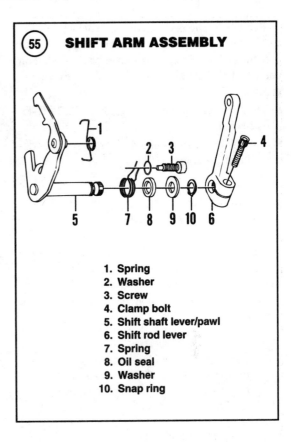

(55) SHIFT ARM ASSEMBLY

1. Spring
2. Washer
3. Screw
4. Clamp bolt
5. Shift shaft lever/pawl
6. Shift rod lever
7. Spring
8. Oil seal
9. Washer
10. Snap ring

Inspection

1. Check the shift pawl for wear. Replace the pawl if it is damaged.
2. Check the springs for wear or damage.
3. Check the shift shaft lever for wear or damage. Check the end splines for wear or damage.
4. Check the shift rod lever for wear or damage. Check the internal splines for wear or damage.

Assembly/Installation

1. Check that the sleeve is still in place in the transmission case.
2. Slide the shift shaft lever spring over the shift shaft lever. Align the opening on the spring with the tab on the lever.
3. Place the spring on the shift shaft lever/pawl.
4. Install the shift shaft lever assembly into the transmission case.
5. Align the spring with the screw in the case (**Figure 56**).
6. Install washer and snap ring onto the shaft. Make sure the snap ring is correctly seated in the shaft.

15

7. Refer to the alignment marks made in Step 1 of *Removal/Disassembly* and install the shift rod lever onto the end of the shift shaft lever/pawl. Push it on until the bolt hole aligns with the shaft lever/pawl groove.

8. Install the clamp bolt and tighten to 18-24 ft.-lb. (24-32 N•m).

98. Install the transmission side door assembly as described in this chapter.

SHIFT LINKAGE ADJUSTMENT (ALL MODELS)

The shift linkage assembly connects the transmission shift rod lever to the foot-operated shift lever. The shift linkage does not require adjustment unless it is replaced or the transmission gears do not engage properly.

> *NOTE*
> *On models so equipped, always disarm the optional TSSM security system prior to disconnecting the battery or the siren will sound.*

1. Disconnect the negative battery cable as described in Chapter Eight.

2. Loosen the two shift linkage rod locknuts (A, **Figure 57**).

3. Turn the shift linkage rod (B, **Figure 57**) as necessary to change the linkage adjustment.

4. Tighten the locknuts to 80-120 in.-lb. (9.0-13.6 N•m).

5. Recheck the shifting. Readjust if necessary.

6. If this adjustment does not correct the shifting, check the shift linkage for interference problems.

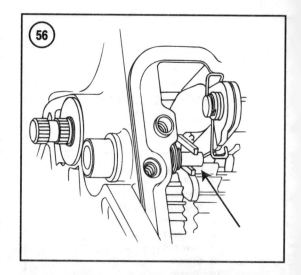

TRANSMISSION SIDE DOOR AND TRANSMISSION SHAFT ASSEMBLIES

Removal/Installation (FLHTCSE2 Models)

This is the same in all aspects, except, the oil slinger assembly is not equipped on these models.

Table 11 TRANSMISSION TORQUE SPECIFICATIONS

Item	ft.-lb.	in.-lb.	N•m
Shift rod lever clamp bolt	18-24	–	24-32
Shift rod linkage locknuts	–	80-120	9.0-13.6

CHAPTER SEVEN

FUEL, EXHAUST AND EMISSION CONTROL SYSTEMS

FUEL TANK CONSOLE

Removal/Installation (FLHRS/FLHRSI Models)

Refer to **Figure 58**.

The removal and installation procedure is the same as on FLHR, FLHRI and FLHRCI models with the exception of the rear mounting fastener. Removing the fuel tank rear bolt also releases the mounting bracket attached to the rear of console.

Tighten the acorn nut to 50-90 in.-lb. (5.7-10.2 N•m), and the fuel tank rear mounting bolt to 15-20 ft.-lbs. (20-27 N•m).

Removal/Installation (FLHTCSE2 Models)

Refer to **Figure 59**.

The removal and installation procedure is the same as on the FLHT and FLTR models in Chapter Seven.

FUEL TANK (CARBURETED MODELS)

WARNING
Some fuel may spill from the fuel tank hose when performing this procedure. Because gasoline is extremely flammable and explosive, perform this procedure away from all open flames, including appliance pilot lights, and sparks. Do not allow anyone to smoke in the work area. Always work in a well-ventilated area. Wipe up any spills immediately.

WARNING
Route the fuel tank vapor hoses so that they cannot contact any hot engine or exhaust component. These hoses contain flammable vapors. If a hose melts from contacting a hot part, leaking vapors may ignite, causing a fire.

Removal/Installation

The fuel hoses are secured to the fuel tank (**Figure 60** or **Figure 61**) with a non-reusable clamp. Purchase *new* ones before servicing the fuel tank.

1. Remove the fuel tank console as described under *Fuel Tank Console* in Chapter Seven.
2. Turn the fuel valve to the OFF position (A, **Figure 62**, typical).
3. Remove the hose clamp and disconnect the fuel hose (B, **Figure 62**) from the valve.

NOTE
A crossover tube connects the two fuel tank compartments. Drain both sides of the tank before removing the tank in the following steps.

4. Drain the fuel tank as follows:

NOTE
A vacuum-operated fuel valve is installed on all carbureted models. A hand-operated vacuum pump is required to drain the fuel tank.

   a. Connect the drain hose to the fuel valve and secure it with a hose clamp. Insert the end of the drain hose into a gas can.
   b. Disconnect the vacuum hose from the fuel valve.

15

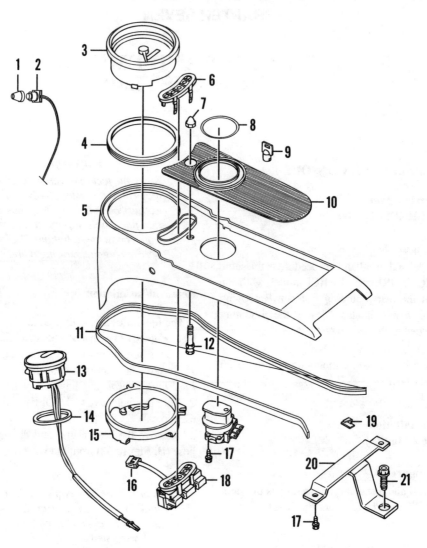

**FUEL TANK CONSOLE
(2004-2005 FLHRS, FLHRSI)**

1. Rubber boot
2. Odometer reset switch
3. Speedometer
4. Gasket
5. Console
6. Bezel
7. Acorn nut
8. Name plate
9. Key
10. Trim insert
11. Trim gasket
12. Threaded stud
13. Fuel gauge
14. Gasket
15. Lower clamp
16. Connector
17. Bolt
18. Indicator lamp housing
19. Clip
20. Mounting bracket
21. Fuel tank mounting bolt

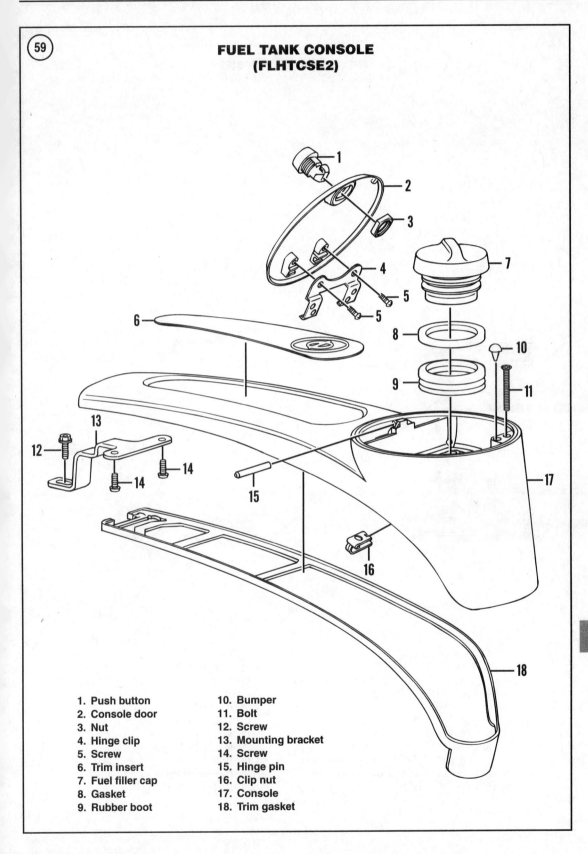

FUEL TANK CONSOLE
(FLHTCSE2)

59

1. Push button
2. Console door
3. Nut
4. Hinge clip
5. Screw
6. Trim insert
7. Fuel filler cap
8. Gasket
9. Rubber boot
10. Bumper
11. Bolt
12. Screw
13. Mounting bracket
14. Screw
15. Hinge pin
16. Clip nut
17. Console
18. Trim gasket

15

60

FUEL TANK
(FLHT, FLHTC, FLTR)

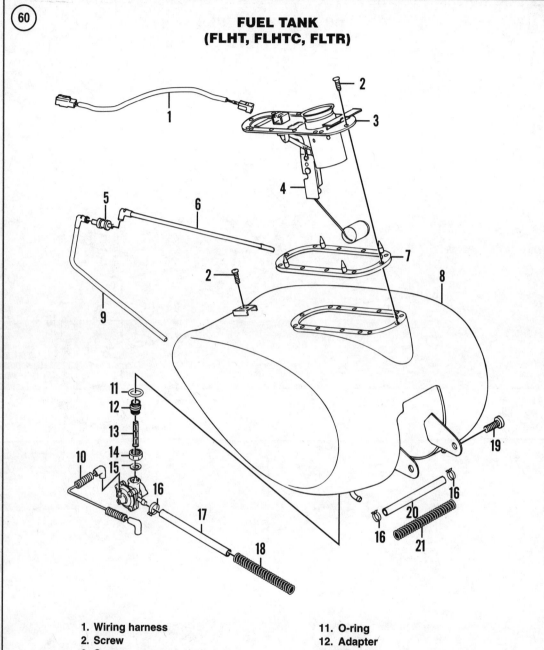

1. Wiring harness
2. Screw
3. Canopy
4. Fuel level sending unit
5. Vapor valve
6. Fuel hose-fuel
   tank-to-valve
7. Gasket
8. Fuel tank
9. Fuel hose-valve-to-atmosphere
10. Vacuum hose

11. O-ring
12. Adapter
13. Filter
14. Nut
15. Gasket
16. Hose clamp
17. Fuel hose
18. Insulator
19. Bolt
20. Crossover hose
21. Insulator

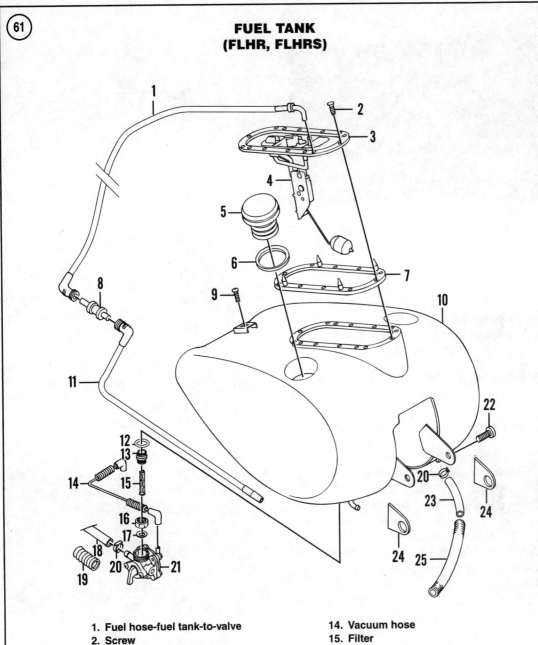

61

FUEL TANK
(FLHR, FLHRS)

1. Fuel hose-fuel tank-to-valve
2. Screw
3. Canopy
4. Fuel level sending unit
5. Fuel filter cap
6. Gasket
7. Gasket
8. Vapor valve
9. Bolt
10. Fuel tank
11. Fuel hose-valve-to-atmosphere
12. O-ring
13. Adapter

14. Vacuum hose
15. Filter
16. Nut
17. Gasket
18. Fuel hose
19. Insulator
20. Hose clamp
21. Fuel shutoff valve
22. Bolt
23. Crossover valve
24. Trim tab
25. Insulator

15

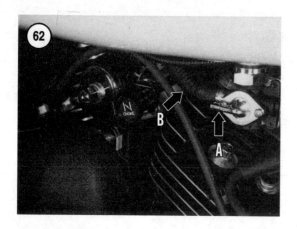

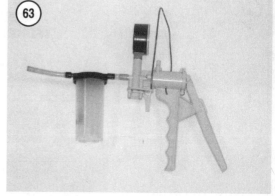

c. Connect a hand-operated vacuum pump (**Figure 63**) to the fuel valve vacuum hose fitting.

d. Turn the fuel valve to the RES position.

CAUTION
In the following step, do not apply more vacuum than 25 in. (635 mm) Hg or the fuel valve diaphragm will be damaged.

e. Gently operate the vacuum pump handle and apply up to a *maximum* of 25 in. (635 mm) Hg of vacuum. Once the vacuum is applied the fuel will start to flow into the gas can.

f. When fuel stops flowing through the hose, turn the fuel valve off and release the vacuum. Disconnect the vacuum pump and drain hose.

5. Disconnect the vent hose from the fuel tank.

6. Disconnect the crossover hose (**Figure 64**) from one side of the fuel tank. Plug the tank opening and plug to the crossover hose.

7. At the front of the fuel tank, remove the T40 Torx bolt and washer (**Figure 65**) on each side securing the fuel tank to the frame.

8. At the rear of the fuel tank, remove the bolt and washer securing the fuel tank to the frame.

9. Lift off and remove the fuel tank.

NOTE
Store the fuel tank in a safe place—away from open flames or where it could be damaged.

10. Drain any remaining fuel left in the tank into a gas can.

NOTE
*The fuel level sender units are different as shown in **Figure 60** and **Figure 61***

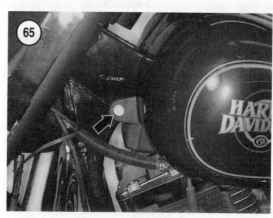

but the removal and installation is the same as on prior models.

11. Installation is the reverse of these steps while noting the following:

a. Tighten the front and rear bolts and nuts to 15-20 ft.-lbs. (20-27 N•m).

b. Reconnect the fuel hose to the fuel valve and secure it with a *new* hose clamps.

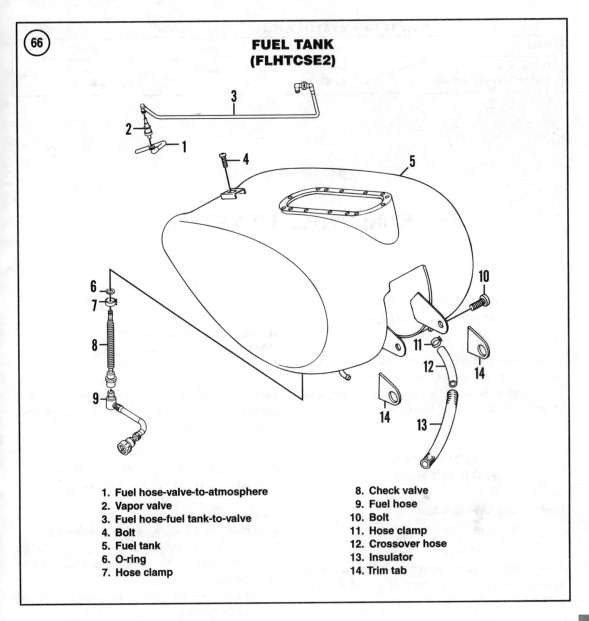

**FUEL TANK
(FLHTCSE2)**

1. Fuel hose-valve-to-atmosphere
2. Vapor valve
3. Fuel hose-fuel tank-to-valve
4. Bolt
5. Fuel tank
6. O-ring
7. Hose clamp
8. Check valve
9. Fuel hose
10. Bolt
11. Hose clamp
12. Crossover hose
13. Insulator
14. Trim tab

c. Connect the crossover hose and secure it with *new* hose clamps.

d. Refill the tank and check for leaks.

FUEL TANK
(FUEL INJECTED MODELS)

**Removal/Installation
(All Models-Except FLHTCSE2)**

The removal and installation procedure is the same as on prior models with the following exception.

Tighten the front and rear mounting bolts and nuts to 15-20 ft.-lbs. (20-27 N•m).

**Removal/Installation
(FLHTCSE2 Models)**

Refer to **Figure 66**.

The removal and installation procedure is the same as on 2002 fuel injected models. Tighten the bolts front and rear mounting bolts and nuts to 15-20 ft.-lbs. (20-27 N•m).

15

Table 12 FUEL SYSTEM TORQUE SPECIFICATIONS

Item	ft.-lb.	in.-lb.	N•m
Fuel tank acorn nut	–	50-90	5.7-10.2
Fuel tank mounting bolts	15-20	–	20-27

CHAPTER EIGHT

ELECTRICAL SYSTEM

CHARGING SYSTEM (FLHTCSE2 MODELS)

The charging system is identical to all other models with the exception of the voltage regulator's wiring socket housing, pin terminal housing and secondary lock as shown in **Figure 67**.

ALTERNATOR (FLHTCSE2 MODELS)

Rotor Removal/Installation

The removal and installation procedure is the same as on all other models, except the washer previously used outside of the rotor has been eliminated. Refer to **Figure 67**.

IGNITION SYSTEM (2004-2005 CARBURETED MODELS)

Ignition Module Removal/Installation

The removal and installation procedure is the same as on all other models, except the prior two 12-pin gray and black electrical connectors have been replaced with a single 12-pin black electrical connector. Refer to **Figure 68**.

LIGHTING SYSTEM

Headlight Bulb Replacement (2004-2005 FLHR Series Models)

The removal and installation procedure is the same as on prior FLHT and FLHR models, except of slight cosmetic variations of the some of the components. Refer to **Figure 69**.

Passing Light and Front Turn Signal Bulb Replacement (FLHTCSE2 Models)

Refer to **Figure 70**.
1. Remove the passing light bulb as follows:
   a. Loosen the clamping screw at the base of the trim bezel and remove the trim bezel from the passing light housing.
   b. Carefully pull the sealed beam unit partially out of the housing.
   c. Disconnect the electrical connector from the backside of the sealed beam and remove the sealed beam unit.
   d. Push the sealed beam unit into the housing and install the trim bezel.
   e. Tighten the clamping screw securely.
2. Remove the front turn signal bulb as follows:
   a. Locate the notch in the lens cap.
   b. Insert a coin into the notch and carefully twist the coin until the lens cap come off the housing (A, **Figure 71**).
   c. Push in on the bulb (B, **Figure 71**), rotate it and remove it.

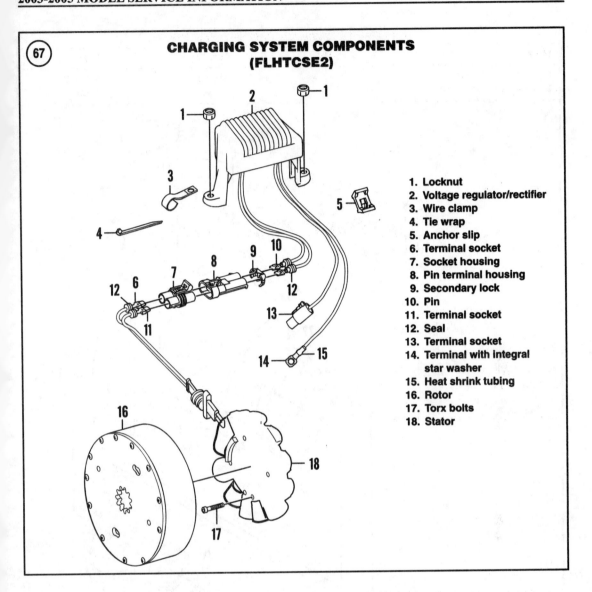

CHARGING SYSTEM COMPONENTS (FLHTCSE2)

1. Locknut
2. Voltage regulator/rectifier
3. Wire clamp
4. Tie wrap
5. Anchor slip
6. Terminal socket
7. Socket housing
8. Pin terminal housing
9. Secondary lock
10. Pin
11. Terminal socket
12. Seal
13. Terminal socket
14. Terminal with integral star washer
15. Heat shrink tubing
16. Rotor
17. Torx bolts
18. Stator

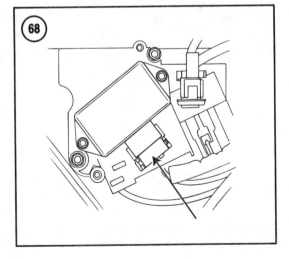

d. Install a new bulb and lens.

e. Push the lens cap into the housing until is snaps into place.

Passing Light Adjustment (FLHTCSE2 Models)

Refer to **Figure 70**.

1. Check the headlight aim and adjust if necessary.

2. Park the motorcycle on a level surface approximately 25 ft. (7.6 m) from the wall.

3. Check tire inflation pressure. Readjust it if necessary, as described in Chapter Three.

15

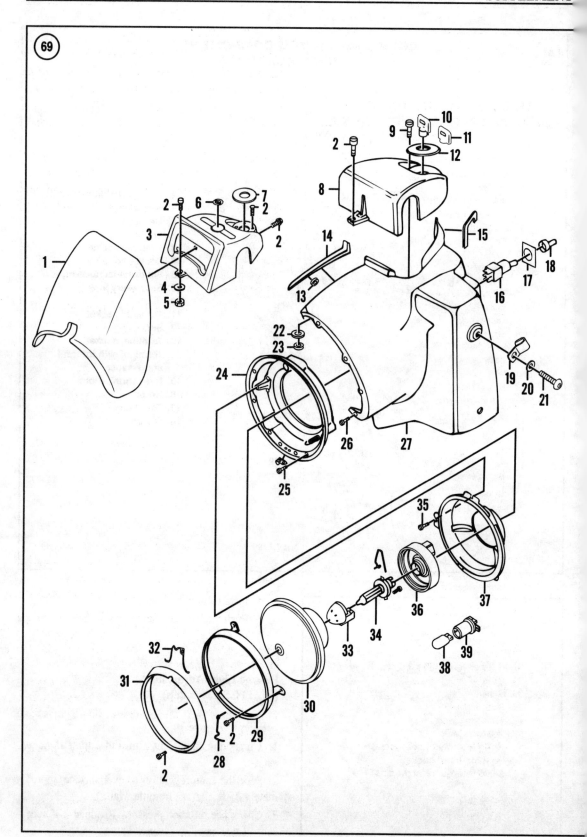

HEADLIGHT AND NACELLE
(2004-2005 FLHR SERIES MODELS)

1. Deflector wing
   (FLHRS, FLHRSI models only)
2. Screw
3. Handlebar cover–chrome
   (FLHRS, FLHRSI models only)
4. Washer
5. Nut with washer
6. Label
7. Trim plate
   (FLHRS, FLHRSI models only)
8. Handlebar cover
   (other than FLHRS, FLHRSI models)
9. Screw
10. Key
11. Key cover
12. Trim plate
    (other than FLHRS, FLHRSI models)
13. Speed nut
14. Trim
15. Trim
16. Switch
17. Label
18. Rubber boot
19. Clamp
20. Washer
21. Screw
22. Washer
23. Nut with washer
24. Headlight housing
25. Screw
26. Screw
27. Headlight nacelle
    (left side shown)
28. Spring
29. Retaining ring
30. Headlight lens
31. Trim bezel
32. Top spring
33. Bulb cover (2005 models)
34. Bulb
35. Screw
36. Rubber boot
37. Mounting ring
38. Position lamp
    (2005 International models)
39. Position lamp socket
    (2005 International models)

4. Have an assistant (with the same approximate weight as the vehicle's owner) sit on the seat.

5. Draw a horizontal line on the wall the same height as the center of the headlight (**Figure 72**).

6. Aim the headlight at the wall. Switch the headlight to the HIGH beam. Point the front wheel straight ahead.

7. Check the headlight beam alignment. The broad, flat pattern of light (main beam of light) must be centered on the horizontal line with an equal area of light above and below line. Mark this location on the wall (A, **Figure 73**).

8. Turn off the headlight.

9. Measure the distance from the horizontal centerline of the headlight to the horizontal centerline of the left side passing light. Note the dimension.

10. Measure the distance from the headlight vertical centerline out to the vertical centerline of the passing light. Note the dimension.

11. Repeat Steps 9 and 10 for the right side passing light. Note both dimensions.

12. Refer to the dimensions taken in Steps 9-11 and mark these locations on the wall. Refer to B and C, **Figure 73**.

13. Have the same assistant used in Step 4, sit on the seat and turn the headlight to HIGH beam. Verify that the headlight beam is still correctly aligned with the vertical and horizontal centerlines on the wall.

14. Turn the headlight to LOW beam.

15. Completely cover the headlight and the right side passing light so their beam is not visible on the wall.

16. Observe the location of the left side passing light on the wall. It should be within the area indicated in D, **Figure 73**. If the location is incorrect perform Step 20.

17. Remove the cover from the right side passing light and place it over the left side passing light.

18. Leave the headlight on LOW beam and still covered so their beam is not visible on the wall.

19. Observe the location of the right side passing light on the wall. It should be within the area indicated in E, **Figure 73**. If the location is incorrect perform Step 20.

20A. On 2005 models, adjust the passing lamp as follows:

     a. Turn off the headlight and passing lights.

     b. Remove the two screws securing the turn signal lamp assembly to the mounting bracket, and lower the turn signal lamp assembly.

15

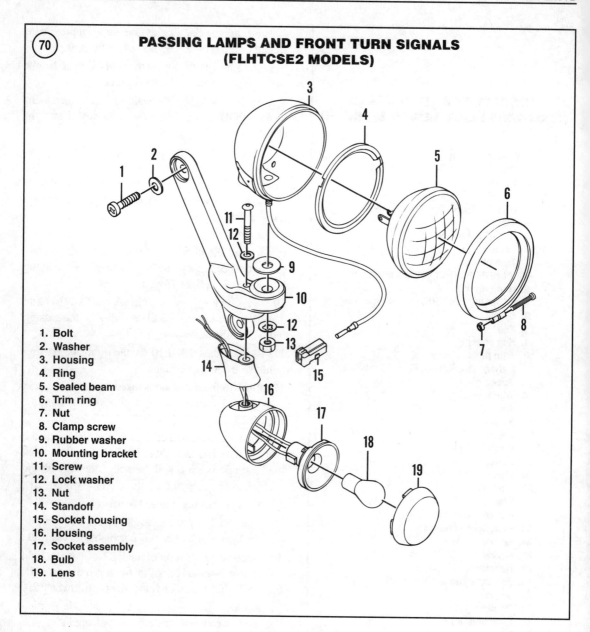

⑦ PASSING LAMPS AND FRONT TURN SIGNALS
(FLHTCSE2 MODELS)

1. Bolt
2. Washer
3. Housing
4. Ring
5. Sealed beam
6. Trim ring
7. Nut
8. Clamp screw
9. Rubber washer
10. Mounting bracket
11. Screw
12. Lock washer
13. Nut
14. Standoff
15. Socket housing
16. Housing
17. Socket assembly
18. Bulb
19. Lens

c. Insert a flare nut socket (Snap-on FRX181), or an equivalent, into the bottom of the turn signal mounting bracket and loosen the locknut.

d. Move the housing in the desired direction to correct the aim.

e. Tighten the locknut to 18 ft.-lb. (24 N•m).

f. Recheck alignment and repeat if necessary.

20B. On FLHTCSE2 models adjust the passing lamp as follows:

a. Loosen the nut securing the passing lamp to the mounting bracket.

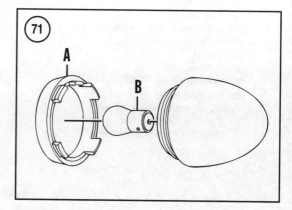

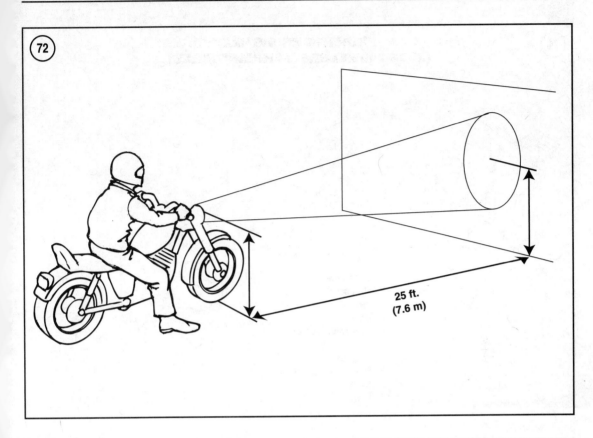

25 ft.
(7.6 m)

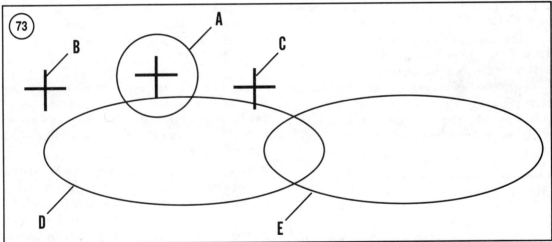

15

b. Move the housing in the desired direction to correct the aim.

c. Tighten the nut to 15-18 ft.-lb. (20-24 N•m).

**Front Turn Signal Replacement
(2004-2005 FLHRS, FLHRSI Models)**

Refer to **Figure 74**.

1. Support the motorcycle with the front wheel off the ground. See *Motorcycle Stands* in Chapter Nine.

2. Remove the fuel tank as described in this Supplement.

3. Follow each front turn signal wiring harness to the main wiring harness. Disconnect the two-pin electrical connector for each front turn signal assembly.

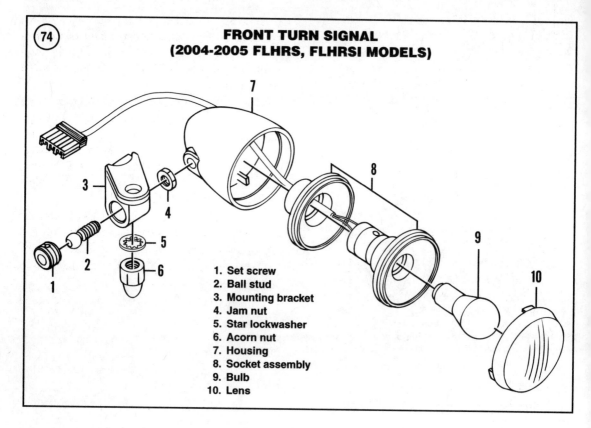

FRONT TURN SIGNAL
(2004-2005 FLHRS, FLHRSI MODELS)

1. Set screw
2. Ball stud
3. Mounting bracket
4. Jam nut
5. Star lockwasher
6. Acorn nut
7. Housing
8. Socket assembly
9. Bulb
10. Lens

4. Loosen the Acorn nut securing the turn signal assembly to the passing light assembly above it.
5. Hold onto the turn signal assembly and remove the Acorn nut and toothed lockwasher.
6. Remove the turn signal assembly.
7. Reinstall the lockwasher and acorn nut to hold the passing light assembly in place on the bracket.
8. Repeat for the other turn signal assemblies.
9. Tighten the Acorn nut securely.

Front Turn Signal Replacement
(FLHTCSE2 Models)

Refer to **Figure 70**.
1. Remove the front fairing and windshield as described under *Front Outer Fairing (FLHT Models)* in Chapter Fourteen.
2. Locate the six-pin electrical connector for the front turn signal located on the inboard side of the left fairing bracket. Depress the locking button and disconnect the connector.

NOTE
The six-pin electrical connector contains the wires for both turn signals. If

only removing one turn signal assembly, refer to the wiring diagrams for the appropriate wire colors for the side being worked on.

3. Disconnect the appropriate terminals from within the socket housing. Refer to *Amp Multilock Connectors* in Chapter Eight. Note the wire color location within the connector as they must be installed in the correct location.

4. Securely attach a piece of flexible mechanics wire to each wire terminal. Make each length of wire long enough to run from the connector under the front fairing, through the wiring conduit, to the front turn signal assembly. Apply liquid glass cleaner, or an equivalent, to the mechanics wire and wiring to assist in pulling the wires through the conduit,

5. Remove the screw and lockwasher securing the turn signal assembly to the mounting bracket and slowly lower the assembly from the mounting bracket.

6. Carefully pull one wire at a time out from the conduit and withdraw all three wires.

7. Withdraw the wires from the mounting bracket and standoff.

8. Install by reversing these removal steps. Note the following:

   a. Make sure none of the wires cannot be pinched when tighten the assembly mounting screw.

   b. Tighten the assembly mounting screw to 96-120 in.-lb. (11-14 N•m).

   c. Check operation of the turn signal(s) prior to installing the front fairing and windshield.

**Front Turn Signal Replacement
(All 2004-2005 Models Except FLHTCSE2)**

1A. On FLHR and FLHRC models, perform the following:

   a. Remove the headlight lens assembly as described in Chapter Eight.

   b. Locate the six-pin electrical connector for the front turn signal located within the headlight housing. Depress the locking button and disconnect the connector.

1B. On all models except FLHR and FLHRC, perform the following:

   a. Remove the front fairing and windshield as described under *Front Fairing and Headlight Assembly* in Chapter Fourteen.

   b. Locate the six-pin electrical connector for the front turn signal located on the inboard side of the left fairing bracket. Depress the locking button and disconnect the connector.

NOTE
The six-pin electrical connector contains the wires for both turn signals. If only removing one turn signal assembly, refer to the wiring diagrams for the appropriate wire colors for the specific side and model being worked on.

3. Disconnect the appropriate terminals from with in the socket housing. Refer to *Amp Multilock Connectors* in Chapter Eight. Note the wire color location within the connector as they must be installed in the correct location.

4. Securely attach a piece of flexible mechanics wire to each wire terminal. Make each length of wire long enough to run from the connector under the front fairing, through the wiring conduit, to the front turn signal assembly. Apply liquid glass cleaner, or an equivalent, to the mechanics wire and wiring to assist in pulling the wires through the conduit,

5. Remove the screws and lockwashers securing the turn signal assembly to the mounting bracket and slowly lower the assembly from the mounting bracket.

6. Carefully pull one wire at a time out from the conduit and withdraw all three wires.

7. Withdraw the wires from the mounting bracket and standoff.

8. Install by reversing these removal steps. Note the following:

   a. Make sure the wires cannot be pinched when tighten the assembly mounting screws.

   b. Tighten the assembly mounting screws to 36-60 in.-lb. (4-7 N•m).

   c. Check operation of the turn signal(s) prior to installing the front fairing and windshield.

Taillight/Brake Light Replacement

Taillight/Brake light bulb replacement is the same as on previous models with the following exception. On early 2003 models, rotate the blown bulb and remove it from the socket assembly (**Figure 75**), then install a new bulb. On later 2003 and the 2004-2005 models, pull the bulb straight out from the socket assembly, and install a new bulb.

SWITCHES

**Ignition/Light Switch Removal/Installation
(FLHT Series International Models)**

Refer to **Figure 76**.

1. Remove the outer fairing as described in Chapter Fourteen.

2. To remove the ignition switch knob, perform the following:

15

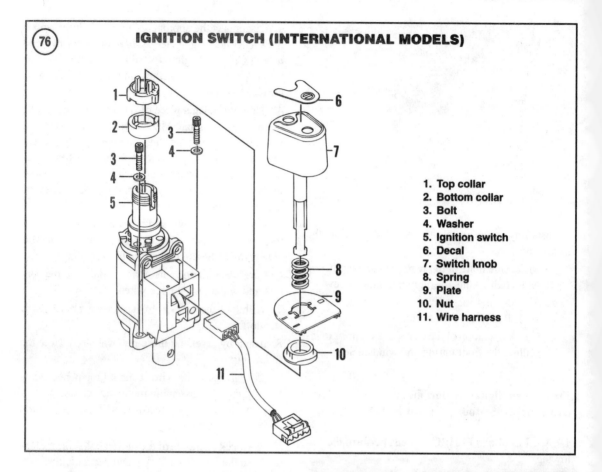

IGNITION SWITCH (INTERNATIONAL MODELS)

1. Top collar
2. Bottom collar
3. Bolt
4. Washer
5. Ignition switch
6. Decal
7. Switch knob
8. Spring
9. Plate
10. Nut
11. Wire harness

a. Using the ignition key, turn the ignition switch to the UNLOCK position. Leave the key in the ignition switch knob.

b. Turn the handlebar to the full left side fork stop.

c. Turn the ignition switch knob to the FORK LOCK position.

d. Insert a small flat-bladed screwdriver under the left side of the switch knob (A, **Figure 77**) and depress the release button. Keep it depressed.

e. Push the ignition key down, turn the ignition key 60° *counterclockwise* (B, **Figure 77**), then lift up and remove the switch knob. Do not lose the spring located below the knob.

3. If necessary, temporarily reinstall the ignition switch knob to move the switch to another position.

4. Turn the handlebar to the full right side fork stop.

5. Use a 7/8 in. open end wrench and loosen the ignition switch nut (**Figure 78**). Unscrew and remove the nut from the threaded post.

6. Remove the top and bottom collars (**Figure 79**) from the threaded post.

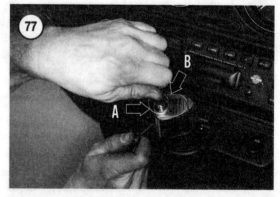

7. Pull on the tabs and remove the decal plate (**Figure 80**) from the slots in the fairing cap or instrument console.

8. Remove the T27 Torx screws and washers (**Figure 81**) on each side securing the fairing cap on each side of the inner fairing.

9. Carefully disengage the firing cap (**Figure 82**) and pull it down. Disconnect the auxiliary switch electrical connector from the harness (A, **Figure 83**).

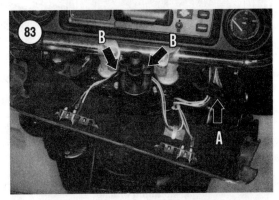

15

10. Carefully remove the auxiliary switch wiring harness (B, **Figure 83**) from around the ignition switch and remove the fairing cap from the front fairing inner panel.

11. Working at the front of the motorcycle, locate the ignition switch black four-pin Packard electrical connector next to the fork bracket. Disconnect the four-pin connector.

12. Use pliers and remove the remaining portions of the break-away screws (A, **Figure 84**) securing the ignition switch to the upper fork bracket. If necessary,

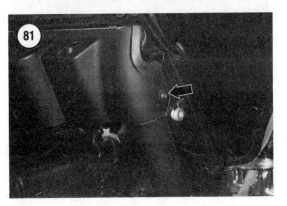

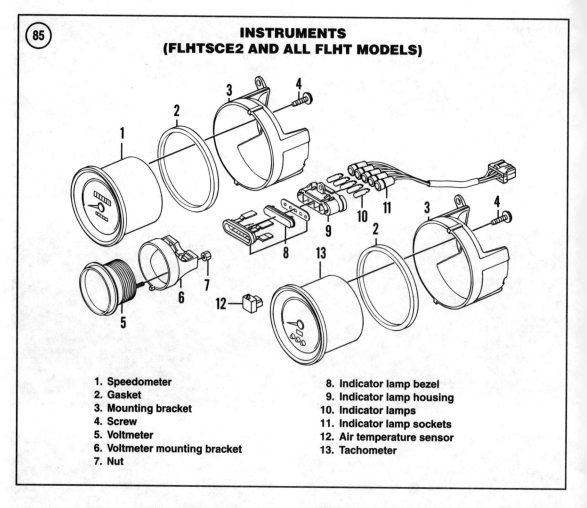

⑧⑤

INSTRUMENTS
(FLHTSCE2 AND ALL FLHT MODELS)

1. Speedometer
2. Gasket
3. Mounting bracket
4. Screw
5. Voltmeter
6. Voltmeter mounting bracket
7. Nut

8. Indicator lamp bezel
9. Indicator lamp housing
10. Indicator lamps
11. Indicator lamp sockets
12. Air temperature sensor
13. Tachometer

drill out the screws and use an easy-out to remove the screws.

13. Carefully remove the ignition switch (B, **Figure 84**) and wiring harness from the inner fairing.

14. Installation is the reverse of removal, while noting the following:

    a. Apply a light coat of dielectric compound to the electrical connectors prior to connecting them.

    b. Install the ignition switch to the upper fork bracket. Install *new* break-away screws and tighten until the heads snap off.

    c. Check the switch in each of its operating positions.

INSTRUMENTS
(FLHTSCE2 AND ALL FLHT MODELS)

Removal and installation is the same as on prior models with the exception of the shape of the gasket

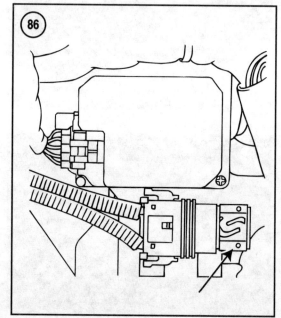

⑧⑥

and the speedometer and tachometer mounting brackets as shown in **Figure 85**.

MAXI-FUSE REPLACEMENT
(2004-2005 MODELS)

On all 2004-2005 models, the 40 amp circuit breaker has been replaced with the 40 amp maxi-fuse.
1. Remove the left side saddlebag as described in Chapter Fourteen.

2. Gently pull the side cover from the frame down tube and remove it.

3. Depress the latch on the maxi-fuse holder, slide the cover toward the rear and remove the cover.

4. Full the maxi-fuse straight back and out of the holder (**Figure 86**).

5. Install by reversing these removal steps. Make sure the cover is locked into place.

Table 13 ELECTRICAL SYSTEM TORQUE SPECIFICATIONS

Item	ft.-lb.	in.-lb.	N•m
Turn signal mounting bracket locknut	18	–	24
Passing lamp-to-mounting bracket	15-18	–	20-24
Turn signal assembly screws			
FLHTCSE2 models	–	96-120	10.8-13.6
All 2004-2005 models			
(except FLHTCSE2)	–	36-60	4-7

CHAPTER NINE

WHEEL, HUBS AND TIRES

FRONT WHEEL

Removal/Installation
(FLHTCSE2 Models)

Refer to **Figure 87**.
Removal and installation is the same as on prior models with the exception of the chrome cover on the front axle on each side. Loosen the set screw on the cover and remove the cover from each side. Apply medium strength thread locking compound to the set screws and tighten to 60-84 in.-lb. (6.8-9.5 N•m).

FRONT AND REAR HUBS
(FLHTCSE2 AND 2004-2005 MODELS)

Refer to *Front and Rear Hubs* in Chapter Nine and to **Figures 87-90**.

15

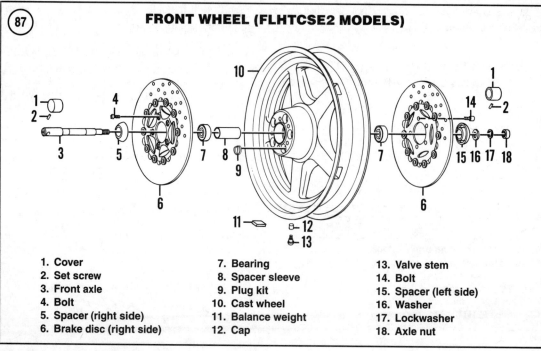

FRONT WHEEL (FLHTCSE2 MODELS)

1. Cover
2. Set screw
3. Front axle
4. Bolt
5. Spacer (right side)
6. Brake disc (right side)
7. Bearing
8. Spacer sleeve
9. Plug kit
10. Cast wheel
11. Balance weight
12. Cap
13. Valve stem
14. Bolt
15. Spacer (left side)
16. Washer
17. Lockwasher
18. Axle nut

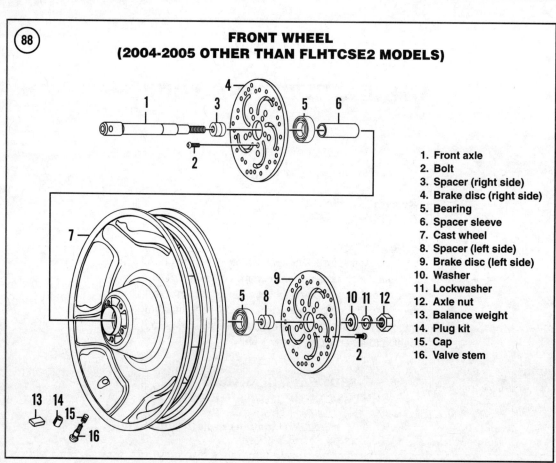

**FRONT WHEEL
(2004-2005 OTHER THAN FLHTCSE2 MODELS)**

1. Front axle
2. Bolt
3. Spacer (right side)
4. Brake disc (right side)
5. Bearing
6. Spacer sleeve
7. Cast wheel
8. Spacer (left side)
9. Brake disc (left side)
10. Washer
11. Lockwasher
12. Axle nut
13. Balance weight
14. Plug kit
15. Cap
16. Valve stem

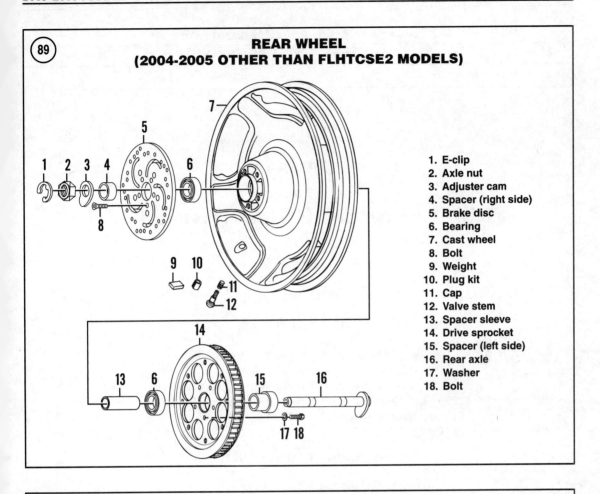

89 REAR WHEEL
(2004-2005 OTHER THAN FLHTCSE2 MODELS)

1. E-clip
2. Axle nut
3. Adjuster cam
4. Spacer (right side)
5. Brake disc
6. Bearing
7. Cast wheel
8. Bolt
9. Weight
10. Plug kit
11. Cap
12. Valve stem
13. Spacer sleeve
14. Drive sprocket
15. Spacer (left side)
16. Rear axle
17. Washer
18. Bolt

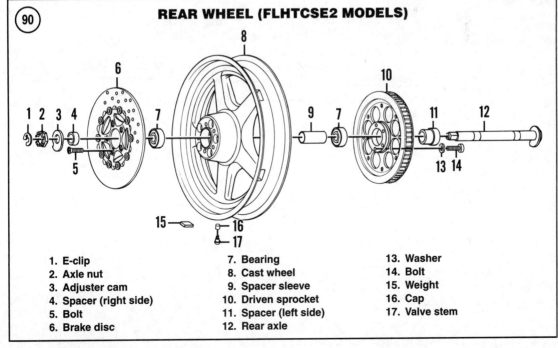

90 REAR WHEEL (FLHTCSE2 MODELS)

1. E-clip
2. Axle nut
3. Adjuster cam
4. Spacer (right side)
5. Bolt
6. Brake disc
7. Bearing
8. Cast wheel
9. Spacer sleeve
10. Driven sprocket
11. Spacer (left side)
12. Rear axle
13. Washer
14. Bolt
15. Weight
16. Cap
17. Valve stem

15

Table 14 WHEEL TORQUE SPECIFICATIONS

Item	ft.-lb.	in.-lb.	N•m
Axle cover set screw	–	60-84	6.8-9.5

CHAPTER TEN

FRONT SUSPENSION AND STEERING

FRONT FORK—CARTRIDGE-TYPE

Front Fork Service—Fork Oil Level

Service to the cartridge-type front fork is the same as on prior models with the exception of the fork oil level. Adjust the fork oil level as described in Chapter Ten so it is 4.21 in. (107 mm) from the top surface of the left fork tube.

STEERING HEAD AND STEM

Removal/Installation

Removal and installation of the steering stem is the same as on prior models with the exception of the two brackets attached to it.

If necessary, remove the screws securing the bracket cover (FLHRS and FLHRSI models) and/or the dust shield (all models) to the steering stem/lower fork bracket.

CHAPTER ELEVEN

REAR SUSPENSION

SHOCK ABSORBERS

Removal/Installation

Removal and installation is the same as on prior models with the exception of the hose routing and connections as shown in **Figure 91**. There is no longer a rear manifold and valve assembly.

Refer to **Table 15** for recommended air pressure.

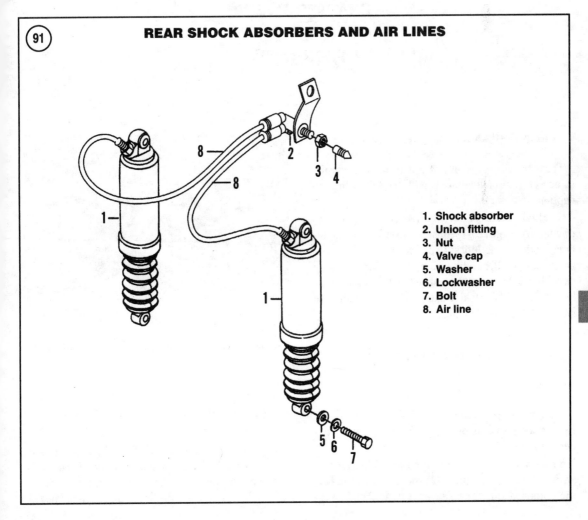

REAR SHOCK ABSORBERS AND AIR LINES

1. Shock absorber
2. Union fitting
3. Nut
4. Valve cap
5. Washer
6. Lockwasher
7. Bolt
8. Air line

15

Table 15 AIR SUSPENSION ADJUSTMENTS

| | Recommended Air Pressure PSI (kPa) | |
Load	Standard rear shock absorber	Low profile rear shock absorber*
Solo rider weight Up to 150 lbs. (68 kg)	0 (0)	0-5 (0-35)
Solo rider weight 150-200 lbs. (68-91 kg)	0-10 (0-69)	0-10 (0-69)
Solo rider weight 200-250 lbs. (91-113 kg)	5-15 (35-103)	5-10 (35-69)
Rider with passenger Up to 150 lbs. (66 kg)	10-15 (69-103)	20-30 (138-207)
Rider with passenger Up to 200 lbs. (91 kg)	20-25 (138-172)	25-35 (172-241)
Maximum GVWR	20-35 (138-241)	40-50 (276-345)
*Equipped on FLHRS and FLHRSI models only.		

CHAPTER TWELVE

BRAKES

FRONT BRAKE PAD REPLACEMENT

Front brake pad removal and installation is the same as on previous models with the following exception.

The brake pads are not symmetrical. The pad with one tab (A, **Figure 92**) must be installed on the inboard side of the left side caliper and on the outboard side of the right side caliper. The pad with two tabs (B, **Figure 92**) must be installed on the outboard side of the left side caliper and on the inboard side of the right side caliper.

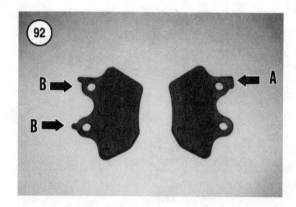

REAR BRAKE PAD REPLACEMENT

All Models

Rear brake pad removal and installation is the same as on previous models with the following exception.

The brake pads are not symmetrical. The pad with one tab (A, **Figure 92**) must be installed on the outboard side. The pad with two tabs (B, **Fig-**

ure 92) must be installed on the inboard side of the caliper.

FLHTCSE2 Models

Follow the *Rear Brake Pad Replacement* procedure in Chapter Twelve. Once the brake pad pins are removed, rotate the brake pads up and toward the rear following the arc the brake disc. This is neces-

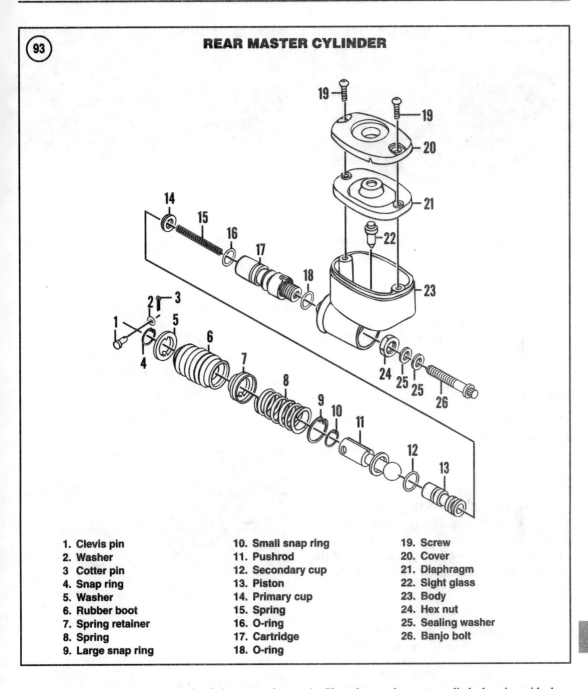

REAR MASTER CYLINDER

1. Clevis pin
2. Washer
3. Cotter pin
4. Snap ring
5. Washer
6. Rubber boot
7. Spring retainer
8. Spring
9. Large snap ring
10. Small snap ring
11. Pushrod
12. Secondary cup
13. Piston
14. Primary cup
15. Spring
16. O-ring
17. Cartridge
18. O-ring
19. Screw
20. Cover
21. Diaphragm
22. Sight glass
23. Body
24. Hex nut
25. Sealing washer
26. Banjo bolt

15

sary for the pads to clear the raised rivets on the floating brake disc.

REAR MASTER CYLINDER AND REAR BRAKE PEDAL

Disassembly

Refer to **Figure 93**.

1. Clean the exterior master cylinder housing with clean DOT 5 brake fluid or isopropyl alcohol and dry.

2. Store the master cylinder components in a divided container, such as a restaurant-size egg carton, to help maintain their correct alignment position.

3. If still installed, remove the master cylinder cover and diaphragm.

4. Compress the spring, rubber boot and washer.

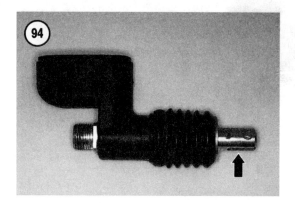

5. Remove the snap ring from the pushrod (**Figure 94**)
6. Remove the washer, rubber boot, spring retainer and spring (**Figure 95**).
7. Depress the pushrod (A, **Figure 96**) and remove the large snap ring (B).
8. Remove the pushrod (**Figure 97**).
9. Remove the piston assembly (A, **Figure 98**) and spring (B) from the cartridge.

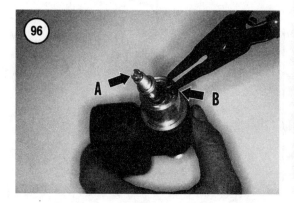

Inspection

The inspection procedure is the same as on previous models as described in Chapter Twelve.

Assembly

1. Coat all parts with clean DOT 5 brake fluid.
2. Soak the primary cup, O-ring and piston assembly in clean DOT 5 brake fluid for at least 15 minutes to make them pliable. Coat the inside of the cartridge bore with clean brake fluid prior to the assembly of parts.

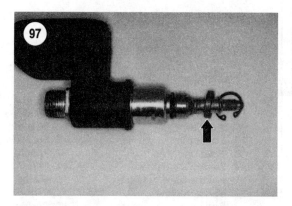

> *CAUTION*
> *When installing the piston assembly, do not allow the primary cup to turn inside out as it will be damaged and allow brake fluid leakage within the cartridge cylinder bore.*

3. Install the spring (B, **Figure 98**) into the cartridge.
4. Position the piston assembly with the primary cup (A, **Figure 98**) end going in first. Make sure the piston cup does not tear as it passes through the bore entrance (**Figure 99**).
5. Turn the reservoir on end on a shop cloth. Carefully push the piston assembly into the cartridge with a Phillips screwdriver. Push the piston assembly in and

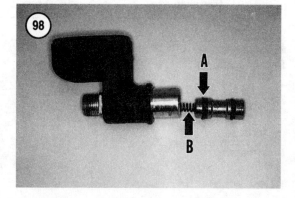

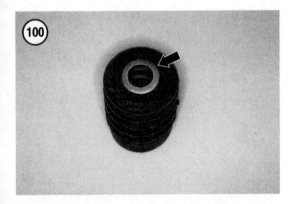

then let it move out several times and check for ease of movement.

6. Position the pushrod onto the end of the piston (**Figure 97**) and push the piston into the cartridge. Hold the push rod in place (A, **Figure 96**) and install the large snap ring (B). Make sure the large snap ring is correctly seated in the cartridge groove.

7. Install the spring and spring seat (**Figure 95**) onto the pushrod and cartridge.

8. Install the washer into the boot and push it all the way to the end (**Figure 100**).

9. Install the boot (**Figure 101**) onto the pushrod and cartridge.

10. Install the washer and snap ring onto the pushrod. Make sure the snap ring is properly seated in the pushrod groove.

11. Install the diaphragm and reservoir cover (**Figure 102**). Tighten the screws finger tight at this time.

BRAKE DISC (FLHTCSE2 MODELS)

Inspection

Check the floating disc fasteners (**Figure 103**) for damage or looseness. If any are loose or damaged, replace the disc.

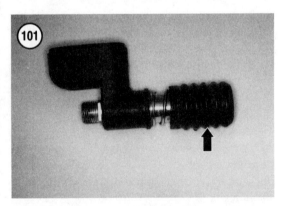

REAR BRAKE PEDAL (2004-2005 MODELS)

Removal/Installation

Removal and installation the rear brake pedal is the same as on all previous models with the addition of two O-ring seals outboard of the bushings as shown in **Figure 104**. Replace the O-rings every time the rear brake pedal is removed.

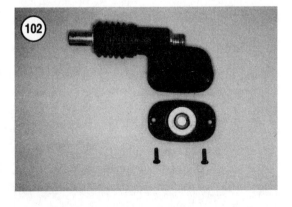

15

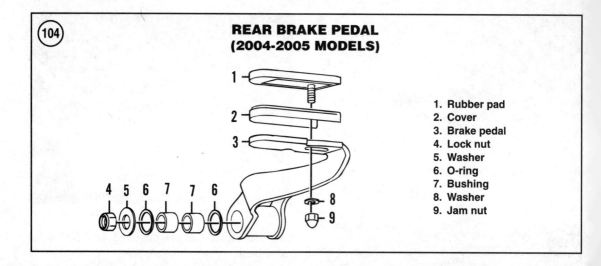

(104)

**REAR BRAKE PEDAL
(2004-2005 MODELS)**

1. Rubber pad
2. Cover
3. Brake pedal
4. Lock nut
5. Washer
6. O-ring
7. Bushing
8. Washer
9. Jam nut

CHAPTER FOURTEEN

BODY

PASSENGER BACKREST (FLHTCSE2 MODELS)

Removal/Installation

Refer to **Figure 105**.

1. Remove the saddlebags as described in Chapter Fourteen.
2. Push in on the spring-loaded locking latch and pull the latch toward the rear.
3. Lift the backrest upward and then toward the rear and remove it from the motorcycle.

NOTE
The following steps are only necessary to remove the mounting hardware.

4. Remove the bolt, washer and front docking bushing.
5. Remove the bolt, washer, rear docking bushing, washer, locknut and the docking bracket.
6. Remove the screw, lockwasher and washer securing the docking assembly mounting bracket.
7. Remove the screw, lockwasher, Tour-Pak docking bushing and spacer.

8. Remove the screw and washer securing the docking assembly mounting bracket and remove the docking assembly mounting bracket.
9. If necessary, remove the bolts, washers and locknuts securing the Tour-Pak mounting bracket to the frame. Remove the mounting bracket.
10. Repeat Steps 5-10 for the components on the opposite side, if necessary.
11. Inspect all parts for wear or damage and replace as necessary.
12. Install by reversing these removal steps. Note the following:
    a. Tighten all fasteners finger-tight until all have been installed, then tighten all to15-20 ft.-lb. (20-27 N•m).
    b. After installing the backrest, pull on it from front-to-back and sideways to make sure it is secure.

HEADLIGHT AND NACELLE (2004-2005 FLHR MODELS)

Removal and installation of the headlight and nacelle are the same as on all previous models with the

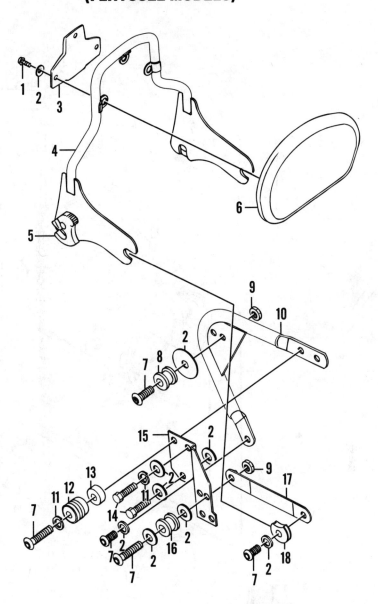

105

PASSENGER BACKREST
(FLHTCSE2 MODELS)

1. Bolt
2. Washer
3. Insert
4. Backrest mounting bracket
5. Spring loaded latch
6. Backrest pad
7. Bolt
8. Tour pack docking–rear
9. Locknut
10. Tour packing mounting bracket

11. Lockwasher
12. Tour pack docking
    bushing–front
13. Spacer
14. Hex bolt
15. Docking assembly mounting
    bracket
16. Tour Pak docking bushing–rear
17. Docking bracket
18. Front docking bushing

15

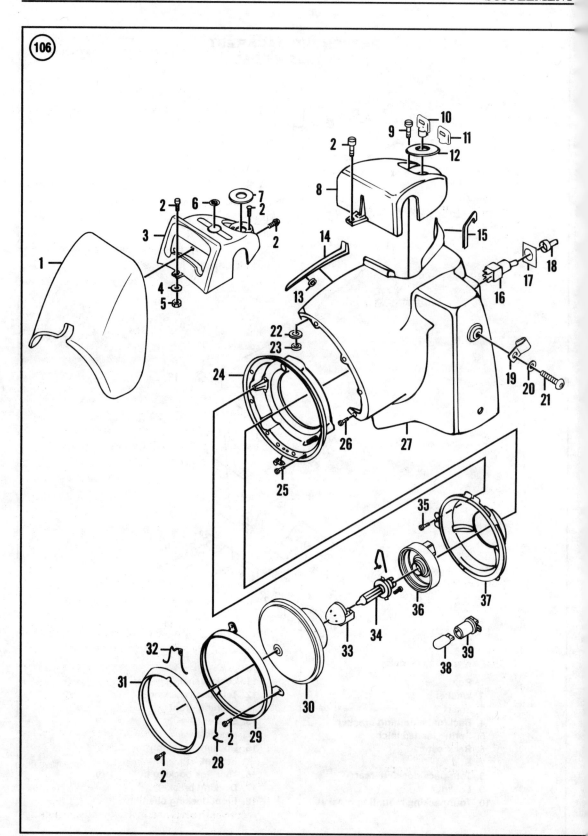

HEADLIGHT AND NACELLE
(2004-2005 FLHR SERIES MODELS)

1. Deflector wing
   (FLHRS, FLHRSI models only)
2. Screw
3. Handlebar cover–chrome
   (FLHRS, FLHRSI models only)
4. Washer
5. Nut with washer
6. Label
7. Trim plate
   (FLHRS, FLHRSI models only)
8. Handlebar cover
   (other than FLHRS, FLHRSI models)
9. Screw
10. Key
11. Key cover
12. Trim plate
   (other than FLHRS, FLHRSI models)
13. Speed nut
14. Trim
15. Trim
16. Switch
17. Label
18. Rubber boot
19. Clamp
20. Washer
21. Screw
22. Washer
23. Nut with washer
24. Headlight housing
25. Screw
26. Screw
27. Headlight nacelle
   (left side shown)
28. Spring
29. Retaining ring
30. Headlight lens
31. Trim bezel
32. Top spring
33. Bulb cover (2005 models)
34. Bulb
35. Screw
36. Rubber boot
37. Mounting ring
38. Position lamp
   (2005 International models)
39. Position lamp socket
   (2005 International models)

exception of the deflector and chrome handlebar cover on FLHRS models as shown in **Figure 106**.

LOWER FAIRING
(FLHTCSE2 AND 2005 FLHTCUI MODELS)

Removal

Refer to **Figure 107**.

1. Position the front wheel in the straight ahead position to protect finish on the fender and lower firing during removal.

2. Carefully pull out and release the door flap push-in snaps. Release all four snaps and remove the door flap.

3. Reach into the glove box and remove the two flange nuts from the clip studs.

4. Push in on end of both studs. Carefully pull straight out and remove the fairing cap from the lower fairing. Do not twist the fairing cap during removal as it will be damaged.

5. Secure the upper portion of the lower fairing to the engine guard with tape or twine.

6. Secure the locknut below the engine guard clamp and remove the T40 Torx screw securing the fairing lower to the engine guard.

7. Carefully remove the lower fairing from the engine guard.

8. Remove and discard the rubber washer located between the lower fairing and the clamp.

9. Repeat for the other side, if necessary.

Installation

1. Make sure the front wheel in the straight ahead position.

2. Install the lower faring onto the engine guard and secure it with tape or twine.

3. Install the T40 Torx screw through the lower fairing, *new* rubber washer and engine guard clamp.

4. Install the locknut onto the Torx screw and tighten finger-tight.

5. Make sure the clip studs are in place on the fairing cap.

6. Position the fairing cap against the engine guard and against the fairing lower while aligning the clips suds with the holes in the lower fairing.

7. Secure both parts and install the flange nuts onto the clip studs.

15

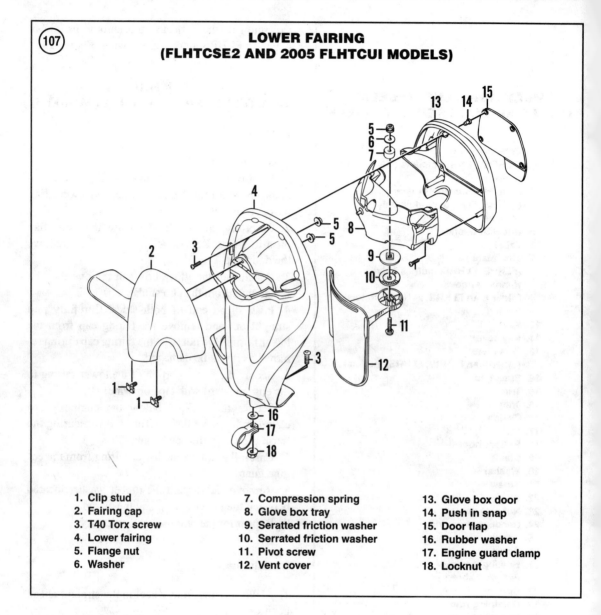

**LOWER FAIRING
(FLHTCSE2 AND 2005 FLHTCUI MODELS)**

107

1. Clip stud
2. Fairing cap
3. T40 Torx screw
4. Lower fairing
5. Flange nut
6. Washer
7. Compression spring
8. Glove box tray
9. Seratted friction washer
10. Serrated friction washer
11. Pivot screw
12. Vent cover
13. Glove box door
14. Push in snap
15. Door flap
16. Rubber washer
17. Engine guard clamp
18. Locknut

8. Make sure the lower fairing is centered on the engine guard, and alternately tighten the flange nuts to 35-40 in.-lb. (4.0-4.5 N•m).

9. Secure the locknut on the engine guard clamp and tighten the T40 Torx screw to 90-100 in.-lb. (10-11 N•m).

10. Repeat for the other side, if necessary.

Disassembly/Assembly

1. To remove the vent door, remove the locknut, washer and compression spring securing the vent

door to the glove box tray. Remove the vent door and serrated fiction washers.

2. To remove the glove box door and tray, remove the T40 Torx screws securing the glove box door and tray to the lower fairing. Separate the parts.

3. To remove the glove box tray, remove the T20 Torx screws securing the glove box tray to the door. Separate the parts.

4. Assemble by reversing these disassembly steps. Tighten the T40 Torx screws securely. Do not overtighten the screws as the screw mounting posts may crack or strip out.

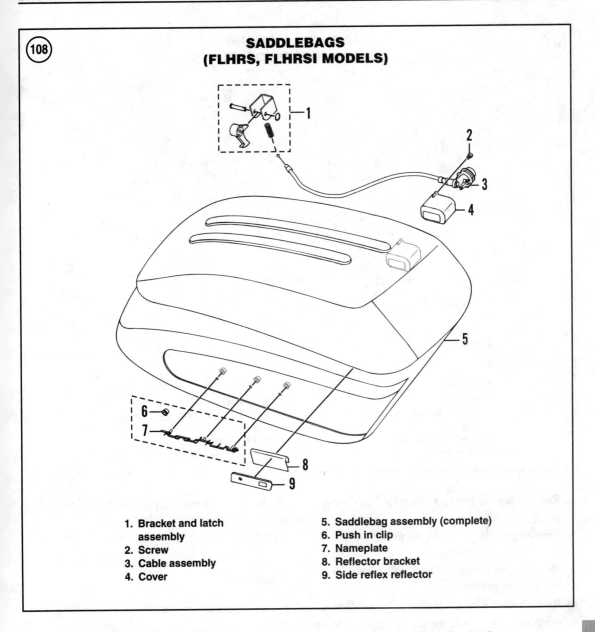

**SADDLEBAGS
(FLHRS, FLHRSI MODELS)**

1. Bracket and latch assembly
2. Screw
3. Cable assembly
4. Cover
5. Saddlebag assembly (complete)
6. Push in clip
7. Nameplate
8. Reflector bracket
9. Side reflex reflector

SADDLEBAGS AND GUARDS

Saddlebags Removal/Installation (FLHRS Models)

1. Place the motorcycle on level ground on the jiffy stand.

2. Depress the button on the front inboard side of the saddlebag.

3. Hold the button down and raise the lid.

4. Within the saddlebag case, grasp the latch bail wire, rotate the latch stud a 1/4 turn counterclockwise and release the stud from the mounting bracket.

5. Repeat Step 4 for the other latch.

6. Carefully pull the saddlebag up and out of the guard.

7. Inspect the latch mounting brackets for damage.

8. Install by reversing these removal steps. Make sure the saddlebag is locked into place.

Cable Assembly and Latch (FLHRS Models)

Removal/installation

Refer to **Figure 108**.

15

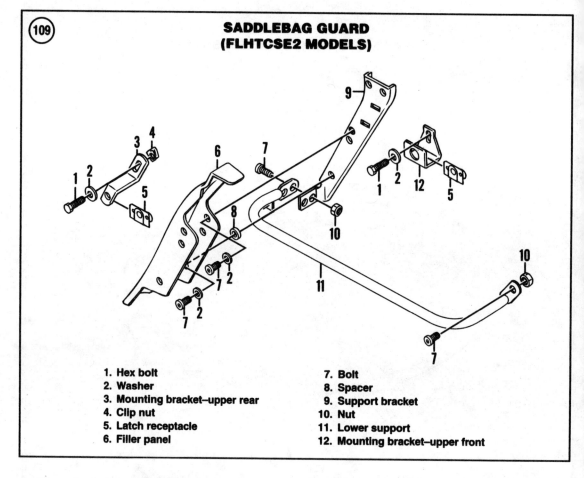

**SADDLEBAG GUARD
(FLHTCSE2 MODELS)**

1. Hex bolt
2. Washer
3. Mounting bracket–upper rear
4. Clip nut
5. Latch receptacle
6. Filler panel
7. Bolt
8. Spacer
9. Support bracket
10. Nut
11. Lower support
12. Mounting bracket–upper front

1. Remove the saddlebag as described in this section.

2. Remove the two screws securing the plastic cover and remove the cover.

3. Depress the wireform and pull button from opening in the saddlebag.

4. Remove sleeve from opening in the saddlebag.

5. On the inboard side of the saddlebag, remove the lock ring from the opening in the end of the latch pin.

6. Pull the latch pin from the metal shroud, the saddlebag bracket and the latch. Remove the metal shroud.

7. Depress the spring and pull and remove the cable ball end from the slot in the latch. Remove the latch.

8. Remove the spring from the cable and remove the e-clip from the groove in the fitting in the end of the cable.

9. Pull the cable end fitting from the opening in the saddlebag bracket.

10. Remove the cable from the channel along the inboard edge of the saddlebag.

11. Install by reversing these removal steps.

Adjustment

1. Open the lid of the saddlebag as previously described.

2. Remove the two screws securing the plastic cover and remove the cover.

3. Loosen the locknut on the cable adjuster hex body.

4. Rotate the adjuster in either direction until the closes part of the latch is approximately 3/8 in. (9.5 mm) form the inboard side of the saddlebag lid.

5. Tighten the locknut securely.

6. Install the plastic cover and tighten the two screws.

7. Close and open the saddlebag lid several times to make sure it locks every time. Readjust if necessary.

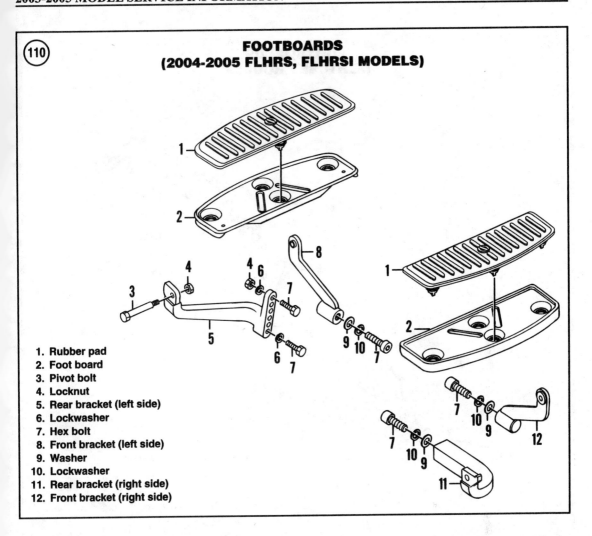

FOOTBOARDS
(2004-2005 FLHRS, FLHRSI MODELS)

1. Rubber pad
2. Foot board
3. Pivot bolt
4. Locknut
5. Rear bracket (left side)
6. Lockwasher
7. Hex bolt
8. Front bracket (left side)
9. Washer
10. Lockwasher
11. Rear bracket (right side)
12. Front bracket (right side)

Saddlebag Guard Removal/Installation
(FLHTCSE2 Models)

Refer to **Figure 109**.
1. Remove the saddlebag.
2. Remove the frame side cover.
3. Remove the two screws, washers and spacers securing the filler panel to the support bracket.
4. Remove the two screws and lockwashers securing the saddlebag lower support to the muffler.
5. Remove the muffler mounting bracket and rubber mount from the lower support.
6. Remove the front bolt and locknut securing the saddlebag lower support to the frame.
7. Remove the rear bolt and locknut securing the saddlebag lower support to the support bracket.
8. Remove the saddlebag support bracket.
9. Install by reversing these removal steps. Note the following:

a. Tighten the bolts and locknuts securing the saddlebag lower support to 15-20 ft.-lb. (20-27 N•m).

b. Tighten the screws securing the muffler mounting bracket to 96-144 ft.-lb. 11-16 N•m).

c. Tighten the screws securing the filler panel to 15-20 ft.-lb. (20-27 N•m).

FOOTBOARDS

Removal/Installation
(FLHRS and FLHTCSE2 Models)

Refer to **Figures 110-112** and follow the procedure in Chapter Fourteen.

15

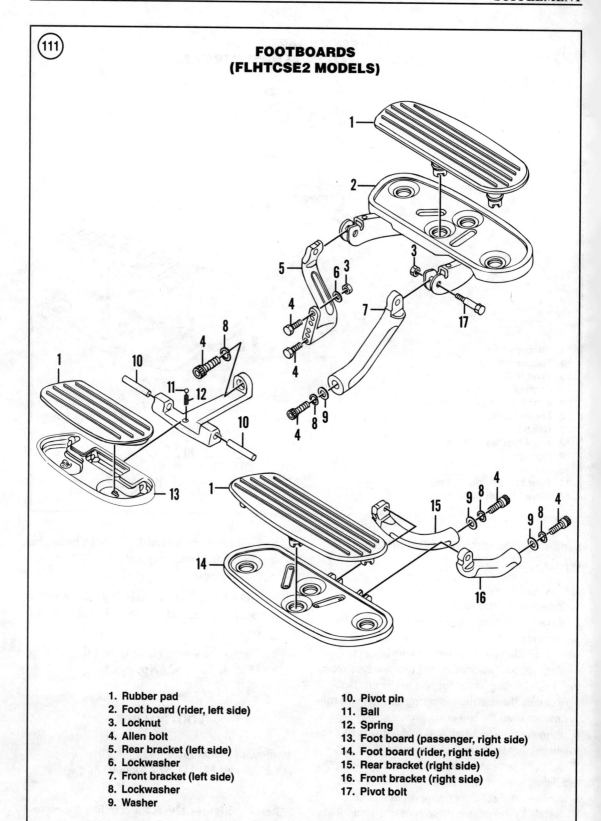

**FOOTBOARDS
(FLHTCSE2 MODELS)**

1. Rubber pad
2. Foot board (rider, left side)
3. Locknut
4. Allen bolt
5. Rear bracket (left side)
6. Lockwasher
7. Front bracket (left side)
8. Lockwasher
9. Washer
10. Pivot pin
11. Ball
12. Spring
13. Foot board (passenger, right side)
14. Foot board (rider, right side)
15. Rear bracket (right side)
16. Front bracket (right side)
17. Pivot bolt

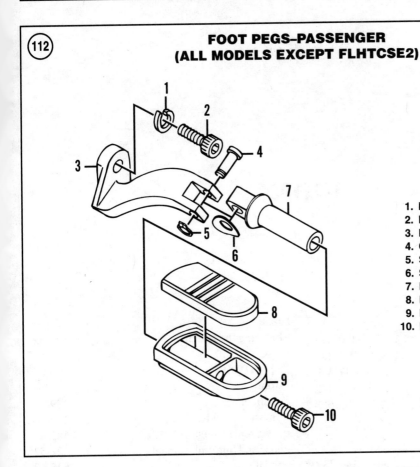

**FOOT PEGS–PASSENGER
(ALL MODELS EXCEPT FLHTCSE2)**

1. Lockwasher
2. Bolt
3. Bracket (left side shown)
4. Clevis pin
5. Snap ring
6. Spring washer
7. Foot peg mount
8. Pad
9. Foot peg
10. Bolt

Table 16 BODY TORQUE SPECIFICATIONS

Item	ft.-lb.	in.-lb.	N•m
Saddle bag			
Filler panel screws	15-20	–	20-27
Lower support	15-20	–	20-27
Muffler mounting bracket	96-144	–	11-16
Passenger backrest fasteners	15-20	–	20-27
Lower fairing flange nuts	–	35-40	4.0-4.5
Lower fairing T40 Torx screw	–	90-100	10-11

15

INDEX

16

16

WIRING
DIAGRAMS

1999 FLHR SERIES

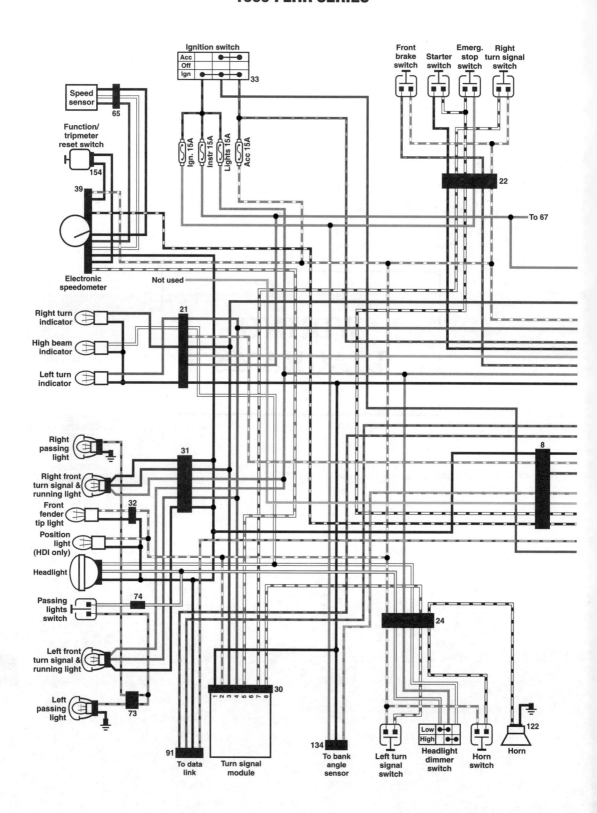

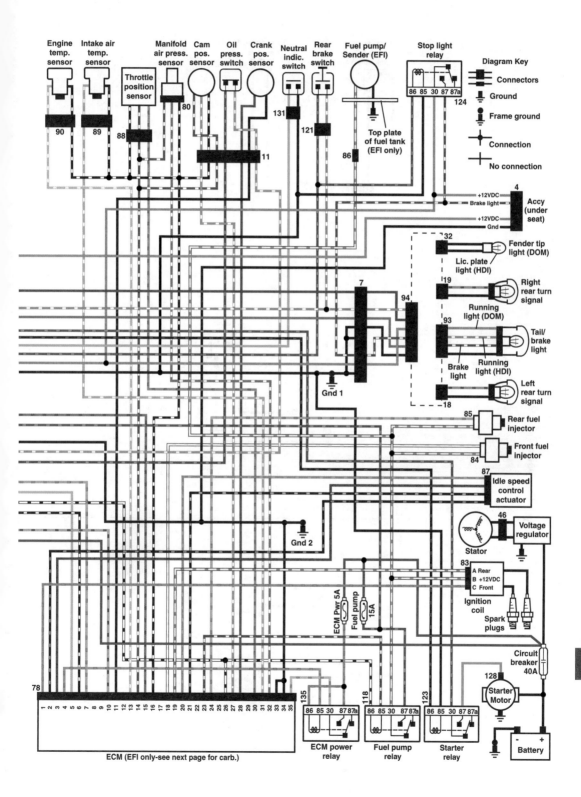

ECM (EFI only-see next page for carb.)

1999 FLHR SERIES

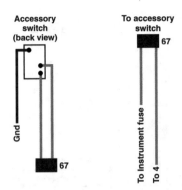

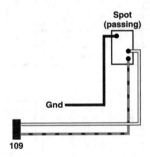

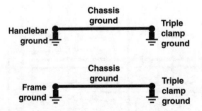

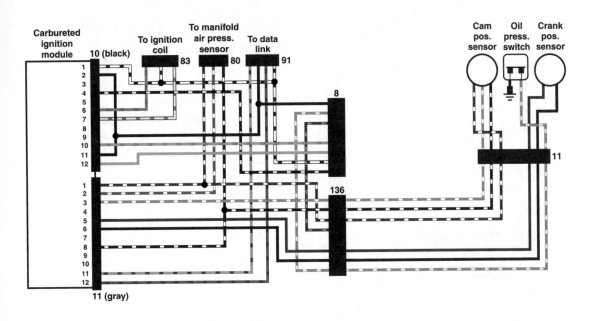

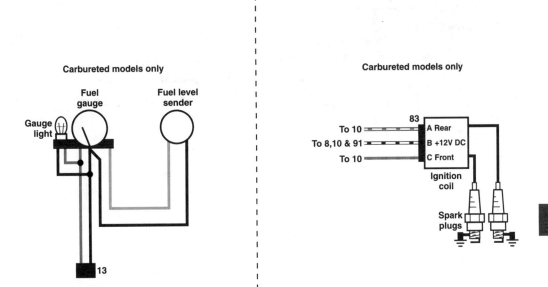

17

1999 FLHT AND FLTR SERIES

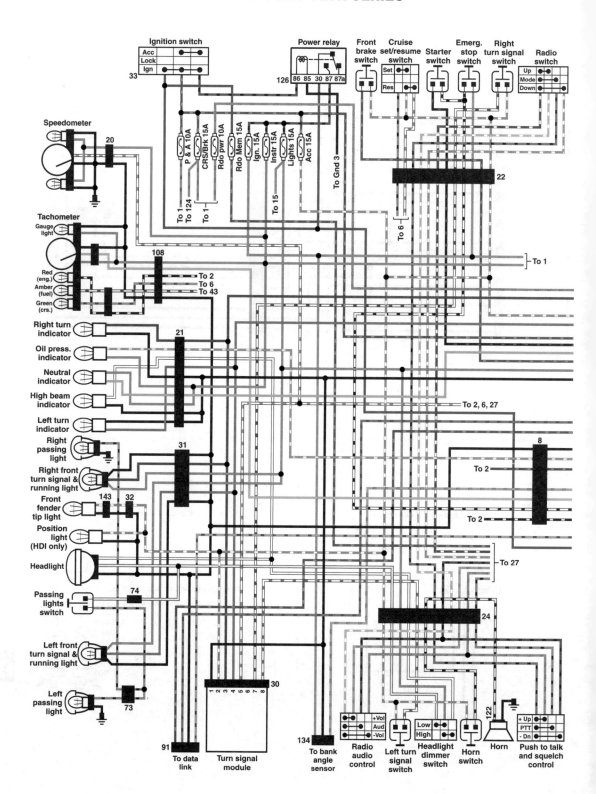

Engine temp. sensor

Intake air temp. sensor

Manifold air press. sensor

Cam pos. sensor

Oil press. switch

Crank pos. sensor

Neutral indic. switch

Rear brake switch

Fuel pump/ Sender

Stop light relay

To tour pack

Throttle position sensor

Diagram Key

Connectors

Ground

Frame ground

Connection

No connection

90

89

88

80

131

121

141

86

13

86 85 30 87 87a

124

11

12

To 2

To Crs/Brk fuse

+12VDC

Brake light

+12VDC

Gnd

4

Accy (under seat)

To 2

45

Fender tip light (DOM)

Lic. plate light (HDI)

119

Right rear turn signal

Running light (DOM)

7

94

93

Tail/ brake light

Brake light

Running light (HDI)

Gnd 1

18

Left rear turn signal

85

Rear fuel injector

84

Front fuel injector

87

Idle speed control actuator

Gnd 2

46

Voltage regulator

Stator

83

A Front
B +12VDC
C Rear

Ignition coil

Spark plugs

ECM Pwr 5A

Fuel pump 15A

Circuit breaker 40A

128

Starter Motor

78

135

118

123

1 2 3 4 5 6 7 8 9 10 11 12 13 14 15 16 17 18 19 20 21 22 23 24 25 26 27 28 29 30 31 32 33 34 35

86 85 30 87 87a

86 85 30 87 87a

86 85 30 87 87a

- +

Battery

ECM (EFI only-see next page for carb.)

ECM power relay

Fuel pump relay

Starter relay

17

1999 FLHT AND FLTR SERIES

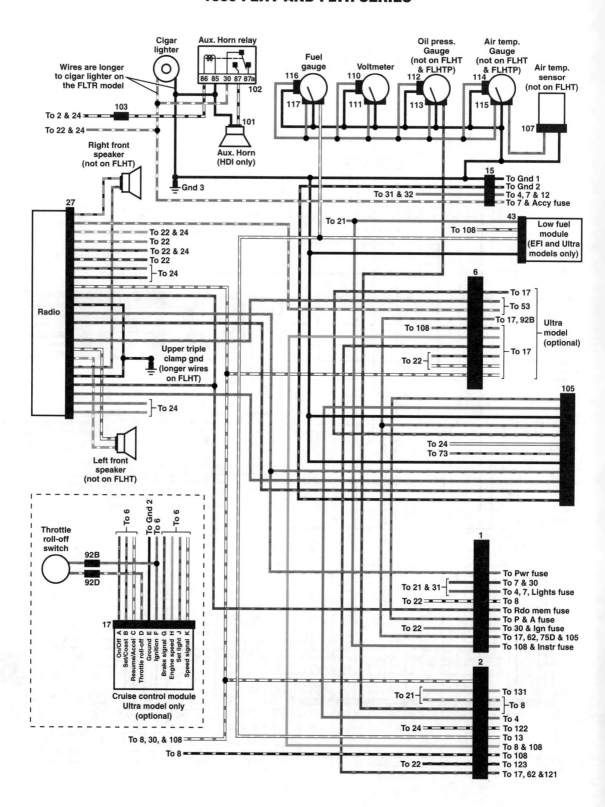

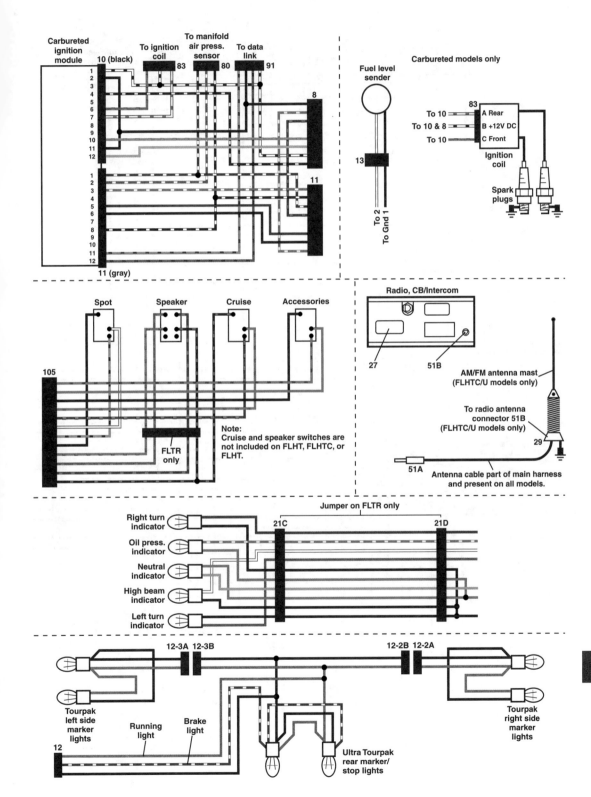

2000 FLHR SERIES

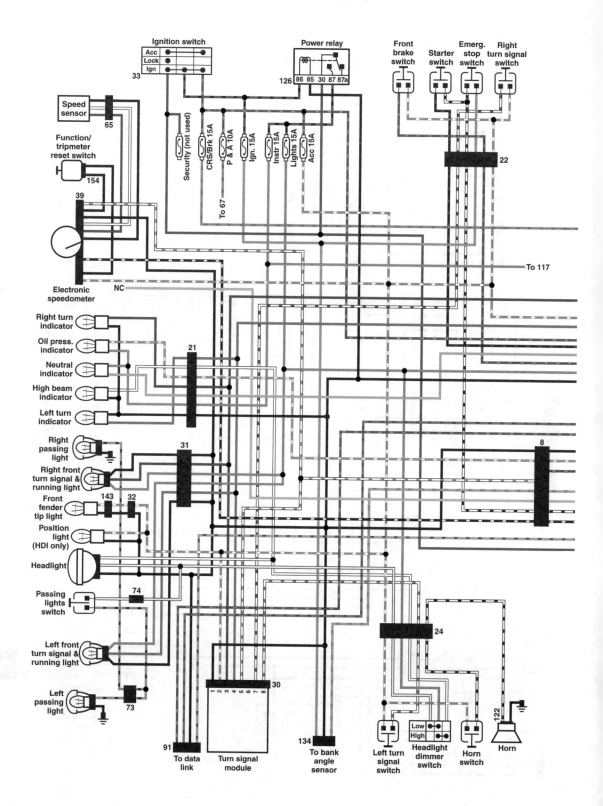

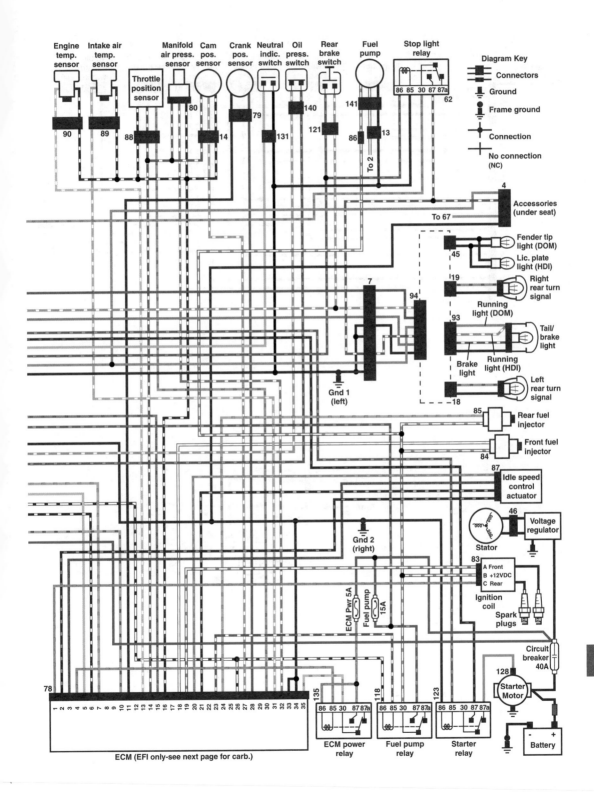

2000 FLHR SERIES (CONTINUED)

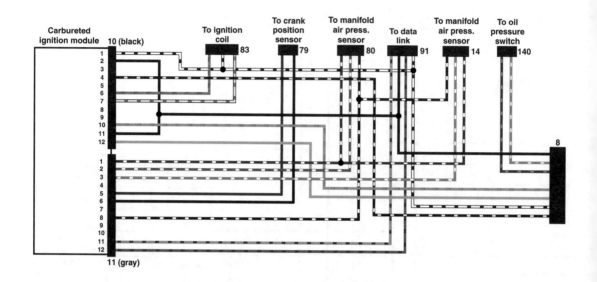

Carbureted models only

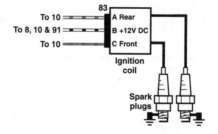

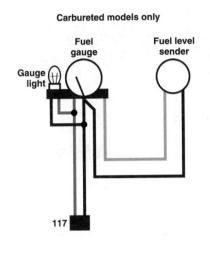

Carbureted models only

Fuel gauge

Fuel level sender

Gauge light

117

Fuel gauge (EFI model)

117

To 21 & Instr fuse
To 13
To gnd 1

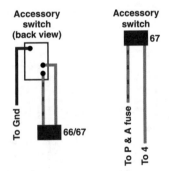

Accessory switch (back view)

Accessory switch

67

To Gnd

66/67

To P & A fuse
To 4

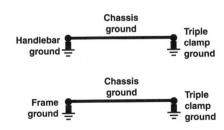

Chassis ground

Handlebar ground

Triple clamp ground

Chassis ground

Frame ground

Triple clamp ground

17

2000 FLHT AND FLTR SERIES

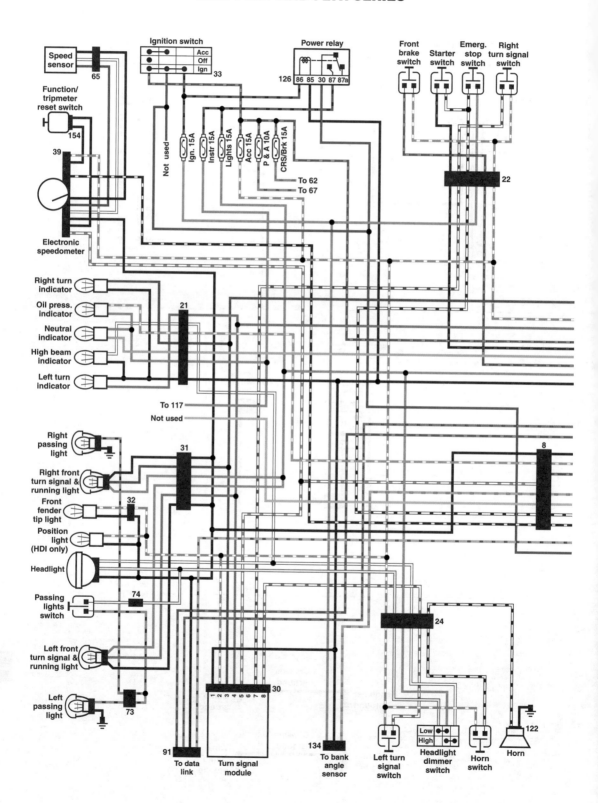

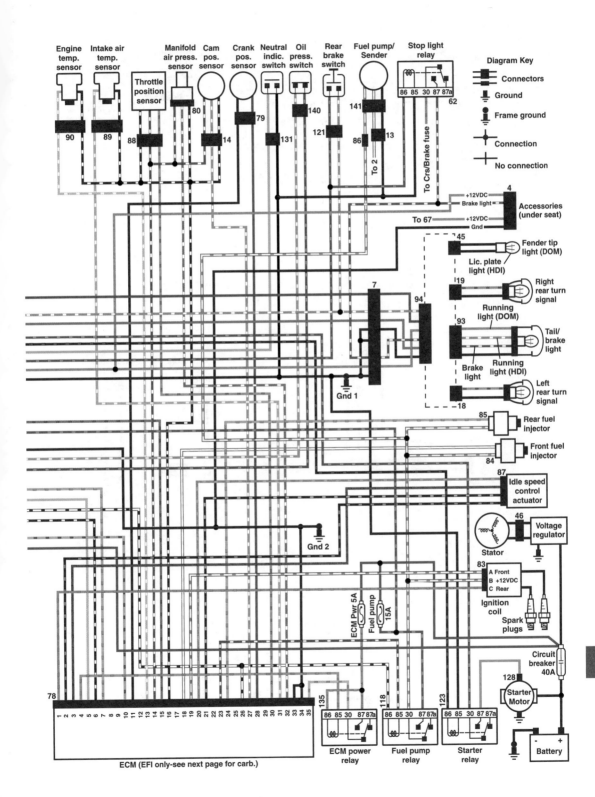

ECM (EFI only-see next page for carb.)

17

2000 FLHT AND FLTR SERIES (CONTINUED)

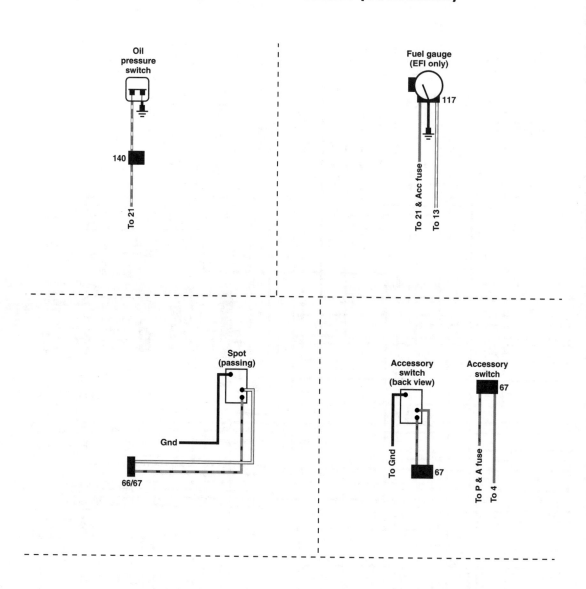

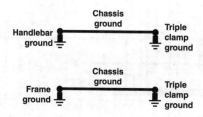

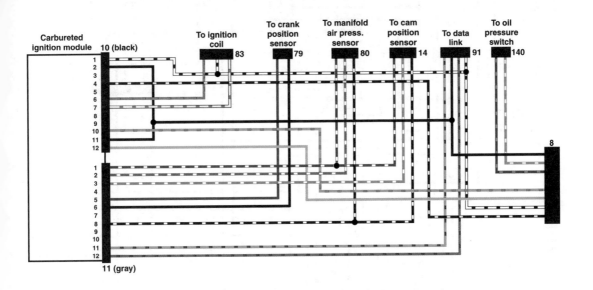

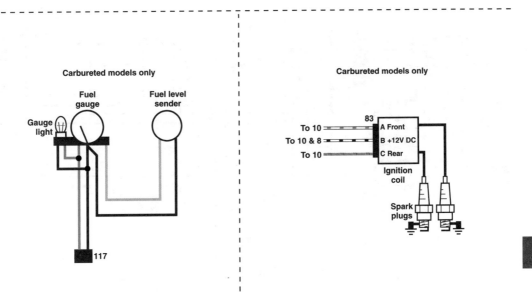

17

2001 FLHR SERIES

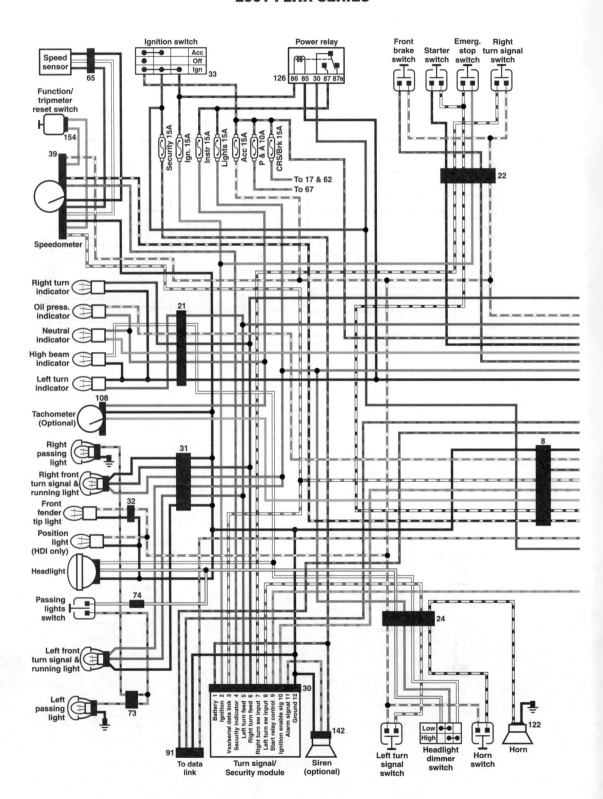

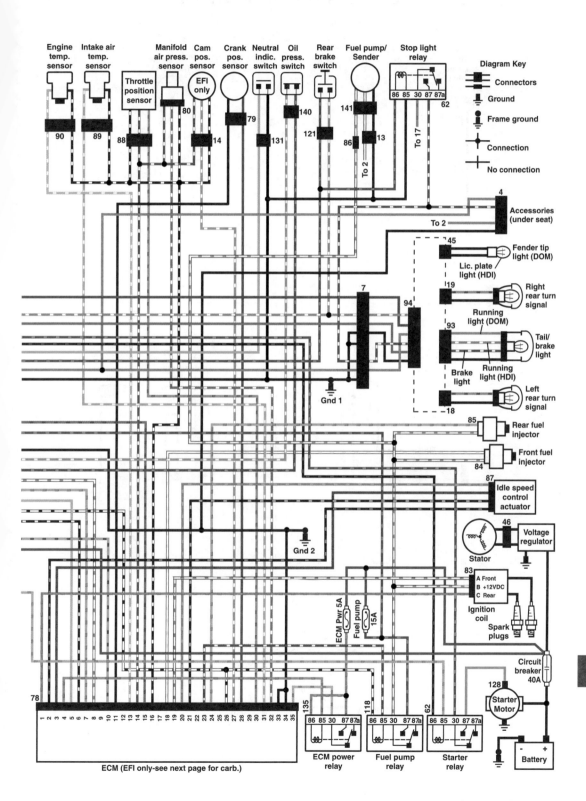

2001 FLHR SERIES (CONTINUED)

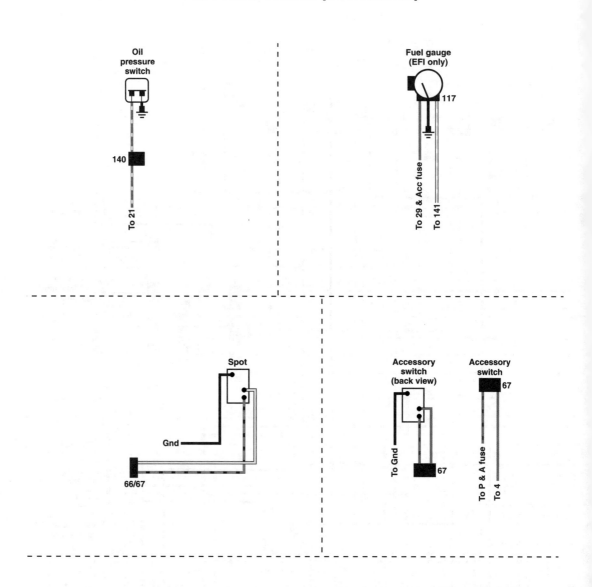

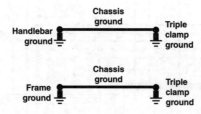

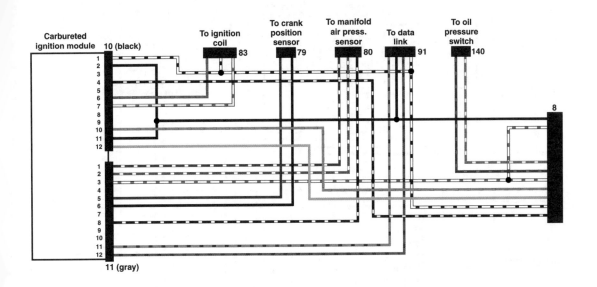

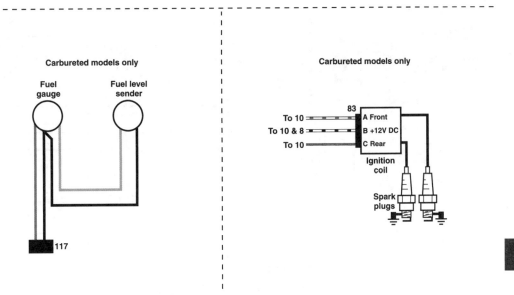

17

2001 FLHT AND FLTR SERIES

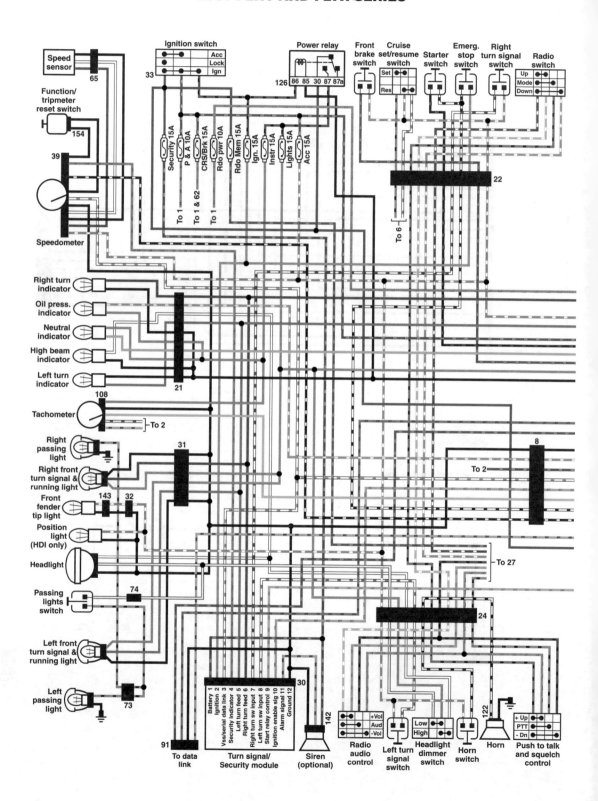

Engine temp. sensor

Intake air temp. sensor

Throttle position sensor

Manifold air press. sensor

Cam pos. sensor

EFI only

Crank pos. sensor

Neutral indic. switch

Oil press. switch

Rear brake switch

Fuel pump/ Sender

Stop light relay

To tour pack

90 89 88 14 80 79 131 121 140 141 86 13

Diagram Key

- Connectors
- Ground
- Frame ground
- Connection
- No connection

12

86 85 30 87 87a 62

To 2

To 17

4

Accessories (under seat)

To 2

Fender tip light (DOM)

Lic. plate light (HDI)

45

Right rear turn signal

19

Running light (DOM)

93

Tail/ brake light

Brake light

Running light (HDI)

Left rear turn signal

18

7

94

Gnd 1

85 Rear fuel injector

84 Front fuel injector

87 Idle speed control actuator

46 Voltage regulator

Stator

83

A Front
B +12VDC
C Rear

Ignition coil

Spark plugs

Gnd 2

Circuit breaker 40A

128 Starter Motor

ECM Pwr 5A

Fuel pump 15A

78

1 2 3 4 5 6 7 8 9 10 11 12 13 14 15 16 17 18 19 20 21 22 23 24 25 26 27 28 29 30 31 32 33 34 35

135

118

62

ECM (EFI only-see next page for carb.)

86 85 30 87 87a
ECM power relay

86 85 30 87 87a
Fuel pump relay

86 85 30 87 87a
Starter relay

- + Battery

17

2001 FLHT AND FLTR SERIES (CONTINUED)

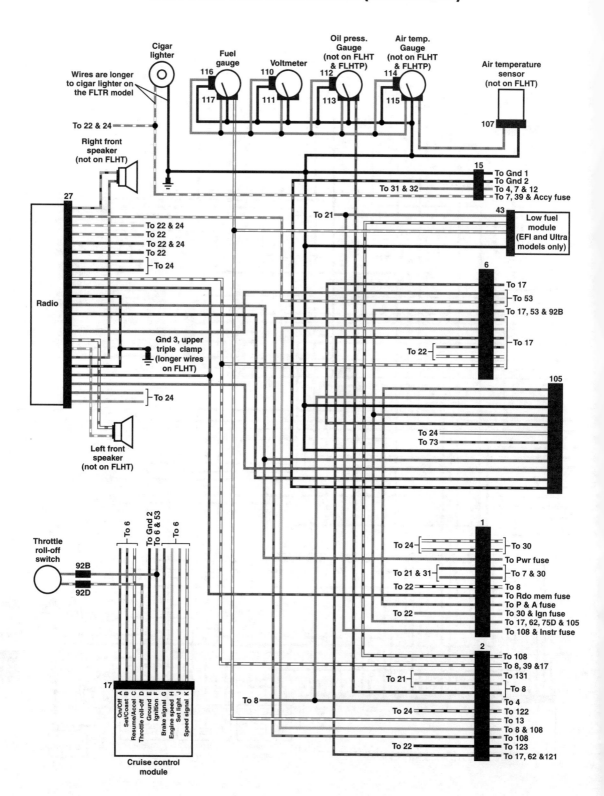

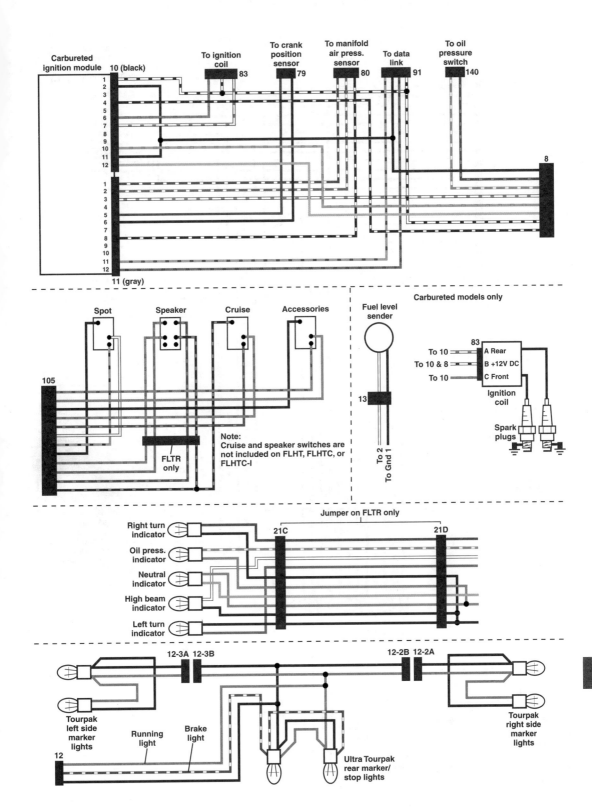

Carbureted ignition module   10 (black)

To ignition coil   83

To crank position sensor   79

To manifold air press. sensor   80

To data link   91

To oil pressure switch   140

11 (gray)

Spot   Speaker   Cruise   Accessories

105

FLTR only

Note:
Cruise and speaker switches are not included on FLHT, FLHTC, or FLHTC-I

Fuel level sender

13

To 2
To Gnd 1

Carbureted models only

To 10   A Rear
To 10 & 8   B +12V DC
To 10   C Front

83

Ignition coil

Spark plugs

Right turn indicator

Oil press. indicator

Neutral indicator

High beam indicator

Left turn indicator

Jumper on FLTR only

21C   21D

12-3A 12-3B   12-2B 12-2A

Tourpak left side marker lights

Running light

Brake light

Ultra Tourpak rear marker/ stop lights

Tourpak right side marker lights

12

17

2001 FLHT AND FLTR SERIES (CONTINUED)

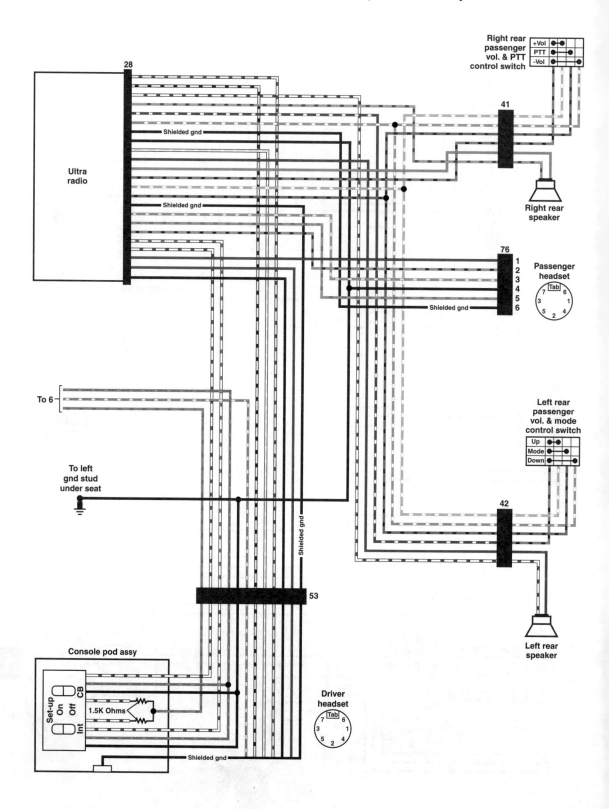

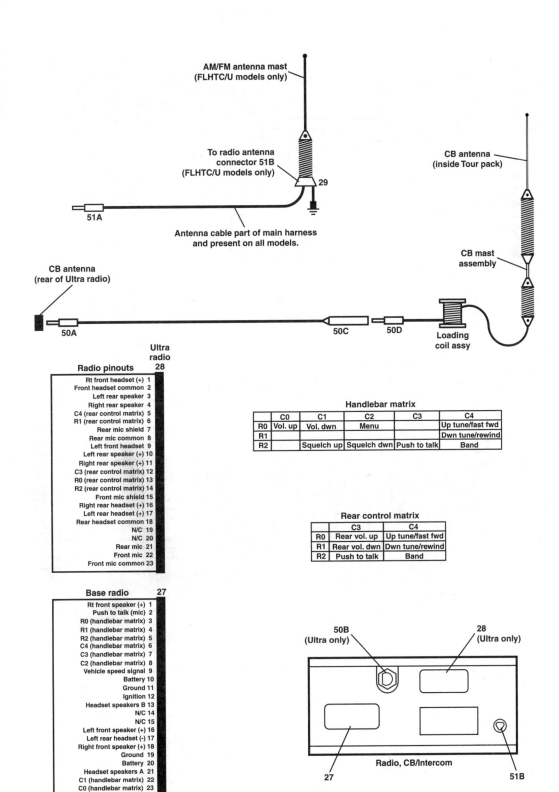

AM/FM antenna mast
(FLHTC/U models only)

To radio antenna
connector 51B
(FLHTC/U models only)

29

51A

Antenna cable part of main harness
and present on all models.

CB antenna
(inside Tour pack)

CB mast
assembly

CB antenna
(rear of Ultra radio)

50A   50C   50D

Loading
coil assy

Ultra
radio
Radio pinouts   **28**

Rt front headset (+) 1
Front headset common 2
Left rear speaker 3
Right rear speaker 4
C4 (rear control matrix) 5
R1 (rear control matrix) 6
Rear mic shield 7
Rear mic common 8
Left front headset 9
Left rear speaker (+) 10
Right rear speaker (+) 11
C3 (rear control matrix) 12
R0 (rear control matrix) 13
R2 (rear control matrix) 14
Front mic shield 15
Right rear headset (+) 16
Left rear headset (+) 17
Rear headset common 18
N/C 19
N/C 20
Rear mic 21
Front mic 22
Front mic common 23

Handlebar matrix

	C0	C1	C2	C3	C4
R0	Vol. up	Vol. dwn	Menu		Up tune/fast fwd
R1					Dwn tune/rewind
R2		Squelch up	Squelch dwn	Push to talk	Band

Rear control matrix

	C3	C4
R0	Rear vol. up	Up tune/fast fwd
R1	Rear vol. dwn	Dwn tune/rewind
R2	Push to talk	Band

Base radio   **27**

Rt front speaker (+) 1
Push to talk (mic) 2
R0 (handlebar matrix) 3
R1 (handlebar matrix) 4
R2 (handlebar matrix) 5
C4 (handlebar matrix) 6
C3 (handlebar matrix) 7
C2 (handlebar matrix) 8
Vehicle speed signal 9
Battery 10
Ground 11
Ignition 12
Headset speakers B 13
N/C 14
N/C 15
Left front speaker (+) 16
Left rear headset (-) 17
Right front speaker (+) 18
Ground 19
Battery 20
Headset speakers A 21
C1 (handlebar matrix) 22
C0 (handlebar matrix) 23

50B
(Ultra only)

28
(Ultra only)

17

Radio, CB/Intercom

27   51B

2002 FLHR SERIES

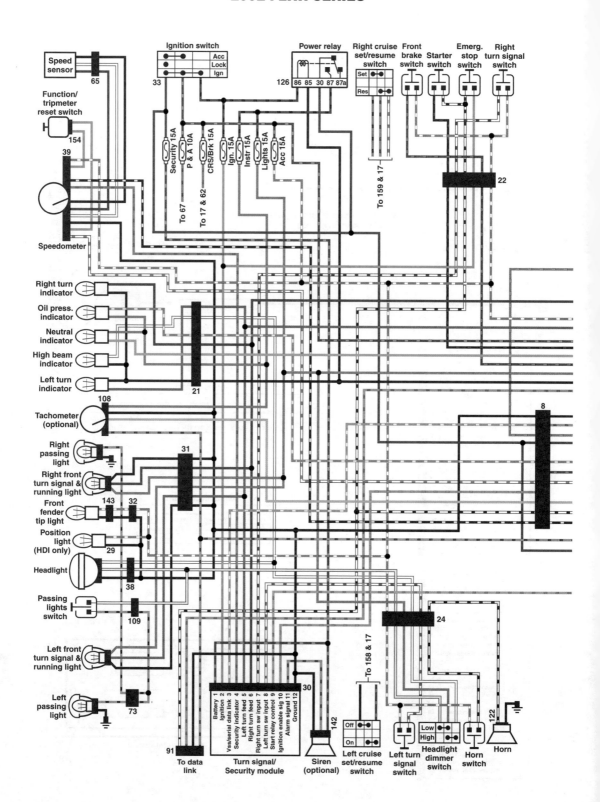

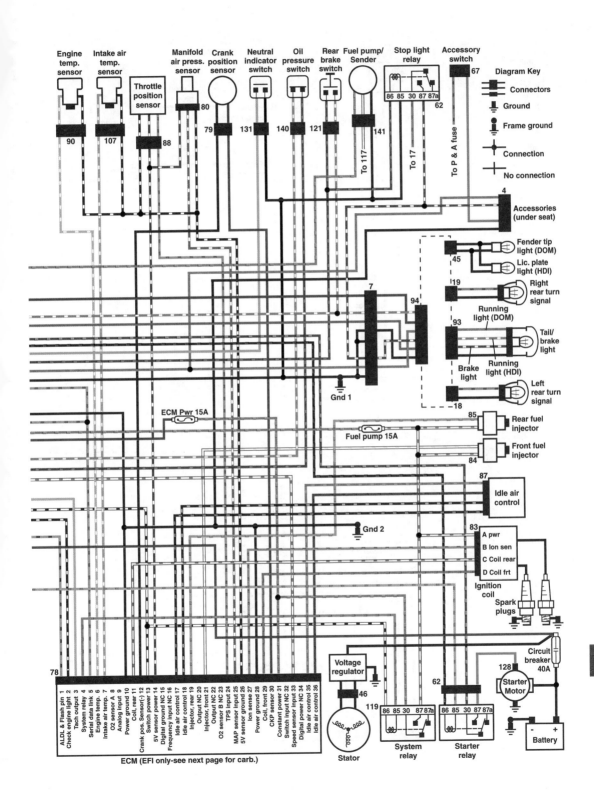

2002 FLHR SERIES (CONTINUED)

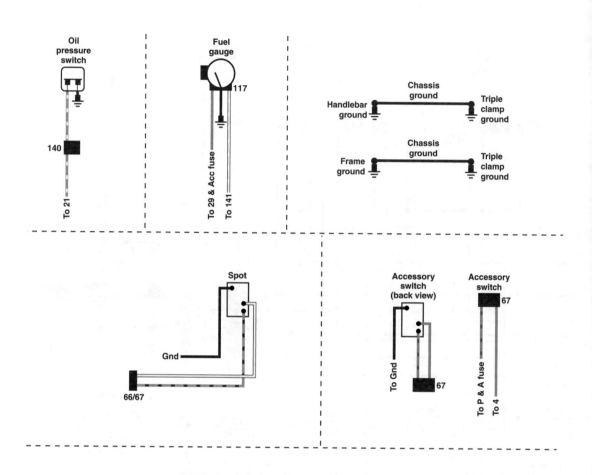

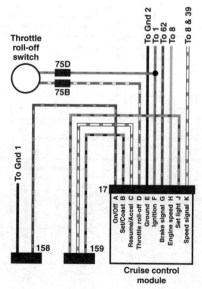

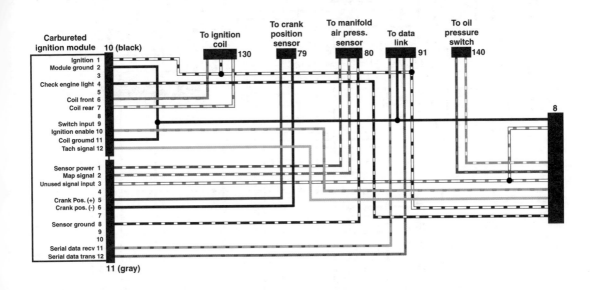

Carbureted
ignition module 10 (black)

To ignition
coil
130

To crank
position
sensor
79

To manifold
air press.
sensor
80

To data
link
91

To oil
pressure
switch
140

Ignition	1
Module ground	2
	3
Check engine light	4
	5
Coil front	6
Coil rear	7
	8
Switch input	9
Ignition enable	10
Coil groumd	11
Tach signal	12

8

Sensor power	1
Map signal	2
Unused signal input	3
	4
Crank Pos. (+)	5
Crank pos. (-)	6
	7
Sensor ground	8
	9
	10
Serial data recv	11
Serial data trans	12

11 (gray)

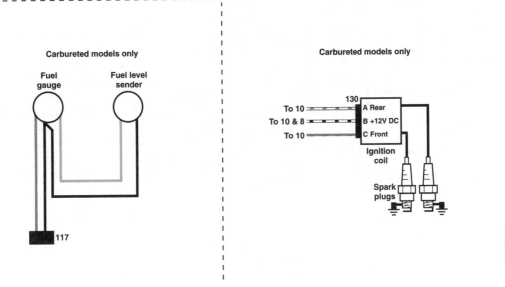

Carbureted models only

Fuel
gauge

Fuel level
sender

117

Carbureted models only

To 10 ▬ 130
To 10 & 8 ▬ A Rear
To 10 ▬ B +12V DC
C Front

Ignition
coil

Spark
plugs

17

2002 FLHT AND FLTR SERIES

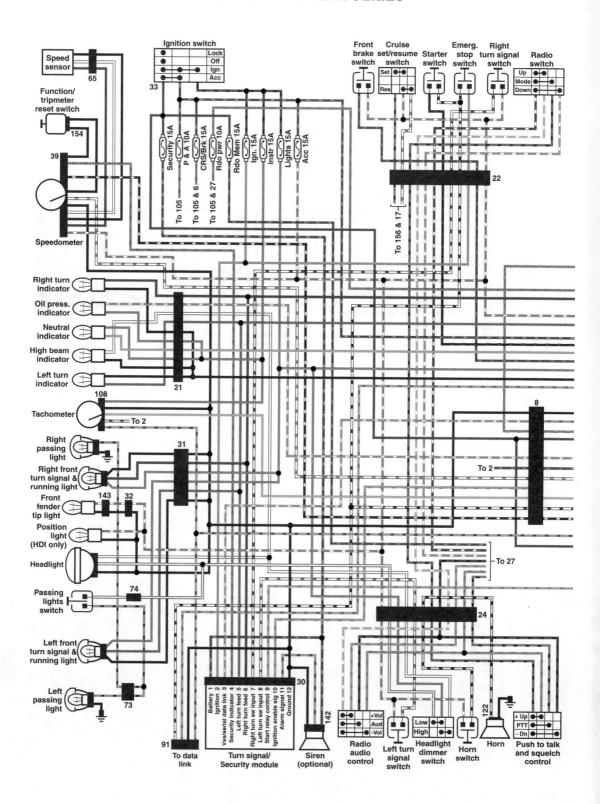

Engine temp. sensor

Intake air temp. sensor

Throttle position sensor

Manifold air press. sensor

Crank position sensor

Neutral indicator switch

Oil pressure switch

Rear brake switch

Fuel pump/ Sender

Stop light relay

To tour pack

Diagram Key

Connectors

Ground

Frame ground

Connection

No connection

90

107

88

80

79

131

140

121

141

13

86 85 30 87 87a

62

12

To 17

To 2

4

Accessories (under seat)

To 2

Fender tip light (DOM)

45

Lic. plate light (HDI)

19

Right rear turn signal

93

Running light (DOM)

Tail/ brake light

Brake light

Running light (HDI)

18

Left rear turn signal

7

94

Gnd 1

ECM Pwr 15A

Fuel pump 15A

85

Rear fuel injector

84

Front fuel injector

87

Idle air control

Gnd 2

83

A pwr

B Ion sen

C Coil rear

D Coil frt

Ignition coil

Spark plugs

Circuit breaker 40A

128

Starter Motor

78

Voltage regulator

46

119

123

Stator

System relay

86 85 30 87 87a

Starter relay

86 85 30 87 87a

Battery

- +

ECM (EFI only-see next page for carb.)

ALDL & Flash pin 1
Check engine light 2
Tach output 3
System relay 4
Serial data link 5
Engine temp. 6
Intake air temp. 7
O2 sensor A 8
Analog input 9
Power ground 10
Coil, rear 11
Crank pos. Sensor(-) 12
Switch power 13
Switch ground 14
Digital ground NC 15
Frequency input NC 16
Idle air control 17
Idle air control 18
Injector, rear 19
Output NC 20
Injector, front 21
Output NC 22
O2 sensor B NC 23
TPS Input 24
MAP sensor input 25
5V sensor ground 26
Ion sense 27
Power ground 28
Coil, front 29
CKP sensor 30
Constant power 31
Switch input NC 32
Speed sensor input 33
Digital power NC 34
Idle air control 35
Idle air control 36

17

2002 FLHT AND FLTR SERIES (CONTINUED)

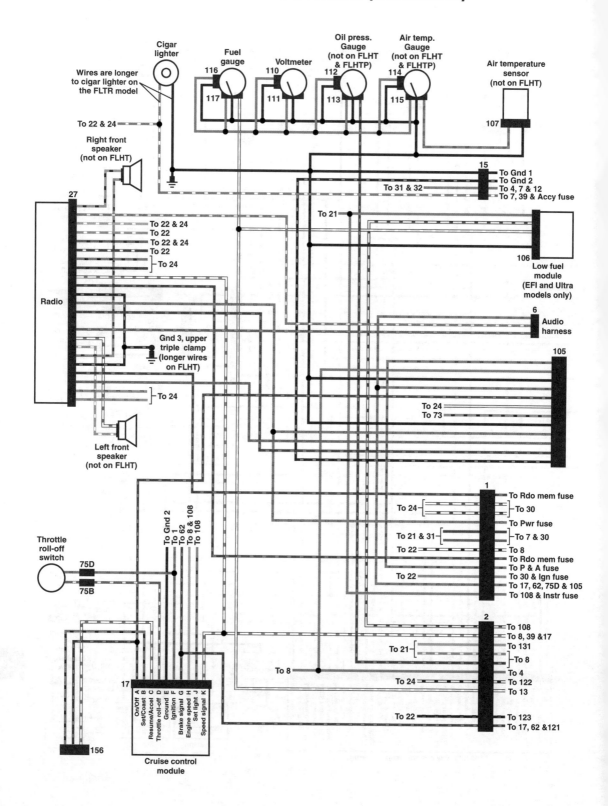

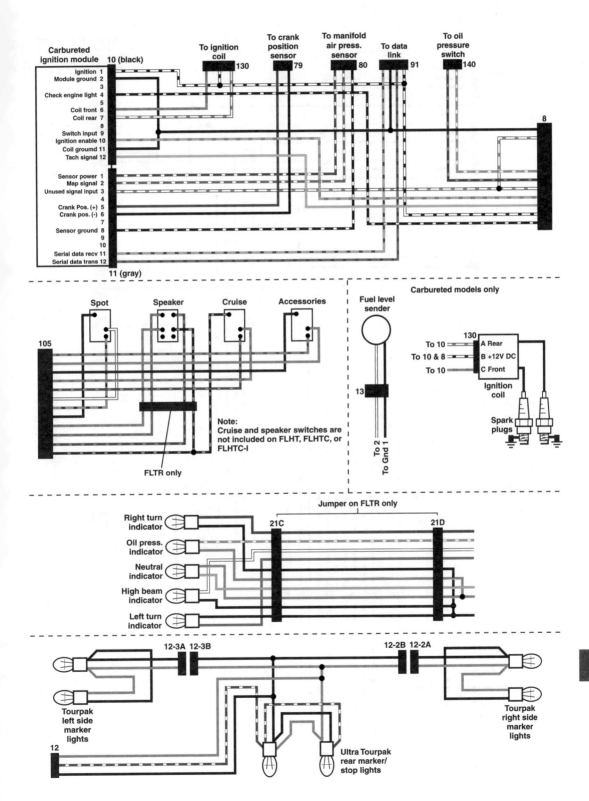

2002 FLHT AND FLTR SERIES (CONTINUED)

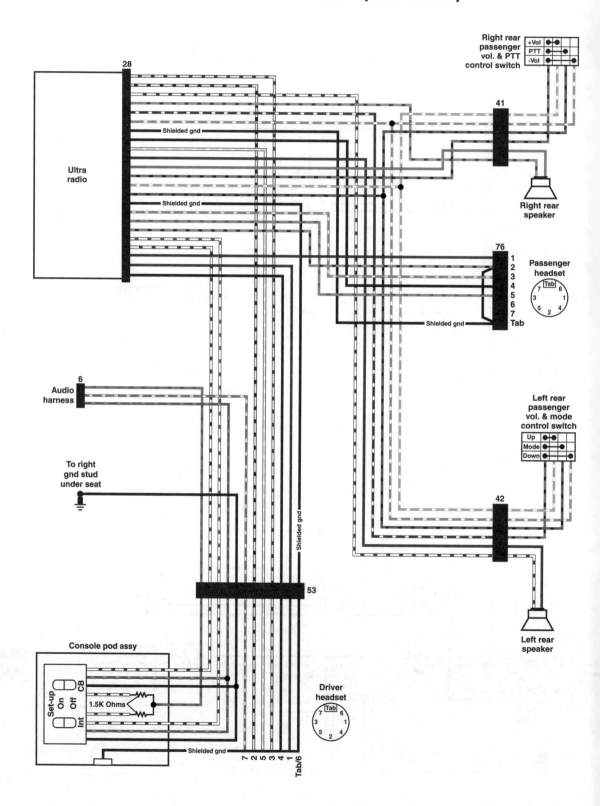

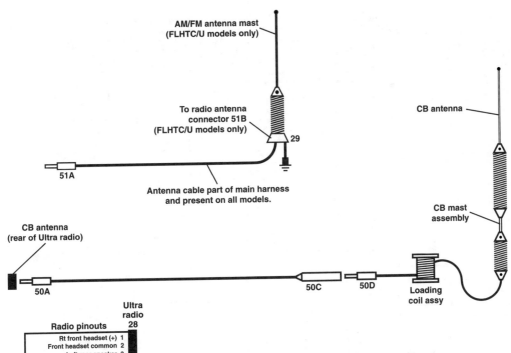

Radio pinouts

Ultra radio 28

- Rt front headset (+) 1
- Front headset common 2
- Left rear speaker 3
- Right rear speaker 4
- C4 (rear control matrix) 5
- R1 (rear control matrix) 6
- Rear mic shield 7
- Rear mic common 8
- Left front headset 9
- Left rear speaker (+) 10
- Right rear speaker (+) 11
- C3 (rear control matrix) 12
- R0 (rear control matrix) 13
- R2 (rear control matrix) 14
- Front mic shield 15
- Right rear headset (+) 16
- Left rear headset (+) 17
- Rear headset common 18
- N/C 19
- N/C 20
- Rear mic 21
- Front mic 22
- Front mic common 23

Handlebar matrix

	C0	C1	C2	C3	C4
R0	Vol. up	Vol. dwn	Menu		Up tune/fast fwd
R1					Dwn tune/rewind
R2		Squelch up	Squelch dwn	Push to talk	Band

Rear control matrix

	C3	C4
R0	Rear vol. up	Up tune/fast fwd
R1	Rear vol. dwn	Dwn tune/rewind
R2	Push to talk	Band

Base radio 27

- Rt front speaker (+) 1
- Push to talk (mic) 2
- R0 (handlebar matrix) 3
- R1 (handlebar matrix) 4
- R2 (handlebar matrix) 5
- C4 (handlebar matrix) 6
- C3 (handlebar matrix) 7
- C2 (handlebar matrix) 8
- Vehicle speed signal 9
- Battery 10
- Ground 11
- Ignition 12
- Headset speakers B 13
- N/C 14
- N/C 15
- Left front speaker (+) 16
- Left rear headset (-) 17
- Right front speaker (+) 18
- Ground 19
- Battery 20
- Headset speakers A 21
- C1 (handlebar matrix) 22
- C0 (handlebar matrix) 23

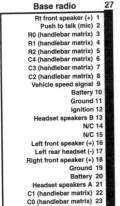
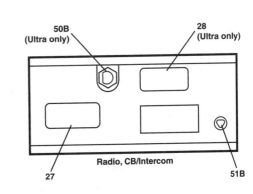

Radio, CB/Intercom

17

2003 FLHR SERIES

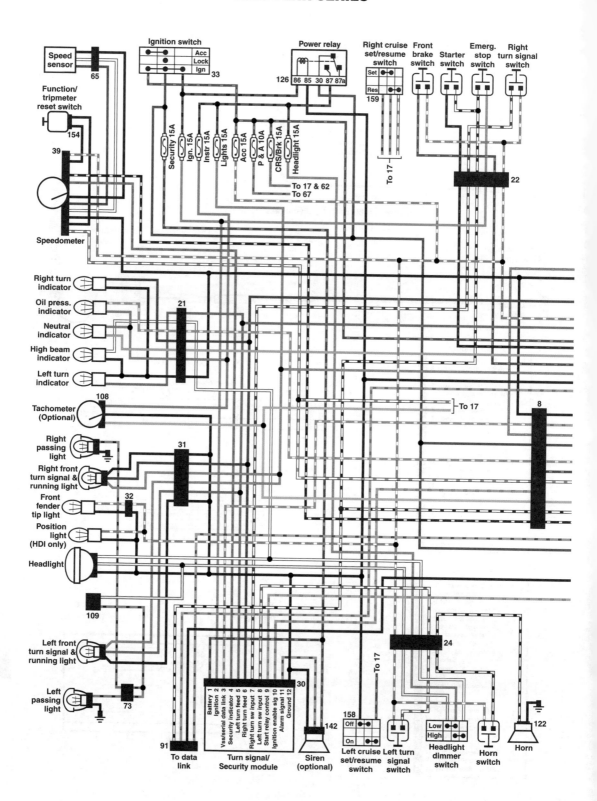

Engine temp. sensor

Intake air temp. sensor

Throttle position sensor

Manifold air press. sensor

Crank pos. sensor

Neutral indic. switch

Oil press. switch

Rear brake switch

Fuel Sender

Stop light relay

Diagram Key

- Connectors
- Ground
- Frame ground
- Connection
- No connection (NC)

90

89

88

80

79

131

140

121

141

To 117

To 17

62

86 85 30 87 87a

4

Accessories (under seat)

To 67

Gnd 2 (right)

45

Fender tip light (DOM)

Lic. plate light (HDI)

19

Right rear turn signal

Running light (DOM)

7

94

93

Tail/ brake light

Brake light

Running light (HDI)

18

Left rear turn signal

Gnd 1 (left)

ECM Pwr 15A

85

Rear fuel injector

Fuel pump 15A

84

Front fuel injector

87

Idle speed control actuator

46

Voltage regulator

Stator

83

A Power
B Ion sen
C Coil Rr
D Coil Frt

Ignition coil

Spark plugs

Circuit breaker 40A

128

Starter solenoid/ Motor

78

ALDL & Flash pin 1
Check engine LP 2
Tach output 3
System relay 4
Serial data link 5
Engine temp. 6
Intake air temp. 7
O2 sensor A 8
Analog input 9
Power ground 10
Coil, rear 11
Crank pos. Sensor(-) 12
Switch power 13
5V sensor power 14
Digital ground NC 15
Frequency input NC 16
Idle air control 17
Injector, rear 18
Idle air control 19
Output NC 20
Injector, front 21
Output NC 22
O2 sensor B NC 23
TPS input 24
MAP sensor input 25
5V sensor ground 26
Ion sense 27
Power ground 28
Coil, front 29
CKP sensor 30
Constant power 31
Switch input NC 32
Speed sensor input 33
Digital power NC 34
Idle air control 35
Idle air control 36

ECM (EFI only-see next page for carb.)

119

86 85 30 87 87a

System relay

62

86 85 30 87 87a

Starter relay

- +

Battery

17

2003 FLHR SERIES (CONTINUED)

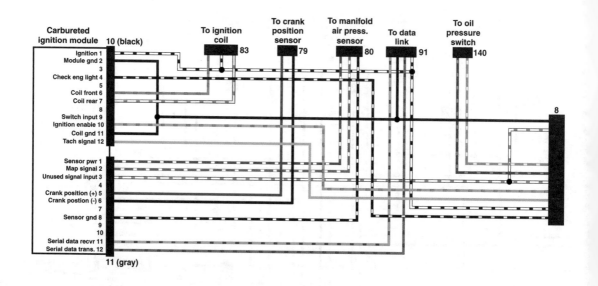

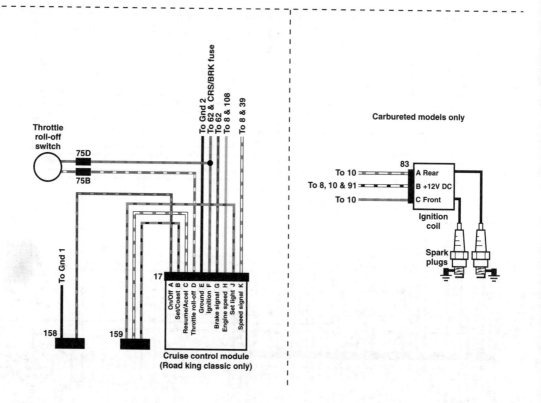

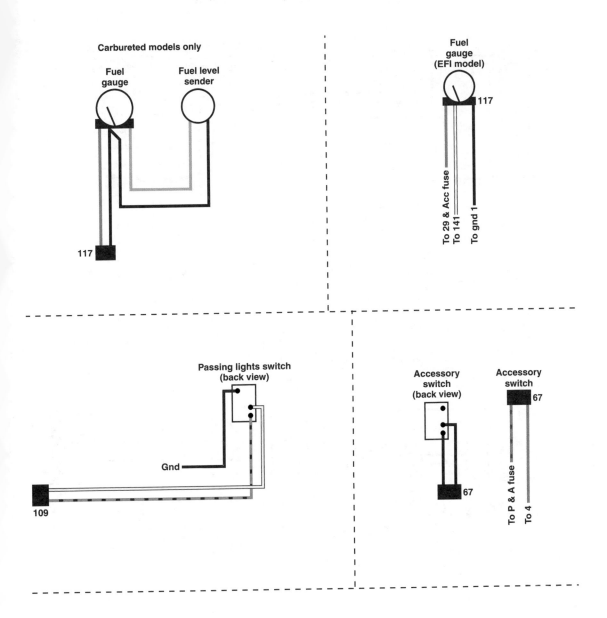

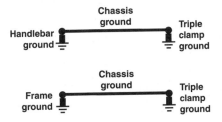

2003 FLHT AND FLTR SERIES

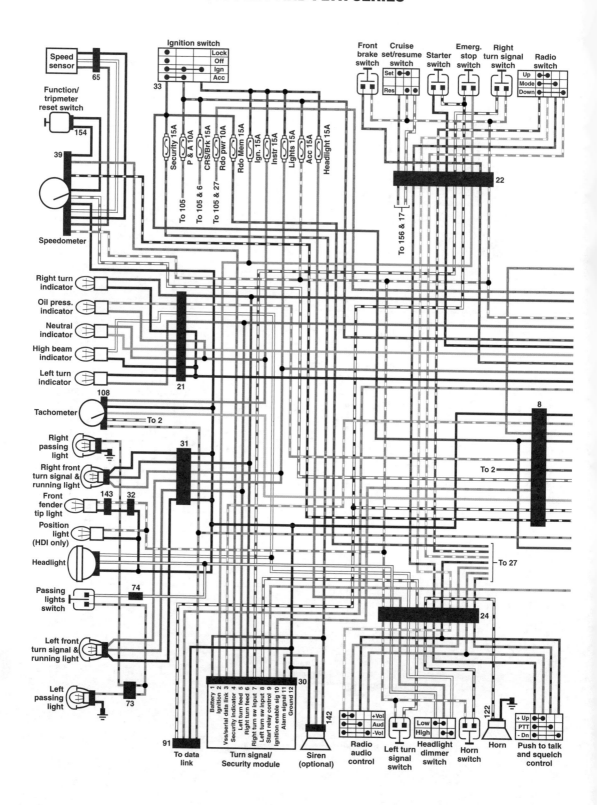

Engine temp. sensor

Intake air temp. sensor

Throttle position sensor

Manifold air press. sensor

Crank position sensor

Neutral indicator switch

Oil pressure switch

Rear brake switch

Fuel pump/ Sender

Stop light relay

To tour pack

12

Diagram Key

Connectors

Ground

Frame ground

Connection

No connection

90

107

88

80

79

131

140

121

141

13

86 85 30 87 87a

62

To 17

To 106

4

Accessories (under seat)

To 2

Fender tip light (DOM)

45

Lic. plate light (HDI)

I19

Right rear turn signal

Running light (DOM)

7

94

93

Tail/ brake light

Brake light

Running light (HDI)

Gnd 1

18

Left rear turn signal

ECM Pwr 15A

85

Rear fuel injector

Fuel pump 15A

84

Front fuel injector

87

Idle air control

Gnd 2

83

A pwr
B Ion sen
C Coil rear
D Coil frt

Ignition coil

Spark plugs

Circuit breaker 40A

128

Voltage regulator

46

123

Starter Motor

Battery

78

Flash pin 1
Check engine light 2
Tach output 3
System relay 4
Serial data link 5
Engine temp. 6
Intake air temp. 7
O2 sensor input NC 8
Bank angle NC 9
Power ground 10
Coil, rear 11
CKP sensor 12
Switch power 13
5V sensor power 14
Digital ground NC 15
Frequency input NC 16
Idle air control 17
Idle air control 18
Injector, rear 19
Flash pin NC 20
Injector, front 21
HDI solenoid NC 22
Analog/O2 input NC 23
TPS input 24
MAP sensor input 25
5V sensor ground 26
Ion sense 27
Power ground 28
Coil, front 29
CKP sensor 30
Constant power 31
Switch input NC 32
Speed sensor input 33
Digital power NC 34
Idle air control 35
Idle air control 36

ECM (EFI only-see next page for carb.)

Stator

86 85 30 87 87a

System relay

86 85 30 87 87a

Starter relay

- +

17

2003 FLHT AND FLTR SERIES (CONTINUED)

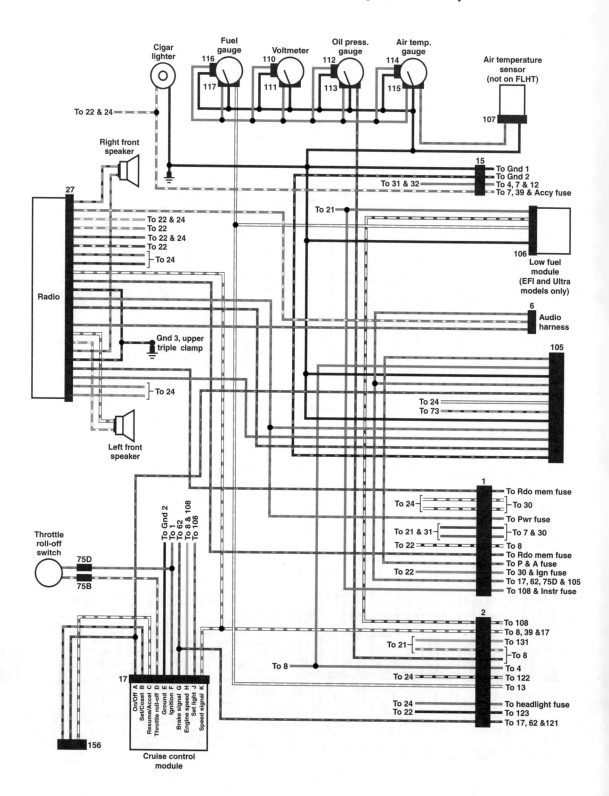

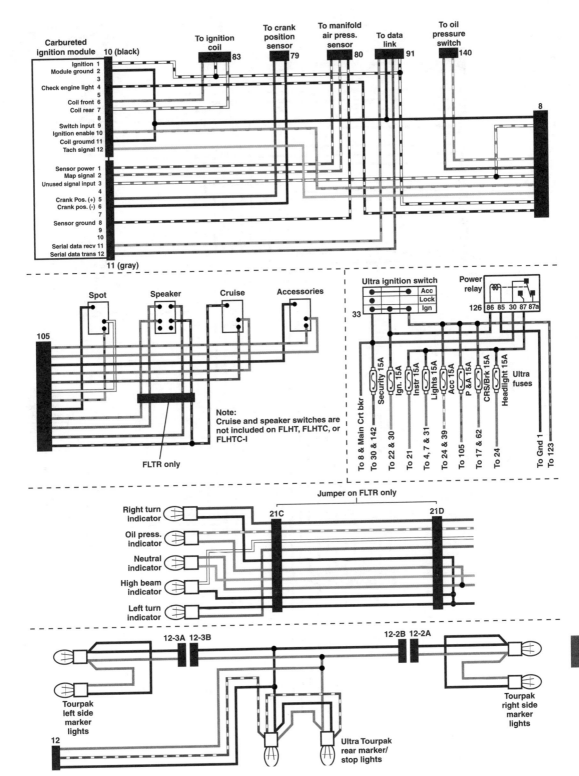

Carbureted ignition module 10 (black)

Pin	Label
1	Ignition
2	Module ground
3	
4	Check engine light
5	
6	Coil front
7	Coil rear
8	
9	Switch input
10	Ignition enable
11	Coil groumd
12	Tach signal

Pin	Label
1	Sensor power
2	Map signal
3	Unused signal input
4	
5	Crank Pos. (+)
6	Crank pos. (-)
7	
8	Sensor ground
9	
10	
11	Serial data recv
12	Serial data trans

11 (gray)

To ignition coil 83
To crank position sensor 79
To manifold air press. sensor 80
To data link 91
To oil pressure switch 140

8

Spot
Speaker
Cruise
Accessories

105

Note:
Cruise and speaker switches are not included on FLHT, FLHTC, or FLHTC-I

FLTR only

Ultra ignition switch
Acc
Lock
Ign
33
126
Power relay
86 85 30 87 87a

Security 15A
Ign. 15A
Instr 15A
Lights 15A
Acc 15A
P &A 15A
CRS/Brk 15A
Headlight 15A
Ultra fuses

To 8 & Main Crt bkr
To 30 & 142
To 22 & 30
To 21
To 4, 7 & 31
To 24 & 39
To 105
To 17 & 62
To 24
To Gnd 1
To 123

Jumper on FLTR only

Right turn indicator
Oil press. indicator
Neutral indicator
High beam indicator
Left turn indicator

21C
21D

12-3A 12-3B
12-2B 12-2A

Tourpak left side marker lights
12

Ultra Tourpak rear marker/ stop lights

Tourpak right side marker lights

17

2003 FLHT AND FLTR SERIES (CONTINUED)

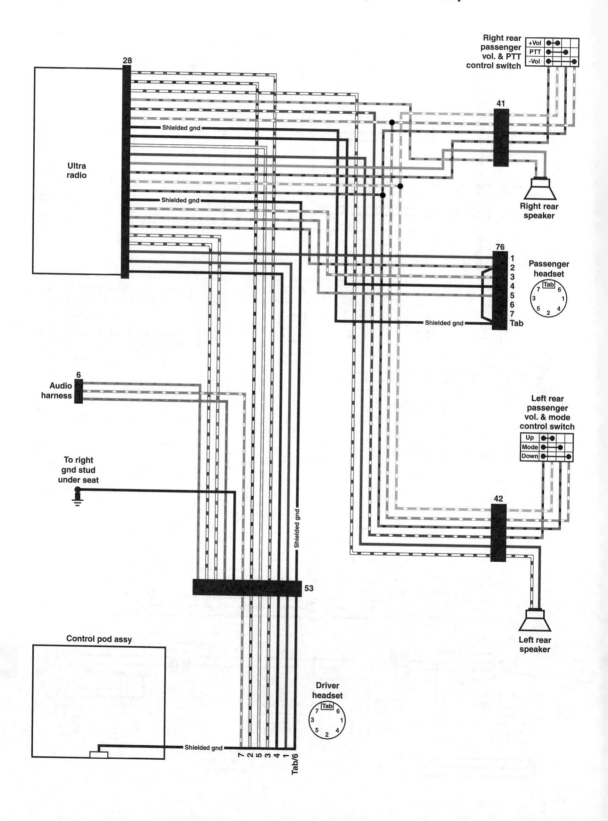

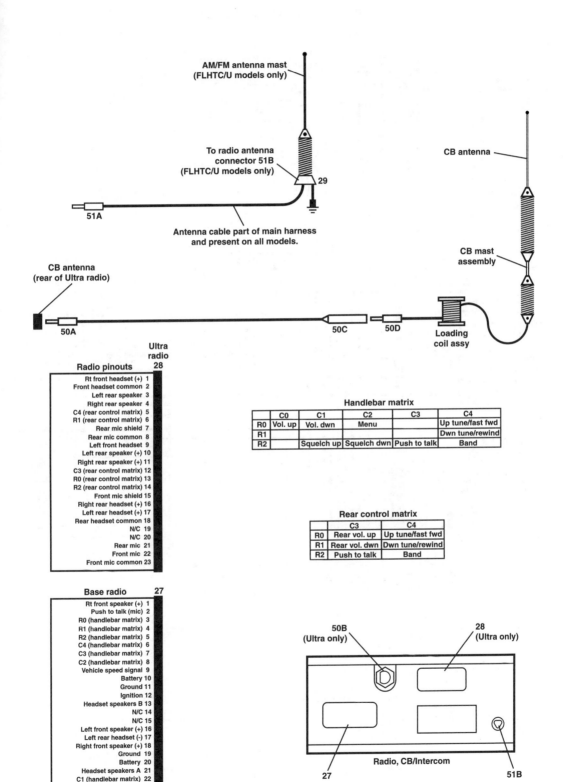

AM/FM antenna mast
(FLHTC/U models only)

To radio antenna
connector 51B
(FLHTC/U models only)

29

51A

Antenna cable part of main harness
and present on all models.

CB antenna

CB mast
assembly

CB antenna
(rear of Ultra radio)

50A

50C

50D

Loading
coil assy

Ultra
radio
28

Radio pinouts

Rt front headset (+)	1
Front headset common	2
Left rear speaker	3
Right rear speaker	4
C4 (rear control matrix)	5
R1 (rear control matrix)	6
Rear mic shield	7
Rear mic common	8
Left front headset	9
Left rear speaker (+)	10
Right rear speaker (+)	11
C3 (rear control matrix)	12
R0 (rear control matrix)	13
R2 (rear control matrix)	14
Front mic shield	15
Right rear headset (+)	16
Left rear headset (+)	17
Rear headset common	18
N/C	19
N/C	20
Rear mic	21
Front mic	22
Front mic common	23

Handlebar matrix

	C0	C1	C2	C3	C4
R0	Vol. up	Vol. dwn	Menu		Up tune/fast fwd
R1					Dwn tune/rewind
R2		Squelch up	Squelch dwn	Push to talk	Band

Rear control matrix

	C3	C4
R0	Rear vol. up	Up tune/fast fwd
R1	Rear vol. dwn	Dwn tune/rewind
R2	Push to talk	Band

Base radio 27

Rt front speaker (+)	1
Push to talk (mic)	2
R0 (handlebar matrix)	3
R1 (handlebar matrix)	4
R2 (handlebar matrix)	5
C4 (handlebar matrix)	6
C3 (handlebar matrix)	7
C2 (handlebar matrix)	8
Vehicle speed signal	9
Battery	10
Ground	11
Ignition	12
Headset speakers B	13
N/C	14
N/C	15
Left front speaker (+)	16
Left rear headset (-)	17
Right front speaker (+)	18
Ground	19
Battery	20
Headset speakers A	21
C1 (handlebar matrix)	22
C0 (handlebar matrix)	23

50B
(Ultra only)

28
(Ultra only)

Radio, CB/Intercom

27

51B

17

2004-2005 FLHR SERIES

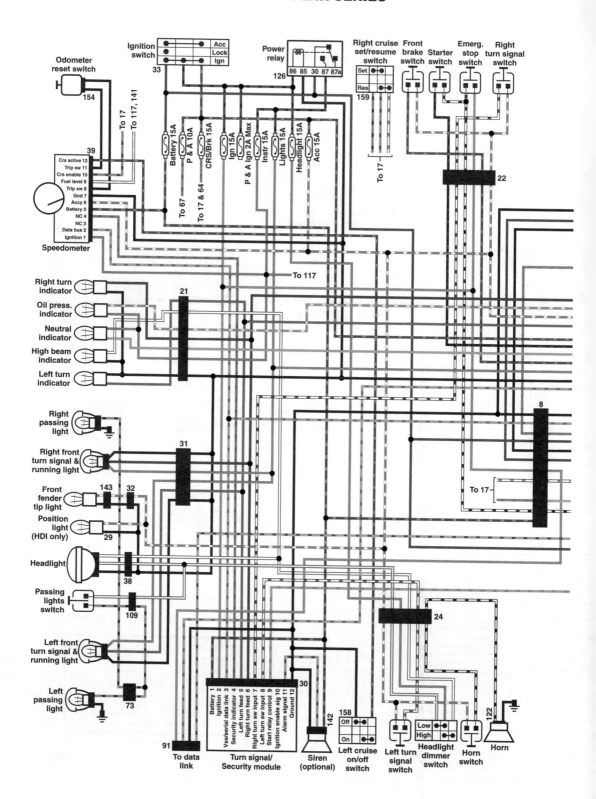

Engine temp. sensor · Intake air temp. sensor · Throttle position sensor · Manifold air press. sensor · Crank position sensor · Speed sensor · Oil press. switch · Rear brake switch · Fuel pump/Sender (EFI only) · Neutral indicator switch · Stop light relay · To accy switch

Diagram Key
Connectors
Ground
Frame ground
Connection
No connection (NC)

To 17
To P & A fuse
Accessory connector
Fender tip light (DOM)
Lic. plate light (HDI)
Right rear turn signal
Running light (DOM)
Tail/brake light
Brake light · Running light (HDI)
Left rear turn signal

Gnd 1 (left)
ECM Pwr 15A
Fuel pump 15A
Rear fuel injector
Front fuel injector
Idle air control actuator
Gnd 2 (right)

A pwr
B Ion sen
C Coil rear
D Coil frt
Ignition coil
Spark plugs

Maxi-fuse 40A
Voltage regulator
Starter Motor
Battery
Stator
System relay
Starter relay

ECM (EFI only-see next page for carb.)

17

2004-2005 FLHR SERIES (CONTINUED)

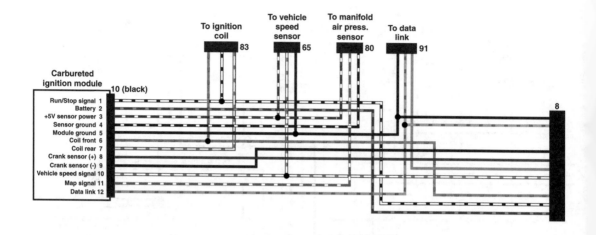

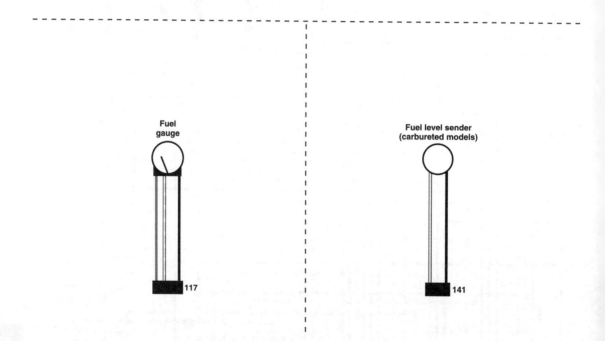

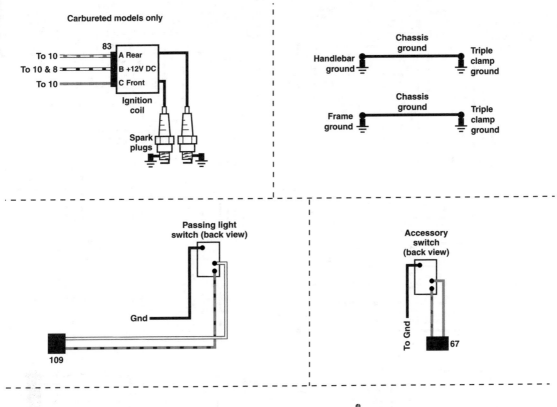

Carbureted models only

To 10
To 10 & 8
To 10

83
A Rear
B +12V DC
C Front

Ignition coil

Spark plugs

Chassis ground

Handlebar ground

Triple clamp ground

Chassis ground

Frame ground

Triple clamp ground

Passing light switch (back view)

Gnd

109

Accessory switch (back view)

To Gnd

67

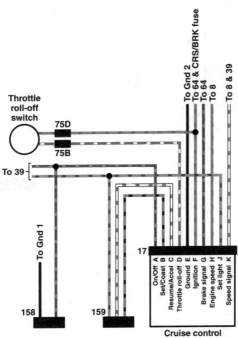

Throttle roll-off switch

75D

75B

To 39

To Gnd 2
To 64 & CRS/BRK fuse
To 64
To 8
To 8 & 39

To Gnd 1

17

On/Off A
Set/Coast B
Resume/Accel C
Throttle roll-off D
Ground E
Ignition F
Brake signal G
Engine speed H
Set light J
Speed signal K

158

159

Cruise control

17

2004-2005 FLHT AND FLTR SERIES

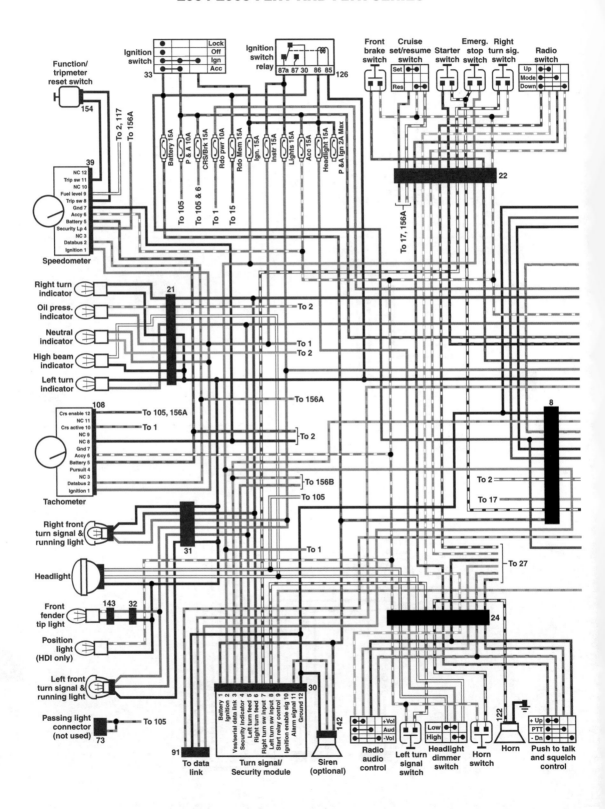

Engine temp. sensor

Intake air temp. sensor

Throttle position sensor

Manifold air press. sensor

Crank position sensor

Speed sensor

Oil press. switch

Rear brake switch

Fuel pump/ Sender

Neutral indicator switch

Stop light relay

To tour pack

12

90

89

88

80

79

65

140

121

141

13

131

64

Diagram Key

Connectors

Ground

Frame ground

Connection

No connection (NC)

To 2

To 2

To 2

To 17

To 1

To 2

4

Accessory connector

Fender tip light (DOM)

Lic. plate light (HDI)

45

19

Right rear turn signal

Running light (DOM)

93

Tail/ brake light

Brake light

Running light (HDI)

Left rear turn signal

18

7

94

Gnd 1 (left)

ECM Pwr 15A

Fuel pump 15A

85

Rear fuel injector

Front fuel injector

84

87

Idle air control actuator

83

Gnd 2 (right)

A pwr
B Ion sen
C Coil rear
D Coil frt

Ignition coil

Spark plugs

B+
106

77

Maxi-fuse 40A

128

Starter Motor

123

78

Voltage regulator

46

119

System relay

Starter relay

Battery

Stator

ECM (EFI only—see next page for carb.)

ALDL & Flash pin 1
Check engine LP 2
Tach output 3
System relay 4
Serial data link 5
Engine temp. 6
Intake air temp. 7
O2 sensor A 8
Analog input 9
Power ground 10
Coil, rear 11
Crank pos. Sensor(-) 12
Switch power 13
5V sensor power 14
Digital ground NC 15
Frequency input NC 16
Idle air control 17
Idle air control 18
Injector, rear 19
Output NC 20
Injector, front 21
Output NC 22
O2 sensor B NC 23
TPS input 24
MAP sensor input 25
5V sensor ground 26
Ion sense 27
Power ground 28
Coil, front 29
Constant power 30
Switch input NC 31
Speed sensor input 32
Digital power NC 34
Idle air control 35
Idle air control 36

1 2 3 5 4

86 85 30 87 87a

- +

2004-2005 FLHT AND FLTR SERIES (CONTINUED)

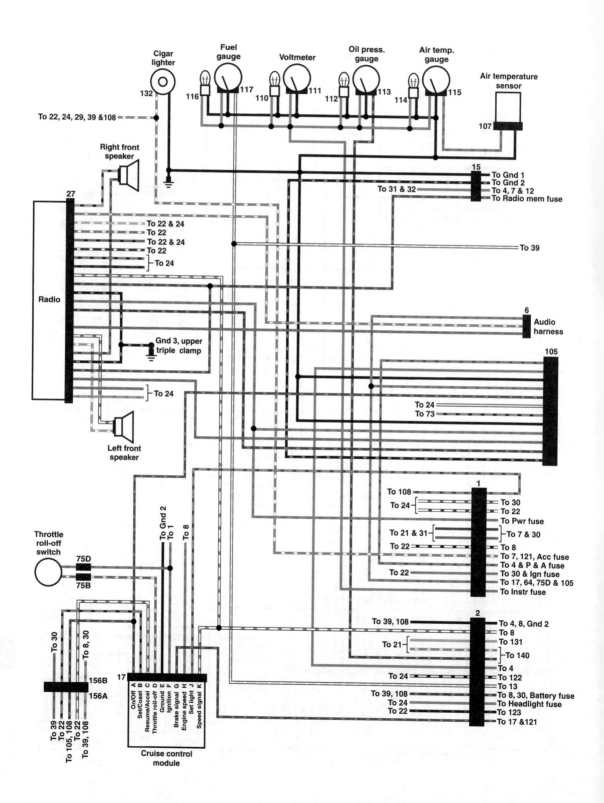

Carbureted ignition module 10 (black)

To ignition coil 83

To vehicle speed sensor 65

To manifold air press. sensor 80

To data link 91

Run/Stop signal 1
Battery 2
+5V sensor power 3
Sensor ground 4
Module ground 5
Coil front 6
Coil rear 7
Crank sensor (+) 8
Crank sensor (-) 9
Vehicle speed signal 10
Map signal 11
Data link 12

8

Spot

Speaker

Cruise

Accessories

105

FLTR only

Note:
Cruise and speaker switches are not included on FLHT, FLHTC, or FLHTC-I.

Fuel level sender

141

To 2
To Gnd 1

Carbureted models only

To 10
83
A Rear
To 8 & 10
B +12V DC
C Front

Ignition coil

Spark plugs

Separate turn signal connectors used on FLTRI model only

31R
Right front turn signal & running light
To 21

To lights fuse

31L
Left front turn signal & running light
To 21

Frame grounds

To 15

Right hand ground stud
To 2, 4, 8, 17, 30, 142

Left hand ground stud
To 7, 12, 13, 64, 122, 126, 131

Ignition switch (international)

Lock
Off
Ign
Acc
33C/D

Jumper harness

33B

12-3A 12-3B

12-2B 12-2A

Tourpak left side marker lights

12

Ultra Tourpak rear marker/ stop lights

Tourpak right side marker lights

17

2004-2005 FLHT AND FLTR SERIES (CONTINUED)

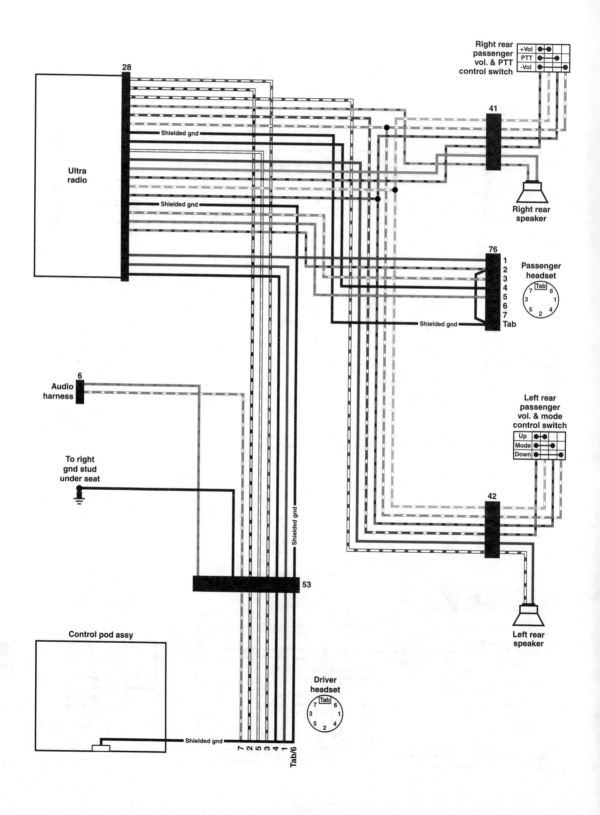

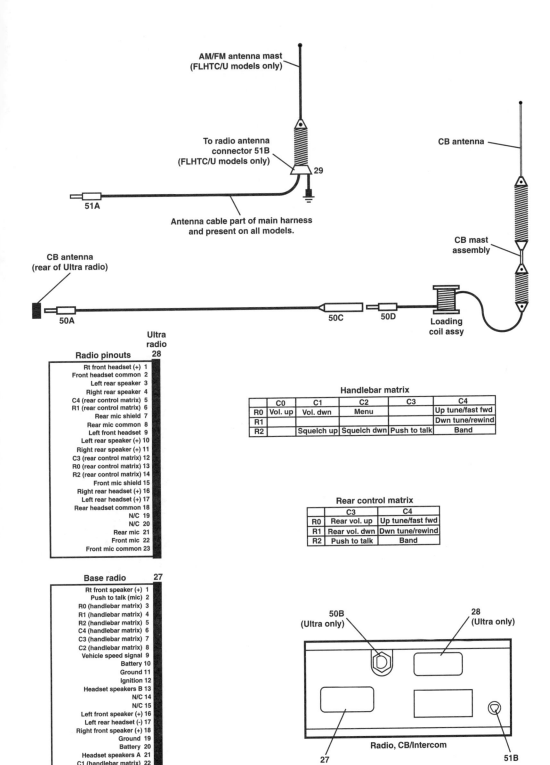

AM/FM antenna mast
(FLHTC/U models only)

To radio antenna
connector 51B
(FLHTC/U models only)

29

51A

Antenna cable part of main harness
and present on all models.

CB antenna

CB antenna
(rear of Ultra radio)

CB mast
assembly

50A

50C

50D

Loading
coil assy

**Ultra
radio
28**

Radio pinouts

Rt front headset (+)	1
Front headset common	2
Left rear speaker	3
Right rear speaker	4
C4 (rear control matrix)	5
R1 (rear control matrix)	6
Rear mic shield	7
Rear mic common	8
Left front headset	9
Left rear speaker (+)	10
Right rear speaker (+)	11
C3 (rear control matrix)	12
R0 (rear control matrix)	13
R2 (rear control matrix)	14
Front mic shield	15
Right rear headset (+)	16
Left rear headset (+)	17
Rear headset common	18
N/C	19
N/C	20
Rear mic	21
Front mic	22
Front mic common	23

Handlebar matrix

	C0	C1	C2	C3	C4
R0	Vol. up	Vol. dwn	Menu		Up tune/fast fwd
R1					Dwn tune/rewind
R2		Squelch up	Squelch dwn	Push to talk	Band

Rear control matrix

	C3	C4
R0	Rear vol. up	Up tune/fast fwd
R1	Rear vol. dwn	Dwn tune/rewind
R2	Push to talk	Band

Base radio   27

Rt front speaker (+)	1
Push to talk (mic)	2
R0 (handlebar matrix)	3
R1 (handlebar matrix)	4
R2 (handlebar matrix)	5
C4 (handlebar matrix)	6
C3 (handlebar matrix)	7
C2 (handlebar matrix)	8
Vehicle speed signal	9
Battery	10
Ground	11
Ignition	12
Headset speakers B	13
N/C	14
N/C	15
Left front speaker (+)	16
Left rear headset (-)	17
Right front speaker (+)	18
Ground	19
Battery	20
Headset speakers A	21
C1 (handlebar matrix)	22
C0 (handlebar matrix)	23

50B
(Ultra only)

28
(Ultra only)

Radio, CB/Intercom

27

51B

17

NOTES

NOTES

NOTES

NOTES

NOTES

MAINTENANCE LOG

Date	Miles	Type of Service

Check out *clymer.com* for our full line of powersport repair manuals.

BMW

M308	500 & 600cc Twins, 55-69
M502-3	BMW R50/5-R100GS PD, 70-96
M500-3	BMW K-Series, 85-97
M501-3	K1200RS, GT & LT, 98-10
M503-3	R850, R1100, R1150 & R1200C, 93-05
M309	F650, 1994-2000

HARLEY-DAVIDSON

M419	Sportsters, 59-85
M429-5	XL/XLH Sportster, 86-03
M427-4	XL Sportster, 04-13
M418	Panheads, 48-65
M420	Shovelheads,66-84
M421-3	FLS/FXS Evolution,84-99
M423-2	FLS/FXS Twin Cam, 00-05
M250	FLS/FXS/FXC Softail, 06-09
M422-3	FLH/FLT/FXR Evolution, 84-98
M430-4	FLH/FLT Twin Cam, 99-05
M252	FLH/FLT, 06-09
M426	VRSC Series, 02-07
M424-2	FXD Evolution, 91-98
M425-3	FXD Twin Cam, 99-05
M254	Dyna Series, 06-11

HONDA

ATVs

M316	Odyssey FL250, 77-84
M311	ATC, TRX & Fourtrax 70-125, 70-87
M433	Fourtrax 90, 93-00
M326	ATC185 & 200, 80-86
M347	ATC200X & Fourtrax 200SX, 86-88
M455	ATC250 & Fourtrax 200/250, 84-87
M342	ATC250R, 81-84
M348	TRX250R/Fourtrax 250R & ATC250R, 85-89
M456-4	TRX250X 87-92; TRX300EX 93-06
M446-3	TRX250 Recon & Recon ES, 97-07
M215-2	TTRX250EX Sportrax and TRX250X, 01-12
M346-3	TRX300/Fourtrax 300 & TRX300FW/Fourtrax 4x4, 88-00
M200-2	TRX350 Rancher, 00-06
M459-3	TRX400 Foreman 95-03
M454-5	TRX400EX Fourtrax & Sportrax 99-13
M201	TRX450R & TRX450ER, 04-09
M205	TRX450 Foreman, 98-04
M210	TRX500 Rubicon, 01-04
M206	TRX500 Foreman, 05-11

Singles

M310-13	50-110cc OHC Singles, 65-99
M315	100-350cc OHC, 69-82
M317	125-250cc Elsinore, 73-80
M442	CR60-125R Pro-Link, 81-88
M431-2	CR80R, 89-95, CR125R, 89-91
M435	CR80R &CR80RB, 96-02
M457-2	CR125R, 92-97; CR250R, 92-96
M464	CR125R, 1998-2002
M443	CR250R-500R Pro-Link, 81-87
M432-3	CR250R, 88-91 & CR500R, 88-01
M437	CR250R, 97-01
M352	CRF250R, CRF250X, CRF450R & CRF450X, 02-05
M319-3	XR50R, CRF50F, XR70R & CRF70F, 97-09
M312-14	XL/XR75-100, 75-91
M222	XR80R, CRF80F, XR100R, & CRF100F, 92-09
M318-4	XL/XR/TLR 125-200, 79-03
M328-4	XL/XR250, 78-00; XL/XR350R 83-85; XR200R, 84-85; XR250L, 91-96
M320-2	XR400R, 96-04
M221	XR600R, 91-07; XR650L, 93-07
M339-8	XL/XR 500-600, 79-90
M225	XR650R, 00-07

Twins

M321	125-200cc Twins, 65-78
M322	250-350cc Twins, 64-74
M323	250-360cc Twins, 74-77
M324-5	Twinstar, Rebel 250 & Nighthawk 250, 78-03
M334	400-450cc Twins, 78-87
M333	450 & 500cc Twins, 65-76
M335	CX & GL500/650, 78-83
M344	VT500, 83-88
M313	VT700 & 750, 83-87
M314-3	VT750 Shadow Chain Drive, 98-06
M440	VT1100C Shadow, 85-96
M460-4	VT1100 Series, 95-07
M230	VTX1800 Series, 02-08
M231	VTX1300 Series, 03-09

Fours

M332	CB350-550, SOHC, 71-78
M345	CB550 & 650, 83-85
M336	CB650,79-82
M341	CB750 SOHC, 69-78
M337	CB750 DOHC, 79-82
M436	CB750 Nighthawk, 91-93 & 95-99
M325	CB900, 1000 & 1100, 80-83
M439	600 Hurricane, 87-90
M441-2	CBR600F2 & F3, 91-98
M445-2	CBR600F4, 99-06
M220	CBR600RR, 03-06
M434-2	CBR900RR Fireblade, 93-99
M329	500cc V-Fours, 84-86
M349	700-1000cc Interceptor, 83-85
M458-2	VFR700F-750F, 86-97
M438	VFR800FI Interceptor, 98-00
M327	700-1100cc V-Fours, 82-88
M508	ST1100/Pan European, 90-02
M340	GL1000 & 1100, 75-83
M504	GL1200, 84-87

Sixes

M505	GL1500 Gold Wing, 88-92
M506-2	GL1500 Gold Wing, 93-00
M507-3	GL1800 Gold Wing, 01-10
M462-2	GL1500C Valkyrie, 97-03

KAWASAKI

ATVs

M465-3	Bayou KLF220 & KLF250, 88-10
M466-4	Bayou KLF300, 86-04
M467	Bayou KLF400, 93-99
M470	Lakota KEF300, 95-99
M385-2	Mojave KSF250, 87-04

Singles

M350-9	80-350cc Rotary Valve, 66-01
M444-2	KX60, 83-02; KX80 83-90
M448-2	KX80, 91-00; KX85, 01-10 & KX100, 89-09
M351	KDX200, 83-88
M447-3	KX125 & KX250, 82-91; KX500, 83-04
M472-2	KX125, 92-00
M473-2	KX250, 92-00
M474-3	KLR650, 87-07
M240-2	KLR650, 08-12

Twins

M355	KZ400, KZ/Z440, EN450 & EN500, 74-95
M241	Ninja 250R (EX250), 88-12
M360-3	EX500, GPZ500S, & Ninja 500R, 87-02
M356-5	Vulcan 700 & 750, 85-06
M354-3	Vulcan 800, 95-05
M246	Vulcan 900, 06-12
M357-2	Vulcan 1500, 87-99
M471-3	Vulcan 1500 Series, 96-08
M245	Vulcan 1600 Series, 03-08

Fours

M449	KZ500/550 & ZX550, 79-85
M450	KZ, Z & ZX750, 80-85
M358	KZ650, 77-83
M359-3	Z & KZ 900-1000cc, 73-81
M451-3	KZ, ZX & ZN 1000 &1100cc, 81-02
M452-3	ZX500 & Ninja ZX600, 85-97
M468-2	Ninja ZX-6, 90-04
M469	Ninja ZX-7, ZX7R & ZX7RR, 91-98
M453-3	Ninja ZX900, ZX1000 & ZX1100, 84-01
M409-2	Concours, 86-06

POLARIS

ATVs

M496	3-, 4- and 6-Wheel Models w/250-425cc Engines, 85-95
M362-2	Magnum & Big Boss, 96-99
M363	Scrambler 500 4X4, 97-00
M365-5	Sportsman/Xplorer, 96-13
M366	Sportsman 600/700/800 Twins, 02-10
M367	Predator 500, 03-07

SUZUKI

ATVs

M381	ALT/LT 125 & 185, 83-87
M475	LT230 & LT250, 85-90
M380-2	LT250R Quad Racer, 85-92
M483-2	LT-4WD, LT-F4WDX & LT-F250, 87-98
M270-2	LT-Z400, 03-08
M343-2	LT-F500F Quadrunner, 98-02

Singles

M369	125-400cc, 64-81
M371	RM50-400 Twin Shock, 75-81
M379	RM125-500 Single Shock, 81-88
M386	RM80-250, 89-95
M400	RM125, 96-00
M401	RM250, 96-02
M476	DR250-350, 90-94
M477-4	DR-Z400E, S & SM, 00-12
M272	DR650, 96-12
M384-5	LS650 Savage/S40, 86-12

Twins

M372	GS400-450 Chain Drive, 77-87
M484-3	GS500E Twins, 89-02
M361	SV650, 1999-2002
M481-6	VS700-800 Intruder/S50, 85-09
M261-2	1500 Intruder/C90, 98-09
M260-3	Volusia/Boulevard C50, 01-11
M482-3	VS1400 Intruder/S83, 87-07

Triple

M368	GT380, 550 & 750, 72-77

Fours

M373	GS550, 77-86
M364	GS650, 81-83
M370	GS750, 77-82
M376	GS850-1100 Shaft Drive, 79-84
M378	GS1100 Chain Drive, 80-81
M383-3	Katana 600, 88-96 GSX-R750-1100, 86-87
M331	GSX-R600, 97-00
M264	GSX-R600, 01-05
M478-2	GSX-R750, 88-92; GSX750F Katana, 89-96
M485	GSX-R750, 96-99
M377	GSX-R1000, 01-04
M266	GSX-R1000, 05-06
M265	GSX1300R Hayabusa, 99-07
M338	Bandit 600, 95-00
M353	GSF1200 Bandit, 96-03

YAMAHA

ATVs

M499-2	YFM80 Moto-4, Badger & Raptor, 85-08
M394	YTM200, 225 & YFM200, 83-86
M488-5	Blaster, 88-05
M489-2	Timberwolf, 89-00
M487-5	Warrior, 87-04
M486-6	Banshee, 87-06
M490-3	Moto-4 & Big Bear, 87-04
M493	Kodiak, 93-98
M287-2	YFZ450, 04-13
M285-2	Grizzly 660, 02-08
M280-2	Raptor 660R, 01-05
M290	Raptor 700R, 06-09
M291	Rhino 700, 2008-2012

Singles

M492-2	PW50 & 80 Y-Zinger & BW80 Big Wheel 80, 81-02
M410	80-175 Piston Port, 68-76
M415	250-400 Piston Port, 68-76
M412	DT & MX Series, 77-83
M414	IT125-490, 76-86
M393	YZ50-80 Monoshock, 78-90
M413	YZ100-490 Monoshock, 76-84
M390	YZ125-250, 85-87 YZ490, 85-90
M391	YZ125-250, 88-93 & WR250Z, 91-93
M497-2	YZ125, 94-01
M498	YZ250, 94-98; WR250Z, 94-97
M406	YZ250F & WR250F, 01-03
M491-2	YZ400F, 98-99 & 426F, 00-02; WR400F, 98-00 & 426F, 00-01
M417	XT125-250, 80-84
M480-3	XT350, 85-00; TT350, 86-87
M405	XT/TT 500, 76-81
M416	XT/TT 600, 83-89

Twins

M403	650cc Twins, 70-82
M395-10	XV535-1100 Virago, 81-03
M495-7	V-Star 650, 98-11
M284	V-Star 950, 09-12
M281-4	V-Star 1100, 99-09
M283	V-Star 1300, 07-10
M282-2	Road Star, 99-07

Triple

M404	XS750 & XS850, 77-81

Fours

M387	XJ550, XJ600 & FJ600, 81-92
M494	XJ600 Seca II/Diversion, 92-98
M388	YX600 Radian & FZ600, 86-90
M396	FZR600, 89-93
M392	FZ700-750 & Fazer, 85-87
M411	XS1100, 78-81
M461	YZF-R6, 99-04
M398	YZF-R1, 98-03
M399	FZ1, 01-05
M397	FJ1100 & 1200, 84-93
M375-2	V-Max, 85-07
M374-2	Royal Star, 96-10

VINTAGE MOTORCYCLES

Clymer® Collection Series

M330	Vintage British Street Bikes, BSA 500–650cc Unit Twins; Norton 750 & 850cc Commandos; Triumph 500-750cc Twins
M300	Vintage Dirt Bikes, V. 1 Bultaco, 125-370cc Singles; Montesa, 123-360cc Singles; Ossa, 125-250cc Singles
M305	Vintage Japanese Street Bikes Honda, 250 & 305cc Twins; Kawasaki, 250-750cc Triples; Kawasaki, 900 & 1000cc Fours